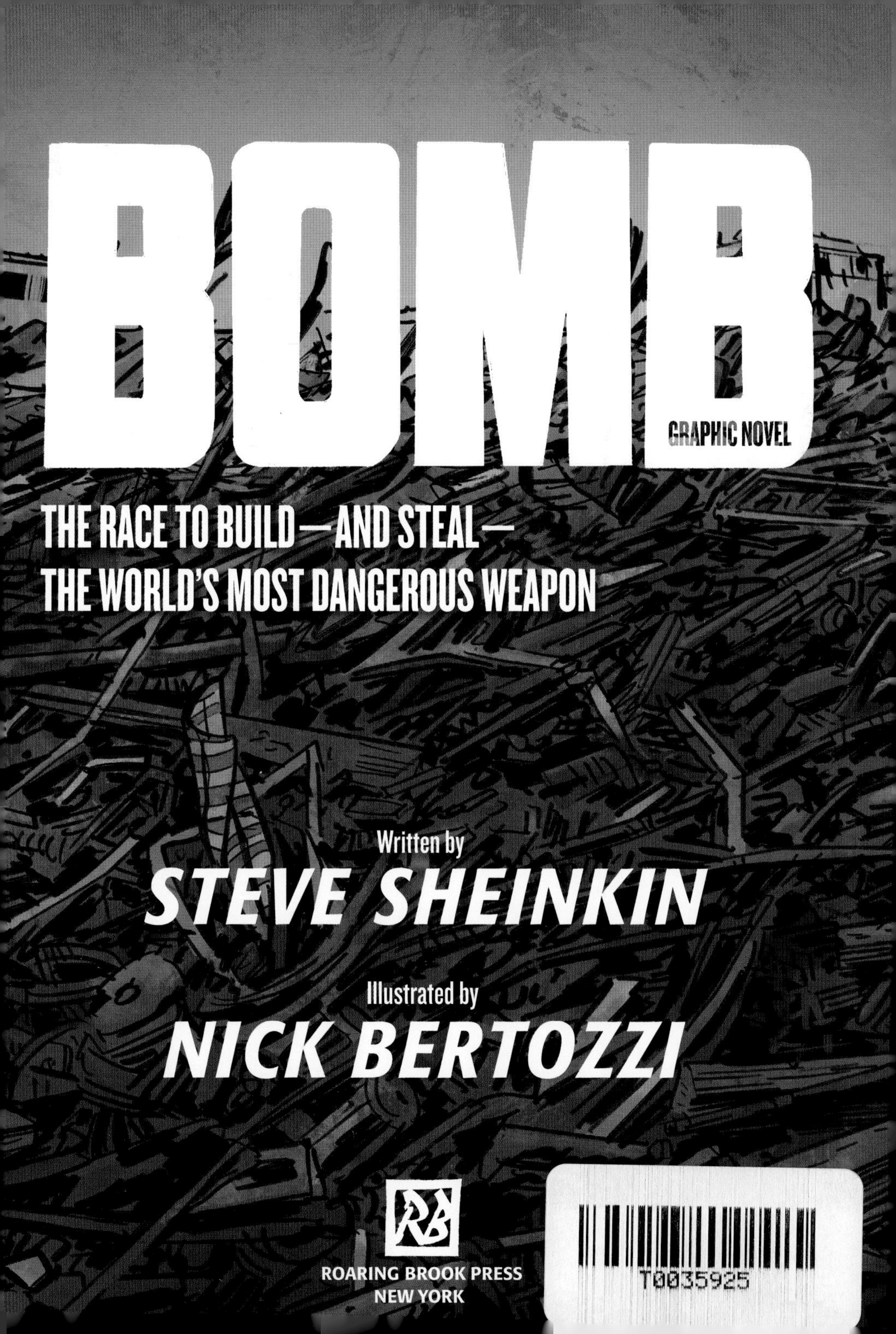

BOMB

GRAPHIC NOVEL

THE RACE TO BUILD—AND STEAL—THE WORLD'S MOST DANGEROUS WEAPON

Written by
STEVE SHEINKIN

Illustrated by
NICK BERTOZZI

ROARING BROOK PRESS
NEW YORK

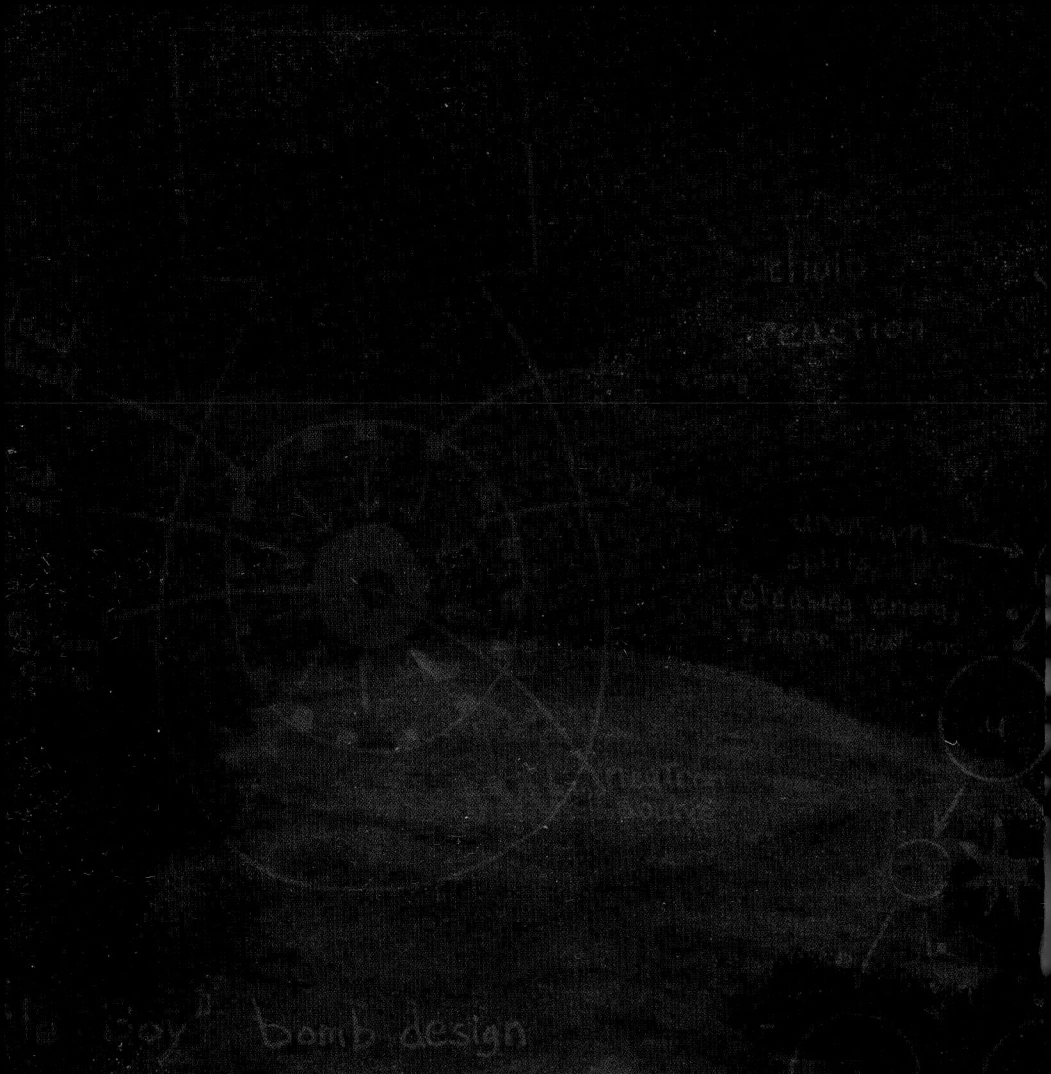

Published by Roaring Brook Press • Roaring Brook Press is a division of Holtzbrinck
Publishing Holdings Limited Partnership • 120 Broadway, NEW YORK, NY 10271 • mackids.com

TeXT © 2023 by STeve Sheinkin • ILLustrations © 2023 by Nick Bertozzi • All rights reserved
Library of Congress Control Number: 2022910304

OUr books may be purchased in bulk for PROmotional, educational, or
business use. PLease contact your local bookseller or the Macmillan Corporate and
Premium SALes Department at (800) 221-7945 EXT. 5442 or by email
at MacmillanSpecialMarkets@MACMILLAN.COM.

First edition, 2023 • Edited by CONNie Hsu • Cover DESIGn by Kirk Benshoff
Cover art by Nick Bertozzi • Interior book design by Sunny Lee • Color by Irene Yeom

Printed in China by Toppan Leefung Printing Ltd., Dongguan City, Guangdong Province

ISBN 978-1-250-20674-9 (PAPERBACK)   ISBN 978-1-250-20673-2 (HARDCOVER)
1 3 5 7 9 10 8 6 4 2   1 3 5 7 9 10 8 6 4 2

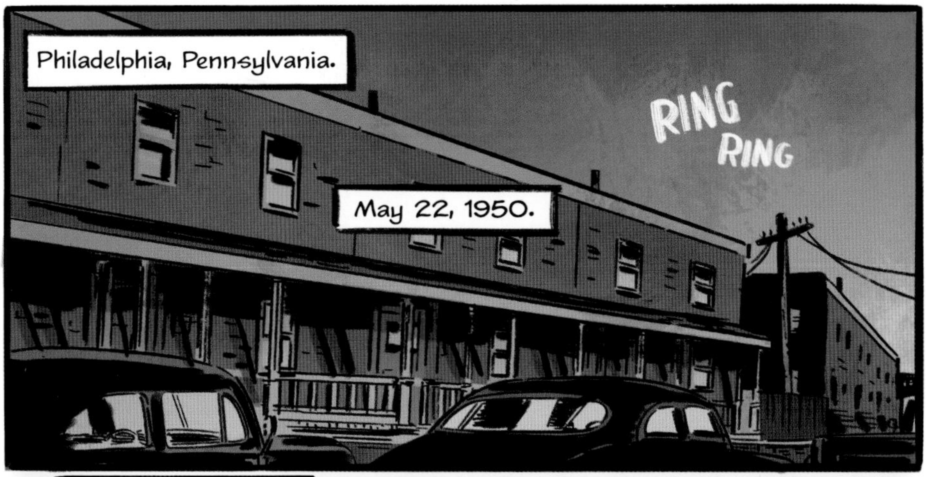
Philadelphia, Pennsylvania.
May 22, 1950.
RING
RING

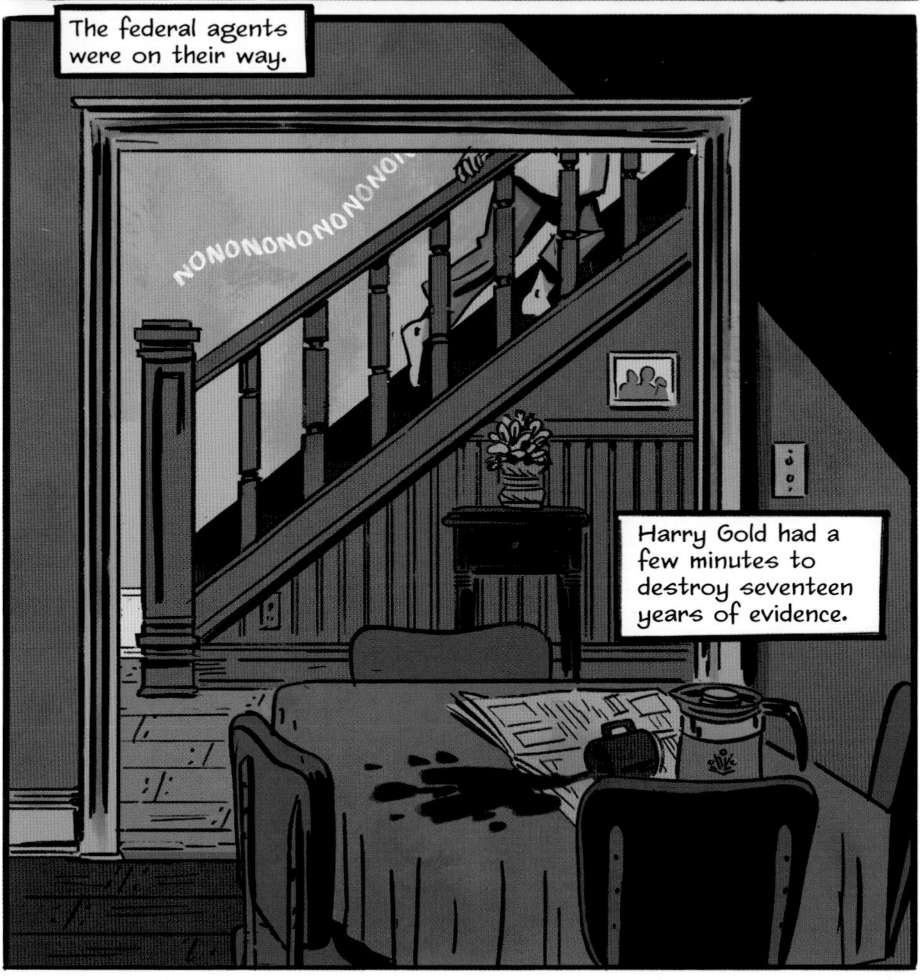
The federal agents were on their way.
NONONONONONONONO
Harry Gold had a few minutes to destroy seventeen years of evidence.

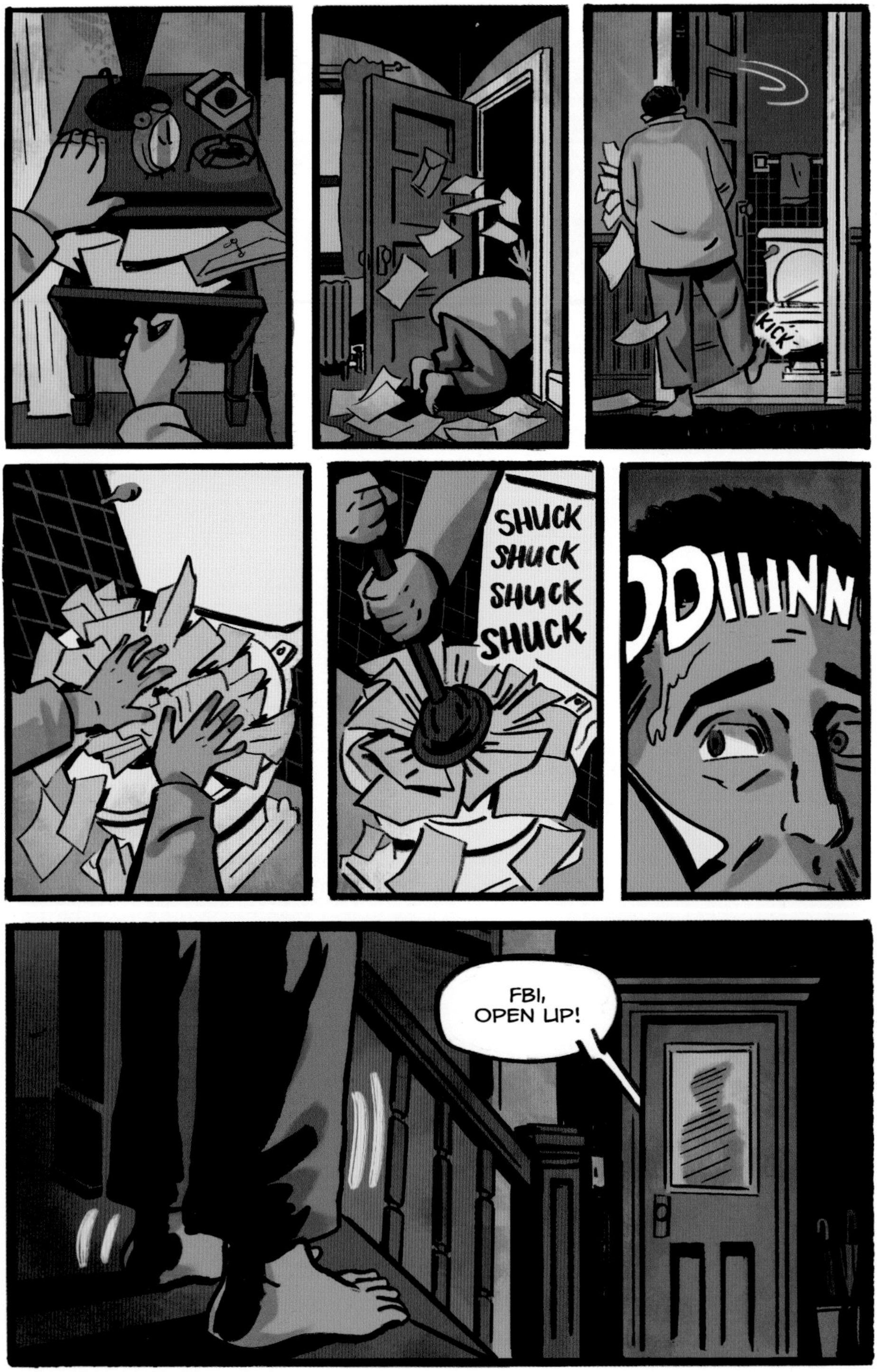
KICK
SHUCK
SHUCK
SHUCK
SHUCK
DIIIINN
FBI, OPEN UP!

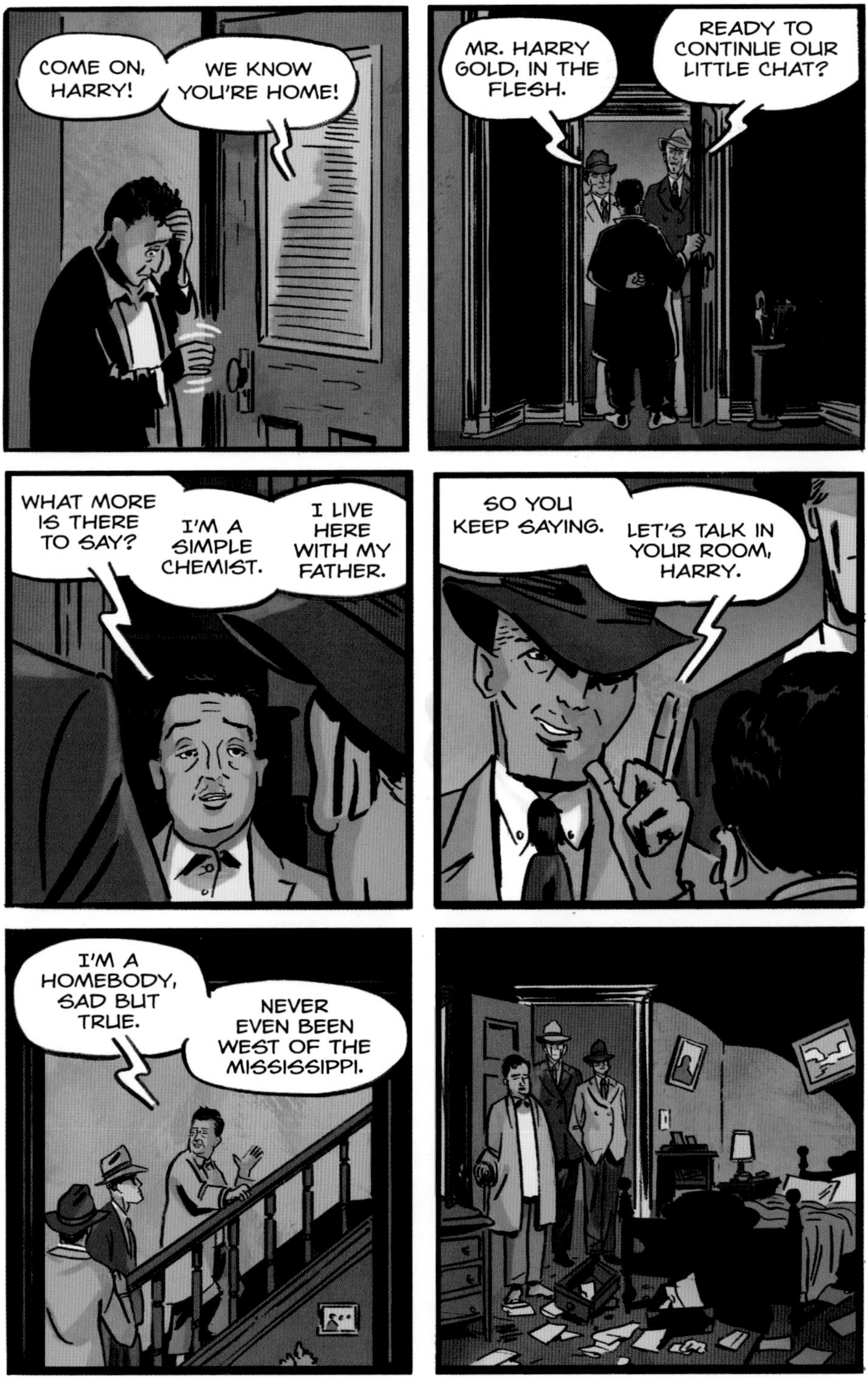
COME ON, HARRY!
WE KNOW YOU'RE HOME!
MR. HARRY GOLD, IN THE FLESH.
READY TO CONTINUE OUR LITTLE CHAT?
WHAT MORE IS THERE TO SAY?
I'M A SIMPLE CHEMIST.
I LIVE HERE WITH MY FATHER.
SO YOU KEEP SAYING.
LET'S TALK IN YOUR ROOM, HARRY.
I'M A HOMEBODY, SAD BUT TRUE.
NEVER EVEN BEEN WEST OF THE MISSISSIPPI.

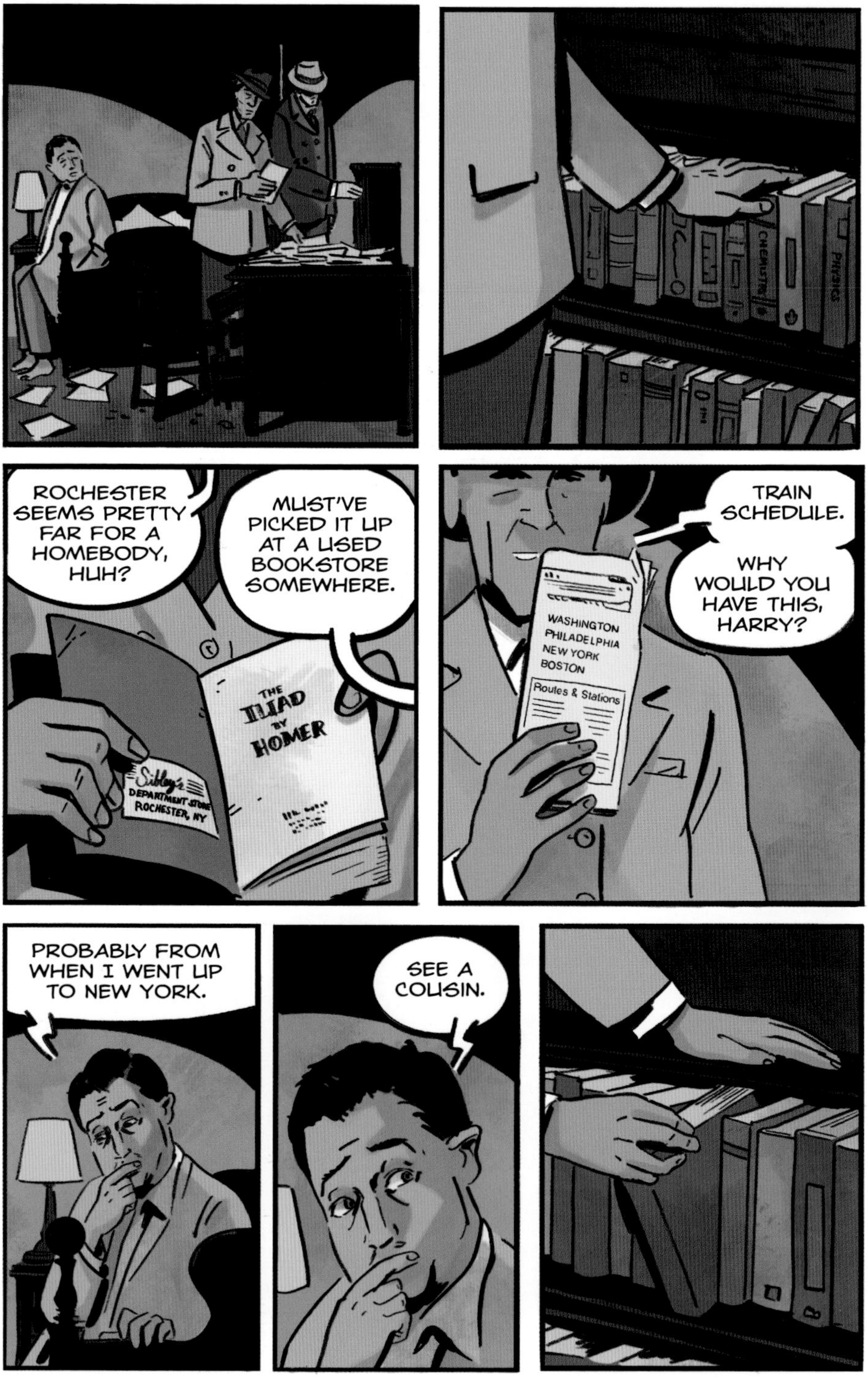
CHEMISTRY
PHYSICS
ROCHESTER SEEMS PRETTY FAR FOR A HOMEBODY, HUH?
MUST'VE PICKED IT UP AT A USED BOOKSTORE SOMEWHERE.
Sibley's DEPARTMENT STORE ROCHESTER, NY
THE ILIAD BY HOMER
TRAIN SCHEDULE.
WHY WOULD YOU HAVE THIS, HARRY?
WASHINGTON PHILADELPHIA NEW YORK BOSTON
Routes & Stations
PROBABLY FROM WHEN I WENT UP TO NEW YORK.
SEE A COUSIN.

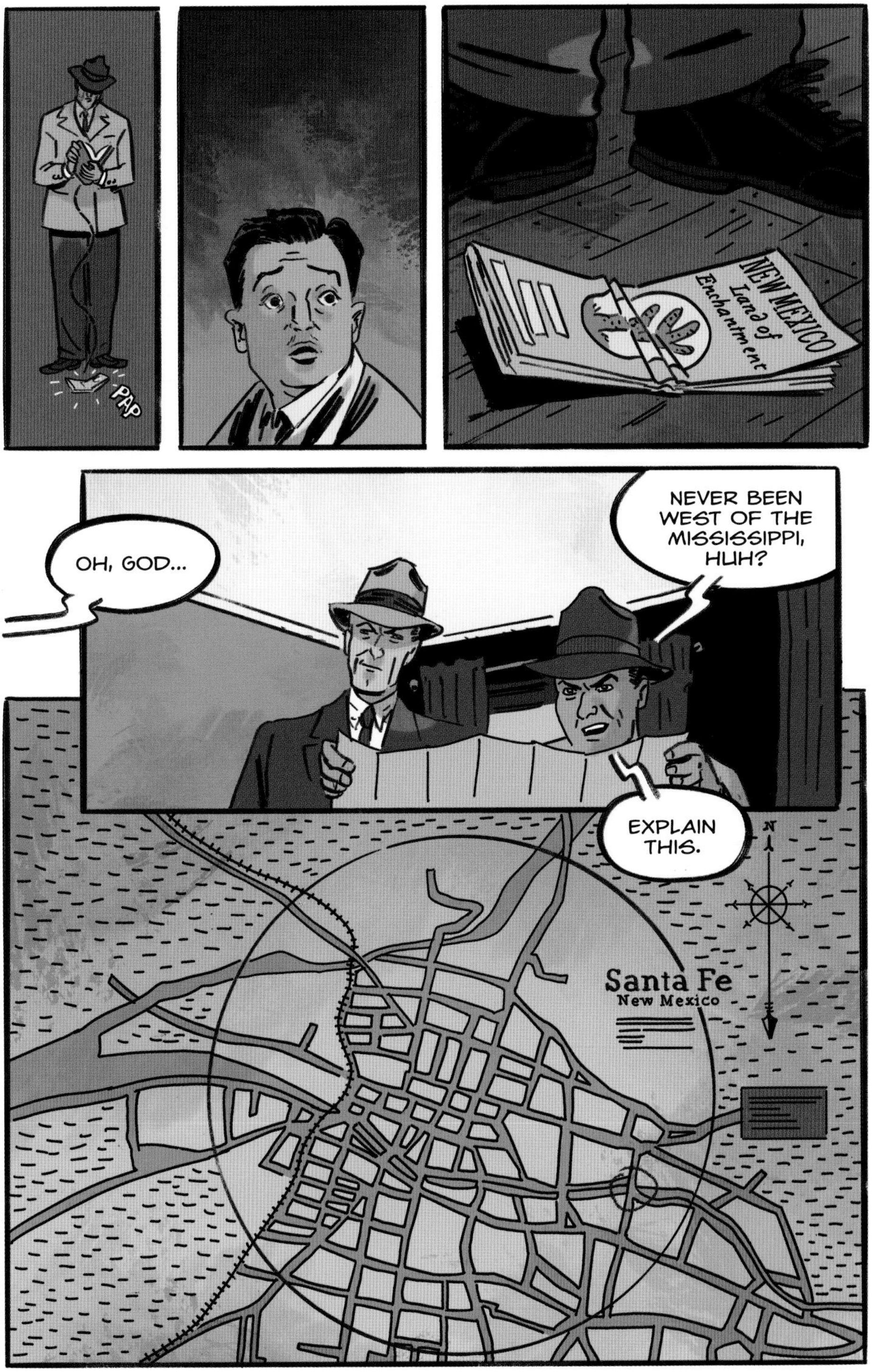
PAP
NEW MEXICO
Land of Enchantment
OH, GOD...
NEVER BEEN WEST OF THE MISSISSIPPI, HUH?
EXPLAIN THIS.
N
Santa Fe
New Mexico

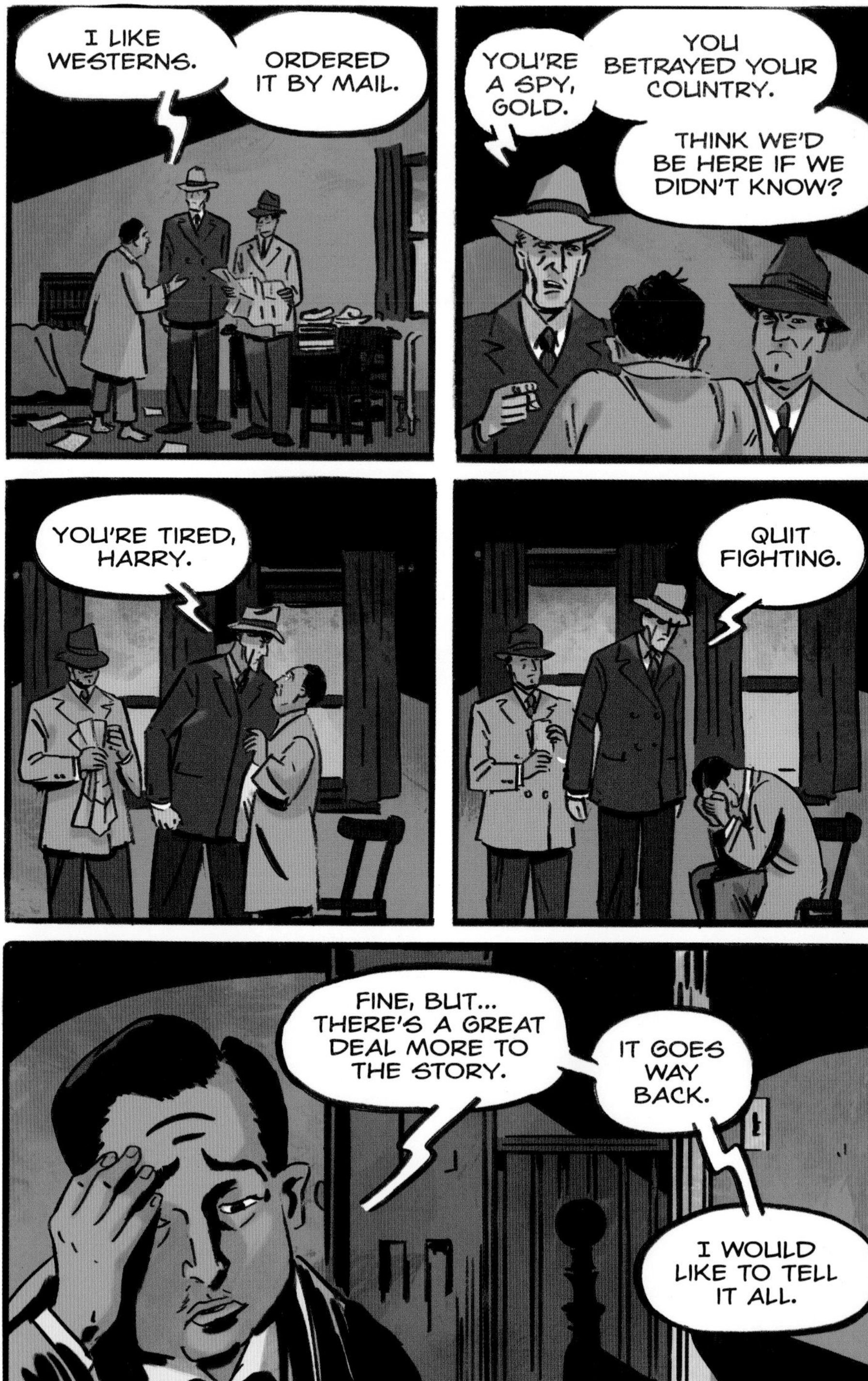
I LIKE WESTERNS.
ORDERED IT BY MAIL.
YOU'RE A SPY, GOLD.
YOU BETRAYED YOUR COUNTRY.
THINK WE'D BE HERE IF WE DIDN'T KNOW?
YOU'RE TIRED, HARRY.
QUIT FIGHTING.
FINE, BUT... THERE'S A GREAT DEAL MORE TO THE STORY.
IT GOES WAY BACK.
I WOULD LIKE TO TELL IT ALL.

Chapter 1

Skinny Superhero

the "liquid drop" theory

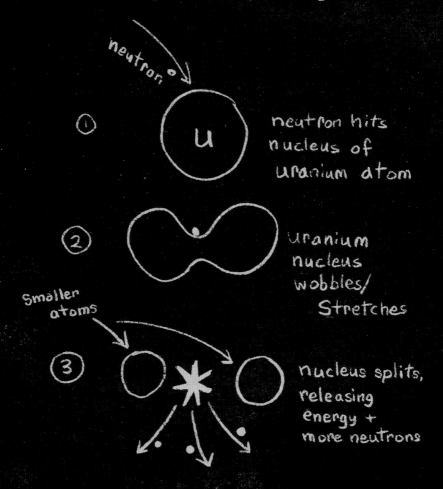

neutron

① neutron hits nucleus of uranium atom

② uranium nucleus wobbles/ Stretches

Smaller atoms

③ nucleus splits, releasing energy + more neutrons

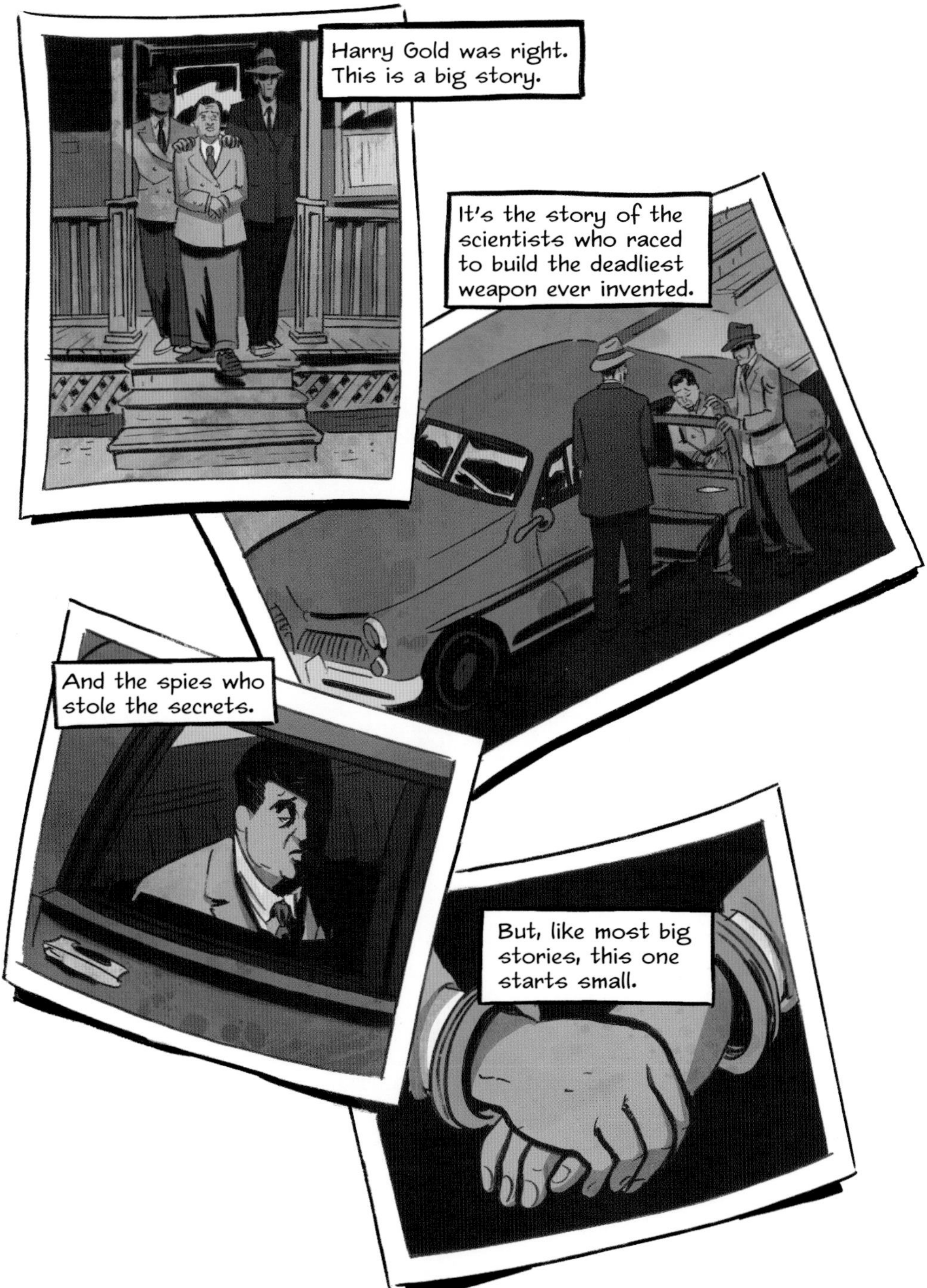
Harry Gold was right. This is a big story.
It's the story of the scientists who raced to build the deadliest weapon ever invented.
And the spies who stole the secrets.
But, like most big stories, this one starts small.

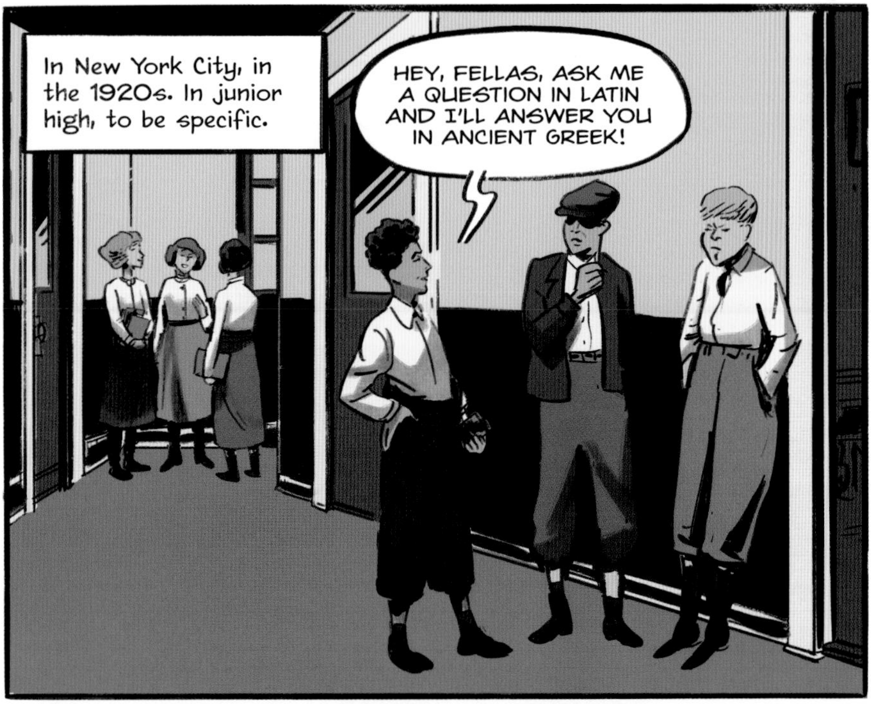
In New York City, in the 1920s. In junior high, to be specific.
HEY, FELLAS, ASK ME A QUESTION IN LATIN AND I'LL ANSWER YOU IN ANCIENT GREEK!

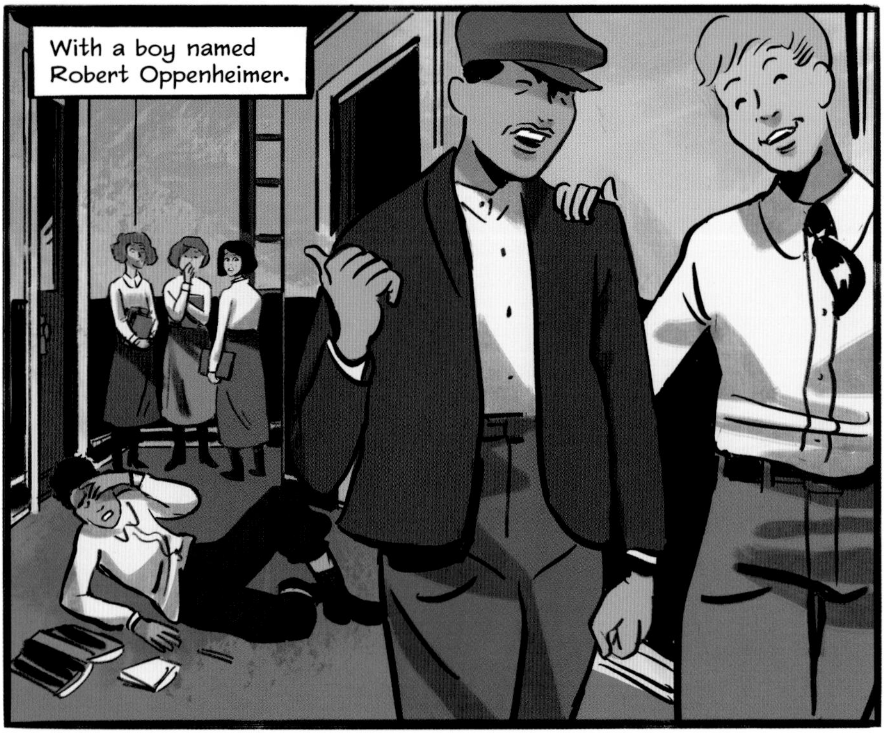
With a boy named Robert Oppenheimer.

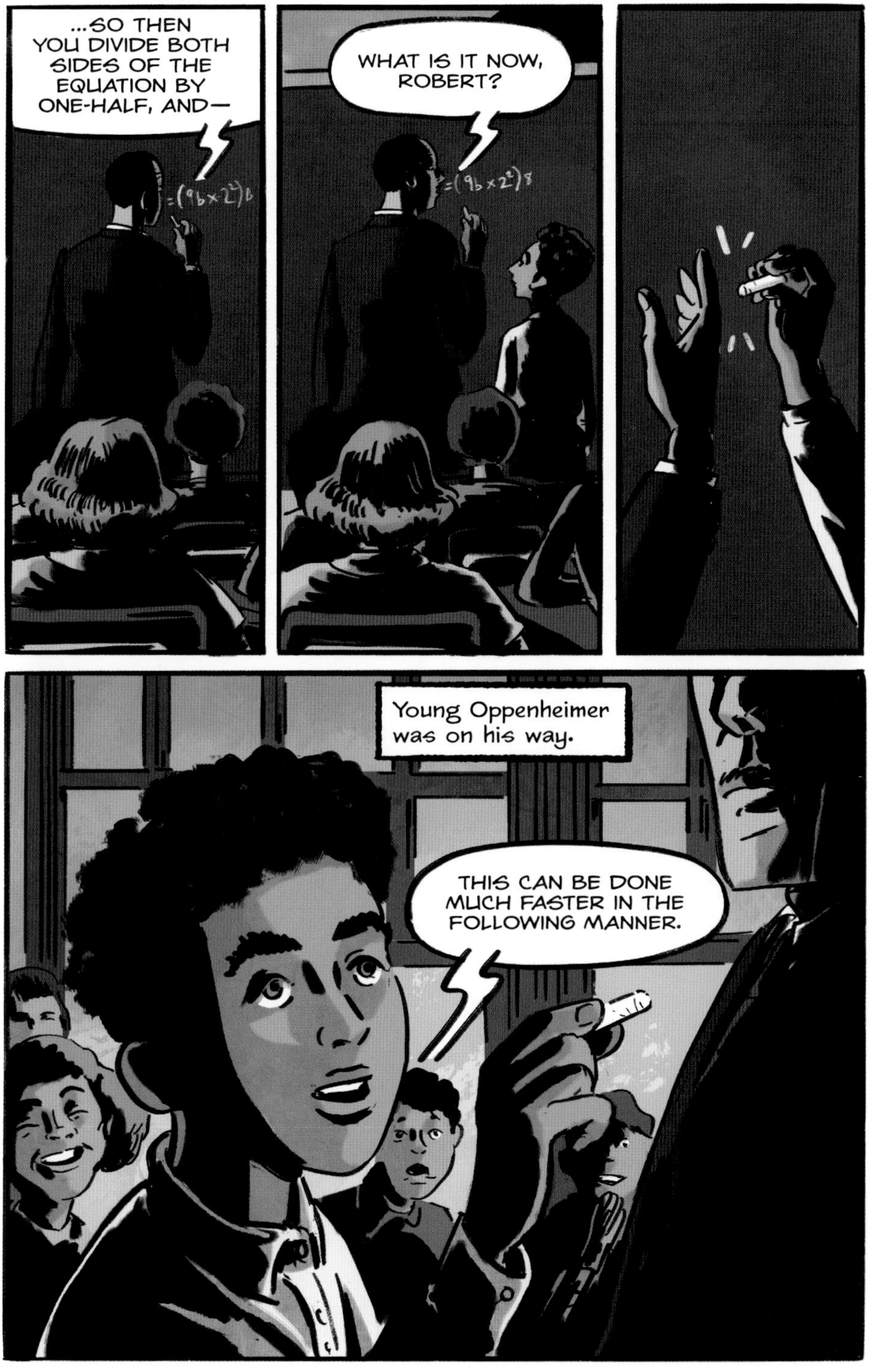
...SO THEN YOU DIVIDE BOTH SIDES OF THE EQUATION BY ONE-HALF, AND—
WHAT IS IT NOW, ROBERT?
Young Oppenheimer was on his way.
THIS CAN BE DONE MUCH FASTER IN THE FOLLOWING MANNER.

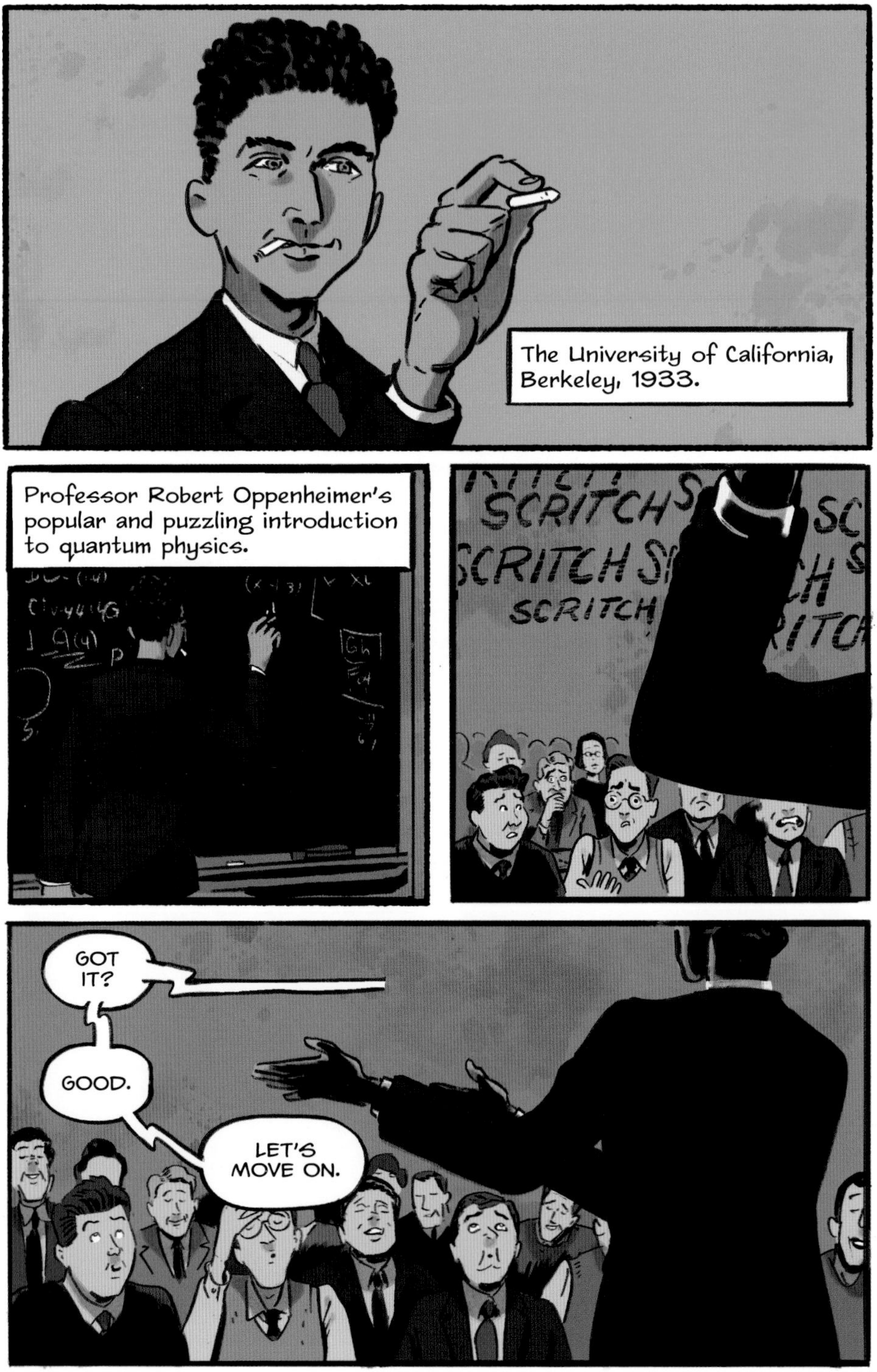
The University of California, Berkeley, 1933.
Professor Robert Oppenheimer's popular and puzzling introduction to quantum physics.
SCRITCH
SCRITCH
SCRITCH
GOT IT?
GOOD.
LET'S MOVE ON.

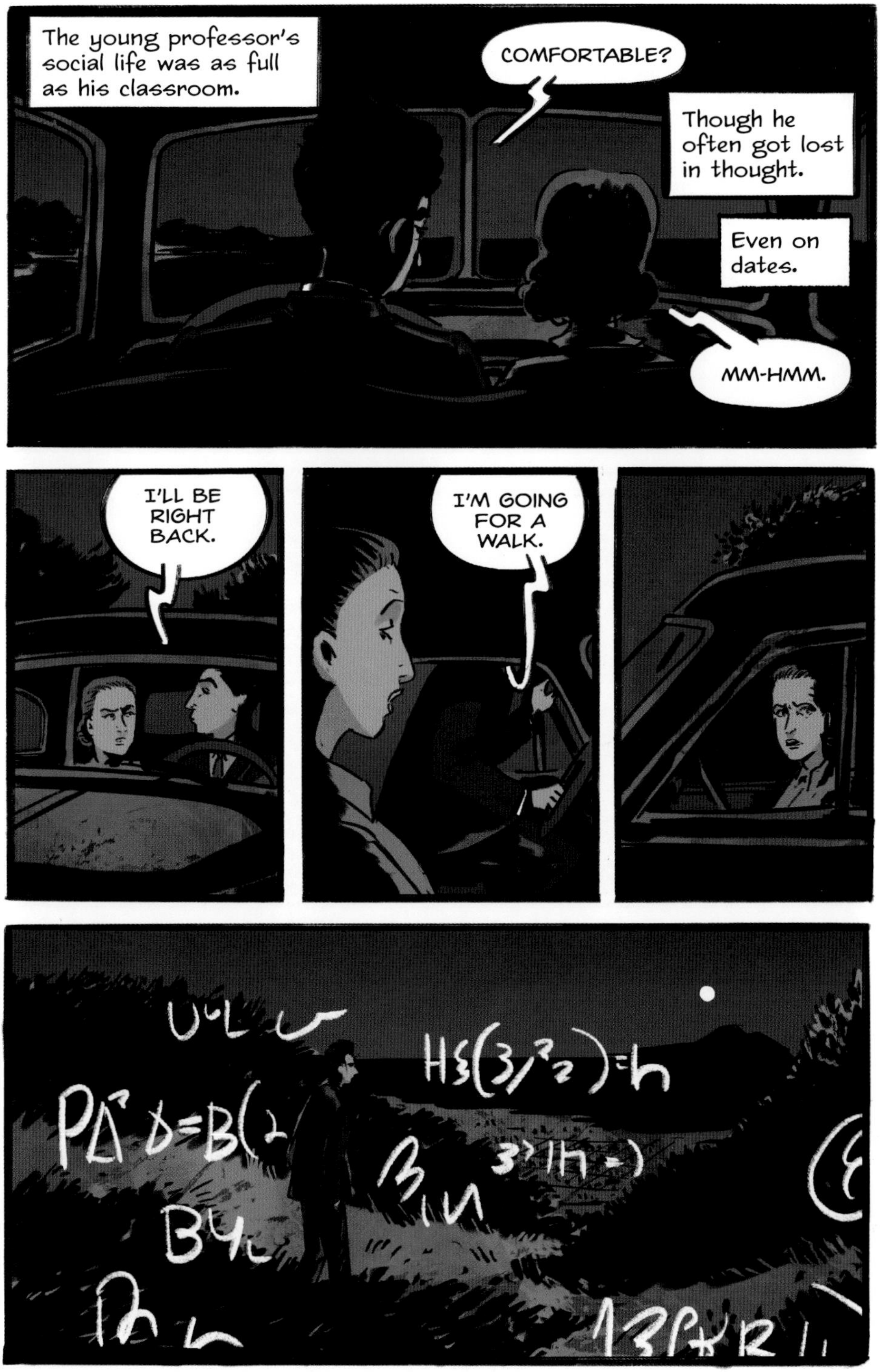
The young professor's social life was as full as his classroom.
COMFORTABLE?
Though he often got lost in thought.
Even on dates.
MM-HMM.
I'LL BE RIGHT BACK.
I'M GOING FOR A WALK.

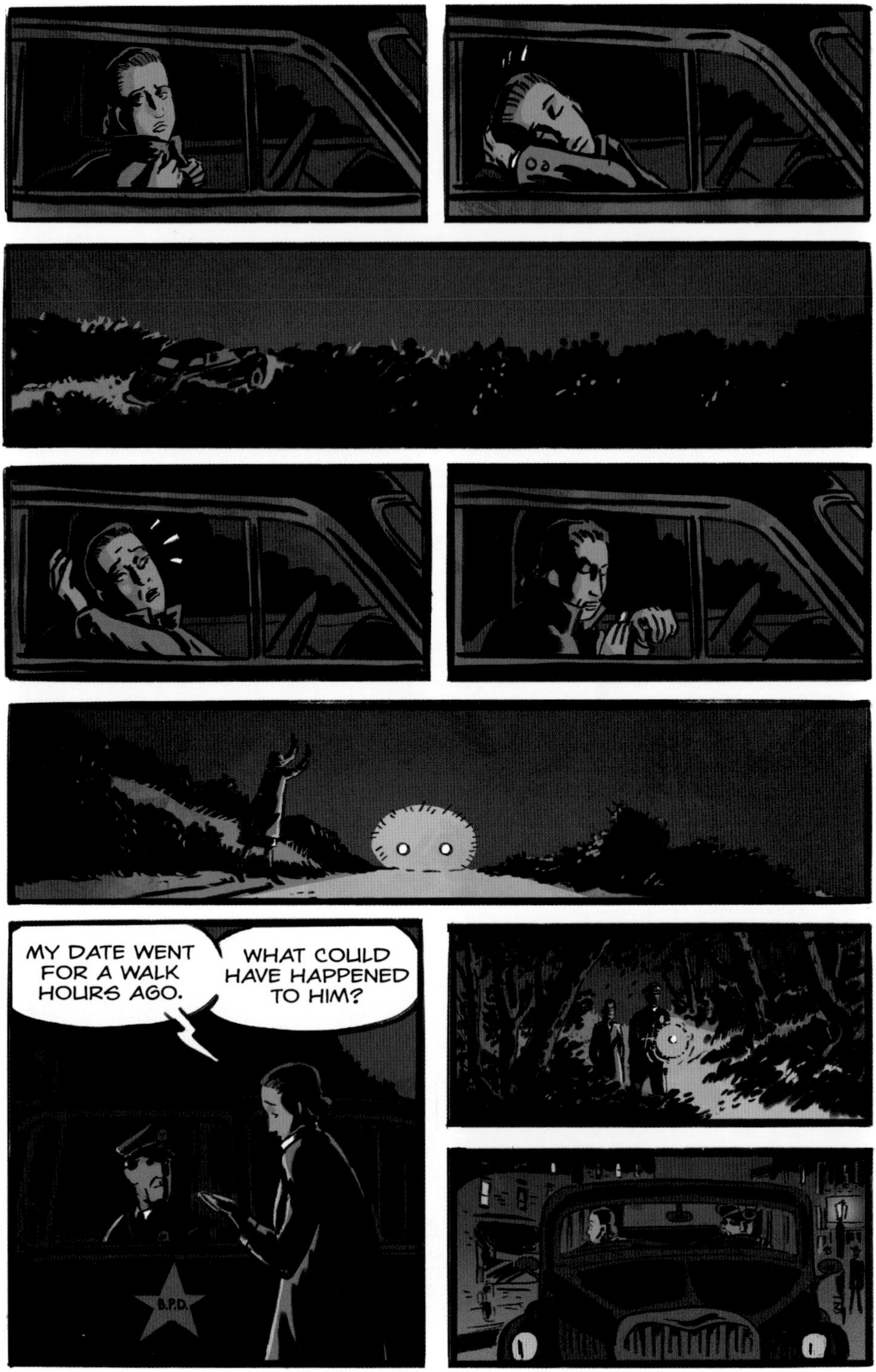
MY DATE WENT FOR A WALK HOURS AGO.
WHAT COULD HAVE HAPPENED TO HIM?
B.P.D.

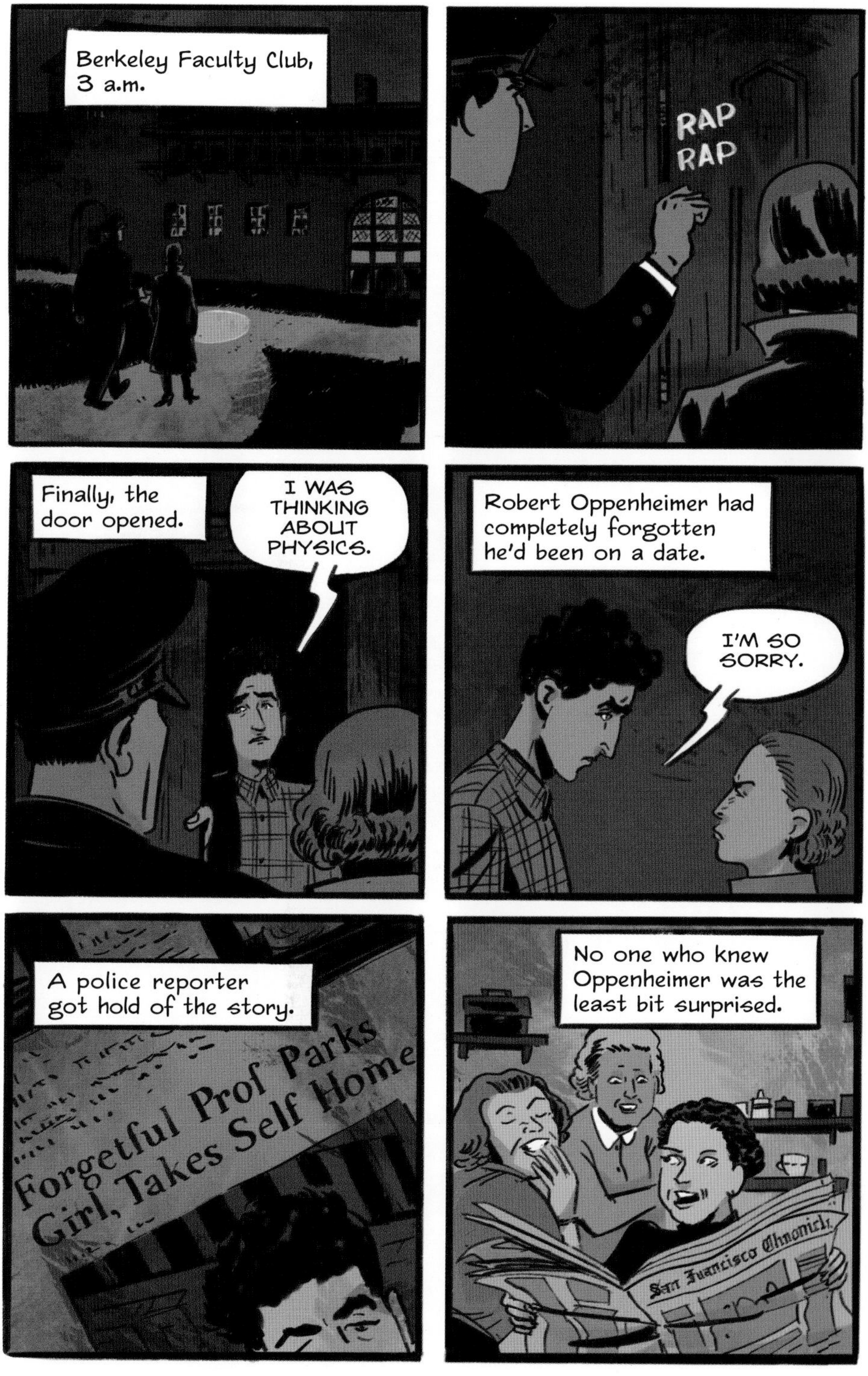
Berkeley Faculty Club, 3 a.m.
RAP RAP
Finally, the door opened.
I WAS THINKING ABOUT PHYSICS.
Robert Oppenheimer had completely forgotten he'd been on a date.
I'M SO SORRY.
A police reporter got hold of the story.
Forgetful Prof Parks Girl, Takes Self Home
No one who knew Oppenheimer was the least bit surprised.
San Francisco Chronicle

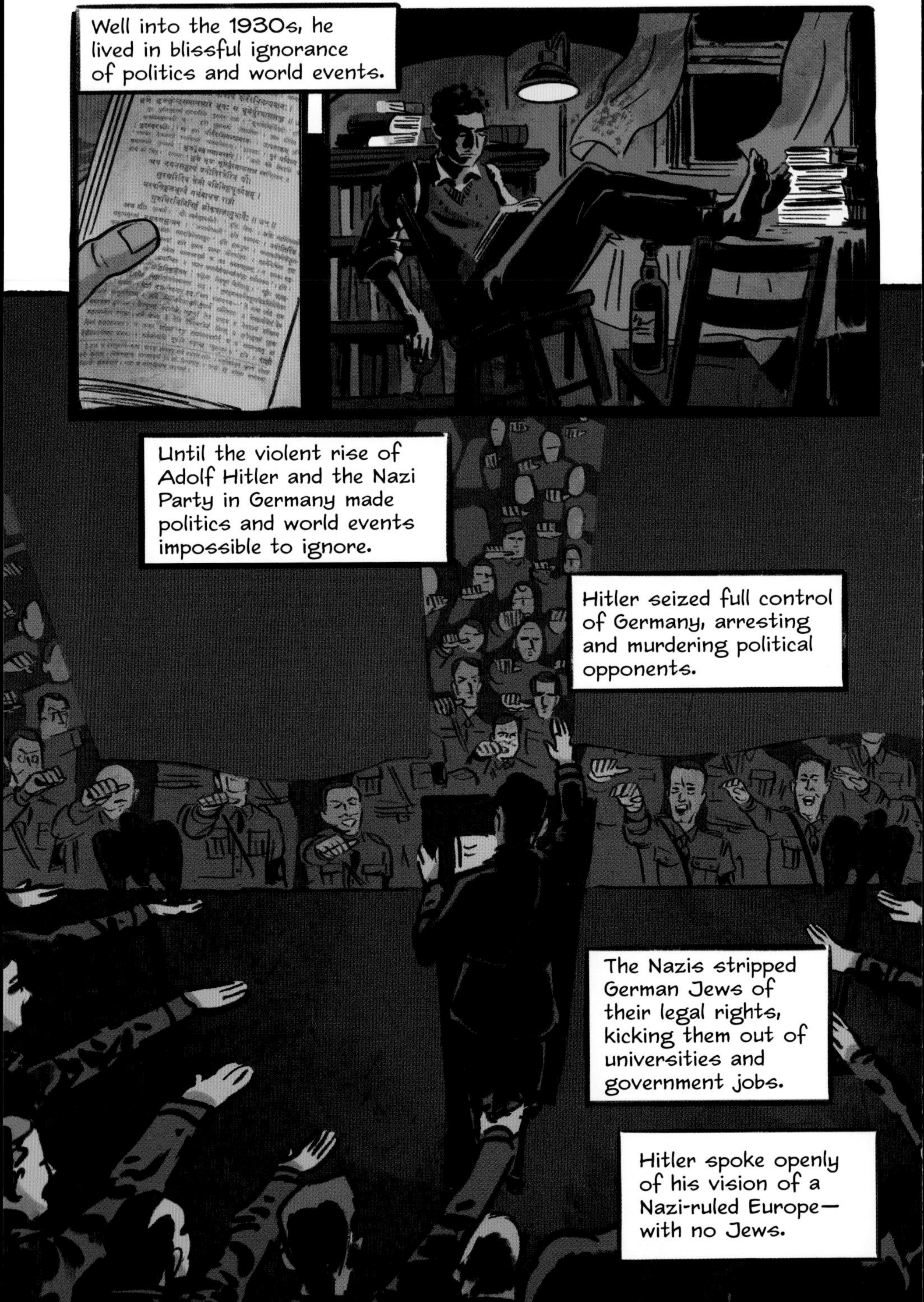
Well into the 1930s, he lived in blissful ignorance of politics and world events.
Until the violent rise of Adolf Hitler and the Nazi Party in Germany made politics and world events impossible to ignore.
Hitler seized full control of Germany, arresting and murdering political opponents.
The Nazis stripped German Jews of their legal rights, kicking them out of universities and government jobs.
Hitler spoke openly of his vision of a Nazi-ruled Europe—with no Jews.

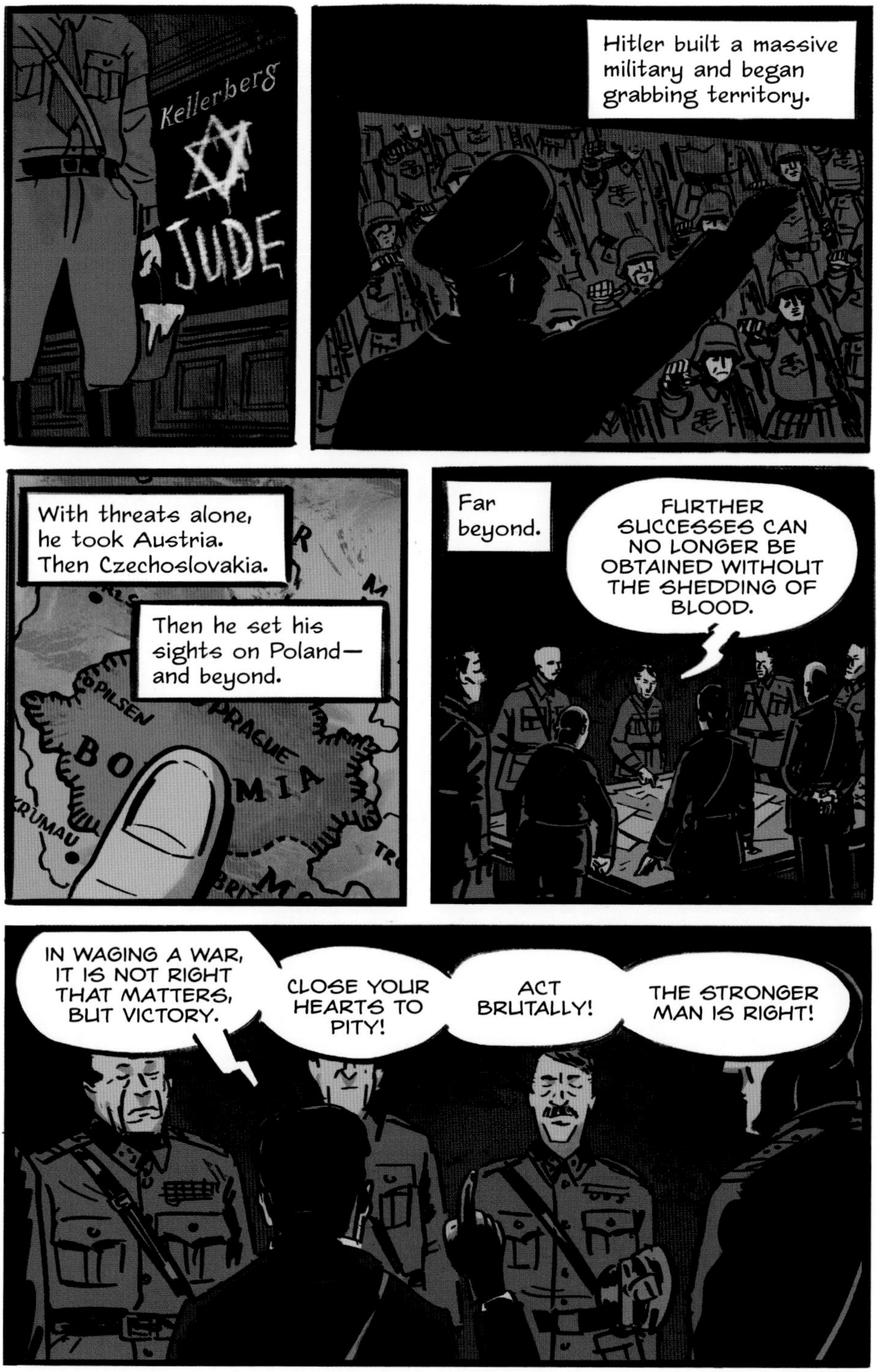
Kellerberg
JUDE
Hitler built a massive military and began grabbing territory.
With threats alone, he took Austria. Then Czechoslovakia.
Then he set his sights on Poland— and beyond.
PILSEN
PRAGUE
BOHEMIA
KRUMAU
Far beyond.
FURTHER SUCCESSES CAN NO LONGER BE OBTAINED WITHOUT THE SHEDDING OF BLOOD.
IN WAGING A WAR, IT IS NOT RIGHT THAT MATTERS, BUT VICTORY.
CLOSE YOUR HEARTS TO PITY!
ACT BRUTALLY!
THE STRONGER MAN IS RIGHT!

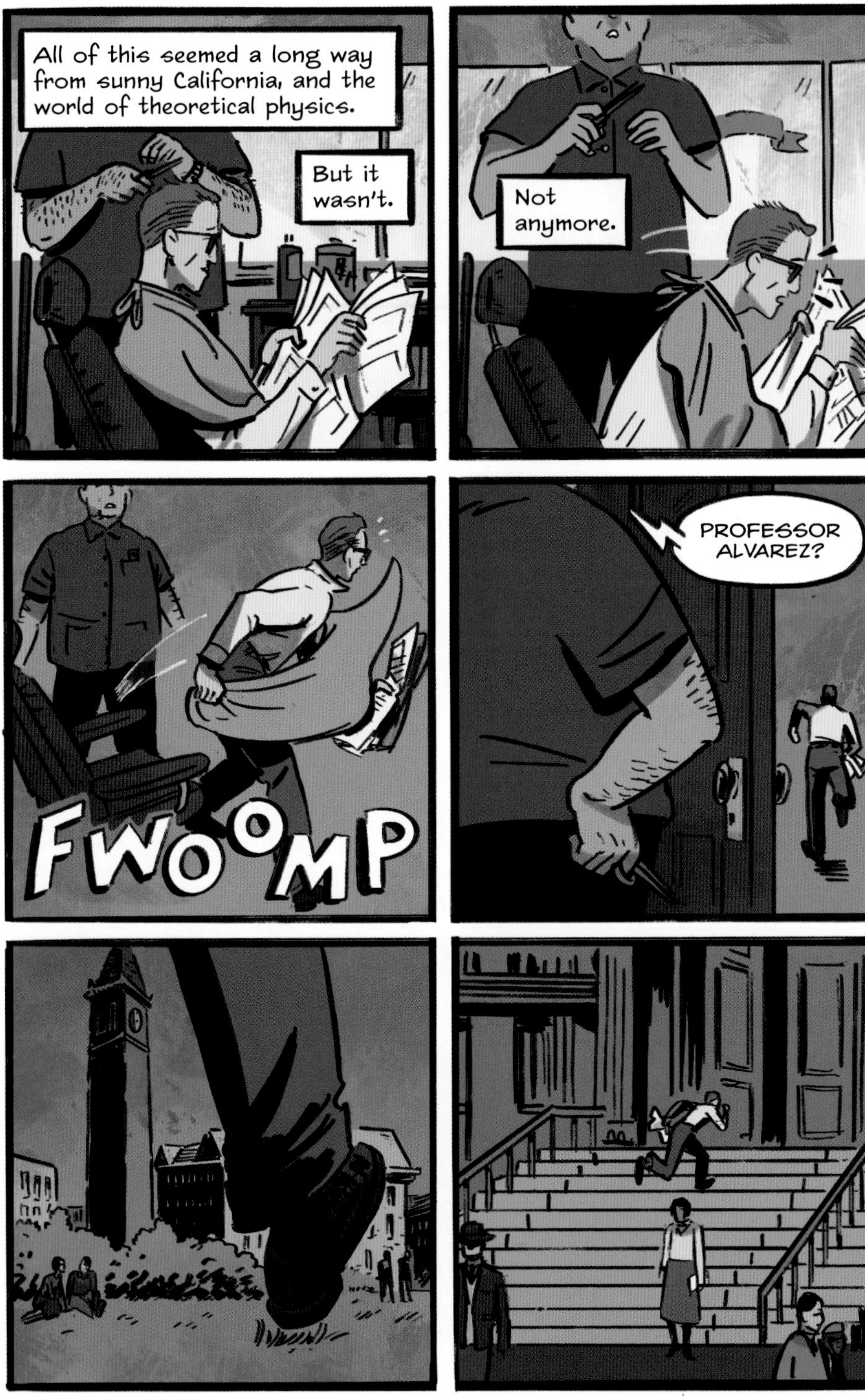
All of this seemed a long way from sunny California, and the world of theoretical physics.
But it wasn't.
Not anymore.
FWOOMP
PROFESSOR ALVAREZ?

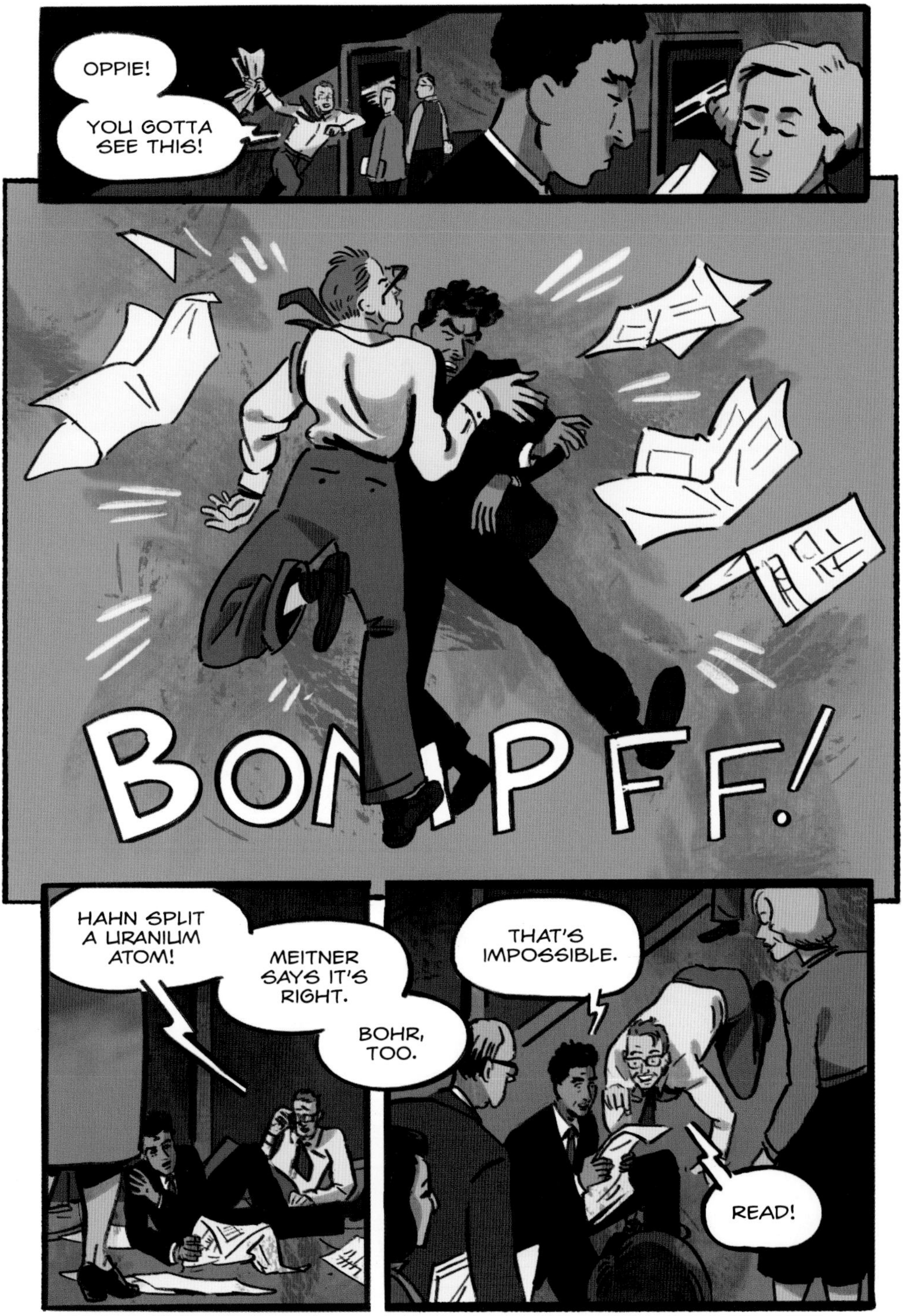
OPPIE!
YOU GOTTA SEE THIS!
BOMPFF!
HAHN SPLIT A URANIUM ATOM!
MEITNER SAYS IT'S RIGHT.
BOHR, TOO.
THAT'S IMPOSSIBLE.
READ!

"IN WHAT SCIENTISTS ARE DESCRIBING AS A WORLD-CHANGING EXPERIMENT"...

..."OTTO HAHN, IN HIS LAB IN BERLIN, GERMANY, HAS SPLIT AN ATOM."

"THIS WAS NOT THOUGHT TO BE POSSIBLE."

"SCIENTISTS HAVE LONG UNDERSTOOD THAT ATOMS ARE COMPOSED OF EVEN TINIER PARTICLES"...

"ATOMS HAVE A CENTRAL CORE, OR NUCLEUS, MADE UP OF PARTICLES CALLED PROTONS AND NEUTRONS, HELD TOGETHER BY AN ENORMOUSLY STRONG FORCE."

"SURROUNDING THE NUCLEUS ARE PARTICLES CALLED ELECTRONS."

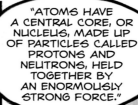

ELECTRON   ELECTRON

NUCLEUS

"IT IS ALSO WELL KNOWN THAT SOME ATOMS ARE RADIOACTIVE."

"THAT IS, THEIR NUCLEUS IS NATURALLY UNSTABLE, SHOOTING OUT PARTICLES AT HIGH SPEEDS."

"THIS IS USEFUL TO EXPERIMENTERS LIKE OTTO HAHN— THEY CAN USE RADIOACTIVE ELEMENTS AS TINY CANNONS."

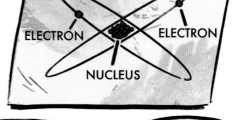

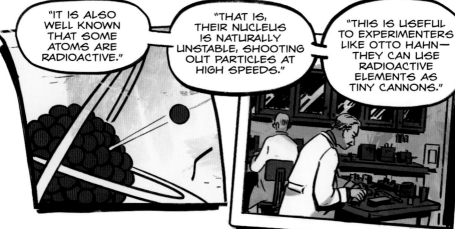

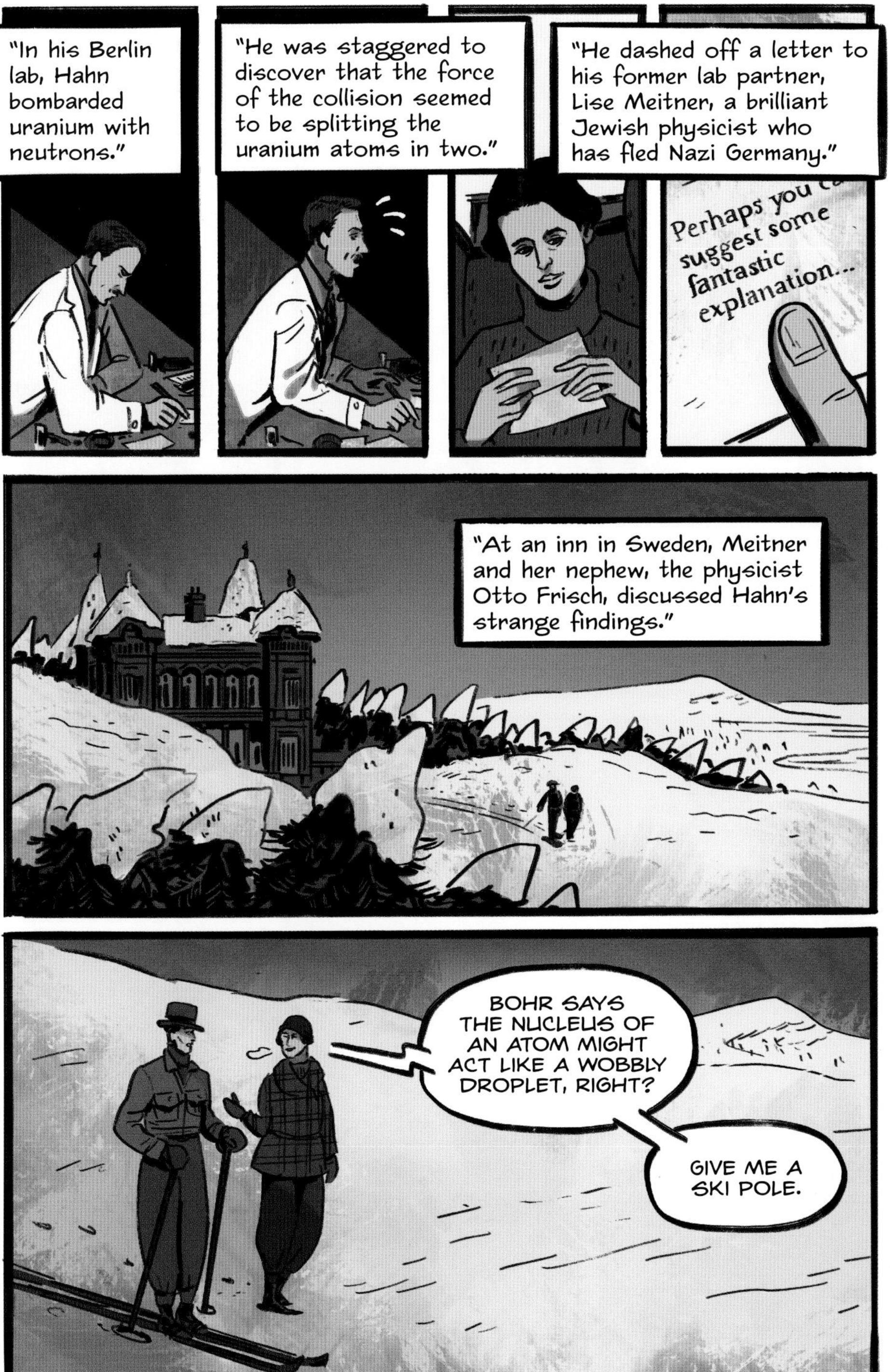
"In his Berlin lab, Hahn bombarded uranium with neutrons."
"He was staggered to discover that the force of the collision seemed to be splitting the uranium atoms in two."
"He dashed off a letter to his former lab partner, Lise Meitner, a brilliant Jewish physicist who has fled Nazi Germany."
Perhaps you
suggest some fantastic explanation...
"At an inn in Sweden, Meitner and her nephew, the physicist Otto Frisch, discussed Hahn's strange findings."
BOHR SAYS THE NUCLEUS OF AN ATOM MIGHT ACT LIKE A WOBBLY DROPLET, RIGHT?
GIVE ME A SKI POLE.

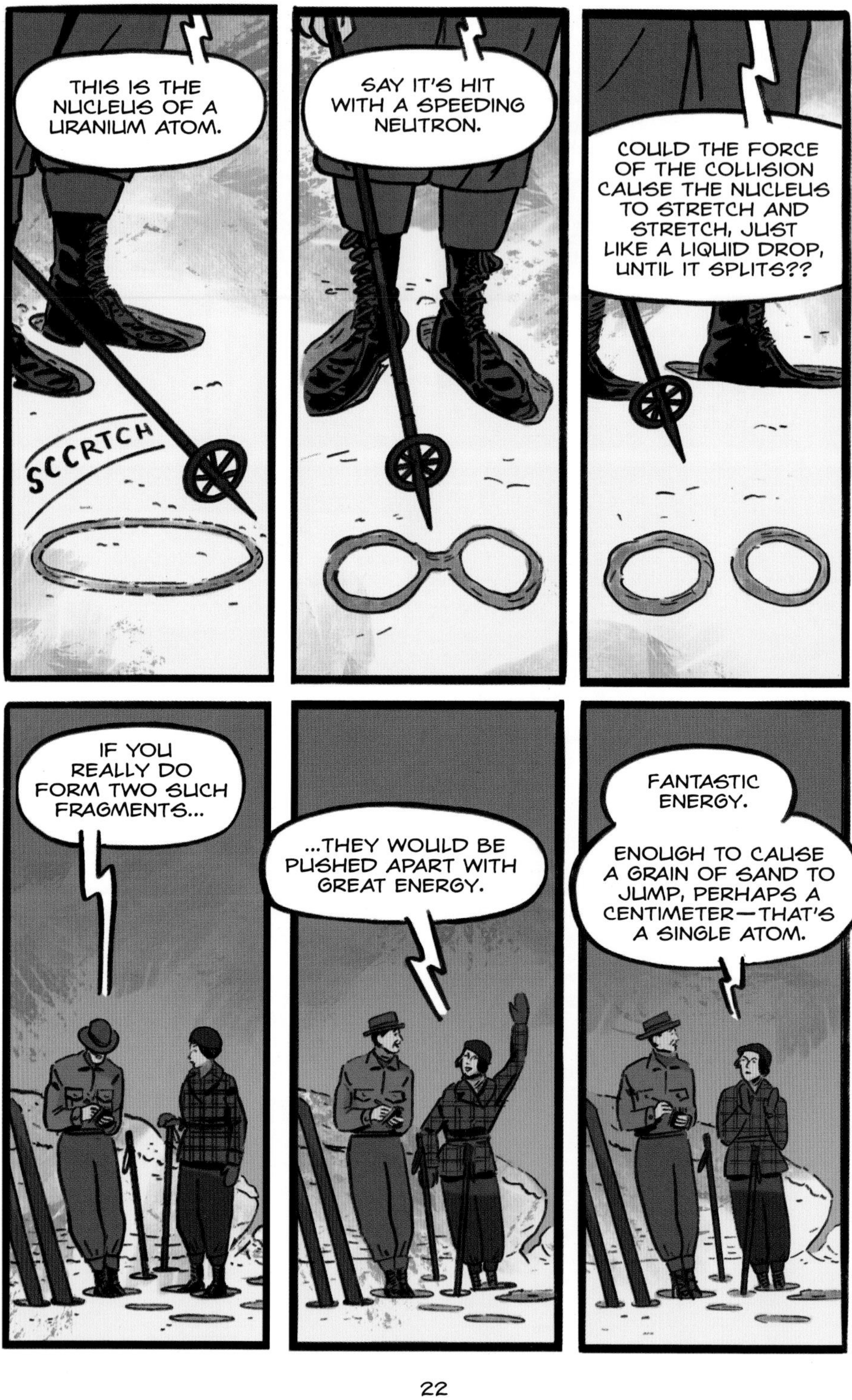
THIS IS THE NUCLEUS OF A URANIUM ATOM.
SCCRTCH
SAY IT'S HIT WITH A SPEEDING NEUTRON.
COULD THE FORCE OF THE COLLISION CAUSE THE NUCLEUS TO STRETCH AND STRETCH, JUST LIKE A LIQUID DROP, UNTIL IT SPLITS??
IF YOU REALLY DO FORM TWO SUCH FRAGMENTS...
...THEY WOULD BE PUSHED APART WITH GREAT ENERGY.
FANTASTIC ENERGY.
ENOUGH TO CAUSE A GRAIN OF SAND TO JUMP, PERHAPS A CENTIMETER—THAT'S A SINGLE ATOM.

"Otto Frisch rushed to Copenhagen, Denmark, where the celebrated physicist Niels Bohr was boarding a ship for America."

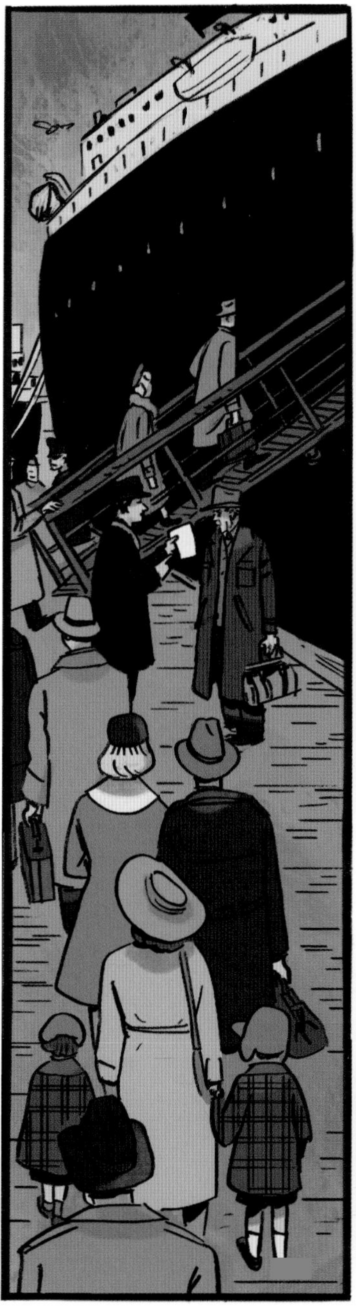

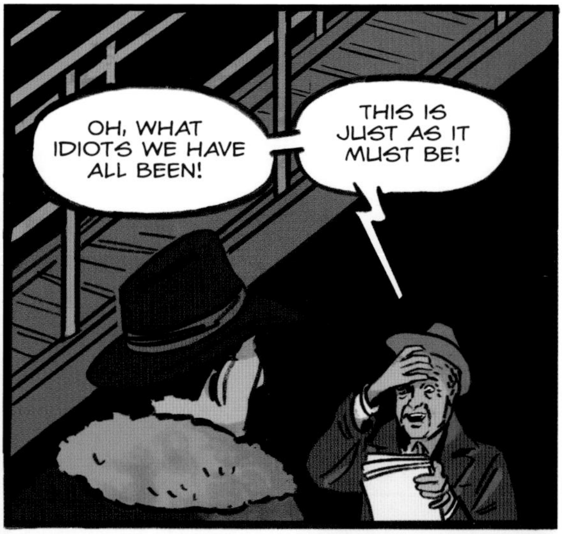
OH, WHAT IDIOTS WE HAVE ALL BEEN!
THIS IS JUST AS IT MUST BE!

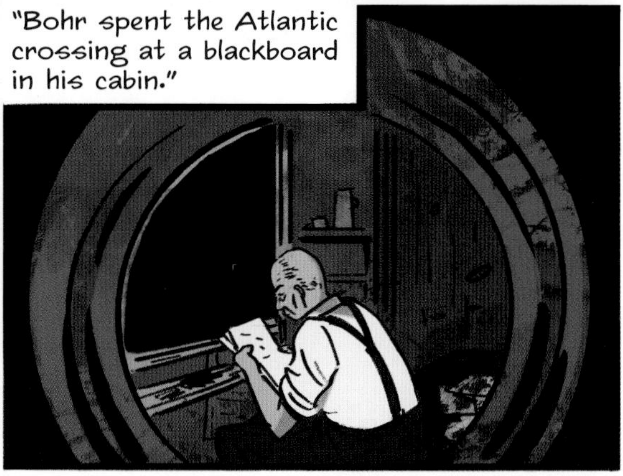
"Bohr spent the Atlantic crossing at a blackboard in his cabin."

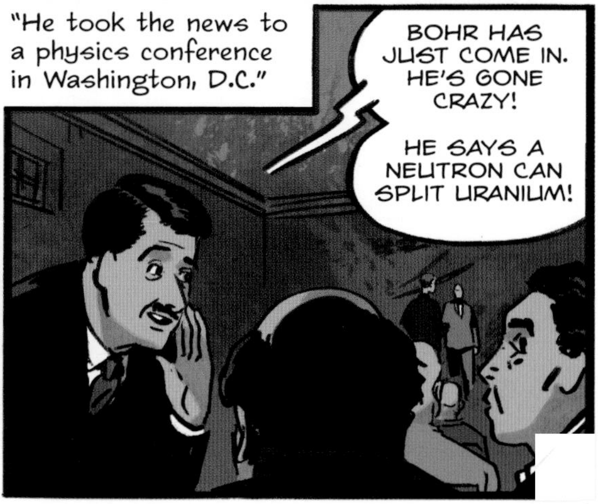
BOHR HAS JUST COME IN. HE'S GONE CRAZY!
HE SAYS A NEUTRON CAN SPLIT URANIUM!
"He took the news to a physics conference in Washington, D.C."

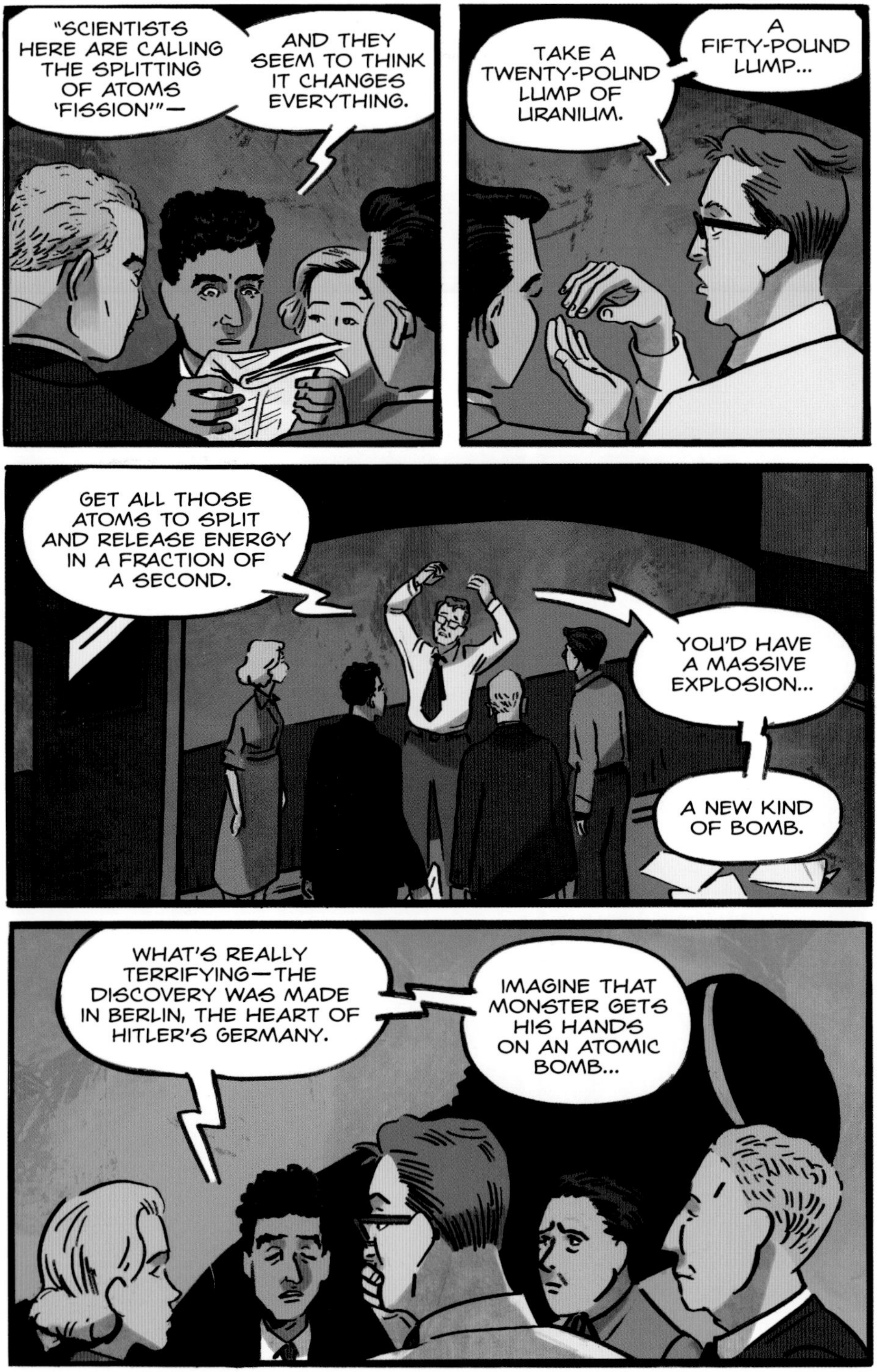
"SCIENTISTS HERE ARE CALLING THE SPLITTING OF ATOMS 'FISSION'"—
AND THEY SEEM TO THINK IT CHANGES EVERYTHING.
TAKE A TWENTY-POUND LUMP OF URANIUM.
A FIFTY-POUND LUMP...
GET ALL THOSE ATOMS TO SPLIT AND RELEASE ENERGY IN A FRACTION OF A SECOND.
YOU'D HAVE A MASSIVE EXPLOSION...
A NEW KIND OF BOMB.
WHAT'S REALLY TERRIFYING—THE DISCOVERY WAS MADE IN BERLIN, THE HEART OF HITLER'S GERMANY.
IMAGINE THAT MONSTER GETS HIS HANDS ON AN ATOMIC BOMB...

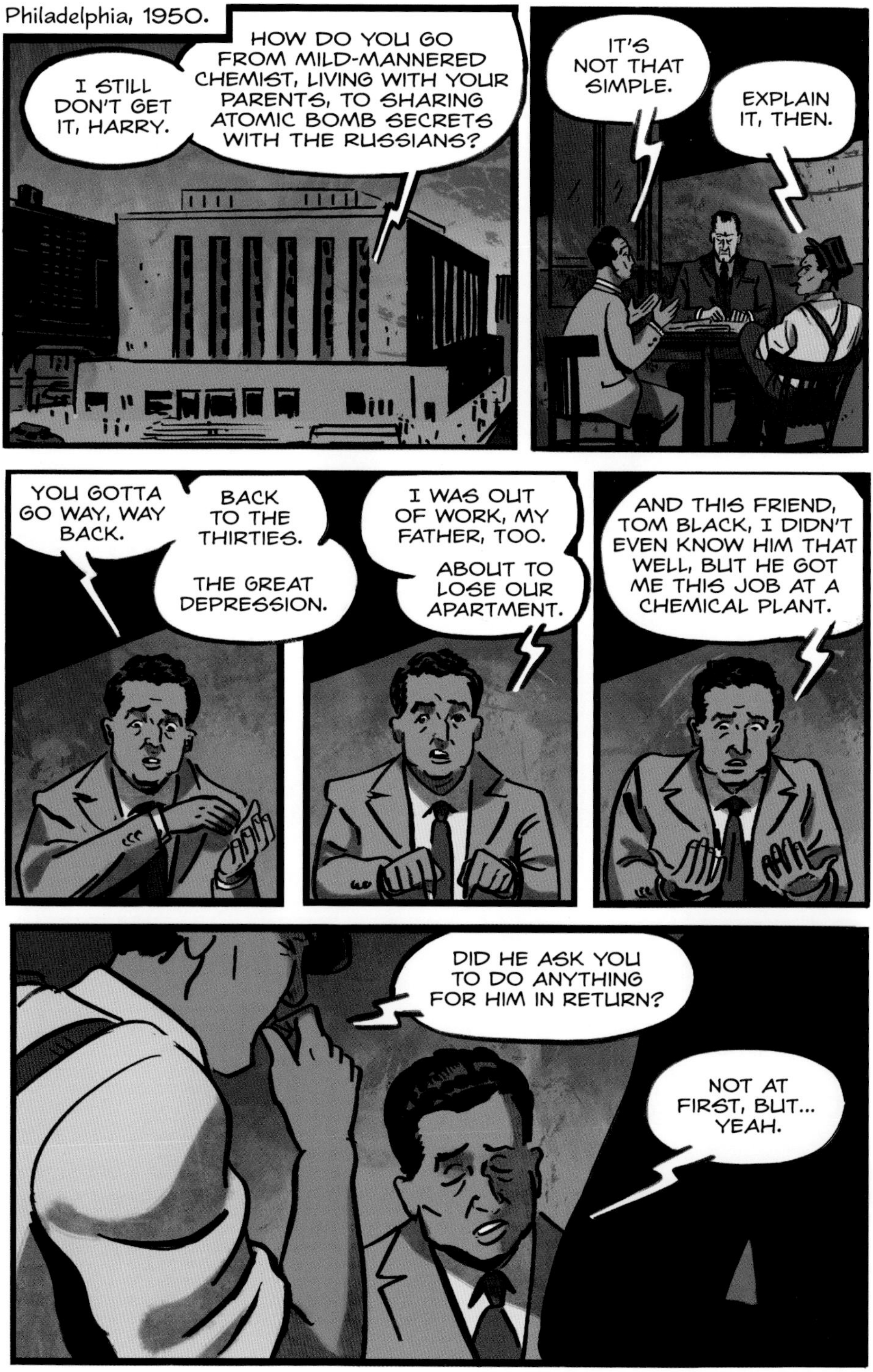
Philadelphia, 1950.
I STILL DON'T GET IT, HARRY.
HOW DO YOU GO FROM MILD-MANNERED CHEMIST, LIVING WITH YOUR PARENTS, TO SHARING ATOMIC BOMB SECRETS WITH THE RUSSIANS?
IT'S NOT THAT SIMPLE.
EXPLAIN IT, THEN.
YOU GOTTA GO WAY, WAY BACK.
BACK TO THE THIRTIES.
THE GREAT DEPRESSION.
I WAS OUT OF WORK, MY FATHER, TOO.
ABOUT TO LOSE OUR APARTMENT.
AND THIS FRIEND, TOM BLACK, I DIDN'T EVEN KNOW HIM THAT WELL, BUT HE GOT ME THIS JOB AT A CHEMICAL PLANT.
DID HE ASK YOU TO DO ANYTHING FOR HIM IN RETURN?
NOT AT FIRST, BUT... YEAH.

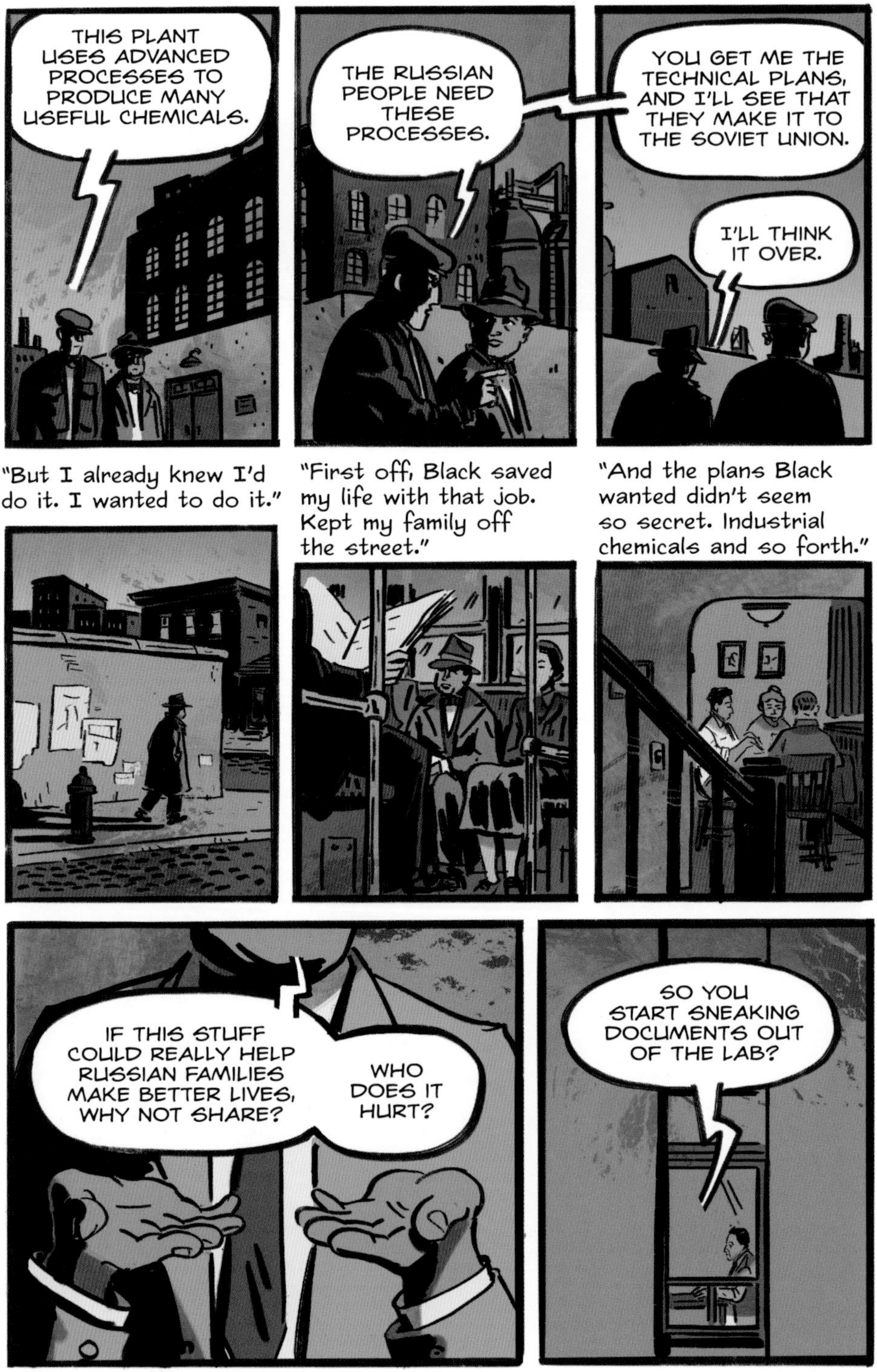
THIS PLANT USES ADVANCED PROCESSES TO PRODUCE MANY USEFUL CHEMICALS.
THE RUSSIAN PEOPLE NEED THESE PROCESSES.
YOU GET ME THE TECHNICAL PLANS, AND I'LL SEE THAT THEY MAKE IT TO THE SOVIET UNION.
I'LL THINK IT OVER.
"But I already knew I'd do it. I wanted to do it."
"First off, Black saved my life with that job. Kept my family off the street."
"And the plans Black wanted didn't seem so secret. Industrial chemicals and so forth."
IF THIS STUFF COULD REALLY HELP RUSSIAN FAMILIES MAKE BETTER LIVES, WHY NOT SHARE?
WHO DOES IT HURT?
SO YOU START SNEAKING DOCUMENTS OUT OF THE LAB?

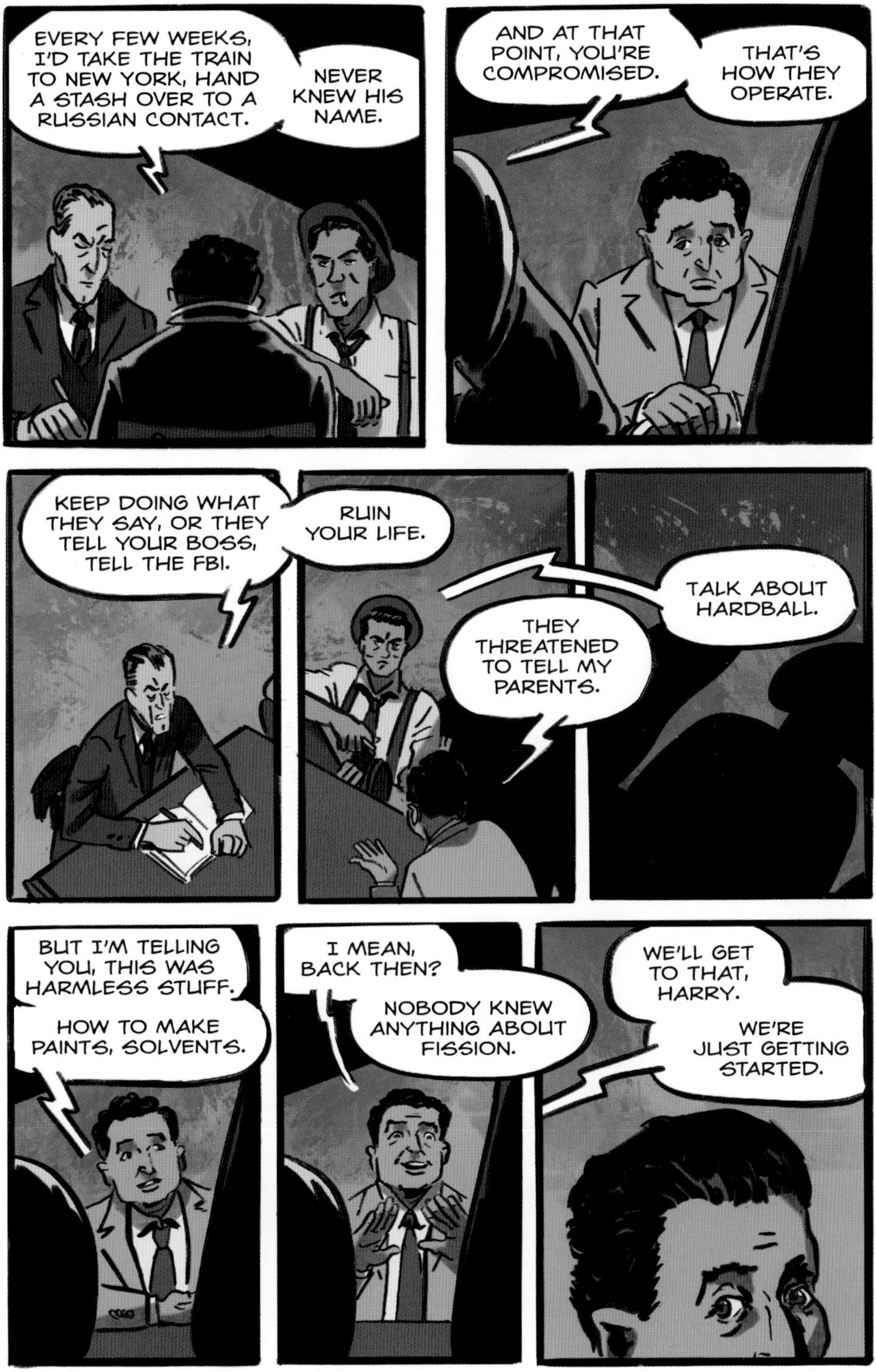
EVERY FEW WEEKS, I'D TAKE THE TRAIN TO NEW YORK, HAND A STASH OVER TO A RUSSIAN CONTACT.
NEVER KNEW HIS NAME.
AND AT THAT POINT, YOU'RE COMPROMISED.
THAT'S HOW THEY OPERATE.
KEEP DOING WHAT THEY SAY, OR THEY TELL YOUR BOSS, TELL THE FBI.
RUIN YOUR LIFE.
THEY THREATENED TO TELL MY PARENTS.
TALK ABOUT HARDBALL.
BUT I'M TELLING YOU, THIS WAS HARMLESS STUFF.
HOW TO MAKE PAINTS, SOLVENTS.
I MEAN, BACK THEN?
NOBODY KNEW ANYTHING ABOUT FISSION.
WE'LL GET TO THAT, HARRY.
WE'RE JUST GETTING STARTED.

Harry Gold was right again.

Not even the president of the United States knew of the discovery of fission.

Hungarian-born physicists Eugene Wigner and Leo Szilard were determined to change that.

Long Island, New York. July 16, 1939.

Step one of their plan: find the world's most famous scientist.

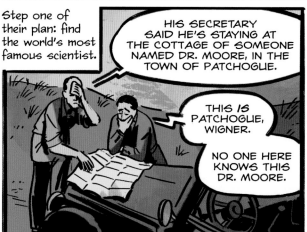

HIS SECRETARY SAID HE'S STAYING AT THE COTTAGE OF SOMEONE NAMED DR. MOORE, IN THE TOWN OF PATCHOGUE.

THIS *IS* PATCHOGUE, WIGNER.

NO ONE HERE KNOWS THIS DR. MOORE.

IT MIGHT HAVE BEEN PECONIC.

WHAT?!

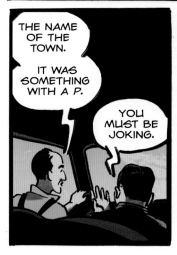

THE NAME OF THE TOWN.

IT WAS SOMETHING WITH A *P*.

YOU MUST BE JOKING.

LET'S GO HOME.

PERHAPS FATE NEVER INTENDED IT.

BUT IT'S OUR DUTY TO TAKE THIS STEP, SZILARD.

OUR CONTRIBUTION TO THE PREVENTION OF A TERRIBLE CALAMITY.

PULL OVER!

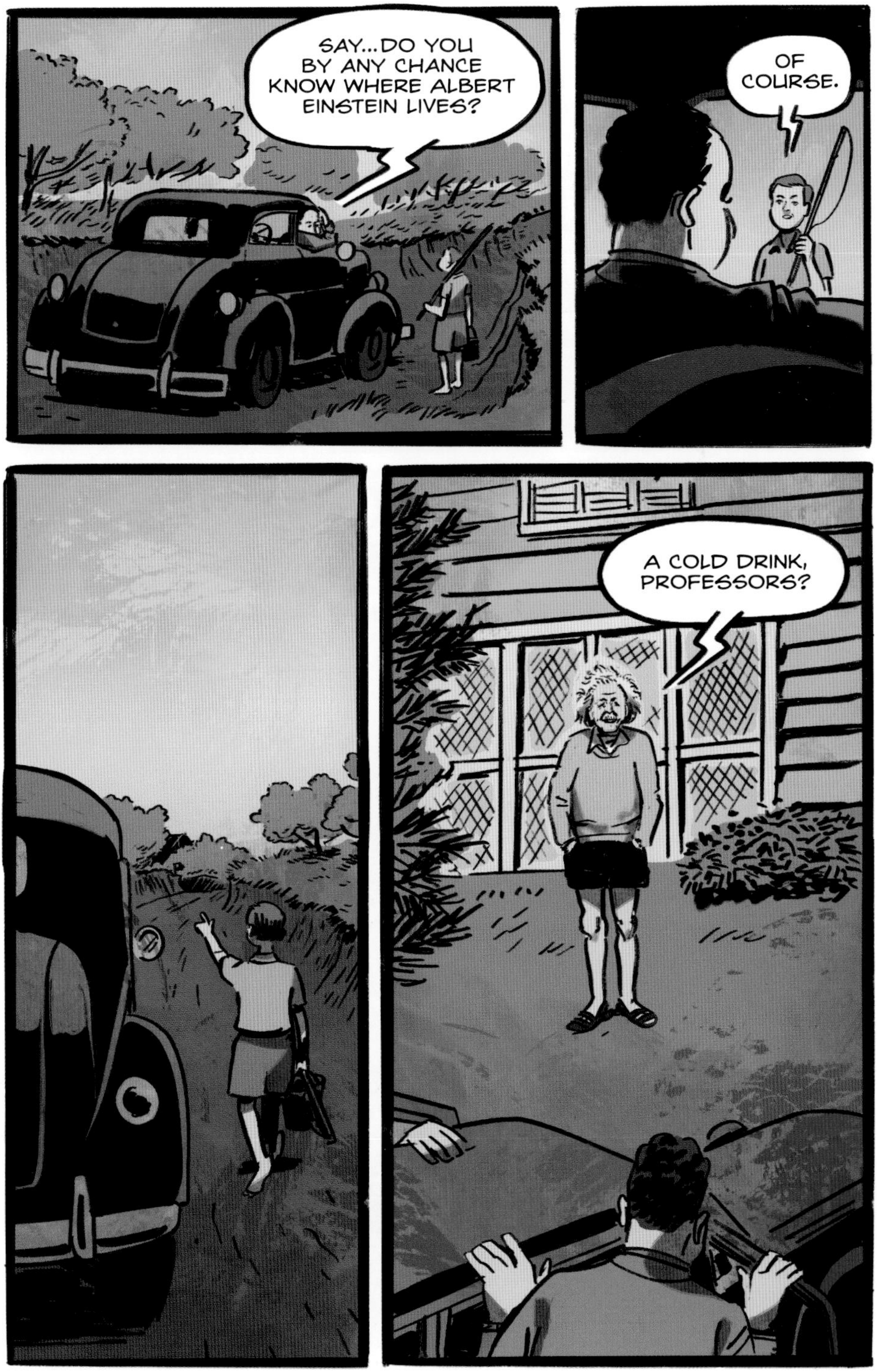
SAY...DO YOU BY ANY CHANCE KNOW WHERE ALBERT EINSTEIN LIVES?
OF COURSE.
A COLD DRINK, PROFESSORS?

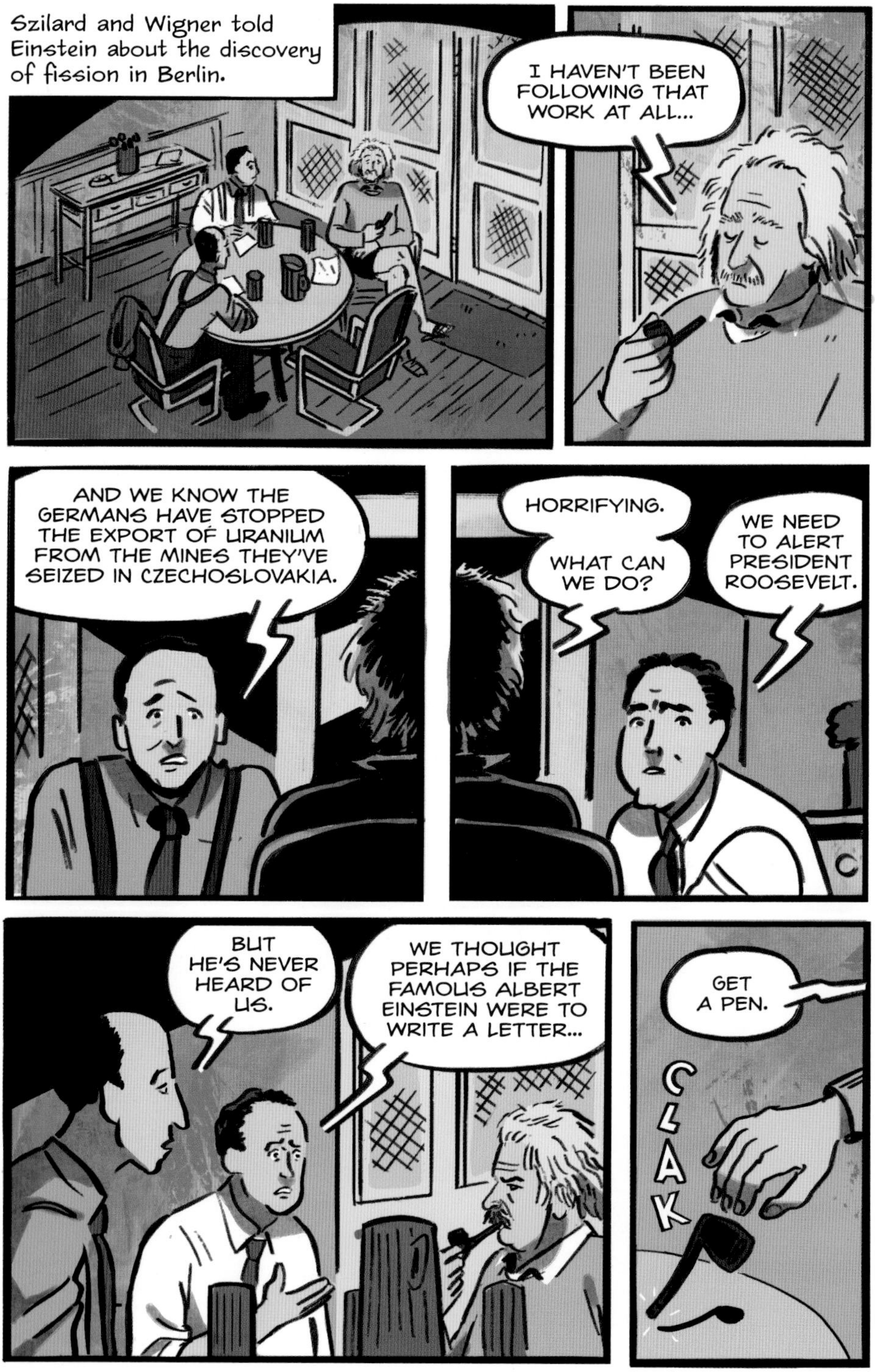
Szilard and Wigner told Einstein about the discovery of fission in Berlin.
I HAVEN'T BEEN FOLLOWING THAT WORK AT ALL...
AND WE KNOW THE GERMANS HAVE STOPPED THE EXPORT OF URANIUM FROM THE MINES THEY'VE SEIZED IN CZECHOSLOVAKIA.
HORRIFYING.
WHAT CAN WE DO?
WE NEED TO ALERT PRESIDENT ROOSEVELT.
BUT HE'S NEVER HEARD OF US.
WE THOUGHT PERHAPS IF THE FAMOUS ALBERT EINSTEIN WERE TO WRITE A LETTER...
GET A PEN.
CLAK

Six weeks later, Germany ignited World War II with a massive invasion of Poland.

Britain and France had promised to protect Poland. They declared war on Germany.

This did nothing to stop the German charge.

Hitler's troops poured into the Polish capital, Warsaw.

It was a hectic time at the White House, in Washington, D.C.

In early October, U.S. President Franklin D. Roosevelt finally had a moment to read Einstein's letter.

"...IT MAY BECOME POSSIBLE TO SET UP A NUCLEAR CHAIN REACTION IN A LARGE MASS OF URANIUM, BY WHICH VAST AMOUNTS OF POWER WOULD BE GENERATED."

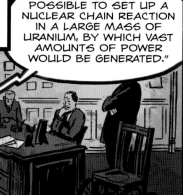

"IT IS CONCEIVABLE, THOUGH NOT CERTAIN, THAT THIS NEW PHENOMENON COULD LEAD TO THE CONSTRUCTION OF EXTREMELY POWERFUL BOMBS."

THIS REQUIRES ACTION!

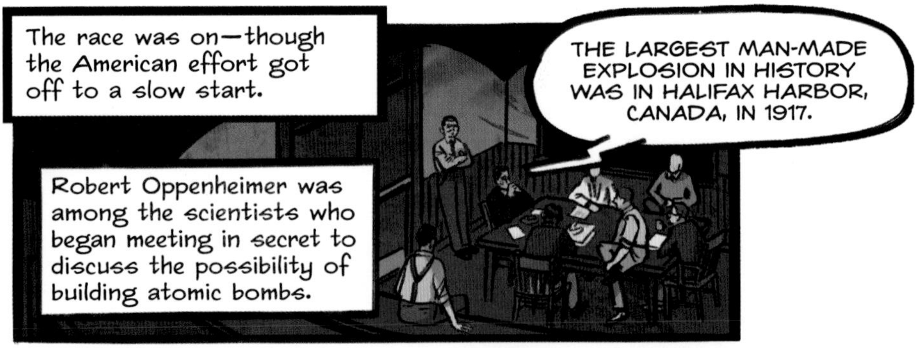
The race was on—though the American effort got off to a slow start.
THE LARGEST MAN-MADE EXPLOSION IN HISTORY WAS IN HALIFAX HARBOR, CANADA, IN 1917.
Robert Oppenheimer was among the scientists who began meeting in secret to discuss the possibility of building atomic bombs.

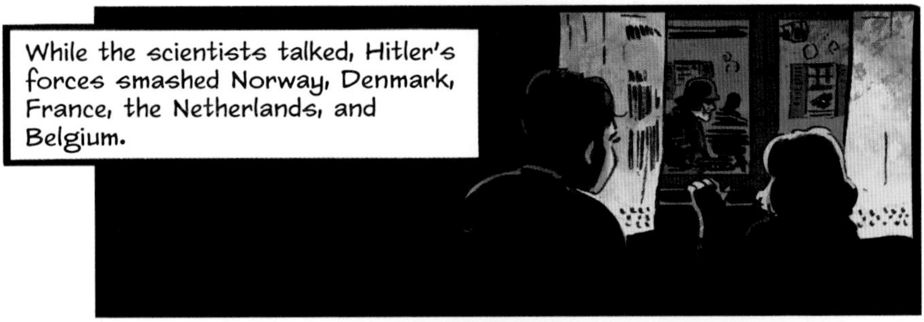
While the scientists talked, Hitler's forces smashed Norway, Denmark, France, the Netherlands, and Belgium.

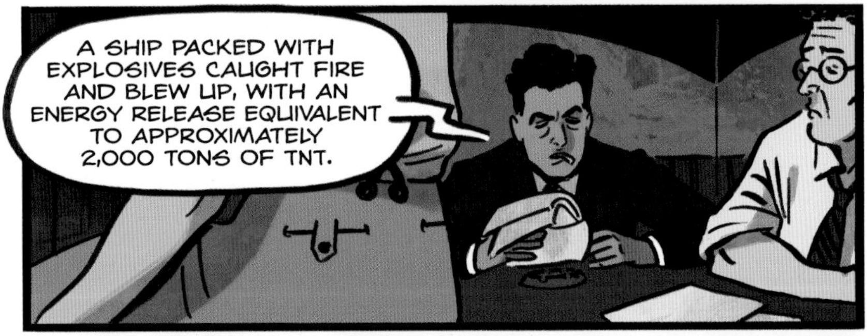
A SHIP PACKED WITH EXPLOSIVES CAUGHT FIRE AND BLEW UP, WITH AN ENERGY RELEASE EQUIVALENT TO APPROXIMATELY 2,000 TONS OF TNT.

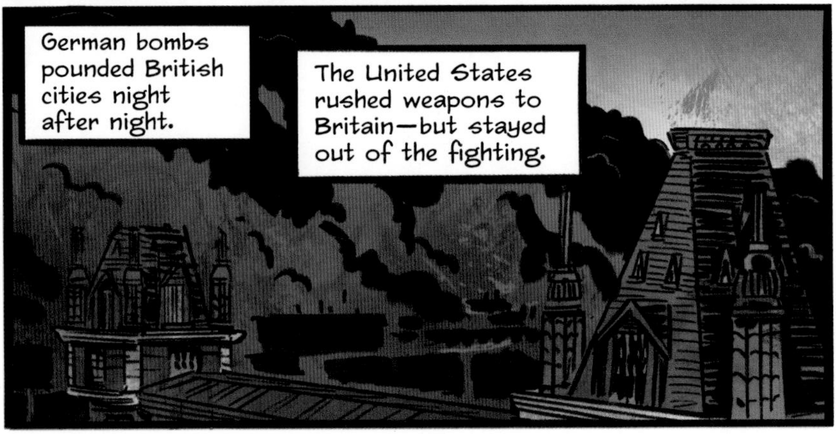
German bombs pounded British cities night after night.
The United States rushed weapons to Britain—but stayed out of the fighting.

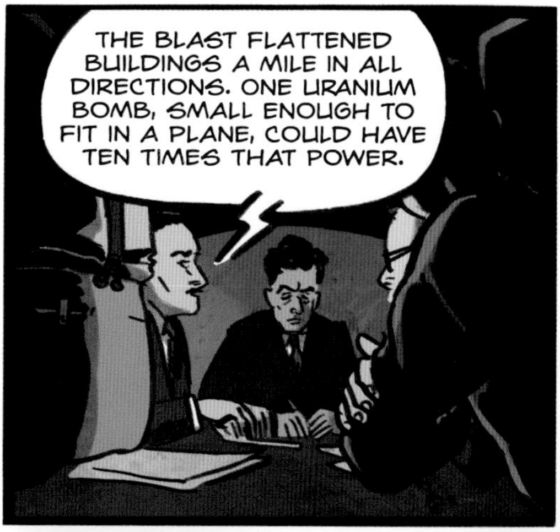
THE BLAST FLATTENED BUILDINGS A MILE IN ALL DIRECTIONS. ONE URANIUM BOMB, SMALL ENOUGH TO FIT IN A PLANE, COULD HAVE TEN TIMES THAT POWER.

In June 1941, Hitler launched a four-million-man invasion force across the Soviet border, driving deep into Russian territory.

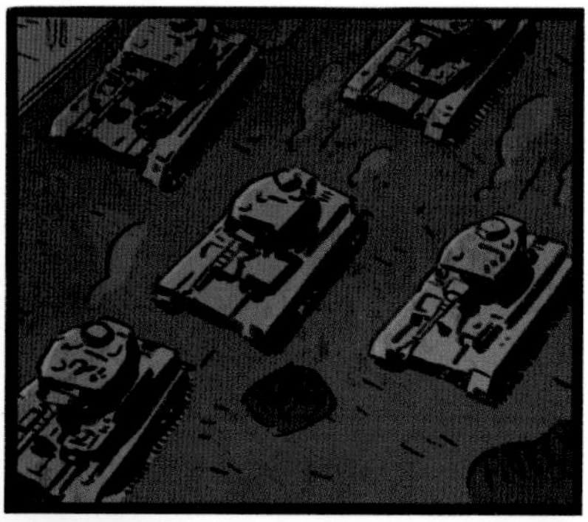

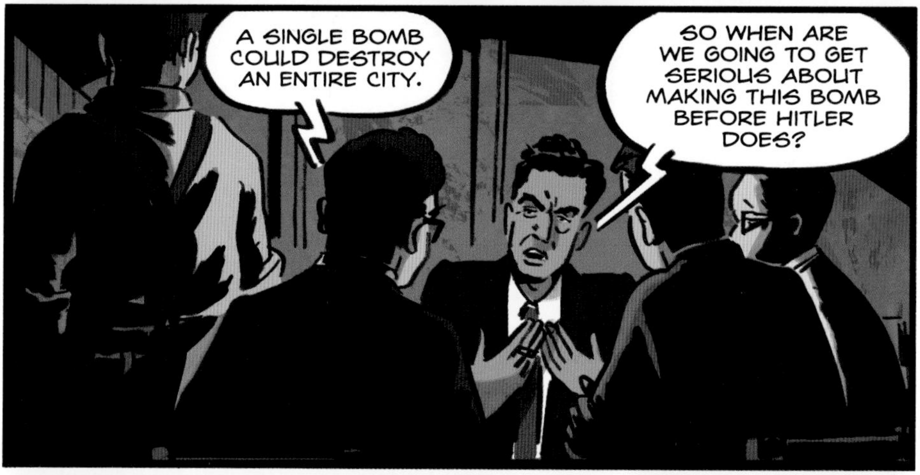
A SINGLE BOMB COULD DESTROY AN ENTIRE CITY.
SO WHEN ARE WE GOING TO GET SERIOUS ABOUT MAKING THIS BOMB BEFORE HITLER DOES?

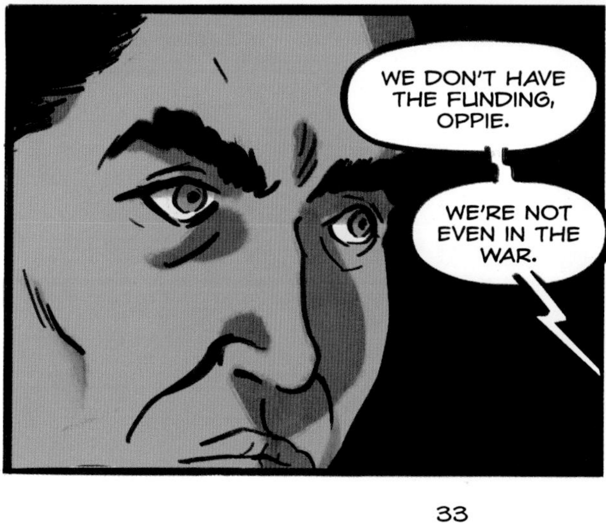
WE DON'T HAVE THE FUNDING, OPPIE.
WE'RE NOT EVEN IN THE WAR.

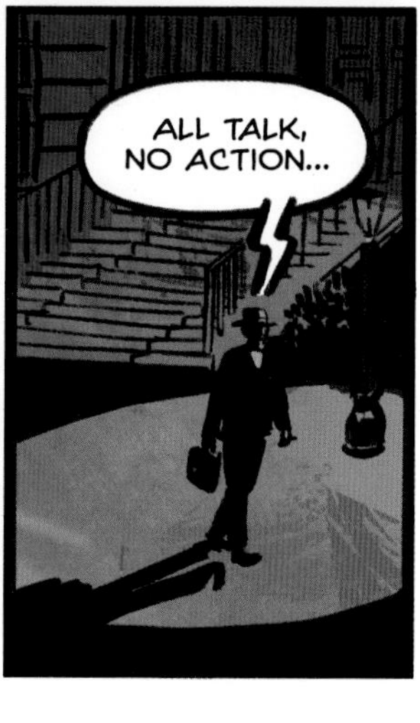
ALL TALK, NO ACTION...

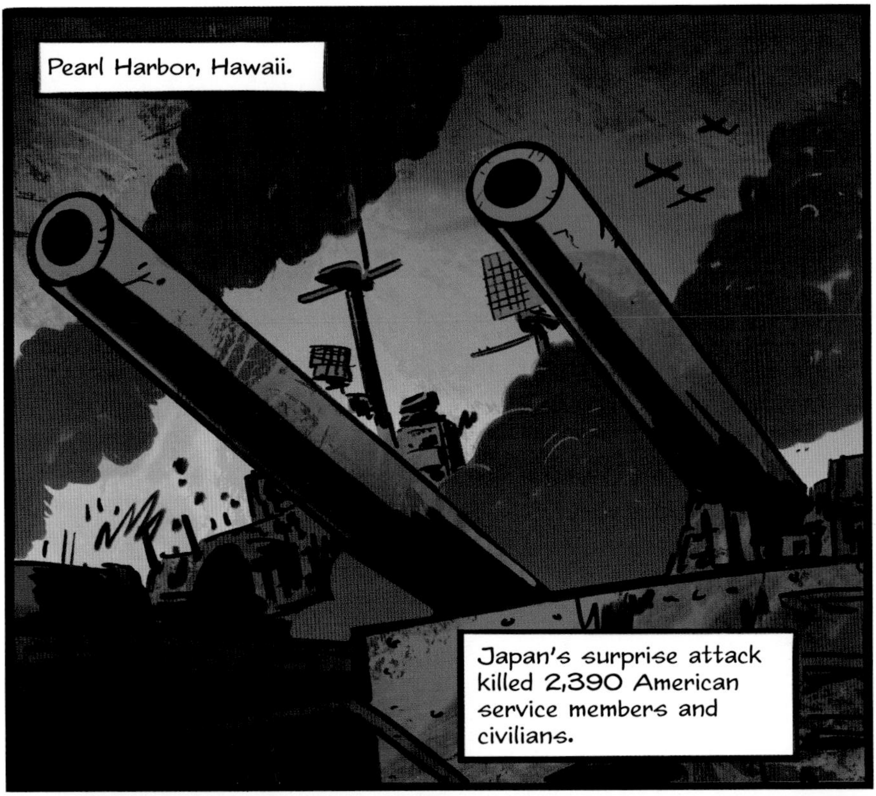
Pearl Harbor, Hawaii.
Japan's surprise attack killed 2,390 American service members and civilians.

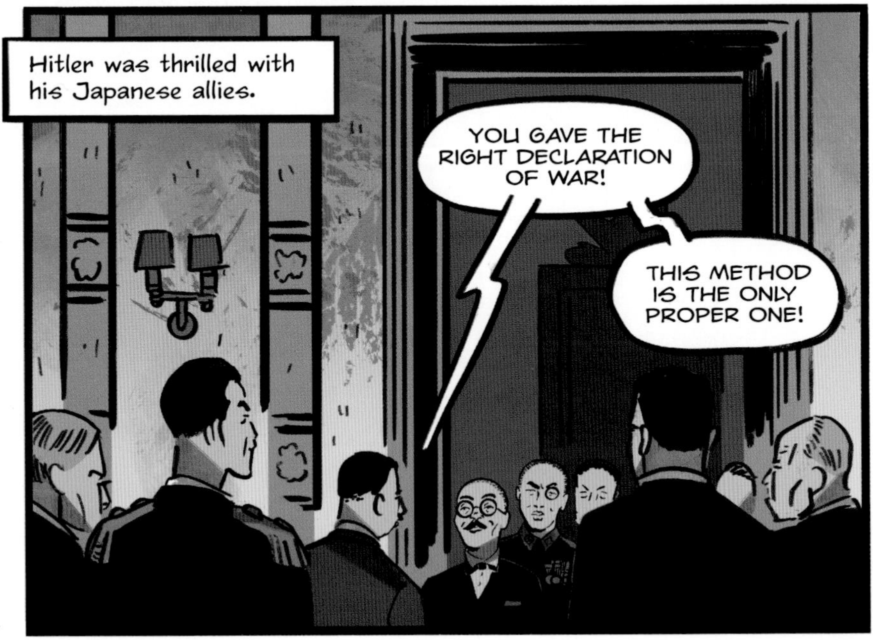
Hitler was thrilled with his Japanese allies.
YOU GAVE THE RIGHT DECLARATION OF WAR!
THIS METHOD IS THE ONLY PROPER ONE!

President Roosevelt addressed Congress the next day.

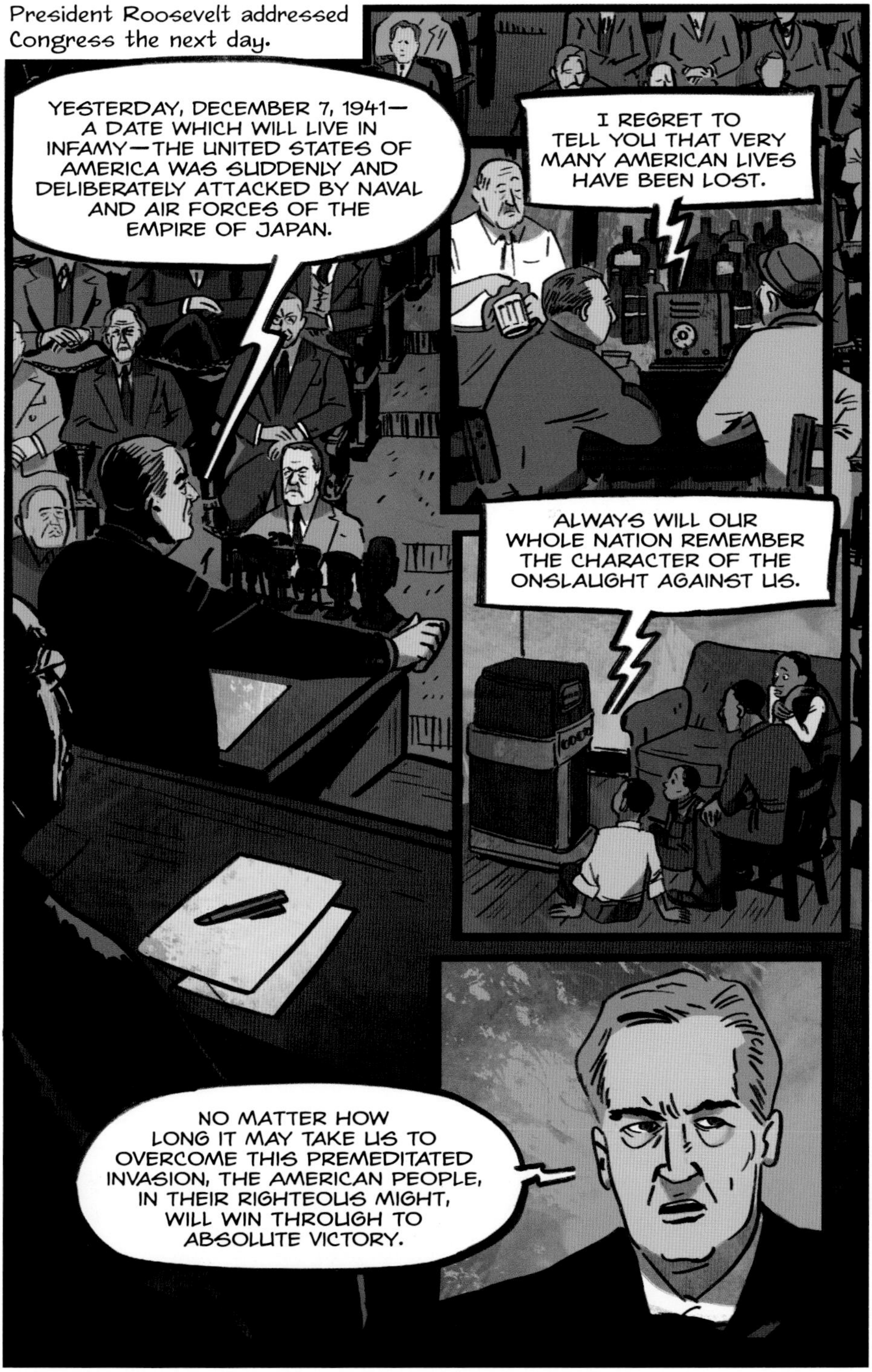

YESTERDAY, DECEMBER 7, 1941—A DATE WHICH WILL LIVE IN INFAMY—THE UNITED STATES OF AMERICA WAS SUDDENLY AND DELIBERATELY ATTACKED BY NAVAL AND AIR FORCES OF THE EMPIRE OF JAPAN.
I REGRET TO TELL YOU THAT VERY MANY AMERICAN LIVES HAVE BEEN LOST.
ALWAYS WILL OUR WHOLE NATION REMEMBER THE CHARACTER OF THE ONSLAUGHT AGAINST US.
NO MATTER HOW LONG IT MAY TAKE US TO OVERCOME THIS PREMEDITATED INVASION, THE AMERICAN PEOPLE, IN THEIR RIGHTEOUS MIGHT, WILL WIN THROUGH TO ABSOLUTE VICTORY.

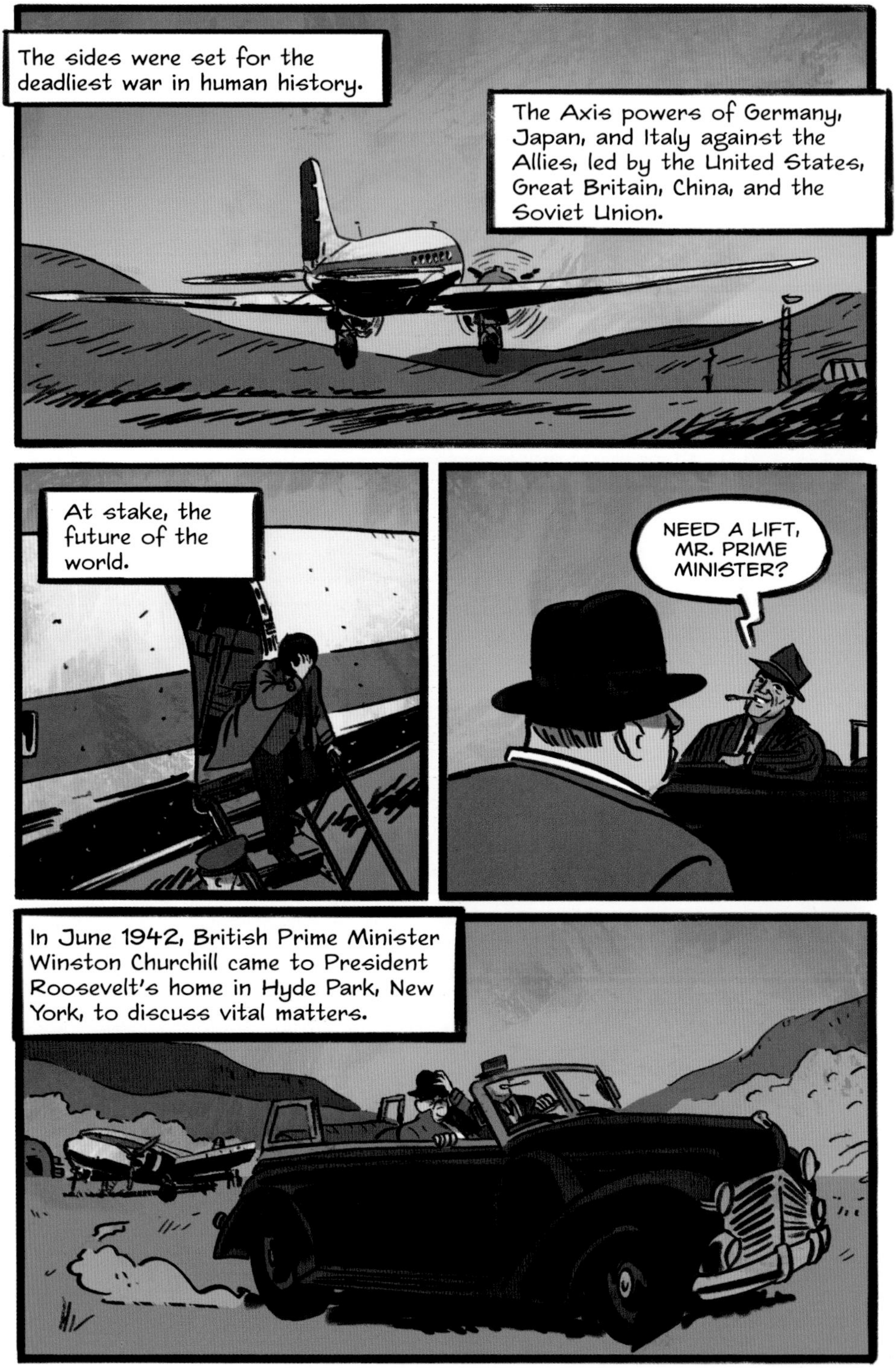
The sides were set for the deadliest war in human history.
The Axis powers of Germany, Japan, and Italy against the Allies, led by the United States, Great Britain, China, and the Soviet Union.
At stake, the future of the world.
NEED A LIFT, MR. PRIME MINISTER?
In June 1942, British Prime Minister Winston Churchill came to President Roosevelt's home in Hyde Park, New York, to discuss vital matters.

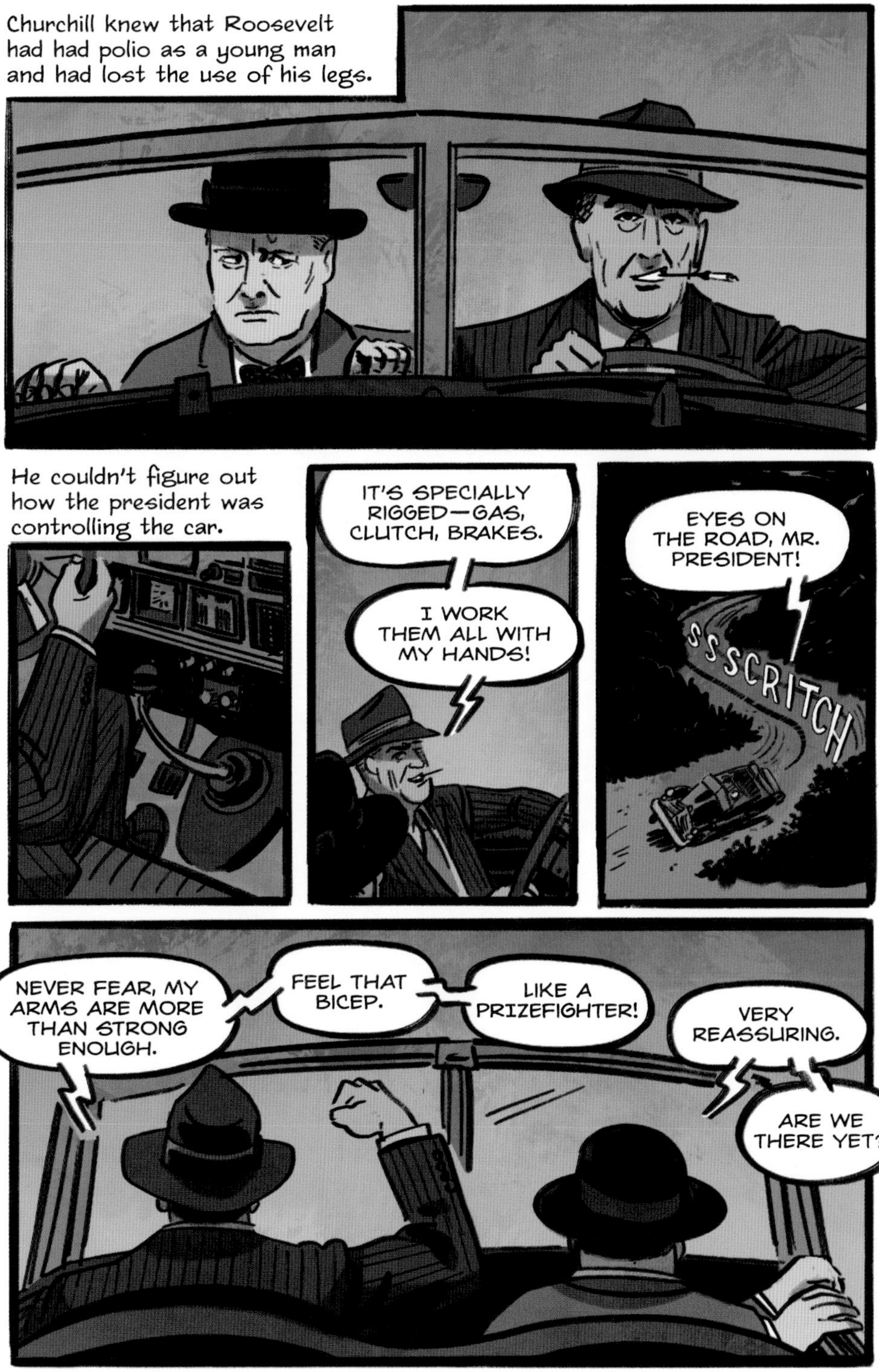
Churchill knew that Roosevelt had had polio as a young man and had lost the use of his legs.
He couldn't figure out how the president was controlling the car.
IT'S SPECIALLY RIGGED—GAS, CLUTCH, BRAKES.
I WORK THEM ALL WITH MY HANDS!
EYES ON THE ROAD, MR. PRESIDENT!
SSSCRITCH
NEVER FEAR, MY ARMS ARE MORE THAN STRONG ENOUGH.
FEEL THAT BICEP.
LIKE A PRIZEFIGHTER!
VERY REASSURING.
ARE WE THERE YET?

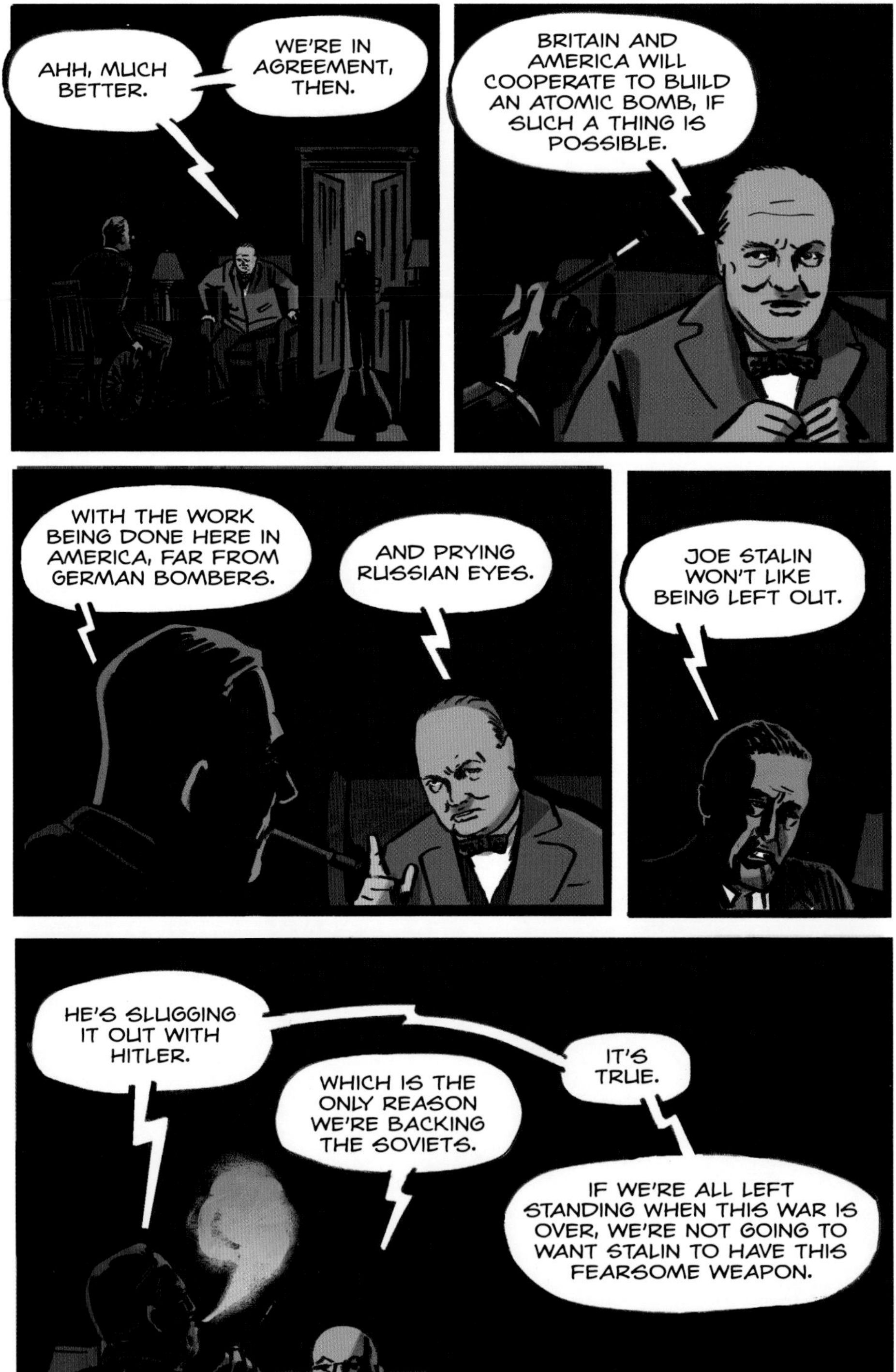

AHH, MUCH BETTER.
WE'RE IN AGREEMENT, THEN.
BRITAIN AND AMERICA WILL COOPERATE TO BUILD AN ATOMIC BOMB, IF SUCH A THING IS POSSIBLE.
WITH THE WORK BEING DONE HERE IN AMERICA, FAR FROM GERMAN BOMBERS.
AND PRYING RUSSIAN EYES.
JOE STALIN WON'T LIKE BEING LEFT OUT.
HE'S SLUGGING IT OUT WITH HITLER.
WHICH IS THE ONLY REASON WE'RE BACKING THE SOVIETS.
IT'S TRUE.
IF WE'RE ALL LEFT STANDING WHEN THIS WAR IS OVER, WE'RE NOT GOING TO WANT STALIN TO HAVE THIS FEARSOME WEAPON.

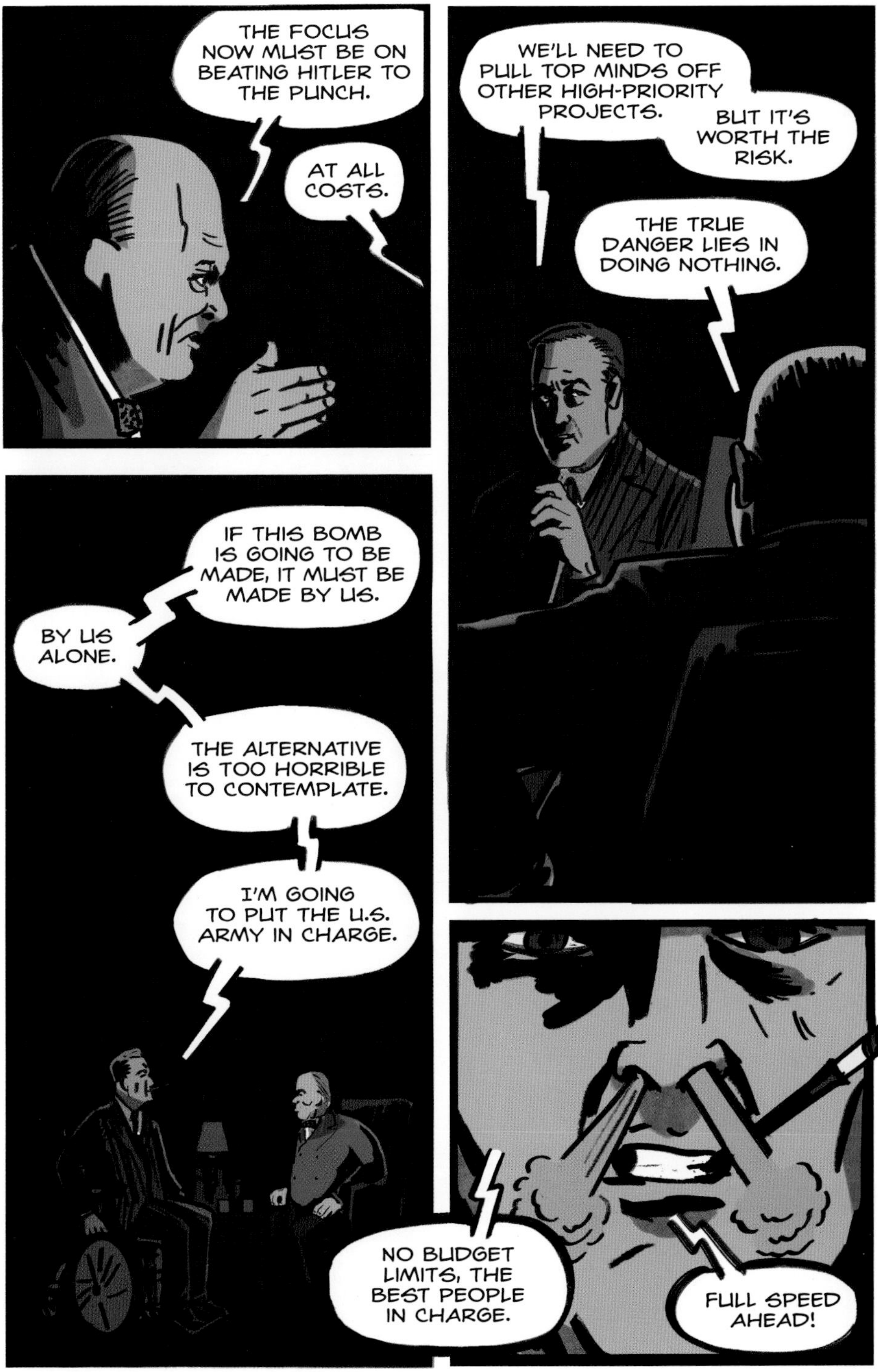
THE FOCUS NOW MUST BE ON BEATING HITLER TO THE PUNCH.
AT ALL COSTS.
WE'LL NEED TO PULL TOP MINDS OFF OTHER HIGH-PRIORITY PROJECTS.
BUT IT'S WORTH THE RISK.
THE TRUE DANGER LIES IN DOING NOTHING.
IF THIS BOMB IS GOING TO BE MADE, IT MUST BE MADE BY US.
BY US ALONE.
THE ALTERNATIVE IS TOO HORRIBLE TO CONTEMPLATE.
I'M GOING TO PUT THE U.S. ARMY IN CHARGE.
NO BUDGET LIMITS, THE BEST PEOPLE IN CHARGE.
FULL SPEED AHEAD!

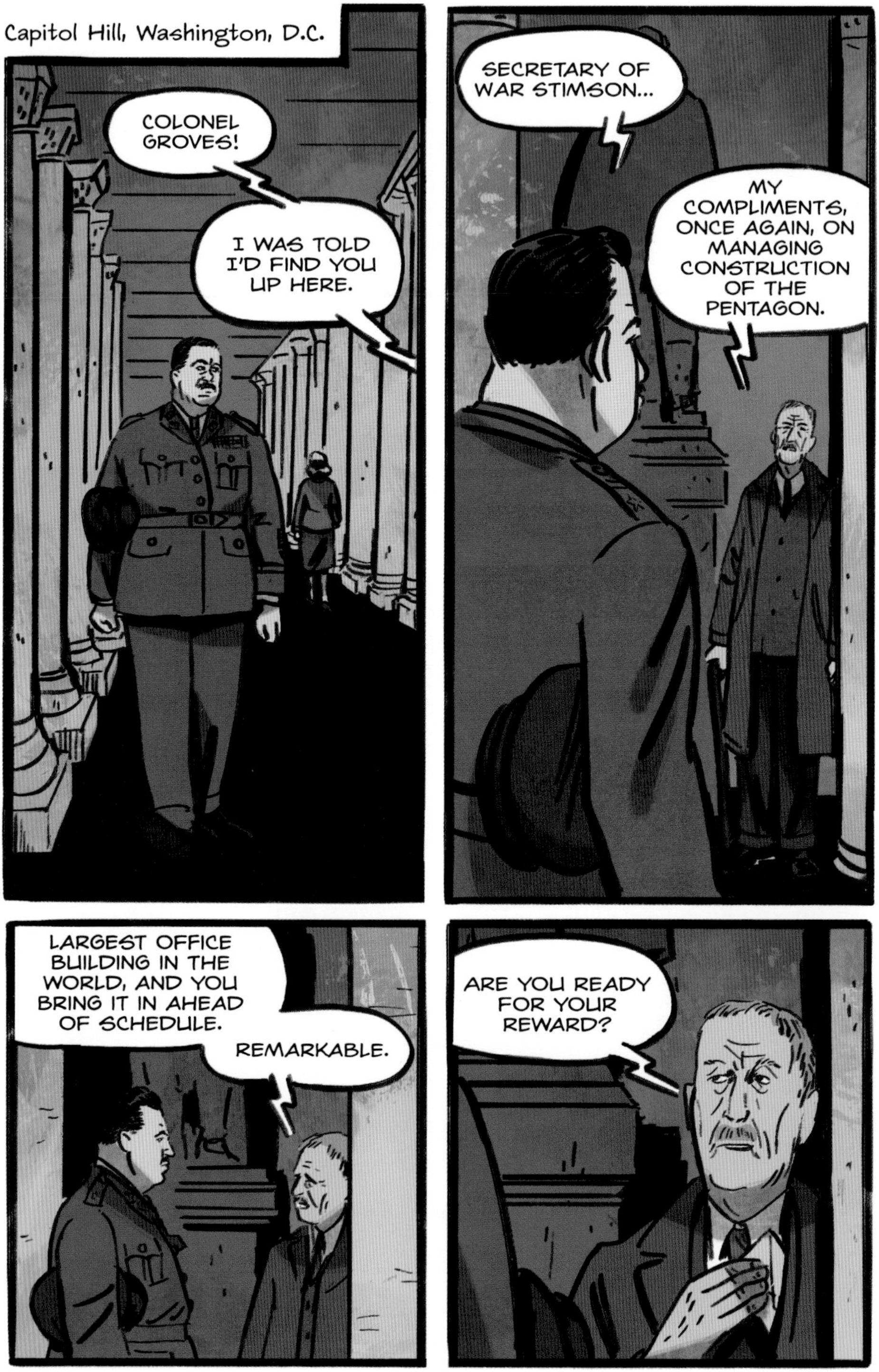
Capitol Hill, Washington, D.C.
COLONEL GROVES!
I WAS TOLD I'D FIND YOU UP HERE.
SECRETARY OF WAR STIMSON...
MY COMPLIMENTS, ONCE AGAIN, ON MANAGING CONSTRUCTION OF THE PENTAGON.
LARGEST OFFICE BUILDING IN THE WORLD, AND YOU BRING IT IN AHEAD OF SCHEDULE.
REMARKABLE.
ARE YOU READY FOR YOUR REWARD?

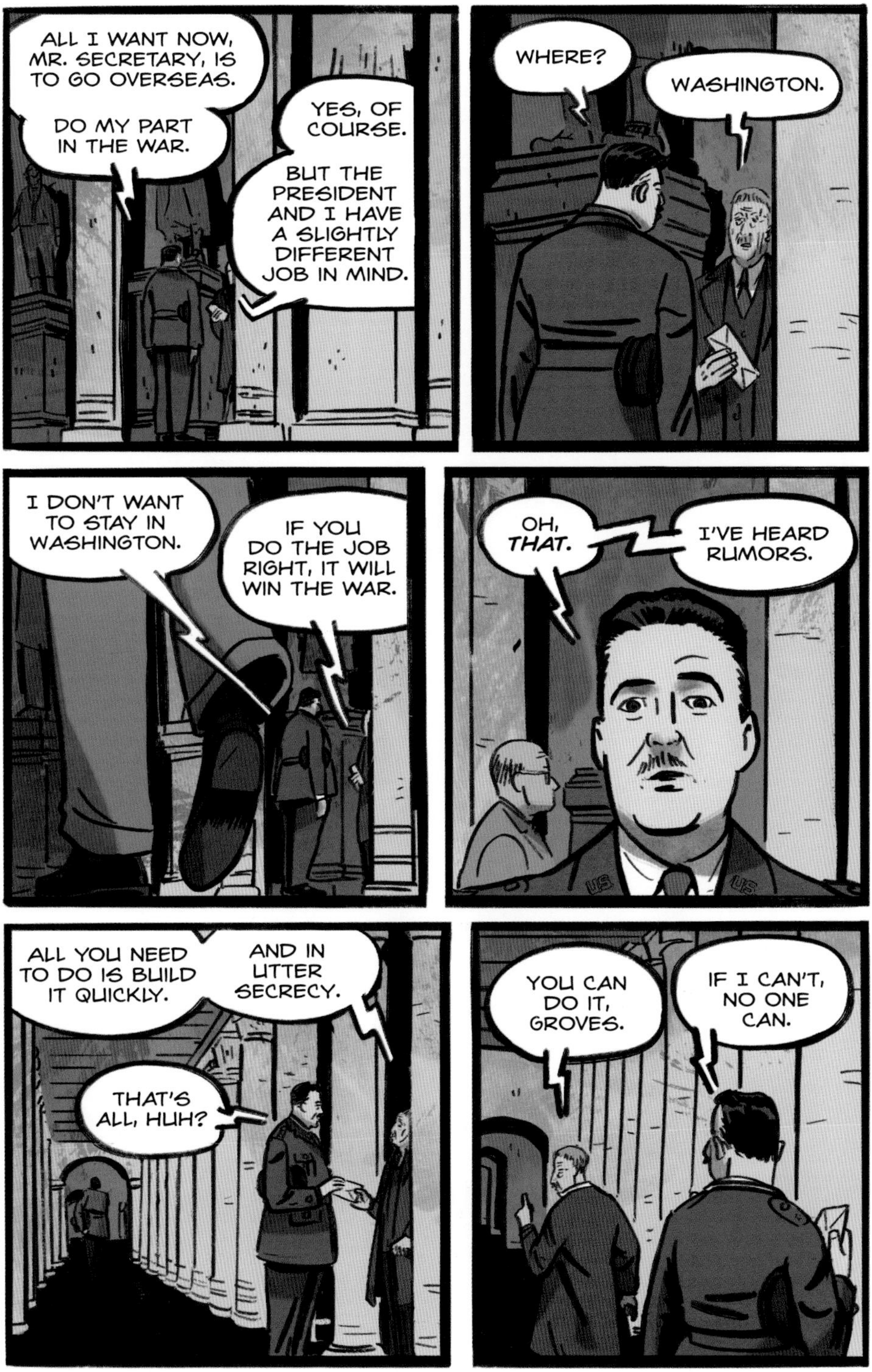

ALL I WANT NOW, MR. SECRETARY, IS TO GO OVERSEAS.
DO MY PART IN THE WAR.
YES, OF COURSE.
BUT THE PRESIDENT AND I HAVE A SLIGHTLY DIFFERENT JOB IN MIND.
WHERE?
WASHINGTON.
I DON'T WANT TO STAY IN WASHINGTON.
IF YOU DO THE JOB RIGHT, IT WILL WIN THE WAR.
OH, *THAT.*
I'VE HEARD RUMORS.
U.S.
U.S.
ALL YOU NEED TO DO IS BUILD IT QUICKLY.
AND IN UTTER SECRECY.
THAT'S ALL, HUH?
YOU CAN DO IT, GROVES.
IF I CAN'T, NO ONE CAN.

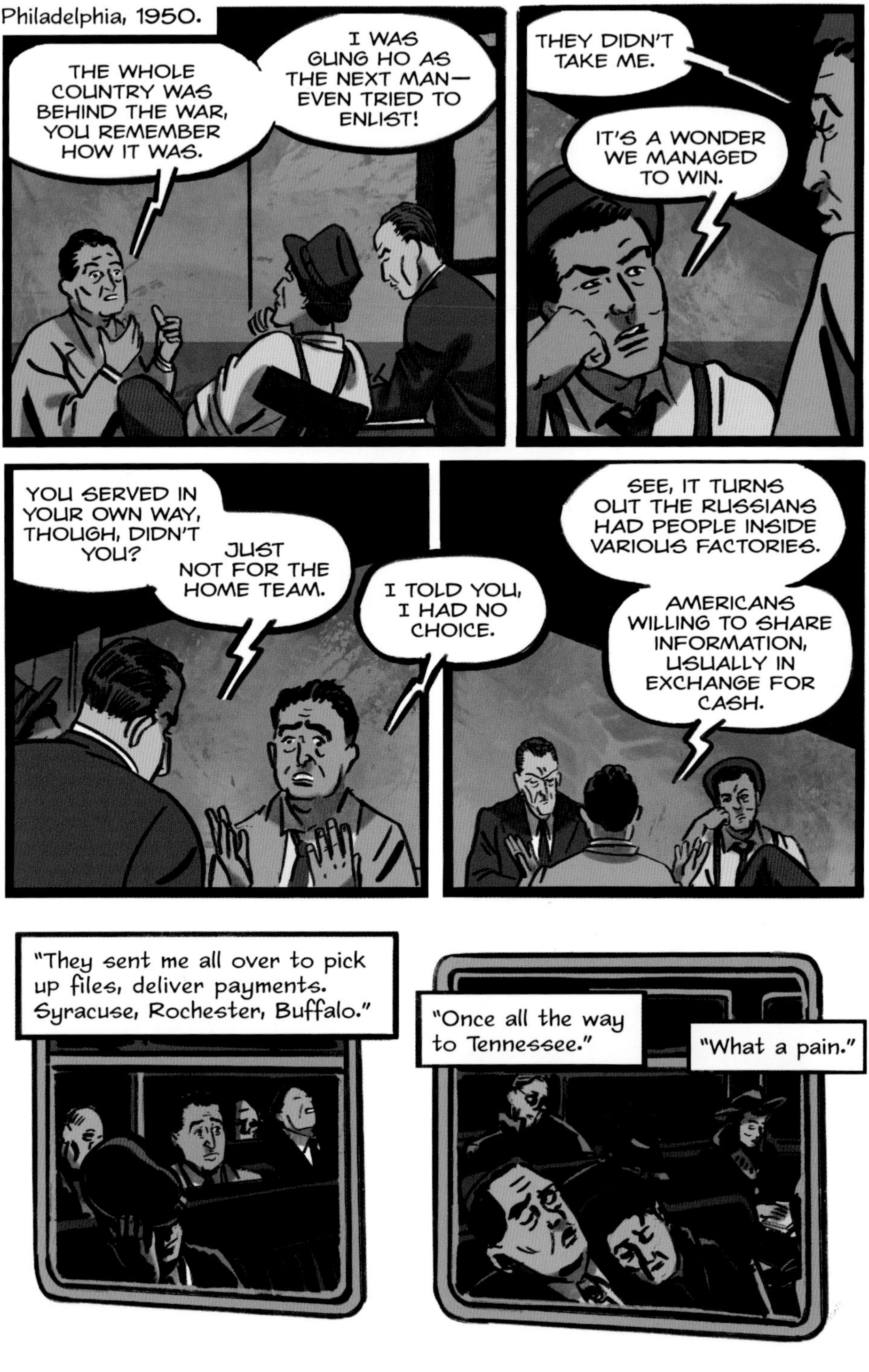
Philadelphia, 1950.
THE WHOLE COUNTRY WAS BEHIND THE WAR, YOU REMEMBER HOW IT WAS.
I WAS GUNG HO AS THE NEXT MAN— EVEN TRIED TO ENLIST!
THEY DIDN'T TAKE ME.
IT'S A WONDER WE MANAGED TO WIN.
YOU SERVED IN YOUR OWN WAY, THOUGH, DIDN'T YOU?
JUST NOT FOR THE HOME TEAM.
I TOLD YOU, I HAD NO CHOICE.
SEE, IT TURNS OUT THE RUSSIANS HAD PEOPLE INSIDE VARIOUS FACTORIES.
AMERICANS WILLING TO SHARE INFORMATION, USUALLY IN EXCHANGE FOR CASH.
"They sent me all over to pick up files, deliver payments. Syracuse, Rochester, Buffalo."
"Once all the way to Tennessee."
"What a pain."

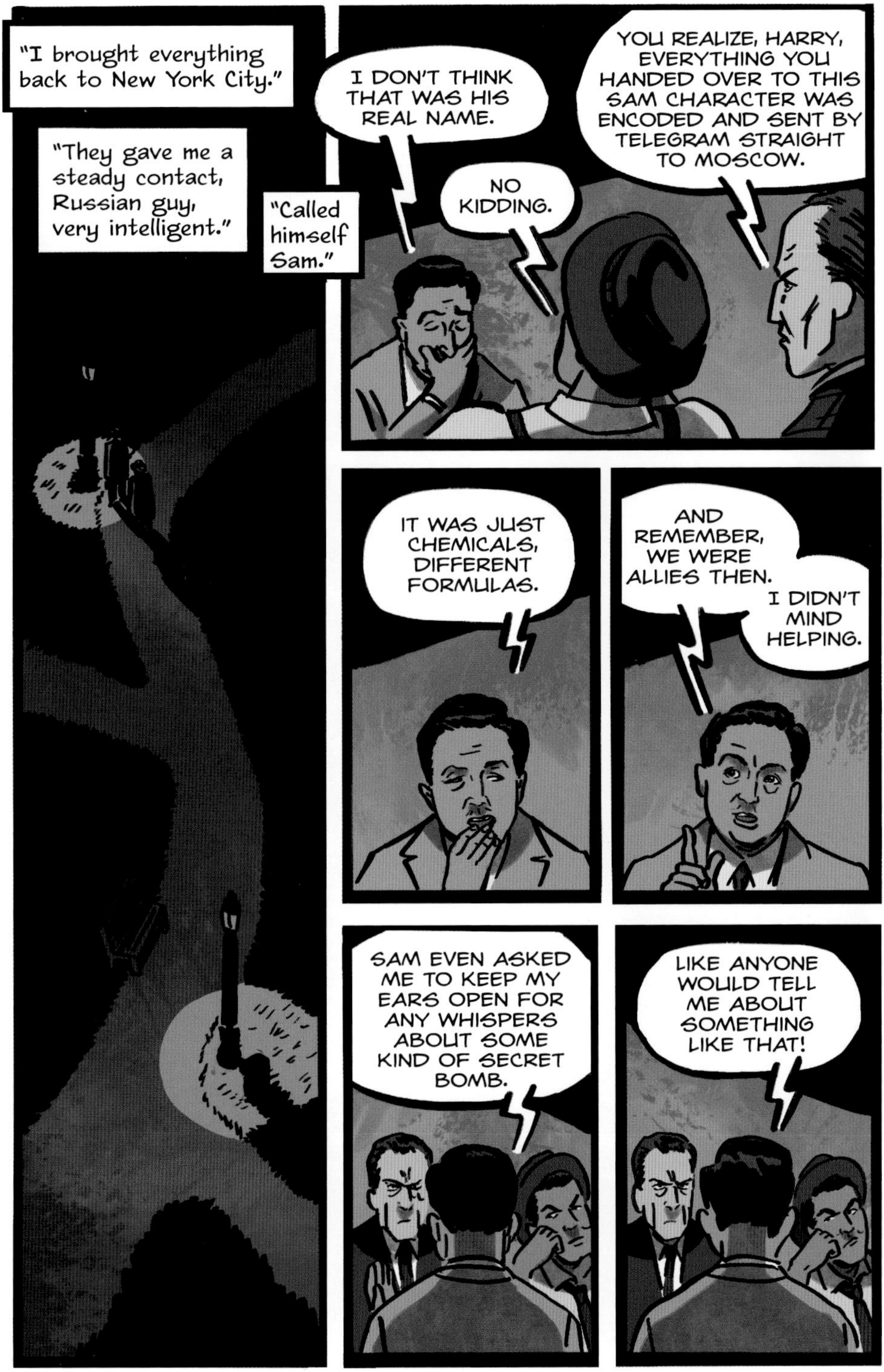
"I brought everything back to New York City."
"They gave me a steady contact, Russian guy, very intelligent."
"Called himself Sam."
I DON'T THINK THAT WAS HIS REAL NAME.
NO KIDDING.
YOU REALIZE, HARRY, EVERYTHING YOU HANDED OVER TO THIS SAM CHARACTER WAS ENCODED AND SENT BY TELEGRAM STRAIGHT TO MOSCOW.
IT WAS JUST CHEMICALS, DIFFERENT FORMULAS.
AND REMEMBER, WE WERE ALLIES THEN.
I DIDN'T MIND HELPING.
SAM EVEN ASKED ME TO KEEP MY EARS OPEN FOR ANY WHISPERS ABOUT SOME KIND OF SECRET BOMB.
LIKE ANYONE WOULD TELL ME ABOUT SOMETHING LIKE THAT!

Leslie Groves—now promoted to general—took command of the effort to build the atomic bomb, code-named the Manhattan Project.

I DON'T UNDERSTAND WHAT YOU PEOPLE HAVE BEEN UP TO!

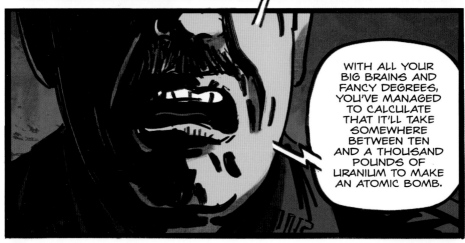

WITH ALL YOUR BIG BRAINS AND FANCY DEGREES, YOU'VE MANAGED TO CALCULATE THAT IT'LL TAKE SOMEWHERE BETWEEN TEN AND A THOUSAND POUNDS OF URANIUM TO MAKE AN ATOMIC BOMB.

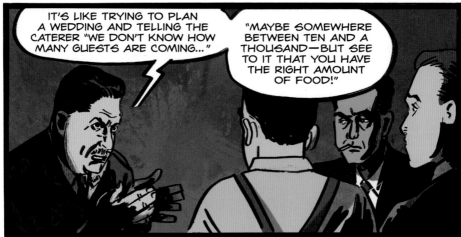

IT'S LIKE TRYING TO PLAN A WEDDING AND TELLING THE CATERER "WE DON'T KNOW HOW MANY GUESTS ARE COMING..."

"MAYBE SOMEWHERE BETWEEN TEN AND A THOUSAND—BUT SEE TO IT THAT YOU HAVE THE RIGHT AMOUNT OF FOOD!"

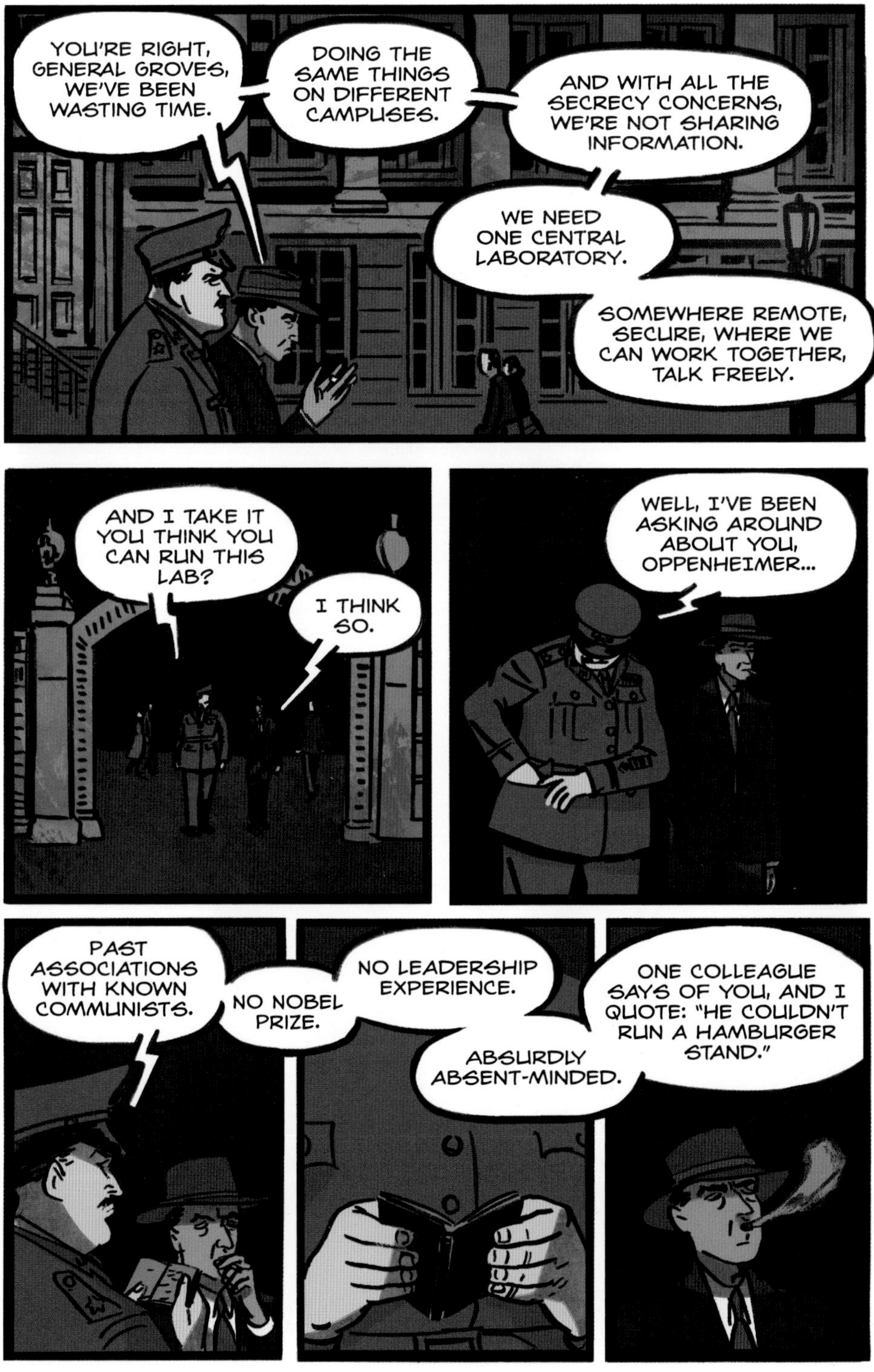
YOU'RE RIGHT, GENERAL GROVES, WE'VE BEEN WASTING TIME.
DOING THE SAME THINGS ON DIFFERENT CAMPUSES.
AND WITH ALL THE SECRECY CONCERNS, WE'RE NOT SHARING INFORMATION.
WE NEED ONE CENTRAL LABORATORY.
SOMEWHERE REMOTE, SECURE, WHERE WE CAN WORK TOGETHER, TALK FREELY.
AND I TAKE IT YOU THINK YOU CAN RUN THIS LAB?
I THINK SO.
WELL, I'VE BEEN ASKING AROUND ABOUT YOU, OPPENHEIMER...
PAST ASSOCIATIONS WITH KNOWN COMMUNISTS.
NO NOBEL PRIZE.
NO LEADERSHIP EXPERIENCE.
ABSURDLY ABSENT-MINDED.
ONE COLLEAGUE SAYS OF YOU, AND I QUOTE: "HE COULDN'T RUN A HAMBURGER STAND."

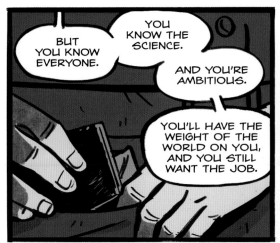

YOU KNOW THE SCIENCE.

BUT YOU KNOW EVERYONE.

AND YOU'RE AMBITIOUS.

YOU'LL HAVE THE WEIGHT OF THE WORLD ON YOU, AND YOU STILL WANT THE JOB.

I RESPECT THAT.

THANK— COUGH COUGH

YOU'RE NOT SOLDIER MATERIAL, OPPENHEIMER.

COUGH

I CONCEDE THE POINT.

BUT YOU JUST MIGHT BE ABLE TO WIN THE WAR.

COUGH

LET'S FIND OURSELVES A LAB.

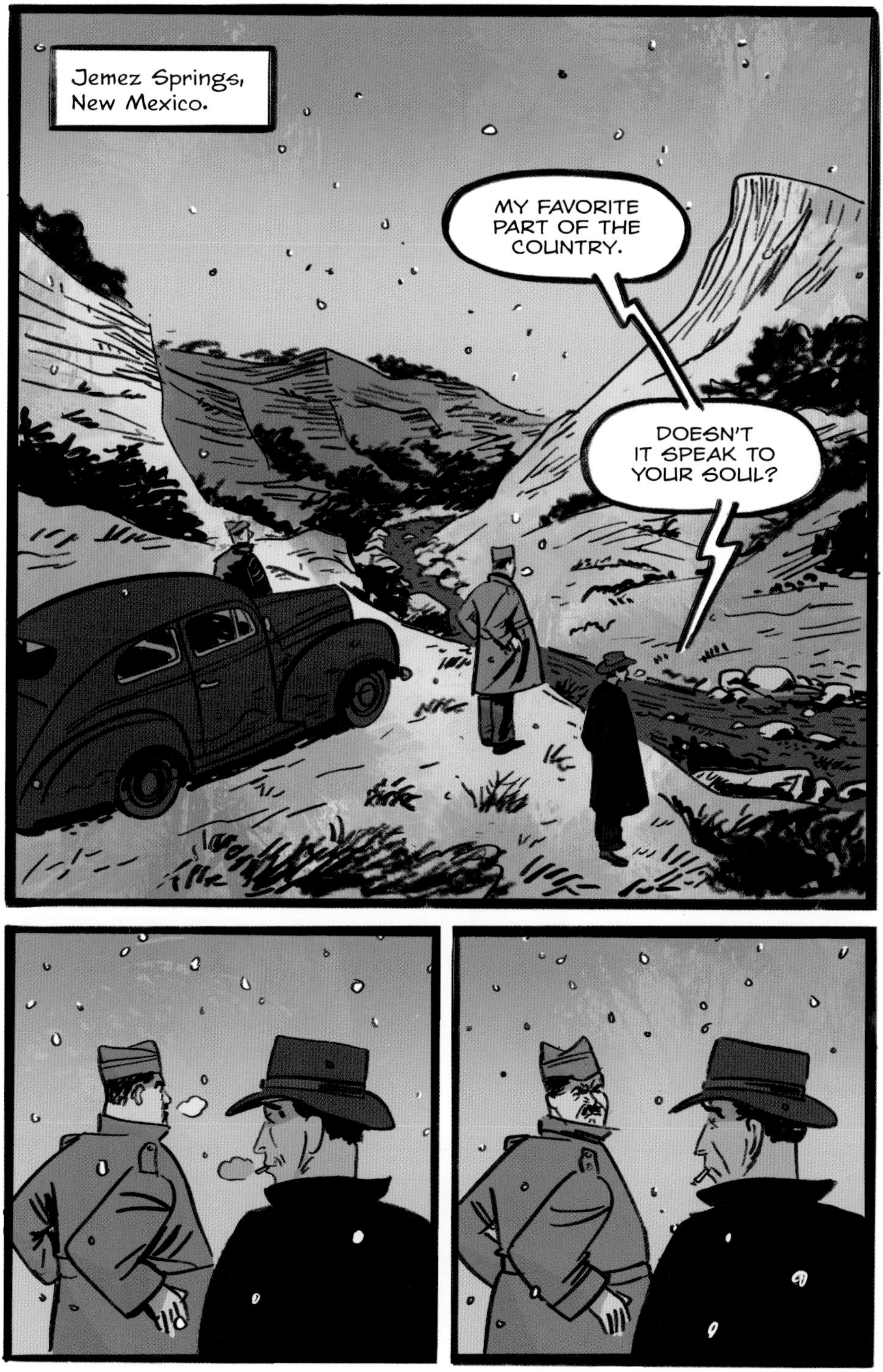
Jemez Springs, New Mexico.
MY FAVORITE PART OF THE COUNTRY.
DOESN'T IT SPEAK TO YOUR SOUL?

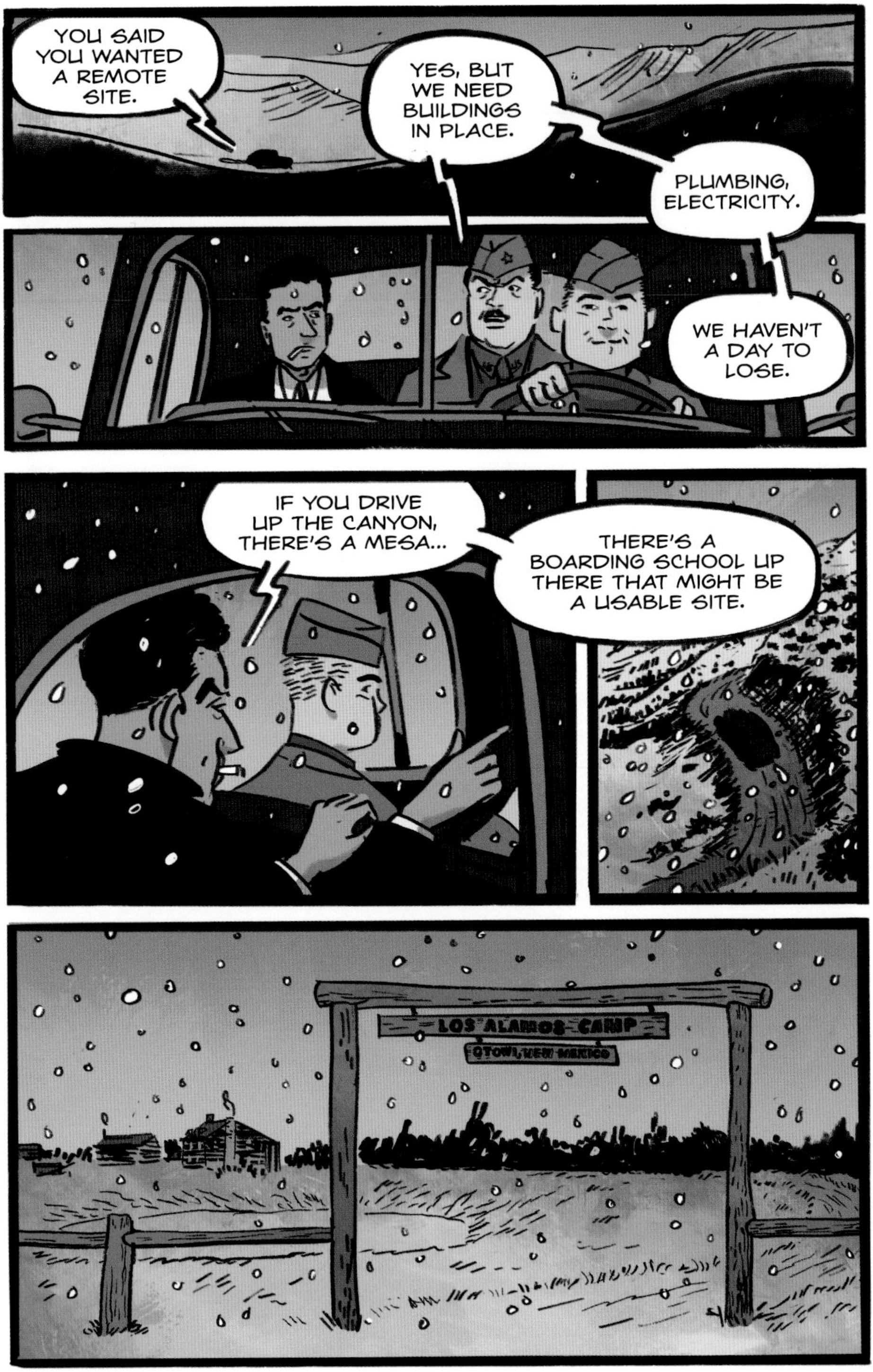
YOU SAID YOU WANTED A REMOTE SITE.
YES, BUT WE NEED BUILDINGS IN PLACE.
PLUMBING, ELECTRICITY.
WE HAVEN'T A DAY TO LOSE.
IF YOU DRIVE UP THE CANYON, THERE'S A MESA...
THERE'S A BOARDING SCHOOL UP THERE THAT MIGHT BE A USABLE SITE.
LOS ALAMOS CAMP
OTOWI, NEW MEXICO

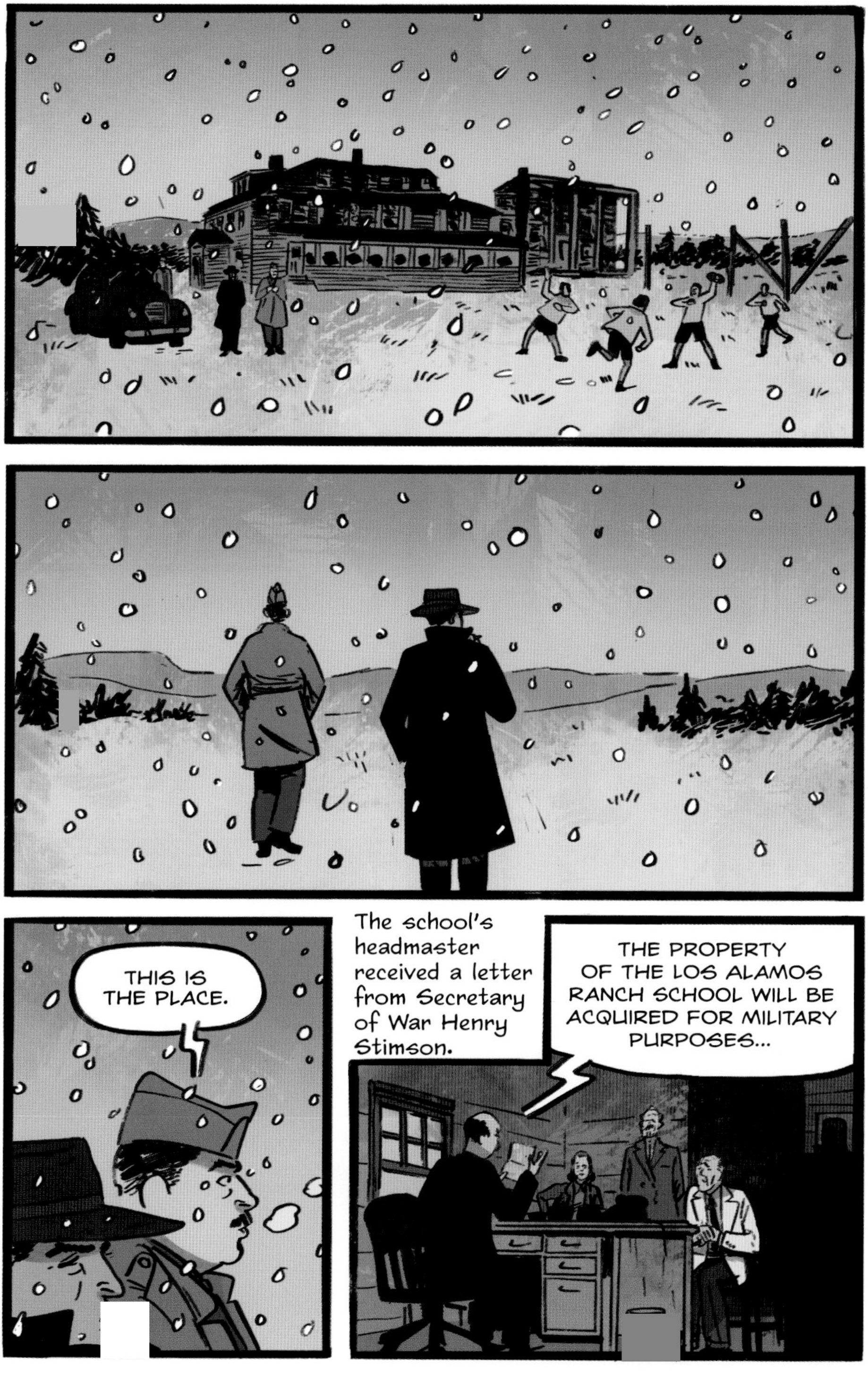
THIS IS THE PLACE.
The school's headmaster received a letter from Secretary of War Henry Stimson.
THE PROPERTY OF THE LOS ALAMOS RANCH SCHOOL WILL BE ACQUIRED FOR MILITARY PURPOSES...

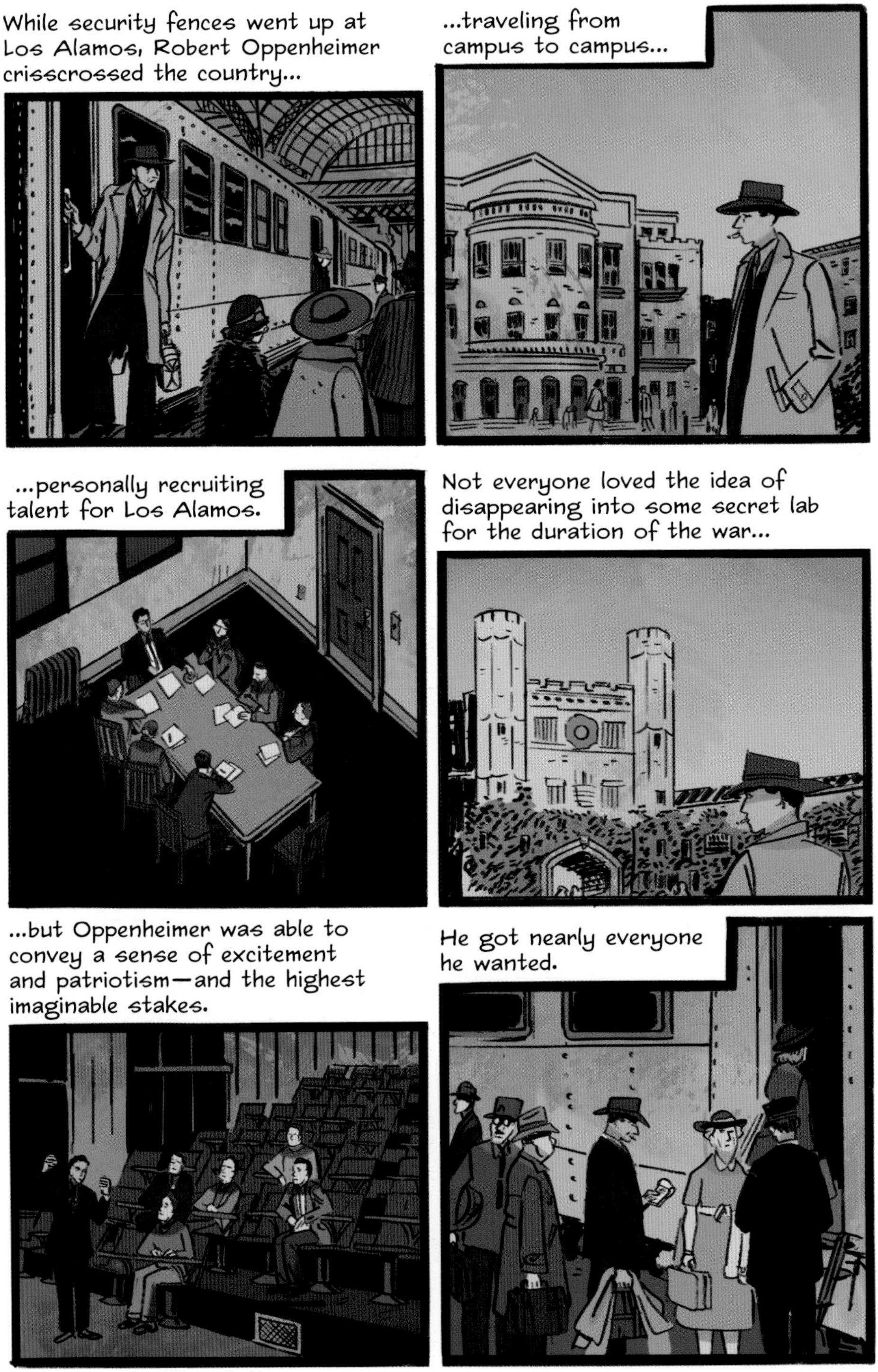
While security fences went up at Los Alamos, Robert Oppenheimer crisscrossed the country...
...traveling from campus to campus...
...personally recruiting talent for Los Alamos.
Not everyone loved the idea of disappearing into some secret lab for the duration of the war...
...but Oppenheimer was able to convey a sense of excitement and patriotism—and the highest imaginable stakes.
He got nearly everyone he wanted.

Including a teenage science prodigy named Theodore Hall.

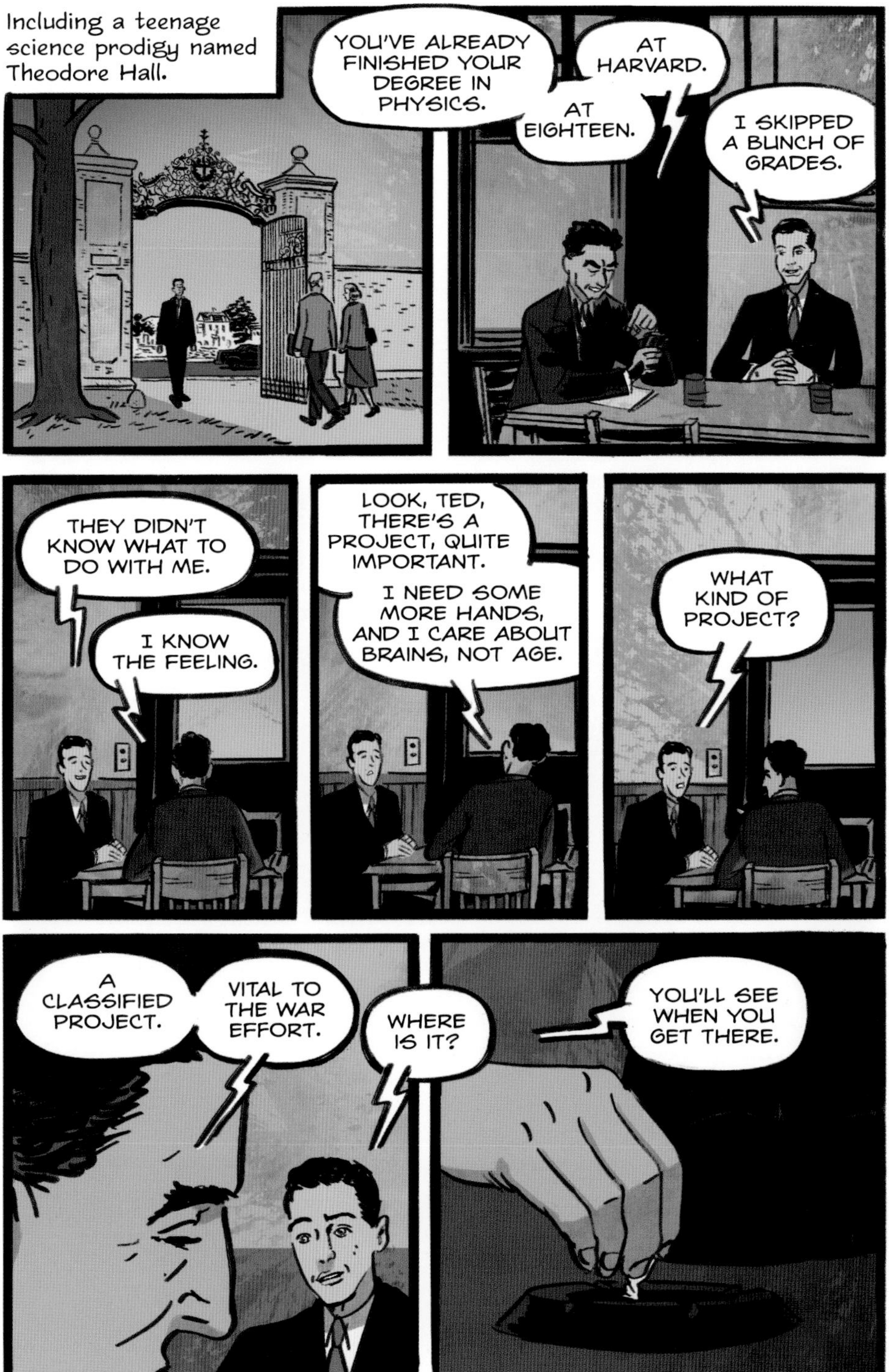
YOU'VE ALREADY FINISHED YOUR DEGREE IN PHYSICS.
AT HARVARD.
AT EIGHTEEN.
I SKIPPED A BUNCH OF GRADES.
THEY DIDN'T KNOW WHAT TO DO WITH ME.
I KNOW THE FEELING.
LOOK, TED, THERE'S A PROJECT, QUITE IMPORTANT.
I NEED SOME MORE HANDS, AND I CARE ABOUT BRAINS, NOT AGE.
WHAT KIND OF PROJECT?
A CLASSIFIED PROJECT.
VITAL TO THE WAR EFFORT.
WHERE IS IT?
YOU'LL SEE WHEN YOU GET THERE.

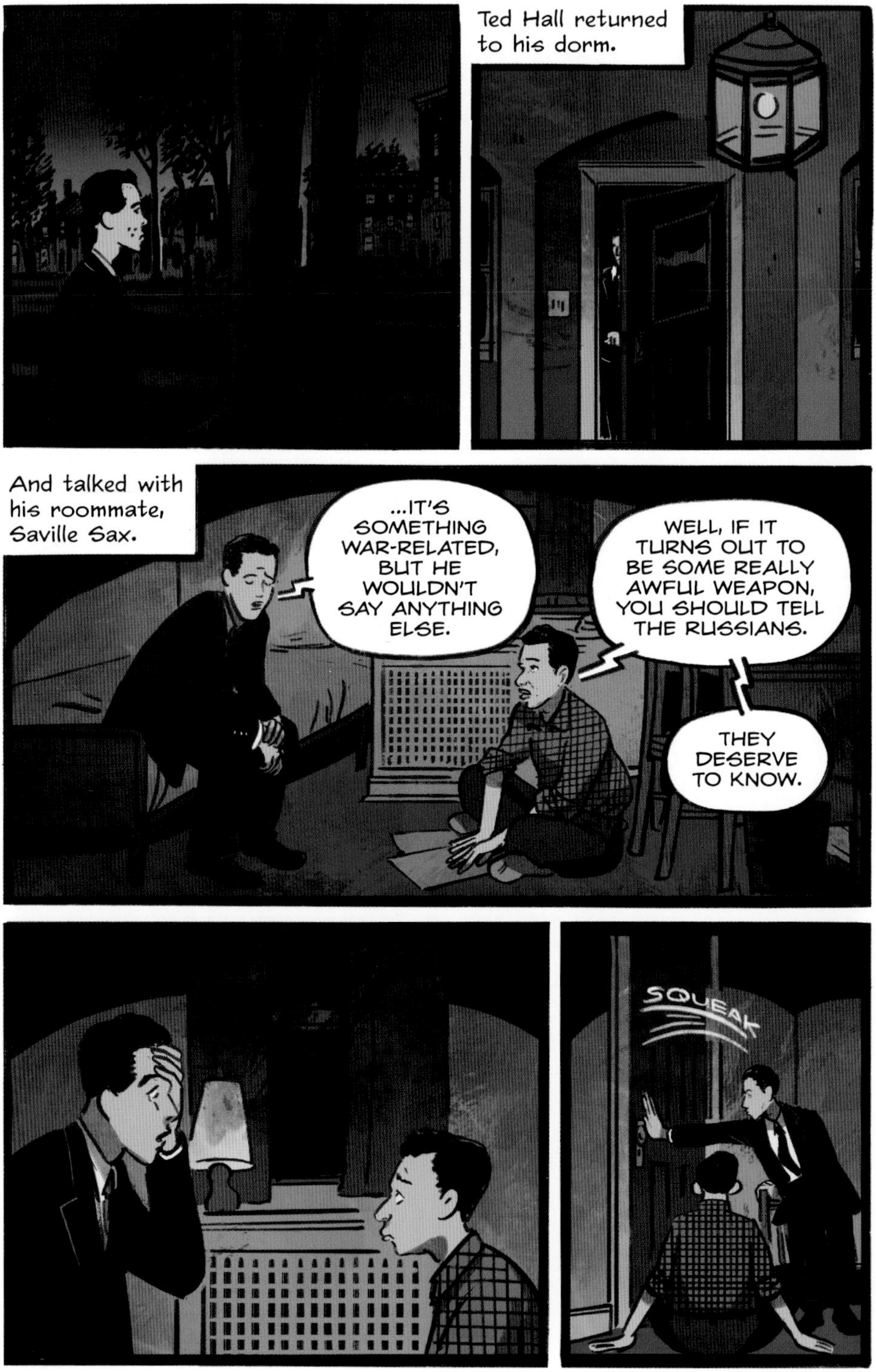
Ted Hall returned to his dorm.
And talked with his roommate, Saville Sax.
...IT'S SOMETHING WAR-RELATED, BUT HE WOULDN'T SAY ANYTHING ELSE.
WELL, IF IT TURNS OUT TO BE SOME REALLY AWFUL WEAPON, YOU SHOULD TELL THE RUSSIANS.
THEY DESERVE TO KNOW.
SQUEAK

Chapter 2

High Concentration

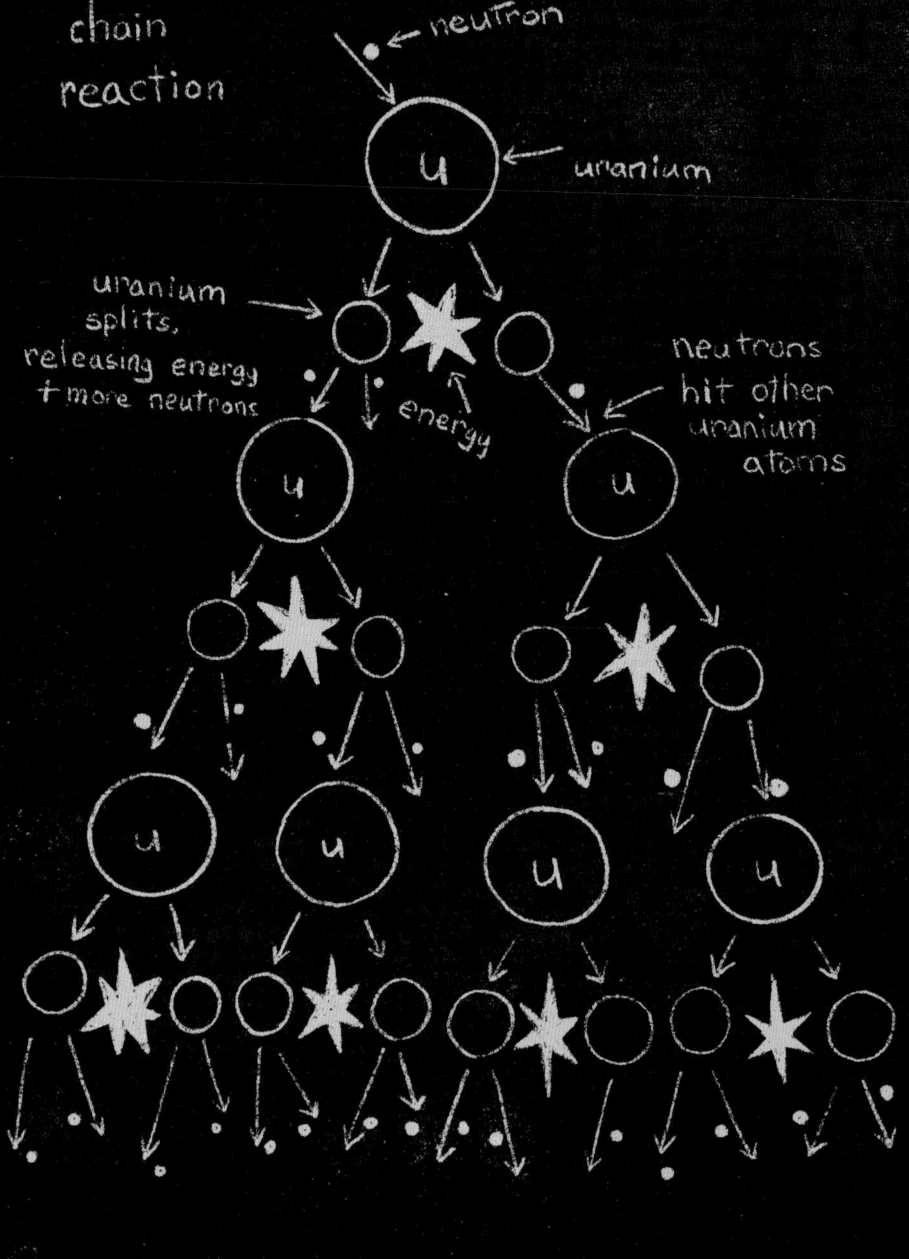

chain reaction
neutron
uranium
u
uranium splits, releasing energy + more neutrons
energy
neutrons hit other uranium atoms

The Pentagon, headquarters of the U.S. Department of War.

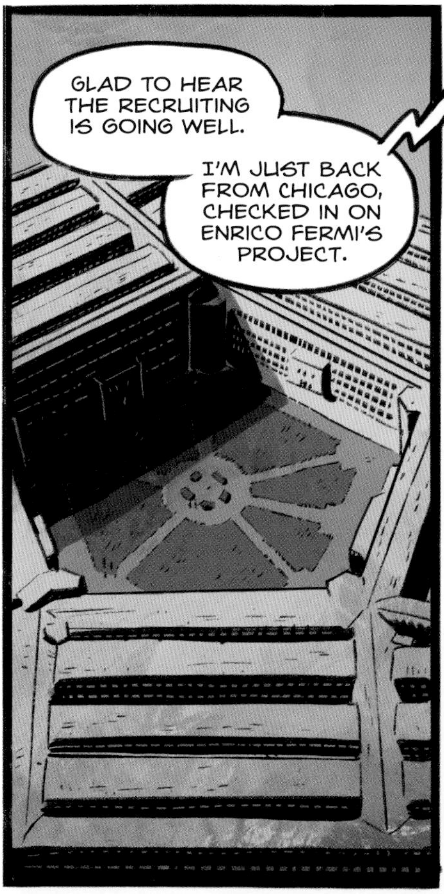
GLAD TO HEAR THE RECRUITING IS GOING WELL.
I'M JUST BACK FROM CHICAGO, CHECKED IN ON ENRICO FERMI'S PROJECT.

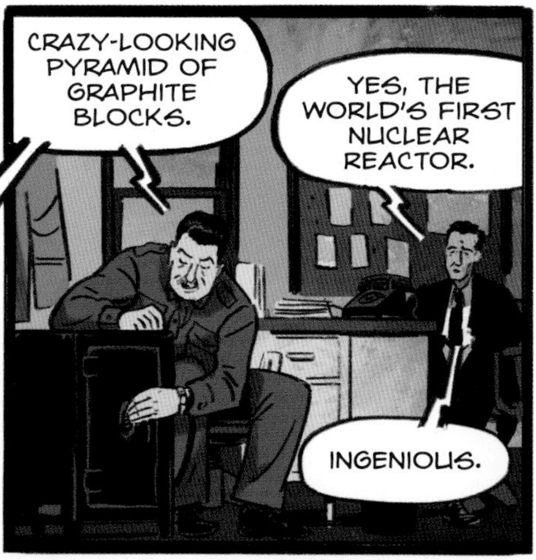
CRAZY-LOOKING PYRAMID OF GRAPHITE BLOCKS.
YES, THE WORLD'S FIRST NUCLEAR REACTOR.
INGENIOUS.

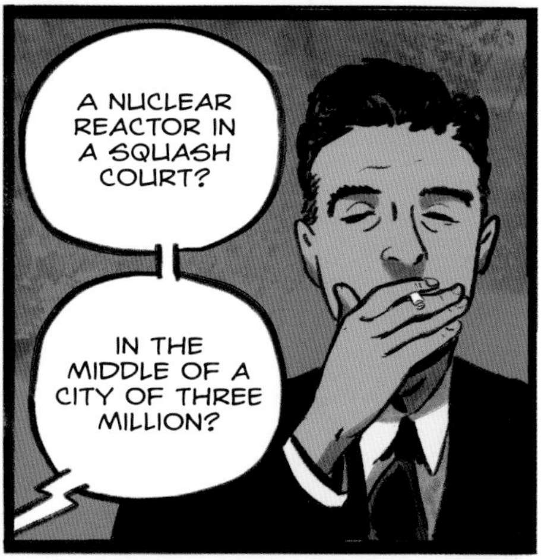
A NUCLEAR REACTOR IN A SQUASH COURT?
IN THE MIDDLE OF A CITY OF THREE MILLION?

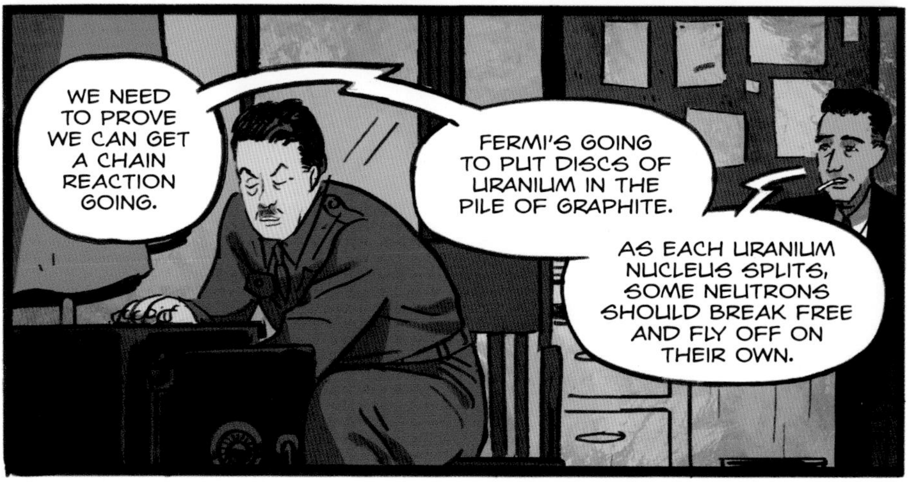
WE NEED TO PROVE WE CAN GET A CHAIN REACTION GOING.
FERMI'S GOING TO PUT DISCS OF URANIUM IN THE PILE OF GRAPHITE.
AS EACH URANIUM NUCLEUS SPLITS, SOME NEUTRONS SHOULD BREAK FREE AND FLY OFF ON THEIR OWN.

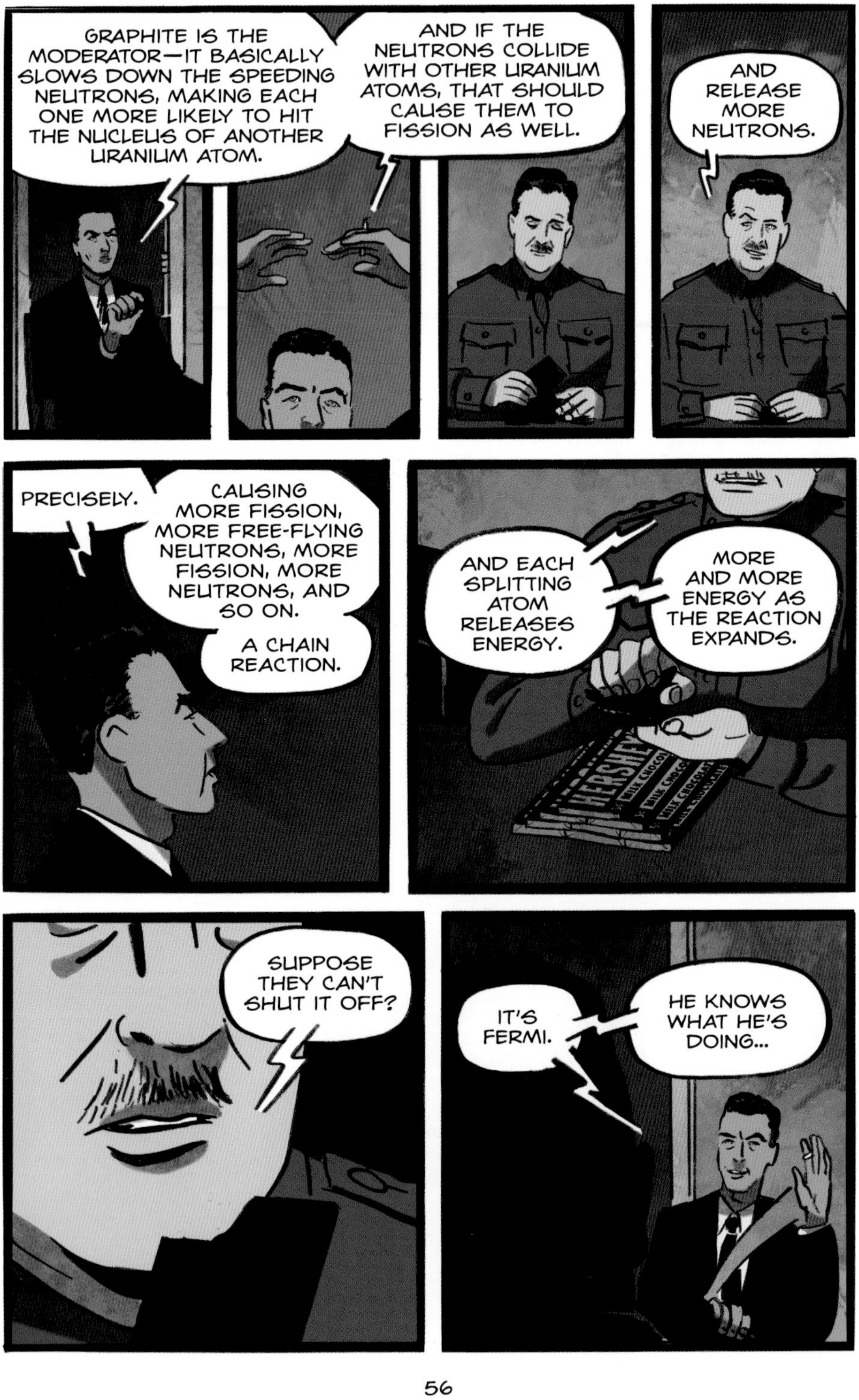

GRAPHITE IS THE MODERATOR—IT BASICALLY SLOWS DOWN THE SPEEDING NEUTRONS, MAKING EACH ONE MORE LIKELY TO HIT THE NUCLEUS OF ANOTHER URANIUM ATOM.
AND IF THE NEUTRONS COLLIDE WITH OTHER URANIUM ATOMS, THAT SHOULD CAUSE THEM TO FISSION AS WELL.
AND RELEASE MORE NEUTRONS.
PRECISELY.
CAUSING MORE FISSION, MORE FREE-FLYING NEUTRONS, MORE FISSION, MORE NEUTRONS, AND SO ON.
A CHAIN REACTION.
AND EACH SPLITTING ATOM RELEASES ENERGY.
MORE AND MORE ENERGY AS THE REACTION EXPANDS.
HERSHEY'S
MILK CHOCOLATE
SUPPOSE THEY CAN'T SHUT IT OFF?
IT'S FERMI.
HE KNOWS WHAT HE'S DOING...

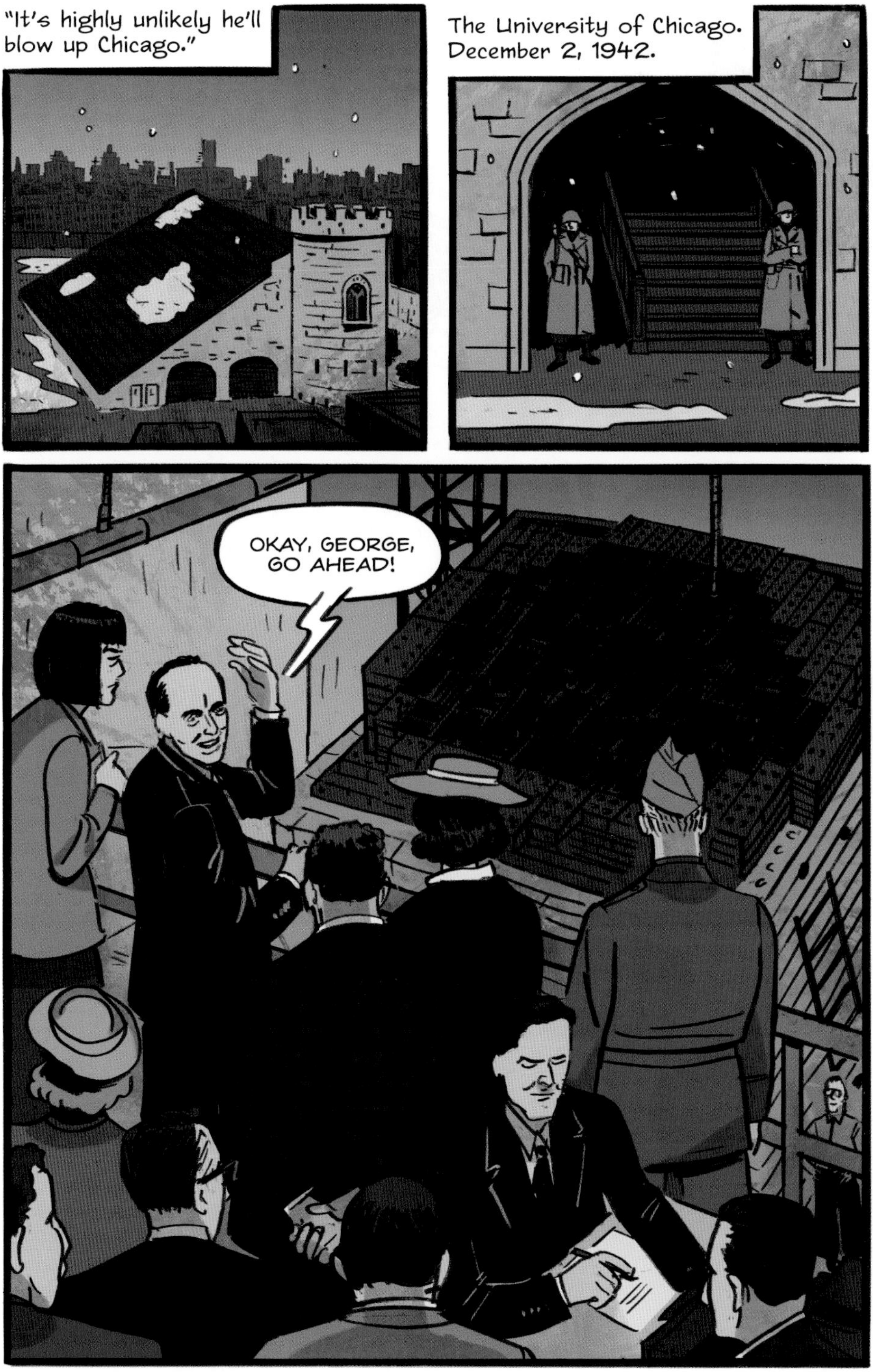
"It's highly unlikely he'll blow up Chicago."
The University of Chicago. December 2, 1942.
OKAY, GEORGE, GO AHEAD!

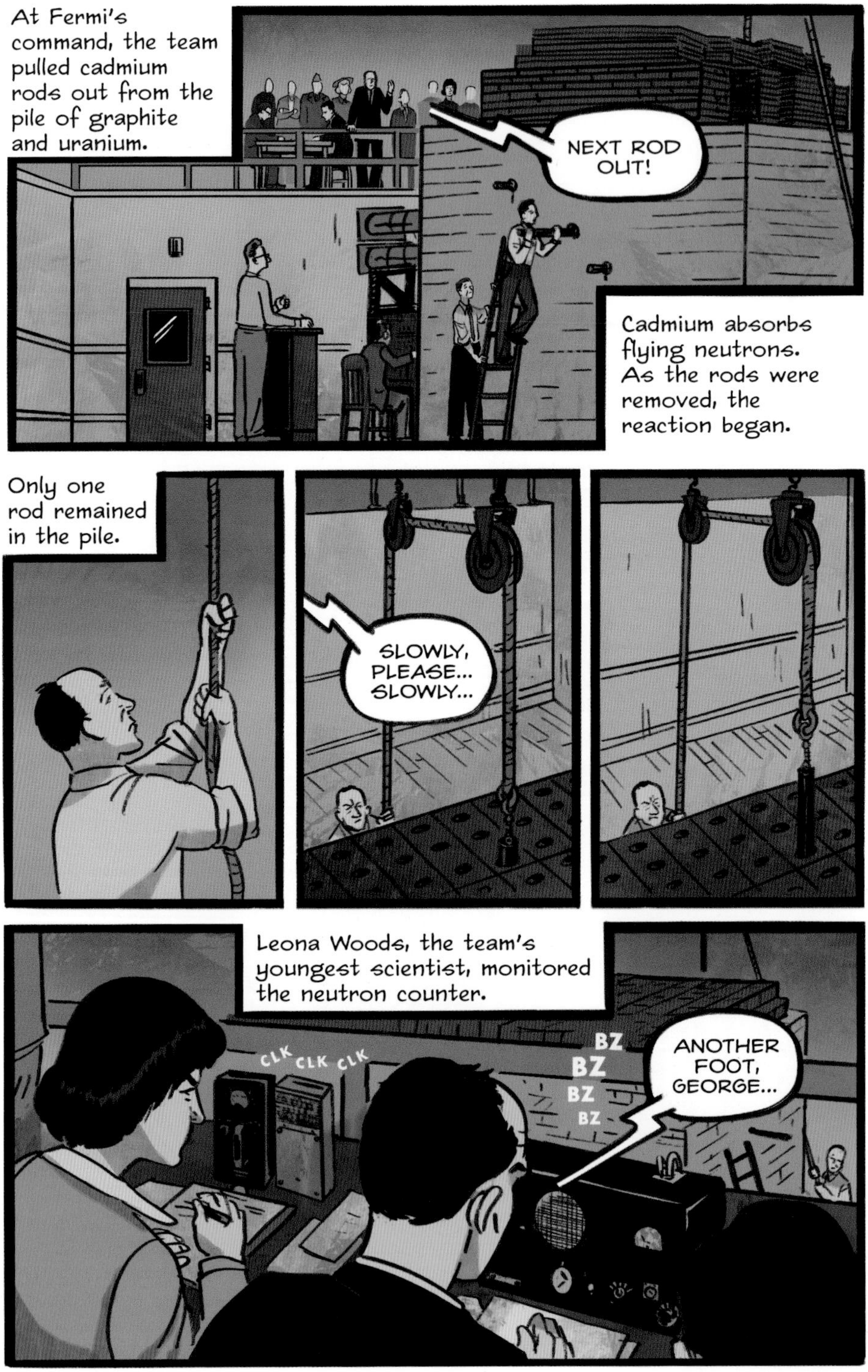
At Fermi's command, the team pulled cadmium rods out from the pile of graphite and uranium.
NEXT ROD OUT!
Cadmium absorbs flying neutrons. As the rods were removed, the reaction began.
Only one rod remained in the pile.
SLOWLY, PLEASE... SLOWLY...
Leona Woods, the team's youngest scientist, monitored the neutron counter.
CLK CLK CLK
BZ BZ BZ BZ
ANOTHER FOOT, GEORGE...

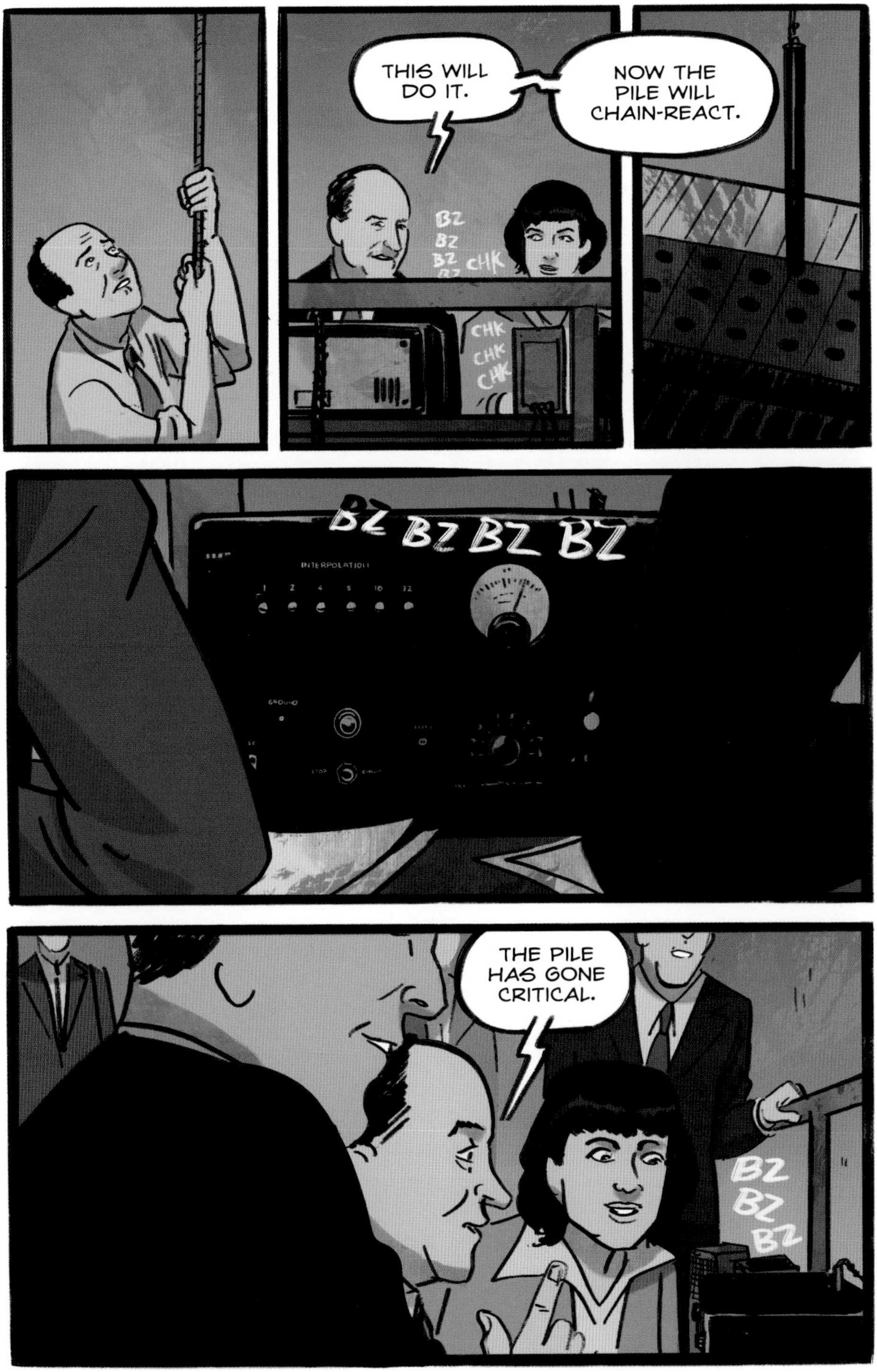
THIS WILL DO IT.
NOW THE PILE WILL CHAIN-REACT.
BZ BZ BZ
CHK
CHK CHK CHK
BZ BZ BZ BZ
INTERPOLATION
THE PILE HAS GONE CRITICAL.
BZ BZ BZ

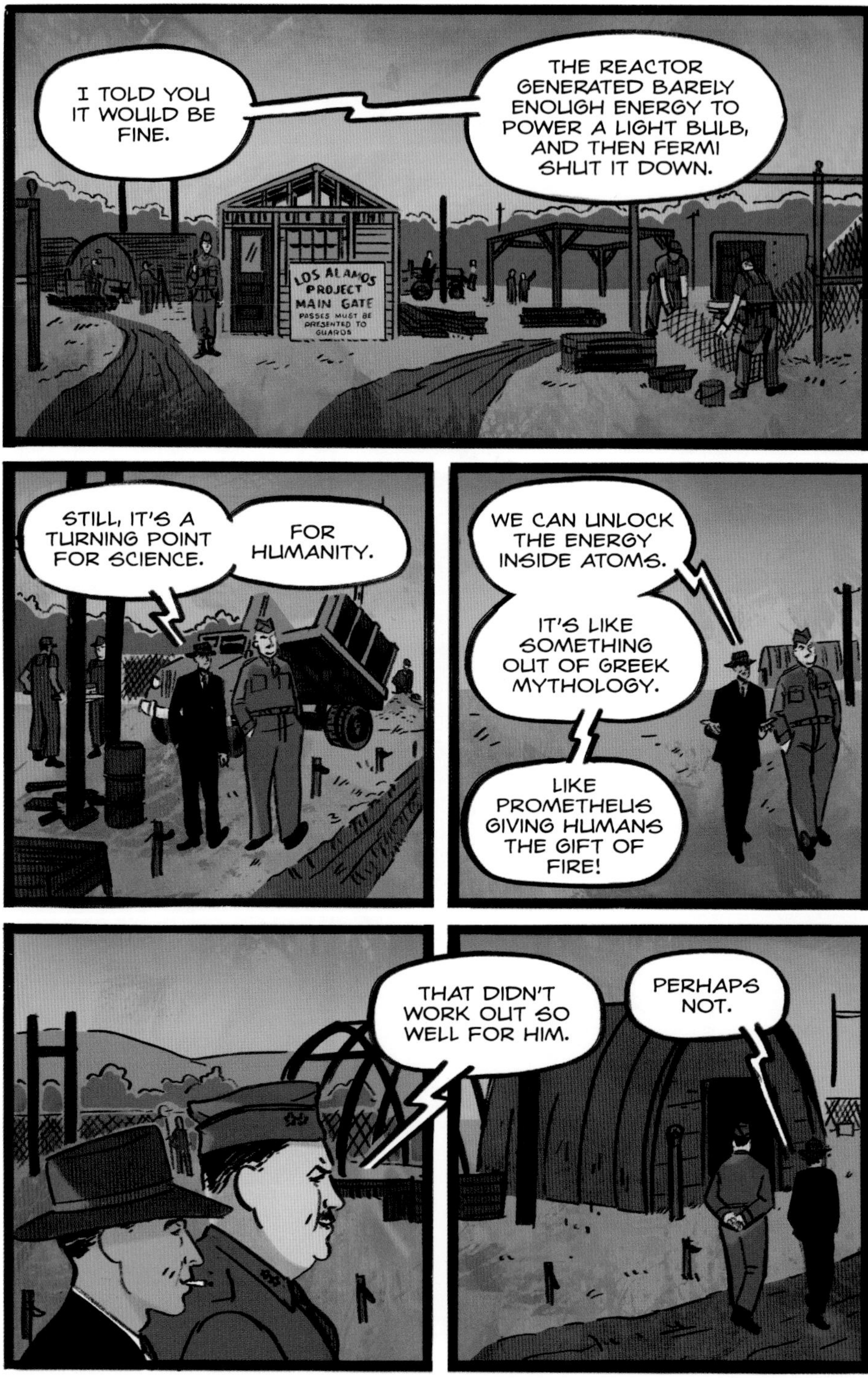
I TOLD YOU IT WOULD BE FINE.
THE REACTOR GENERATED BARELY ENOUGH ENERGY TO POWER A LIGHT BULB, AND THEN FERMI SHUT IT DOWN.
LOS ALAMOS PROJECT MAIN GATE
PASSES MUST BE PRESENTED TO GUARDS
STILL, IT'S A TURNING POINT FOR SCIENCE.
FOR HUMANITY.
WE CAN UNLOCK THE ENERGY INSIDE ATOMS.
IT'S LIKE SOMETHING OUT OF GREEK MYTHOLOGY.
LIKE PROMETHEUS GIVING HUMANS THE GIFT OF FIRE!
THAT DIDN'T WORK OUT SO WELL FOR HIM.
PERHAPS NOT.

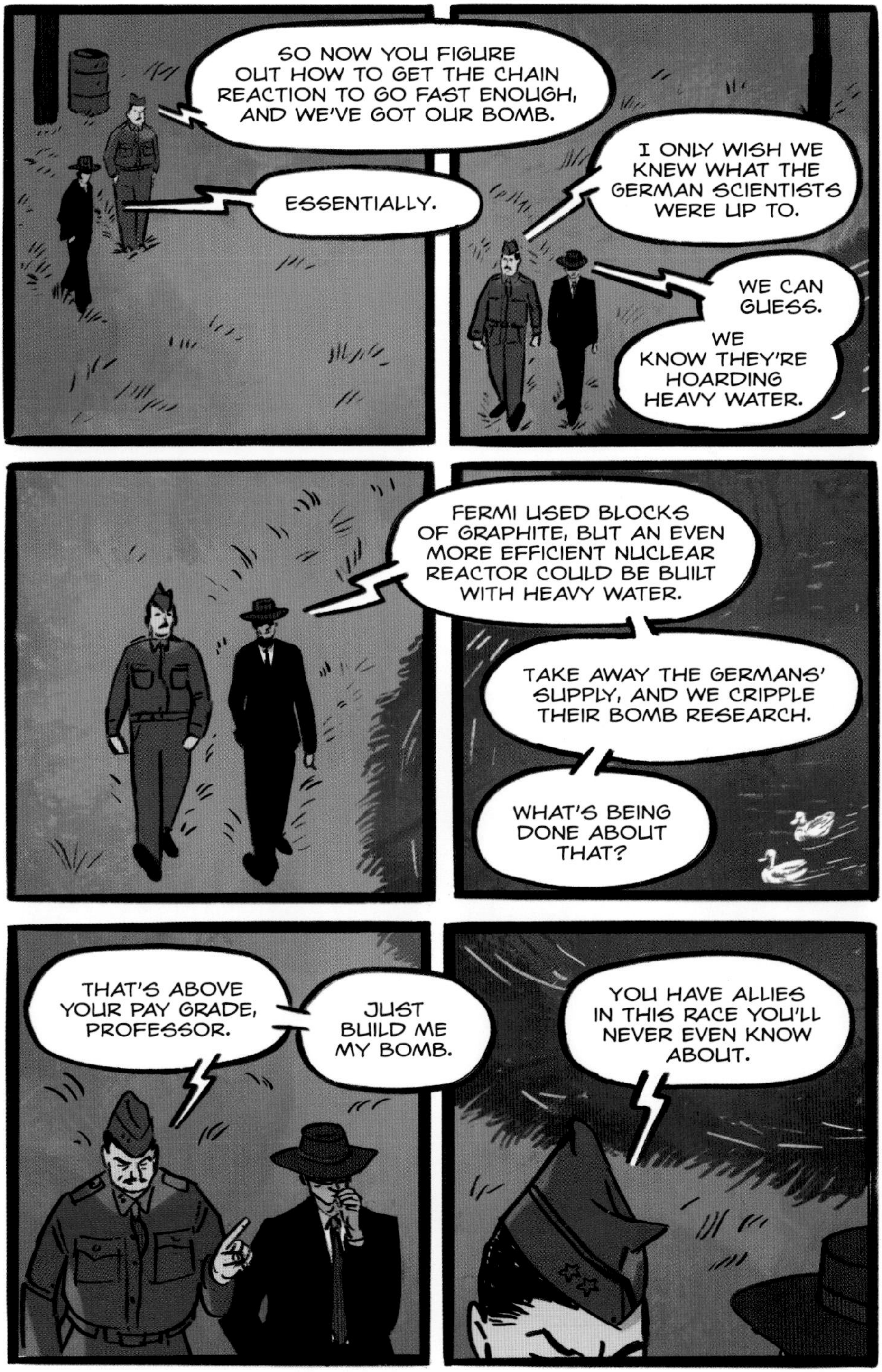
SO NOW YOU FIGURE OUT HOW TO GET THE CHAIN REACTION TO GO FAST ENOUGH, AND WE'VE GOT OUR BOMB.
ESSENTIALLY.
I ONLY WISH WE KNEW WHAT THE GERMAN SCIENTISTS WERE UP TO.
WE CAN GUESS.
WE KNOW THEY'RE HOARDING HEAVY WATER.
FERMI USED BLOCKS OF GRAPHITE, BUT AN EVEN MORE EFFICIENT NUCLEAR REACTOR COULD BE BUILT WITH HEAVY WATER.
TAKE AWAY THE GERMANS' SUPPLY, AND WE CRIPPLE THEIR BOMB RESEARCH.
WHAT'S BEING DONE ABOUT THAT?
THAT'S ABOVE YOUR PAY GRADE, PROFESSOR.
JUST BUILD ME MY BOMB.
YOU HAVE ALLIES IN THIS RACE YOU'LL NEVER EVEN KNOW ABOUT.

Special Training School No. 3. Somewhere in Scotland.

One of Oppenheimer's most valuable allies was a man he would never meet, a young Norwegian named Knut Haukelid.

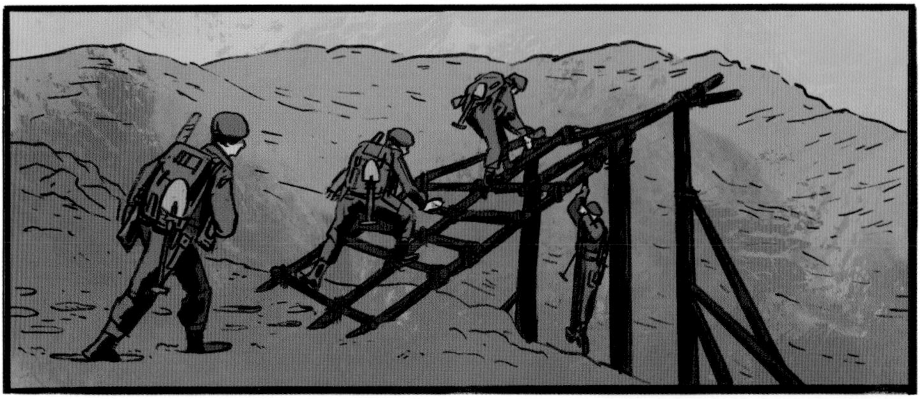

Haukelid was one of a small number of Norwegians who had escaped their country after the German invasion.

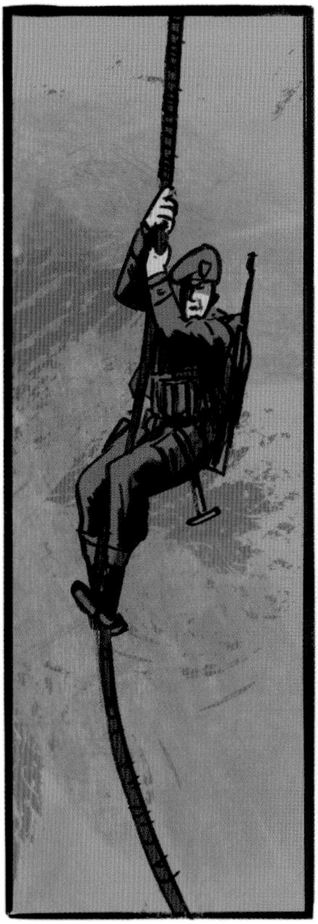

Now he and his fellow countrymen were focused on a single goal.

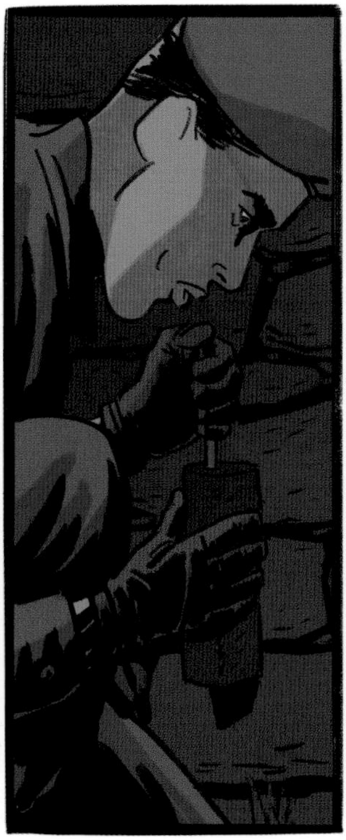

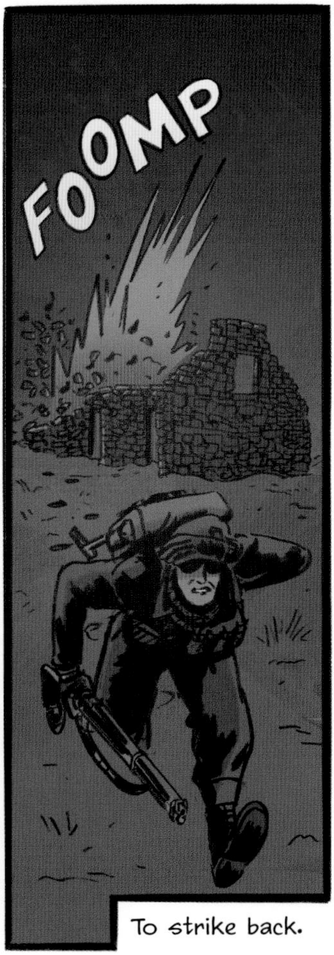
FOOMP

To strike back.

They'd come to the right place, Britain's top secret Special Operations Executive.

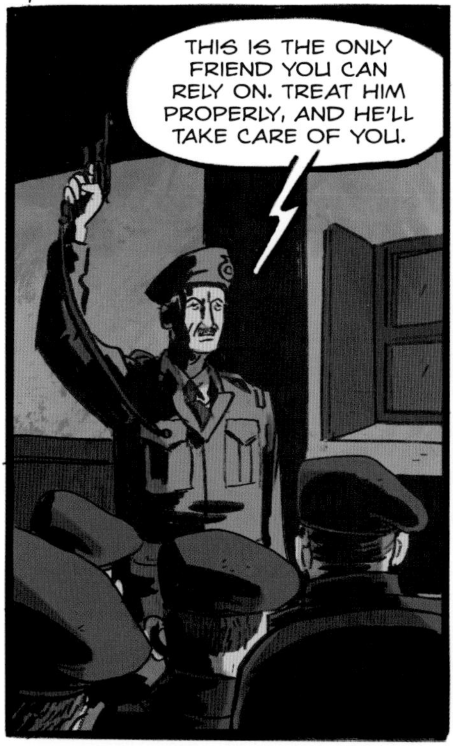
THIS IS THE ONLY FRIEND YOU CAN RELY ON. TREAT HIM PROPERLY, AND HE'LL TAKE CARE OF YOU.

The SOE's mission was to go behind enemy lines and, in Winston Churchill's words, "set Europe ablaze!"

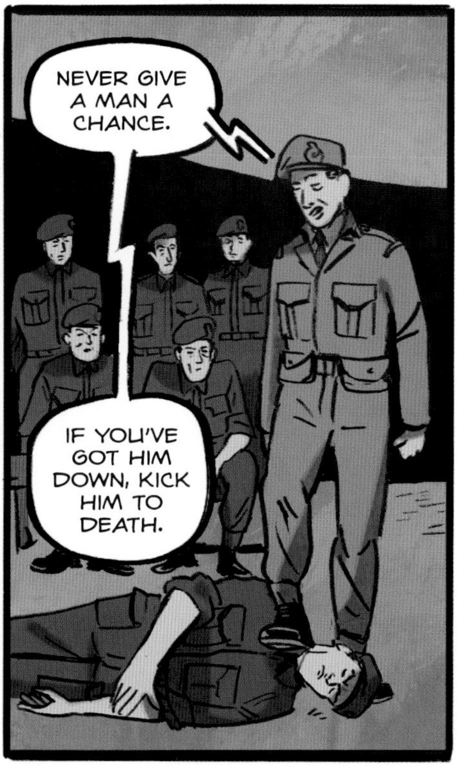
NEVER GIVE A MAN A CHANCE.
IF YOU'VE GOT HIM DOWN, KICK HIM TO DEATH.

Haukelid was not sure what he was being prepared to do.

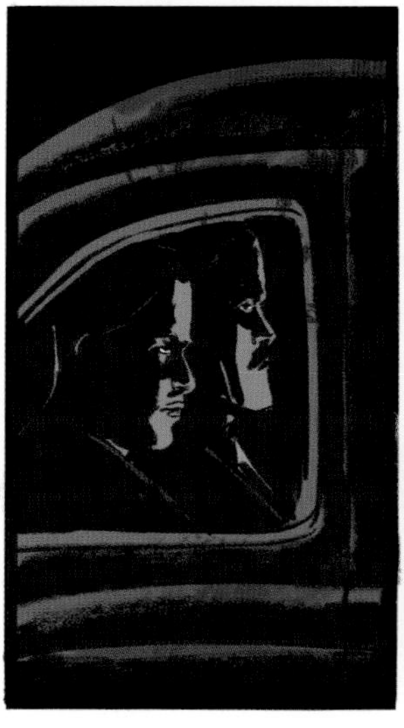

Until a late-night drive to SOE headquarters in London.

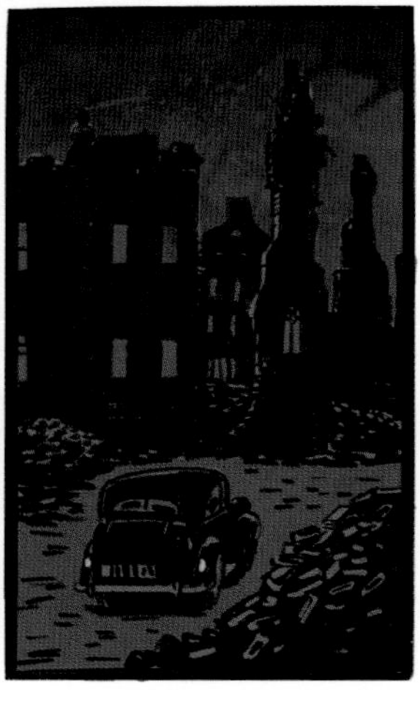

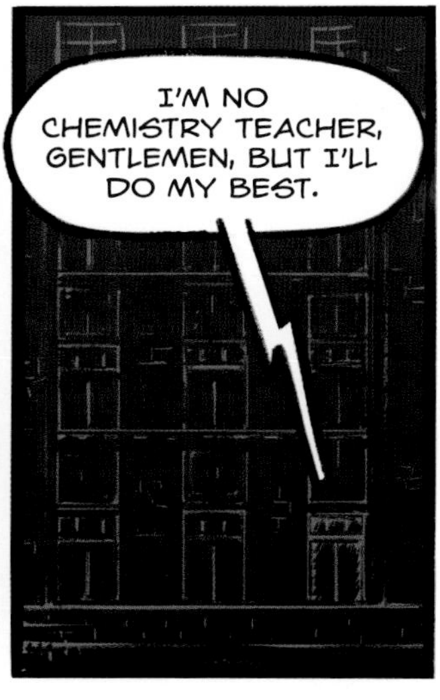
I'M NO CHEMISTRY TEACHER, GENTLEMEN, BUT I'LL DO MY BEST.

A MOLECULE OF WATER IS MADE UP TWO ATOMS OF HYDROGEN AND ONE ATOM OF OXYGEN.

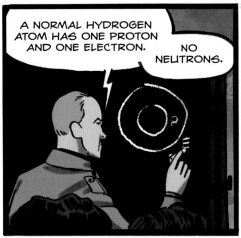

A NORMAL HYDROGEN ATOM HAS ONE PROTON AND ONE ELECTRON.

NO NEUTRONS.

BUT SOME HYDROGEN ATOMS HAVE ONE PROTON AND ONE NEUTRON—MAKING THE ATOM HEAVIER.

WHEN THESE HEAVIER HYDROGEN ATOMS JOIN WITH OXYGEN TO FORM WATER, THE RESULT IS DEUTERIUM OXIDE, OR "HEAVY WATER."

HEAVY WATER OCCURS NATURALLY IN TINY QUANTITIES, AND IT'S PERFECTLY HARMLESS.

SO WHY AM I TELLING YOU THIS?

THE ONE FACILITY ON EARTH CAPABLE OF SEPARATING AND COLLECTING LARGE QUANTITIES OF HEAVY WATER IS HERE, IN YOUR OWN NORWAY.

Bergen

Vemork

Oslo

THE VEMORK POWER PLANT, BUILT INTO THE SIDE OF A MOUNTAIN NEAR THE TOWN OF RJUKAN.

THAT'S MY HOMETOWN.

MOST OF US GREW UP CLIMBING AND SKIING IN THOSE MOUNTAINS.

AND YOU WILL AGAIN, GENTLEMEN.

THE HEAVY WATER EQUIPMENT AT VEMORK MUST BE DESTROYED. THE OUTCOME OF THE WAR MAY DEPEND UPON IT.

WE RECKON YOU'VE GOT A FIFTY-FIFTY CHANCE OF DOING THE JOB. YOU HAVE ONLY A FAIR CHANCE OF GETTING OUT ALIVE.

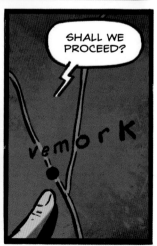

SHALL WE PROCEED?

vemork

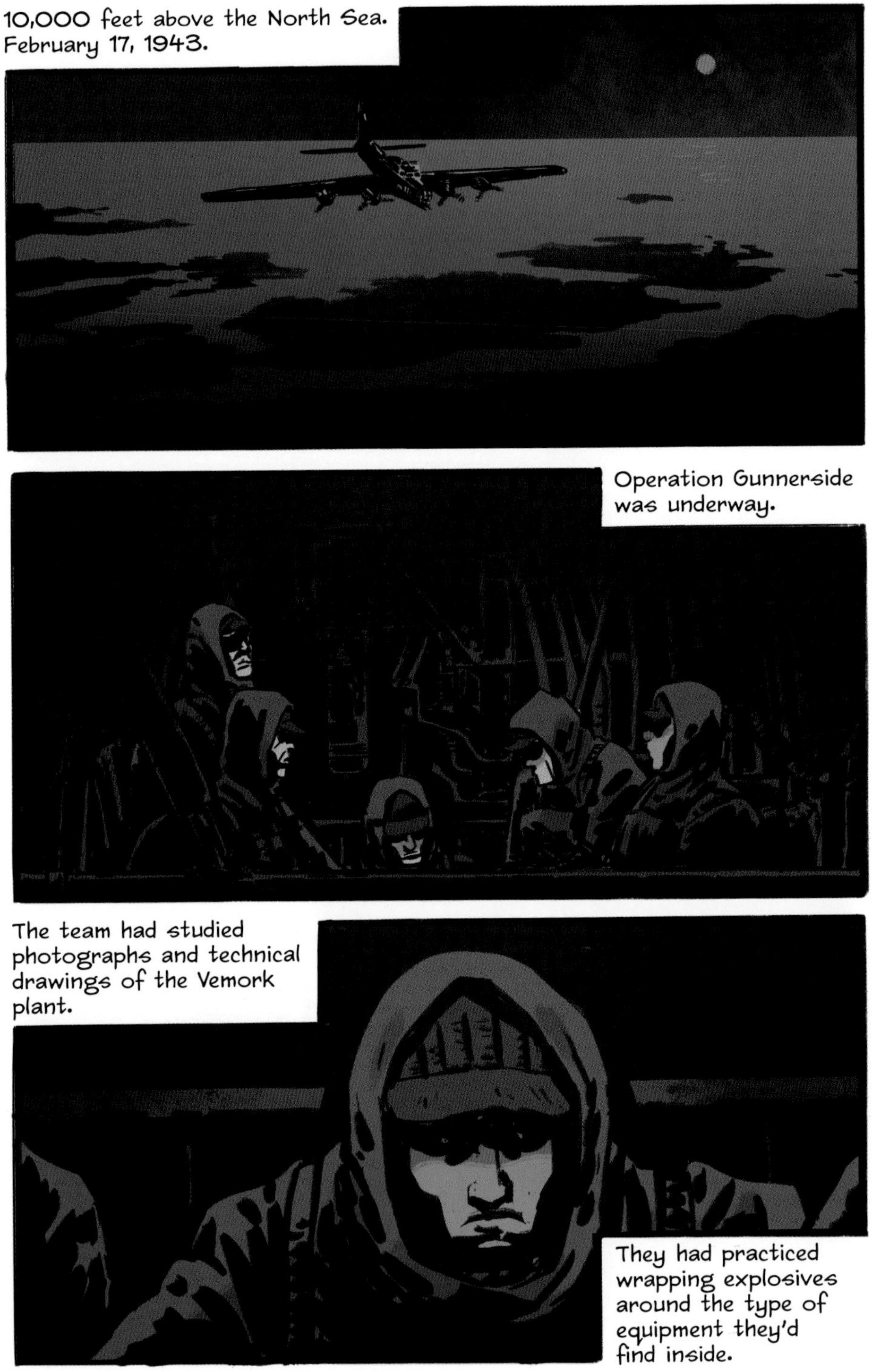
10,000 feet above the North Sea. February 17, 1943.
Operation Gunnerside was underway.
The team had studied photographs and technical drawings of the Vemork plant.
They had practiced wrapping explosives around the type of equipment they'd find inside.

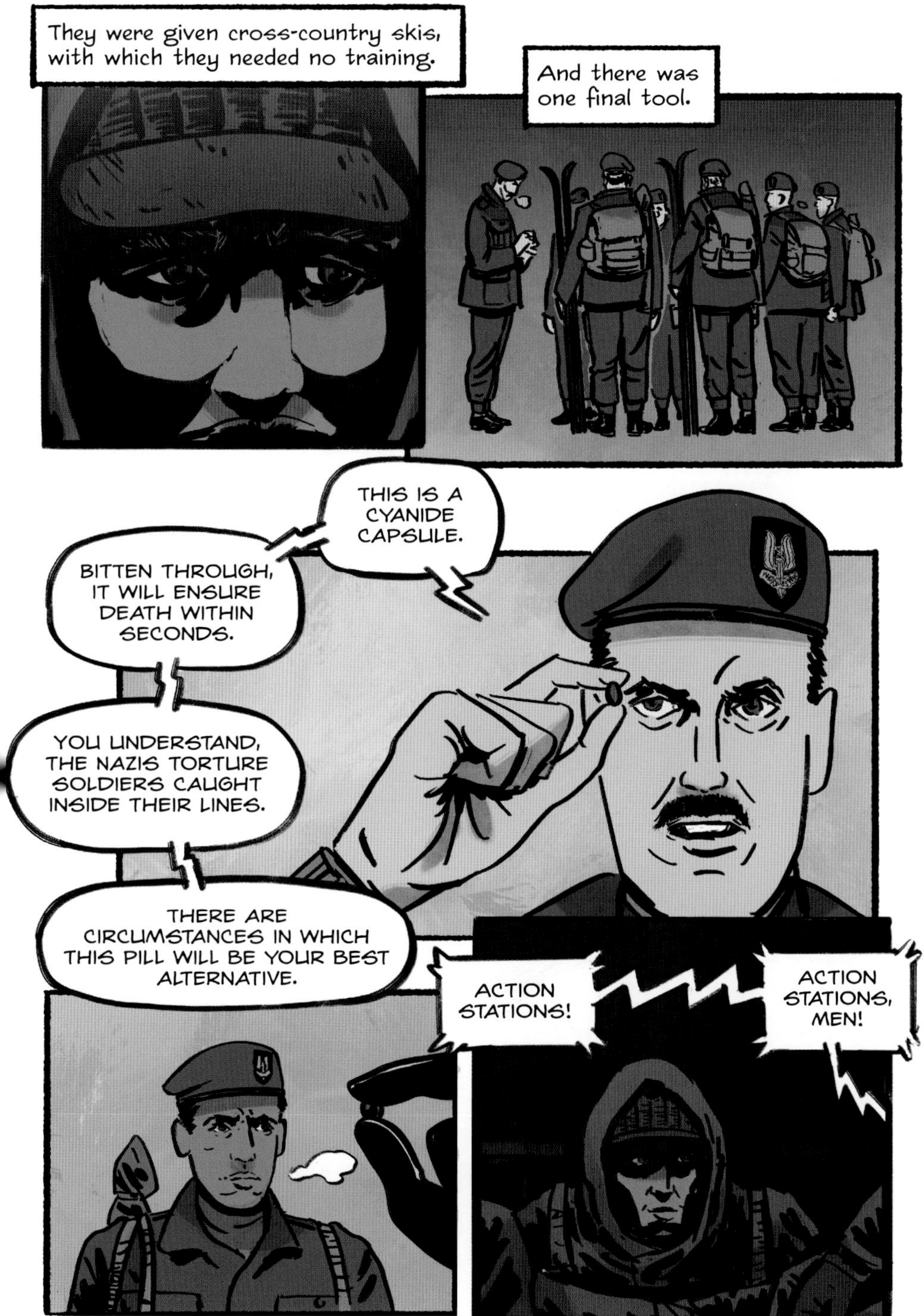

They were given cross-country skis, with which they needed no training.
And there was one final tool.
THIS IS A CYANIDE CAPSULE.
BITTEN THROUGH, IT WILL ENSURE DEATH WITHIN SECONDS.
YOU UNDERSTAND, THE NAZIS TORTURE SOLDIERS CAUGHT INSIDE THEIR LINES.
THERE ARE CIRCUMSTANCES IN WHICH THIS PILL WILL BE YOUR BEST ALTERNATIVE.
ACTION STATIONS!
ACTION STATIONS, MEN!

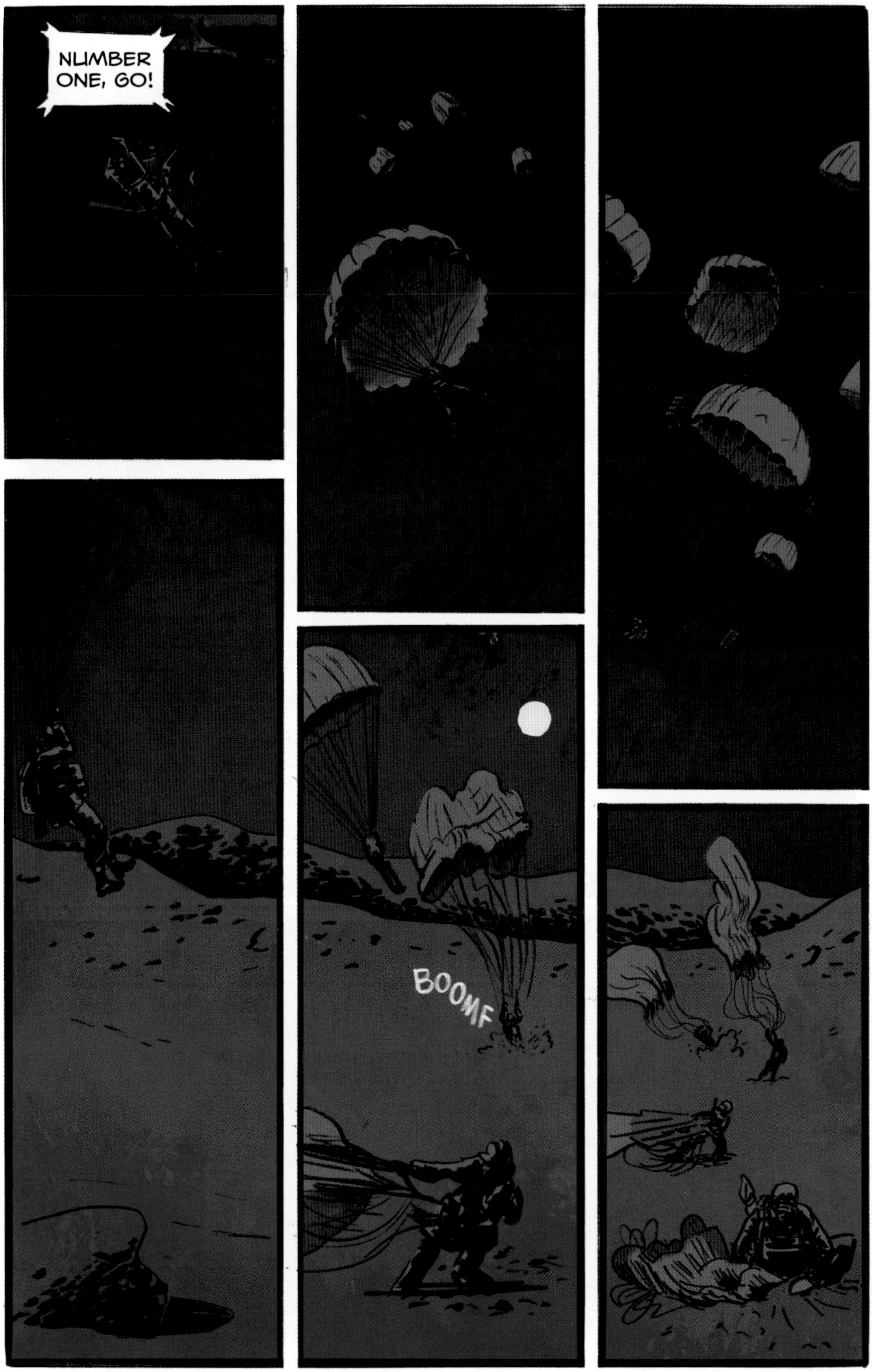
NUMBER ONE, GO!
BOOMF

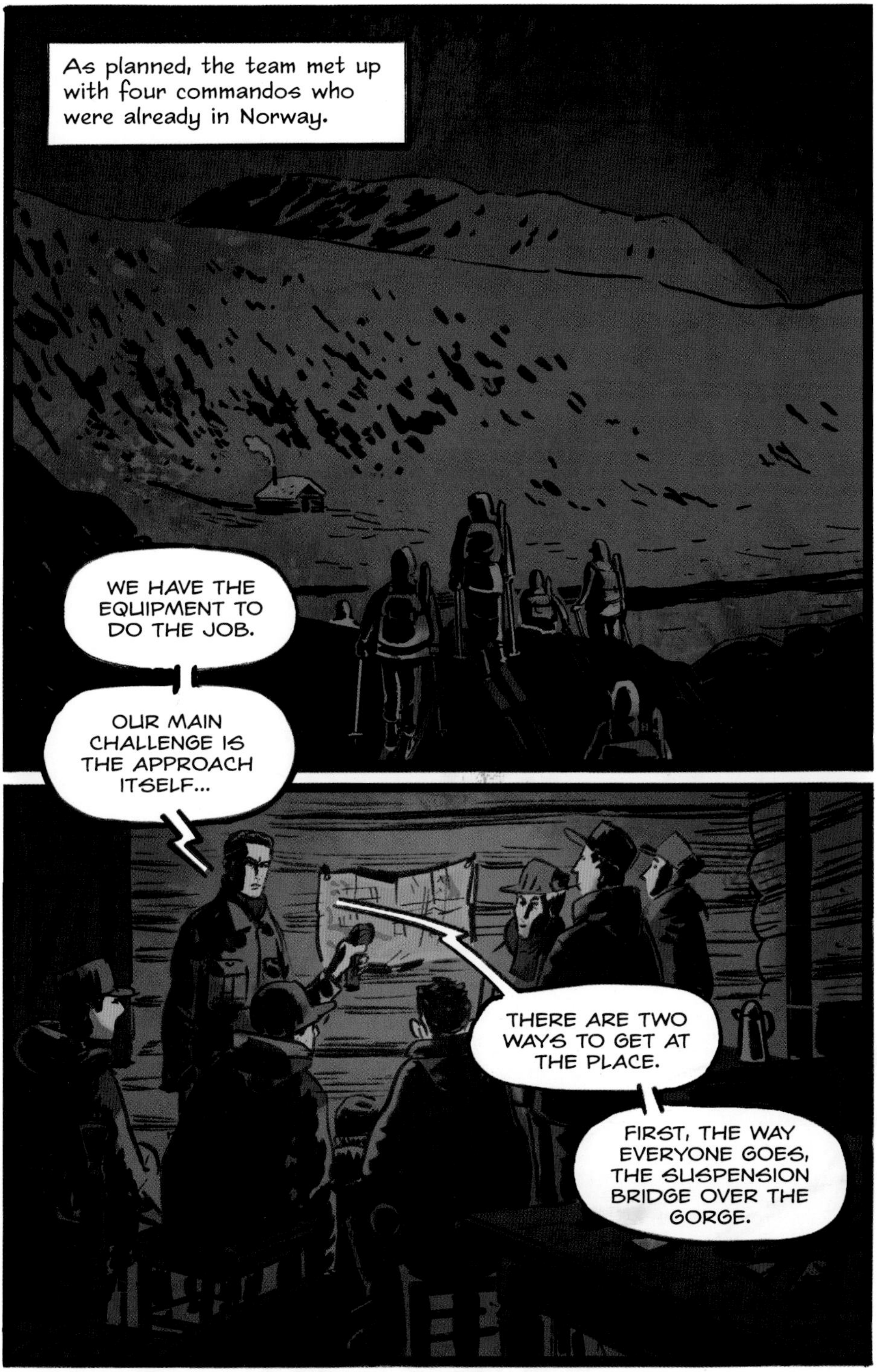

As planned, the team met up with four commandos who were already in Norway.
WE HAVE THE EQUIPMENT TO DO THE JOB.
OUR MAIN CHALLENGE IS THE APPROACH ITSELF...
THERE ARE TWO WAYS TO GET AT THE PLACE.
FIRST, THE WAY EVERYONE GOES, THE SUSPENSION BRIDGE OVER THE GORGE.

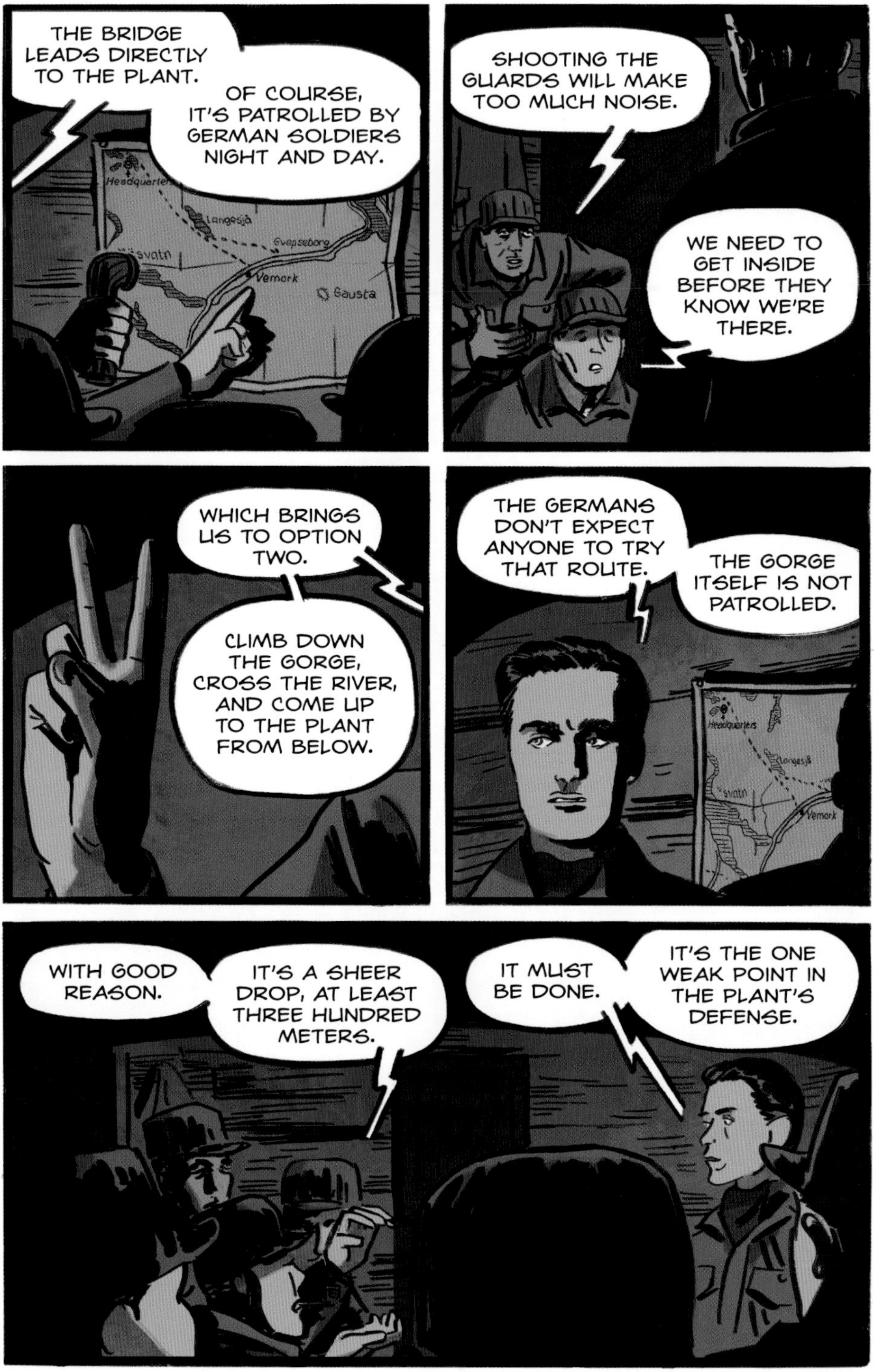
THE BRIDGE LEADS DIRECTLY TO THE PLANT.
OF COURSE, IT'S PATROLLED BY GERMAN SOLDIERS NIGHT AND DAY.
SHOOTING THE GUARDS WILL MAKE TOO MUCH NOISE.
WE NEED TO GET INSIDE BEFORE THEY KNOW WE'RE THERE.
WHICH BRINGS US TO OPTION TWO.
CLIMB DOWN THE GORGE, CROSS THE RIVER, AND COME UP TO THE PLANT FROM BELOW.
THE GERMANS DON'T EXPECT ANYONE TO TRY THAT ROUTE.
THE GORGE ITSELF IS NOT PATROLLED.
WITH GOOD REASON.
IT'S A SHEER DROP, AT LEAST THREE HUNDRED METERS.
IT MUST BE DONE.
IT'S THE ONE WEAK POINT IN THE PLANT'S DEFENSE.

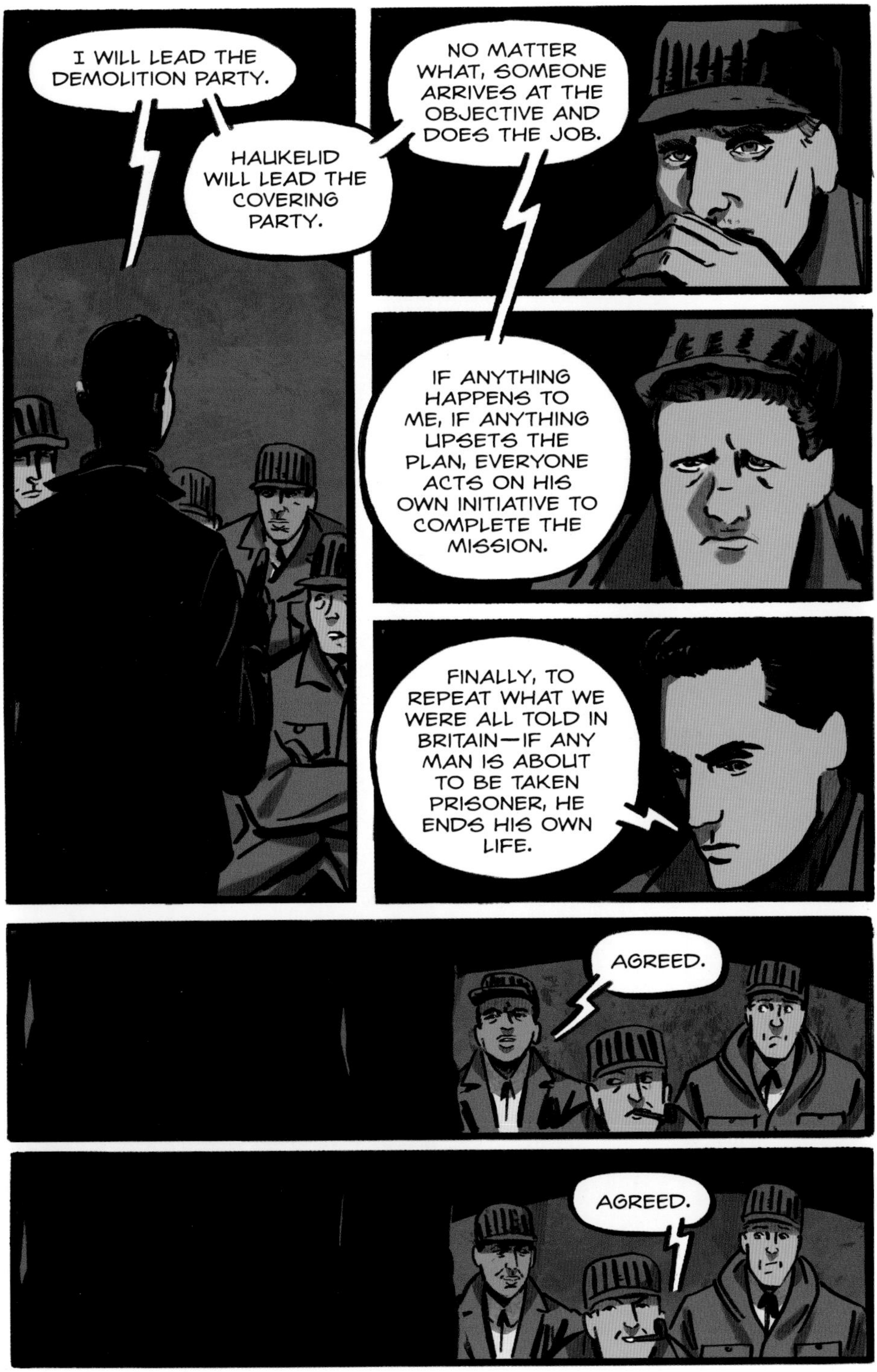
I WILL LEAD THE DEMOLITION PARTY.
HAUKELID WILL LEAD THE COVERING PARTY.
NO MATTER WHAT, SOMEONE ARRIVES AT THE OBJECTIVE AND DOES THE JOB.
IF ANYTHING HAPPENS TO ME, IF ANYTHING UPSETS THE PLAN, EVERYONE ACTS ON HIS OWN INITIATIVE TO COMPLETE THE MISSION.
FINALLY, TO REPEAT WHAT WE WERE ALL TOLD IN BRITAIN—IF ANY MAN IS ABOUT TO BE TAKEN PRISONER, HE ENDS HIS OWN LIFE.
AGREED.
AGREED.

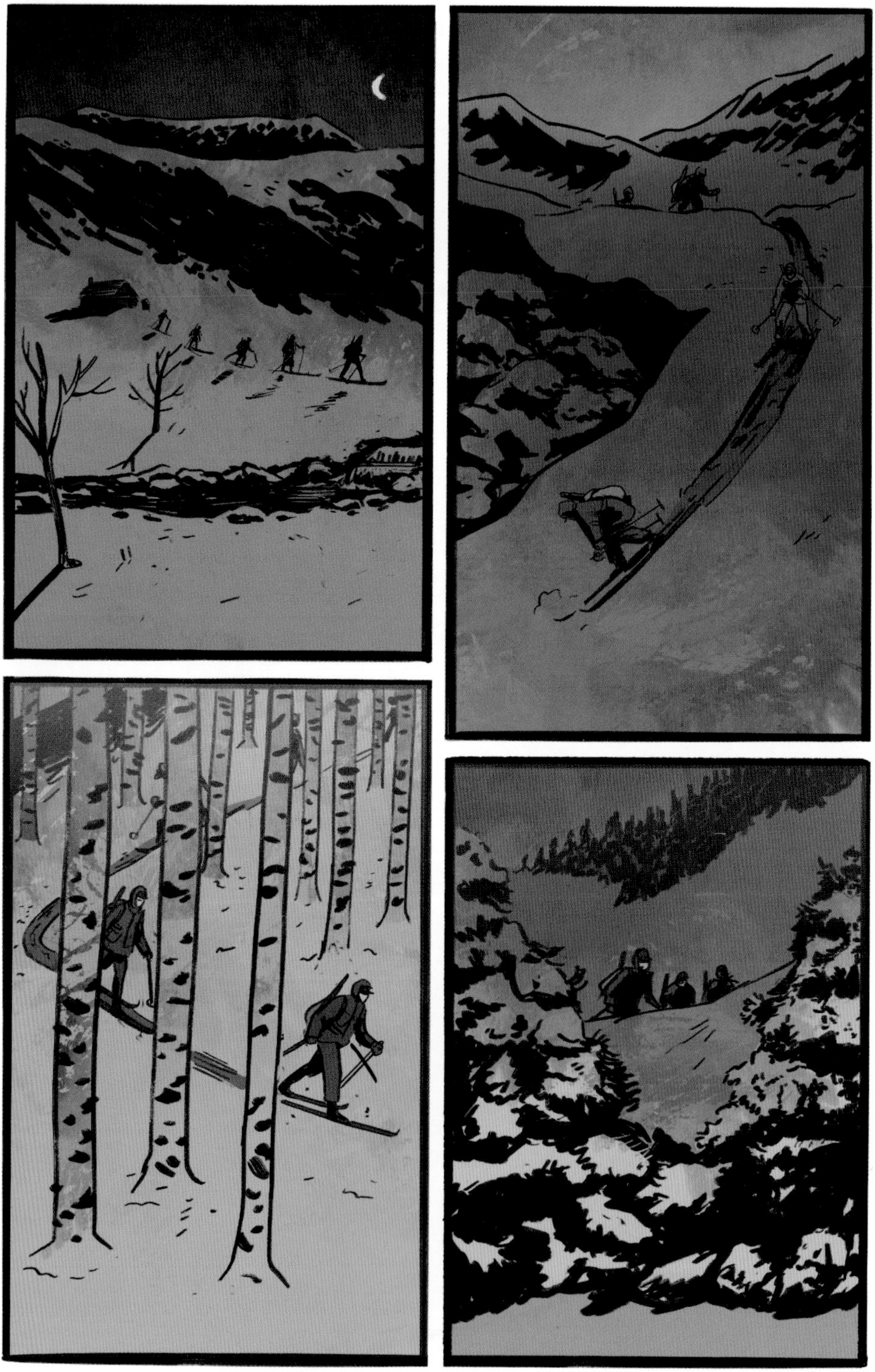

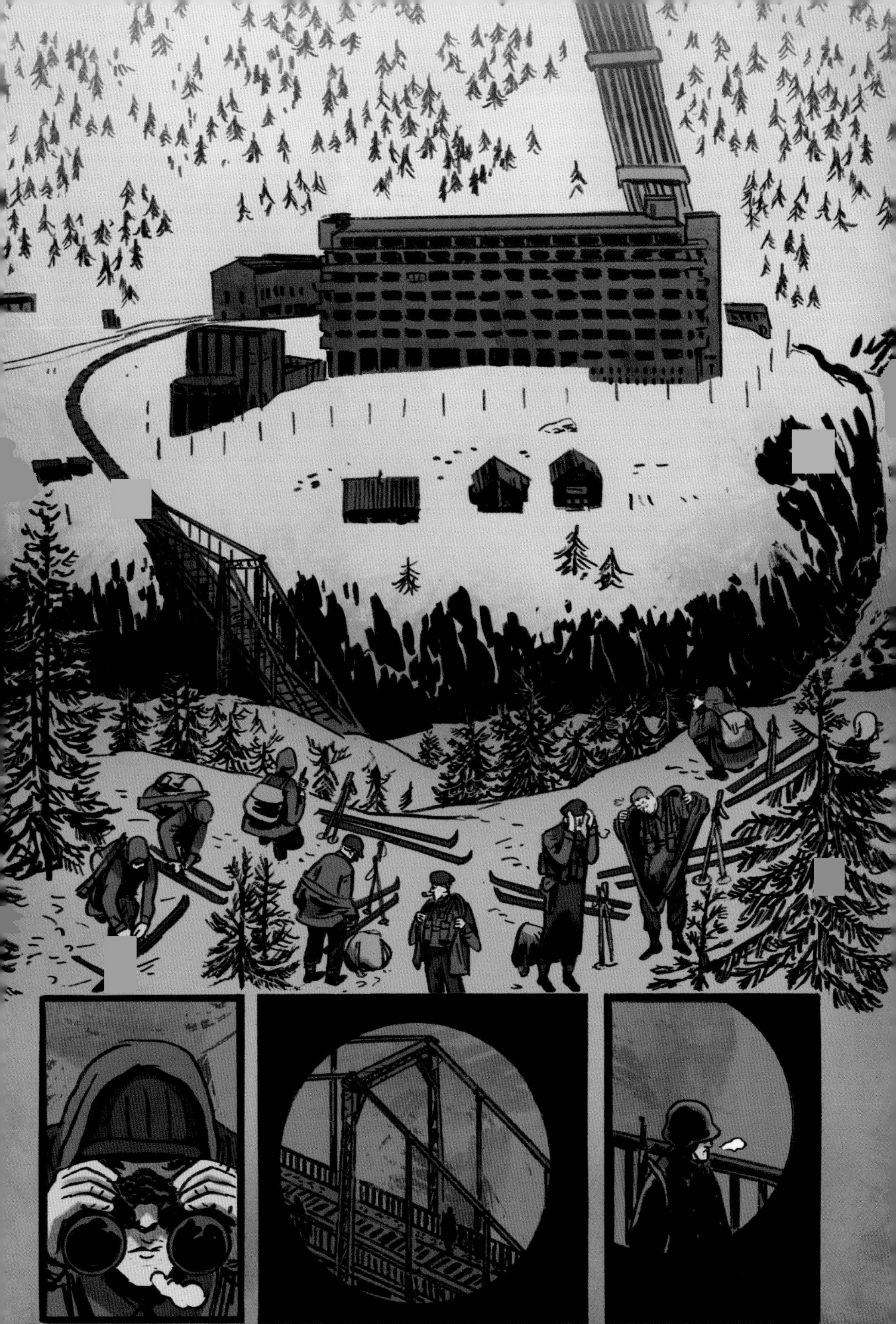

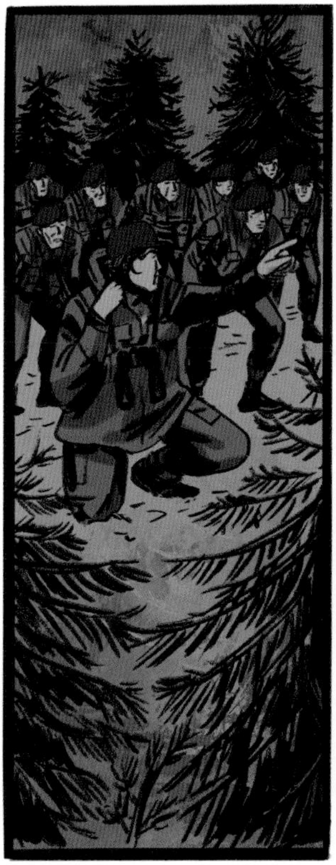

Knut Haukelid remembered a piece of advice from his trainers in Britain.

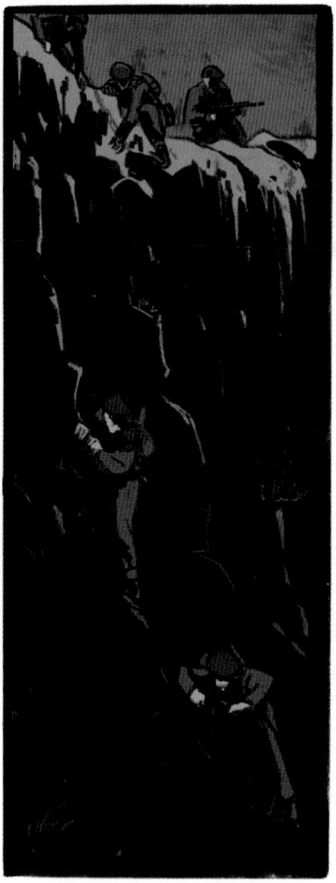

Never look down.

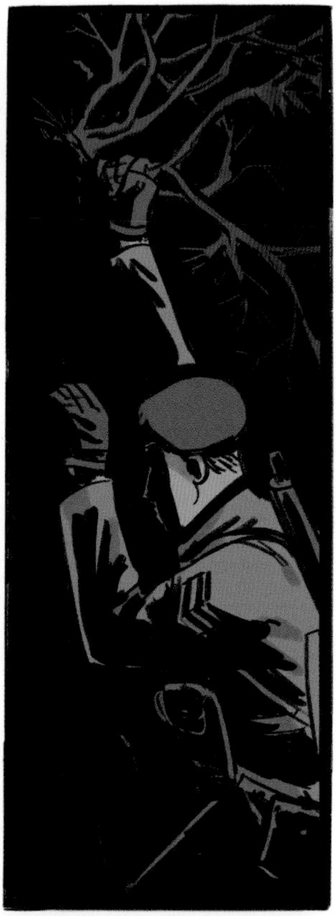

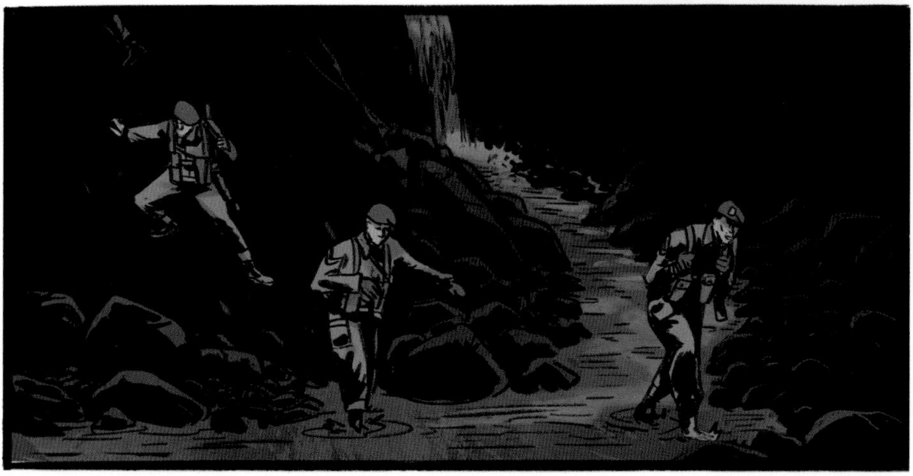

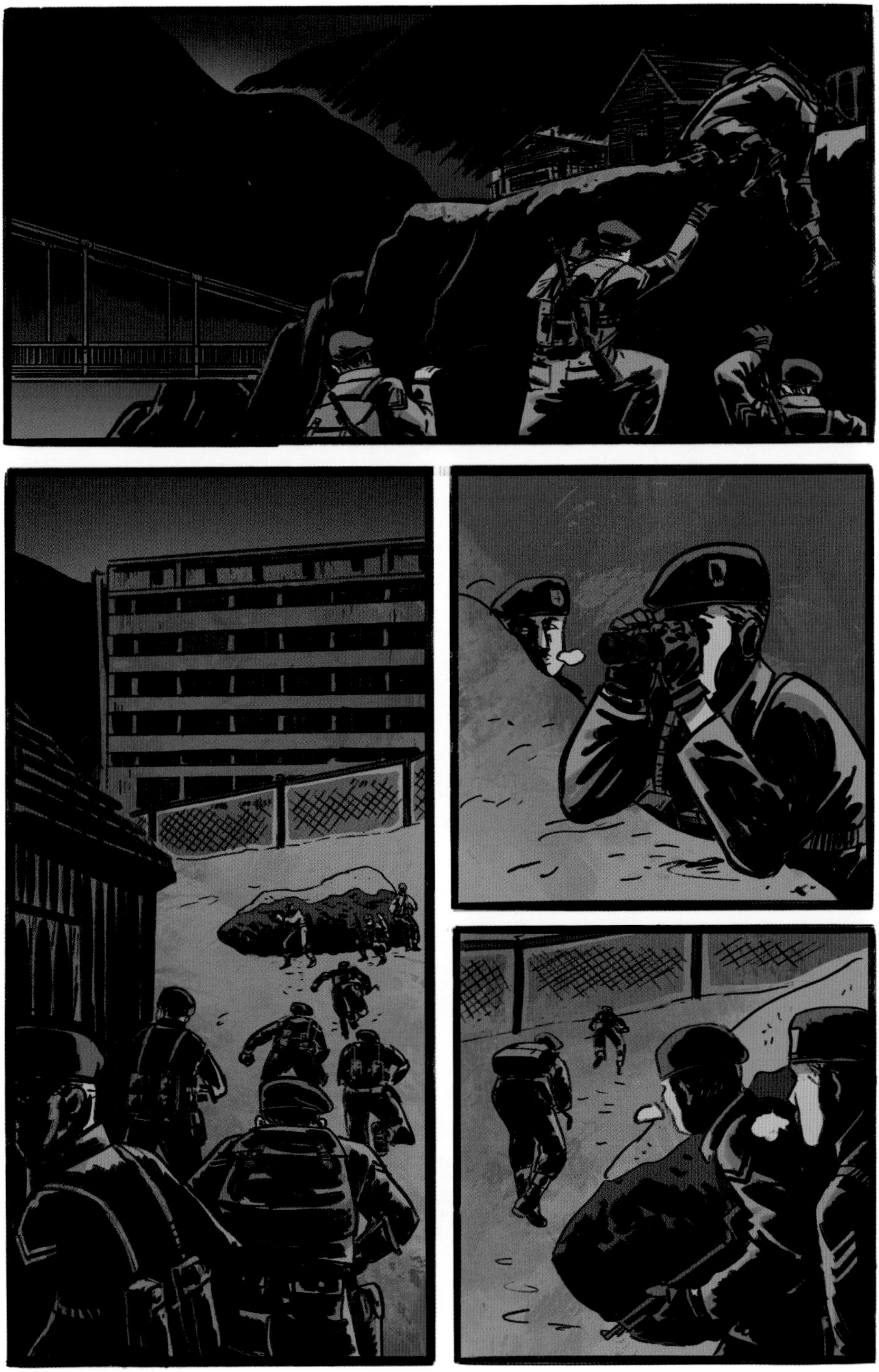

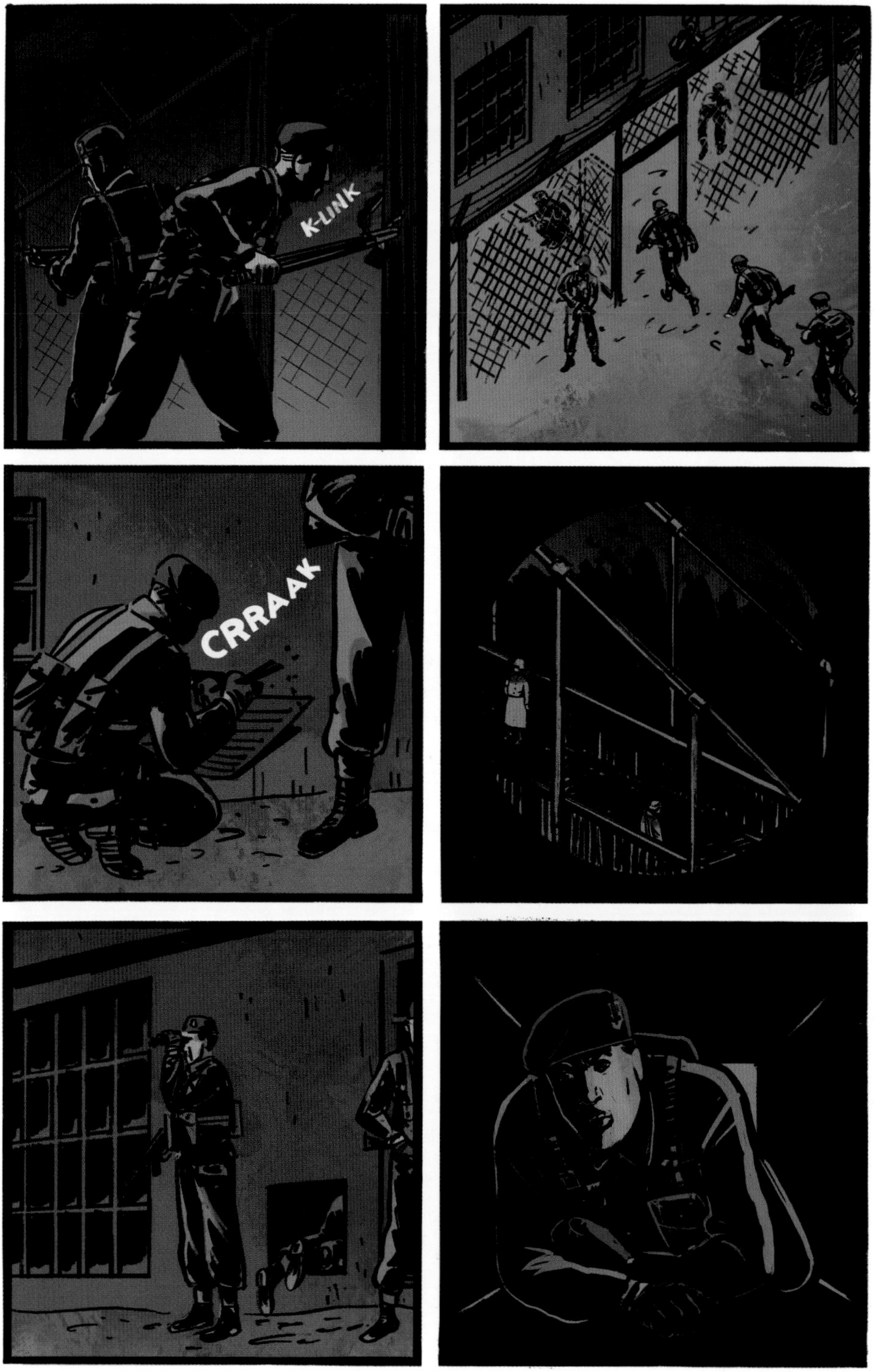
K-LINK
CRRAAK

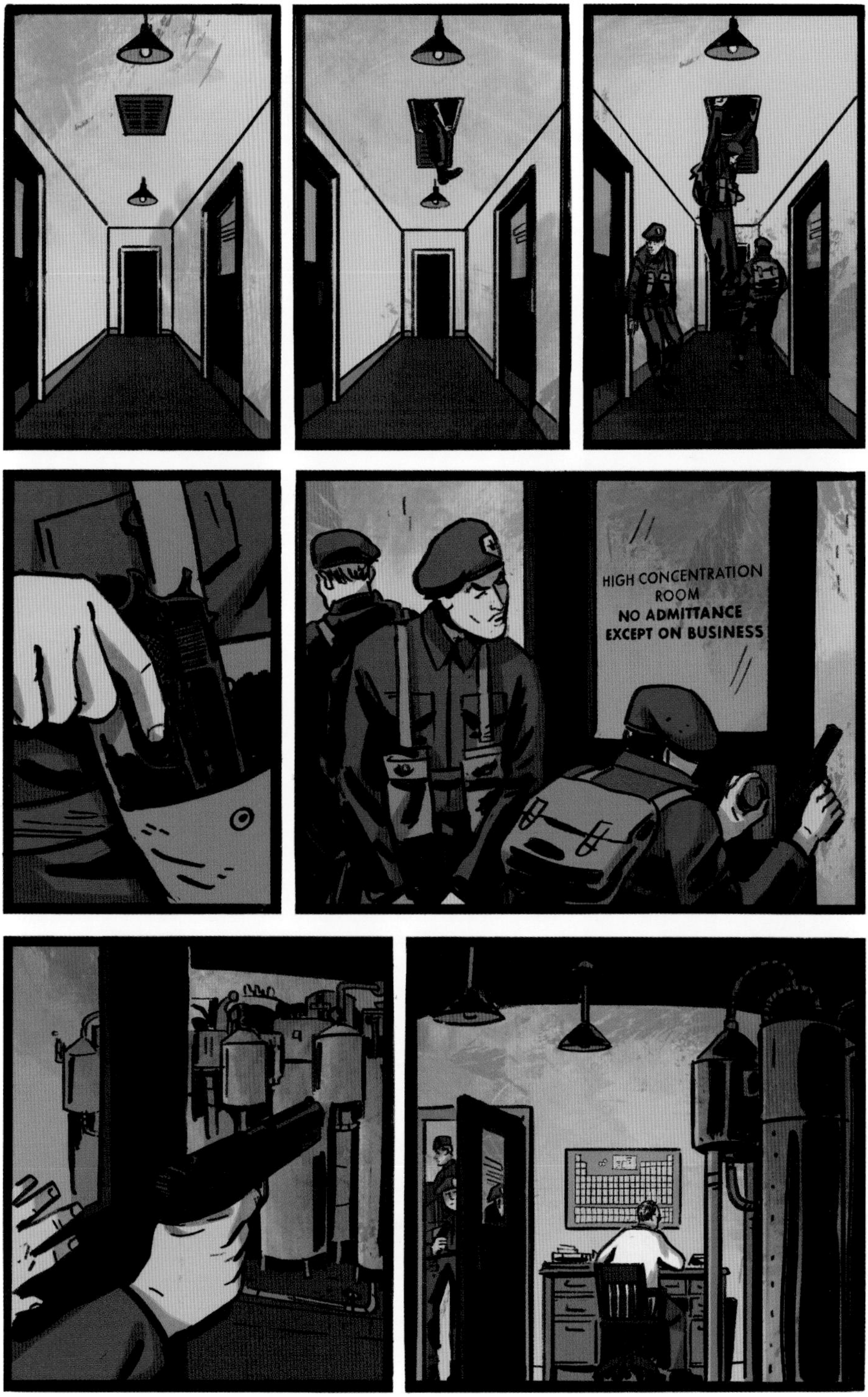
HIGH CONCENTRATION
ROOM
NO ADMITTANCE
EXCEPT ON BUSINESS

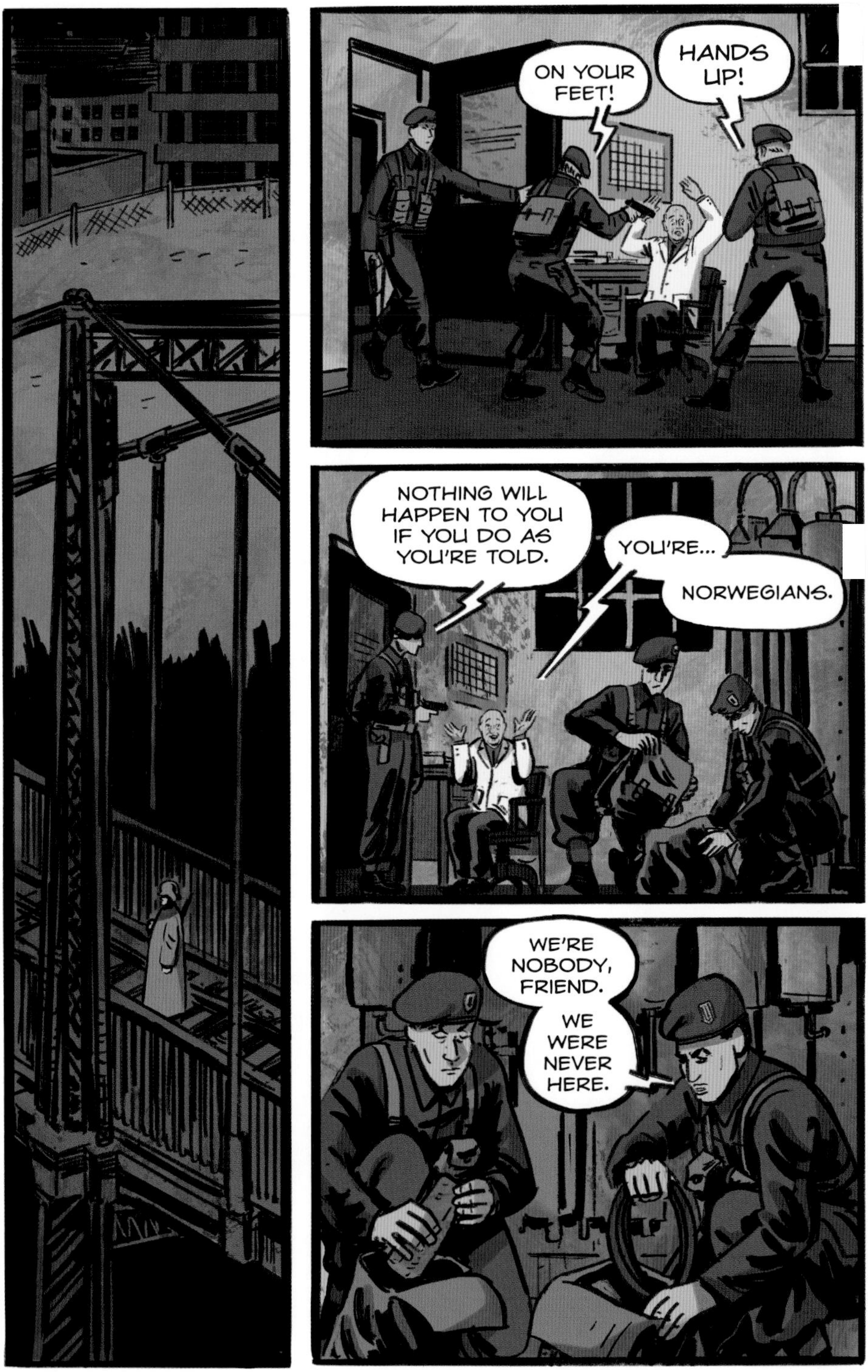
ON YOUR FEET!
HANDS UP!
NOTHING WILL HAPPEN TO YOU IF YOU DO AS YOU'RE TOLD.
YOU'RE...
NORWEGIANS.
WE'RE NOBODY, FRIEND.
WE WERE NEVER HERE.

ALRIGHT, LET'S GET THAT DOOR TO THE YARD UNLOCKED.

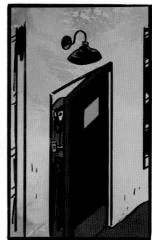

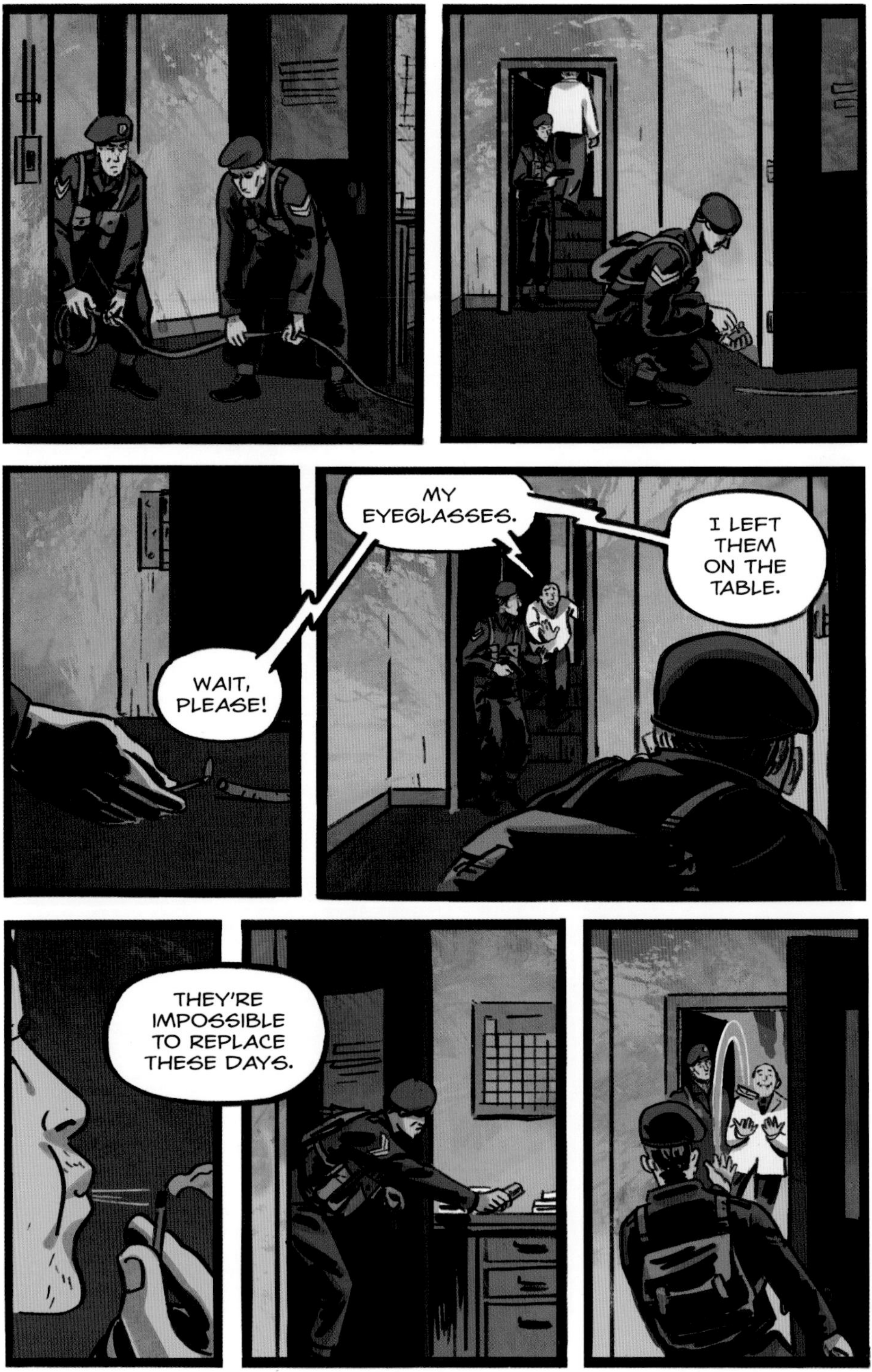
WAIT, PLEASE!
MY EYEGLASSES.
I LEFT THEM ON THE TABLE.
THEY'RE IMPOSSIBLE TO REPLACE THESE DAYS.

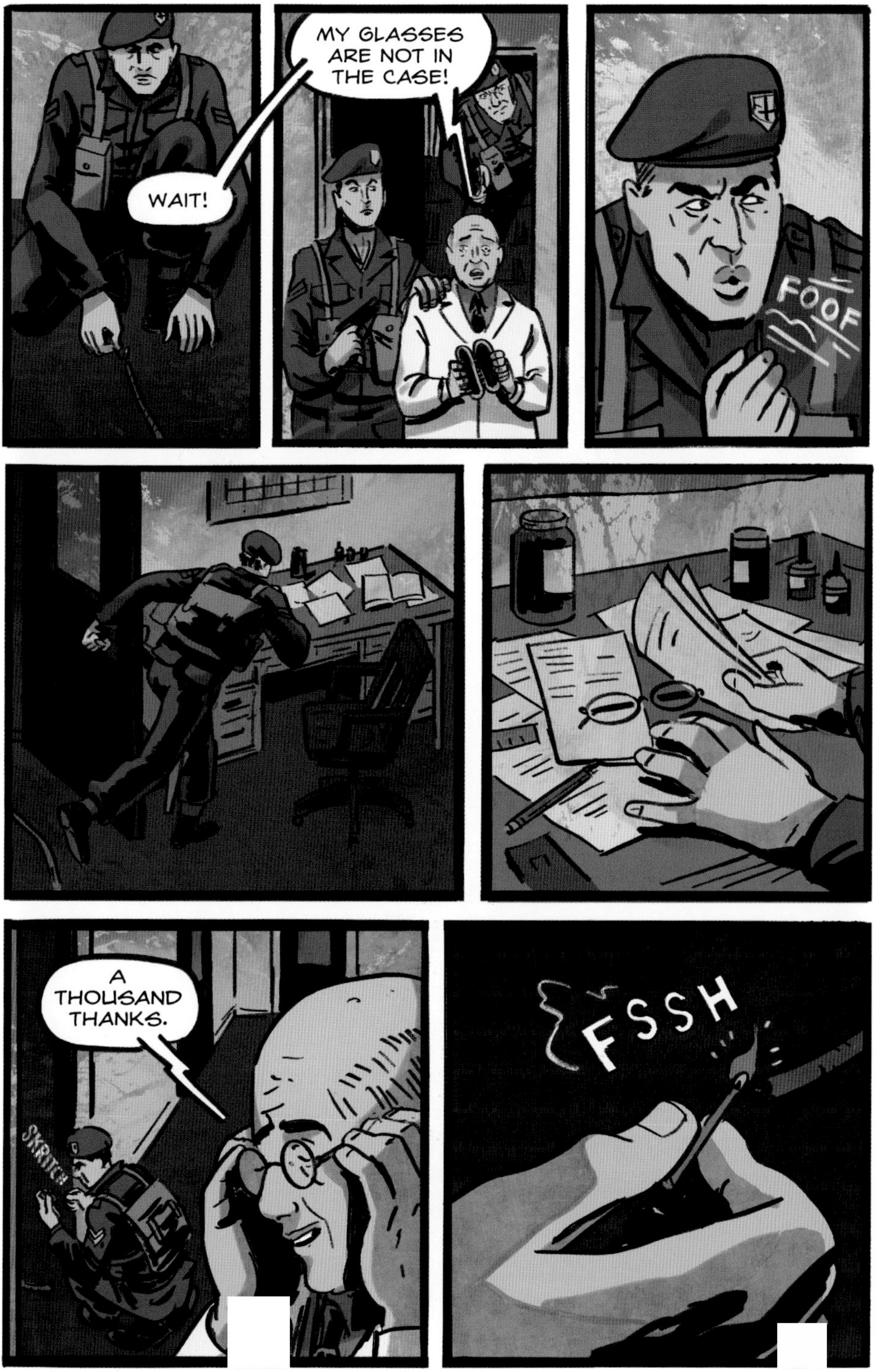
WAIT!
MY GLASSES ARE NOT IN THE CASE!
FOOF
A THOUSAND THANKS.
SKRITCH
FSSH

KOOM

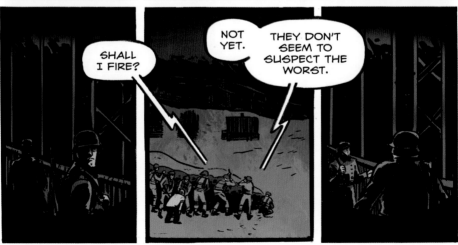

SHALL I FIRE?

NOT YET.

THEY DON'T SEEM TO SUSPECT THE WORST.

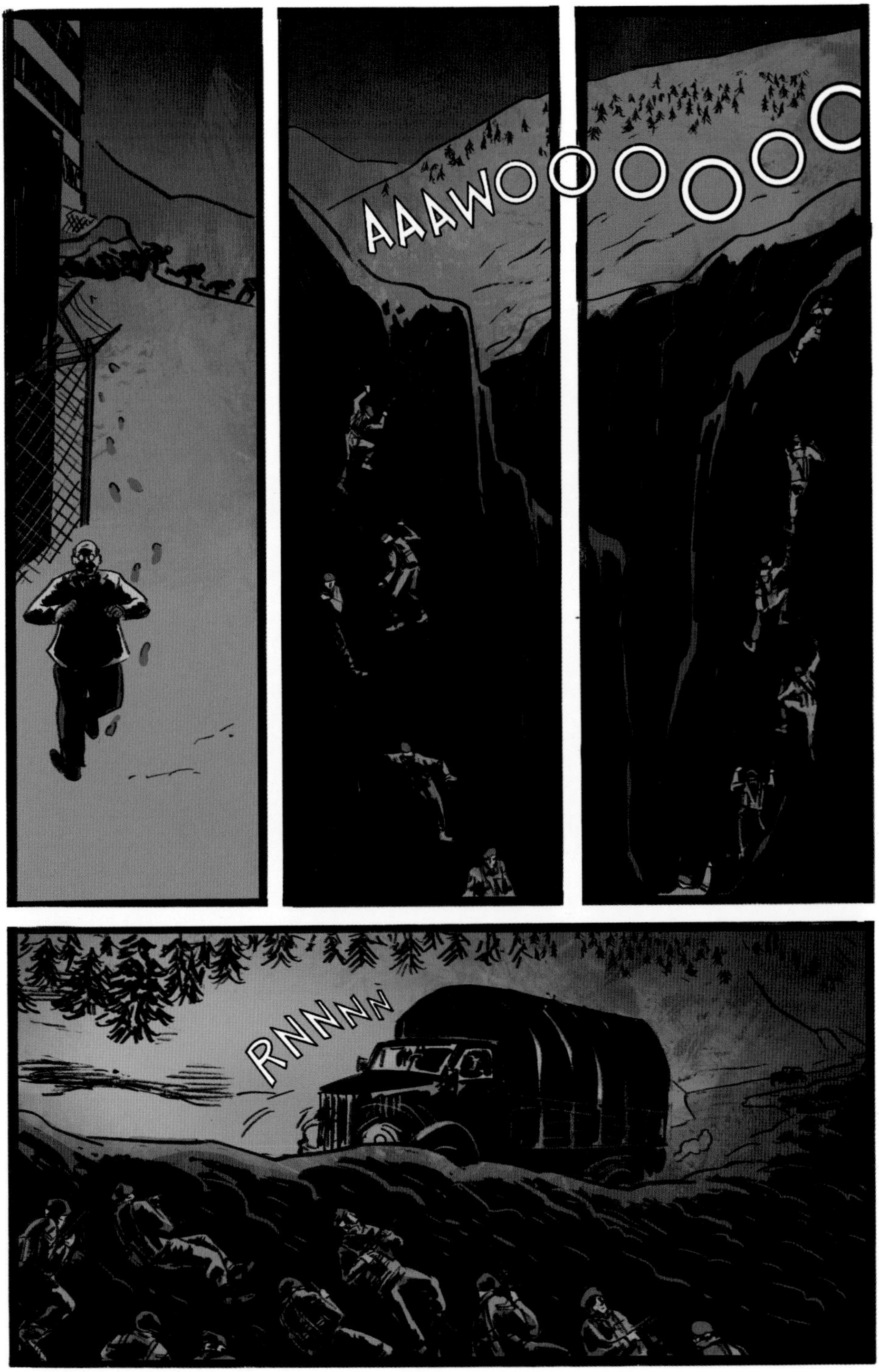
AAAWOOOOOO
RNNNN

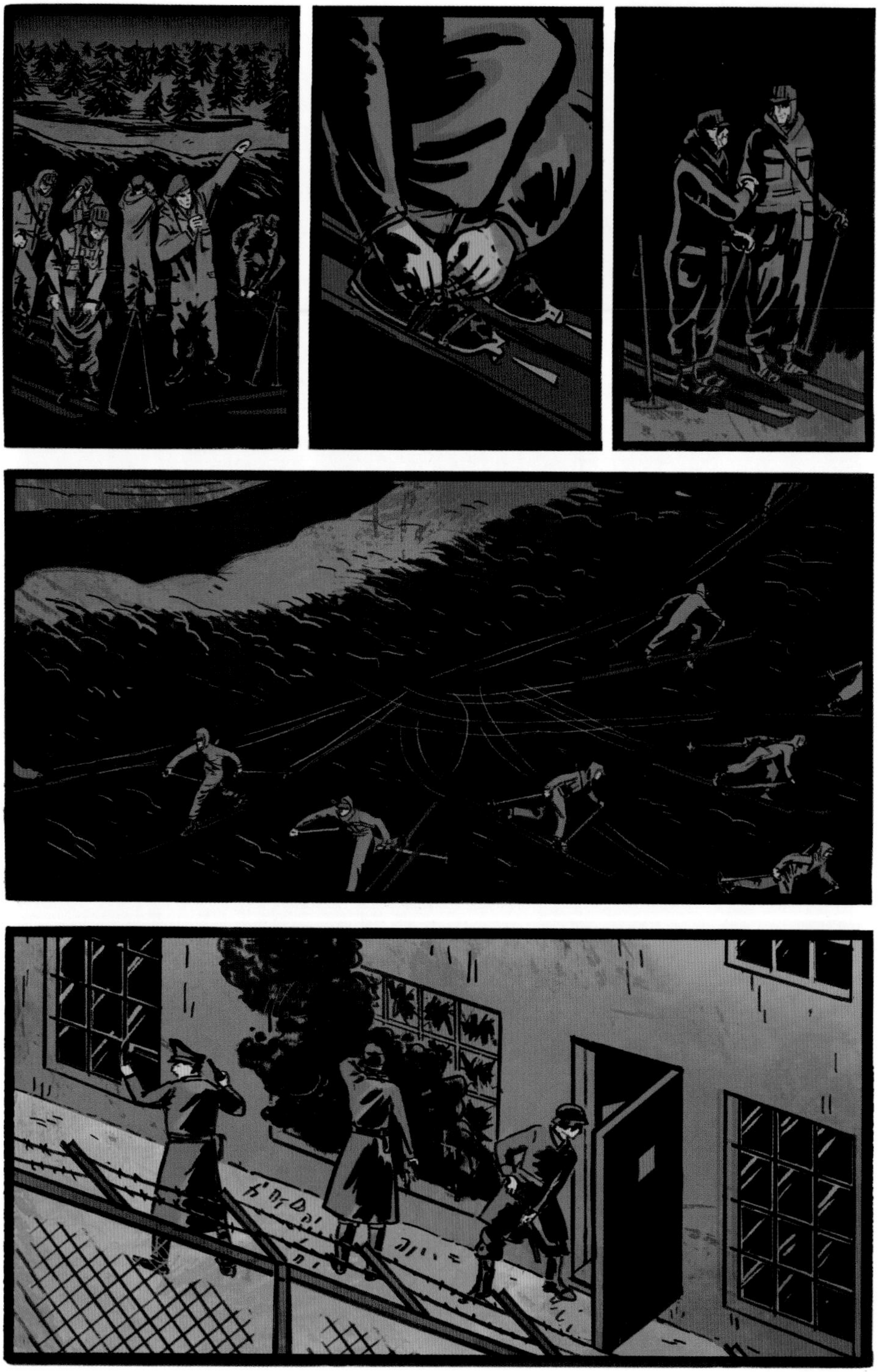

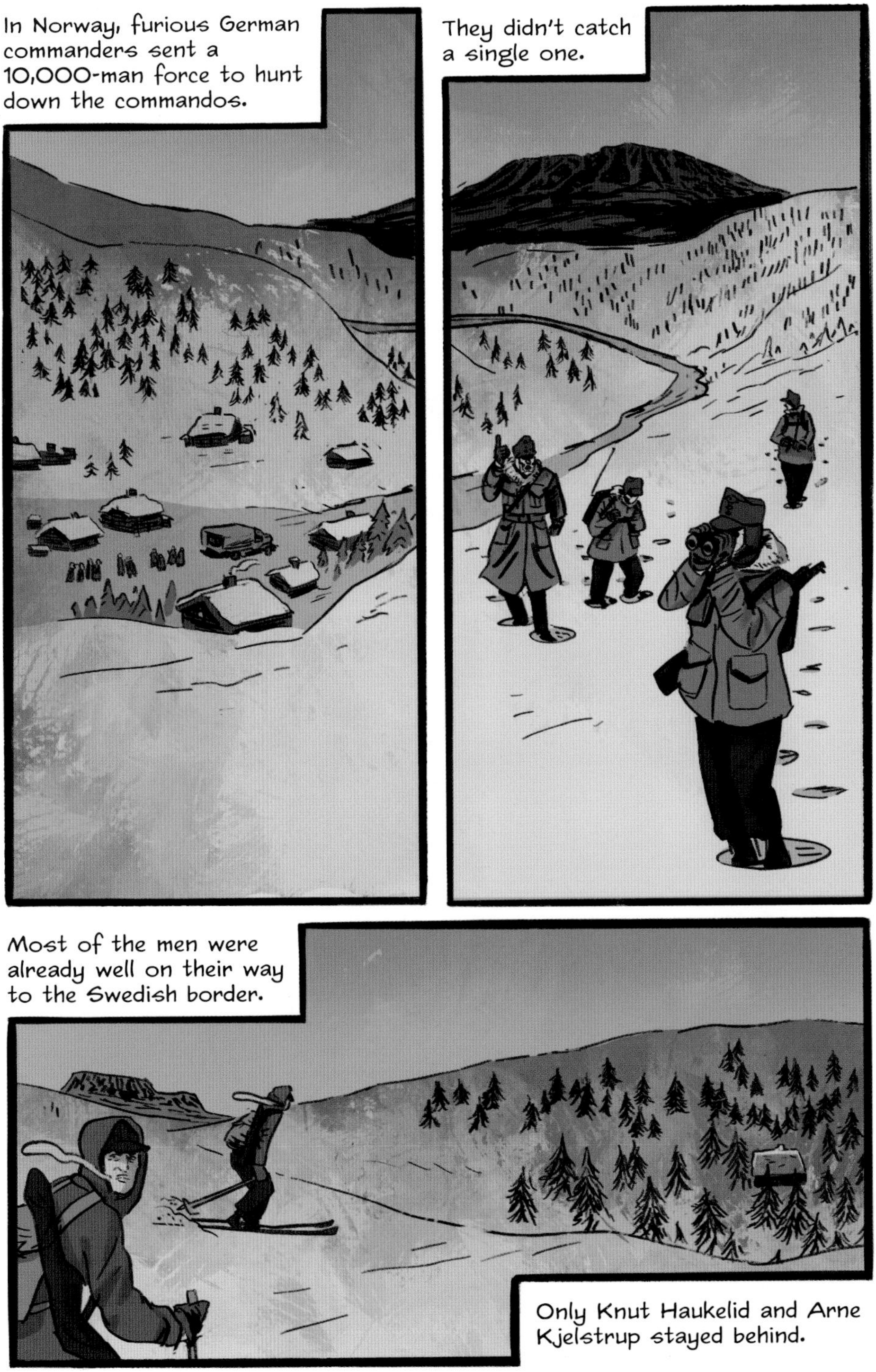
In Norway, furious German commanders sent a 10,000-man force to hunt down the commandos.
They didn't catch a single one.
Most of the men were already well on their way to the Swedish border.
Only Knut Haukelid and Arne Kjelstrup stayed behind.

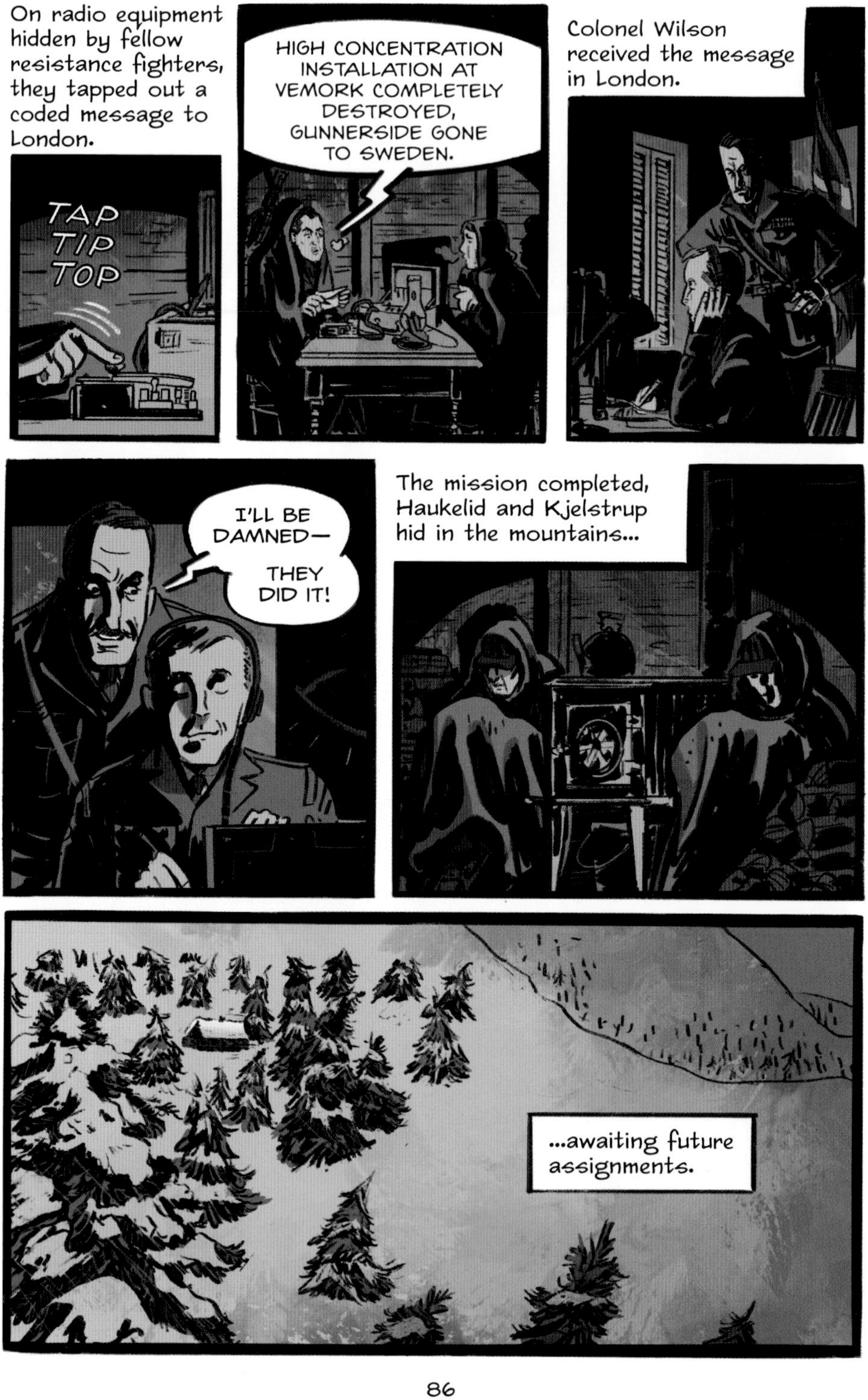
On radio equipment hidden by fellow resistance fighters, they tapped out a coded message to London.
TAP TIP TOP
HIGH CONCENTRATION INSTALLATION AT VEMORK COMPLETELY DESTROYED, GUNNERSIDE GONE TO SWEDEN.
Colonel Wilson received the message in London.
I'LL BE DAMNED—
THEY DID IT!
The mission completed, Haukelid and Kjelstrup hid in the mountains...
...awaiting future assignments.

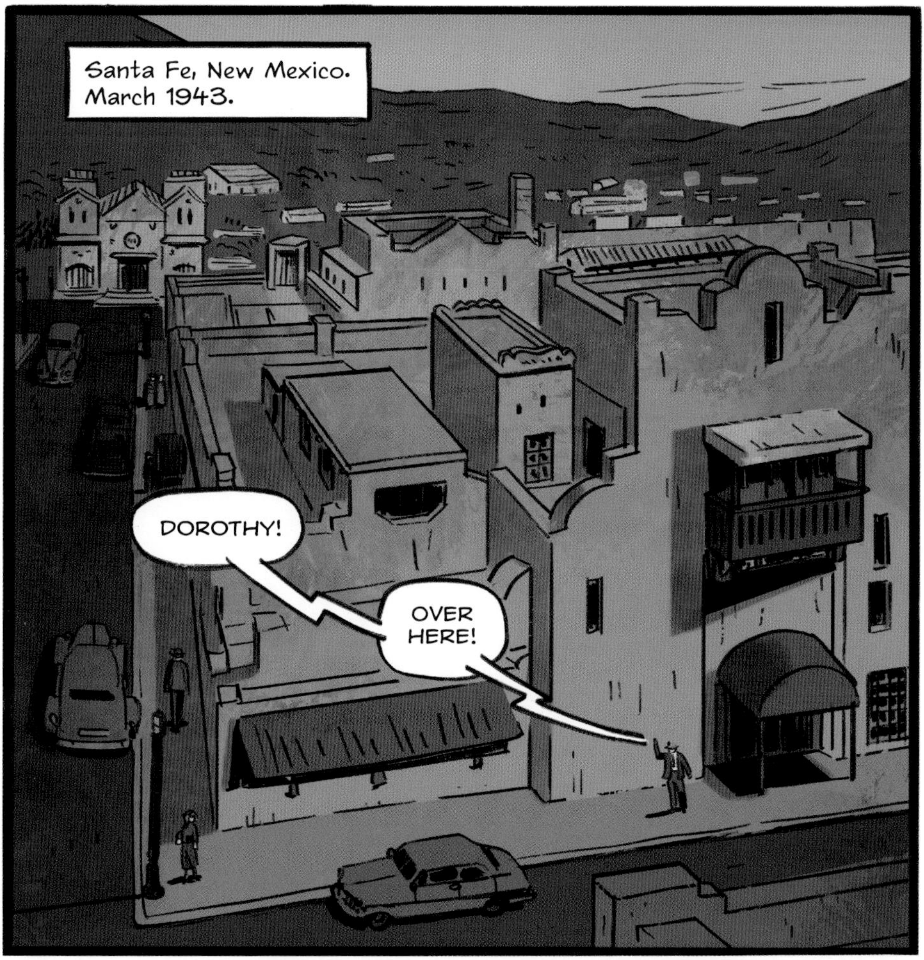
Santa Fe, New Mexico.
March 1943.
DOROTHY!
OVER HERE!

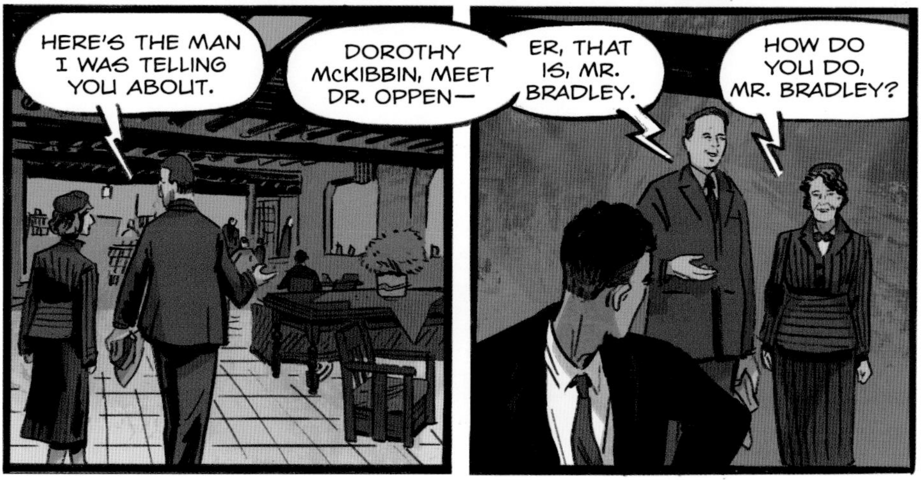
HERE'S THE MAN I WAS TELLING YOU ABOUT.
DOROTHY McKIBBIN, MEET DR. OPPEN—
ER, THAT IS, MR. BRADLEY.
HOW DO YOU DO, MR. BRADLEY?

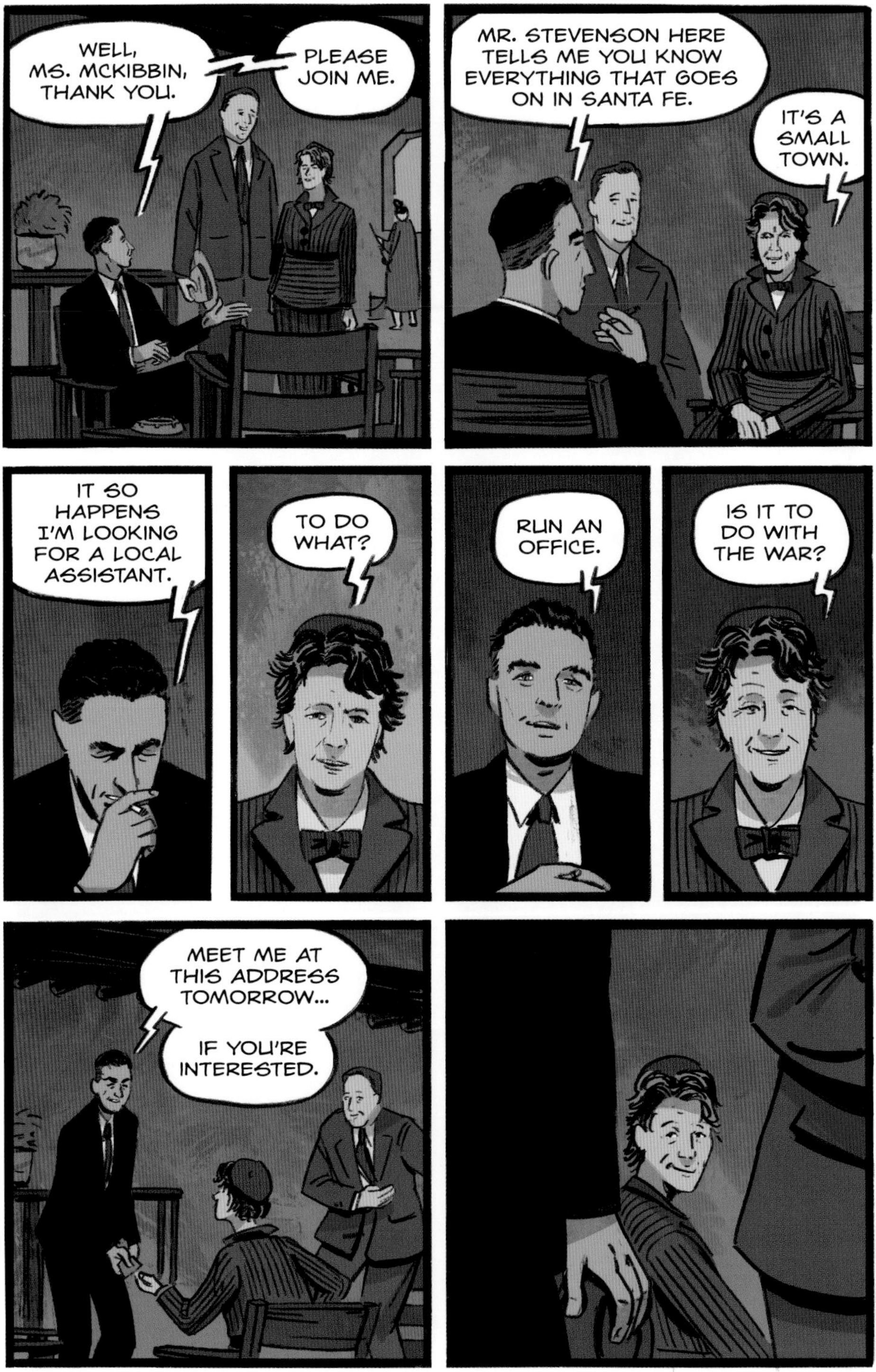
WELL, MS. MCKIBBIN, THANK YOU.
PLEASE JOIN ME.
MR. STEVENSON HERE TELLS ME YOU KNOW EVERYTHING THAT GOES ON IN SANTA FE.
IT'S A SMALL TOWN.
IT SO HAPPENS I'M LOOKING FOR A LOCAL ASSISTANT.
TO DO WHAT?
RUN AN OFFICE.
IS IT TO DO WITH THE WAR?
MEET ME AT THIS ADDRESS TOMORROW...
IF YOU'RE INTERESTED.

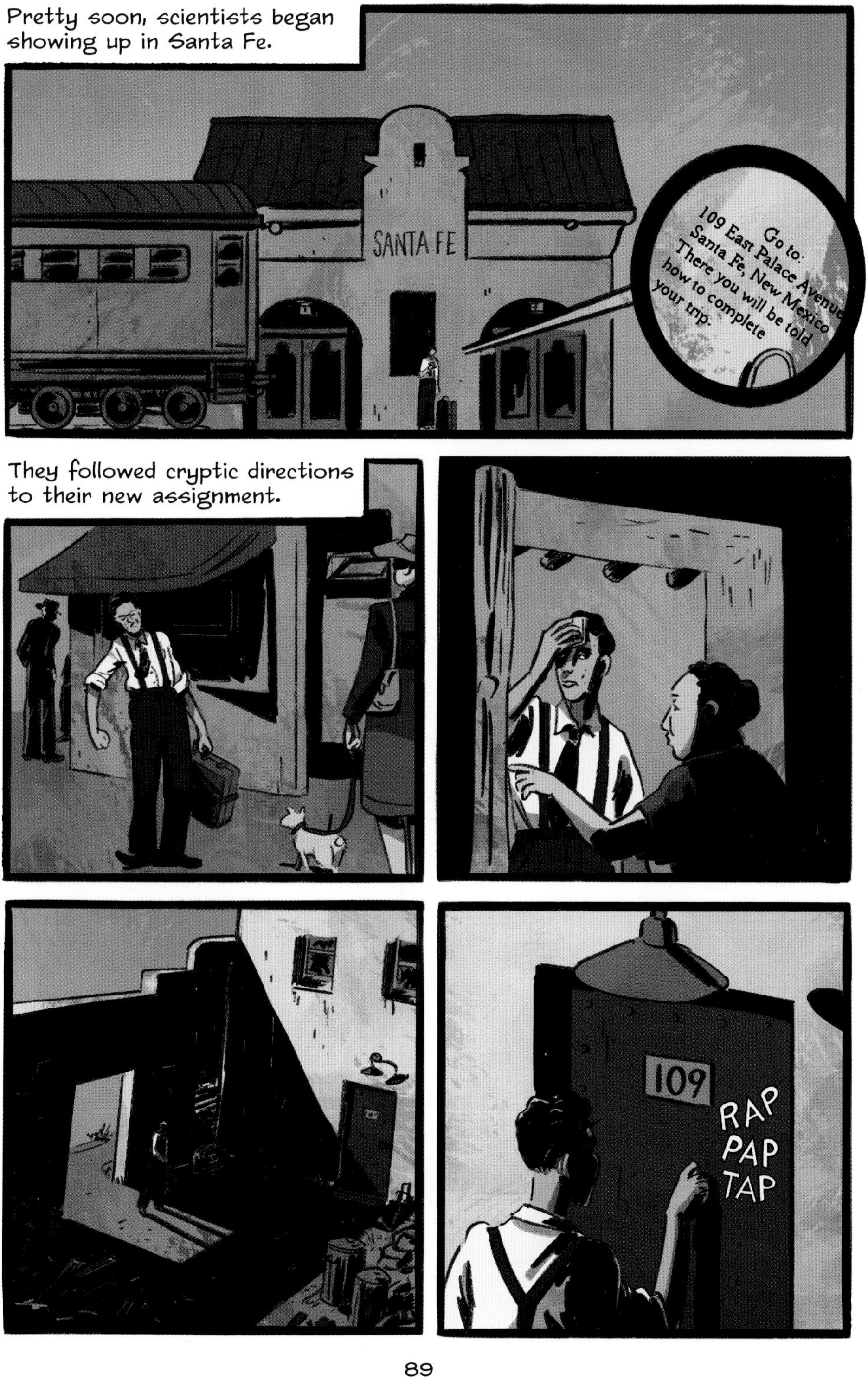
Pretty soon, scientists began showing up in Santa Fe.
SANTA FE
Go to:
109 East Palace Avenue
Santa Fe, New Mexico
There you will be told
how to complete
your trip.
They followed cryptic directions to their new assignment.
109
RAP
PAP
TAP

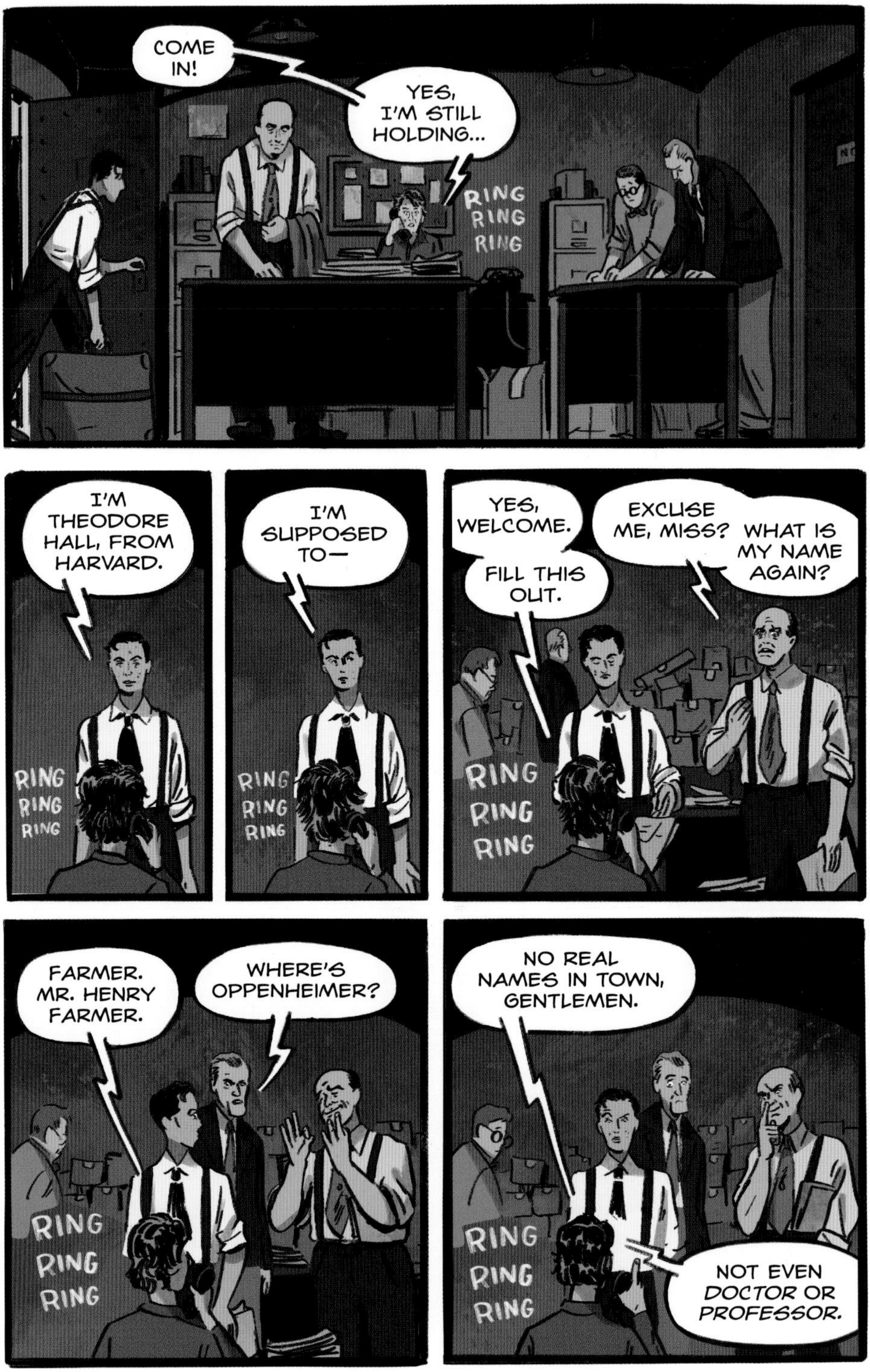
COME IN!
YES, I'M STILL HOLDING...
RING RING RING
I'M THEODORE HALL, FROM HARVARD.
RING RING RING
I'M SUPPOSED TO—
RING RING RING
YES, WELCOME.
FILL THIS OUT.
EXCUSE ME, MISS? WHAT IS MY NAME AGAIN?
RING RING RING
FARMER. MR. HENRY FARMER.
WHERE'S OPPENHEIMER?
RING RING RING
NO REAL NAMES IN TOWN, GENTLEMEN.
NOT EVEN *DOCTOR* OR *PROFESSOR*.
RING RING RING

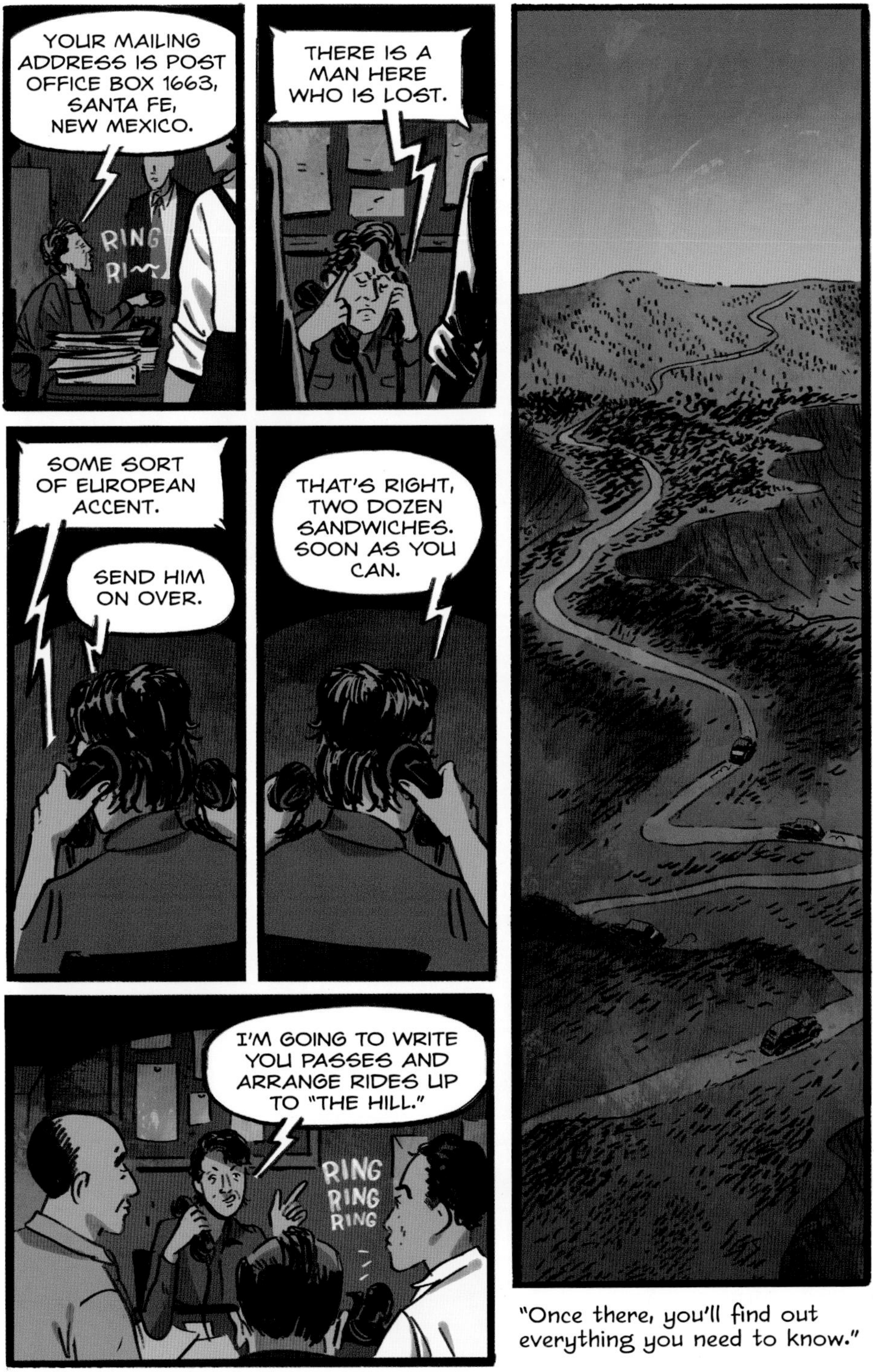
YOUR MAILING ADDRESS IS POST OFFICE BOX 1663, SANTA FE, NEW MEXICO.
RING
RI~~
THERE IS A MAN HERE WHO IS LOST.
SOME SORT OF EUROPEAN ACCENT.
SEND HIM ON OVER.
THAT'S RIGHT, TWO DOZEN SANDWICHES. SOON AS YOU CAN.
I'M GOING TO WRITE YOU PASSES AND ARRANGE RIDES UP TO "THE HILL."
RING
RING
RING

"Once there, you'll find out everything you need to know."

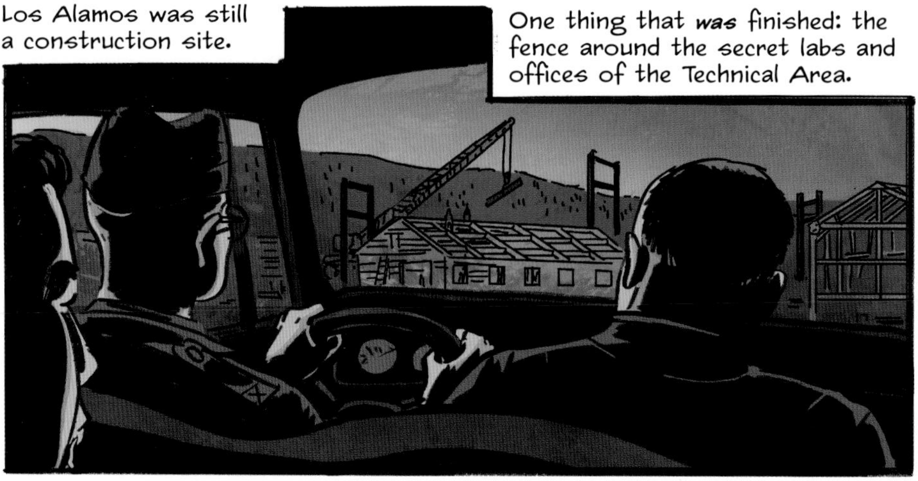
Los Alamos was still a construction site.
One thing that *was* finished: the fence around the secret labs and offices of the Technical Area.

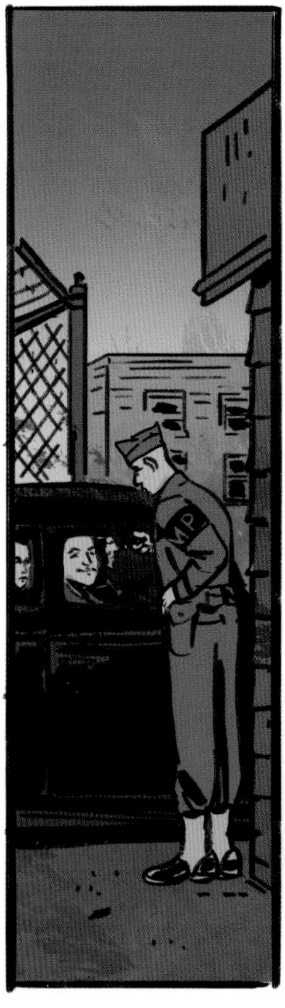
Military police guarded the only gate twenty-four hours a day.
MP

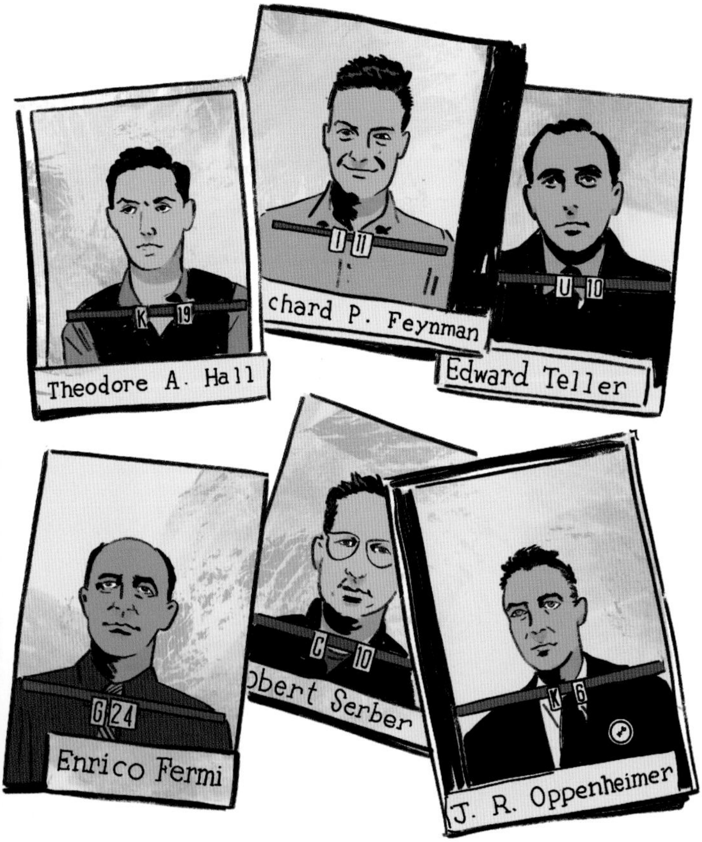
K 19
Theodore A. Hall
U 11
chard P. Feynman
U 10
Edward Teller
G 24
Enrico Fermi
C 10
bert Serber
K 6
J. R. Oppenheimer

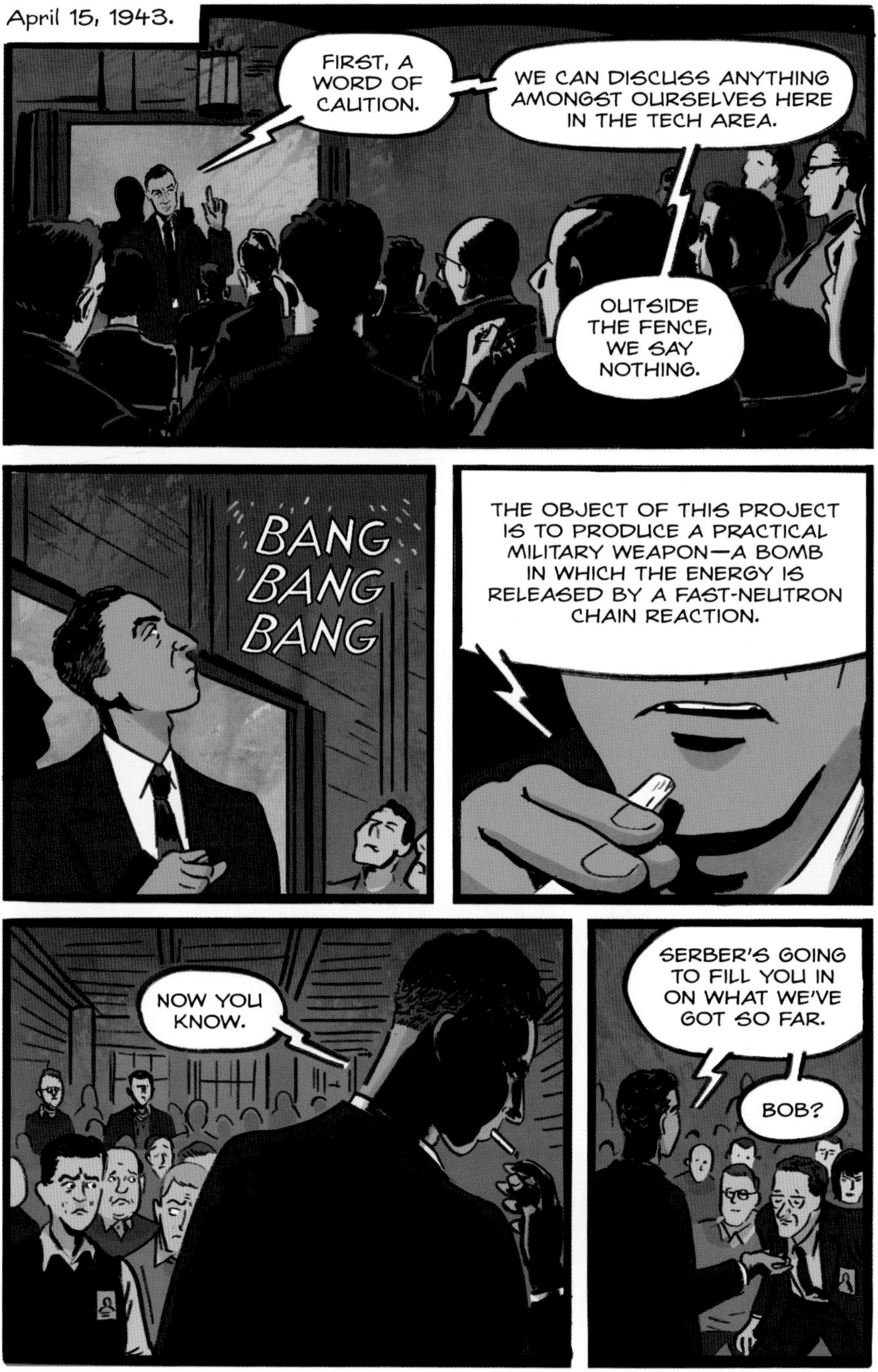
April 15, 1943.
FIRST, A WORD OF CAUTION.
WE CAN DISCUSS ANYTHING AMONGST OURSELVES HERE IN THE TECH AREA.
OUTSIDE THE FENCE, WE SAY NOTHING.
BANG BANG BANG
THE OBJECT OF THIS PROJECT IS TO PRODUCE A PRACTICAL MILITARY WEAPON—A BOMB IN WHICH THE ENERGY IS RELEASED BY A FAST-NEUTRON CHAIN REACTION.
NOW YOU KNOW.
SERBER'S GOING TO FILL YOU IN ON WHAT WE'VE GOT SO FAR.
BOB?

BRING THE DRILL OVER HERE!
UM, OKAY...
THE DIRECT ENERGY RELEASE IN THE FISSION PROCESS IS 170 MEV PER ATOM.
WHICH IS CONSIDERABLY MORE THAN 107 TIMES THE HEAT OF REACTION PER ATOM IN THE CHEMICAL COMBUSTION PROCESS.
SINCE THE MASS OF ONE NUCLEUS OF 235 IS 3.9 X 10-22 GRAMS, THE ENERGY RELEASE IS 8.2 X 1017 ERG/GRAM...
CRACK
#@%&!
...AND SINCE THERE ARE APPROXIMATELY 2.6 X 1024 NUCLEI IN ONE KILOGRAM OF 235, IT WOULD REQUIRE ABOUT N = 80 GENERATIONS TO FISSION THE ENTIRE KILOGRAM.
WE NOW CONSIDER THE ACTUAL MECHANICS OF THE BOMB, THE ASPECT OF THE JOB WE—
HOLD IT THERE, BOB!

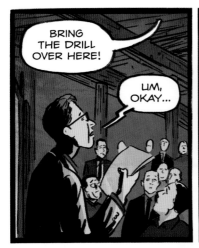

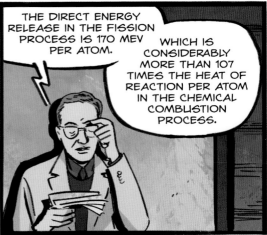

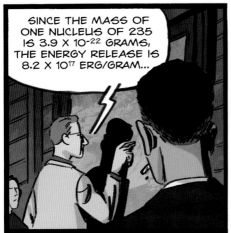

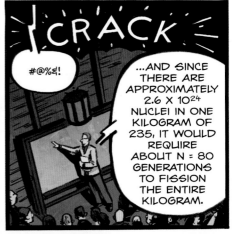

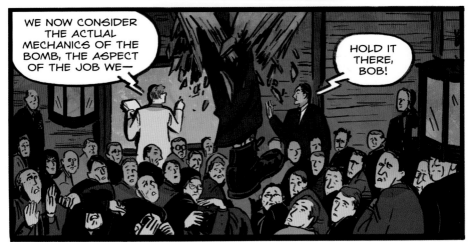

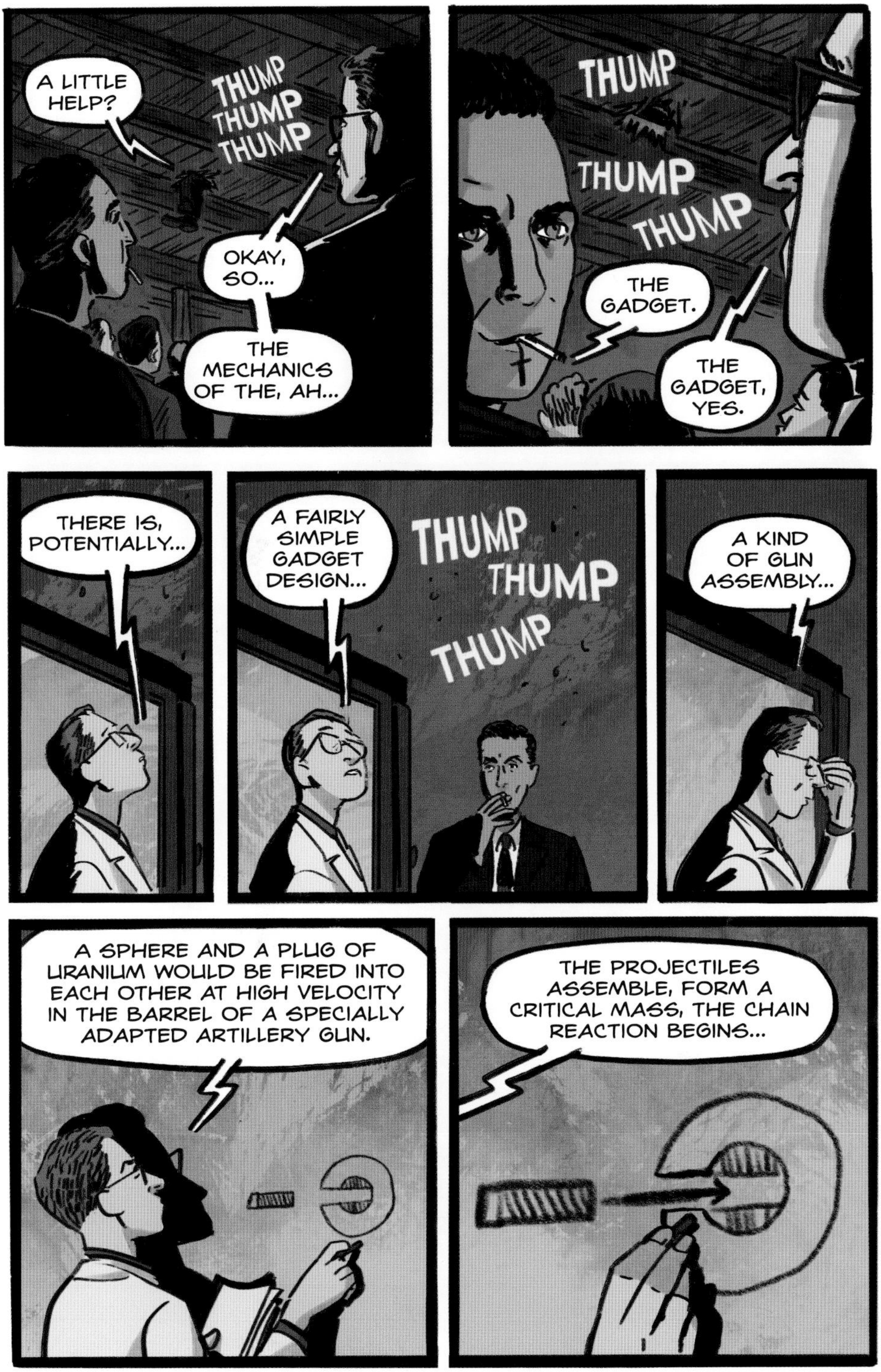
A LITTLE HELP?
THUMP THUMP THUMP
OKAY, SO...
THE MECHANICS OF THE, AH...
THUMP
THUMP
THUMP
THE GADGET.
THE GADGET, YES.
THERE IS, POTENTIALLY...
A FAIRLY SIMPLE GADGET DESIGN...
THUMP THUMP THUMP
A KIND OF GUN ASSEMBLY...
A SPHERE AND A PLUG OF URANIUM WOULD BE FIRED INTO EACH OTHER AT HIGH VELOCITY IN THE BARREL OF A SPECIALLY ADAPTED ARTILLERY GUN.
THE PROJECTILES ASSEMBLE, FORM A CRITICAL MASS, THE CHAIN REACTION BEGINS...

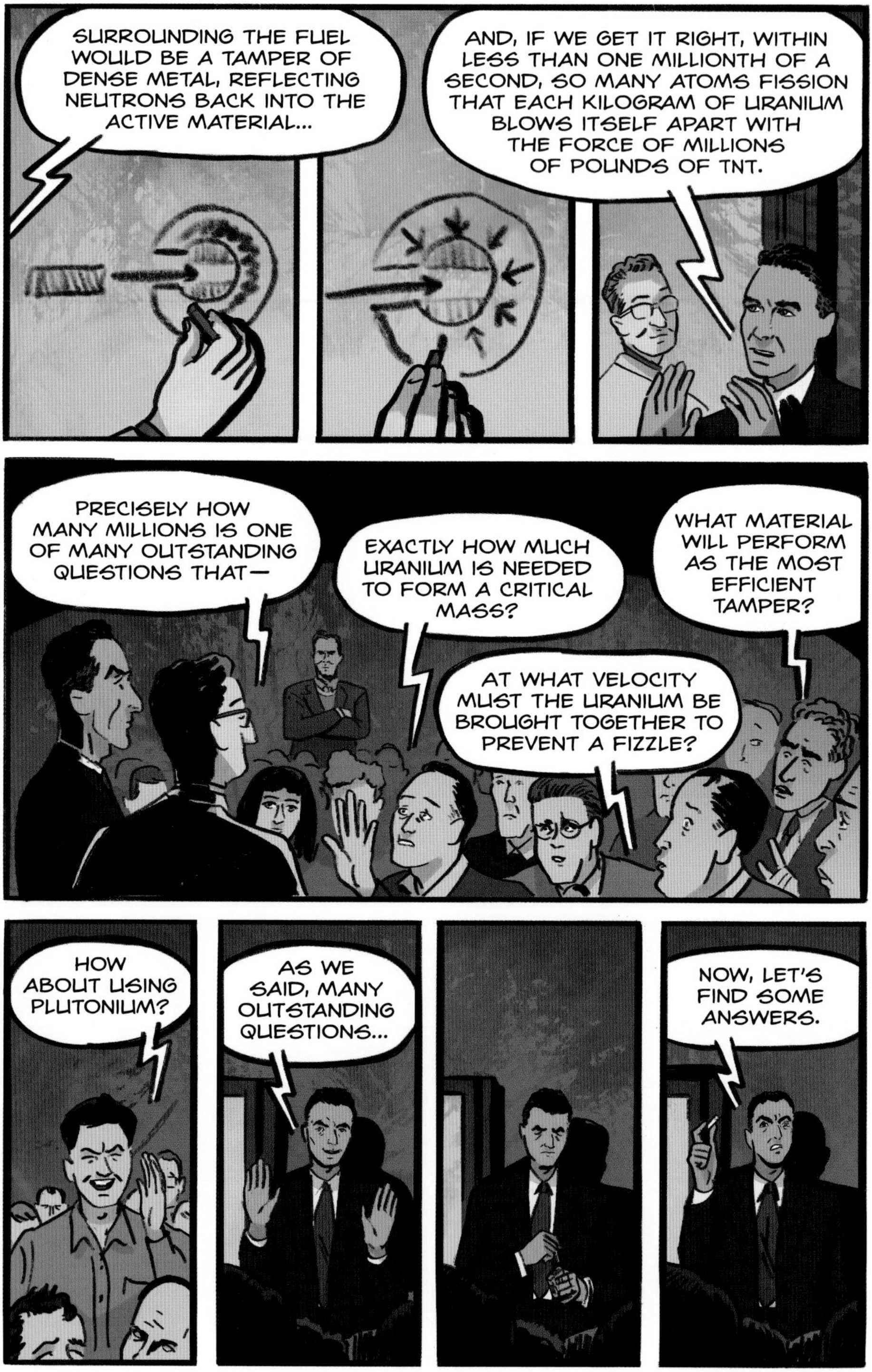
SURROUNDING THE FUEL WOULD BE A TAMPER OF DENSE METAL, REFLECTING NEUTRONS BACK INTO THE ACTIVE MATERIAL...
AND, IF WE GET IT RIGHT, WITHIN LESS THAN ONE MILLIONTH OF A SECOND, SO MANY ATOMS FISSION THAT EACH KILOGRAM OF URANIUM BLOWS ITSELF APART WITH THE FORCE OF MILLIONS OF POUNDS OF TNT.
PRECISELY HOW MANY MILLIONS IS ONE OF MANY OUTSTANDING QUESTIONS THAT—
EXACTLY HOW MUCH URANIUM IS NEEDED TO FORM A CRITICAL MASS?
WHAT MATERIAL WILL PERFORM AS THE MOST EFFICIENT TAMPER?
AT WHAT VELOCITY MUST THE URANIUM BE BROUGHT TOGETHER TO PREVENT A FIZZLE?
HOW ABOUT USING PLUTONIUM?
AS WE SAID, MANY OUTSTANDING QUESTIONS...
NOW, LET'S FIND SOME ANSWERS.

In Norway, the heavy water equipment was repaired.

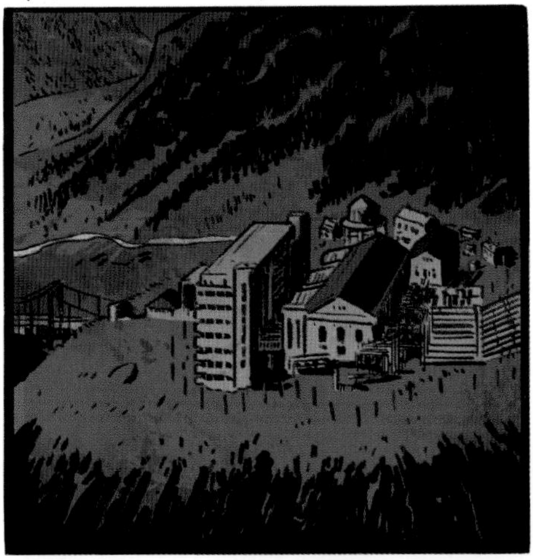

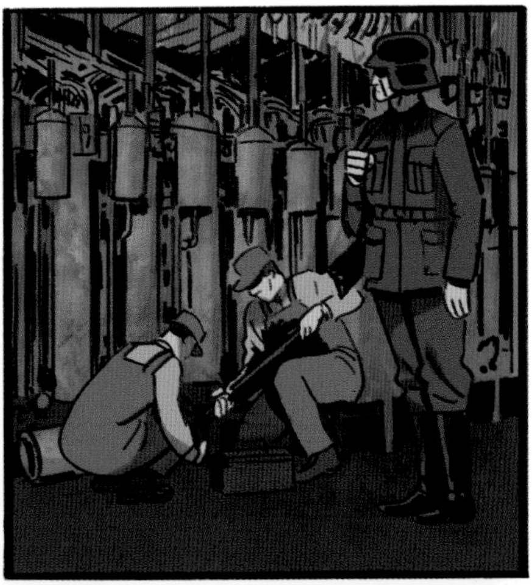

Haukelid and Kjelstrup spent a hard winter in the woods.

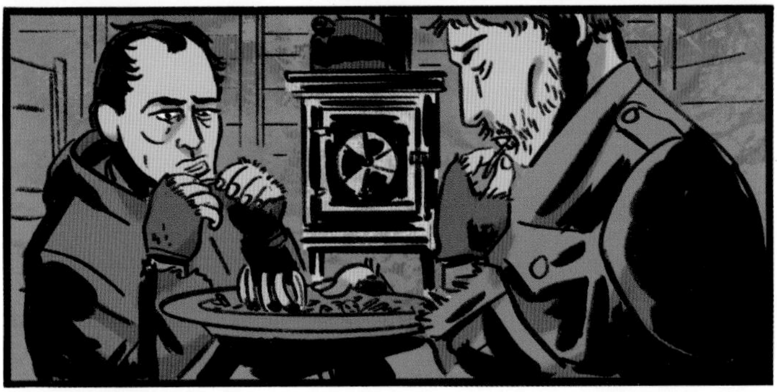

Oppenheimer's team worked long hours at Los Alamos.

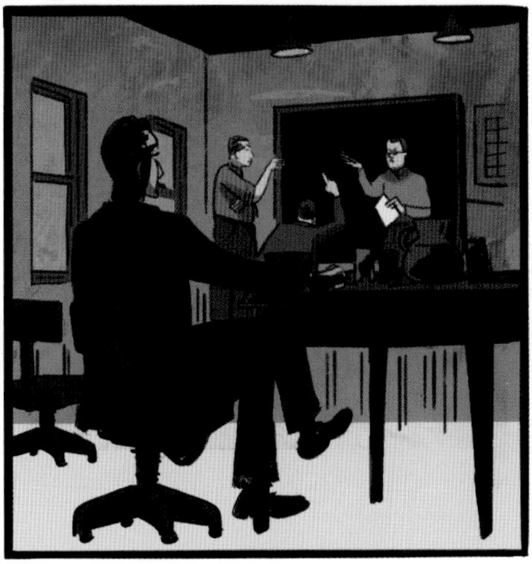

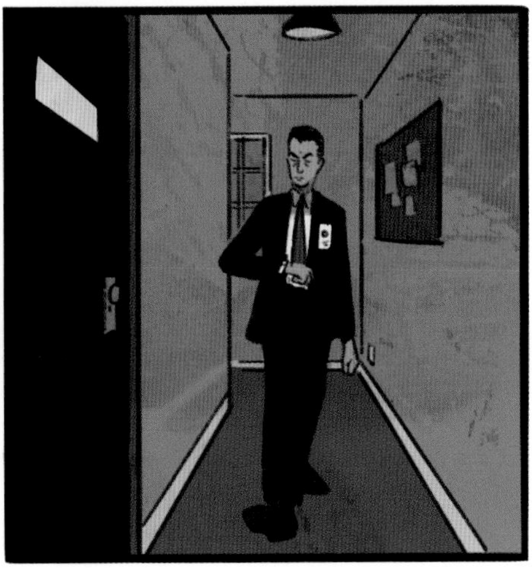

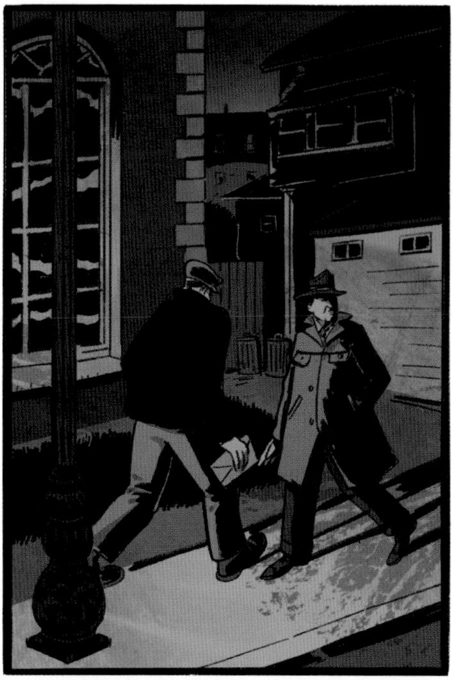

Harry Gold continued his missions for the Russians.

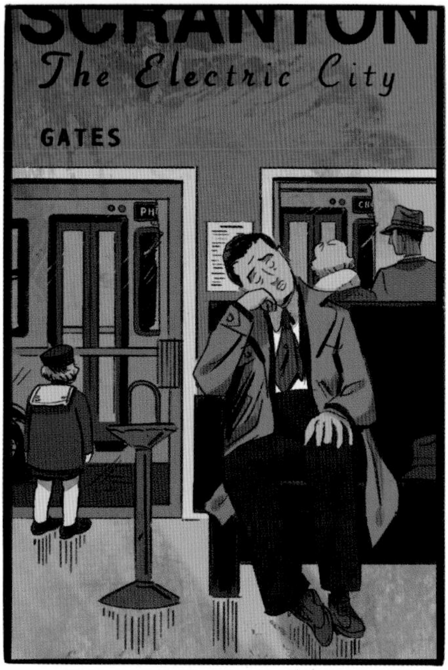
SCRANTON
The Electric City
GATES

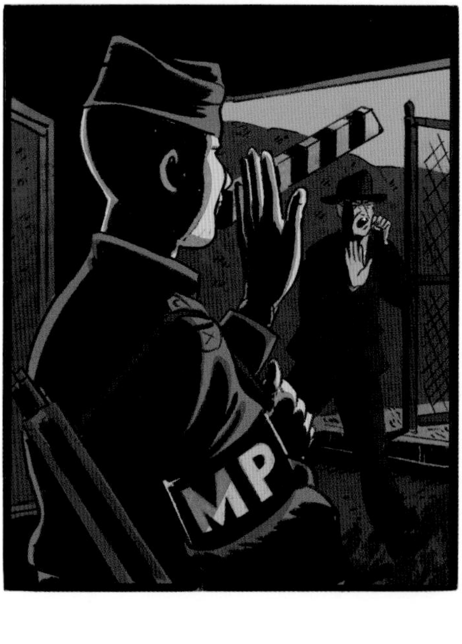
MP

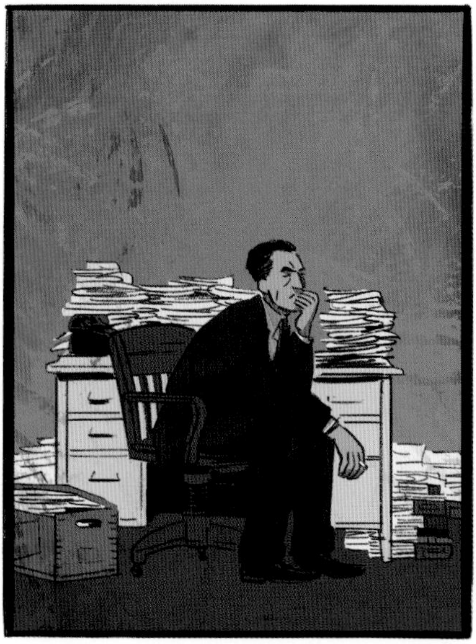

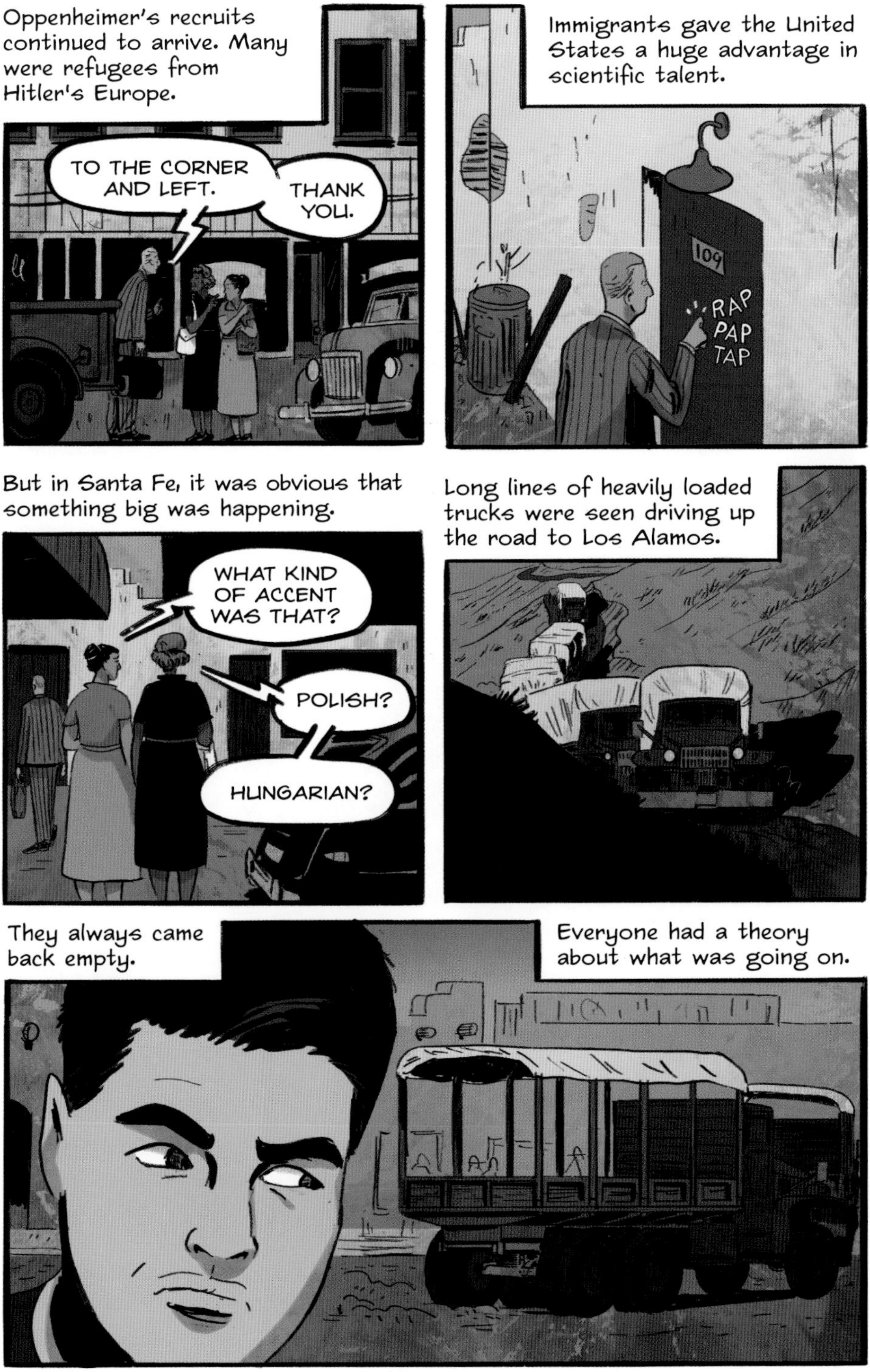

Oppenheimer's recruits continued to arrive. Many were refugees from Hitler's Europe.
TO THE CORNER AND LEFT.
THANK YOU.
Immigrants gave the United States a huge advantage in scientific talent.
109
RAP PAP TAP
But in Santa Fe, it was obvious that something big was happening.
WHAT KIND OF ACCENT WAS THAT?
POLISH?
HUNGARIAN?
Long lines of heavily loaded trucks were seen driving up the road to Los Alamos.
They always came back empty.
Everyone had a theory about what was going on.

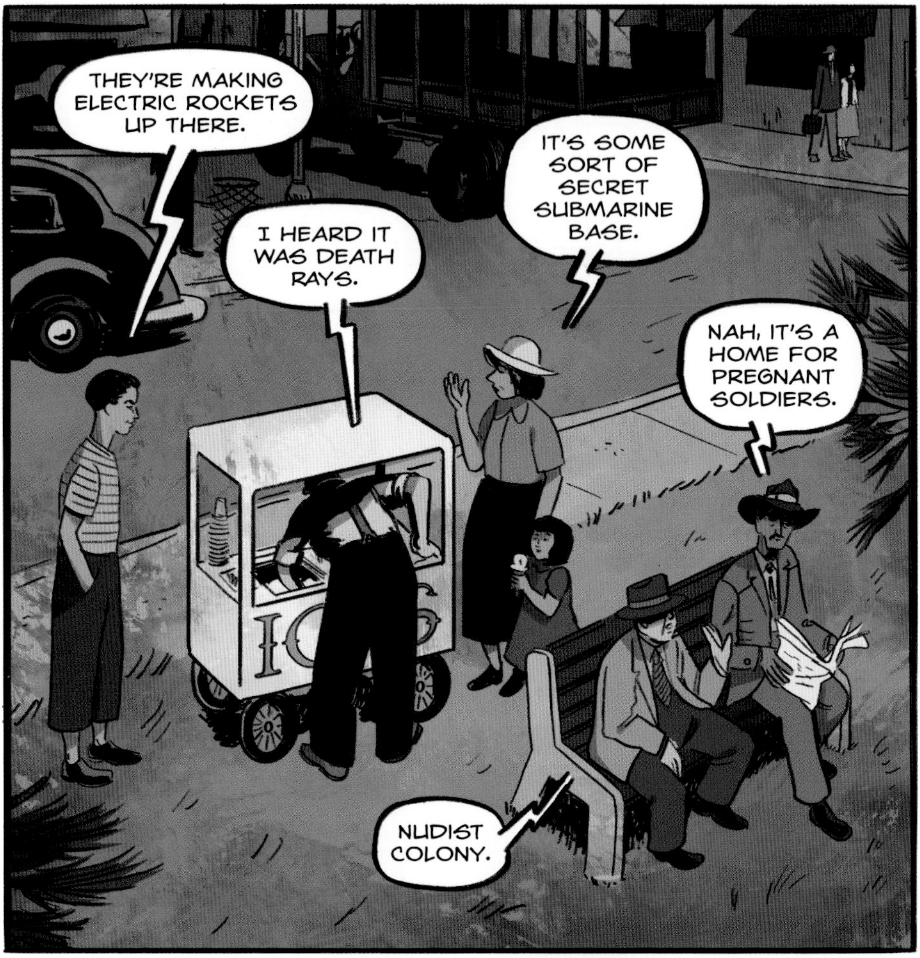
THEY'RE MAKING ELECTRIC ROCKETS UP THERE.
I HEARD IT WAS DEATH RAYS.
IT'S SOME SORT OF SECRET SUBMARINE BASE.
NAH, IT'S A HOME FOR PREGNANT SOLDIERS.
NUDIST COLONY.

Almost every day, someone knocked on the door at 109 East Palace, asking for work.

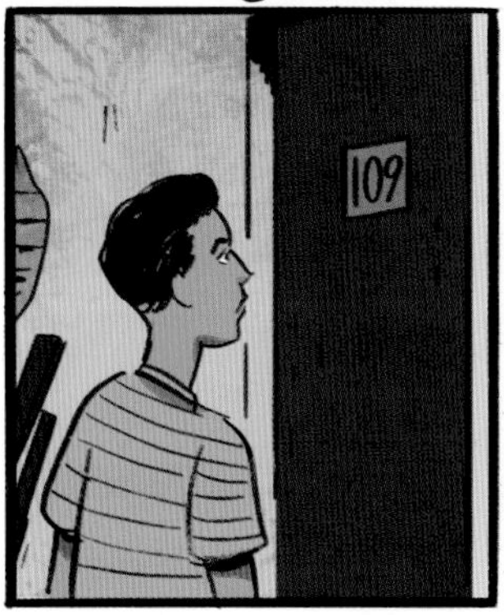
109

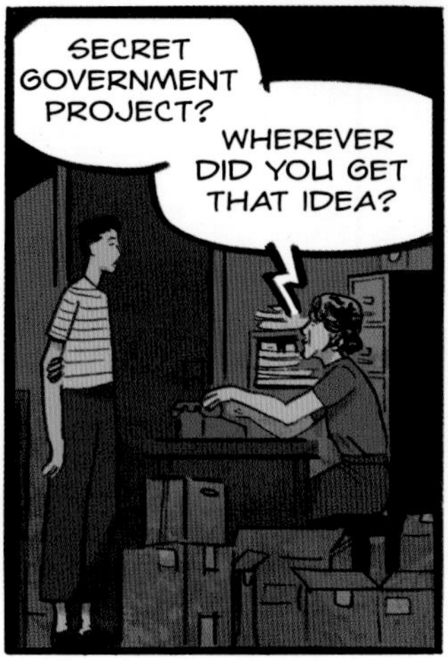
SECRET GOVERNMENT PROJECT?
WHEREVER DID YOU GET THAT IDEA?

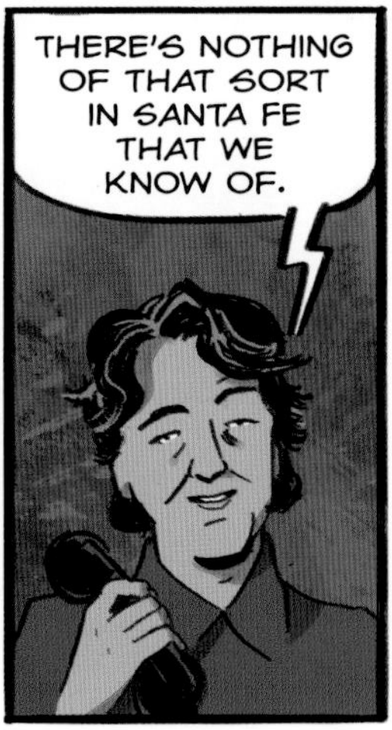
THERE'S NOTHING OF THAT SORT IN SANTA FE THAT WE KNOW OF.

Chapter 3

Two Inside

potential bomb fuels—

uranium vs. plutonium

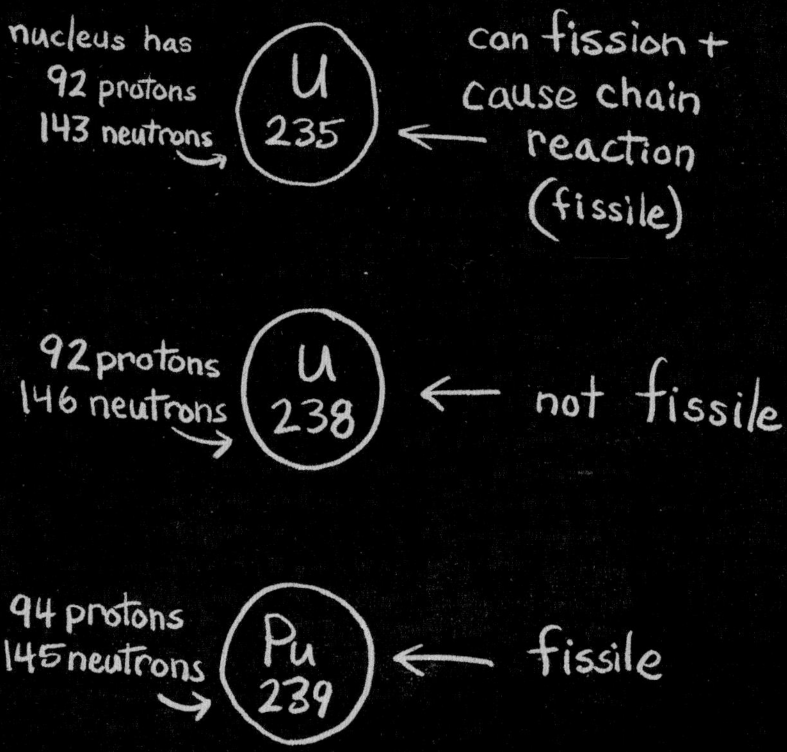
nucleus has
92 protons
143 neutrons
U
235
can fission +
cause chain
reaction
(fissile)
92 protons
146 neutrons
U
238
not fissile
94 protons
145 neutrons
Pu
239
fissile

November 1943.

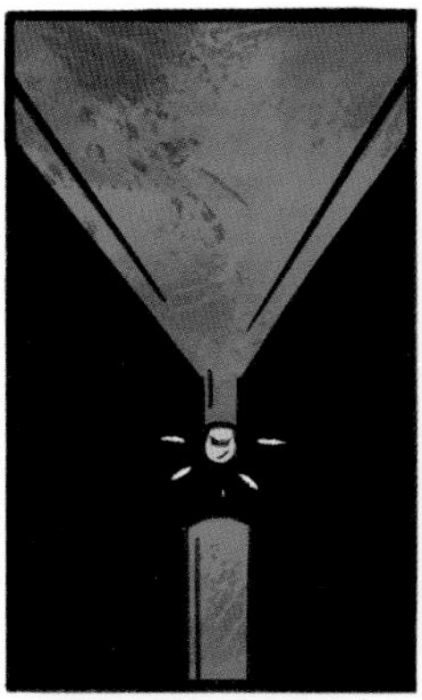

Heavy water production at Vemork was back to full capacity.

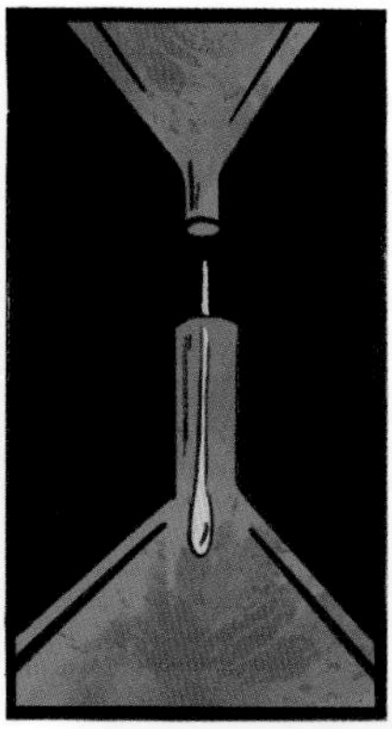

The Norwegian resistance got the information to London. London told Washington.

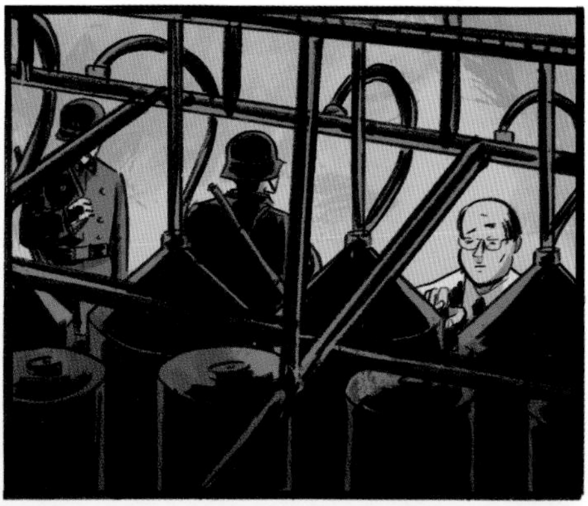

Groves called the U.S. Air Force.

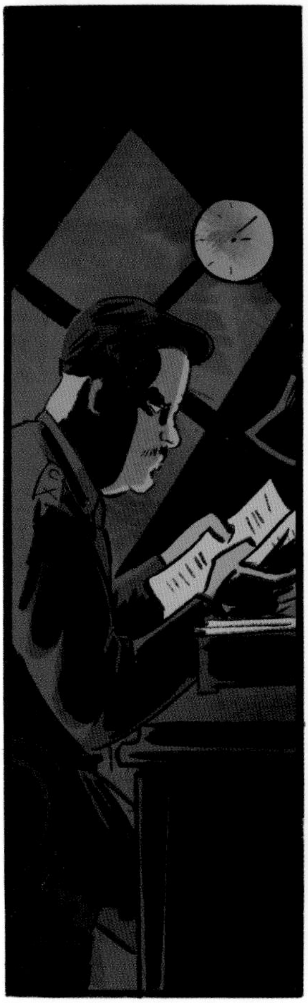

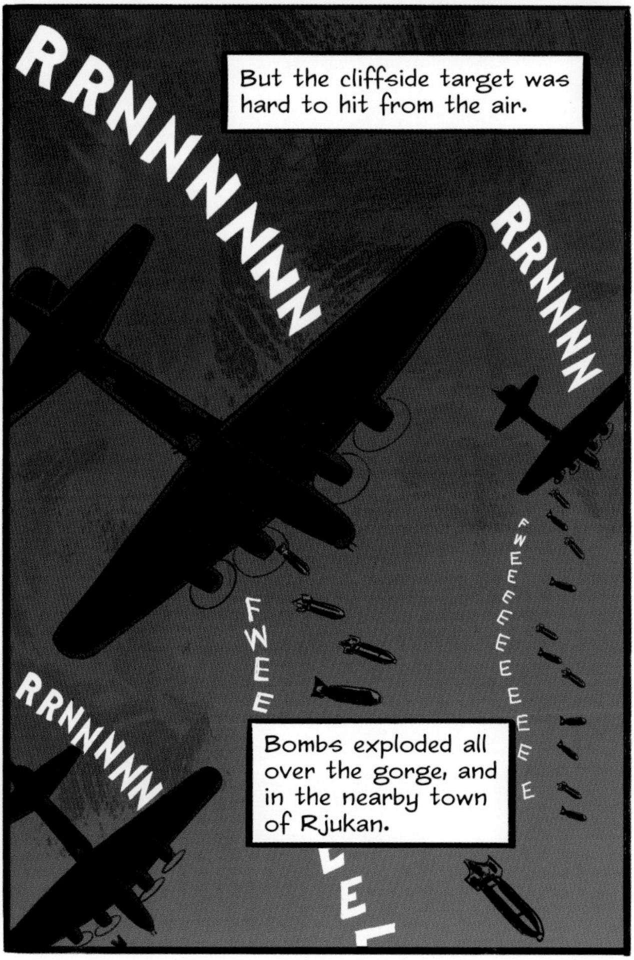
RRNNNNNNN
But the cliffside target was hard to hit from the air.
RRNNNNN
FWEEEEEEEEEE
FWEE
RRNNNNNN
Bombs exploded all over the gorge, and in the nearby town of Rjukan.

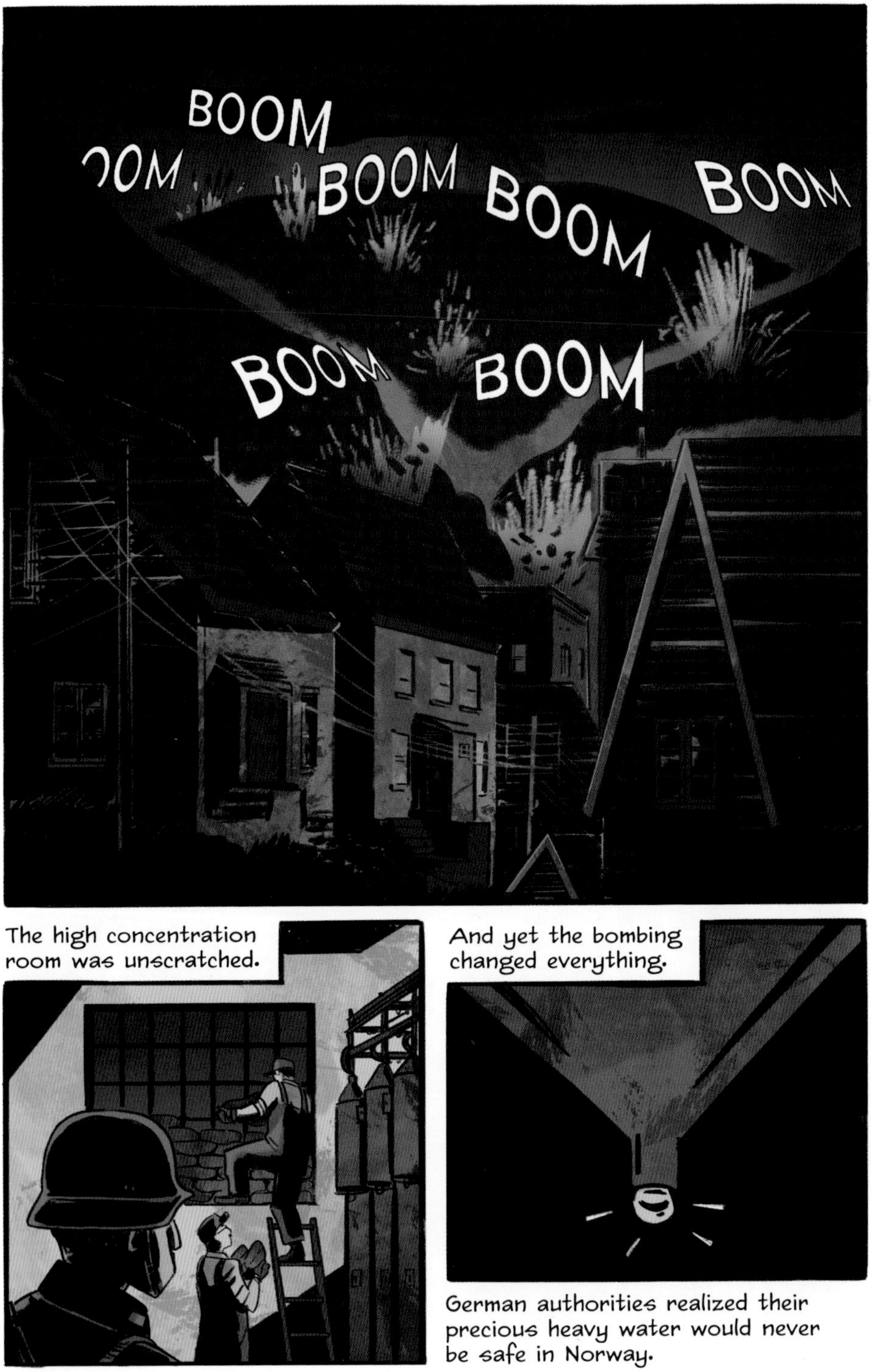
BOOM
OOM
BOOM
BOOM
BOOM
BOOM
BOOM
The high concentration room was unscratched.
And yet the bombing changed everything.
German authorities realized their precious heavy water would never be safe in Norway.

In February 1944, the Germans ordered workers at Vemork to prepare all the heavy water for shipment to Germany.

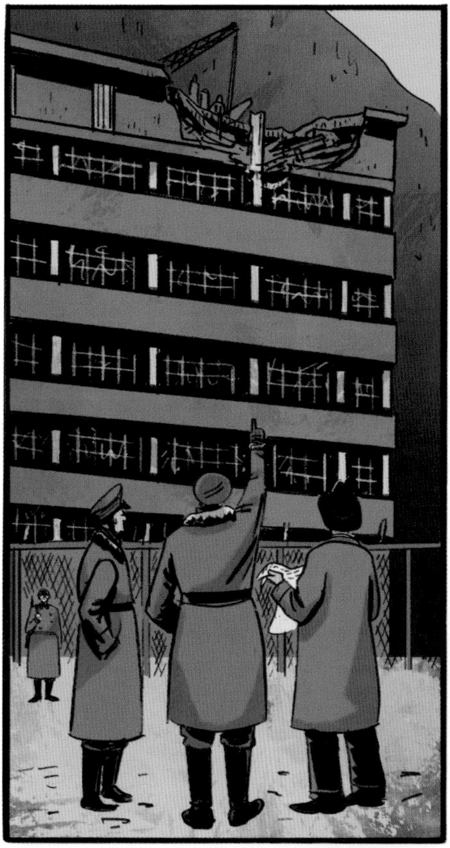

Knut Haukelid soon had a new assignment.

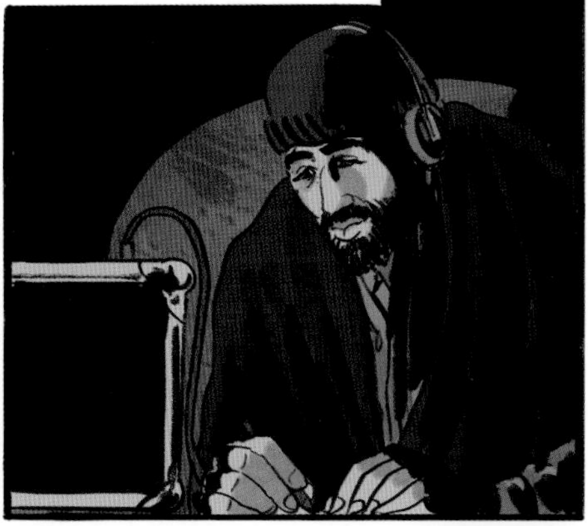

Make sure those barrels never reached German soil.

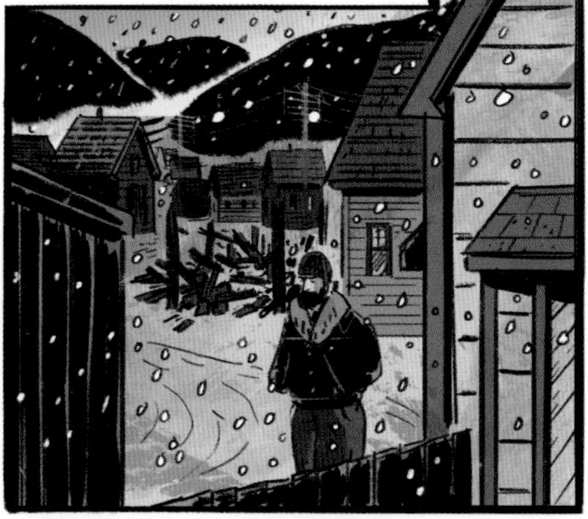

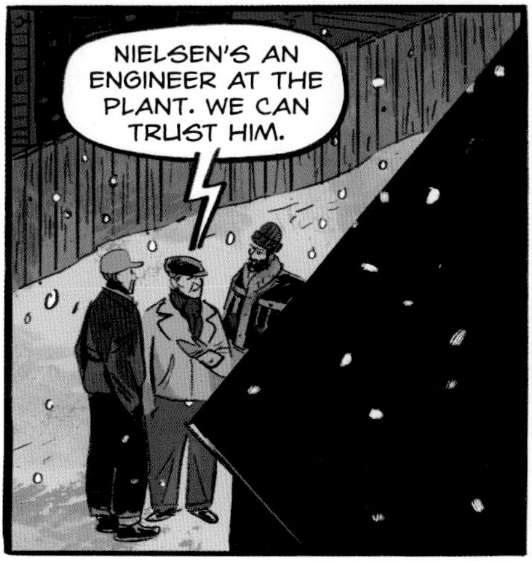
NIELSEN'S AN ENGINEER AT THE PLANT. WE CAN TRUST HIM.

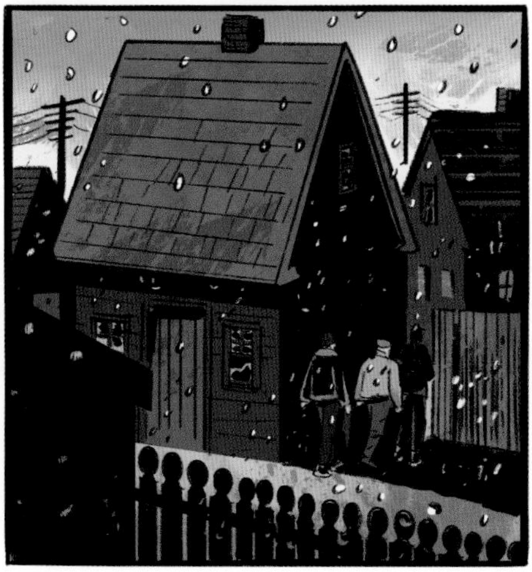

THERE ARE FORTY BARRELS OF DEUTERIUM OXIDE.

IN THREE DAYS, THEY'LL BE LOADED ONTO RAILWAY CARS AND TAKEN AWAY BY TRAIN.

AT LAKE TINN, THE TRAIN CARS WILL SLIDE ONTO A FERRY FOR THE TRIP DOWN THE LAKE.

THEN THEY'LL CONTINUE BY RAIL TO THE COAST...

...WHERE THE BARRELS WILL BE TRANSFERRED TO A GERMAN SHIP AND TAKEN ACROSS THE NORTH SEA.

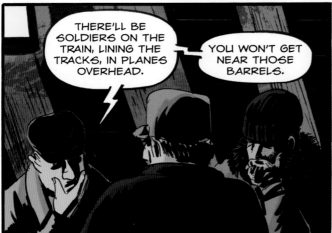

THERE'LL BE SOLDIERS ON THE TRAIN, LINING THE TRACKS, IN PLANES OVERHEAD.

YOU WON'T GET NEAR THOSE BARRELS.

THERE'S ALWAYS A WEAK SPOT.

GO OVER THE ROUTE AGAIN.

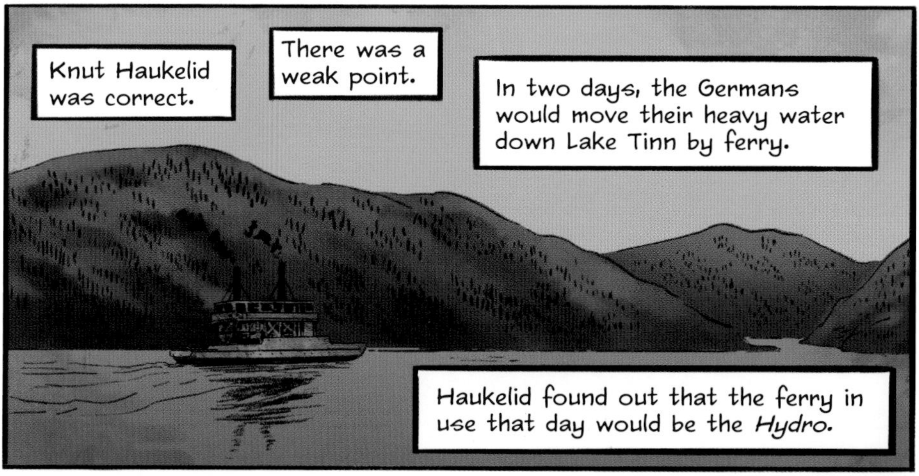
Knut Haukelid was correct.
There was a weak point.
In two days, the Germans would move their heavy water down Lake Tinn by ferry.
Haukelid found out that the ferry in use that day would be the *Hydro*.

Thirty minutes after leaving the dock, the *Hydro* was over the deepest part of the lake.

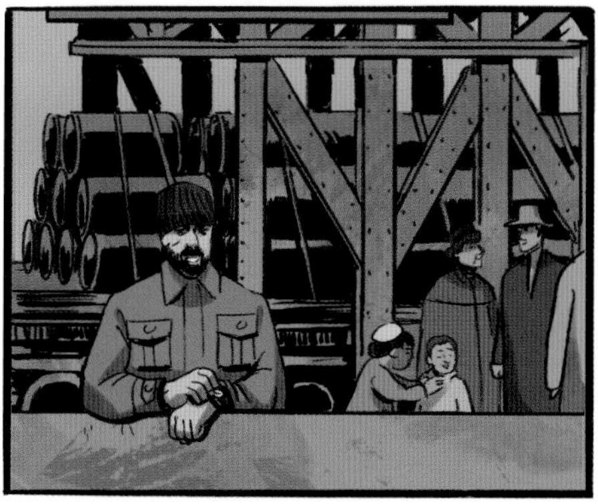

Anything that sank there could not be recovered.

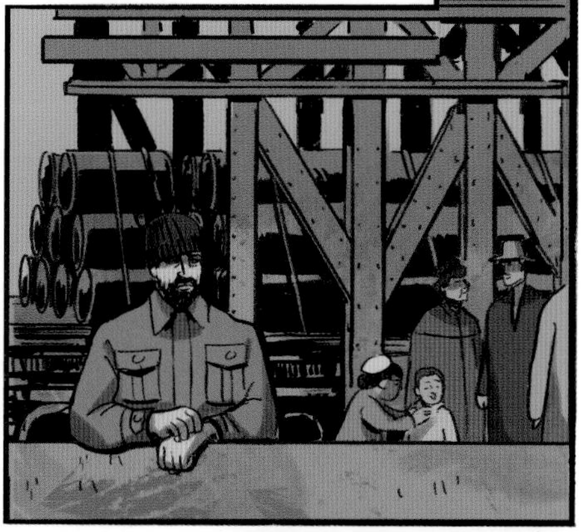

Haukelid relayed his findings to London, warning that the job would almost certainly result in the loss of civilian lives.

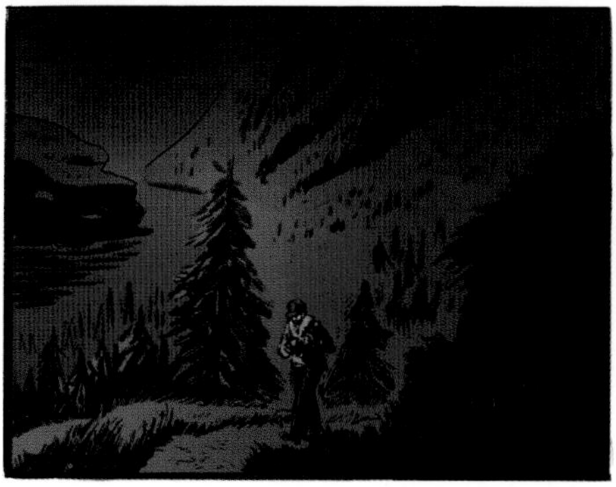

The reply was immediate.

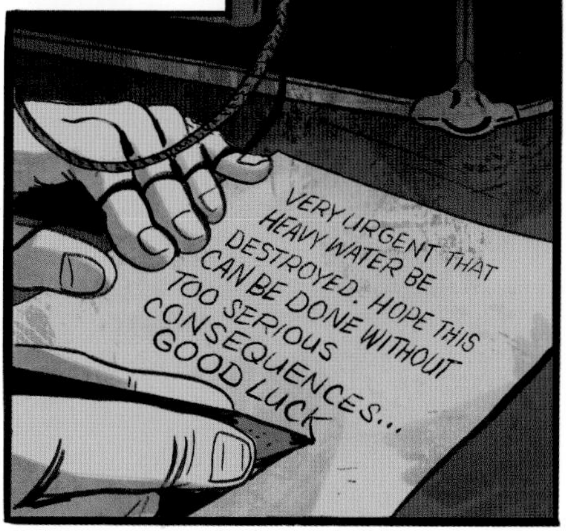
VERY URGENT THAT HEAVY WATER BE DESTROYED. HOPE THIS CAN BE DONE WITHOUT TOO SERIOUS CONSEQUENCES... GOOD LUCK

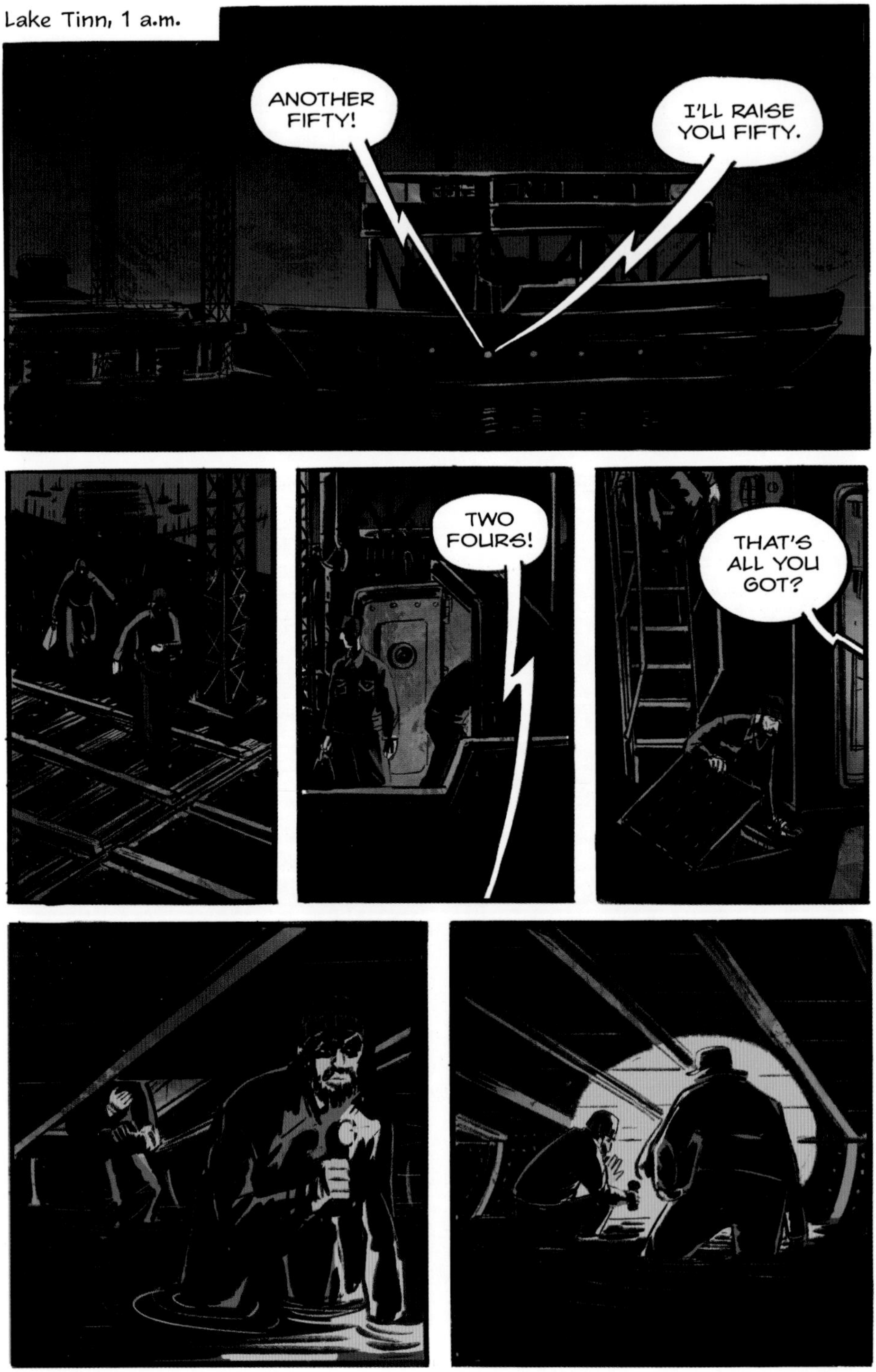
Lake Tinn, 1 a.m.
ANOTHER FIFTY!
I'LL RAISE YOU FIFTY.
TWO FOURS!
THAT'S ALL YOU GOT?

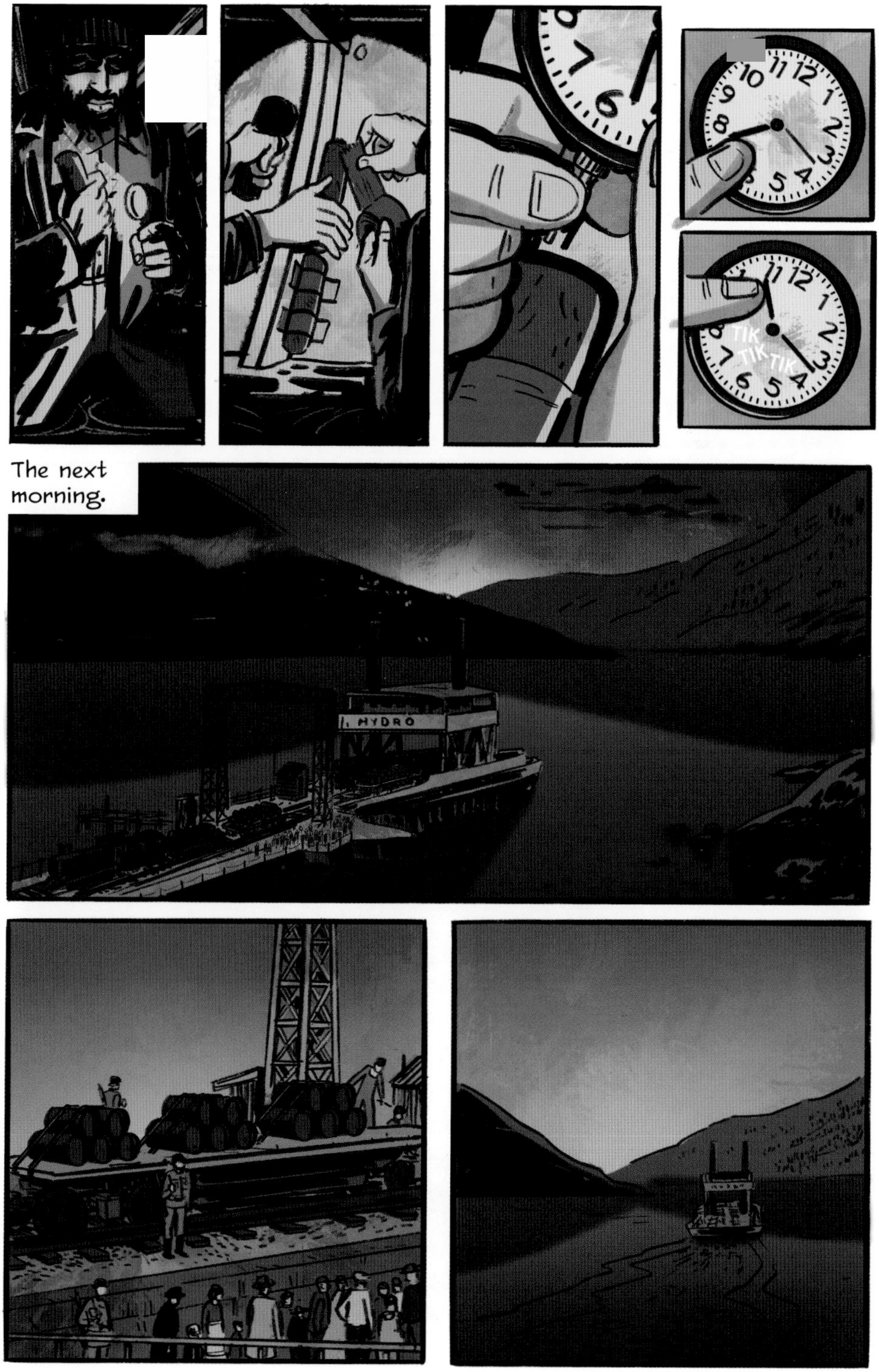
TIK
TIK
TIK
The next morning.
HYDRO

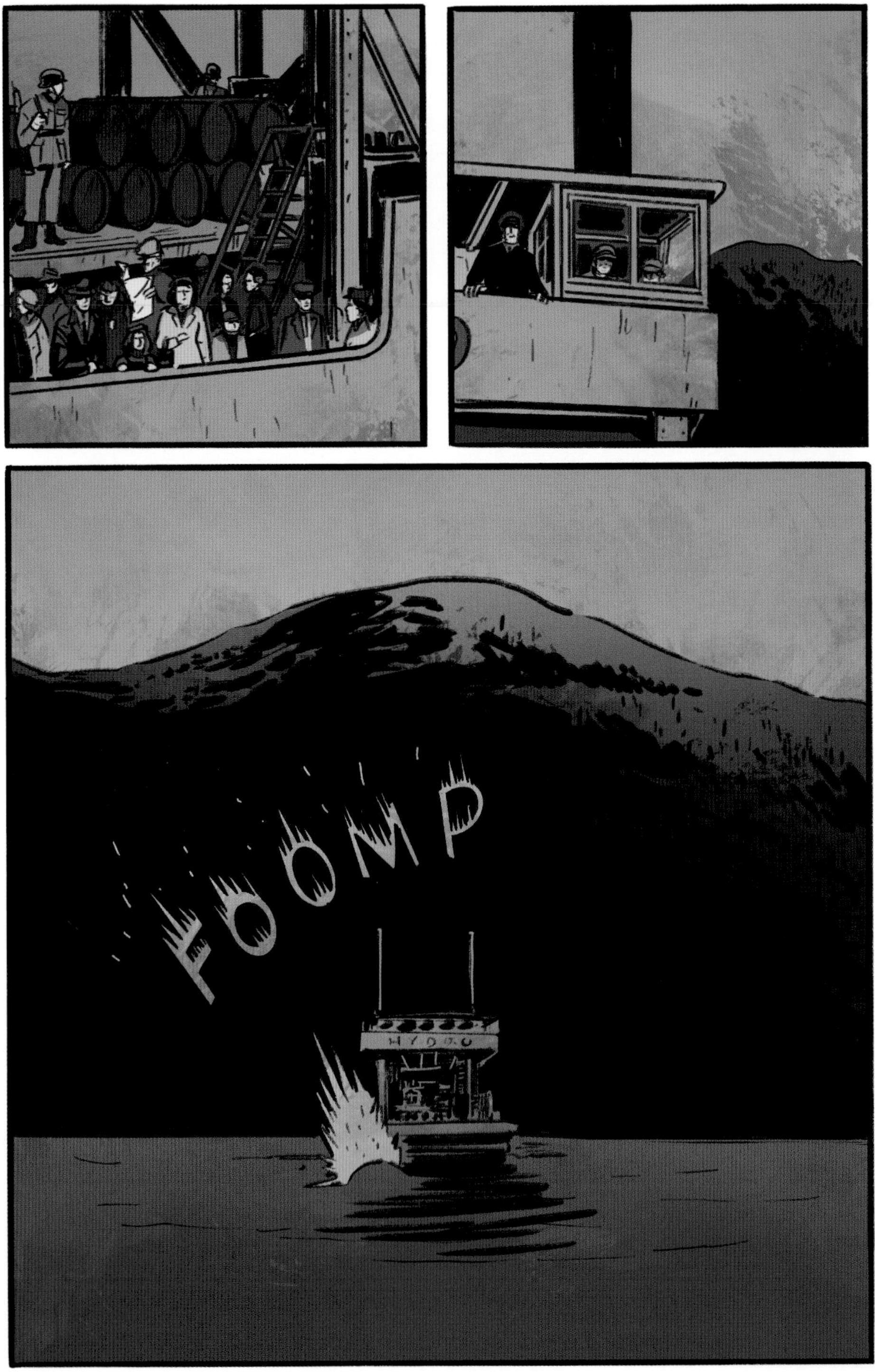
FOOMP

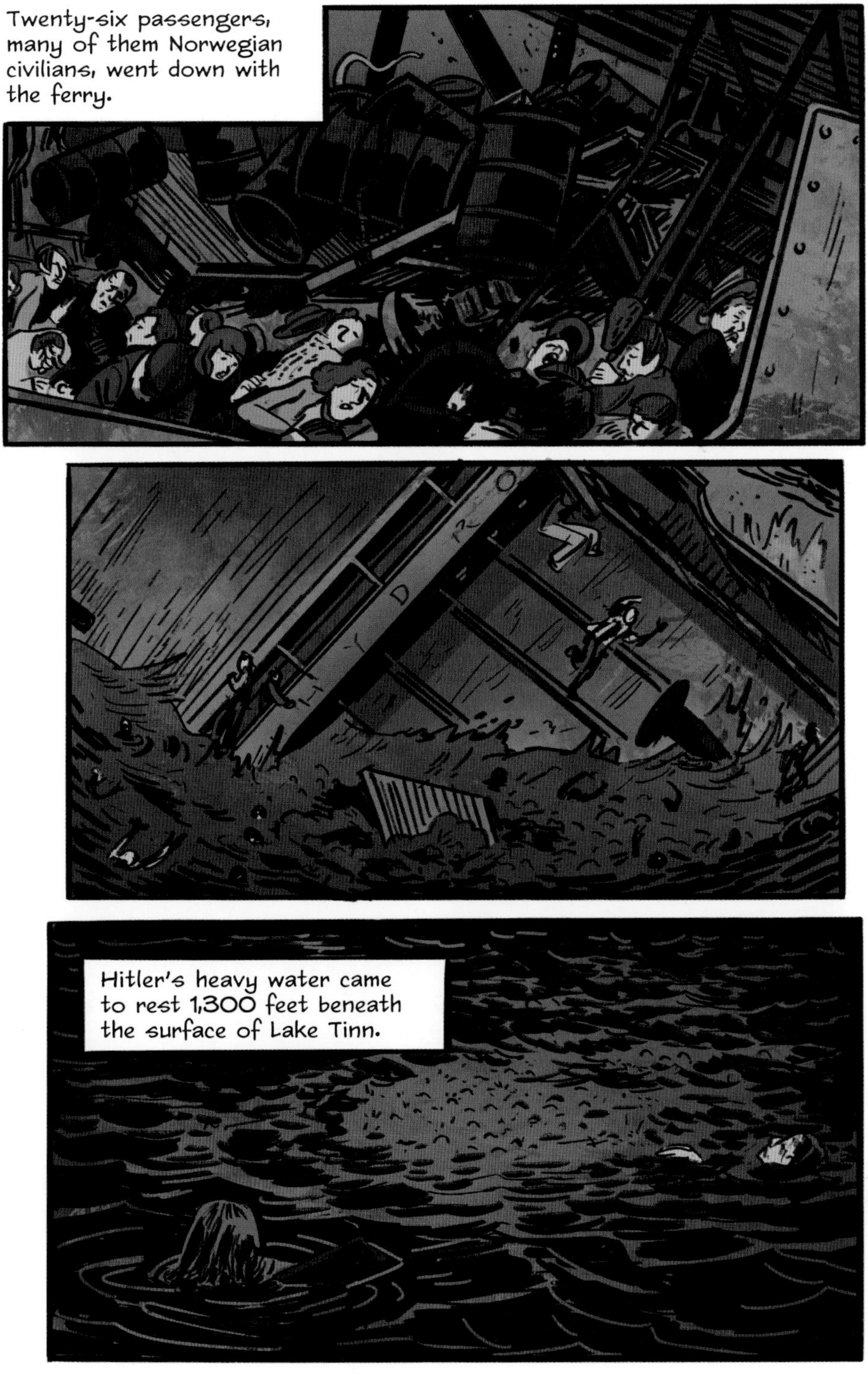
Twenty-six passengers, many of them Norwegian civilians, went down with the ferry.
Hitler's heavy water came to rest 1,300 feet beneath the surface of Lake Tinn.

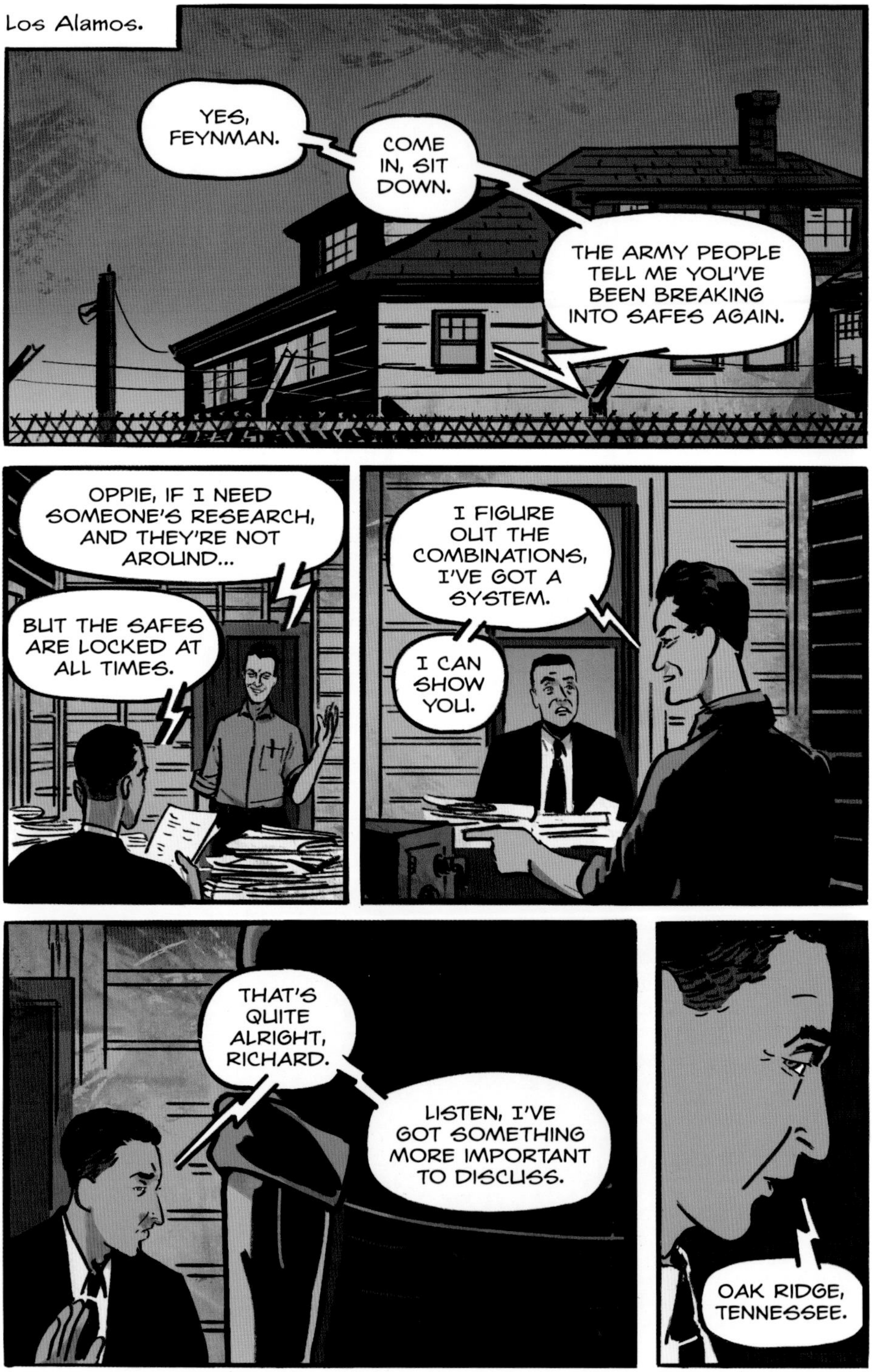

Los Alamos.
YES, FEYNMAN.
COME IN, SIT DOWN.
THE ARMY PEOPLE TELL ME YOU'VE BEEN BREAKING INTO SAFES AGAIN.
OPPIE, IF I NEED SOMEONE'S RESEARCH, AND THEY'RE NOT AROUND...
BUT THE SAFES ARE LOCKED AT ALL TIMES.
I FIGURE OUT THE COMBINATIONS, I'VE GOT A SYSTEM.
I CAN SHOW YOU.
THAT'S QUITE ALRIGHT, RICHARD.
LISTEN, I'VE GOT SOMETHING MORE IMPORTANT TO DISCUSS.
OAK RIDGE, TENNESSEE.

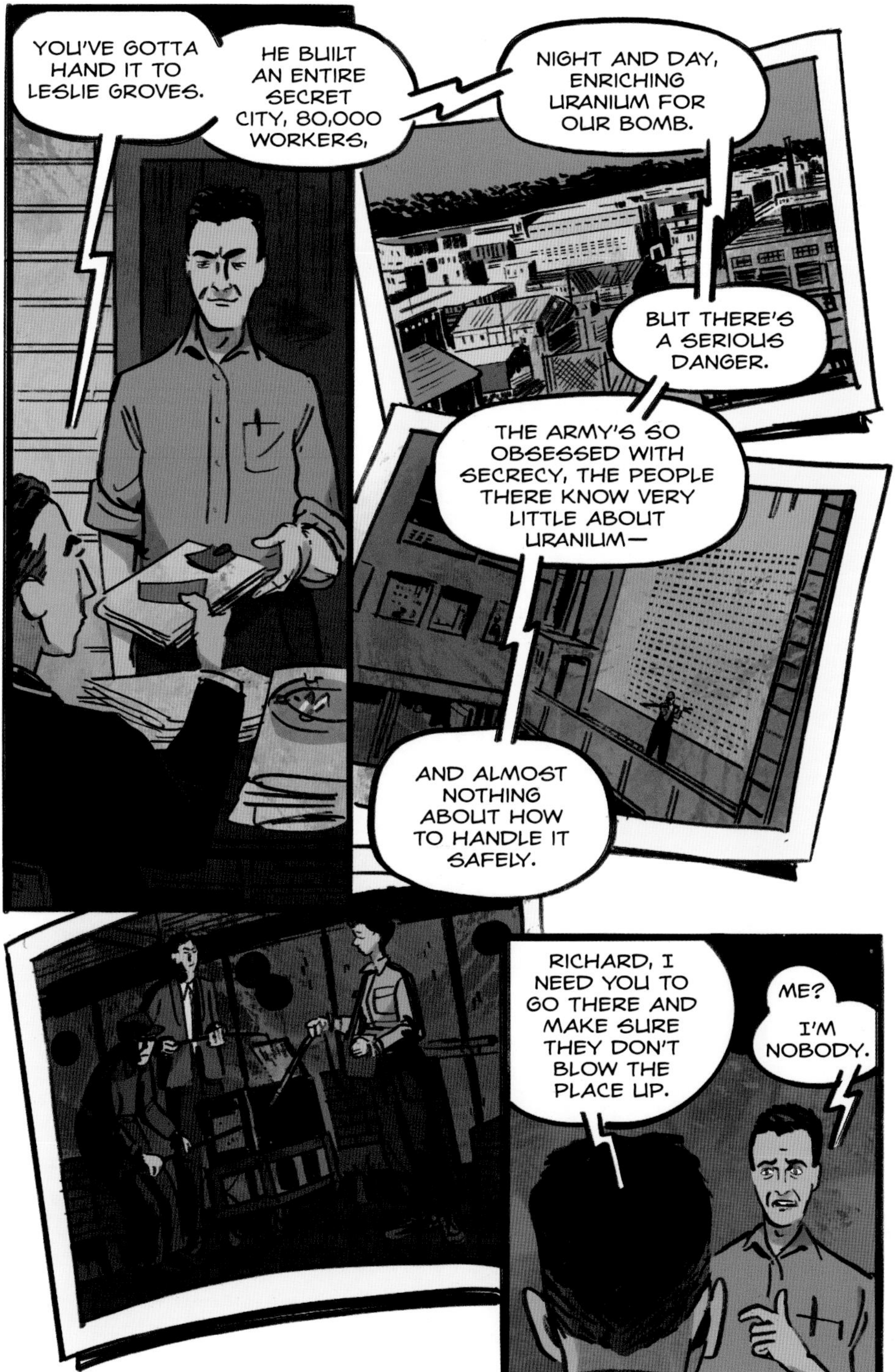
YOU'VE GOTTA HAND IT TO LESLIE GROVES.
HE BUILT AN ENTIRE SECRET CITY, 80,000 WORKERS,
NIGHT AND DAY, ENRICHING URANIUM FOR OUR BOMB.
BUT THERE'S A SERIOUS DANGER.
THE ARMY'S SO OBSESSED WITH SECRECY, THE PEOPLE THERE KNOW VERY LITTLE ABOUT URANIUM—
AND ALMOST NOTHING ABOUT HOW TO HANDLE IT SAFELY.
RICHARD, I NEED YOU TO GO THERE AND MAKE SURE THEY DON'T BLOW THE PLACE UP.
ME?
I'M NOBODY.

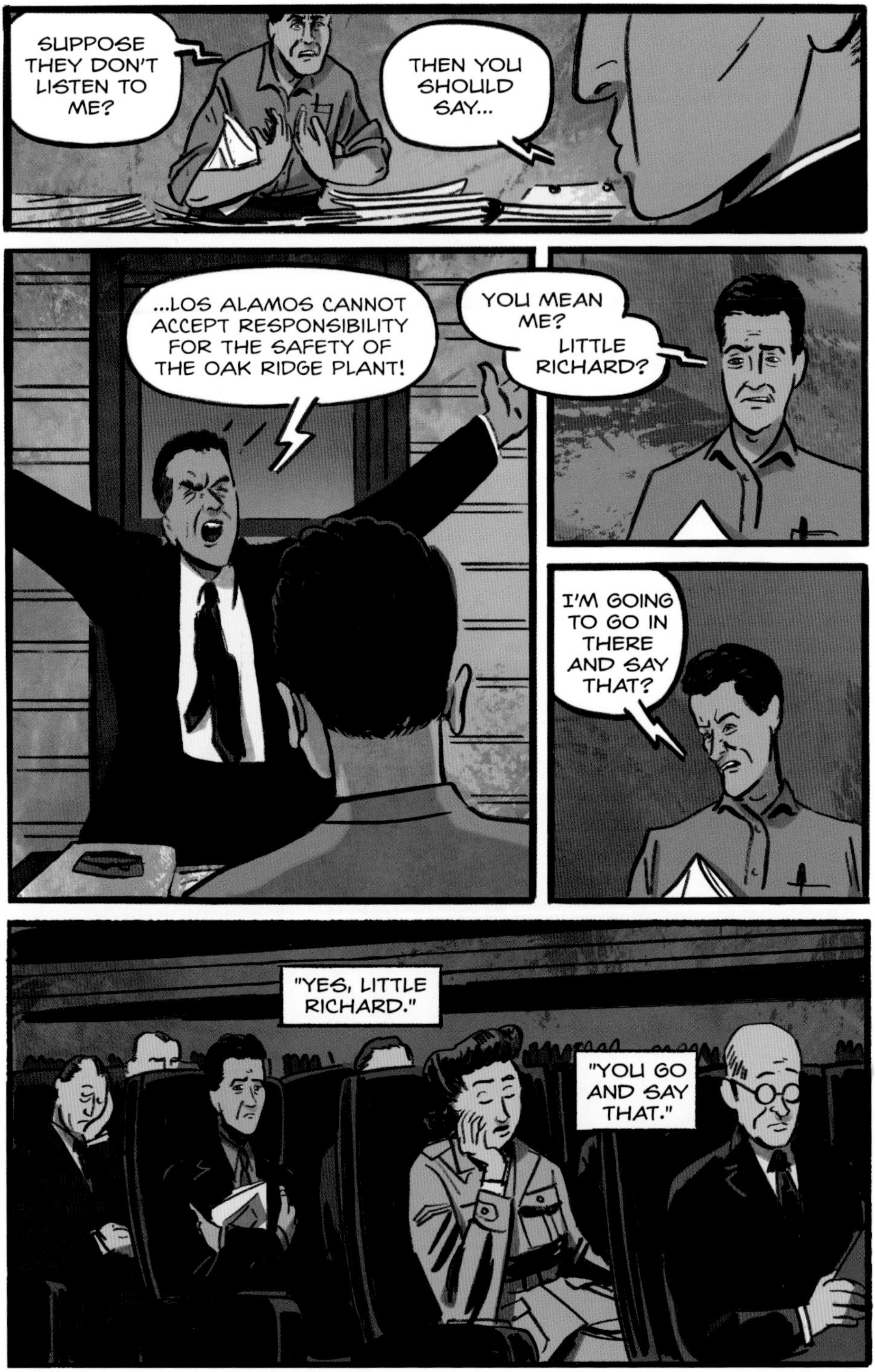
SUPPOSE THEY DON'T LISTEN TO ME?
THEN YOU SHOULD SAY...
...LOS ALAMOS CANNOT ACCEPT RESPONSIBILITY FOR THE SAFETY OF THE OAK RIDGE PLANT!
YOU MEAN ME? LITTLE RICHARD?
I'M GOING TO GO IN THERE AND SAY THAT?
"YES, LITTLE RICHARD."
"YOU GO AND SAY THAT."

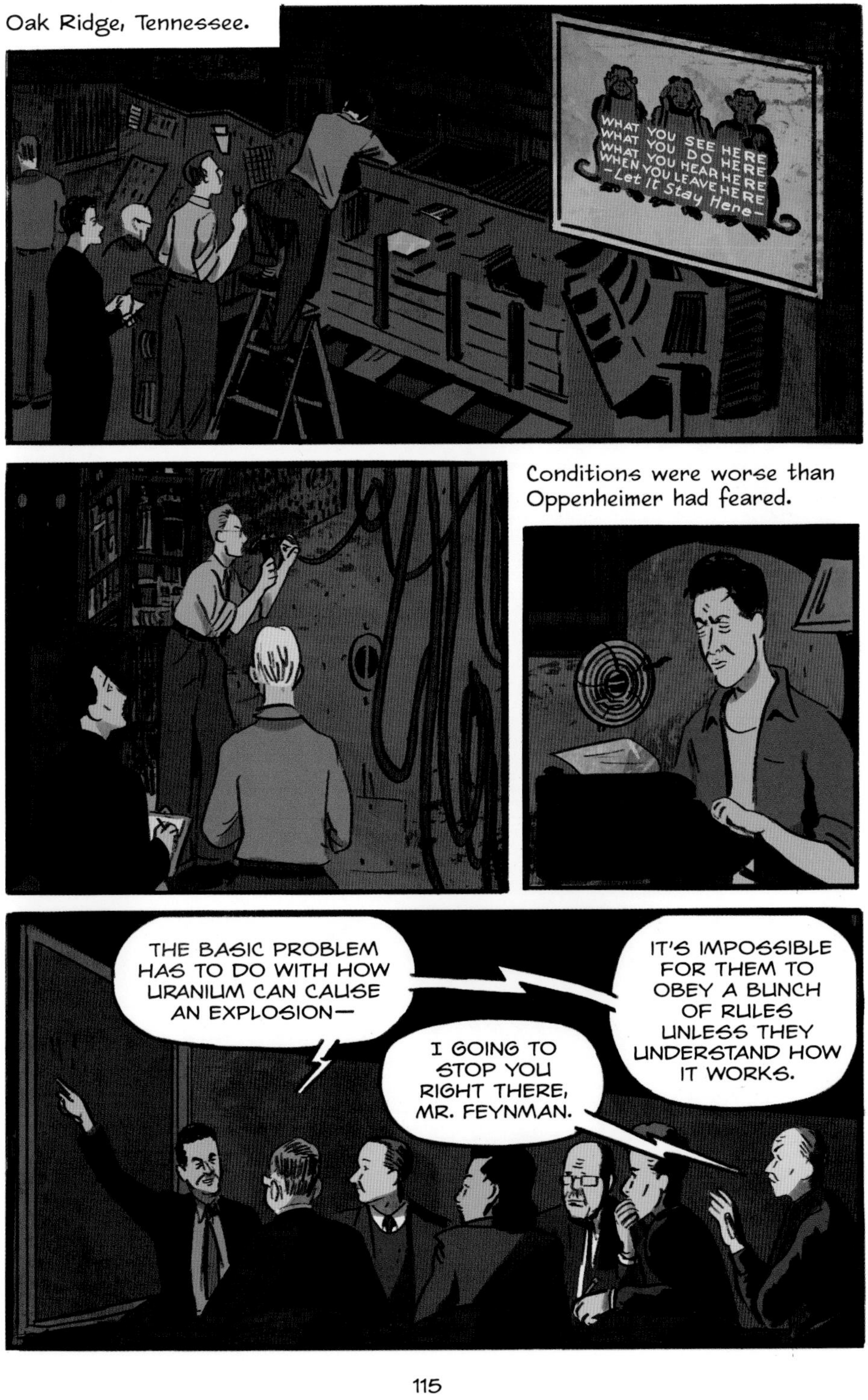
Oak Ridge, Tennessee.
WHAT YOU SEE HERE
WHAT YOU DO HERE
WHAT YOU HEAR HERE
WHEN YOU LEAVE HERE
—Let It Stay Here—
Conditions were worse than Oppenheimer had feared.
THE BASIC PROBLEM HAS TO DO WITH HOW URANIUM CAN CAUSE AN EXPLOSION—
I GOING TO STOP YOU RIGHT THERE, MR. FEYNMAN.
IT'S IMPOSSIBLE FOR THEM TO OBEY A BUNCH OF RULES UNLESS THEY UNDERSTAND HOW IT WORKS.

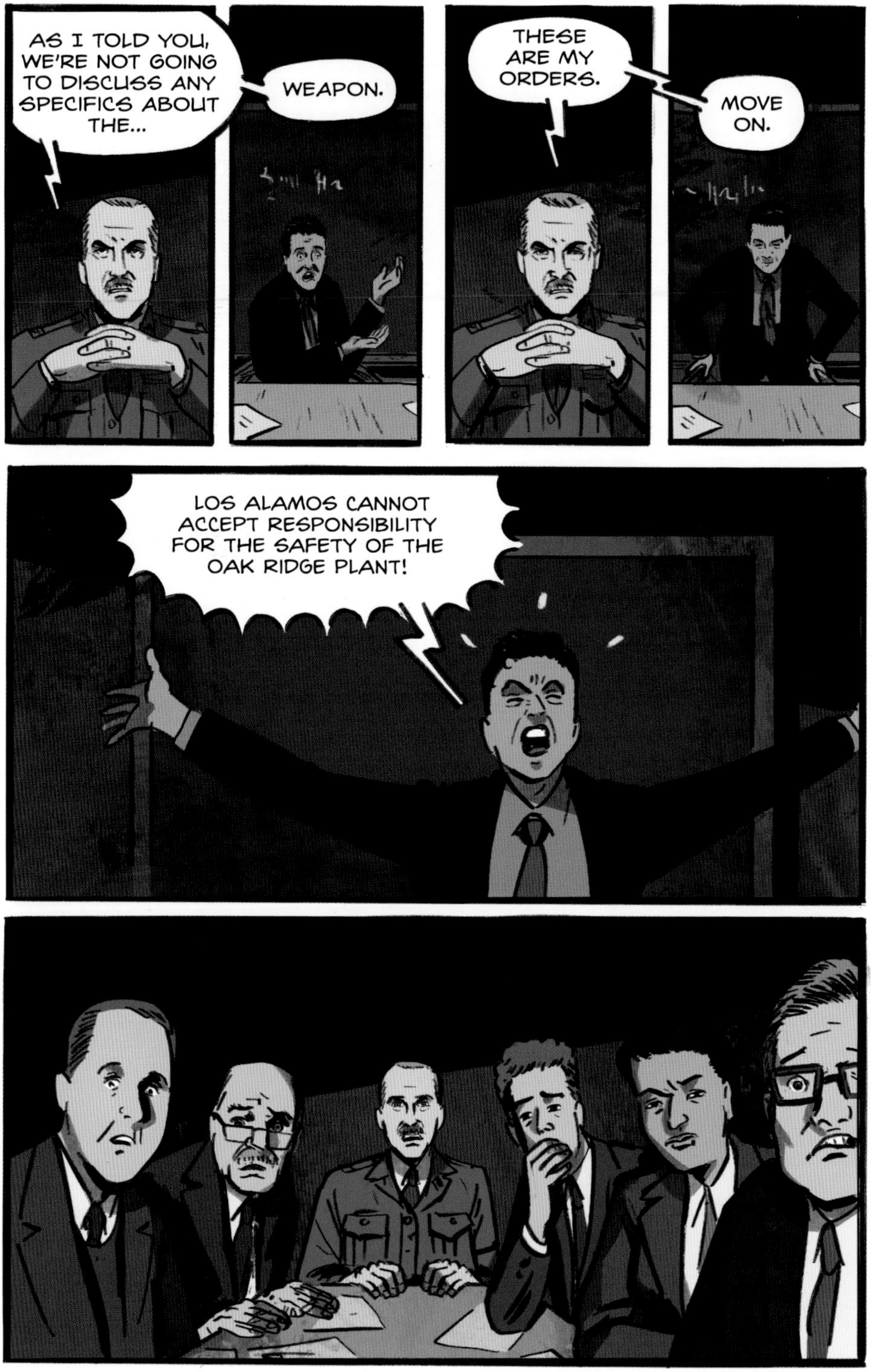
AS I TOLD YOU, WE'RE NOT GOING TO DISCUSS ANY SPECIFICS ABOUT THE...
WEAPON.
THESE ARE MY ORDERS.
MOVE ON.
LOS ALAMOS CANNOT ACCEPT RESPONSIBILITY FOR THE SAFETY OF THE OAK RIDGE PLANT!

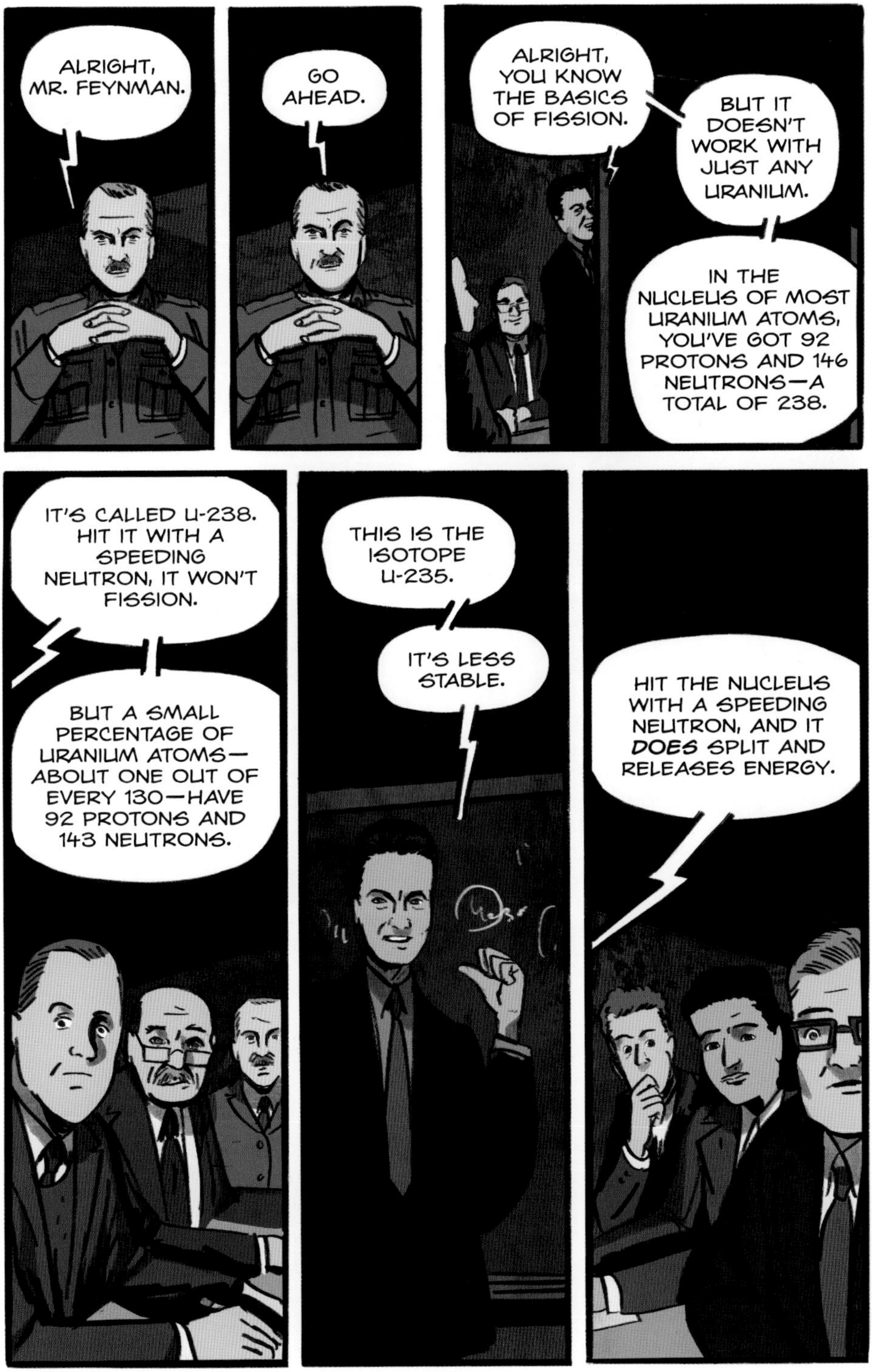
ALRIGHT, MR. FEYNMAN.
GO AHEAD.
ALRIGHT, YOU KNOW THE BASICS OF FISSION.
BUT IT DOESN'T WORK WITH JUST ANY URANIUM.
IN THE NUCLEUS OF MOST URANIUM ATOMS, YOU'VE GOT 92 PROTONS AND 146 NEUTRONS—A TOTAL OF 238.
IT'S CALLED U-238. HIT IT WITH A SPEEDING NEUTRON, IT WON'T FISSION.
BUT A SMALL PERCENTAGE OF URANIUM ATOMS—ABOUT ONE OUT OF EVERY 130—HAVE 92 PROTONS AND 143 NEUTRONS.
THIS IS THE ISOTOPE U-235.
IT'S LESS STABLE.
HIT THE NUCLEUS WITH A SPEEDING NEUTRON, AND IT *DOES* SPLIT AND RELEASES ENERGY.

THE JOB HERE AT OAK RIDGE, INCREDIBLY HARD, IS TO SEPARATE U-235 ATOMS FROM U-238 ATOMS.

"You send the U-235 to Los Alamos."

"And we'll, well..."

"...do the rest."

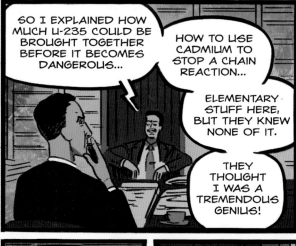

SO I EXPLAINED HOW MUCH U-235 COULD BE BROUGHT TOGETHER BEFORE IT BECOMES DANGEROUS...

HOW TO USE CADMIUM TO STOP A CHAIN REACTION...

ELEMENTARY STUFF HERE, BUT THEY KNEW NONE OF IT.

THEY THOUGHT I WAS A TREMENDOUS GENIUS!

GOOD JOB, RICHARD.

CATASTROPHE AVERTED.

NOW, ABOUT THE SAFES...

After the ferry job, Knut Haukelid slipped across the border to Sweden.

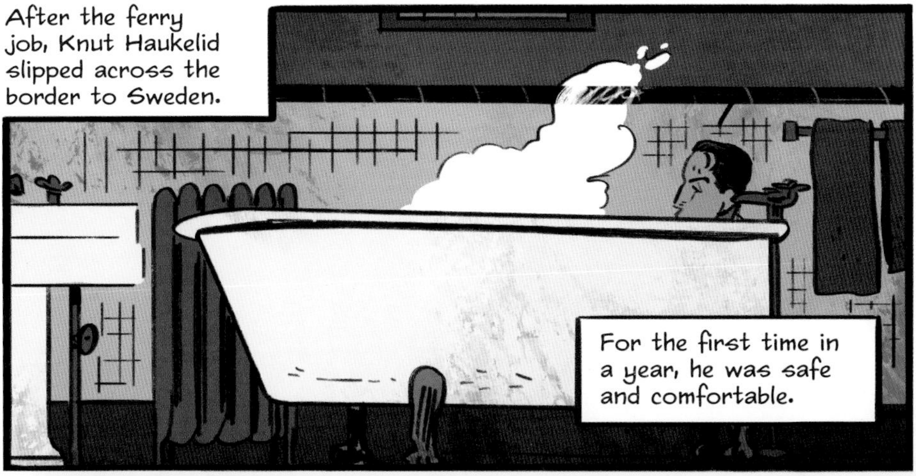
For the first time in a year, he was safe and comfortable.

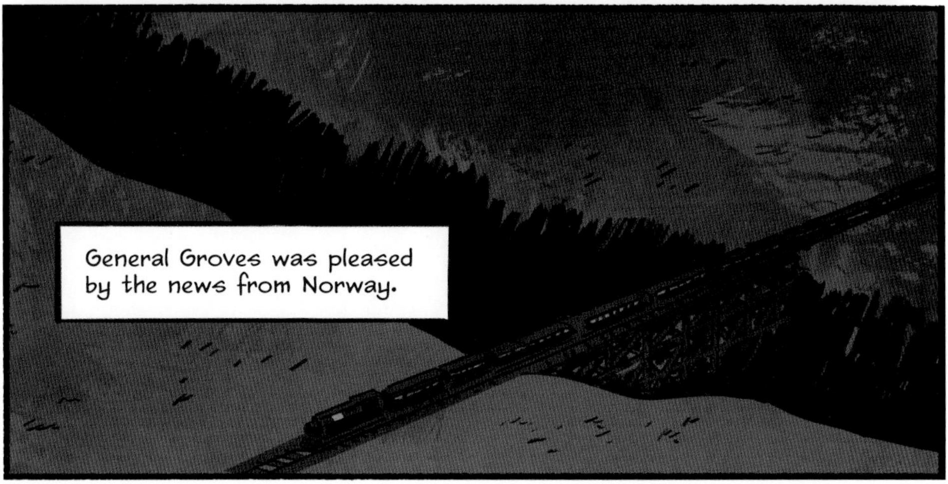
General Groves was pleased by the news from Norway.

Pleased, but not satisfied. This was no time to let up.

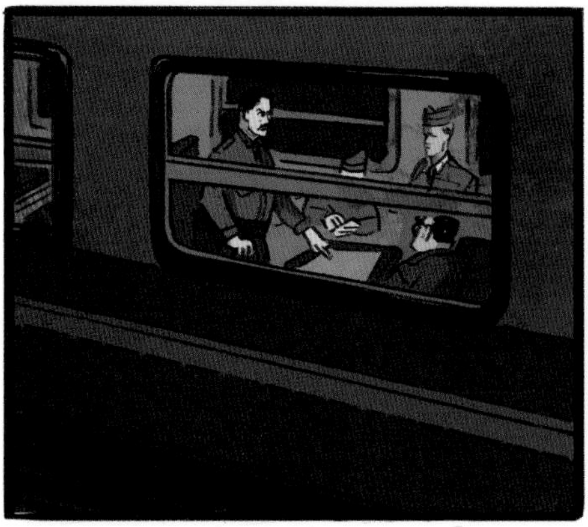

Oak Ridge continued producing U-235. Slowly. If all went well, there might be enough fuel for one bomb by the summer of 1945.

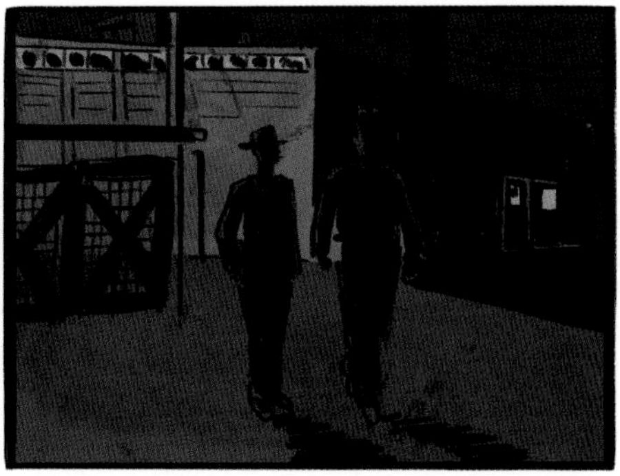

Determined to build a bigger arsenal, Groves ordered the construction of another secret city, this one in Hanford, Washington.

The Hanford plant was based on something scientists had learned about uranium and fission.

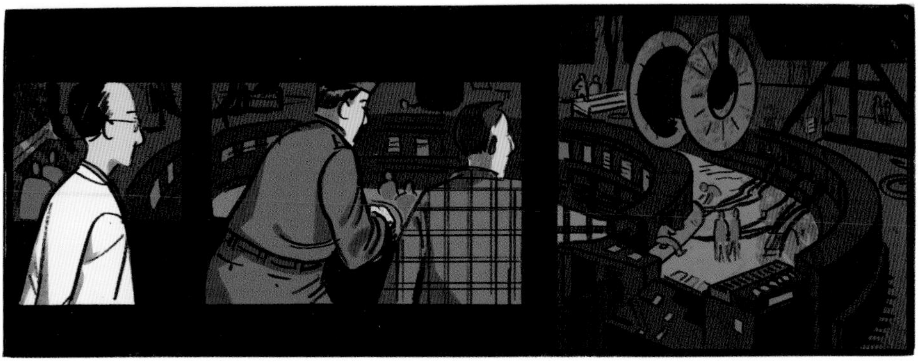

When the nuclei of U-238 atoms are hit with flying neutrons, they absorb the neutrons. That is, the particles stick in the nuclei of the uranium.

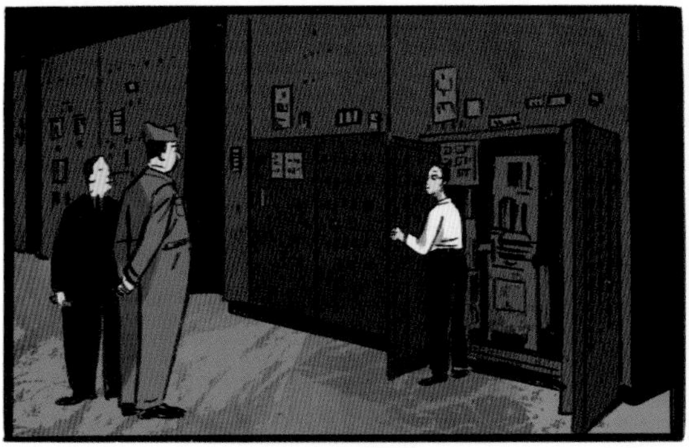

Uranium is transformed into an entirely new element—scientists named it plutonium.

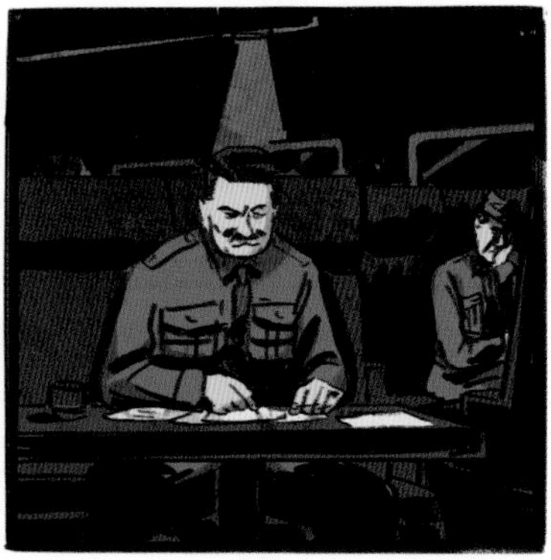

Plutonium will fission even faster than U-235. So, in theory, it could be used to fuel atomic bombs. The job at Hanford was to produce plutonium.

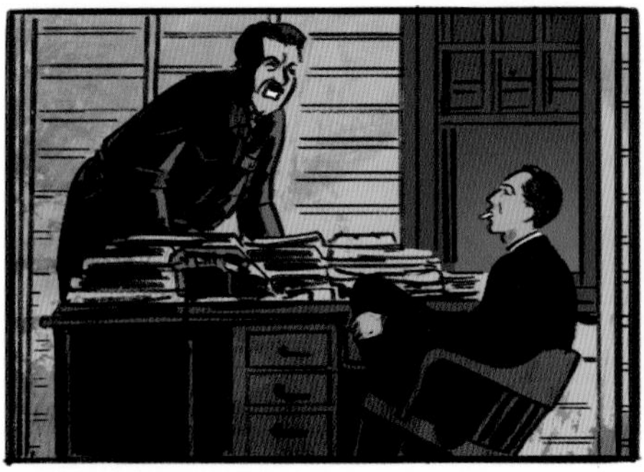

Oppenheimer hoped that the design they were developing for the uranium bomb would work with plutonium as well.

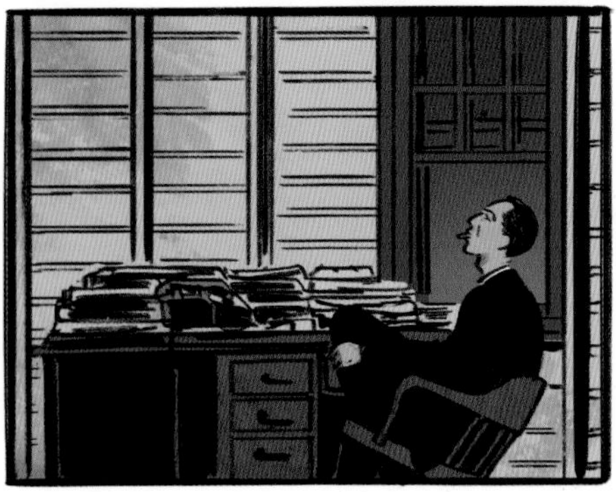

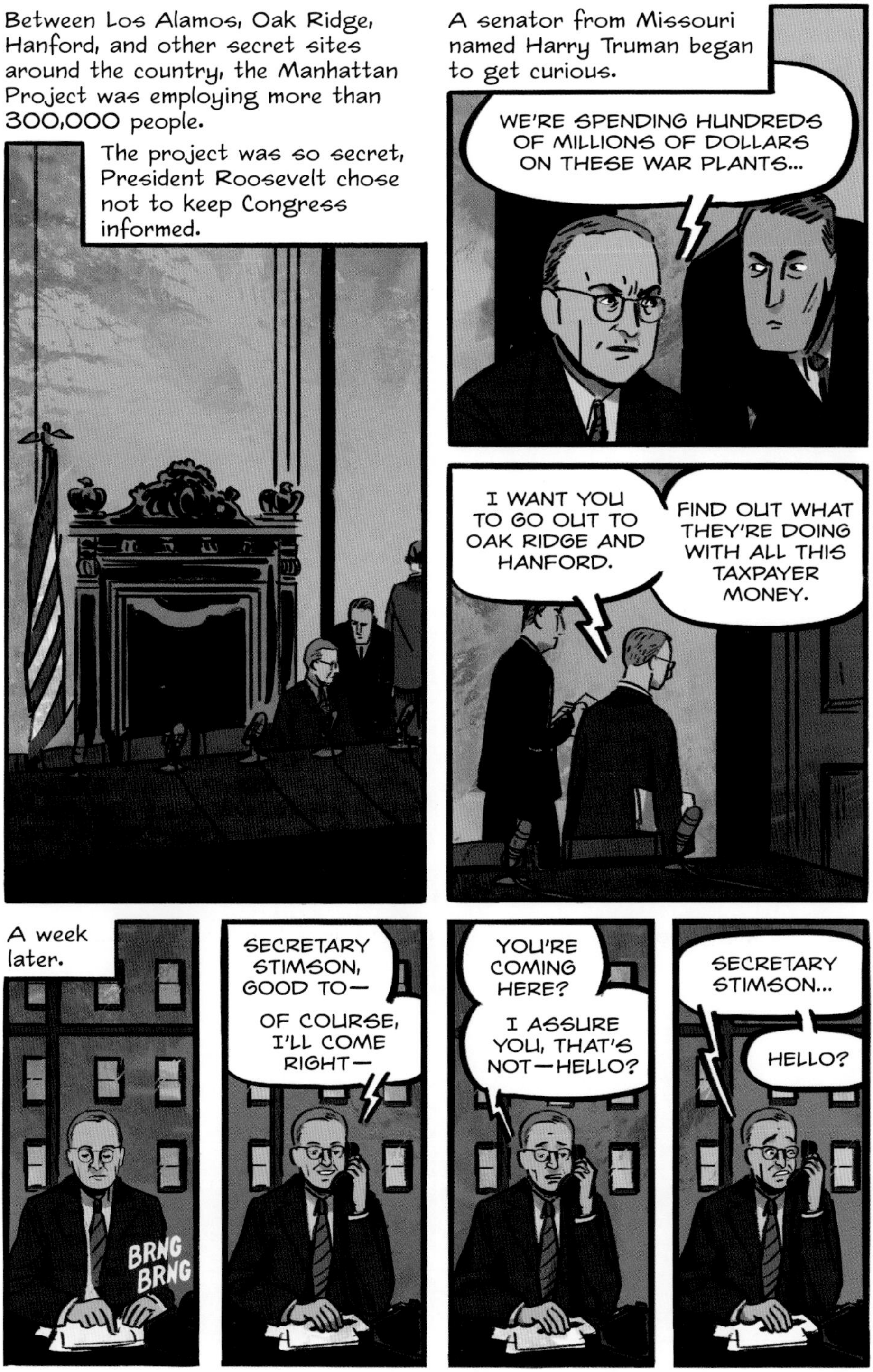
Between Los Alamos, Oak Ridge, Hanford, and other secret sites around the country, the Manhattan Project was employing more than 300,000 people.
The project was so secret, President Roosevelt chose not to keep Congress informed.
A senator from Missouri named Harry Truman began to get curious.
WE'RE SPENDING HUNDREDS OF MILLIONS OF DOLLARS ON THESE WAR PLANTS...
I WANT YOU TO GO OUT TO OAK RIDGE AND HANFORD.
FIND OUT WHAT THEY'RE DOING WITH ALL THIS TAXPAYER MONEY.
A week later.
BRNG BRNG
SECRETARY STIMSON, GOOD TO—
OF COURSE, I'LL COME RIGHT—
YOU'RE COMING HERE?
I ASSURE YOU, THAT'S NOT—HELLO?
SECRETARY STIMSON...
HELLO?

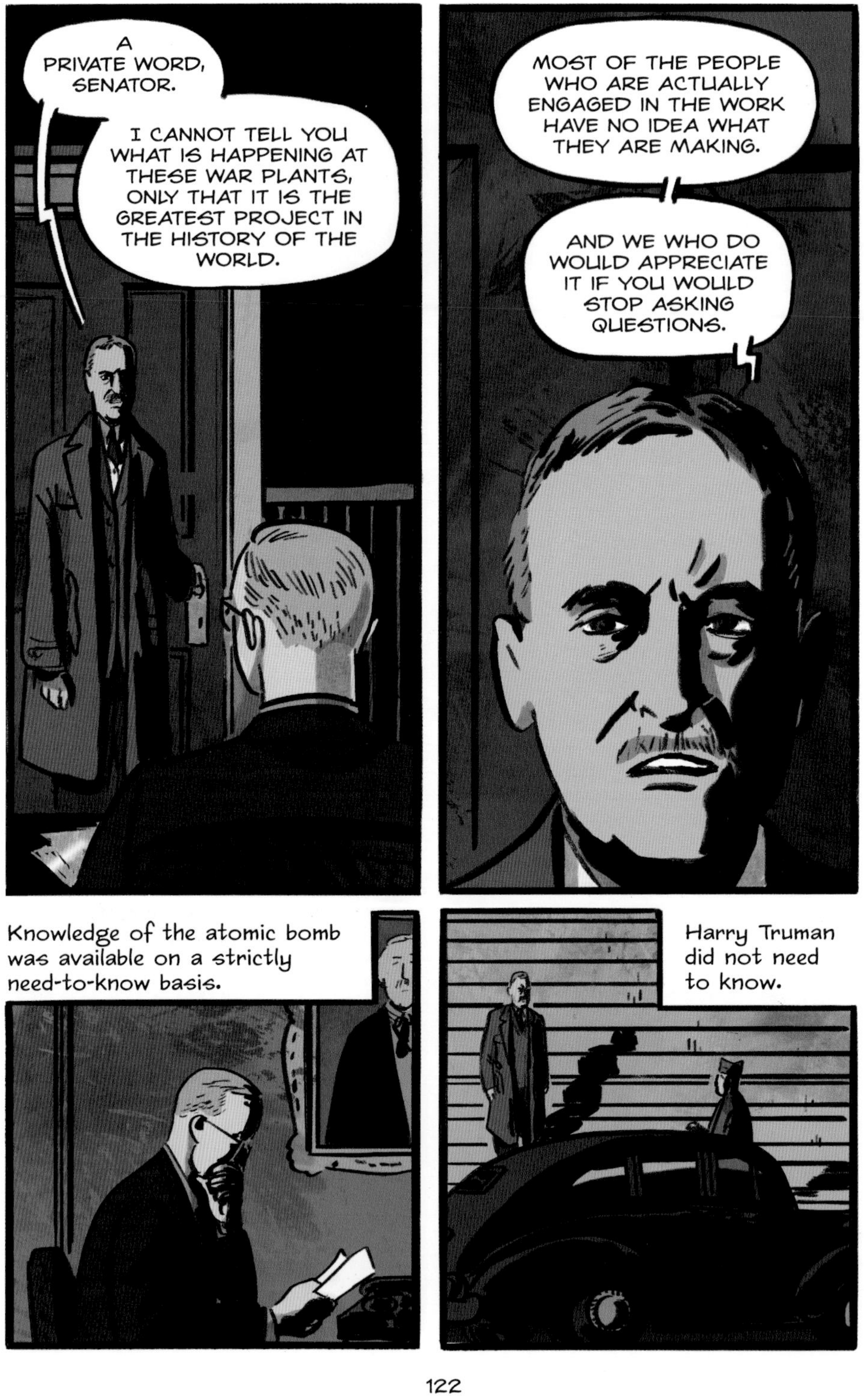
A PRIVATE WORD, SENATOR.
I CANNOT TELL YOU WHAT IS HAPPENING AT THESE WAR PLANTS, ONLY THAT IT IS THE GREATEST PROJECT IN THE HISTORY OF THE WORLD.
MOST OF THE PEOPLE WHO ARE ACTUALLY ENGAGED IN THE WORK HAVE NO IDEA WHAT THEY ARE MAKING.
AND WE WHO DO WOULD APPRECIATE IT IF YOU WOULD STOP ASKING QUESTIONS.
Knowledge of the atomic bomb was available on a strictly need-to-know basis.
Harry Truman did not need to know.

Philadelphia, 1950.

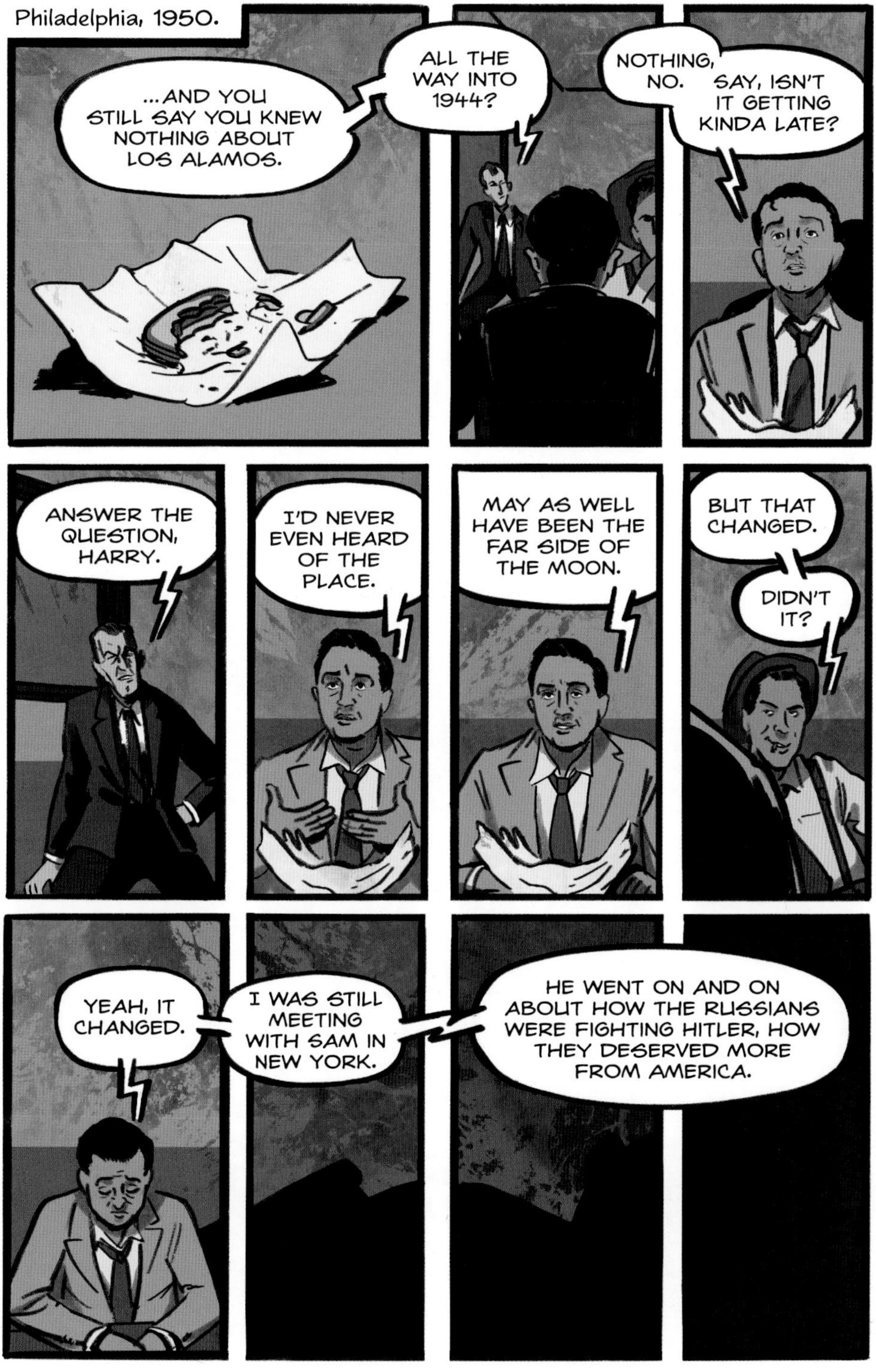
...AND YOU STILL SAY YOU KNEW NOTHING ABOUT LOS ALAMOS.
ALL THE WAY INTO 1944?
NOTHING, NO.
SAY, ISN'T IT GETTING KINDA LATE?
ANSWER THE QUESTION, HARRY.
I'D NEVER EVEN HEARD OF THE PLACE.
MAY AS WELL HAVE BEEN THE FAR SIDE OF THE MOON.
BUT THAT CHANGED.
DIDN'T IT?
YEAH, IT CHANGED.
I WAS STILL MEETING WITH SAM IN NEW YORK.
HE WENT ON AND ON ABOUT HOW THE RUSSIANS WERE FIGHTING HITLER, HOW THEY DESERVED MORE FROM AMERICA.

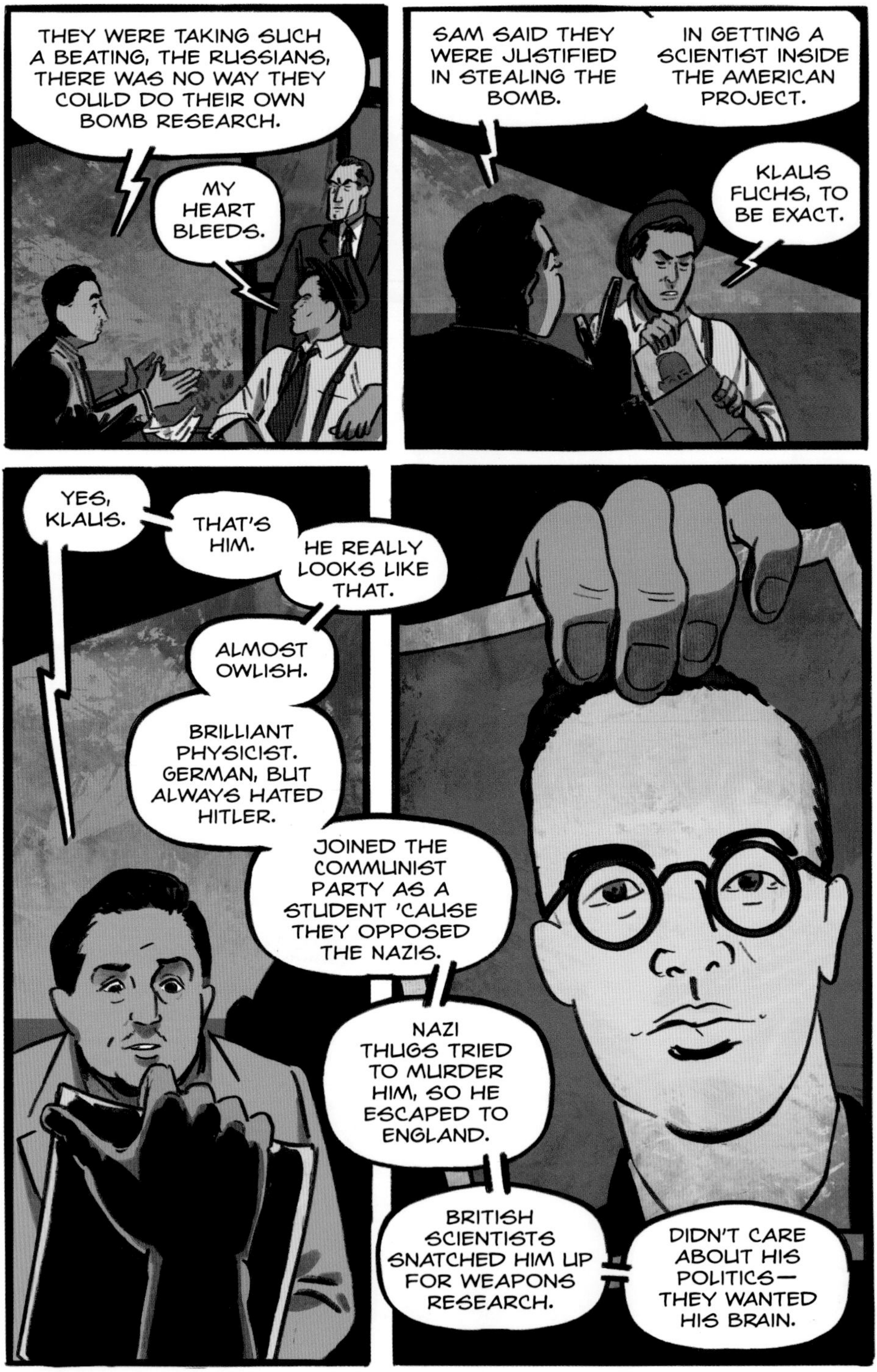
THEY WERE TAKING SUCH A BEATING, THE RUSSIANS, THERE WAS NO WAY THEY COULD DO THEIR OWN BOMB RESEARCH.
MY HEART BLEEDS.
SAM SAID THEY WERE JUSTIFIED IN STEALING THE BOMB.
IN GETTING A SCIENTIST INSIDE THE AMERICAN PROJECT.
KLAUS FUCHS, TO BE EXACT.
YES, KLAUS.
THAT'S HIM.
HE REALLY LOOKS LIKE THAT.
ALMOST OWLISH.
BRILLIANT PHYSICIST. GERMAN, BUT ALWAYS HATED HITLER.
JOINED THE COMMUNIST PARTY AS A STUDENT 'CAUSE THEY OPPOSED THE NAZIS.
NAZI THUGS TRIED TO MURDER HIM, SO HE ESCAPED TO ENGLAND.
BRITISH SCIENTISTS SNATCHED HIM UP FOR WEAPONS RESEARCH.
DIDN'T CARE ABOUT HIS POLITICS— THEY WANTED HIS BRAIN.

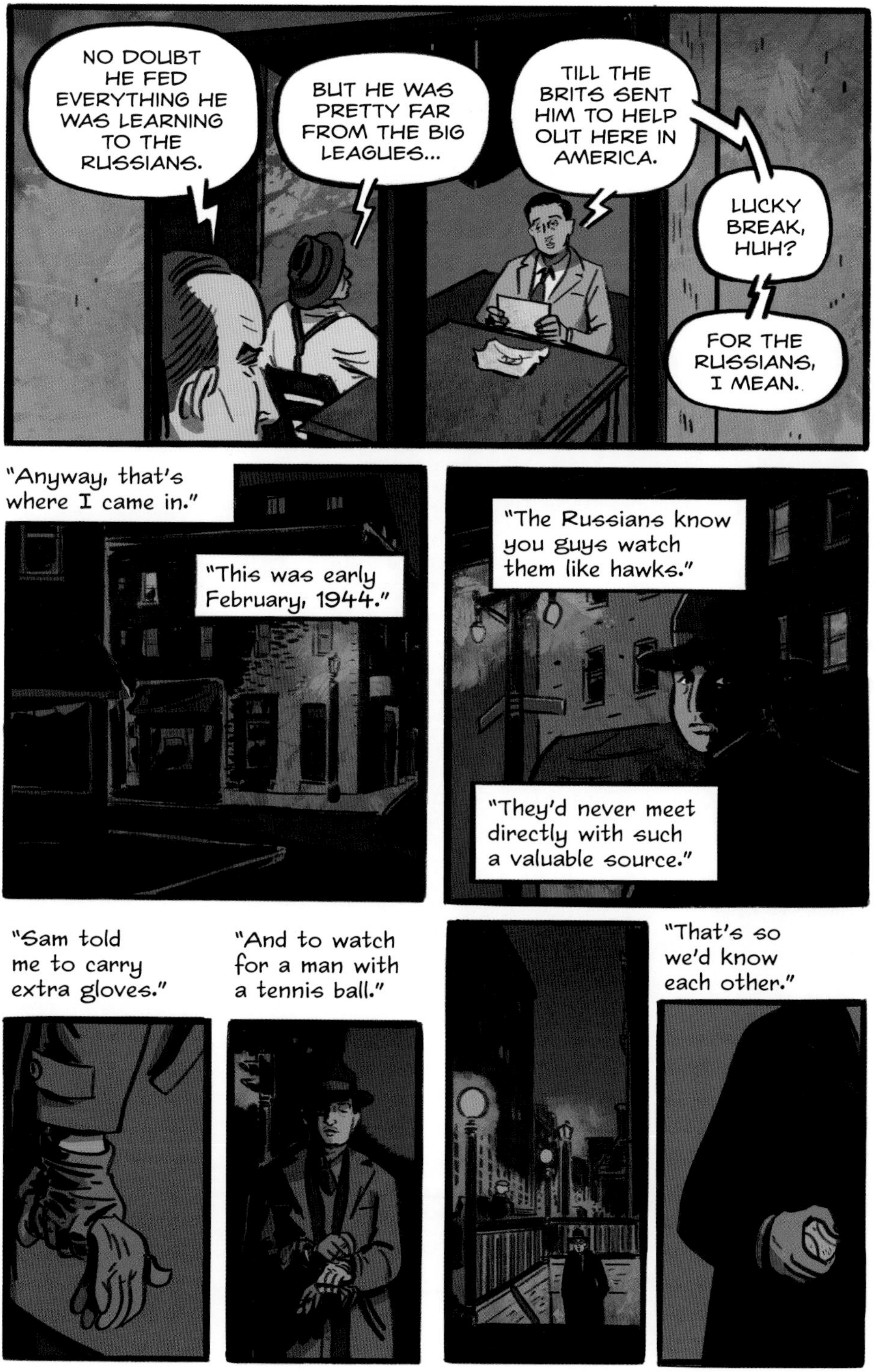
NO DOUBT HE FED EVERYTHING HE WAS LEARNING TO THE RUSSIANS.
BUT HE WAS PRETTY FAR FROM THE BIG LEAGUES...
TILL THE BRITS SENT HIM TO HELP OUT HERE IN AMERICA.
LUCKY BREAK, HUH?
FOR THE RUSSIANS, I MEAN.
"Anyway, that's where I came in."
"This was early February, 1944."
"The Russians know you guys watch them like hawks."
"They'd never meet directly with such a valuable source."
"Sam told me to carry extra gloves."
"And to watch for a man with a tennis ball."
"That's so we'd know each other."

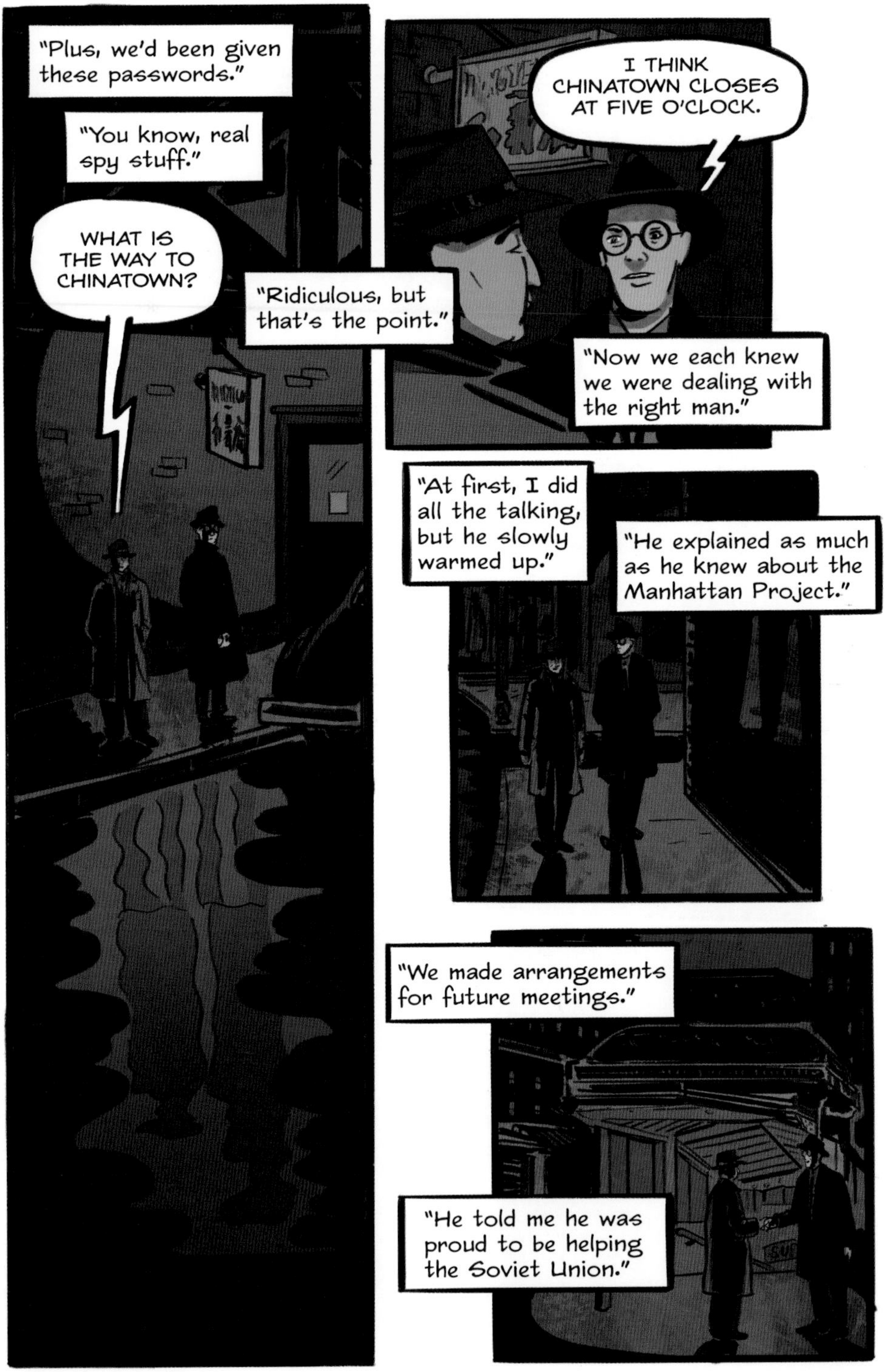
"Plus, we'd been given these passwords."
"You know, real spy stuff."
WHAT IS THE WAY TO CHINATOWN?
"Ridiculous, but that's the point."
I THINK CHINATOWN CLOSES AT FIVE O'CLOCK.
"Now we each knew we were dealing with the right man."
"At first, I did all the talking, but he slowly warmed up."
"He explained as much as he knew about the Manhattan Project."
"We made arrangements for future meetings."
"He told me he was proud to be helping the Soviet Union."

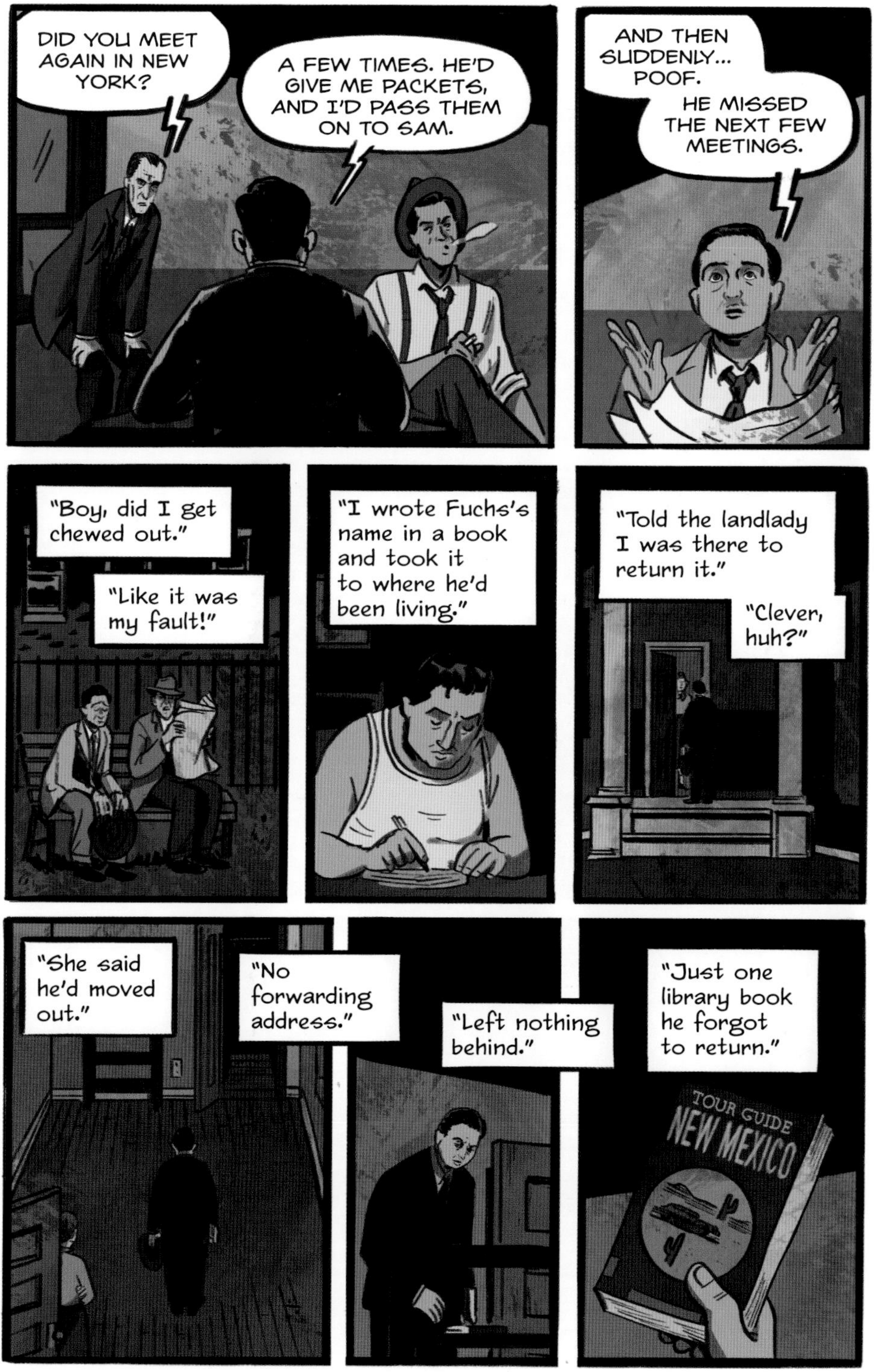
DID YOU MEET AGAIN IN NEW YORK?
A FEW TIMES. HE'D GIVE ME PACKETS, AND I'D PASS THEM ON TO SAM.
AND THEN SUDDENLY... POOF.
HE MISSED THE NEXT FEW MEETINGS.
"Boy, did I get chewed out."
"Like it was my fault!"
"I wrote Fuchs's name in a book and took it to where he'd been living."
"Told the landlady I was there to return it."
"Clever, huh?"
"She said he'd moved out."
"No forwarding address."
"Left nothing behind."
"Just one library book he forgot to return."
TOUR GUIDE
NEW MEXICO

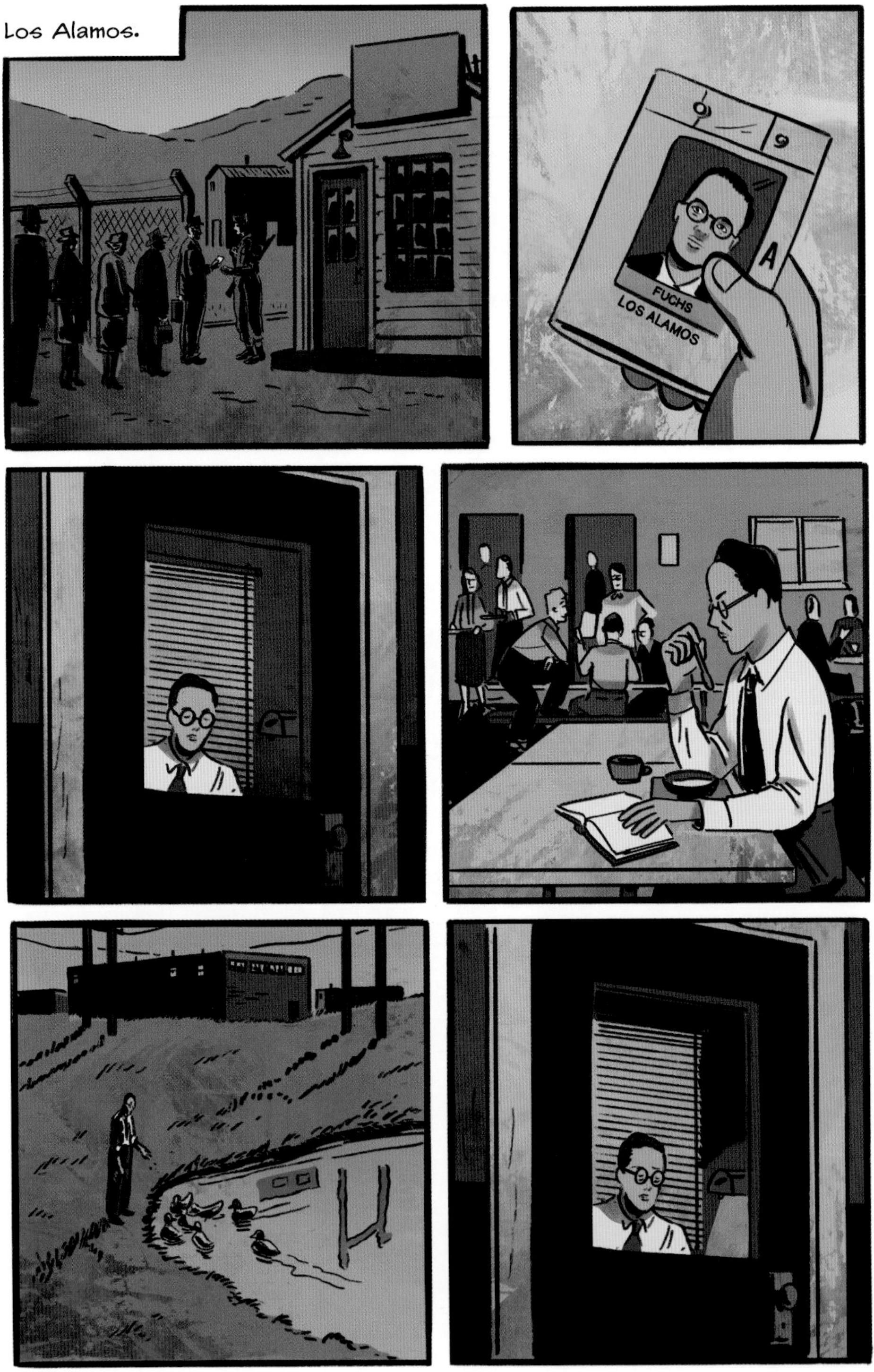
Los Alamos.
9
9
A
FUCHS
LOS ALAMOS

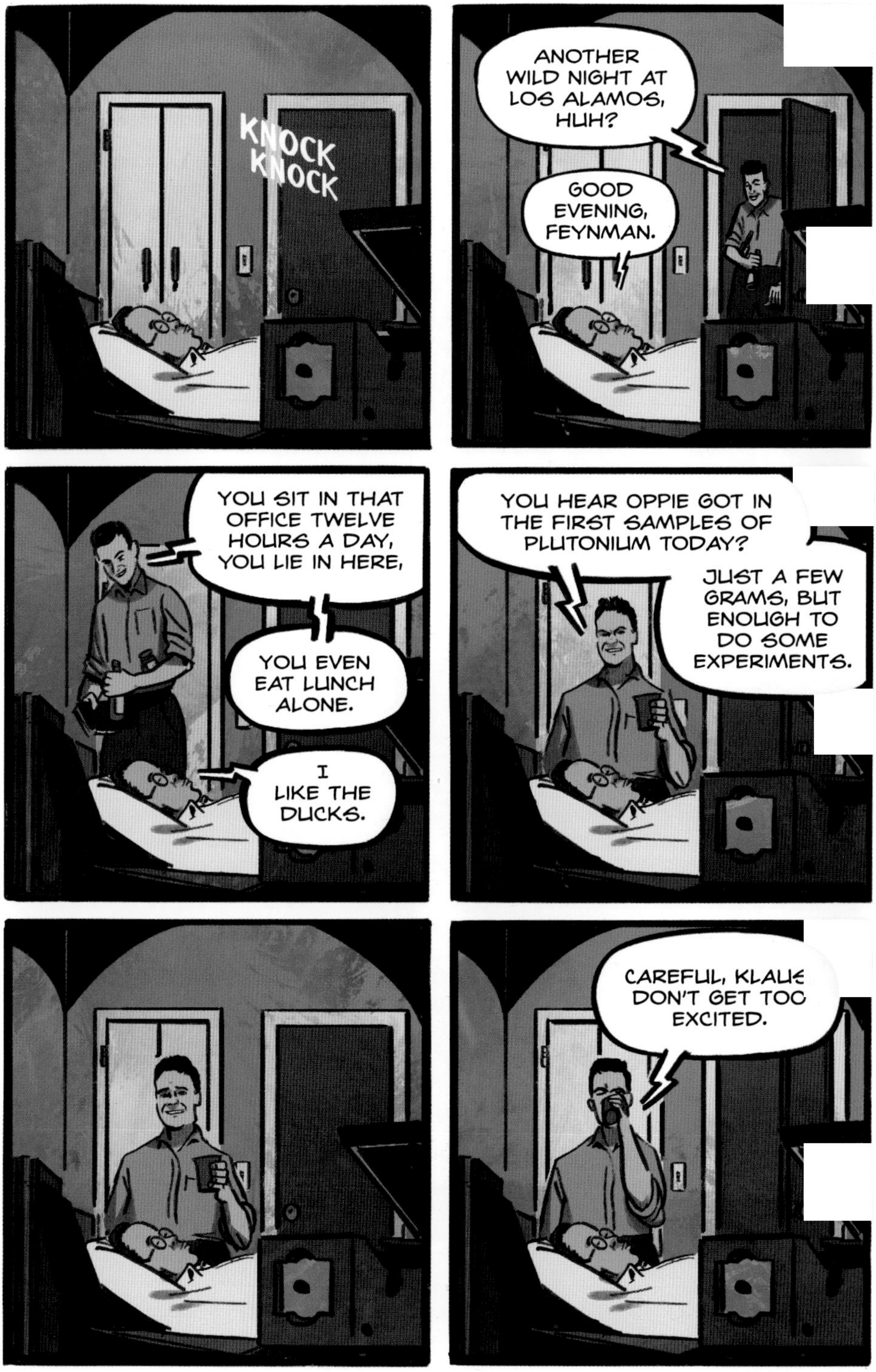
KNOCK KNOCK
ANOTHER WILD NIGHT AT LOS ALAMOS, HUH?
GOOD EVENING, FEYNMAN.
YOU SIT IN THAT OFFICE TWELVE HOURS A DAY, YOU LIE IN HERE,
YOU EVEN EAT LUNCH ALONE.
I LIKE THE DUCKS.
YOU HEAR OPPIE GOT IN THE FIRST SAMPLES OF PLUTONIUM TODAY?
JUST A FEW GRAMS, BUT ENOUGH TO DO SOME EXPERIMENTS.
CAREFUL, KLAUS DON'T GET TOO EXCITED.

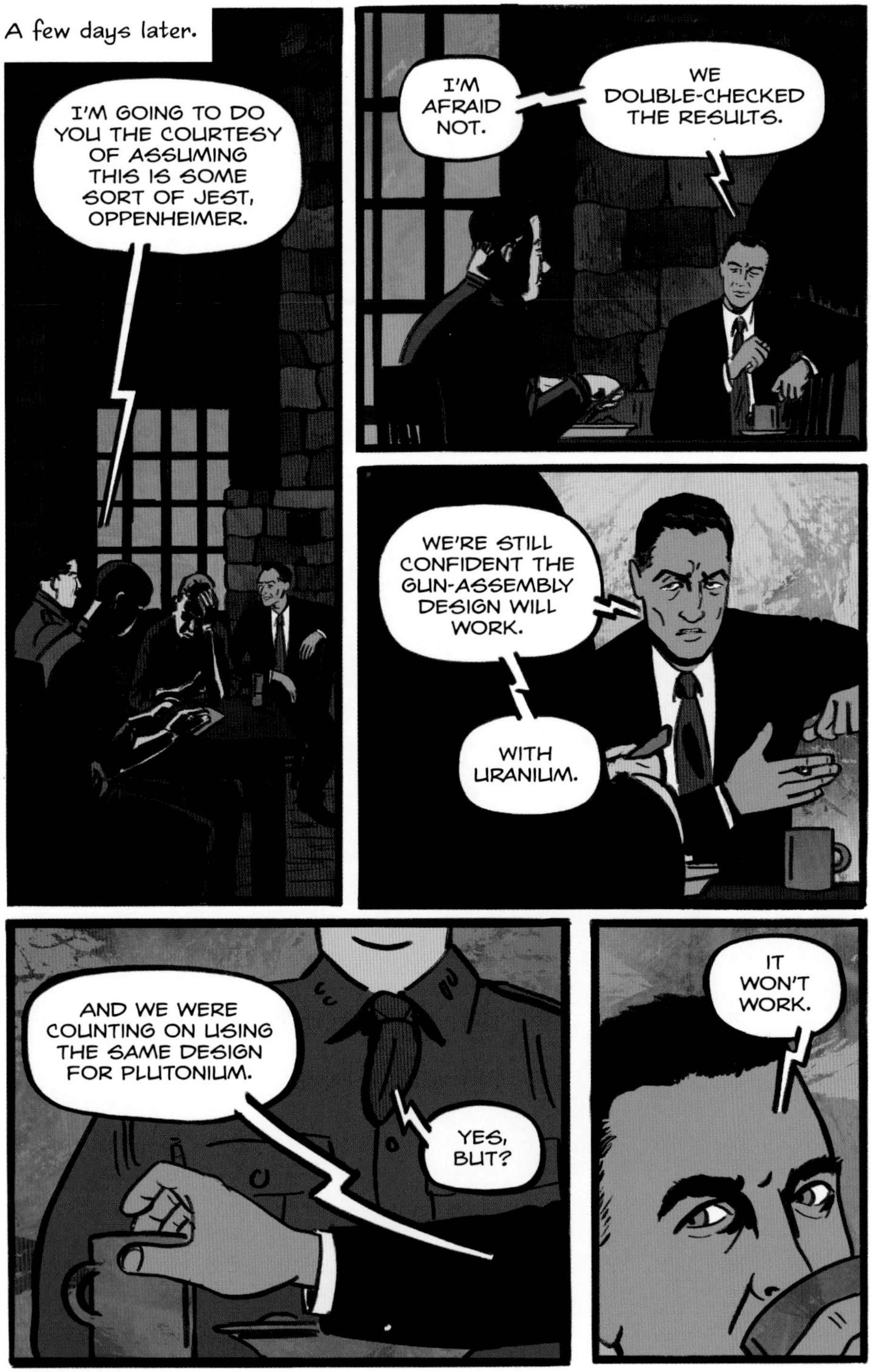
A few days later.
I'M GOING TO DO YOU THE COURTESY OF ASSUMING THIS IS SOME SORT OF JEST, OPPENHEIMER.
I'M AFRAID NOT.
WE DOUBLE-CHECKED THE RESULTS.
WE'RE STILL CONFIDENT THE GUN-ASSEMBLY DESIGN WILL WORK.
WITH URANIUM.
AND WE WERE COUNTING ON USING THE SAME DESIGN FOR PLUTONIUM.
YES, BUT?
IT WON'T WORK.

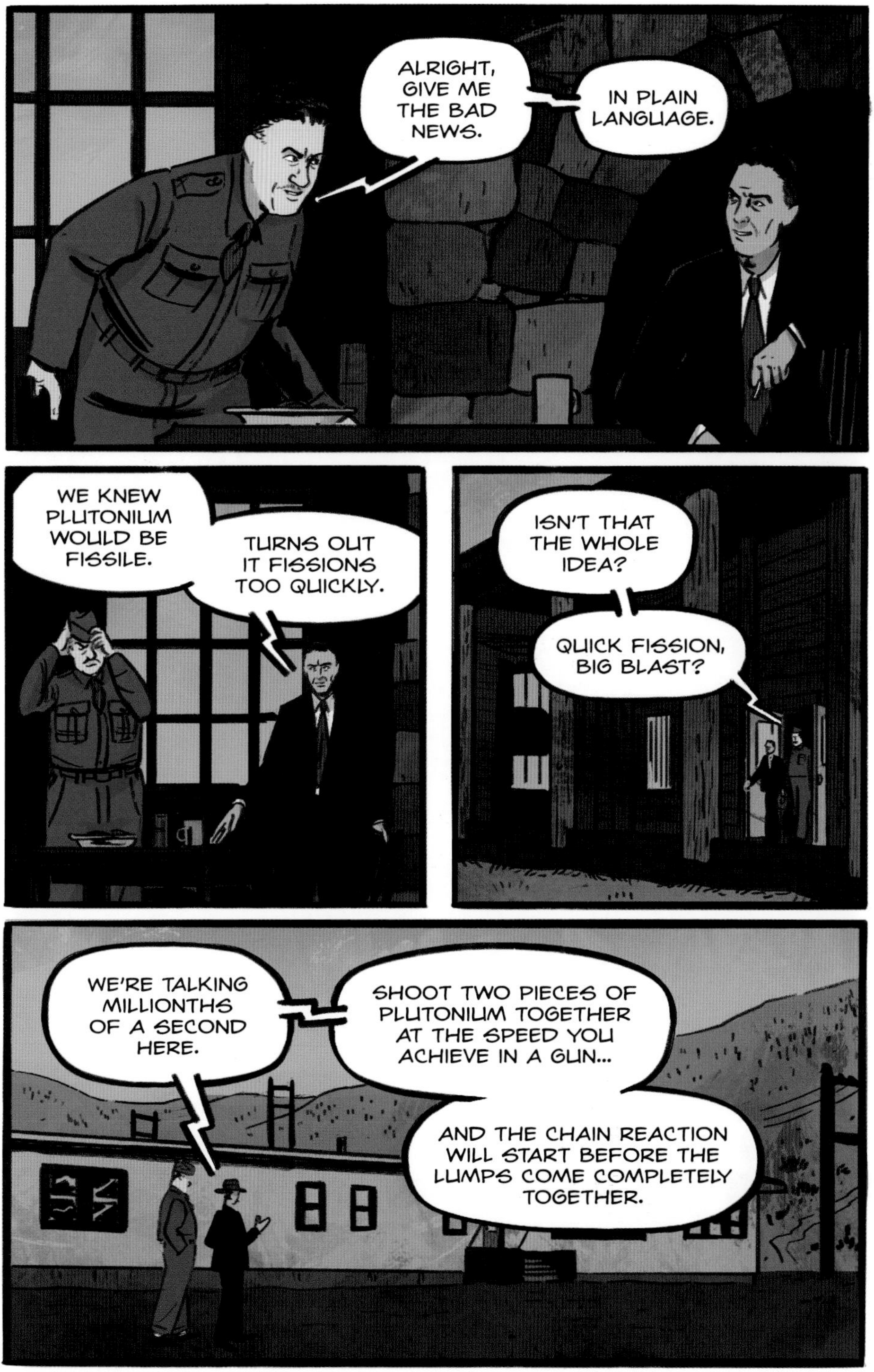
ALRIGHT, GIVE ME THE BAD NEWS.
IN PLAIN LANGUAGE.
WE KNEW PLUTONIUM WOULD BE FISSILE.
TURNS OUT IT FISSIONS TOO QUICKLY.
ISN'T THAT THE WHOLE IDEA?
QUICK FISSION, BIG BLAST?
WE'RE TALKING MILLIONTHS OF A SECOND HERE.
SHOOT TWO PIECES OF PLUTONIUM TOGETHER AT THE SPEED YOU ACHIEVE IN A GUN...
AND THE CHAIN REACTION WILL START BEFORE THE LUMPS COME COMPLETELY TOGETHER.

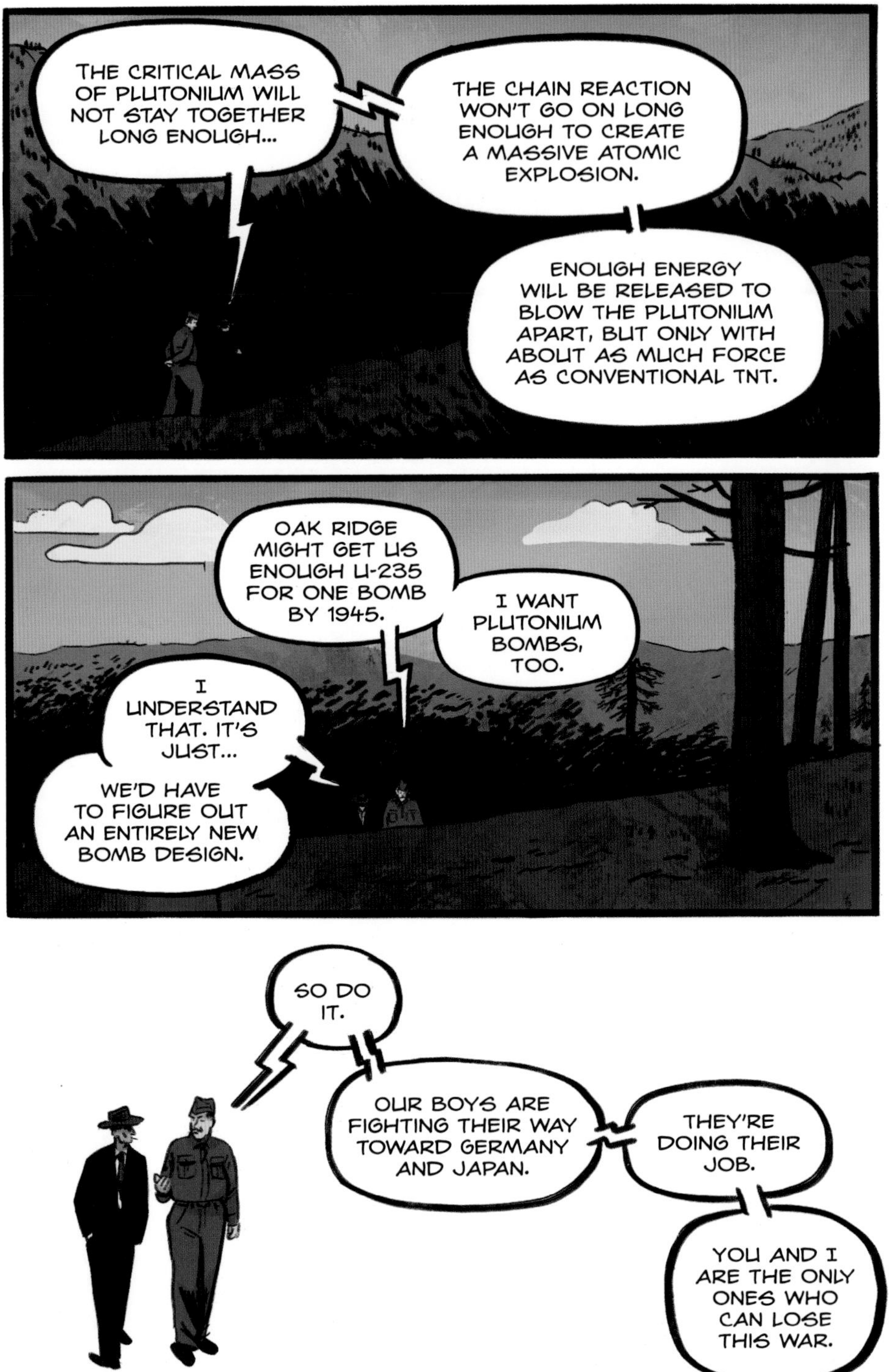
THE CRITICAL MASS OF PLUTONIUM WILL NOT STAY TOGETHER LONG ENOUGH...
THE CHAIN REACTION WON'T GO ON LONG ENOUGH TO CREATE A MASSIVE ATOMIC EXPLOSION.
ENOUGH ENERGY WILL BE RELEASED TO BLOW THE PLUTONIUM APART, BUT ONLY WITH ABOUT AS MUCH FORCE AS CONVENTIONAL TNT.
OAK RIDGE MIGHT GET US ENOUGH U-235 FOR ONE BOMB BY 1945.
I WANT PLUTONIUM BOMBS, TOO.
I UNDERSTAND THAT. IT'S JUST...
WE'D HAVE TO FIGURE OUT AN ENTIRELY NEW BOMB DESIGN.
SO DO IT.
OUR BOYS ARE FIGHTING THEIR WAY TOWARD GERMANY AND JAPAN.
THEY'RE DOING THEIR JOB.
YOU AND I ARE THE ONLY ONES WHO CAN LOSE THIS WAR.

Oppenheimer reorganized Los Alamos to meet the new challenge.

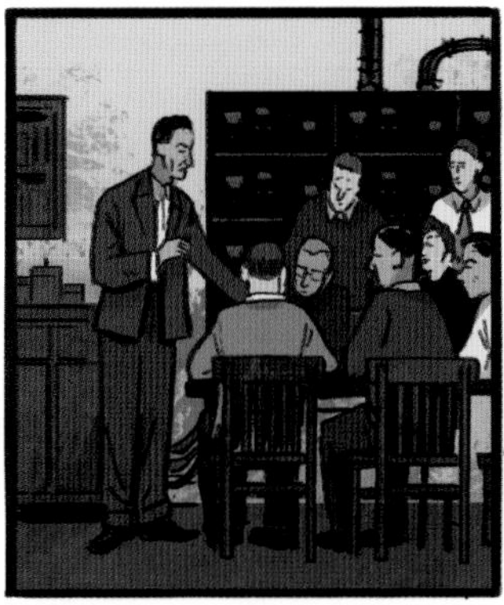

Theodore Hall already knew the basics of the uranium bomb.

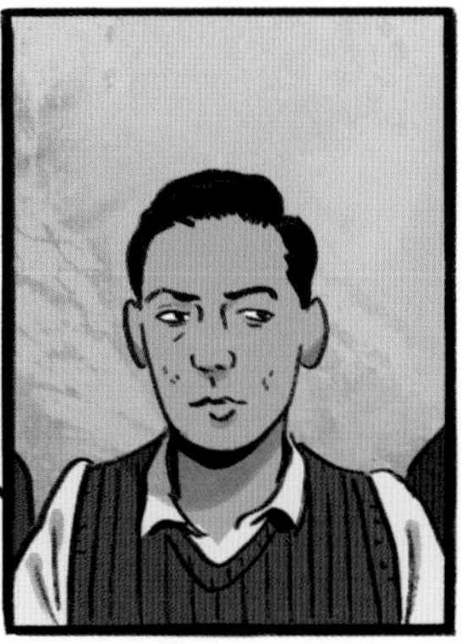

Now he got a new job—testing potential components of a plutonium bomb.

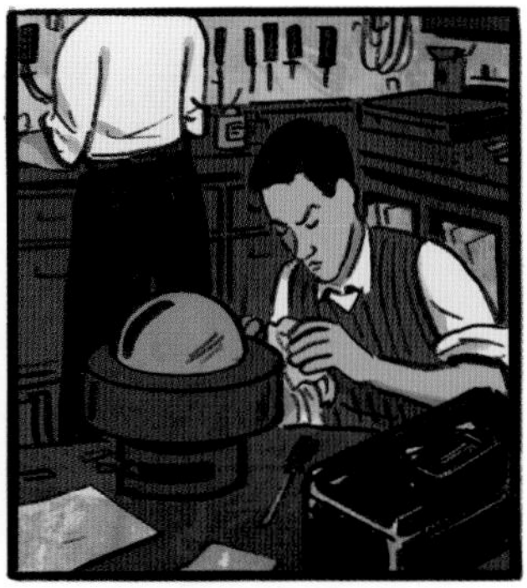

In October 1944, just before his nineteenth birthday, Hall was granted a two-week leave.

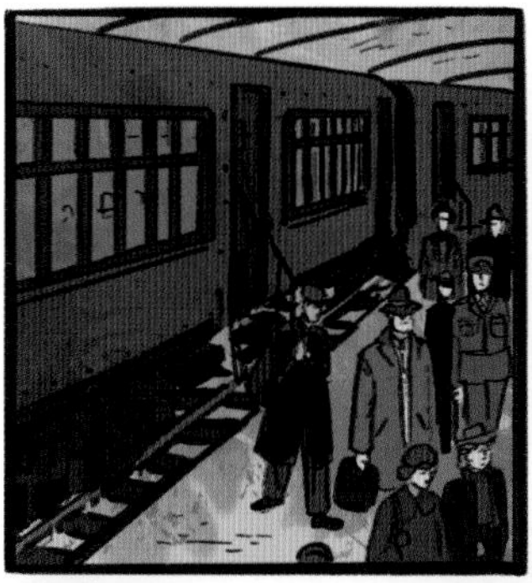

He decided to visit his parents in New York City.

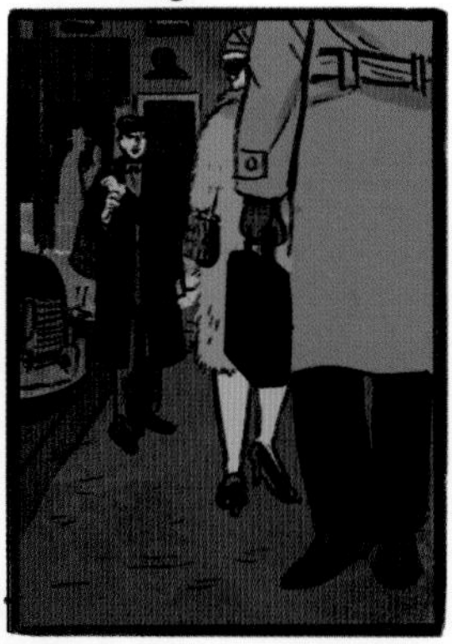

But first he went to see his roommate from Harvard, Saville Sax.

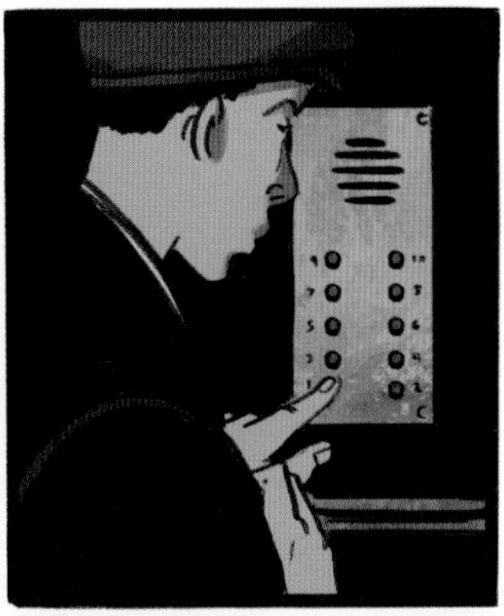

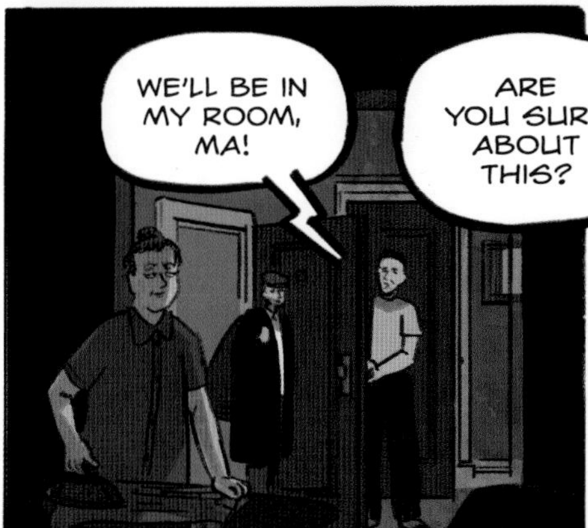
WE'LL BE IN MY ROOM, MA!
ARE YOU SURE ABOUT THIS?

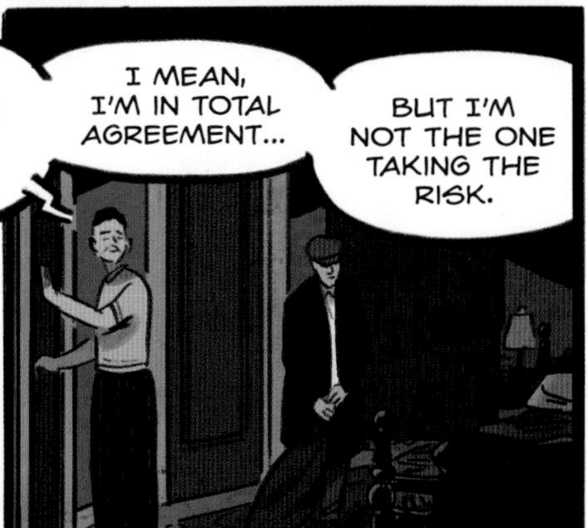
I MEAN, I'M IN TOTAL AGREEMENT...
BUT I'M NOT THE ONE TAKING THE RISK.
PLUMP

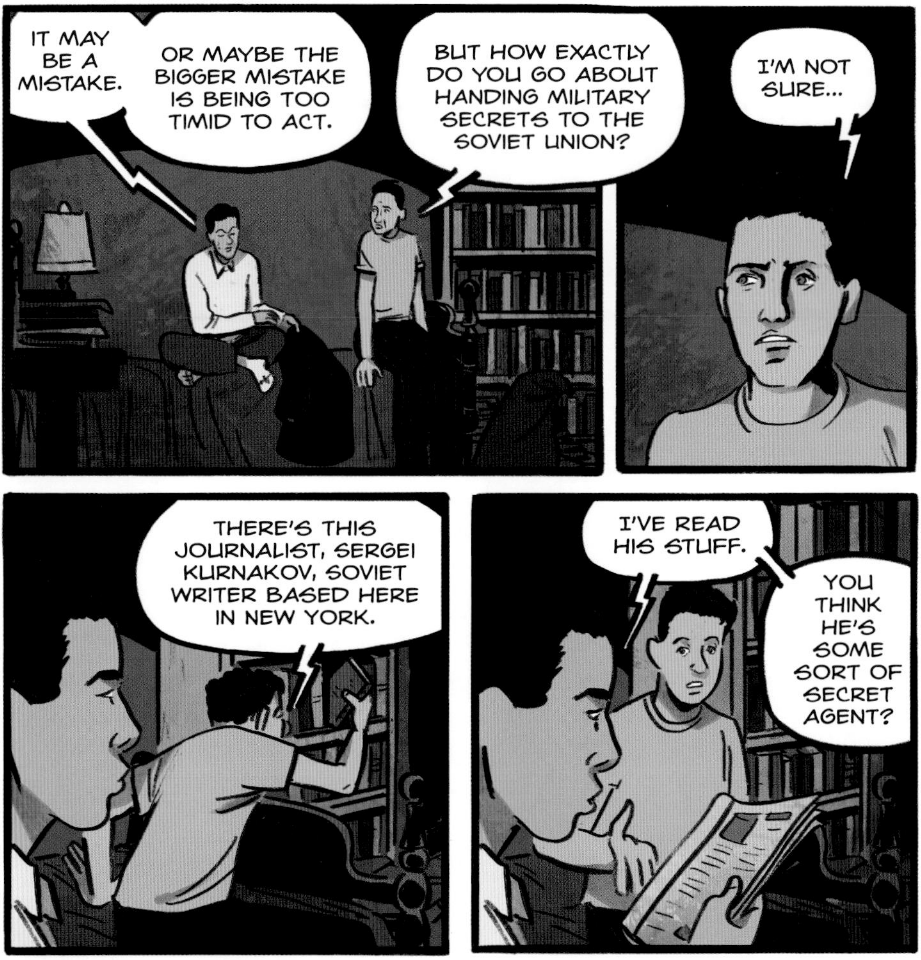
IT MAY BE A MISTAKE.
OR MAYBE THE BIGGER MISTAKE IS BEING TOO TIMID TO ACT.
BUT HOW EXACTLY DO YOU GO ABOUT HANDING MILITARY SECRETS TO THE SOVIET UNION?
I'M NOT SURE...
THERE'S THIS JOURNALIST, SERGEI KURNAKOV, SOVIET WRITER BASED HERE IN NEW YORK.
I'VE READ HIS STUFF.
YOU THINK HE'S SOME SORT OF SECRET AGENT?

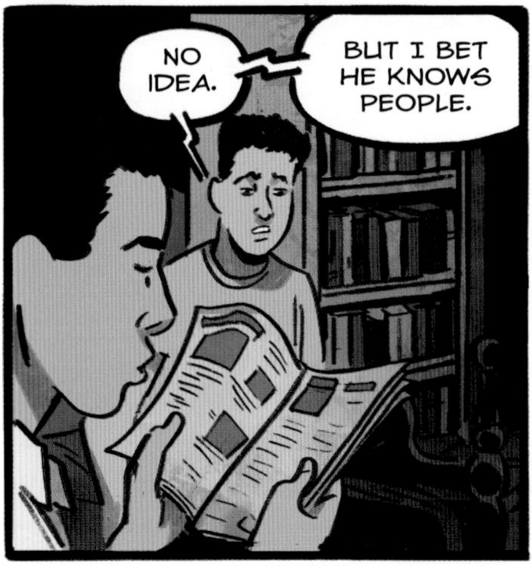
NO IDEA.
BUT I BET HE KNOWS PEOPLE.

Hall phoned Kurnakov.

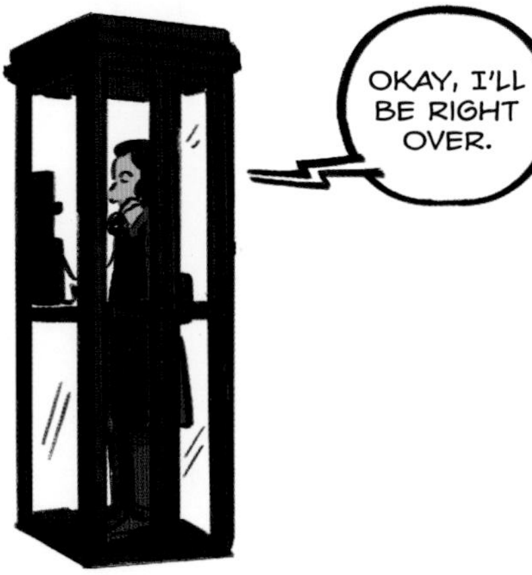
OKAY, I'LL BE RIGHT OVER.

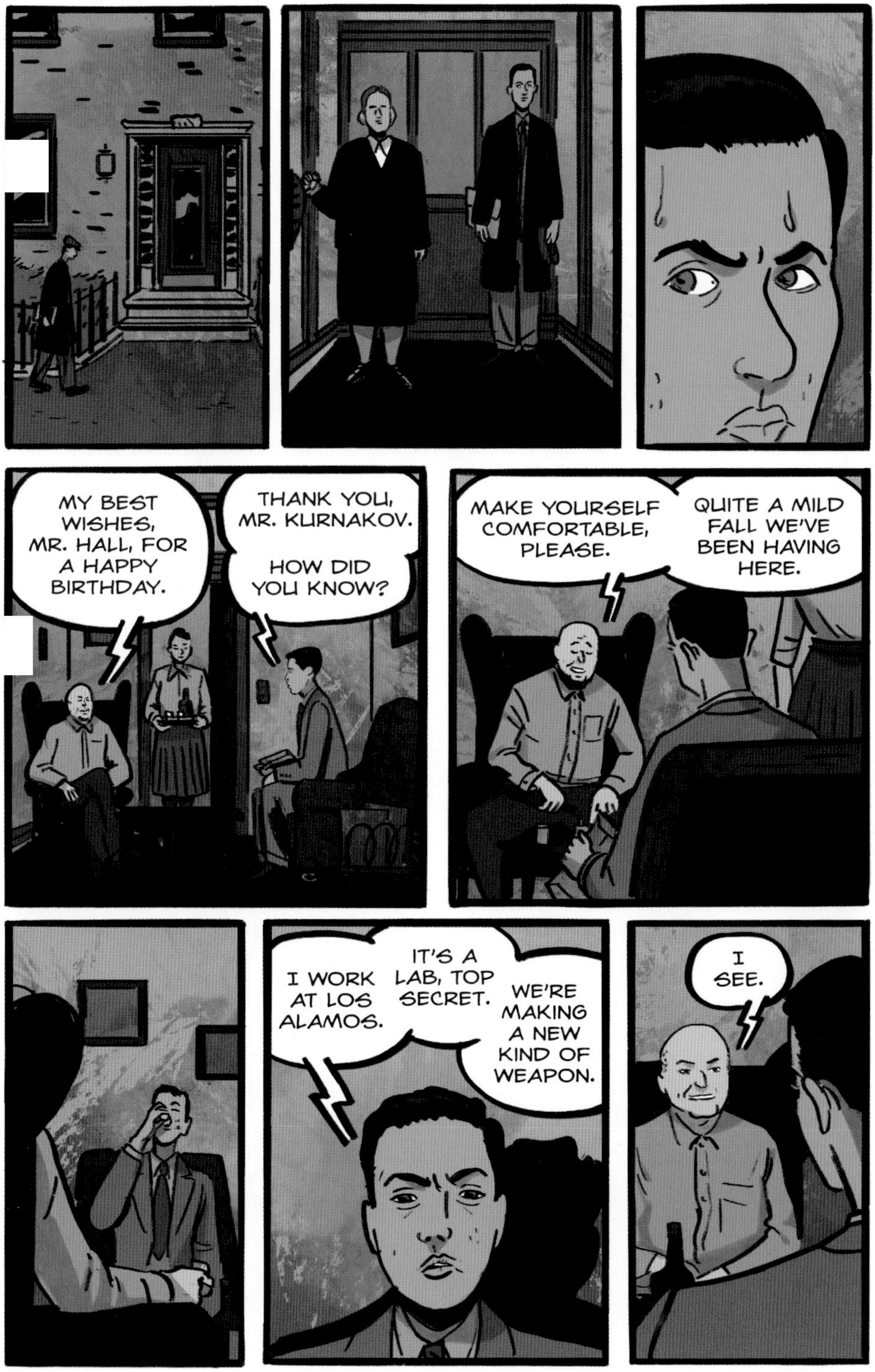
MY BEST WISHES, MR. HALL, FOR A HAPPY BIRTHDAY.
THANK YOU, MR. KURNAKOV.
HOW DID YOU KNOW?
MAKE YOURSELF COMFORTABLE, PLEASE.
QUITE A MILD FALL WE'VE BEEN HAVING HERE.
I WORK AT LOS ALAMOS.
IT'S A LAB, TOP SECRET.
WE'RE MAKING A NEW KIND OF WEAPON.
I SEE.

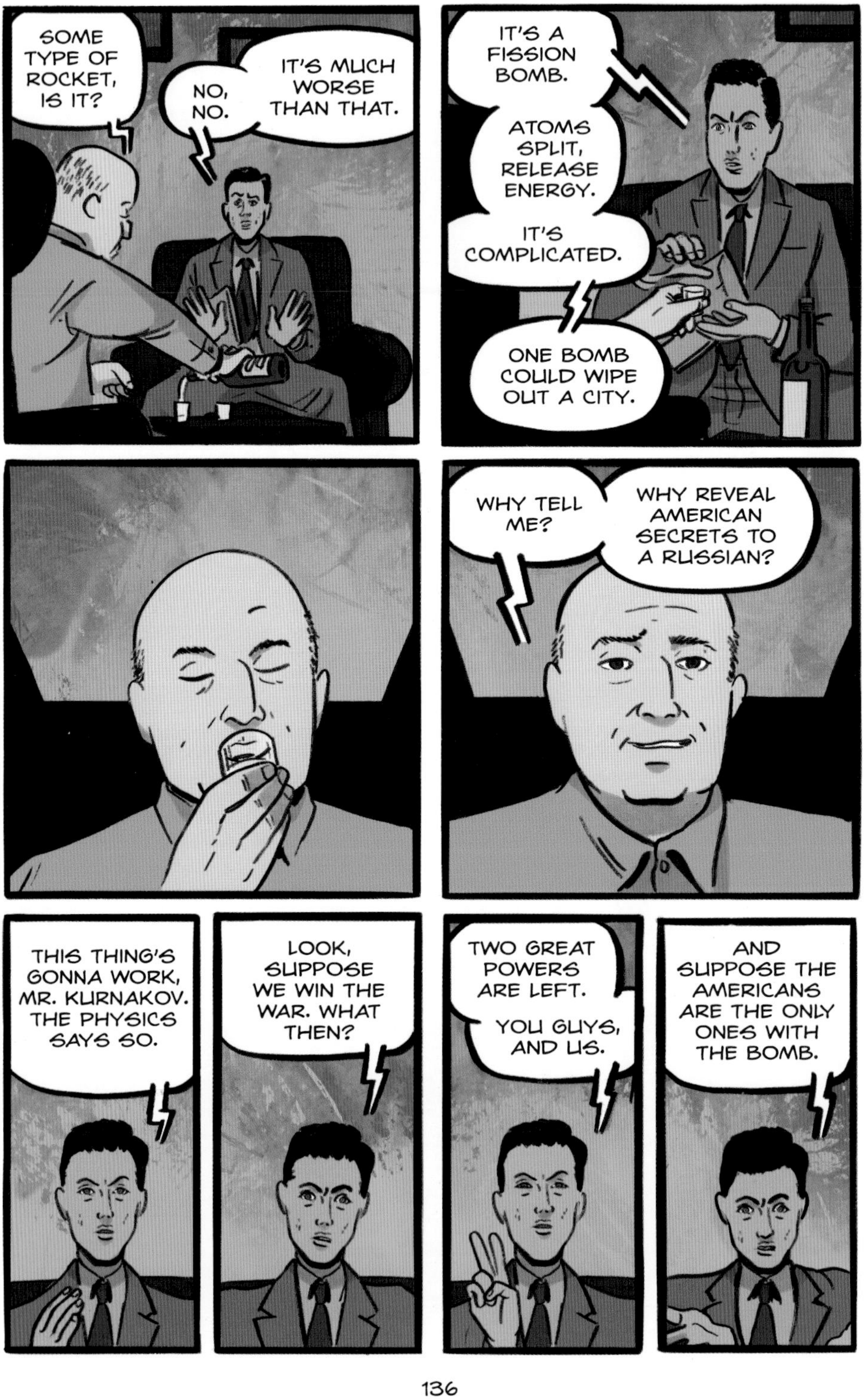
SOME TYPE OF ROCKET, IS IT?
NO, NO.
IT'S MUCH WORSE THAN THAT.
IT'S A FISSION BOMB.
ATOMS SPLIT, RELEASE ENERGY.
IT'S COMPLICATED.
ONE BOMB COULD WIPE OUT A CITY.
WHY TELL ME?
WHY REVEAL AMERICAN SECRETS TO A RUSSIAN?
THIS THING'S GONNA WORK, MR. KURNAKOV. THE PHYSICS SAYS SO.
LOOK, SUPPOSE WE WIN THE WAR. WHAT THEN?
TWO GREAT POWERS ARE LEFT.
YOU GUYS, AND US.
AND SUPPOSE THE AMERICANS ARE THE ONLY ONES WITH THE BOMB.

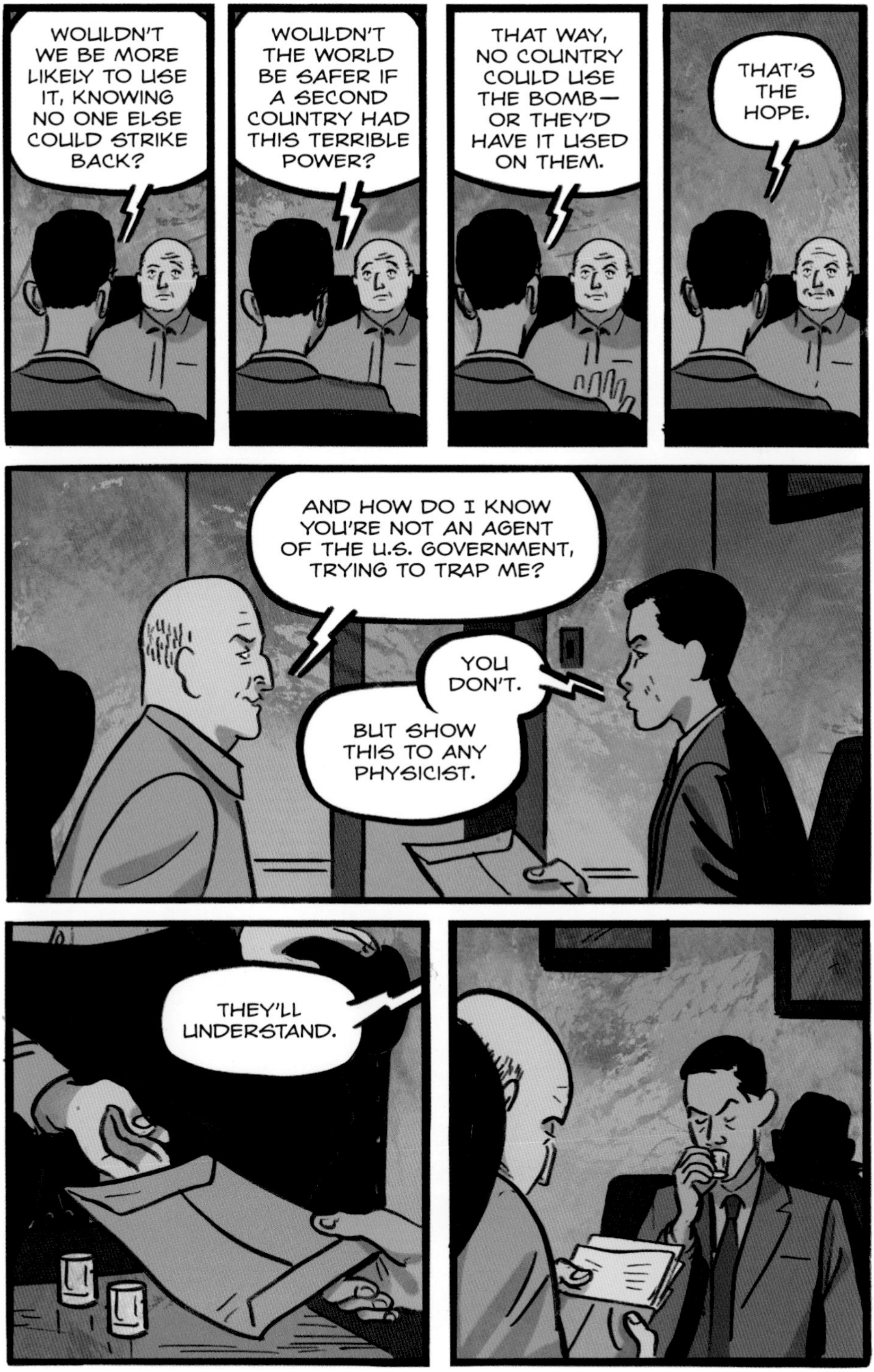
WOULDN'T WE BE MORE LIKELY TO USE IT, KNOWING NO ONE ELSE COULD STRIKE BACK?
WOULDN'T THE WORLD BE SAFER IF A SECOND COUNTRY HAD THIS TERRIBLE POWER?
THAT WAY, NO COUNTRY COULD USE THE BOMB— OR THEY'D HAVE IT USED ON THEM.
THAT'S THE HOPE.
AND HOW DO I KNOW YOU'RE NOT AN AGENT OF THE U.S. GOVERNMENT, TRYING TO TRAP ME?
YOU DON'T.
BUT SHOW THIS TO ANY PHYSICIST.
THEY'LL UNDERSTAND.

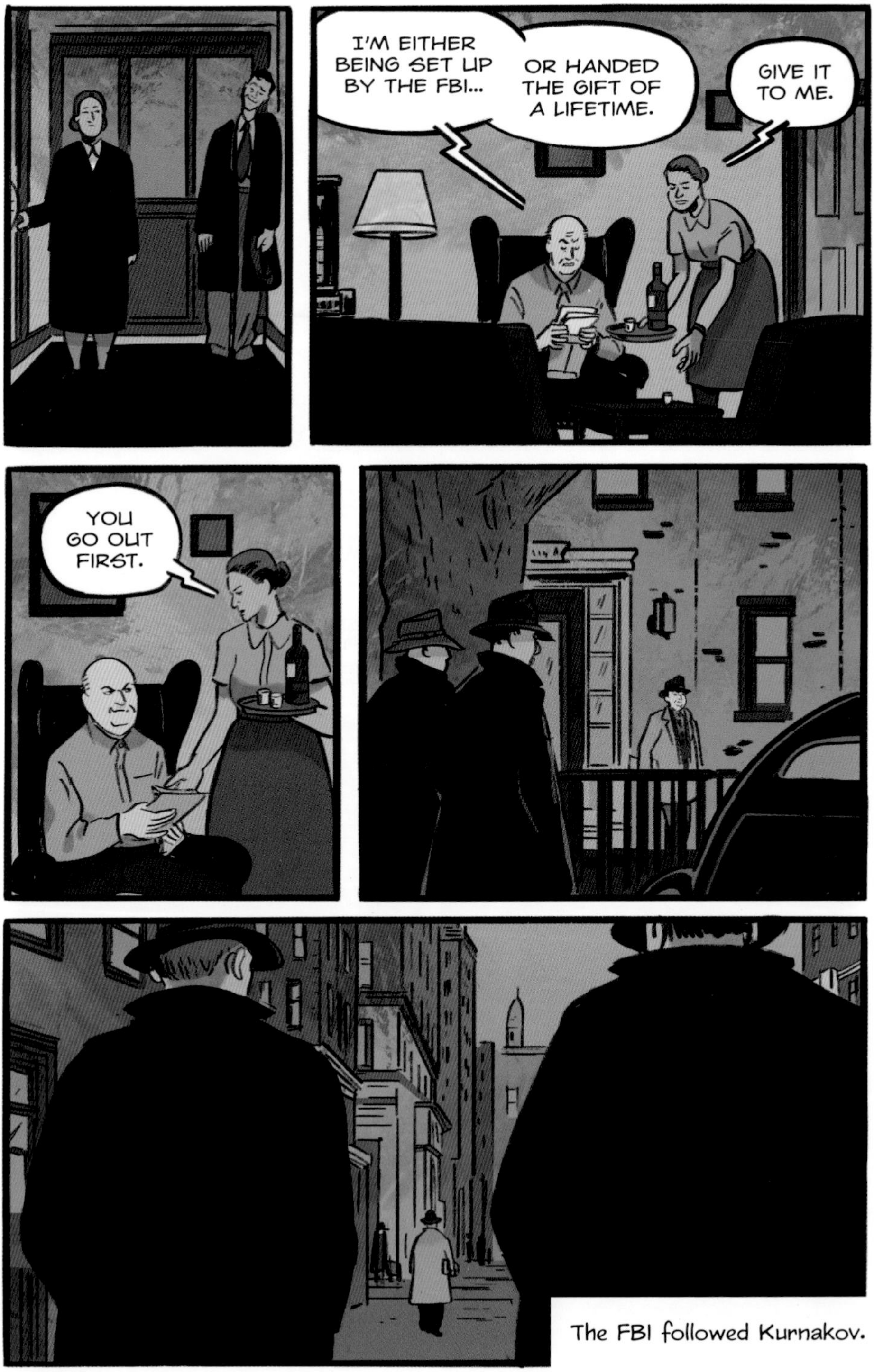
I'M EITHER BEING SET UP BY THE FBI...
OR HANDED THE GIFT OF A LIFETIME.
GIVE IT TO ME.
YOU GO OUT FIRST.
The FBI followed Kurnakov.

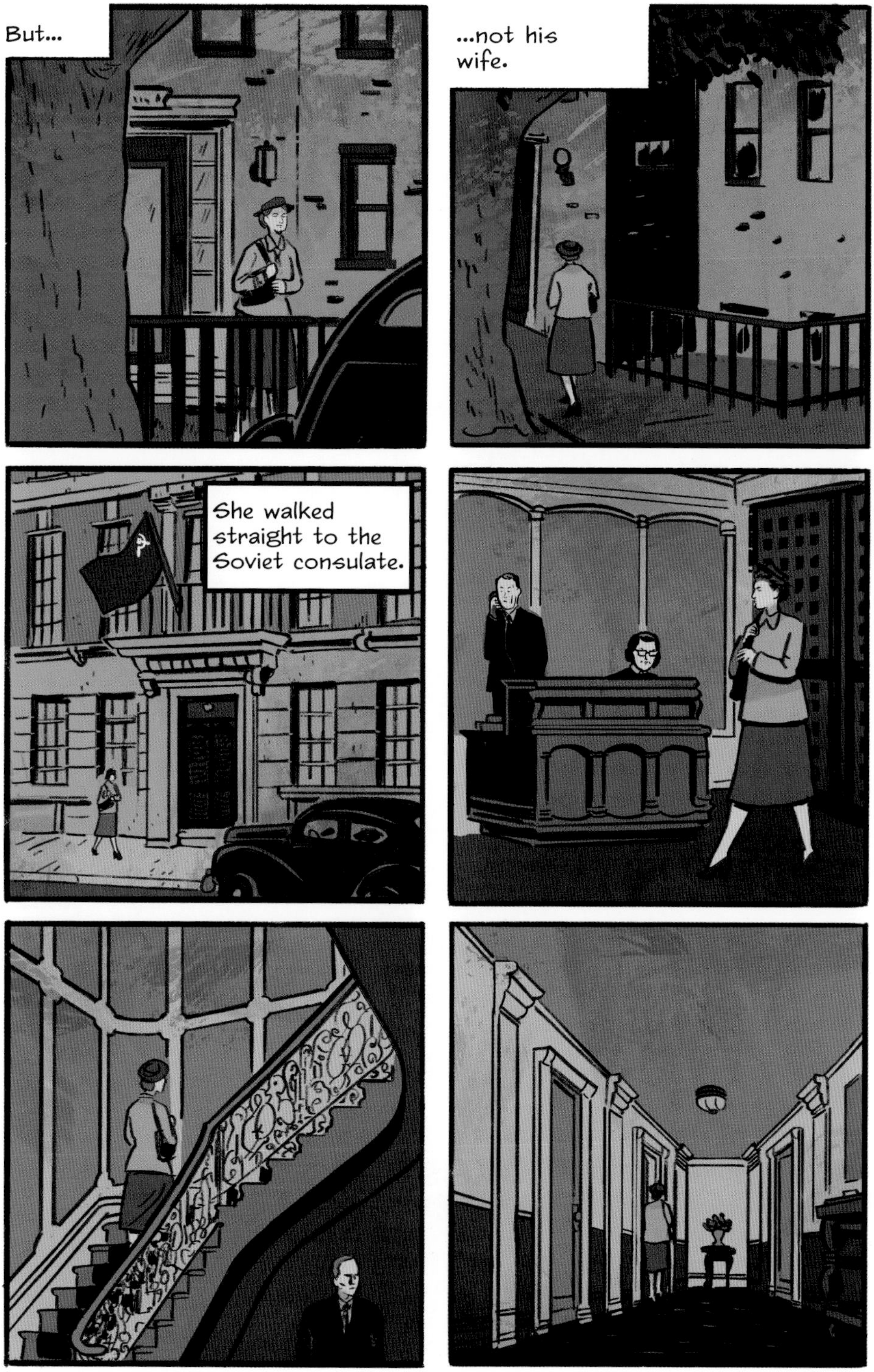
But...
...not his wife.
She walked straight to the Soviet consulate.

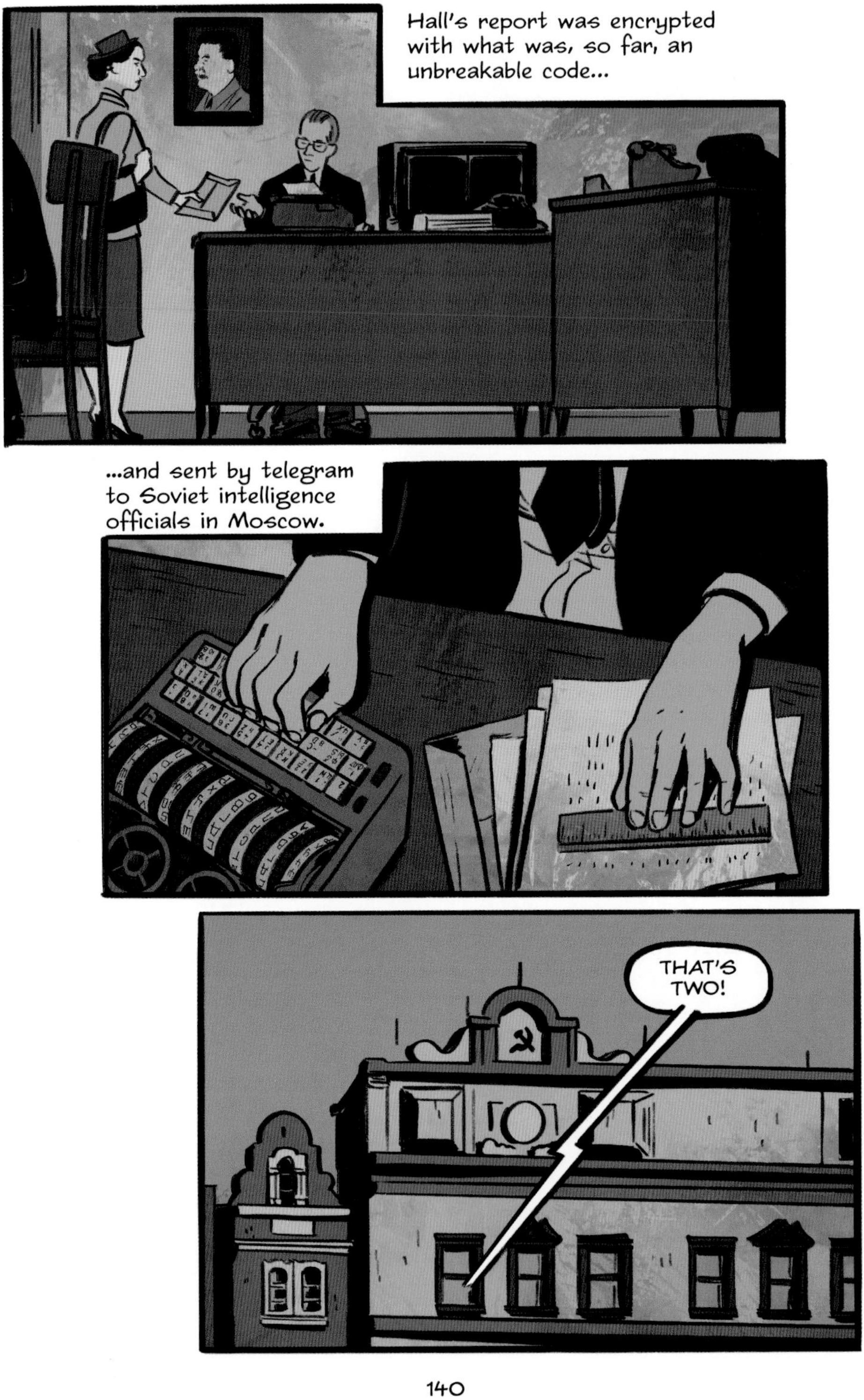
Hall's report was encrypted with what was, so far, an unbreakable code...
...and sent by telegram to Soviet intelligence officials in Moscow.
THAT'S TWO!

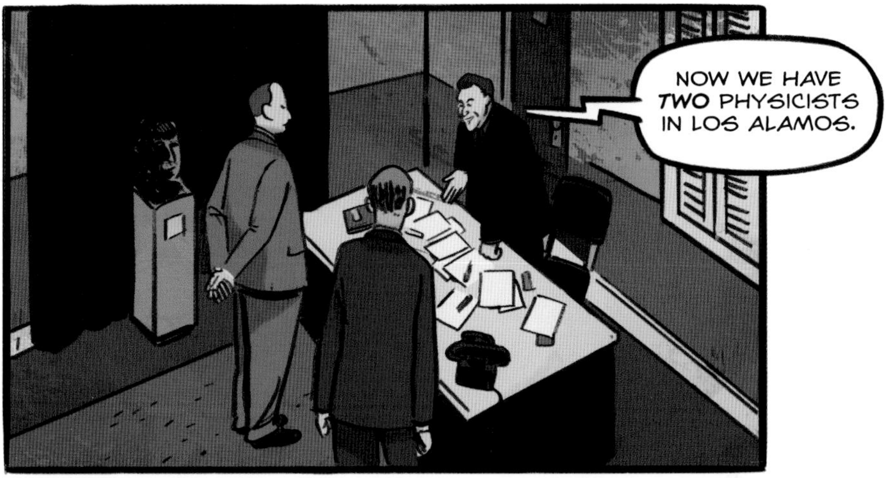
NOW WE HAVE **TWO** PHYSICISTS IN LOS ALAMOS.

From Moscow, the report traveled to Laboratory Number 2—the Soviet answer to Los Alamos.

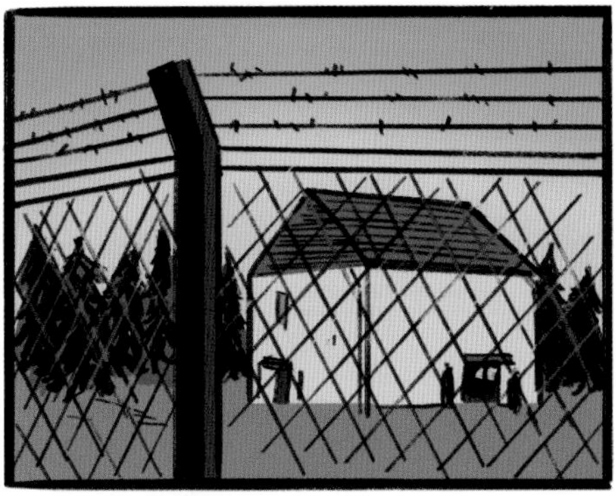

There, the job of building the Soviet bomb was put in the hands of a physicist named Igor Kurchatov.

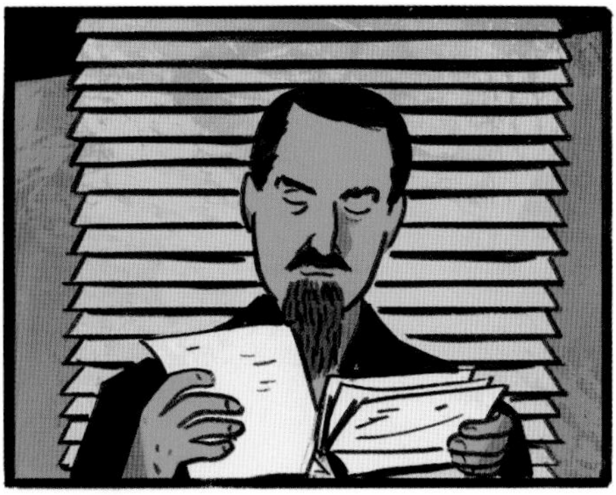

Soviet dictator Joseph Stalin put his head of secret police, Lavrenti Beria, in charge of the project.

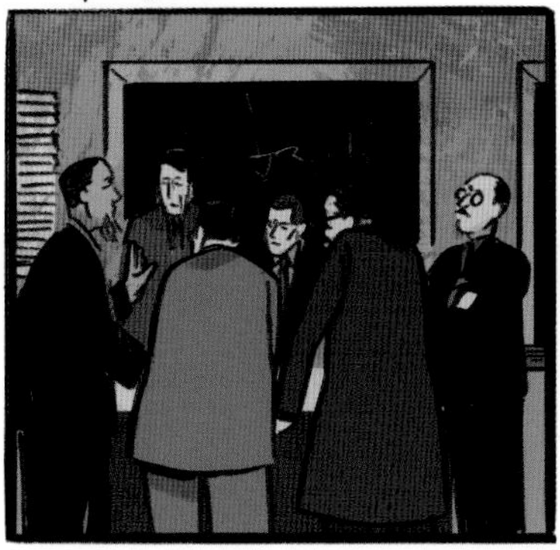

The dreaded Beria was Stalin's Leslie Groves—with additional powers.

One gesture from Beria was enough to make anyone disappear.

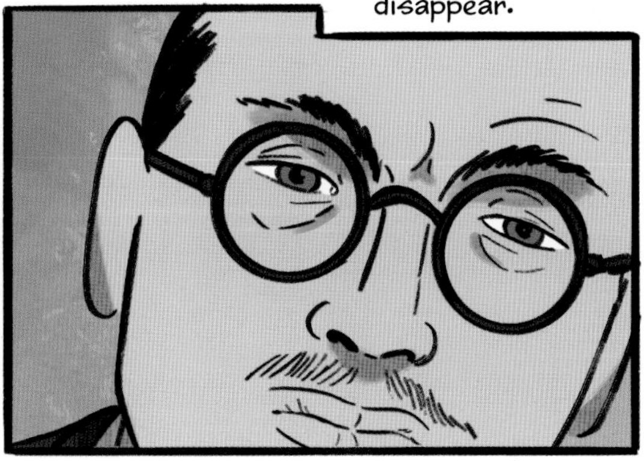

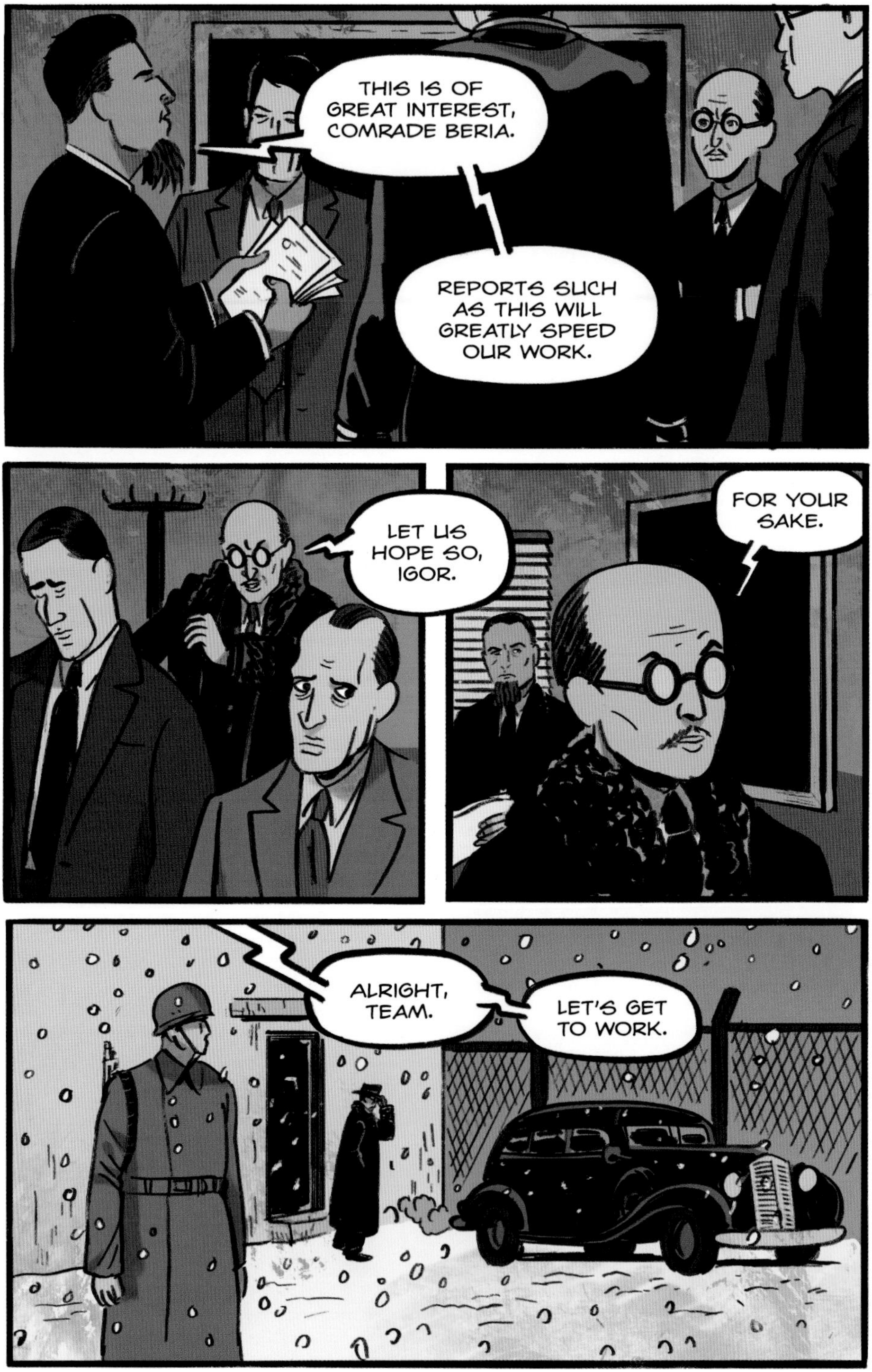
THIS IS OF GREAT INTEREST, COMRADE BERIA.
REPORTS SUCH AS THIS WILL GREATLY SPEED OUR WORK.
LET US HOPE SO, IGOR.
FOR YOUR SAKE.
ALRIGHT, TEAM.
LET'S GET TO WORK.

Chapter 4

Land of Enchantment

implosion bomb design

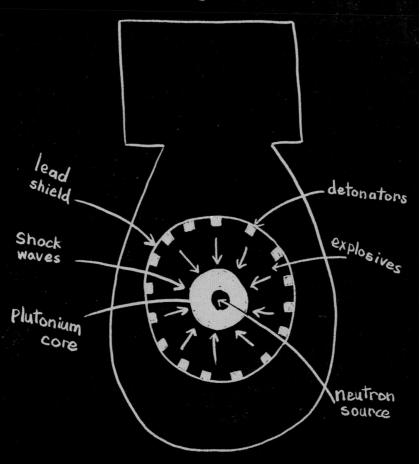

lead shield

Shock waves

Plutonium core

detonators

explosives

neutron source

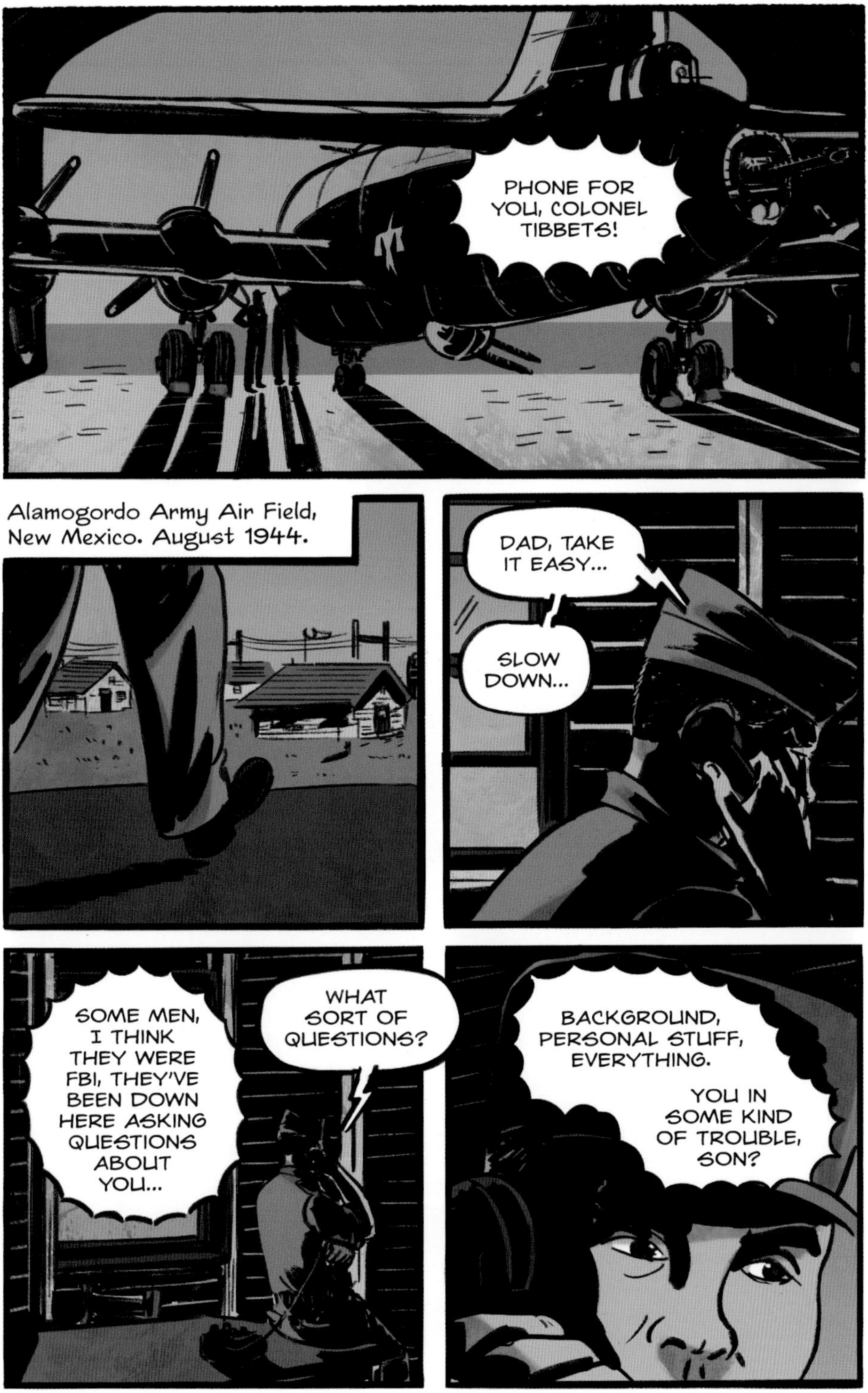
PHONE FOR YOU, COLONEL TIBBETS!
Alamogordo Army Air Field, New Mexico. August 1944.
DAD, TAKE IT EASY...
SLOW DOWN...
SOME MEN, I THINK THEY WERE FBI, THEY'VE BEEN DOWN HERE ASKING QUESTIONS ABOUT YOU...
WHAT SORT OF QUESTIONS?
BACKGROUND, PERSONAL STUFF, EVERYTHING.
YOU IN SOME KIND OF TROUBLE, SON?

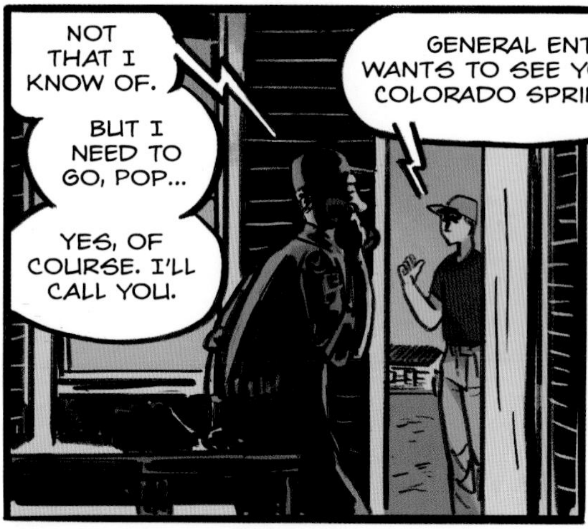
NOT THAT I KNOW OF.
BUT I NEED TO GO, POP...
YES, OF COURSE. I'LL CALL YOU.
GENERAL ENT WANTS TO SEE YOU IN COLORADO SPRINGS.

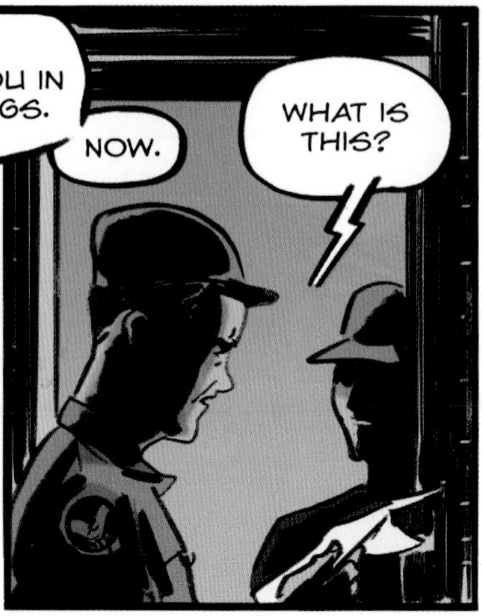
NOW.
WHAT IS THIS?

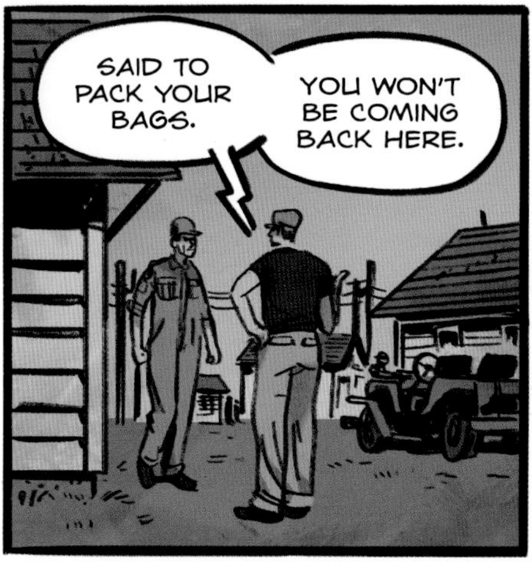
SAID TO PACK YOUR BAGS.
YOU WON'T BE COMING BACK HERE.

At twenty-nine, Paul Tibbets was an experienced pilot who'd flown combat missions over Europe and North Africa.

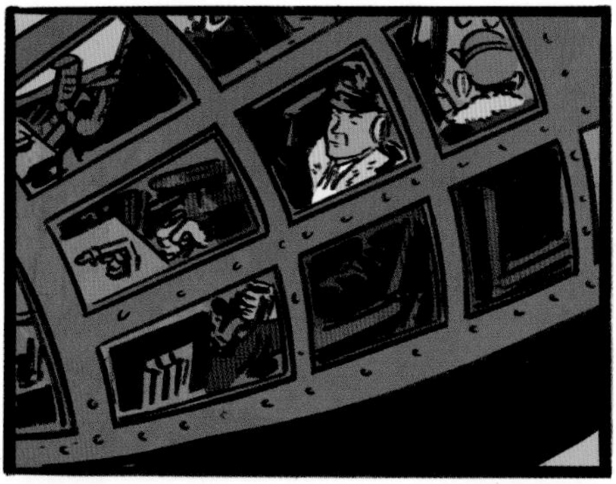

He was cool under fire, a proven leader, and had more flight time in B-29 bombers than any other pilot.

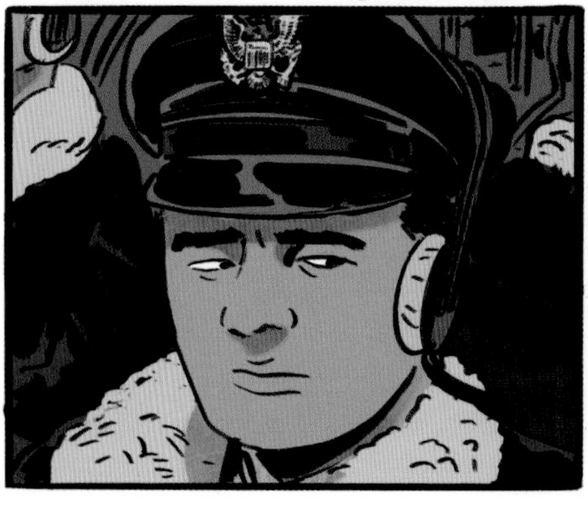

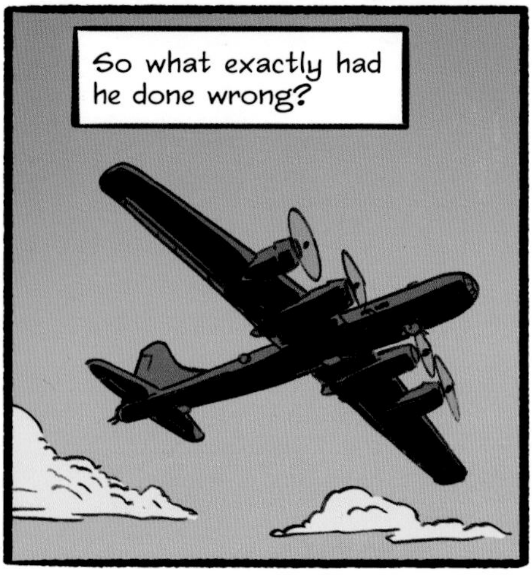
So what exactly had he done wrong?

THE GENERAL'S READY FOR YOU.

THANKS FOR COMING SO QUICKLY.

SHUT THE DOOR, WOULD YOU?

YOU HAVE BEEN CHOSEN FOR A VITAL MISSION, COLONEL TIBBETS.

A TOP SECRET MISSION.

YOU WILL HAVE TO CONCEAL EVERYTHING YOU'RE ABOUT TO HEAR.

EVEN FROM YOUR WIFE, EVEN FROM THE MEN WORKING UNDER YOU.

YOU WILL COMMAND A COMBAT FORCE.

YOUR TASK IS TO DELIVER A NEW TYPE OF EXPLOSIVE, ONE WITH INCREDIBLE DESTRUCTIVE POWER.

YOU'LL NEED TO FIGURE OUT HOW TO DELIVER THESE BOMBS ON-TARGET.

AND HOW TO GET YOUR MEN BACK ALIVE.

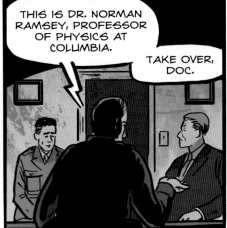

THIS IS DR. NORMAN RAMSEY, PROFESSOR OF PHYSICS AT COLUMBIA.

TAKE OVER, DOC.

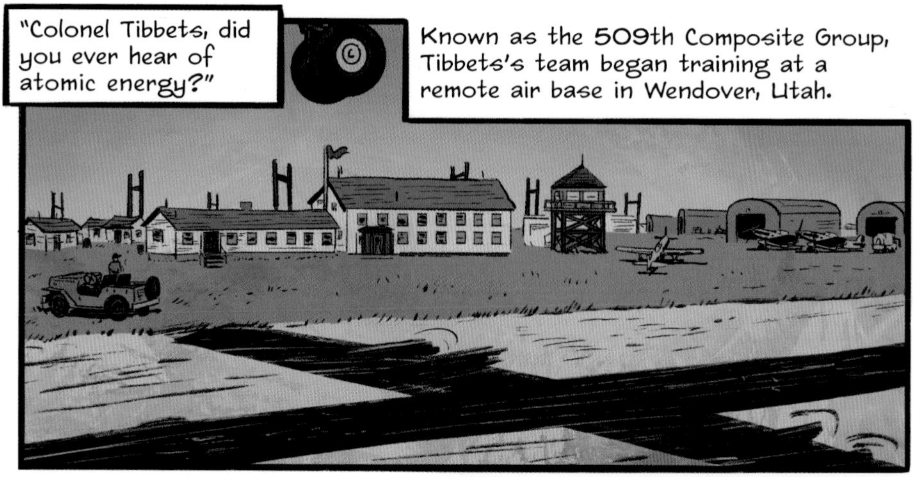
"Colonel Tibbets, did you ever hear of atomic energy?"
Known as the 509th Composite Group, Tibbets's team began training at a remote air base in Wendover, Utah.

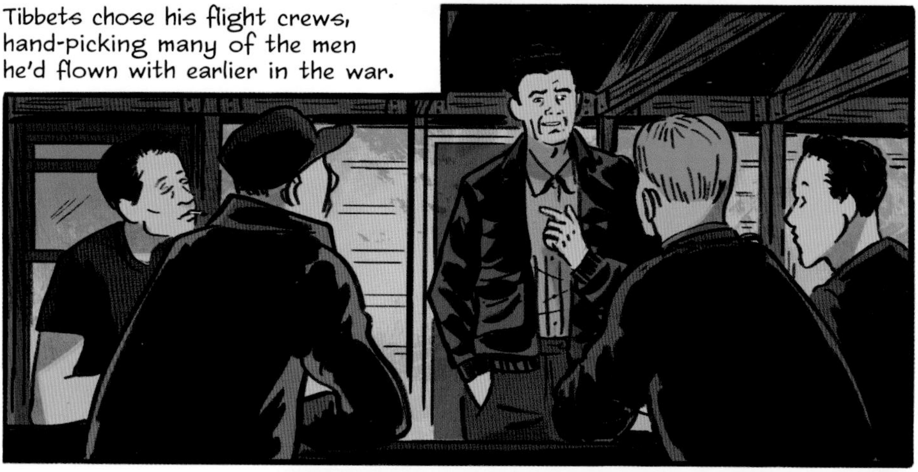
Tibbets chose his flight crews, hand-picking many of the men he'd flown with earlier in the war.

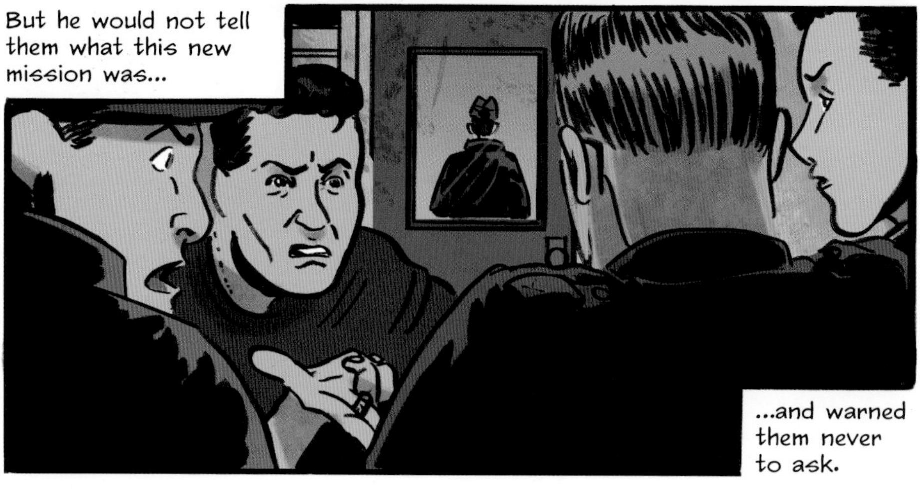
But he would not tell them what this new mission was...
...and warned them never to ask.

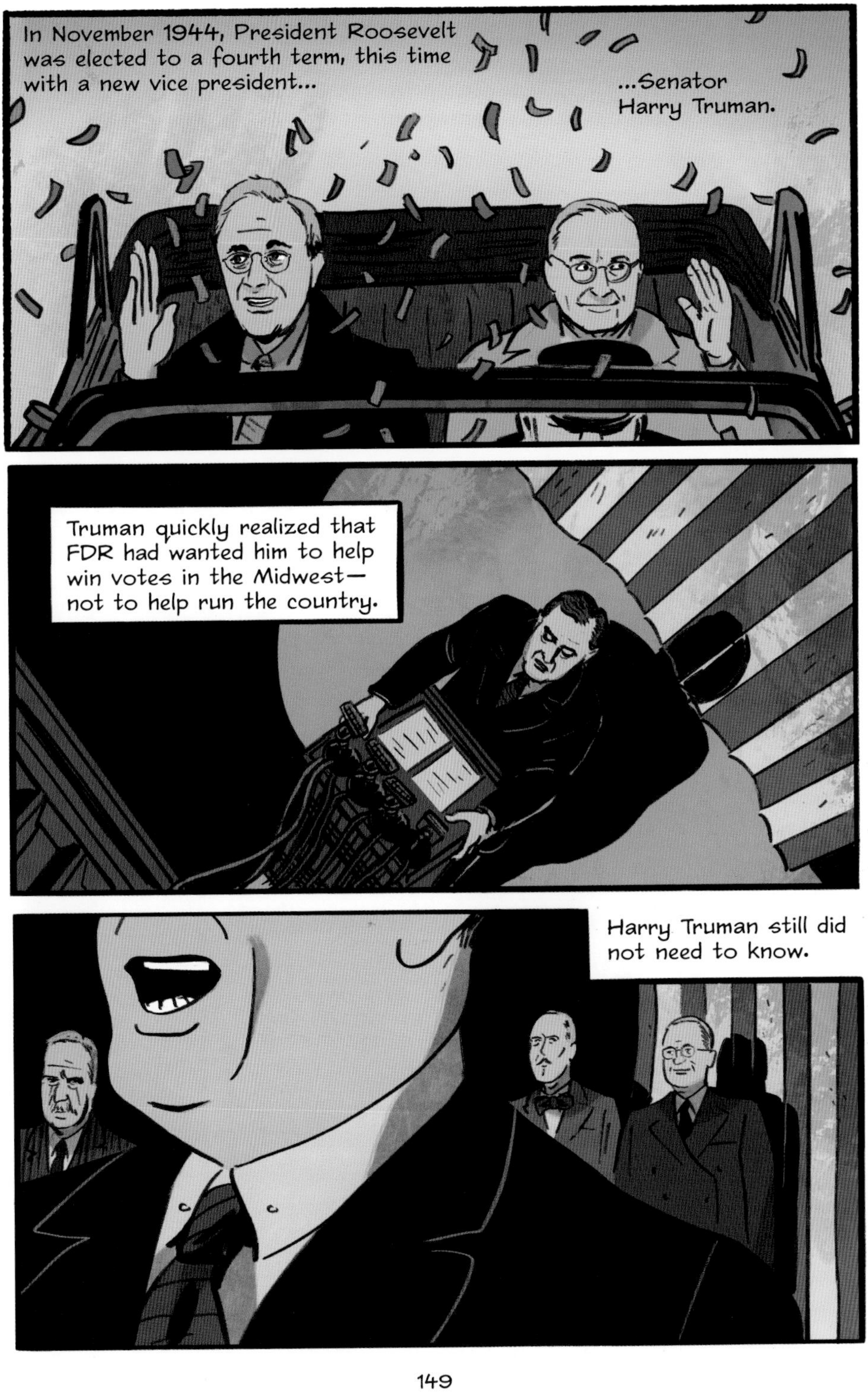

In November 1944, President Roosevelt was elected to a fourth term, this time with a new vice president...
...Senator Harry Truman.
Truman quickly realized that FDR had wanted him to help win votes in the Midwest—not to help run the country.
Harry Truman still did not need to know.

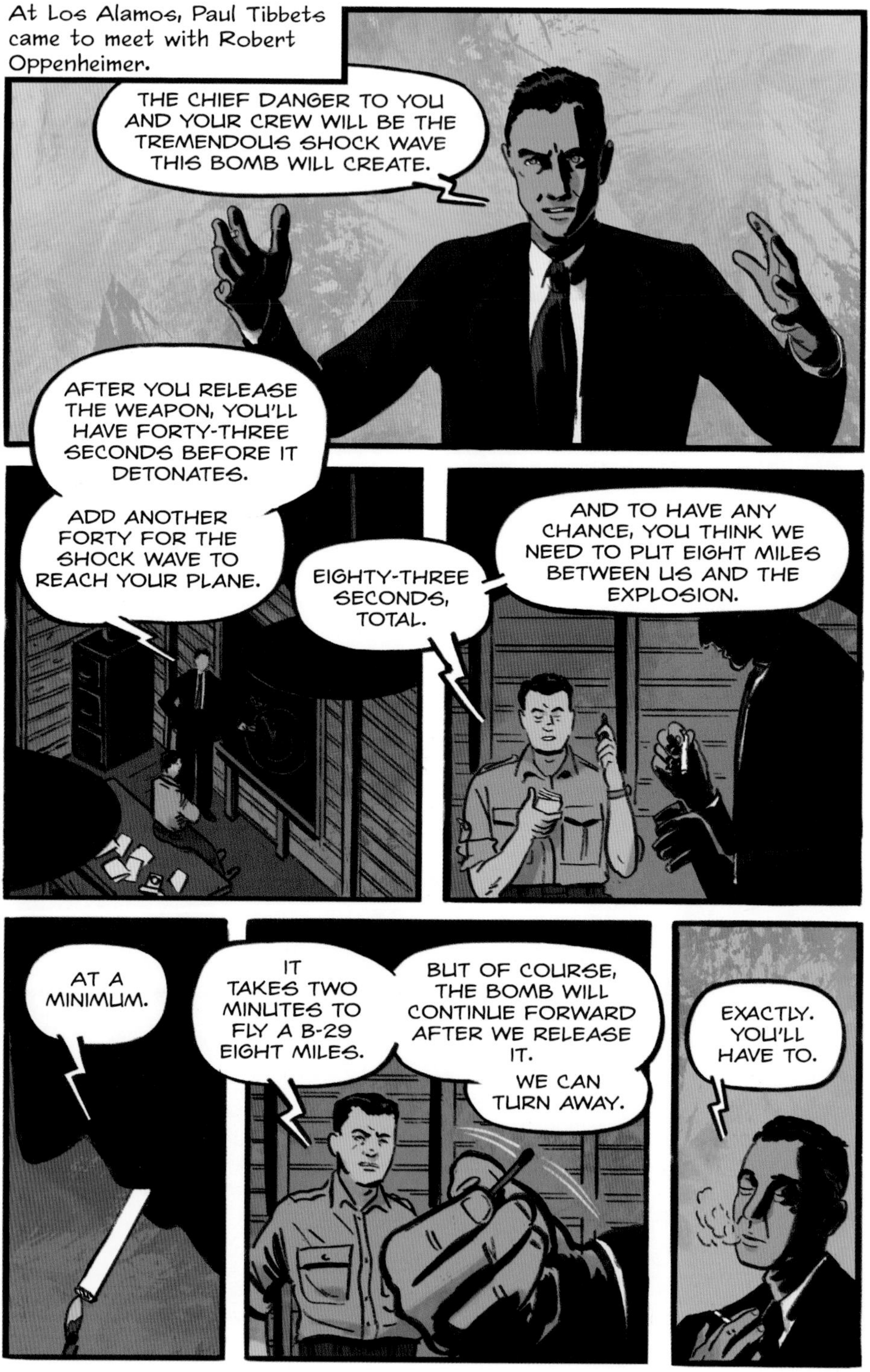
At Los Alamos, Paul Tibbets came to meet with Robert Oppenheimer.
THE CHIEF DANGER TO YOU AND YOUR CREW WILL BE THE TREMENDOUS SHOCK WAVE THIS BOMB WILL CREATE.
AFTER YOU RELEASE THE WEAPON, YOU'LL HAVE FORTY-THREE SECONDS BEFORE IT DETONATES.
ADD ANOTHER FORTY FOR THE SHOCK WAVE TO REACH YOUR PLANE.
EIGHTY-THREE SECONDS, TOTAL.
AND TO HAVE ANY CHANCE, YOU THINK WE NEED TO PUT EIGHT MILES BETWEEN US AND THE EXPLOSION.
AT A MINIMUM.
IT TAKES TWO MINUTES TO FLY A B-29 EIGHT MILES.
BUT OF COURSE, THE BOMB WILL CONTINUE FORWARD AFTER WE RELEASE IT.
WE CAN TURN AWAY.
EXACTLY. YOU'LL HAVE TO.

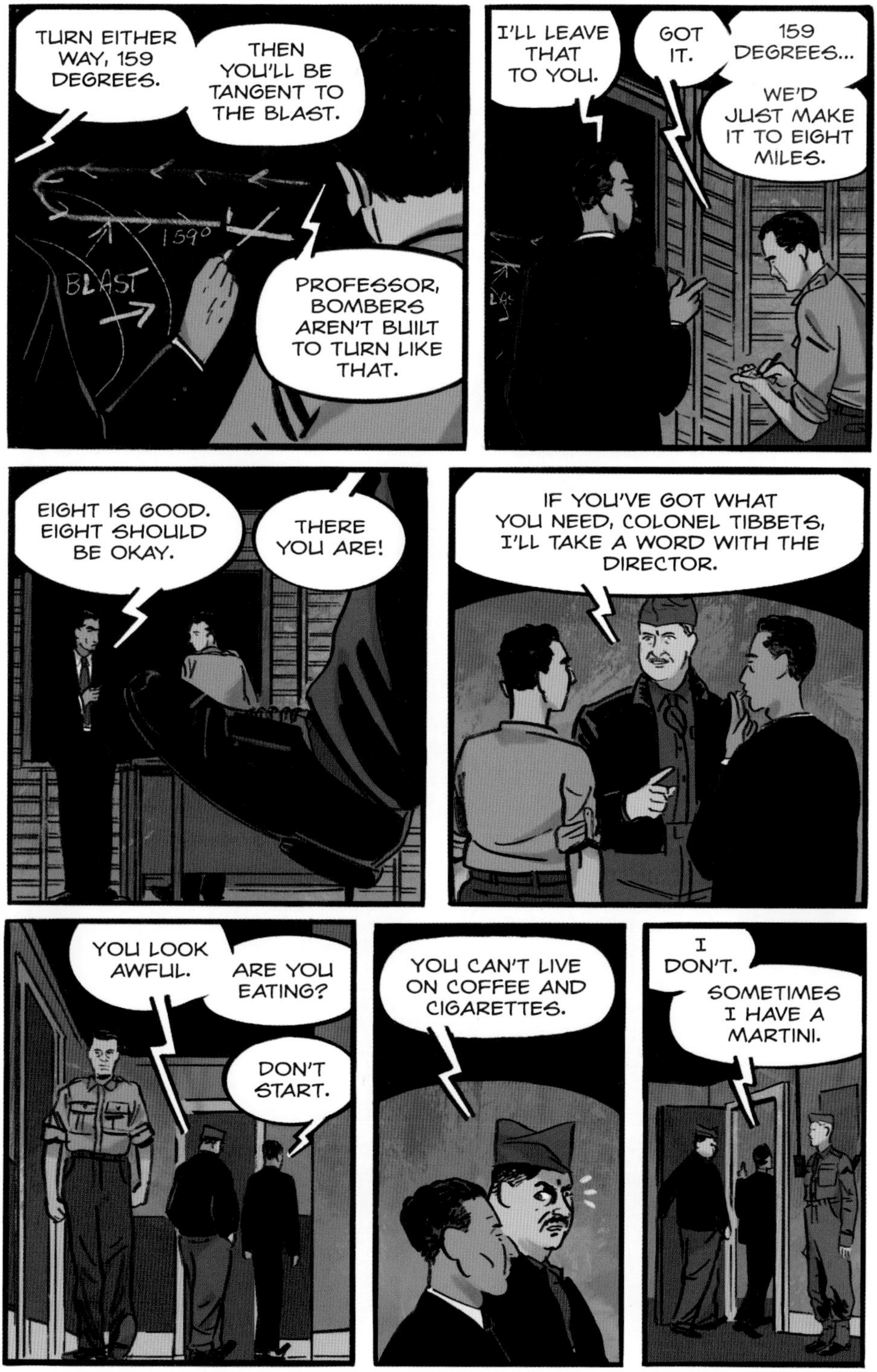
TURN EITHER WAY, 159 DEGREES.
THEN YOU'LL BE TANGENT TO THE BLAST.
159°
BLAST
PROFESSOR, BOMBERS AREN'T BUILT TO TURN LIKE THAT.
I'LL LEAVE THAT TO YOU.
GOT IT.
159 DEGREES...
WE'D JUST MAKE IT TO EIGHT MILES.
EIGHT IS GOOD. EIGHT SHOULD BE OKAY.
THERE YOU ARE!
IF YOU'VE GOT WHAT YOU NEED, COLONEL TIBBETS, I'LL TAKE A WORD WITH THE DIRECTOR.
YOU LOOK AWFUL.
ARE YOU EATING?
DON'T START.
YOU CAN'T LIVE ON COFFEE AND CIGARETTES.
I DON'T.
SOMETIMES I HAVE A MARTINI.

WANT TO SEE WHAT WE'VE GOT ON THE PLUTONIUM GADGET?

I'M NOT HERE FOR THE SCENERY.

OUR BEST BET IS TO BLAST THE PIECES OF PLUTONIUM TOGETHER WITH EXPLOSIVES— IMPLOSION.

BASICALLY, WE TAKE SEVERAL PIECES OF PLUTONIUM, ALL TOGETHER ABOUT THE SIZE OF A GRAPEFRUIT.

ARRANGE EXPLOSIVE LENSES AROUND THE PLUTONIUM.

THE EXPLOSIVES COMPRESS THE PLUTONIUM AT TREMENDOUS SPEED, ASSEMBLING A CRITICAL MASS, SETTING OFF A CHAIN REACTION AND AN ATOMIC EXPLOSION.

NICE THEORY.

WILL IT WORK?

THAT'S WHAT WE'RE TRYING TO FIND OUT.

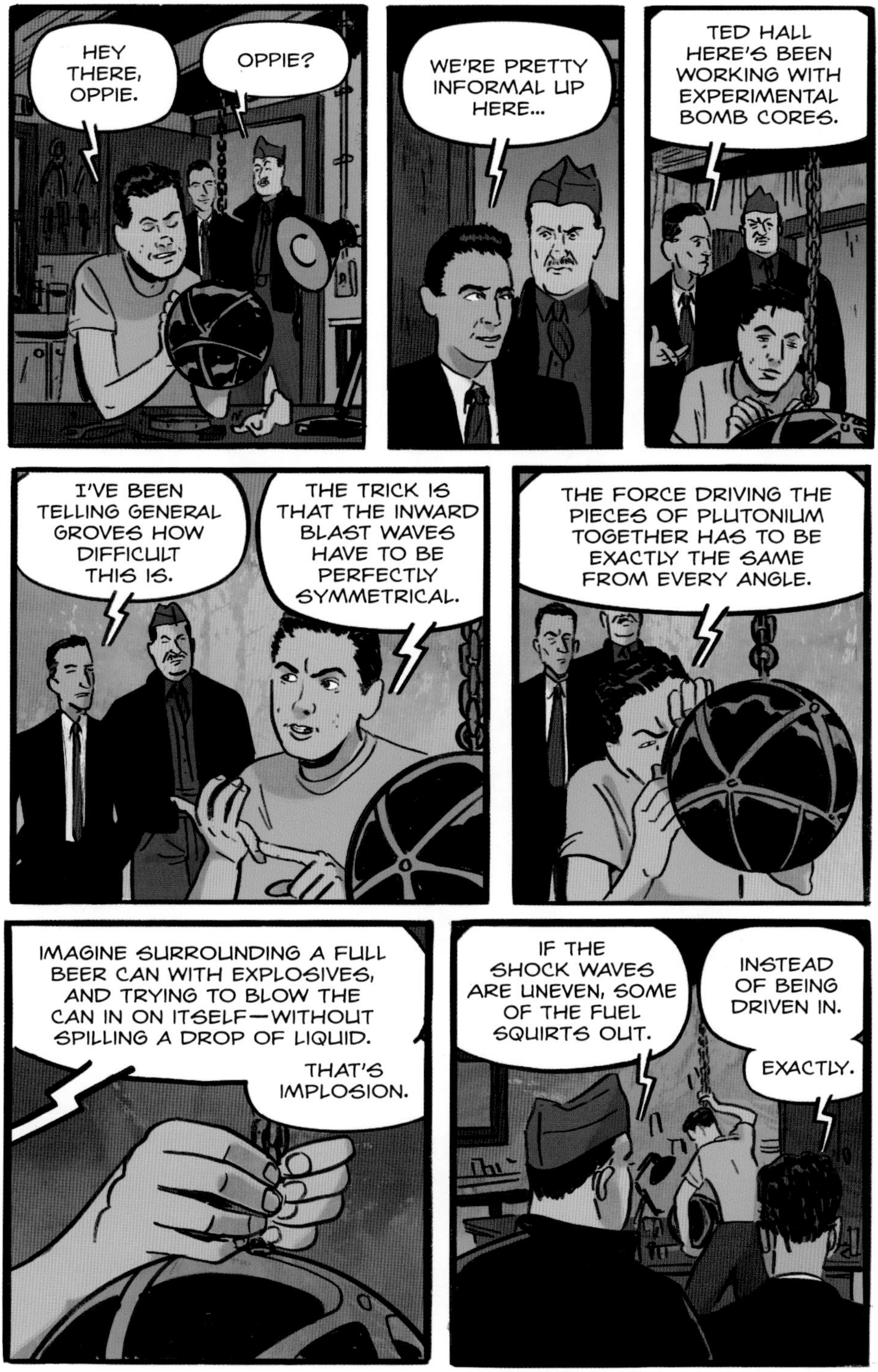
HEY THERE, OPPIE.
OPPIE?
WE'RE PRETTY INFORMAL UP HERE...
TED HALL HERE'S BEEN WORKING WITH EXPERIMENTAL BOMB CORES.
I'VE BEEN TELLING GENERAL GROVES HOW DIFFICULT THIS IS.
THE TRICK IS THAT THE INWARD BLAST WAVES HAVE TO BE PERFECTLY SYMMETRICAL.
THE FORCE DRIVING THE PIECES OF PLUTONIUM TOGETHER HAS TO BE EXACTLY THE SAME FROM EVERY ANGLE.
IMAGINE SURROUNDING A FULL BEER CAN WITH EXPLOSIVES, AND TRYING TO BLOW THE CAN IN ON ITSELF—WITHOUT SPILLING A DROP OF LIQUID.
THAT'S IMPLOSION.
IF THE SHOCK WAVES ARE UNEVEN, SOME OF THE FUEL SQUIRTS OUT.
INSTEAD OF BEING DRIVEN IN.
EXACTLY.

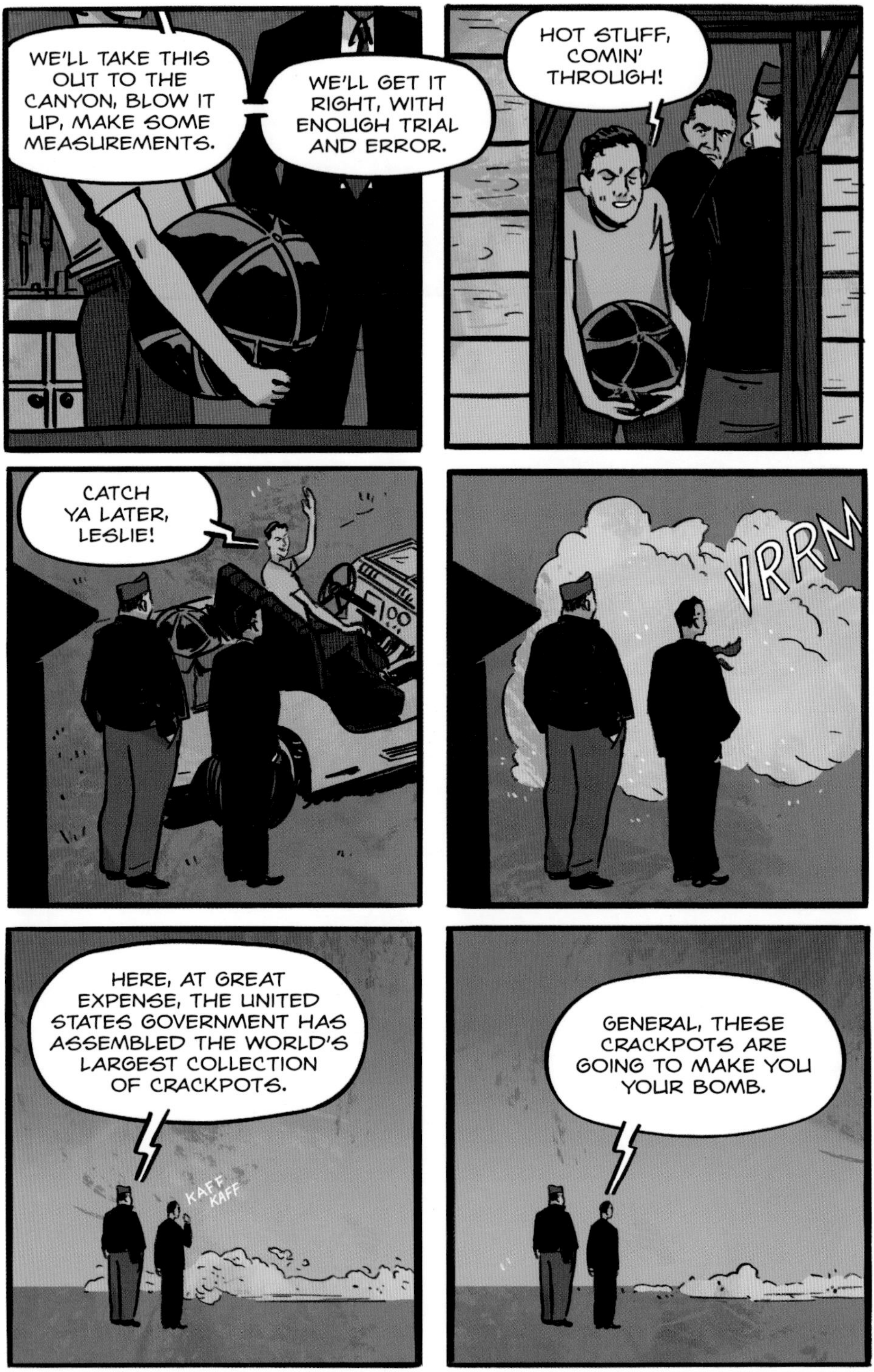
WE'LL TAKE THIS OUT TO THE CANYON, BLOW IT UP, MAKE SOME MEASUREMENTS.
WE'LL GET IT RIGHT, WITH ENOUGH TRIAL AND ERROR.
HOT STUFF, COMIN' THROUGH!
CATCH YA LATER, LESLIE!
VRRM
HERE, AT GREAT EXPENSE, THE UNITED STATES GOVERNMENT HAS ASSEMBLED THE WORLD'S LARGEST COLLECTION OF CRACKPOTS.
KAFF KAFF
GENERAL, THESE CRACKPOTS ARE GOING TO MAKE YOU YOUR BOMB.

Philadelphia, 1950.

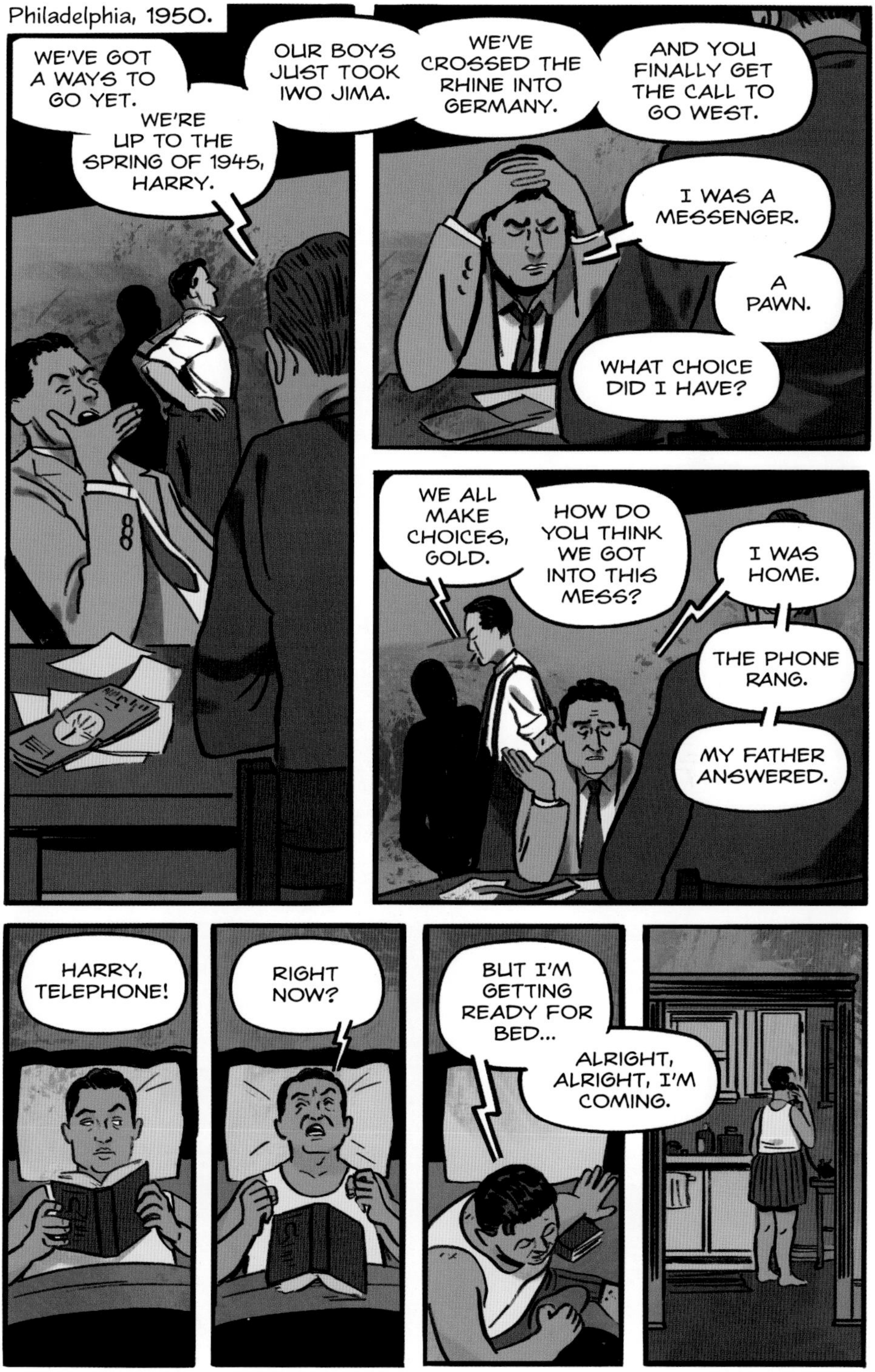
WE'VE GOT A WAYS TO GO YET.
WE'RE UP TO THE SPRING OF 1945, HARRY.
OUR BOYS JUST TOOK IWO JIMA.
WE'VE CROSSED THE RHINE INTO GERMANY.
AND YOU FINALLY GET THE CALL TO GO WEST.
I WAS A MESSENGER.
A PAWN.
WHAT CHOICE DID I HAVE?
WE ALL MAKE CHOICES, GOLD.
HOW DO YOU THINK WE GOT INTO THIS MESS?
I WAS HOME.
THE PHONE RANG.
MY FATHER ANSWERED.
HARRY, TELEPHONE!
RIGHT NOW?
BUT I'M GETTING READY FOR BED...
ALRIGHT, ALRIGHT, I'M COMING.

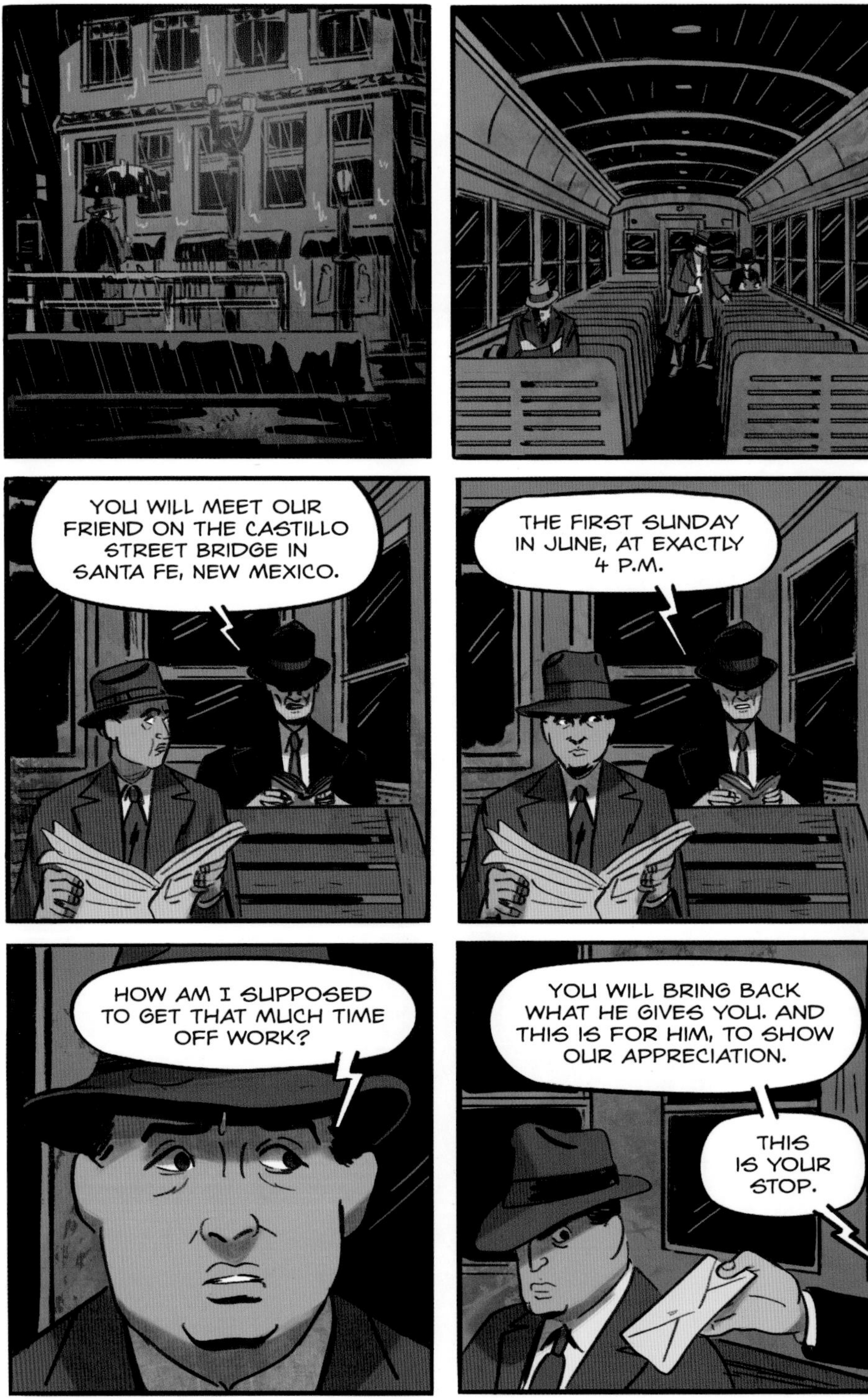
YOU WILL MEET OUR FRIEND ON THE CASTILLO STREET BRIDGE IN SANTA FE, NEW MEXICO.
THE FIRST SUNDAY IN JUNE, AT EXACTLY 4 P.M.
HOW AM I SUPPOSED TO GET THAT MUCH TIME OFF WORK?
YOU WILL BRING BACK WHAT HE GIVES YOU. AND THIS IS FOR HIM, TO SHOW OUR APPRECIATION.
THIS IS YOUR STOP.

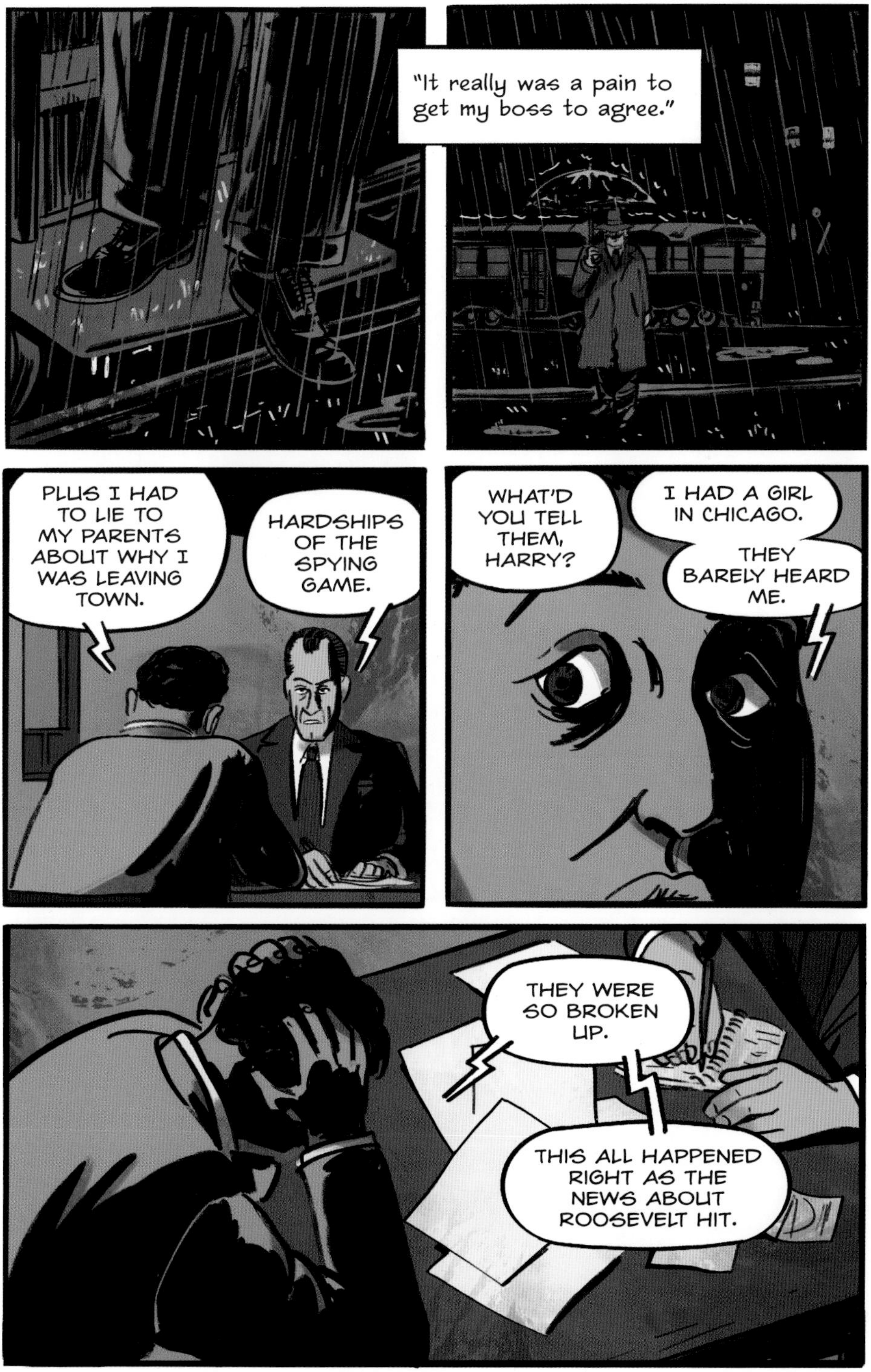
"It really was a pain to get my boss to agree."
PLUS I HAD TO LIE TO MY PARENTS ABOUT WHY I WAS LEAVING TOWN.
HARDSHIPS OF THE SPYING GAME.
WHAT'D YOU TELL THEM, HARRY?
I HAD A GIRL IN CHICAGO.
THEY BARELY HEARD ME.
THEY WERE SO BROKEN UP.
THIS ALL HAPPENED RIGHT AS THE NEWS ABOUT ROOSEVELT HIT.

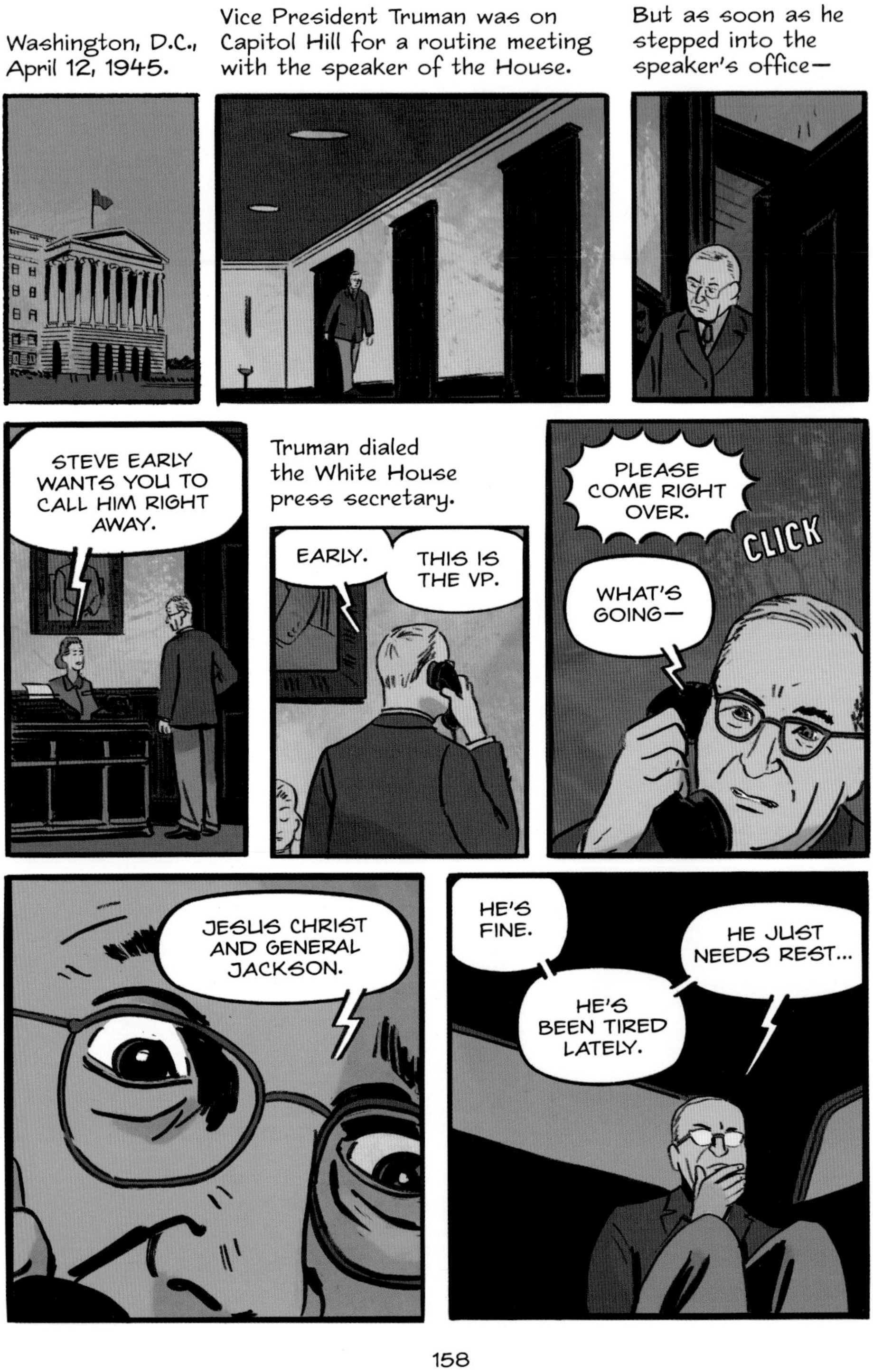
Washington, D.C., April 12, 1945.
Vice President Truman was on Capitol Hill for a routine meeting with the speaker of the House.
But as soon as he stepped into the speaker's office—
STEVE EARLY WANTS YOU TO CALL HIM RIGHT AWAY.
Truman dialed the White House press secretary.
EARLY.
THIS IS THE VP.
PLEASE COME RIGHT OVER.
CLICK
WHAT'S GOING—
JESUS CHRIST AND GENERAL JACKSON.
HE'S FINE.
HE'S BEEN TIRED LATELY.
HE JUST NEEDS REST...

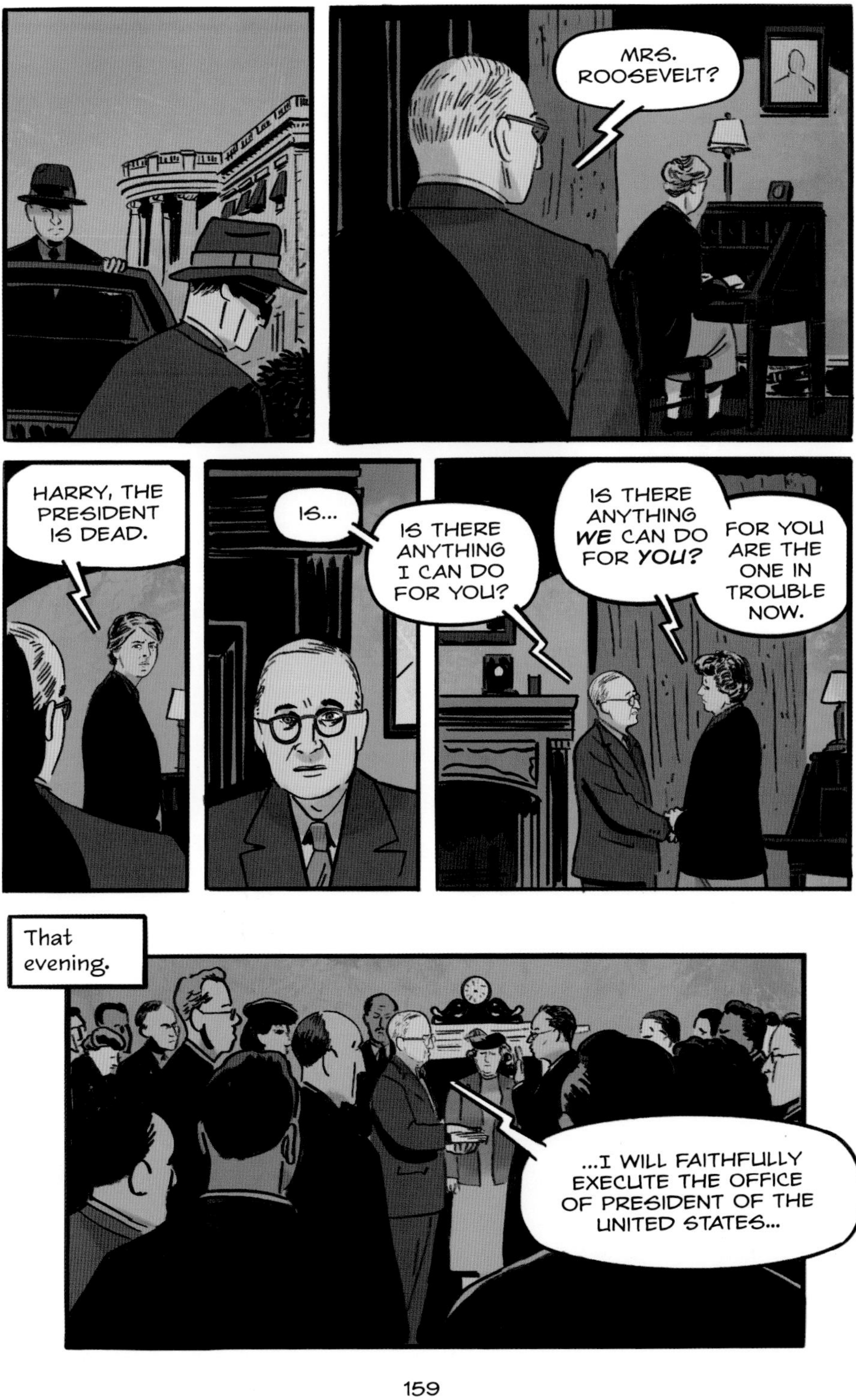
MRS. ROOSEVELT?
HARRY, THE PRESIDENT IS DEAD.
IS...
IS THERE ANYTHING I CAN DO FOR YOU?
IS THERE ANYTHING WE CAN DO FOR YOU?
FOR YOU ARE THE ONE IN TROUBLE NOW.
That evening.
...I WILL FAITHFULLY EXECUTE THE OFFICE OF PRESIDENT OF THE UNITED STATES...

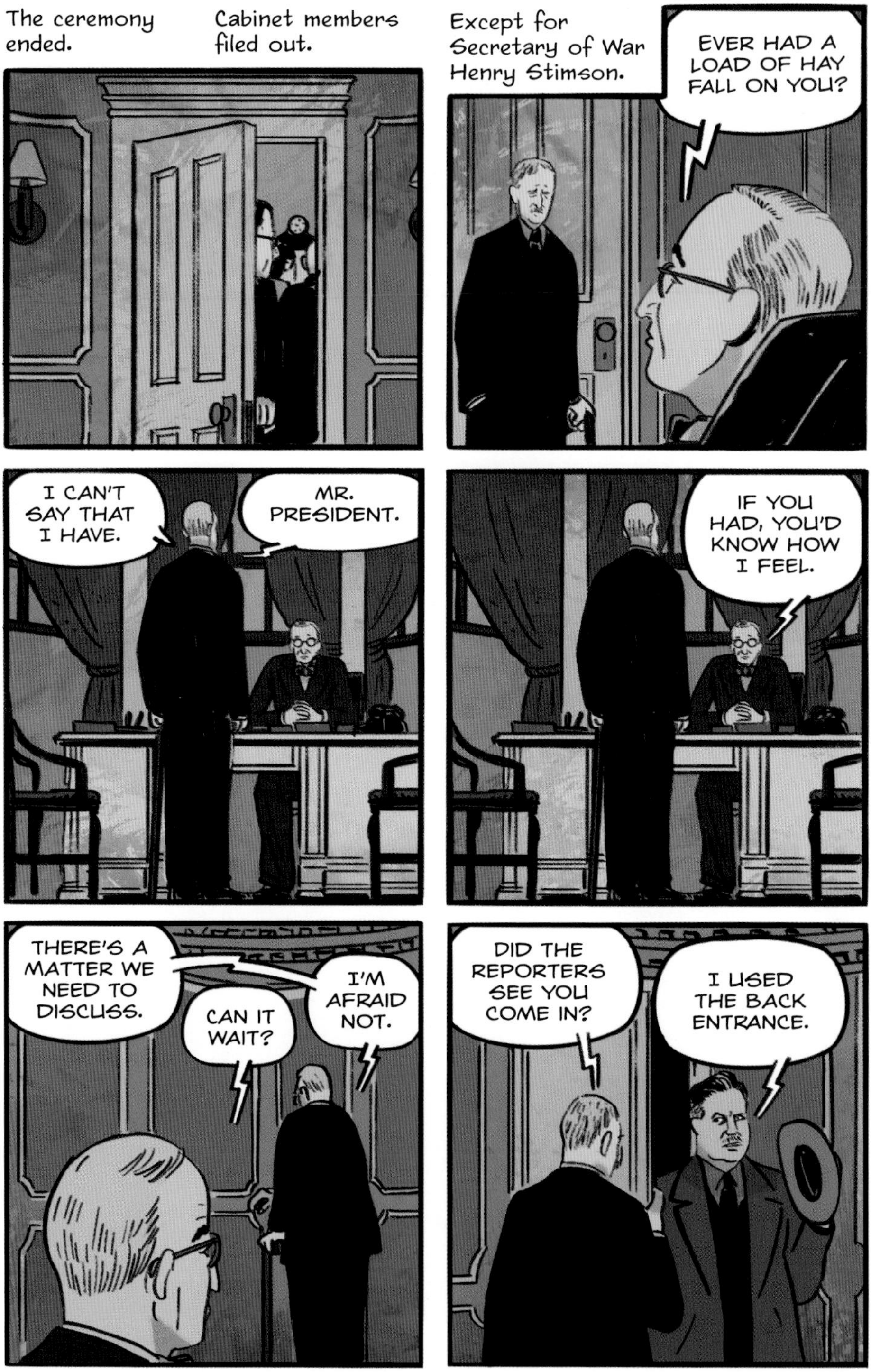
The ceremony ended.
Cabinet members filed out.
Except for Secretary of War Henry Stimson.
EVER HAD A LOAD OF HAY FALL ON YOU?
MR. PRESIDENT.
I CAN'T SAY THAT I HAVE.
IF YOU HAD, YOU'D KNOW HOW I FEEL.
THERE'S A MATTER WE NEED TO DISCUSS.
CAN IT WAIT?
I'M AFRAID NOT.
DID THE REPORTERS SEE YOU COME IN?
I USED THE BACK ENTRANCE.

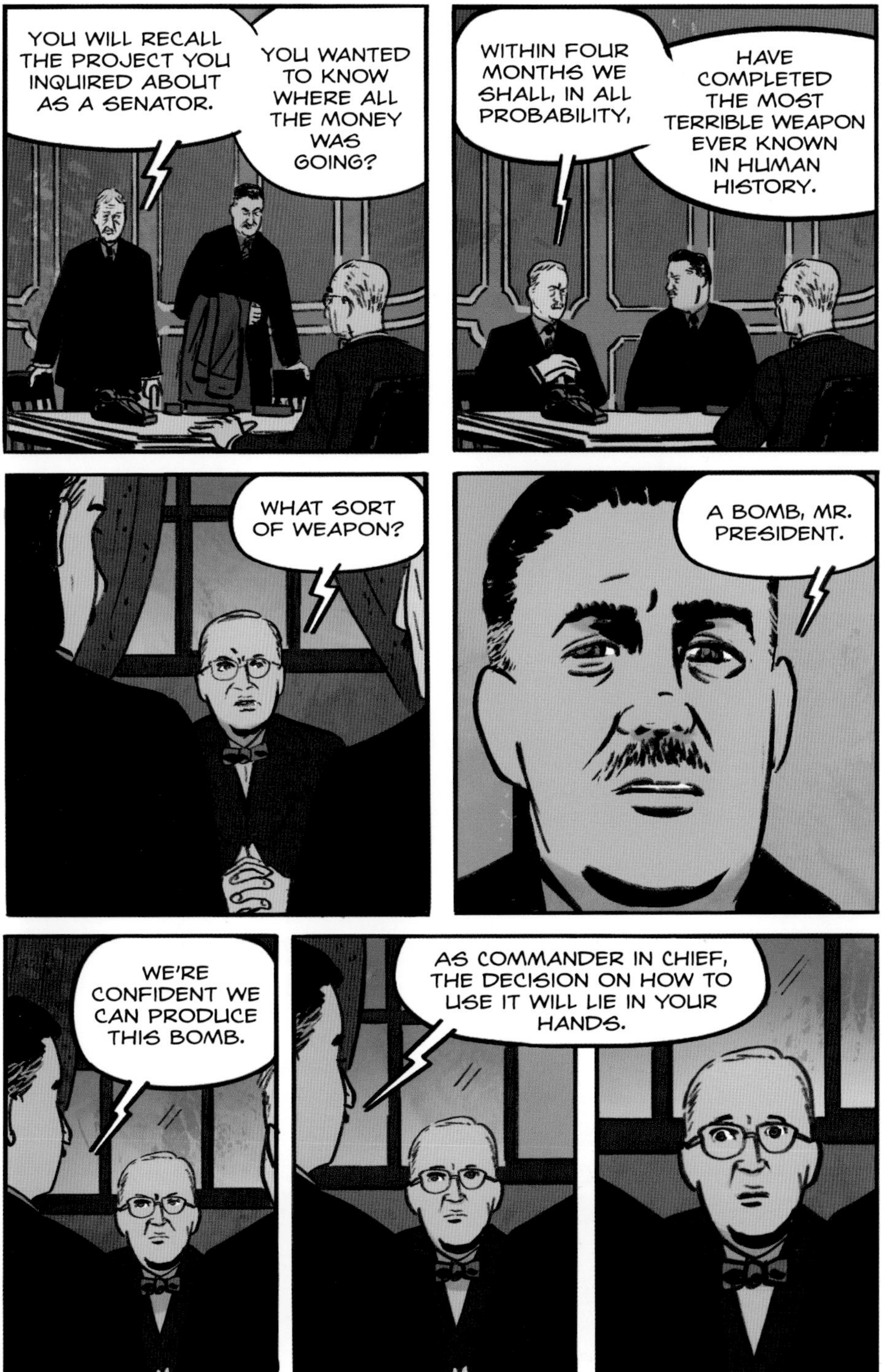
YOU WILL RECALL THE PROJECT YOU INQUIRED ABOUT AS A SENATOR.
YOU WANTED TO KNOW WHERE ALL THE MONEY WAS GOING?
WITHIN FOUR MONTHS WE SHALL, IN ALL PROBABILITY,
HAVE COMPLETED THE MOST TERRIBLE WEAPON EVER KNOWN IN HUMAN HISTORY.
WHAT SORT OF WEAPON?
A BOMB, MR. PRESIDENT.
WE'RE CONFIDENT WE CAN PRODUCE THIS BOMB.
AS COMMANDER IN CHIEF, THE DECISION ON HOW TO USE IT WILL LIE IN YOUR HANDS.

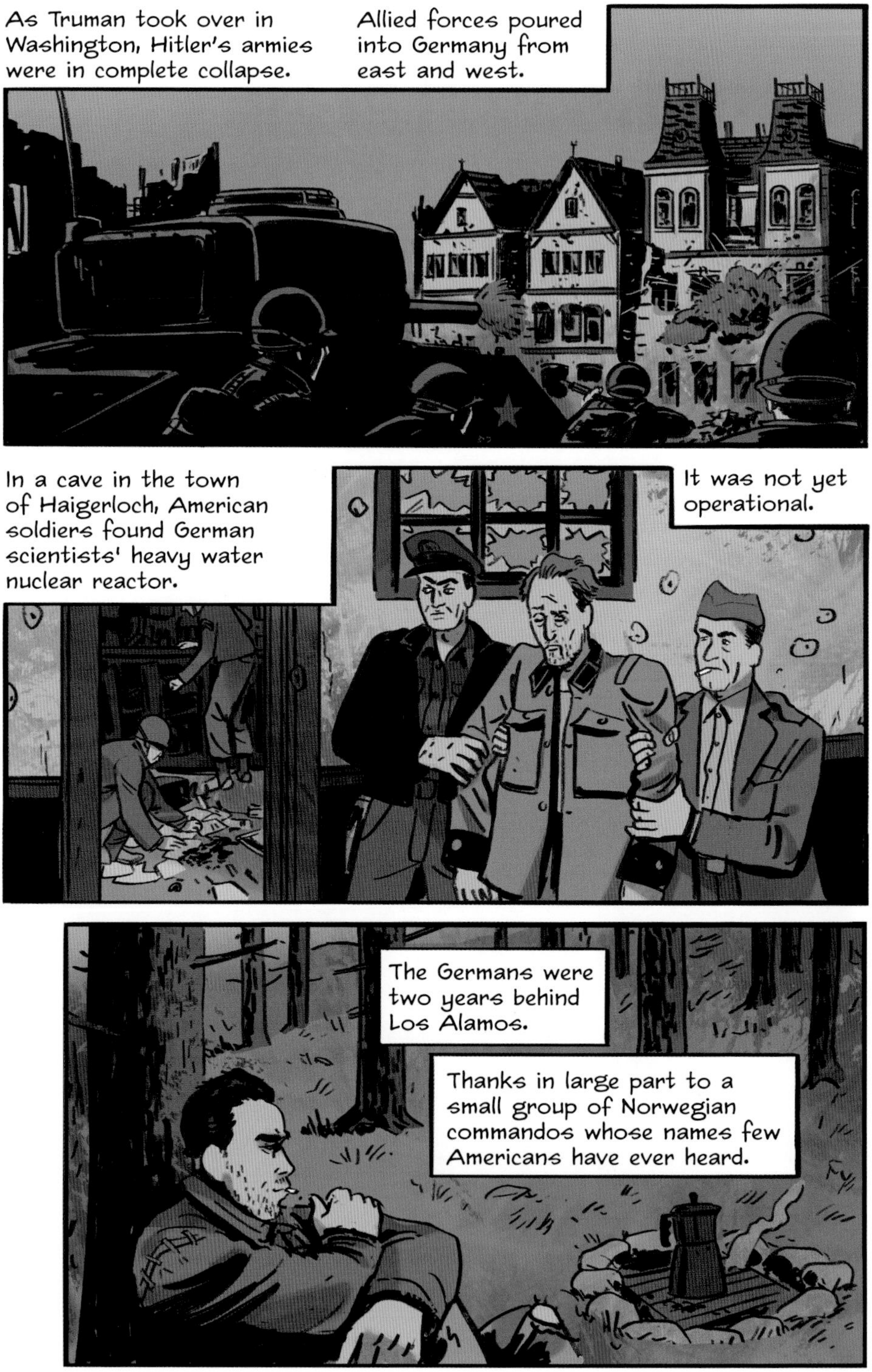
As Truman took over in Washington, Hitler's armies were in complete collapse.
Allied forces poured into Germany from east and west.
In a cave in the town of Haigerloch, American soldiers found German scientists' heavy water nuclear reactor.
It was not yet operational.
The Germans were two years behind Los Alamos.
Thanks in large part to a small group of Norwegian commandos whose names few Americans have ever heard.

Adolf Hitler killed himself.

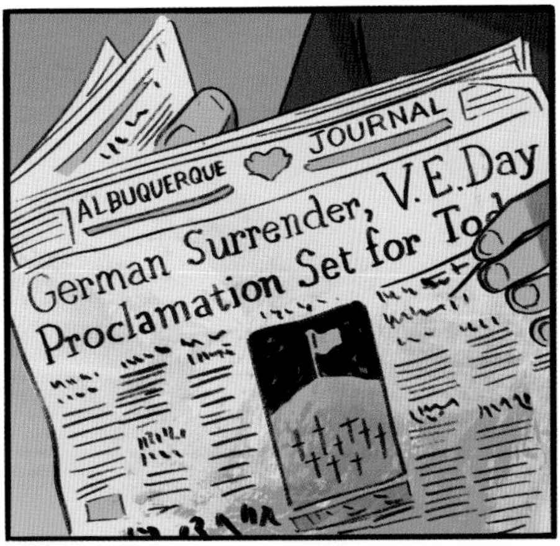
ALBUQUERQUE JOURNAL
German Surrender, V.E. Day
Proclamation Set for To

The news set off a celebration at Los Alamos.

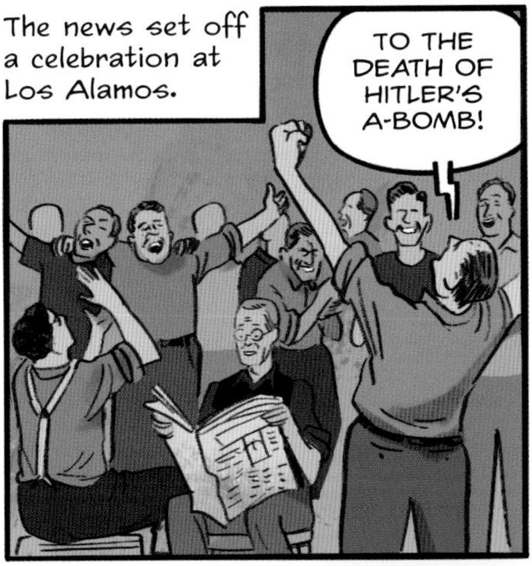
TO THE DEATH OF HITLER'S A-BOMB!

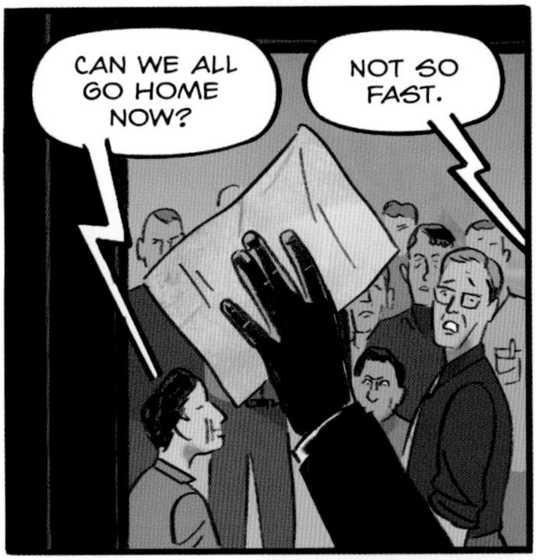
CAN WE ALL GO HOME NOW?
NOT SO FAST.

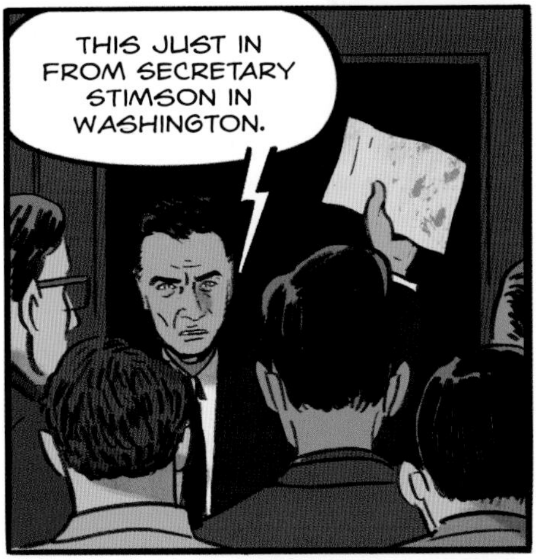
THIS JUST IN FROM SECRETARY STIMSON IN WASHINGTON.

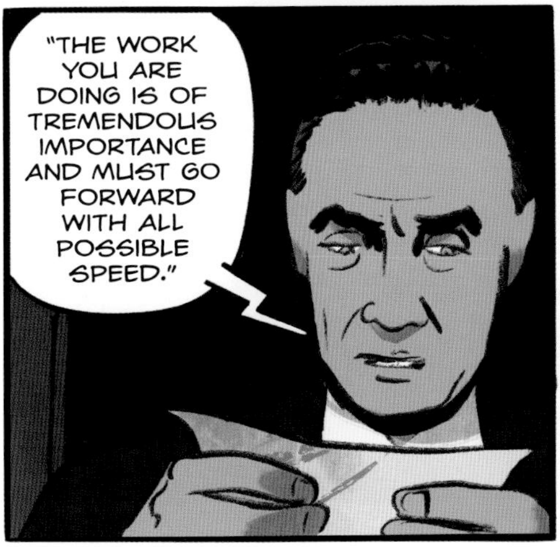
"THE WORK YOU ARE DOING IS OF TREMENDOUS IMPORTANCE AND MUST GO FORWARD WITH ALL POSSIBLE SPEED."

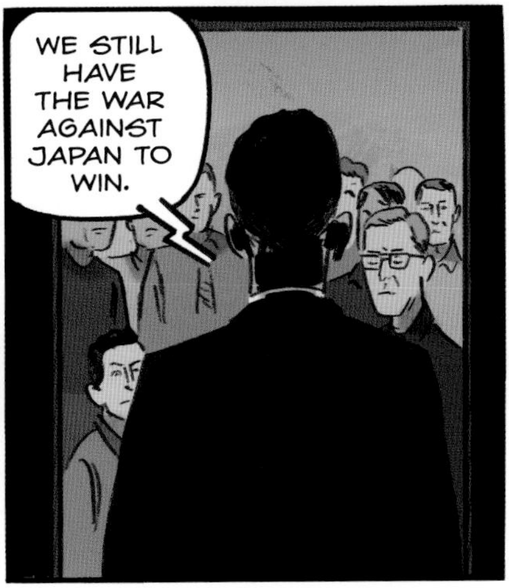
WE STILL HAVE THE WAR AGAINST JAPAN TO WIN.

As ordered, Harry Gold made it to Santa Fe, New Mexico, in June.

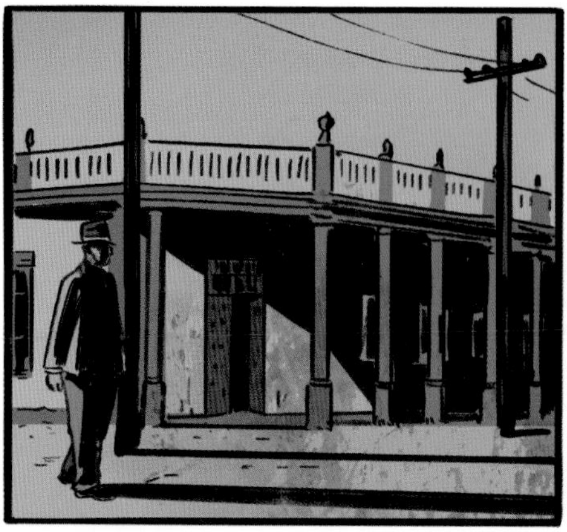

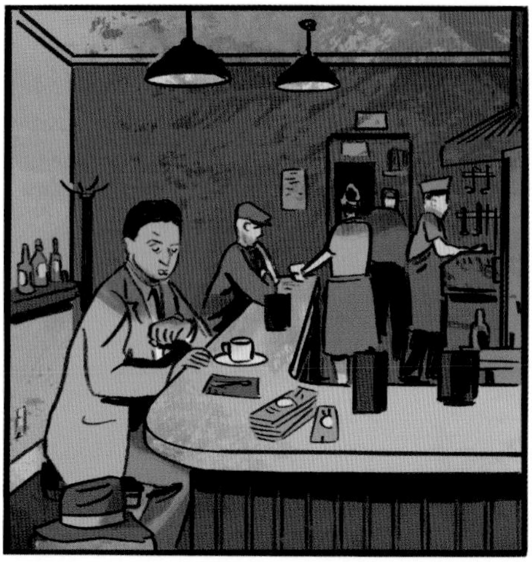

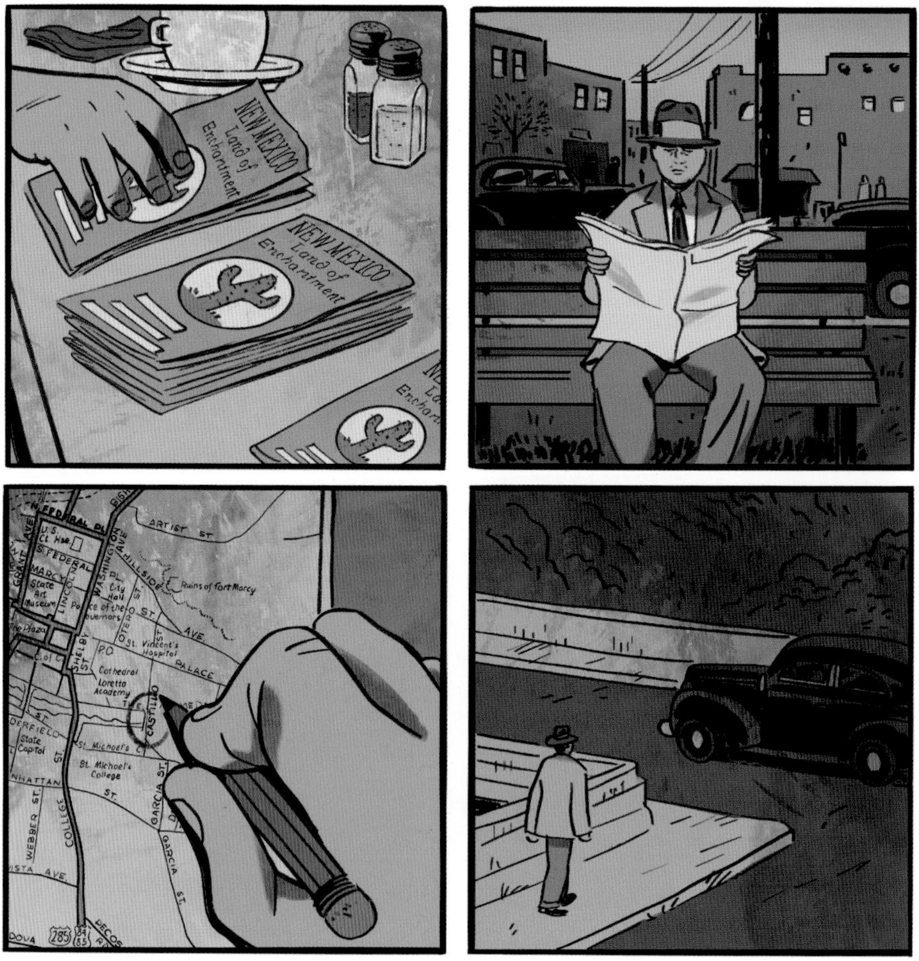
NEW MEXICO
Land of Enchantment
NEW MEXICO
Land of Enchantment
ARTIST ST.
U.S. Ct. Hse.
FEDERAL PL.
MARCY
State Art Museum
LINCOLN
WASHINGTON AVE.
HILLSIDE
Ruins of Fort Marcy
City Hall
The Plaza
SHELBY ST.
P.O.
St. Vincent's Hospital
PALACE
Cathedral
Loretto Academy
CASTILLO
State Capitol
St. Michael's College
GARCIA ST.
WEBBER ST.
COLLEGE
285

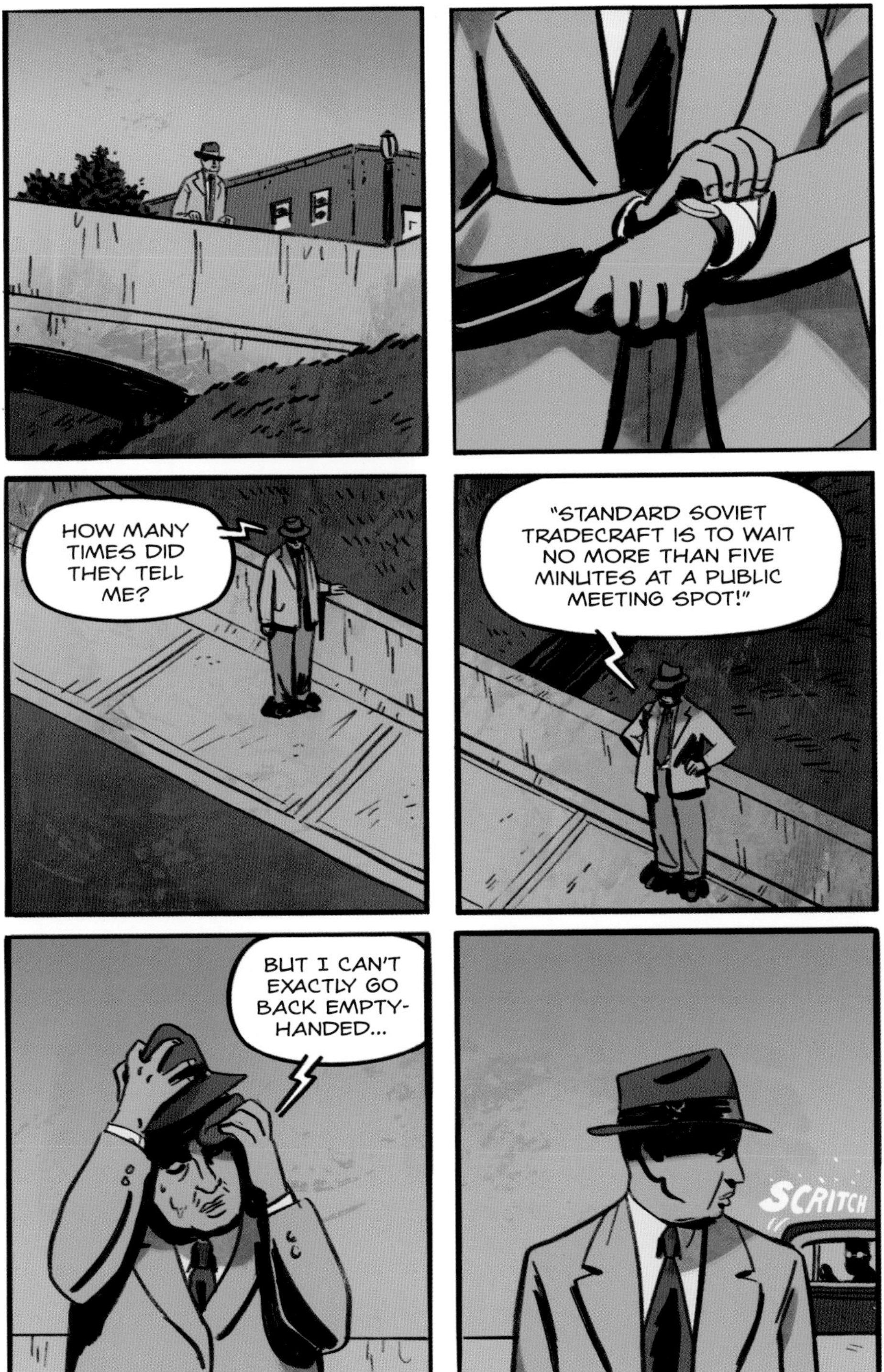
HOW MANY TIMES DID THEY TELL ME?
"STANDARD SOVIET TRADECRAFT IS TO WAIT NO MORE THAN FIVE MINUTES AT A PUBLIC MEETING SPOT!"
BUT I CAN'T EXACTLY GO BACK EMPTY-HANDED...
SCRITCH

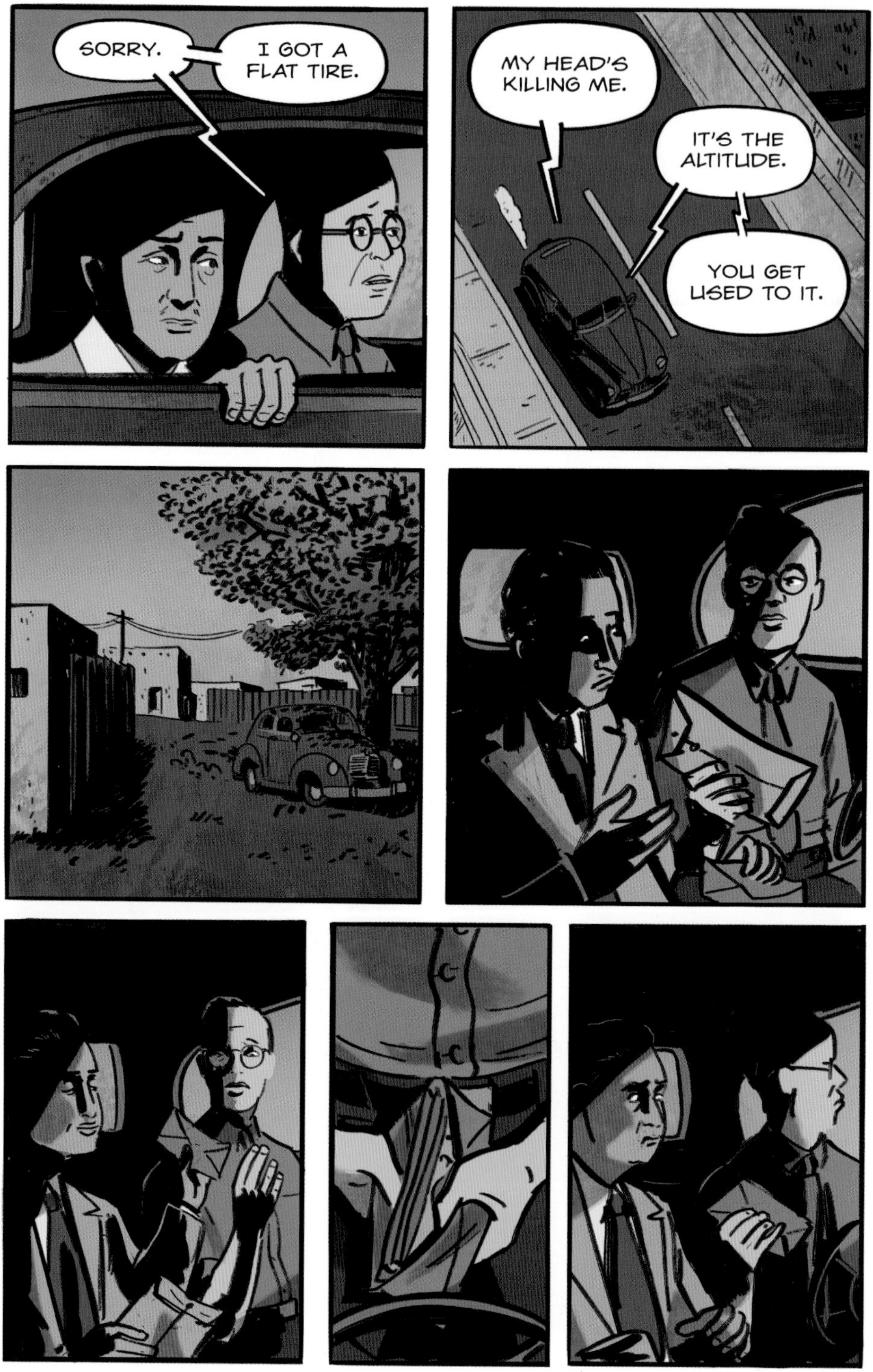
SORRY.
I GOT A FLAT TIRE.
MY HEAD'S KILLING ME.
IT'S THE ALTITUDE.
YOU GET USED TO IT.

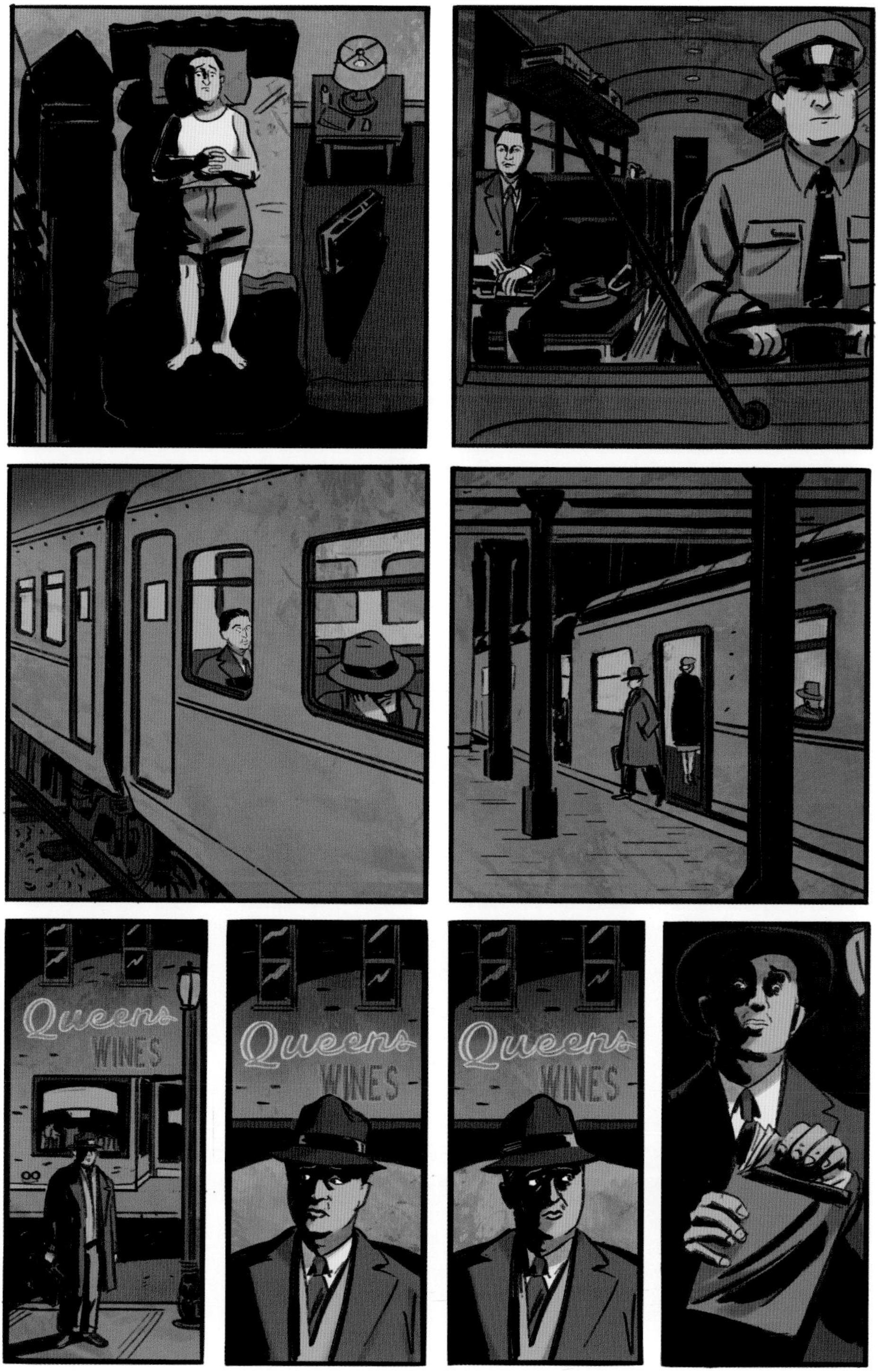
Queens
WINES
Queens
WINES
Queens
WINES

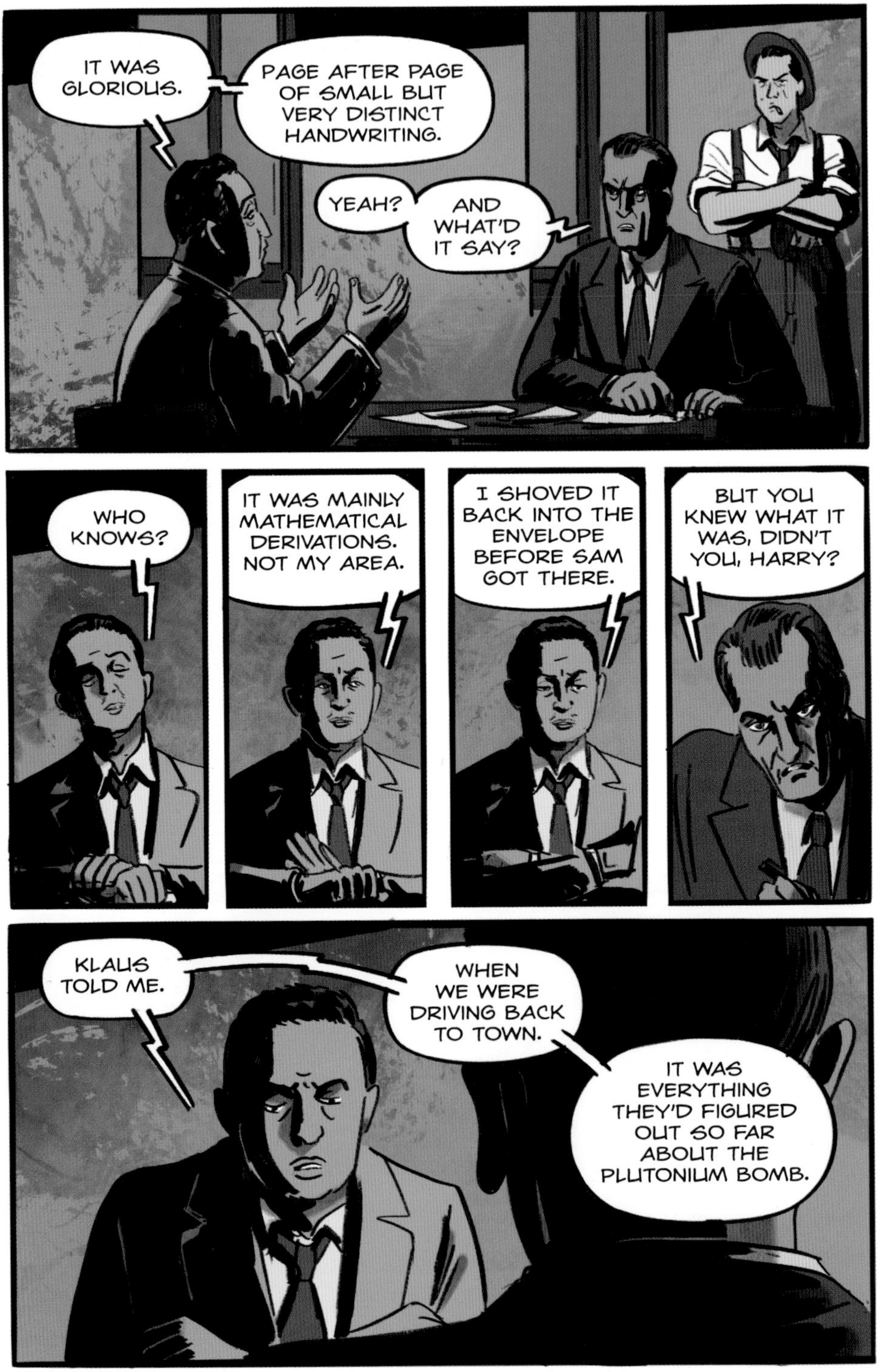
IT WAS GLORIOUS.
PAGE AFTER PAGE OF SMALL BUT VERY DISTINCT HANDWRITING.
YEAH?
AND WHAT'D IT SAY?
WHO KNOWS?
IT WAS MAINLY MATHEMATICAL DERIVATIONS. NOT MY AREA.
I SHOVED IT BACK INTO THE ENVELOPE BEFORE SAM GOT THERE.
BUT YOU KNEW WHAT IT WAS, DIDN'T YOU, HARRY?
KLAUS TOLD ME.
WHEN WE WERE DRIVING BACK TO TOWN.
IT WAS EVERYTHING THEY'D FIGURED OUT SO FAR ABOUT THE PLUTONIUM BOMB.

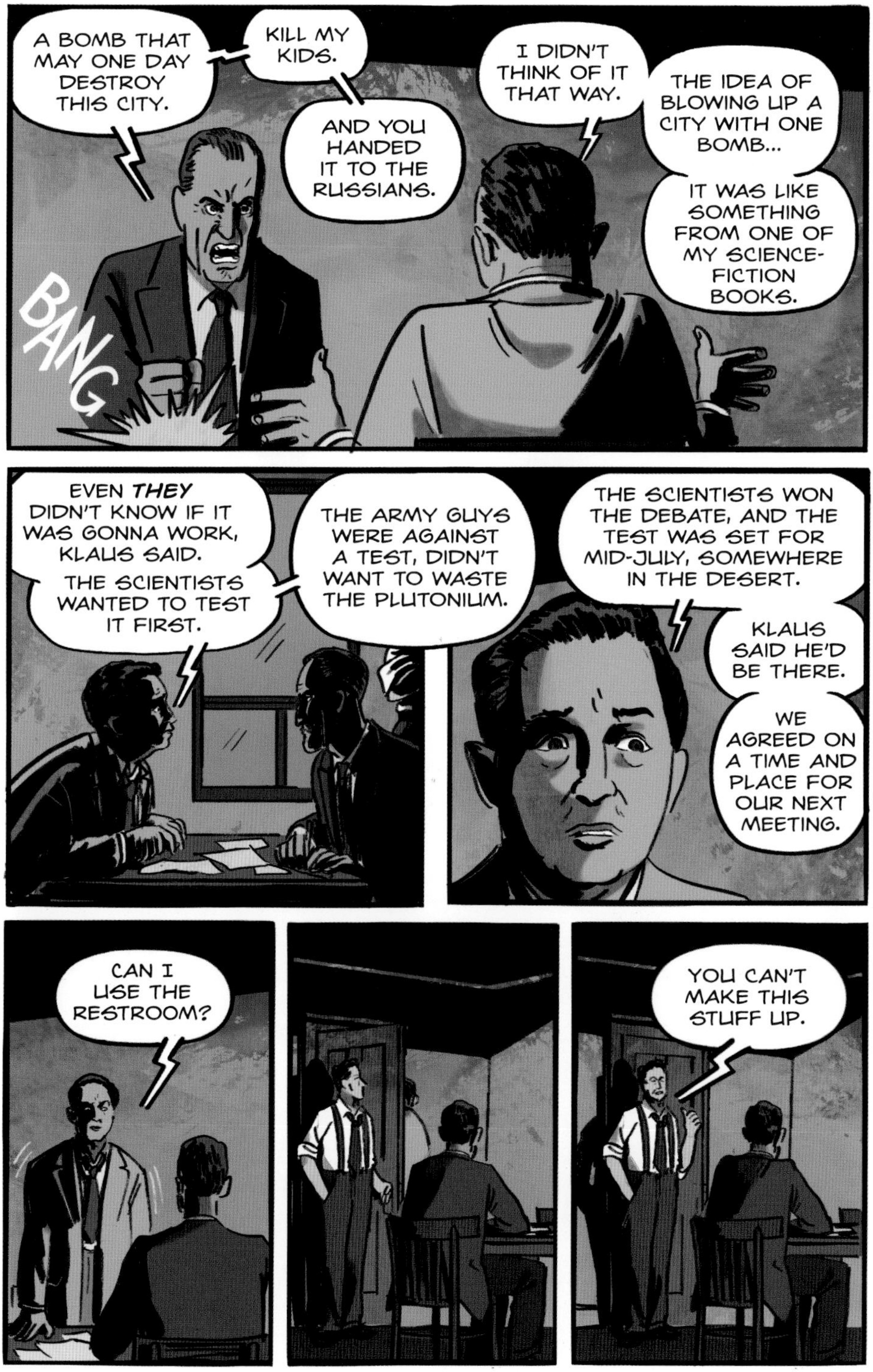
A BOMB THAT MAY ONE DAY DESTROY THIS CITY.
KILL MY KIDS.
AND YOU HANDED IT TO THE RUSSIANS.
BANG
I DIDN'T THINK OF IT THAT WAY.
THE IDEA OF BLOWING UP A CITY WITH ONE BOMB...
IT WAS LIKE SOMETHING FROM ONE OF MY SCIENCE-FICTION BOOKS.
EVEN *THEY* DIDN'T KNOW IF IT WAS GONNA WORK, KLAUS SAID.
THE SCIENTISTS WANTED TO TEST IT FIRST.
THE ARMY GUYS WERE AGAINST A TEST, DIDN'T WANT TO WASTE THE PLUTONIUM.
THE SCIENTISTS WON THE DEBATE, AND THE TEST WAS SET FOR MID-JULY, SOMEWHERE IN THE DESERT.
KLAUS SAID HE'D BE THERE.
WE AGREED ON A TIME AND PLACE FOR OUR NEXT MEETING.
CAN I USE THE RESTROOM?
YOU CAN'T MAKE THIS STUFF UP.

In June 1945, after some of the bloodiest fighting in the history of the American military, U.S. forces captured the Japanese island of Okinawa.

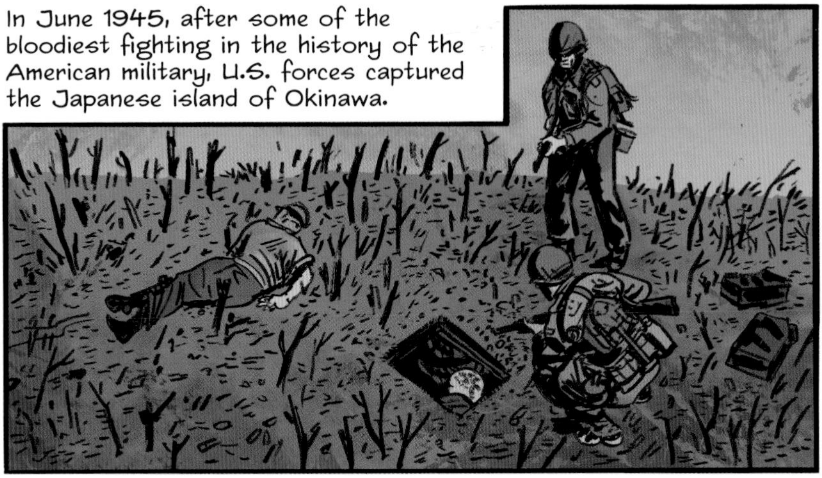

The next step was an all-out invasion of Japan's mainland.

Everyone expected the fighting to become even more ferocious.

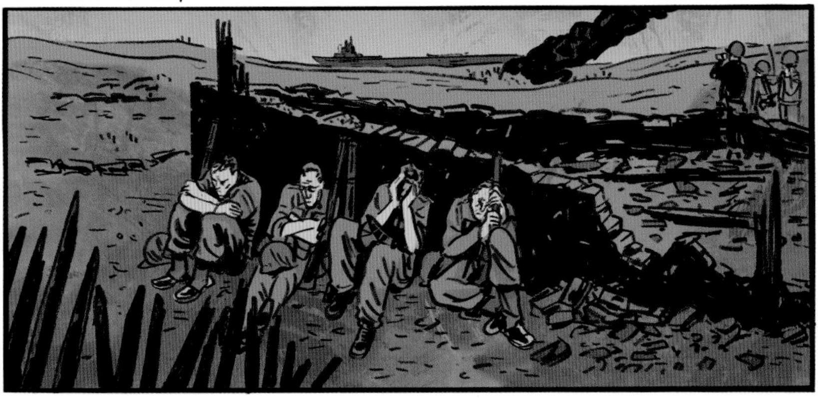

With the test date approaching, Oppenheimer pushed his scientists—and himself—harder than ever to finalize the implosion bomb.

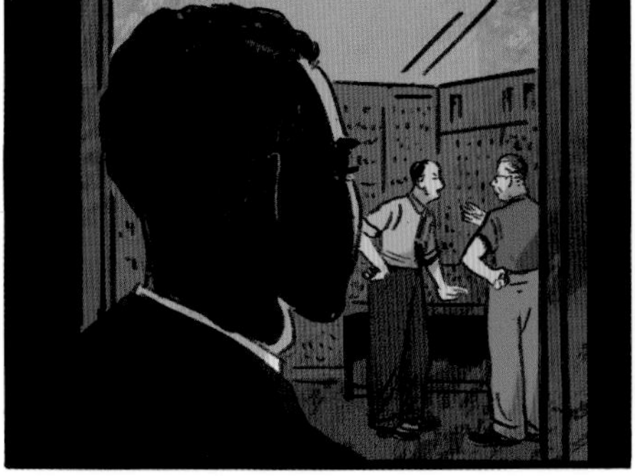

A new crisis erupted nearly every day with at least one of the bomb's 500-plus components.

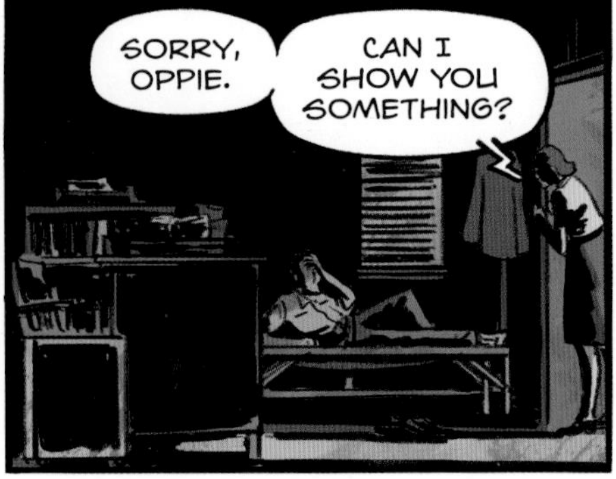
SORRY, OPPIE.
CAN I SHOW YOU SOMETHING?

Explosives expert George Kistiakowsky had the incredibly complex job of designing lenses made of plastic explosives...

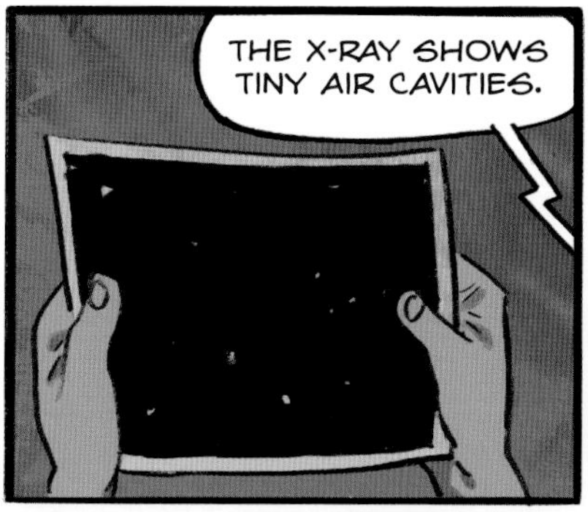
THE X-RAY SHOWS TINY AIR CAVITIES.

...and arranging the lenses to create a perfectly symmetrical blast.

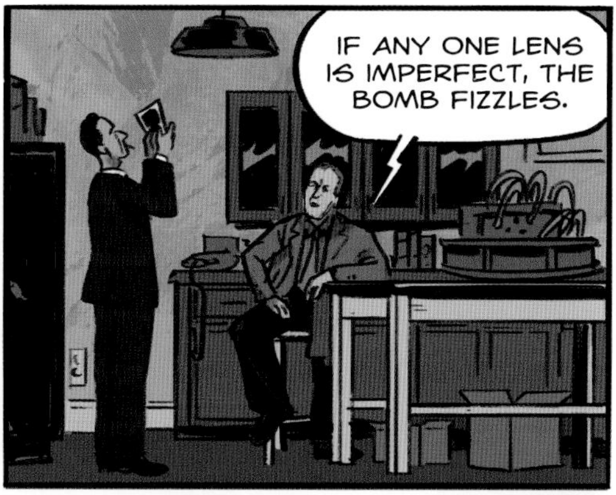
IF ANY ONE LENS IS IMPERFECT, THE BOMB FIZZLES.

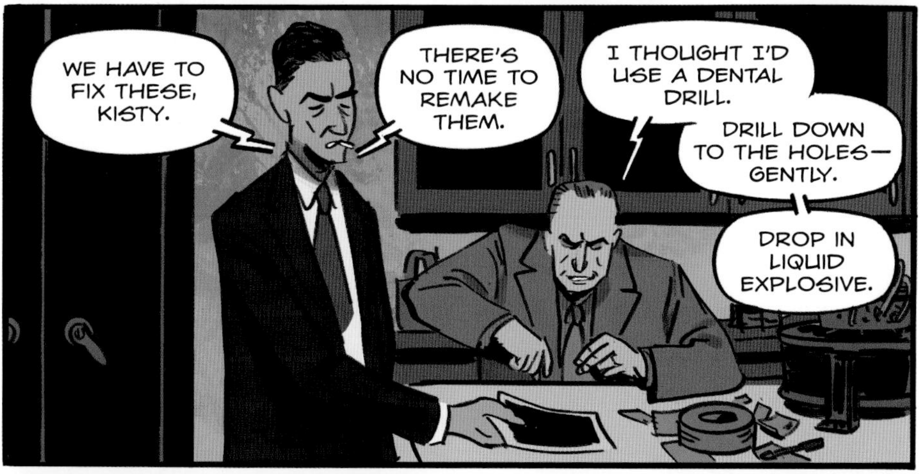
WE HAVE TO FIX THESE, KISTY.
THERE'S NO TIME TO REMAKE THEM.
I THOUGHT I'D USE A DENTAL DRILL.
DRILL DOWN TO THE HOLES—GENTLY.
DROP IN LIQUID EXPLOSIVE.

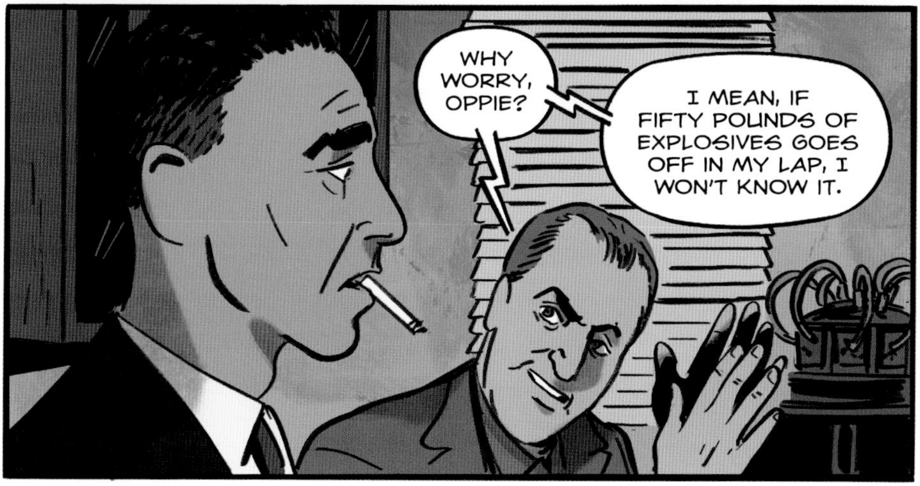
WHY WORRY, OPPIE?
I MEAN, IF FIFTY POUNDS OF EXPLOSIVES GOES OFF IN MY LAP, I WON'T KNOW IT.

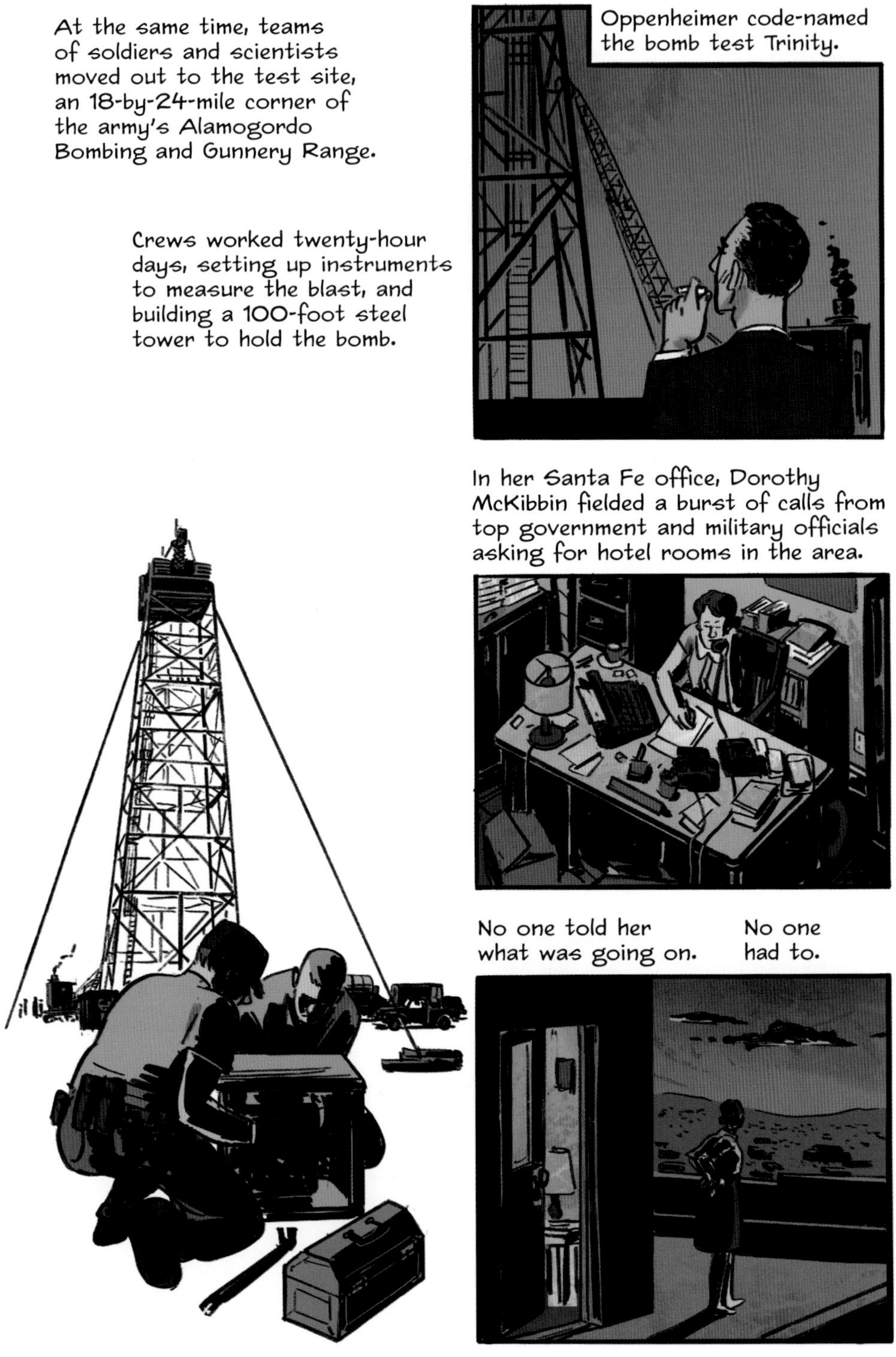
At the same time, teams of soldiers and scientists moved out to the test site, an 18-by-24-mile corner of the army's Alamogordo Bombing and Gunnery Range.
Oppenheimer code-named the bomb test Trinity.
Crews worked twenty-hour days, setting up instruments to measure the blast, and building a 100-foot steel tower to hold the bomb.
In her Santa Fe office, Dorothy McKibbin fielded a burst of calls from top government and military officials asking for hotel rooms in the area.
No one told her what was going on.
No one had to.

July 12, 1945.

The plutonium bomb core made the three-hour trip from Los Alamos to the Trinity site.

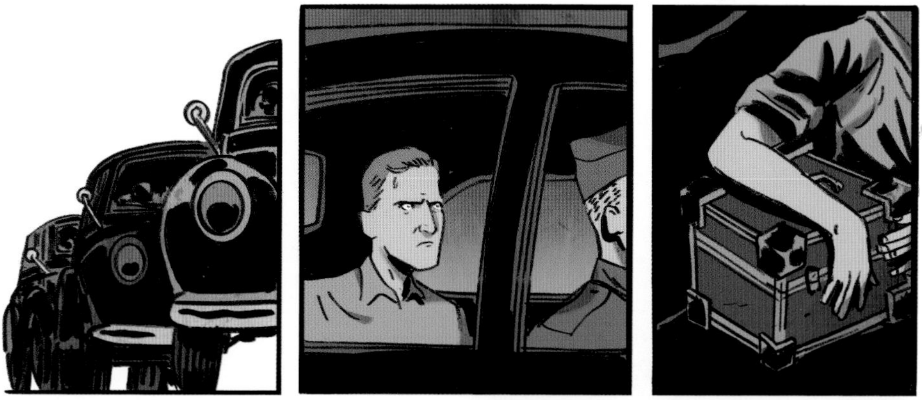

An abandoned ranch house was set up as an assembly lab.

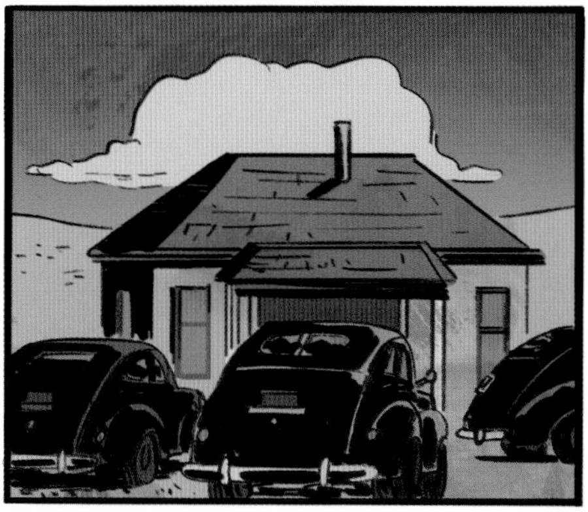

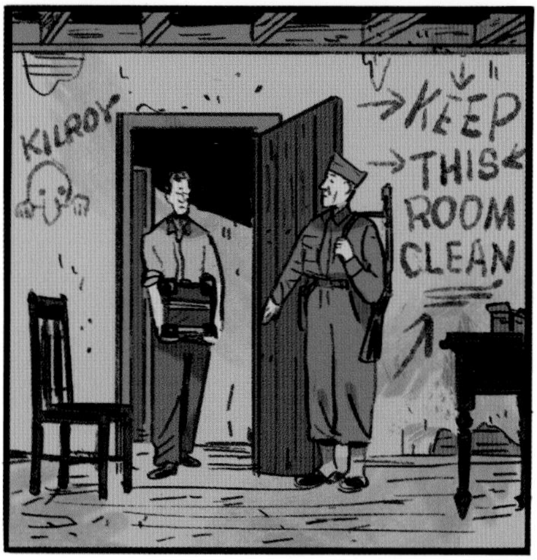
KILROY
KEEP THIS ROOM CLEAN

Very early the next morning, another convoy rolled slowly toward Trinity.

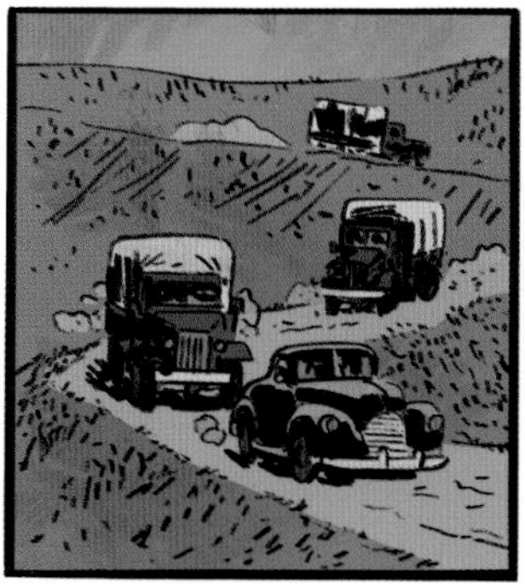

Very slowly.

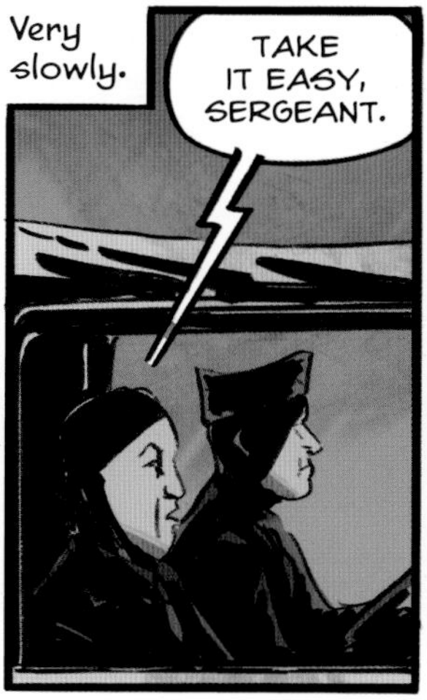
TAKE IT EASY, SERGEANT.

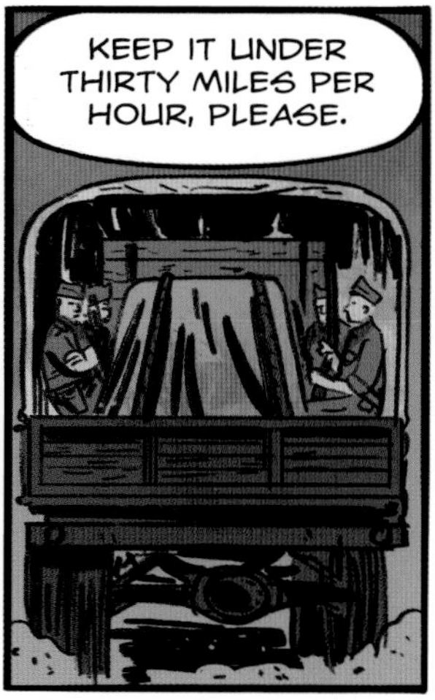
KEEP IT UNDER THIRTY MILES PER HOUR, PLEASE.

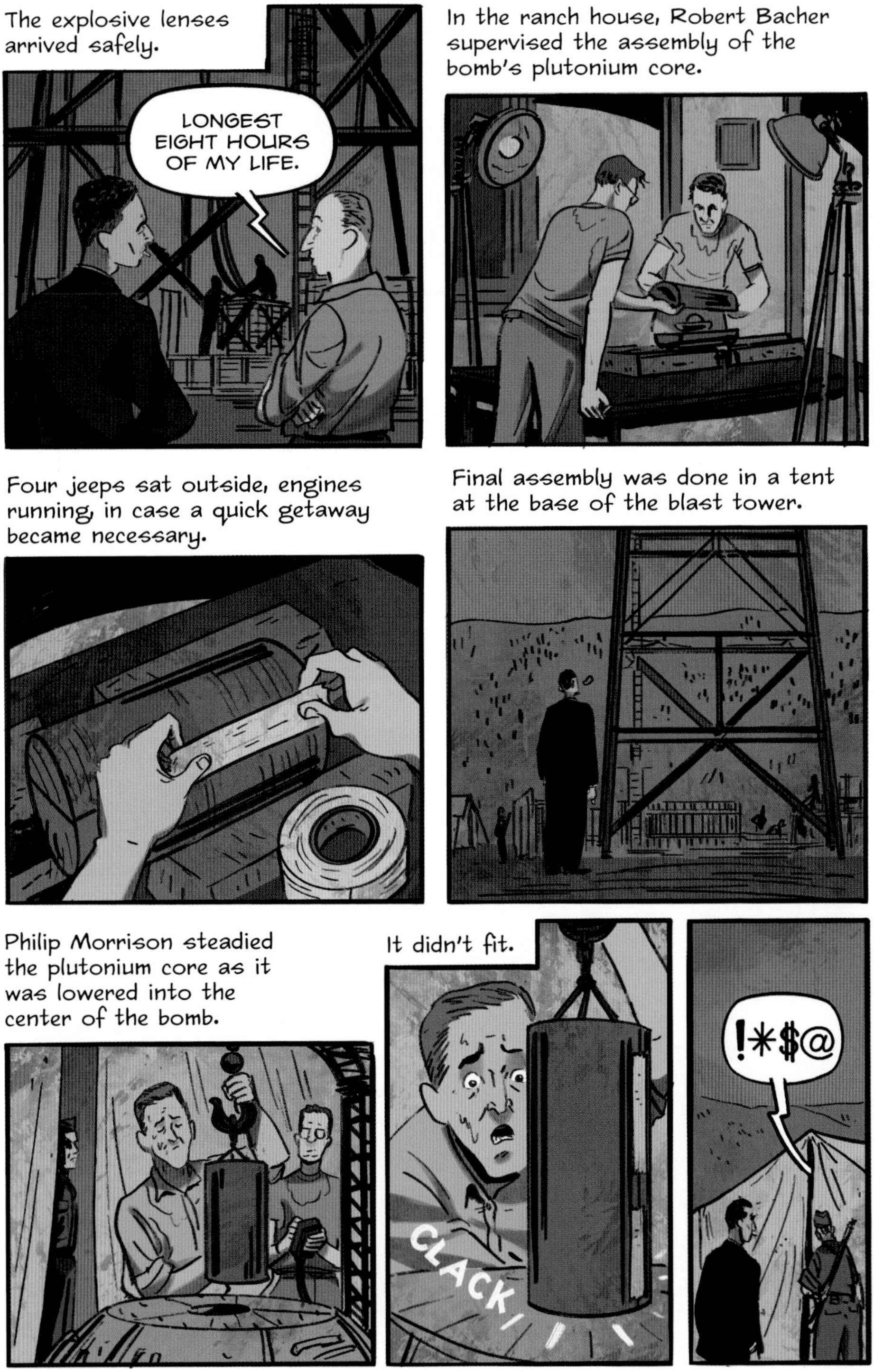
The explosive lenses arrived safely.
LONGEST EIGHT HOURS OF MY LIFE.
In the ranch house, Robert Bacher supervised the assembly of the bomb's plutonium core.
Four jeeps sat outside, engines running, in case a quick getaway became necessary.
Final assembly was done in a tent at the base of the blast tower.
Philip Morrison steadied the plutonium core as it was lowered into the center of the bomb.
It didn't fit.
CLACK
!*$@

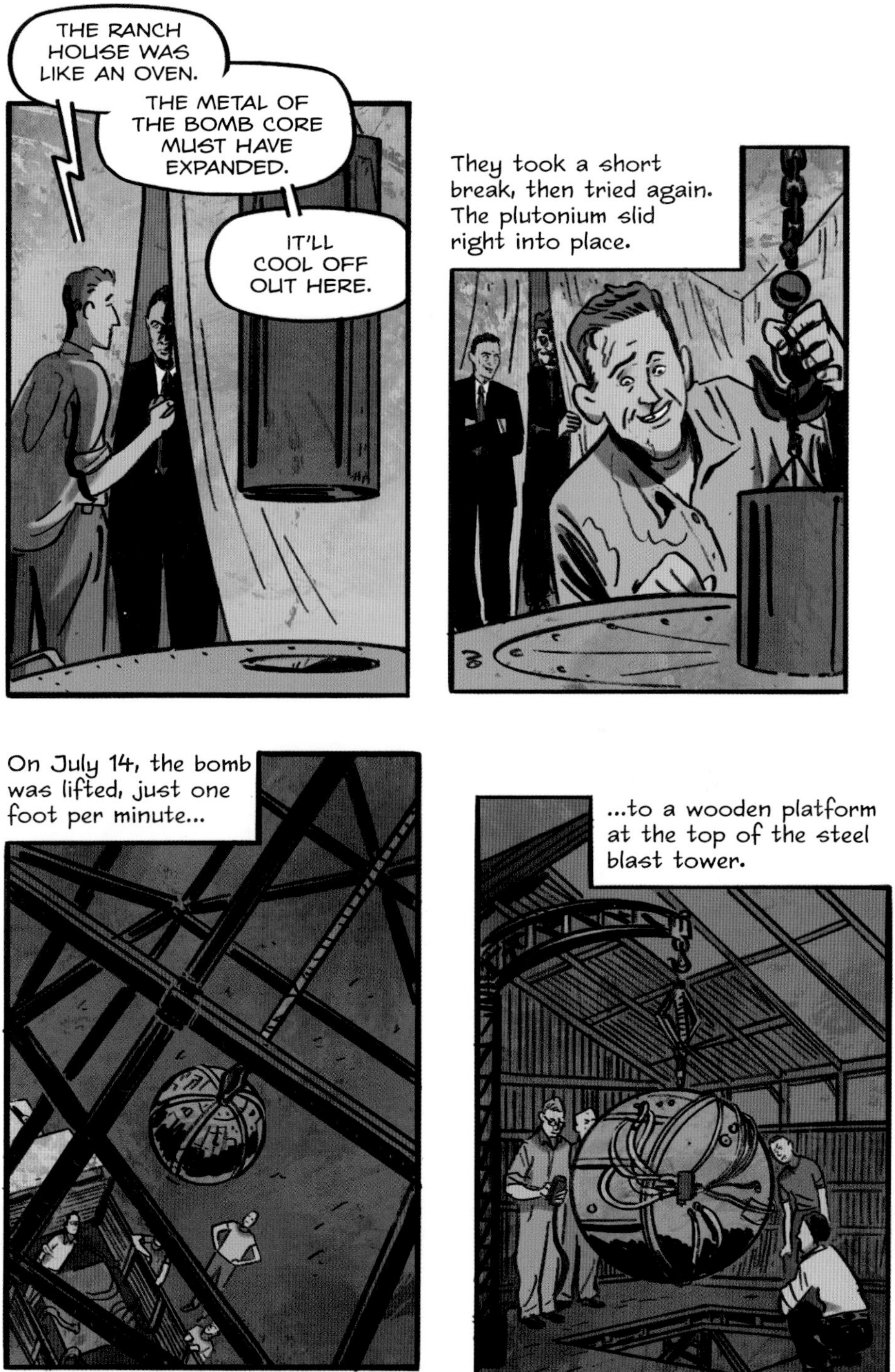
THE RANCH HOUSE WAS LIKE AN OVEN.
THE METAL OF THE BOMB CORE MUST HAVE EXPANDED.
IT'LL COOL OFF OUT HERE.
They took a short break, then tried again. The plutonium slid right into place.
On July 14, the bomb was lifted, just one foot per minute...
...to a wooden platform at the top of the steel blast tower.

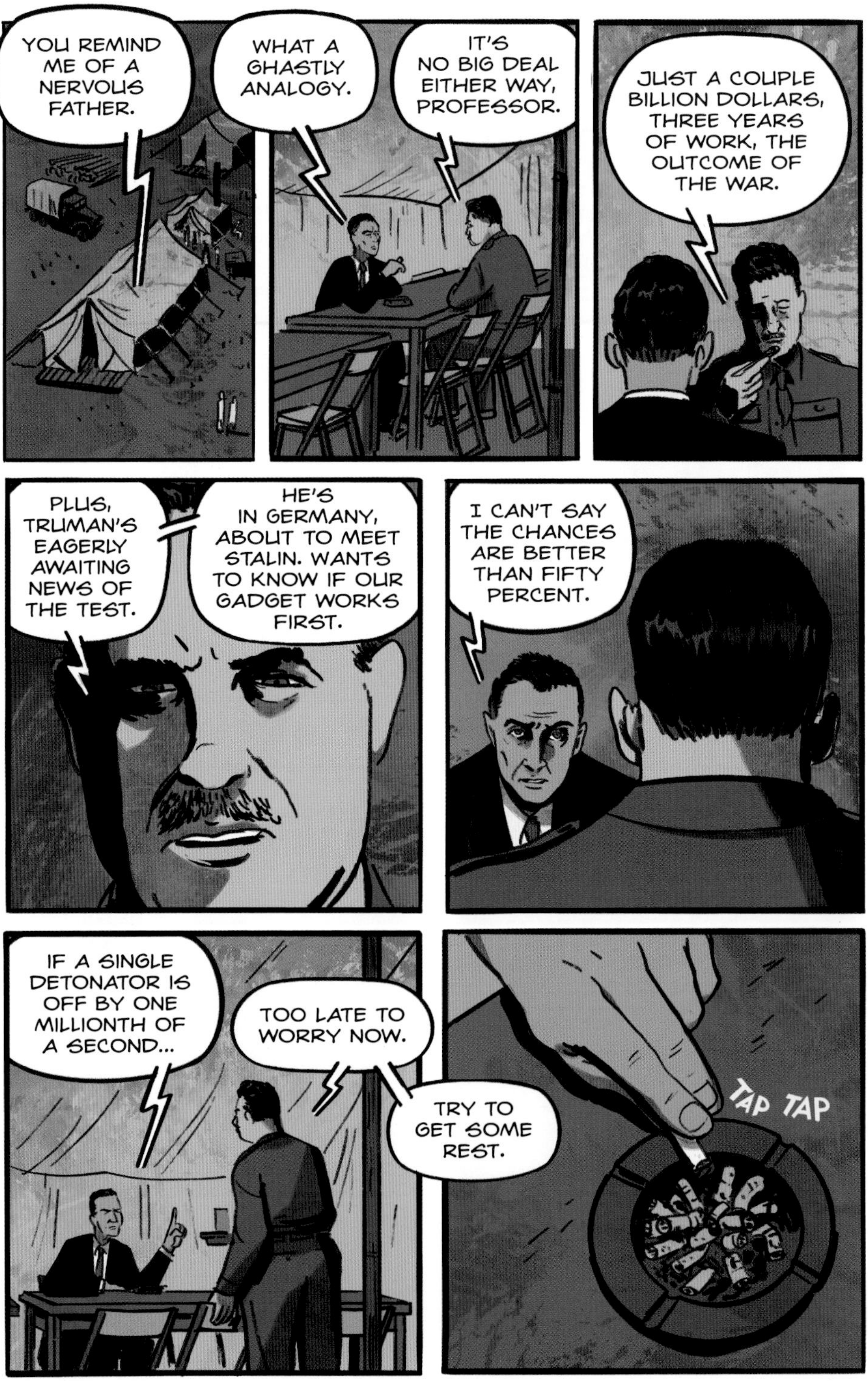
YOU REMIND ME OF A NERVOUS FATHER.
WHAT A GHASTLY ANALOGY.
IT'S NO BIG DEAL EITHER WAY, PROFESSOR.
JUST A COUPLE BILLION DOLLARS, THREE YEARS OF WORK, THE OUTCOME OF THE WAR.
PLUS, TRUMAN'S EAGERLY AWAITING NEWS OF THE TEST.
HE'S IN GERMANY, ABOUT TO MEET STALIN. WANTS TO KNOW IF OUR GADGET WORKS FIRST.
I CAN'T SAY THE CHANCES ARE BETTER THAN FIFTY PERCENT.
IF A SINGLE DETONATOR IS OFF BY ONE MILLIONTH OF A SECOND...
TOO LATE TO WORRY NOW.
TRY TO GET SOME REST.
TAP TAP

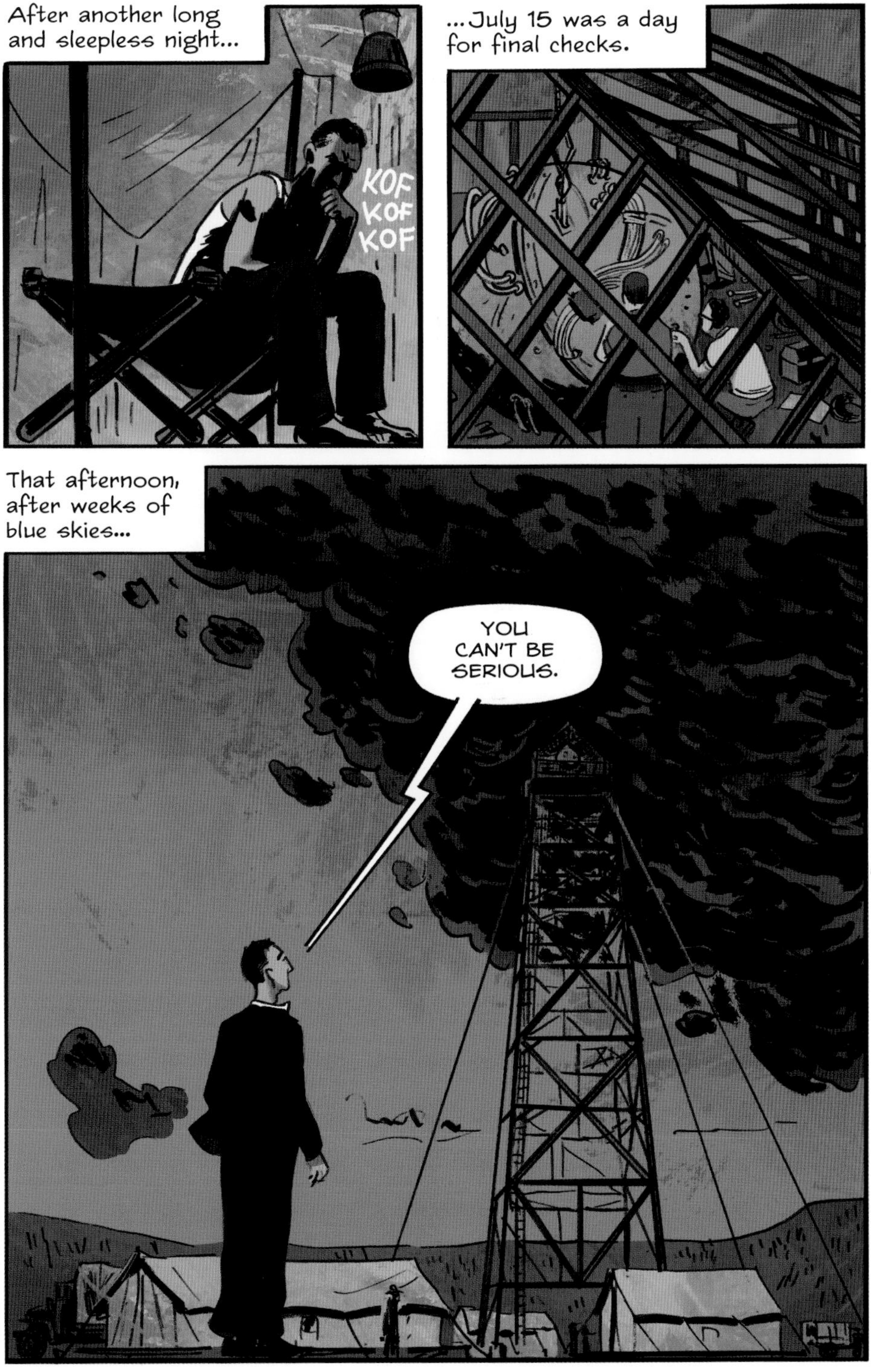
After another long and sleepless night...
KOF KOF KOF
...July 15 was a day for final checks.
That afternoon, after weeks of blue skies...
YOU CAN'T BE SERIOUS.

In Potsdam, Germany, President Truman waited for news from New Mexico.

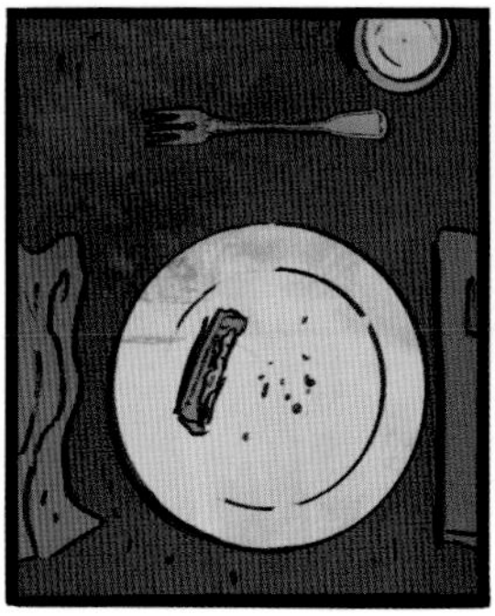

Once the man who did not need to know, Harry Truman was now the most powerful man on Earth.

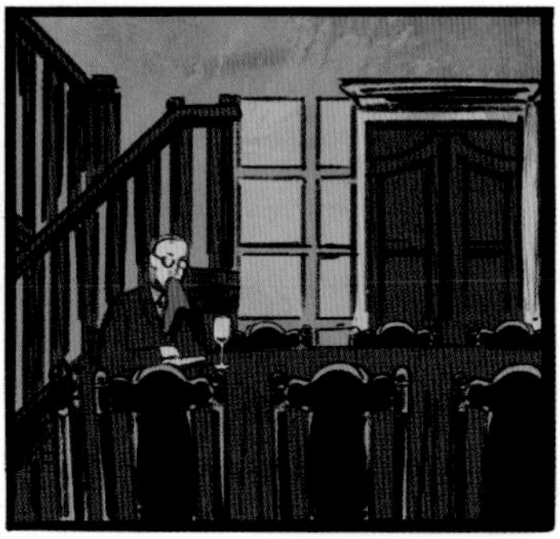

And about to become the most powerful human in history.

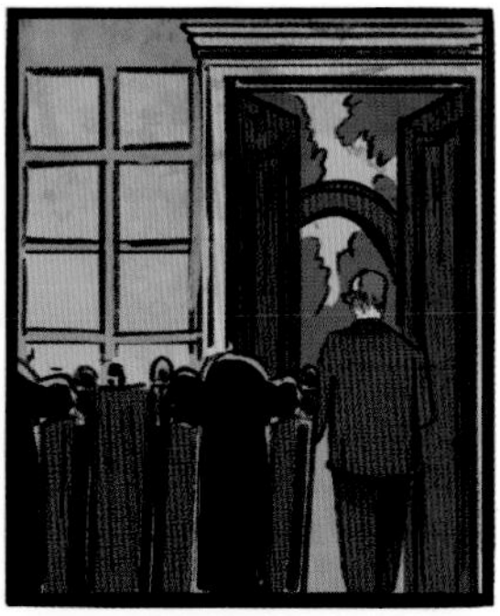

Colonel Paul Tibbets and his crew were already at the American air base on Tinian Island, just 1,500 miles from Japan.

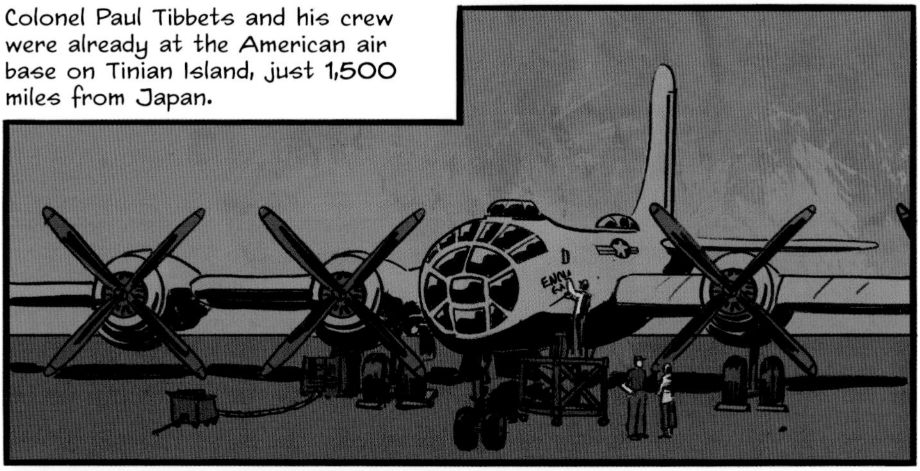

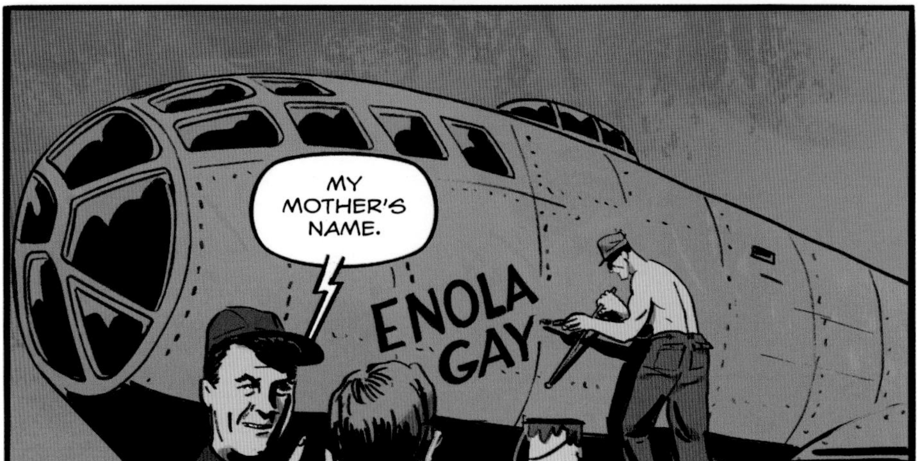
MY MOTHER'S NAME.
ENOLA GAY

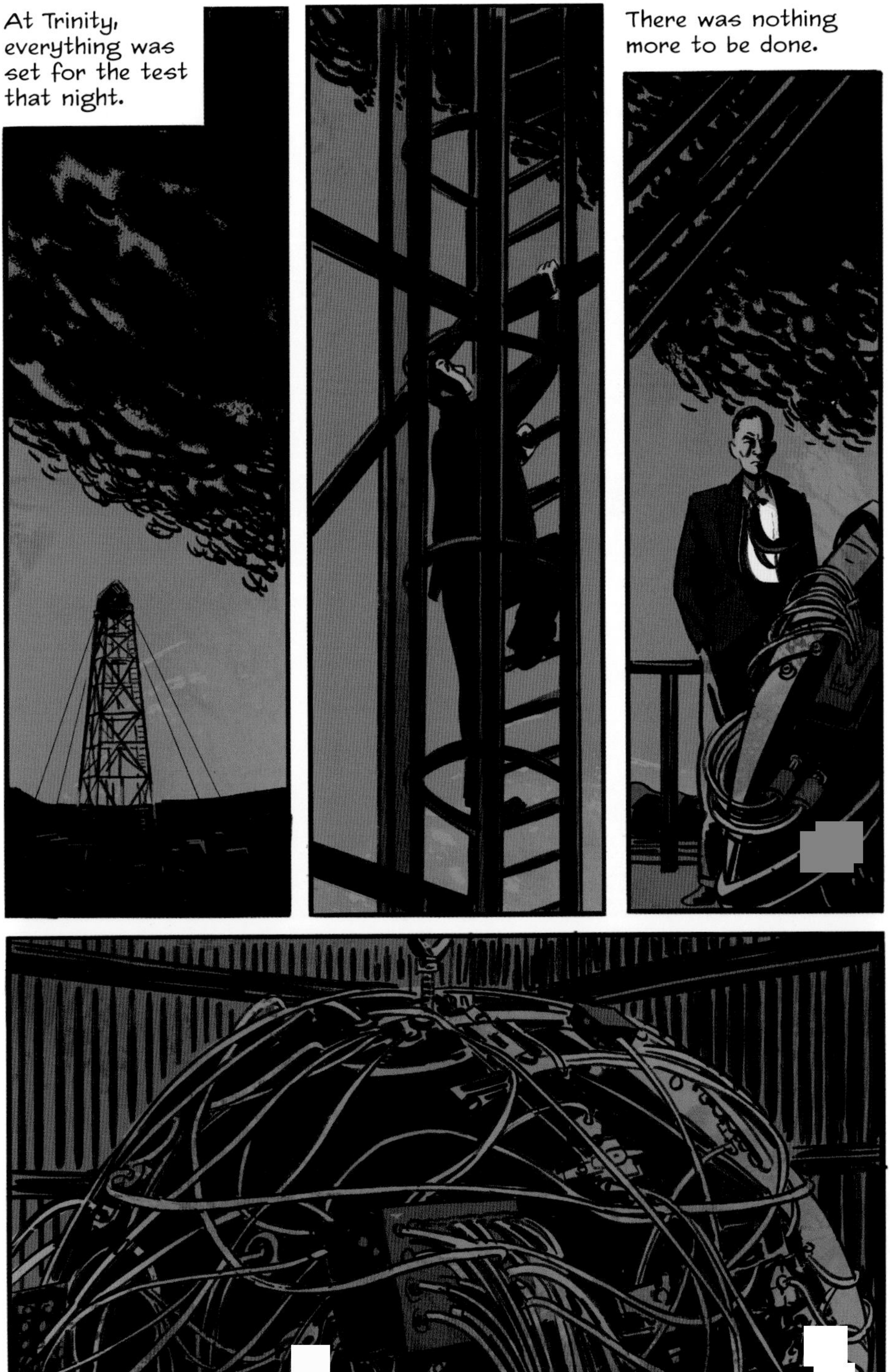
At Trinity, everything was set for the test that night.
There was nothing more to be done.

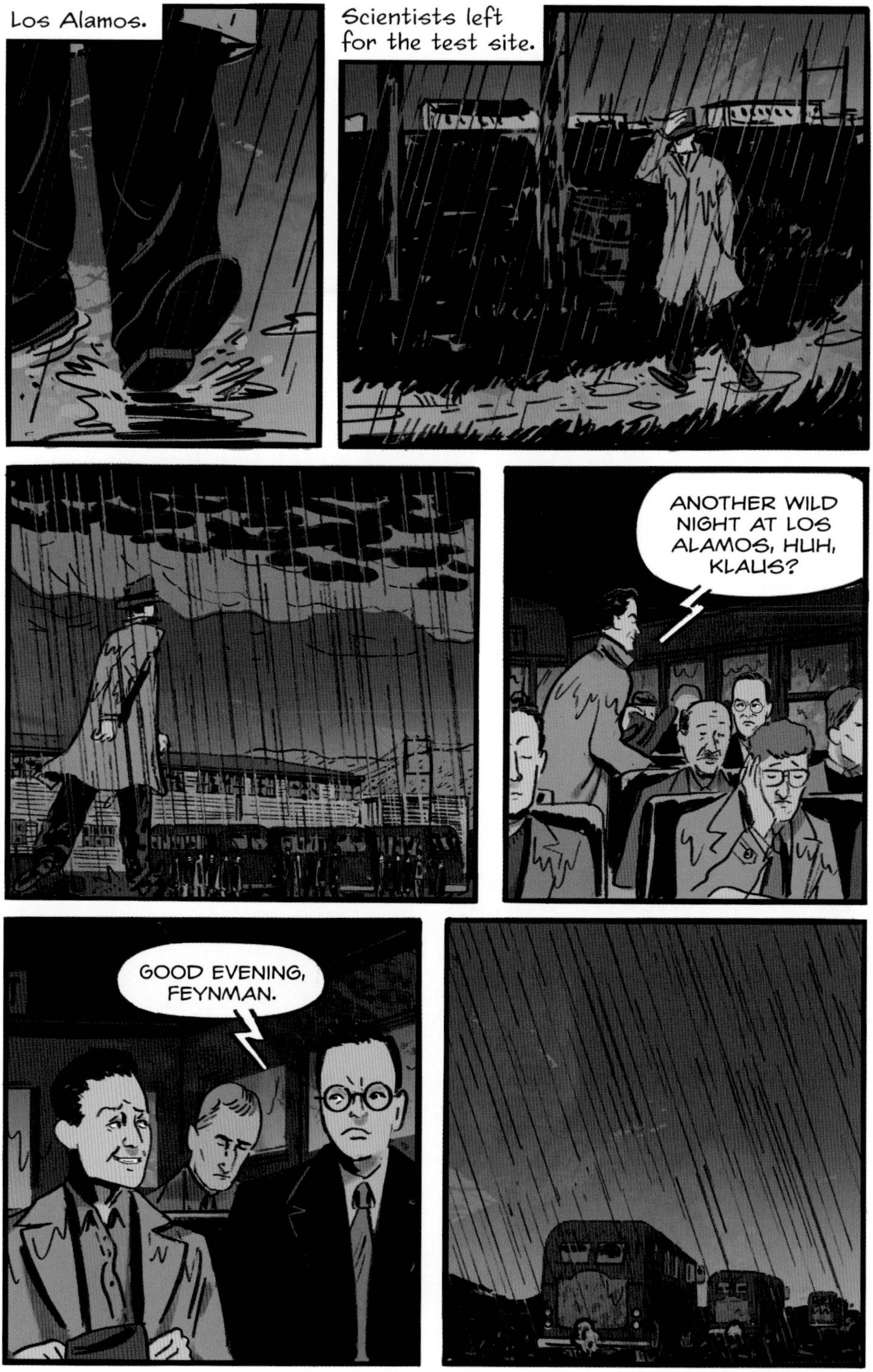
Los Alamos.
Scientists left for the test site.
ANOTHER WILD NIGHT AT LOS ALAMOS, HUH, KLAUS?
GOOD EVENING, FEYNMAN.

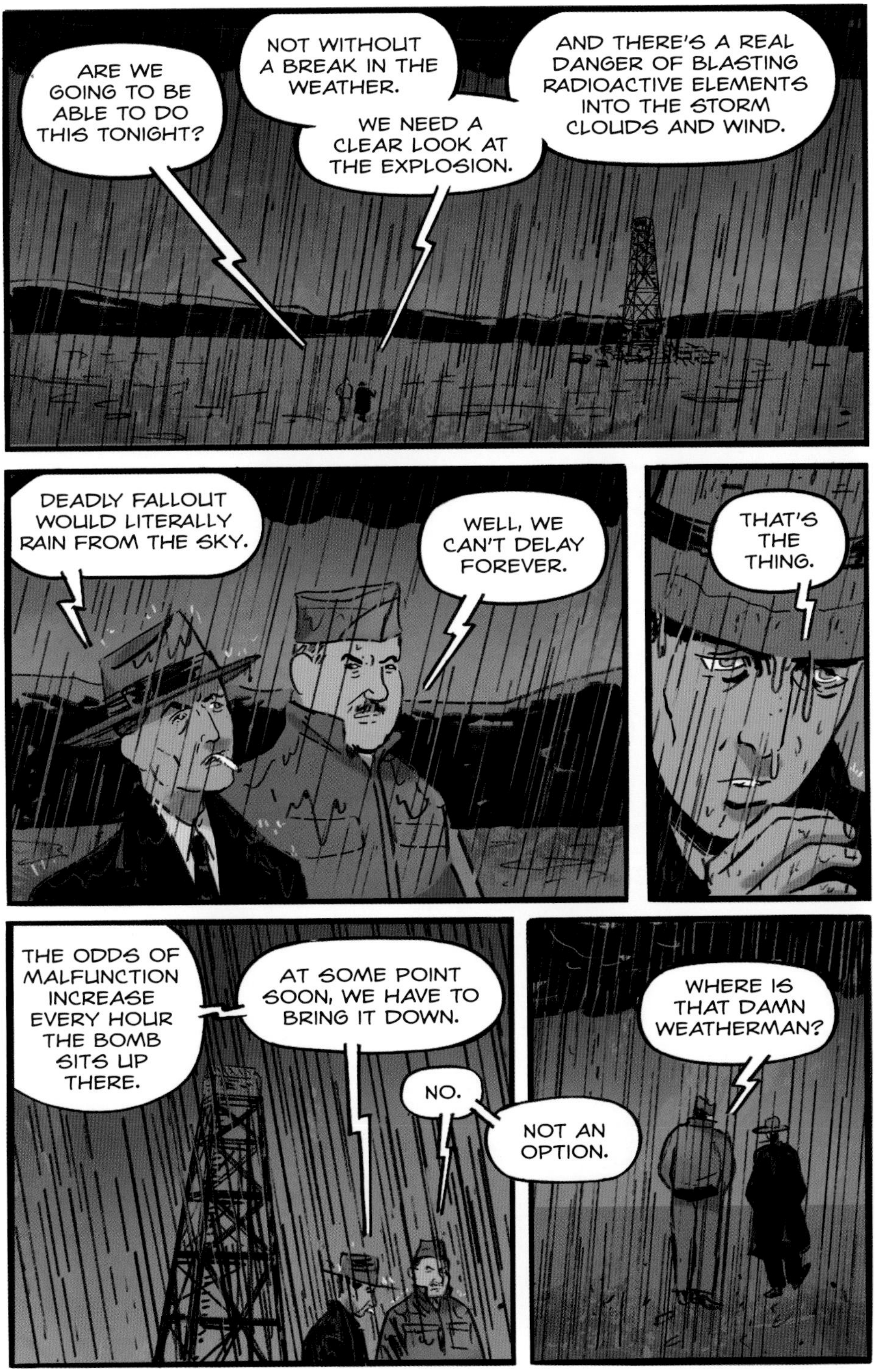
ARE WE GOING TO BE ABLE TO DO THIS TONIGHT?
NOT WITHOUT A BREAK IN THE WEATHER.
WE NEED A CLEAR LOOK AT THE EXPLOSION.
AND THERE'S A REAL DANGER OF BLASTING RADIOACTIVE ELEMENTS INTO THE STORM CLOUDS AND WIND.
DEADLY FALLOUT WOULD LITERALLY RAIN FROM THE SKY.
WELL, WE CAN'T DELAY FOREVER.
THAT'S THE THING.
THE ODDS OF MALFUNCTION INCREASE EVERY HOUR THE BOMB SITS UP THERE.
AT SOME POINT SOON, WE HAVE TO BRING IT DOWN.
NO.
NOT AN OPTION.
WHERE IS THAT DAMN WEATHERMAN?

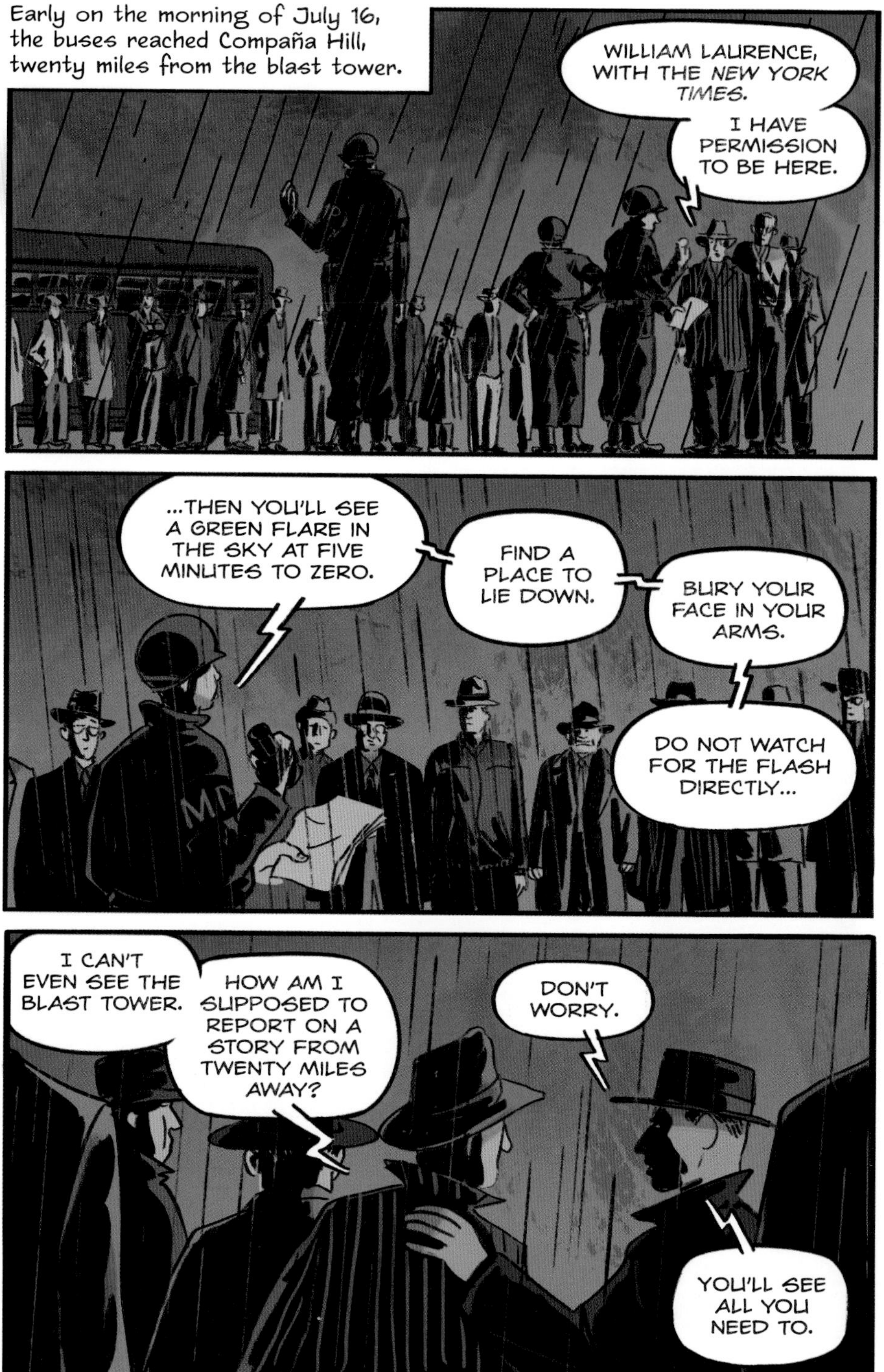
Early on the morning of July 16, the buses reached Compaña Hill, twenty miles from the blast tower.
WILLIAM LAURENCE, WITH THE *NEW YORK TIMES*.
I HAVE PERMISSION TO BE HERE.
...THEN YOU'LL SEE A GREEN FLARE IN THE SKY AT FIVE MINUTES TO ZERO.
FIND A PLACE TO LIE DOWN.
BURY YOUR FACE IN YOUR ARMS.
DO NOT WATCH FOR THE FLASH DIRECTLY...
I CAN'T EVEN SEE THE BLAST TOWER.
HOW AM I SUPPOSED TO REPORT ON A STORY FROM TWENTY MILES AWAY?
DON'T WORRY.
YOU'LL SEE ALL YOU NEED TO.

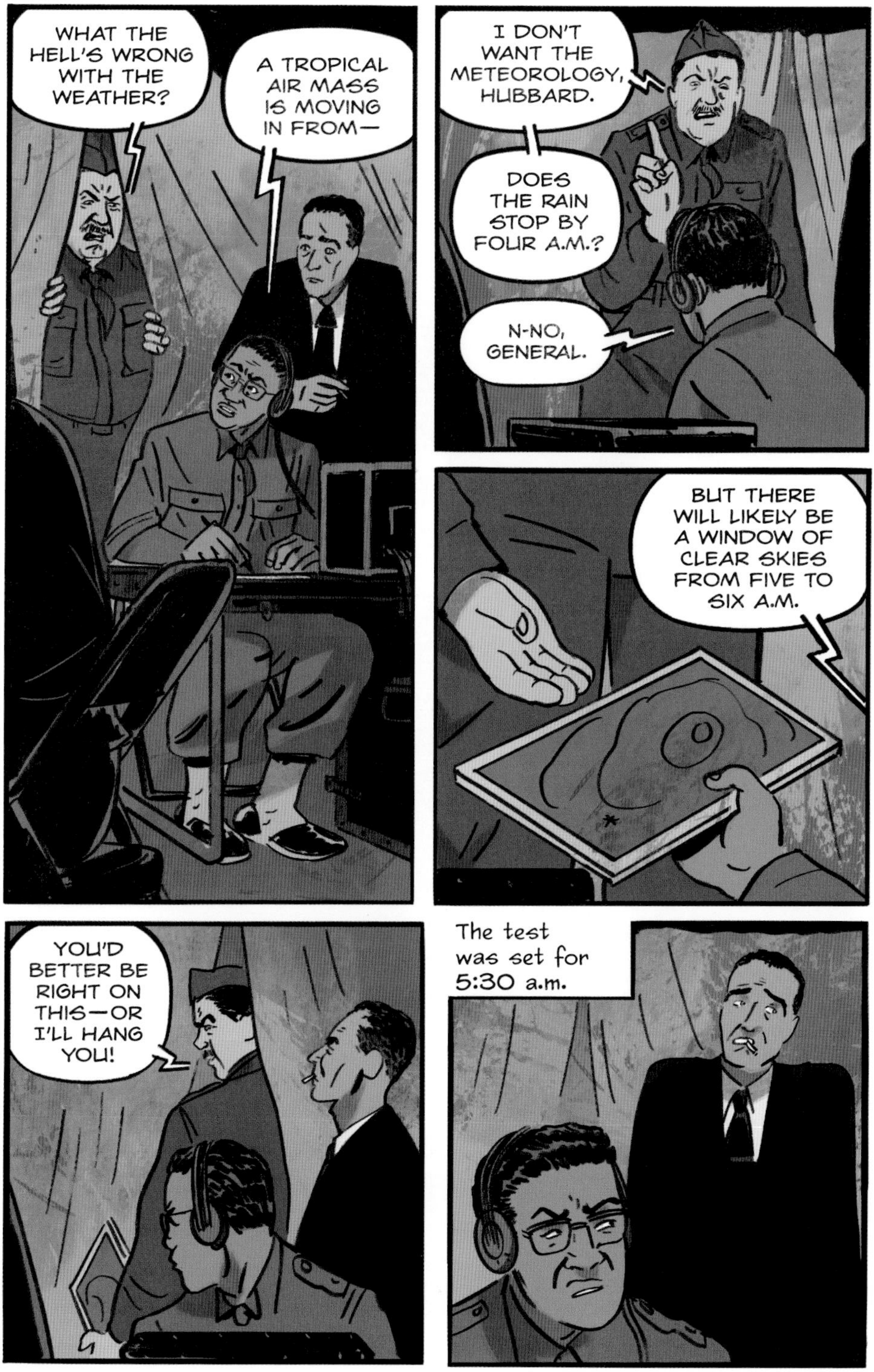
WHAT THE HELL'S WRONG WITH THE WEATHER?
A TROPICAL AIR MASS IS MOVING IN FROM—
I DON'T WANT THE METEOROLOGY, HUBBARD.
DOES THE RAIN STOP BY FOUR A.M.?
N-NO, GENERAL.
BUT THERE WILL LIKELY BE A WINDOW OF CLEAR SKIES FROM FIVE TO SIX A.M.
YOU'D BETTER BE RIGHT ON THIS—OR I'LL HANG YOU!
The test was set for 5:30 a.m.

Ted Hall wasn't considered important enough to see the test up close.

He was assigned to an army rescue crew.

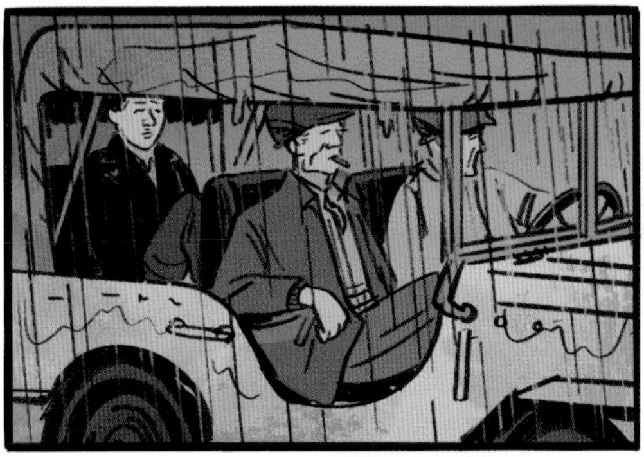

He'd help evacuate nearby farms and villages if radioactive fallout started spreading through the sky.

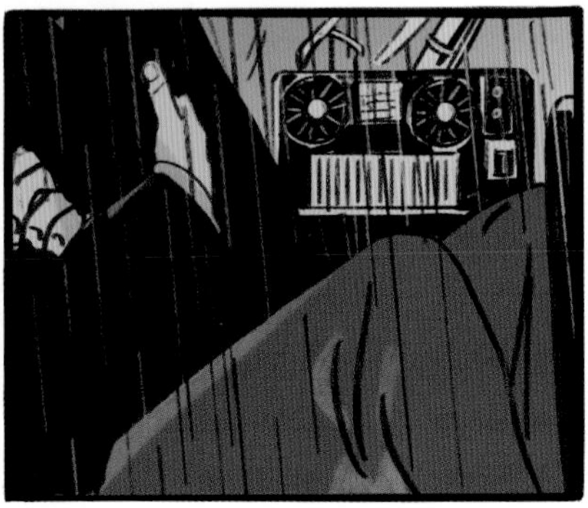

4:55 a.m. The bomb was armed.

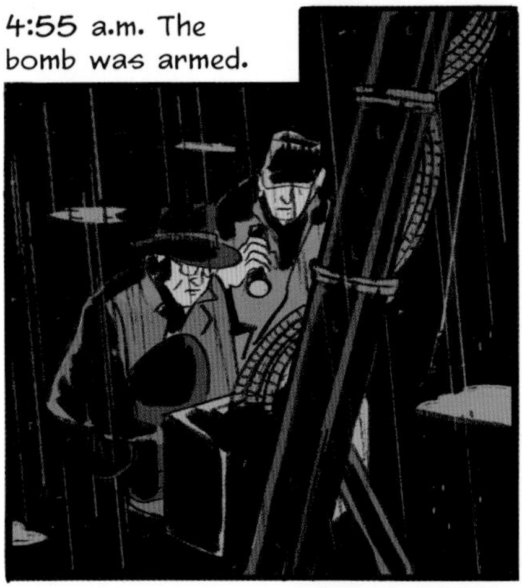

From this point on, everything would be run from concrete bunkers 10,000 yards—about six miles—from the blast site.

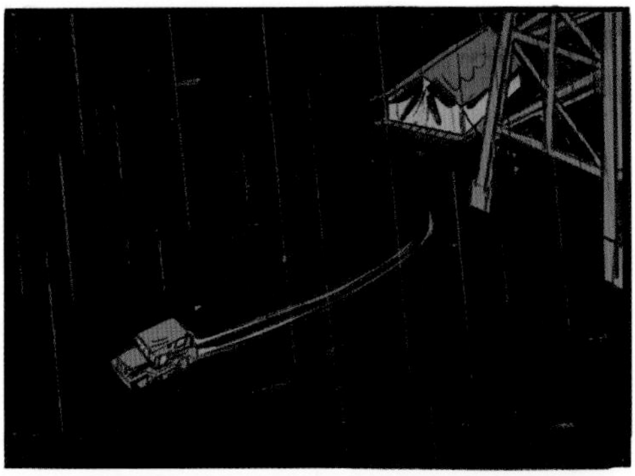

The rain stopped right on schedule.

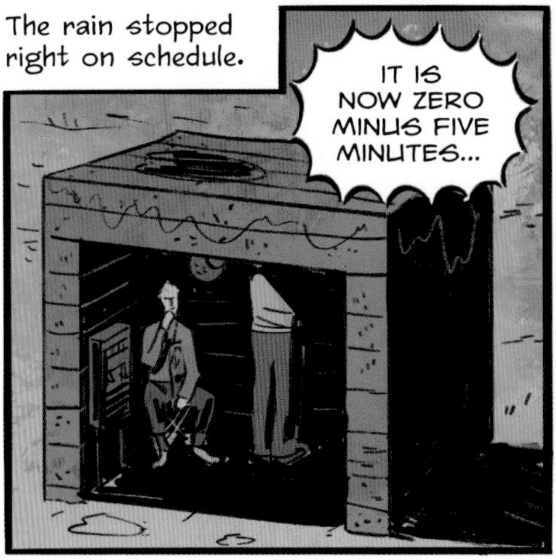
IT IS NOW ZERO MINUS FIVE MINUTES...

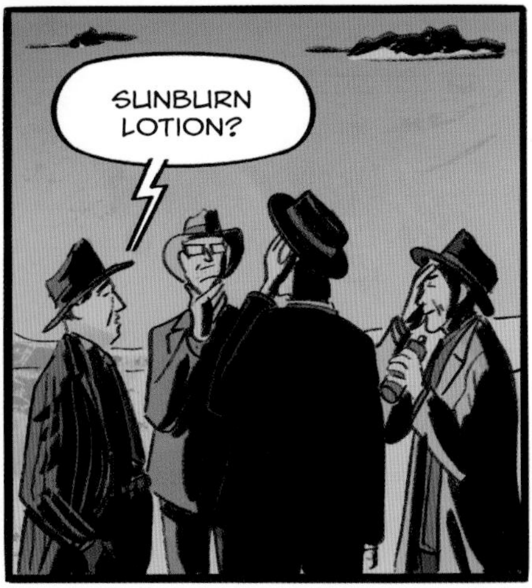
SUNBURN LOTION?

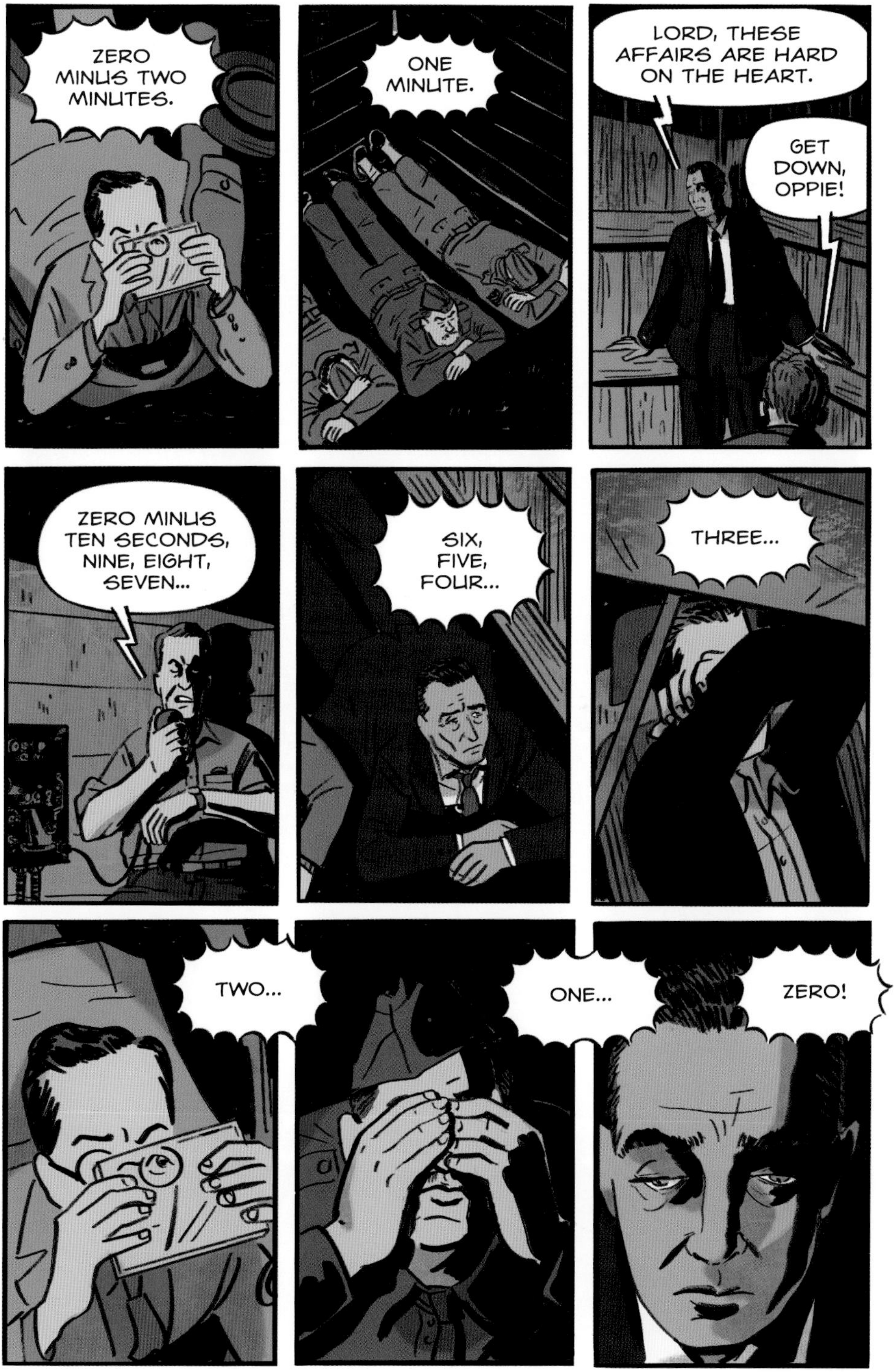

ZERO MINUS TWO MINUTES.
ONE MINUTE.
LORD, THESE AFFAIRS ARE HARD ON THE HEART.
GET DOWN, OPPIE!
ZERO MINUS TEN SECONDS, NINE, EIGHT, SEVEN...
SIX, FIVE, FOUR...
THREE...
TWO...
ONE...
ZERO!

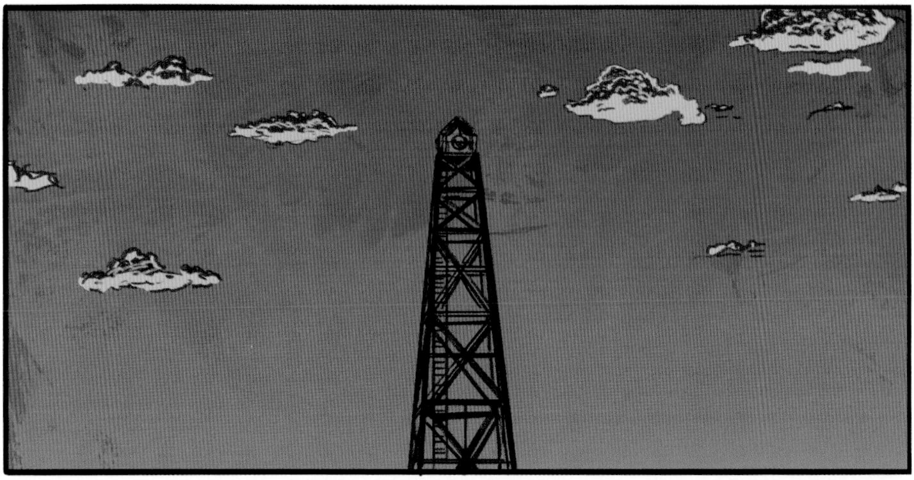

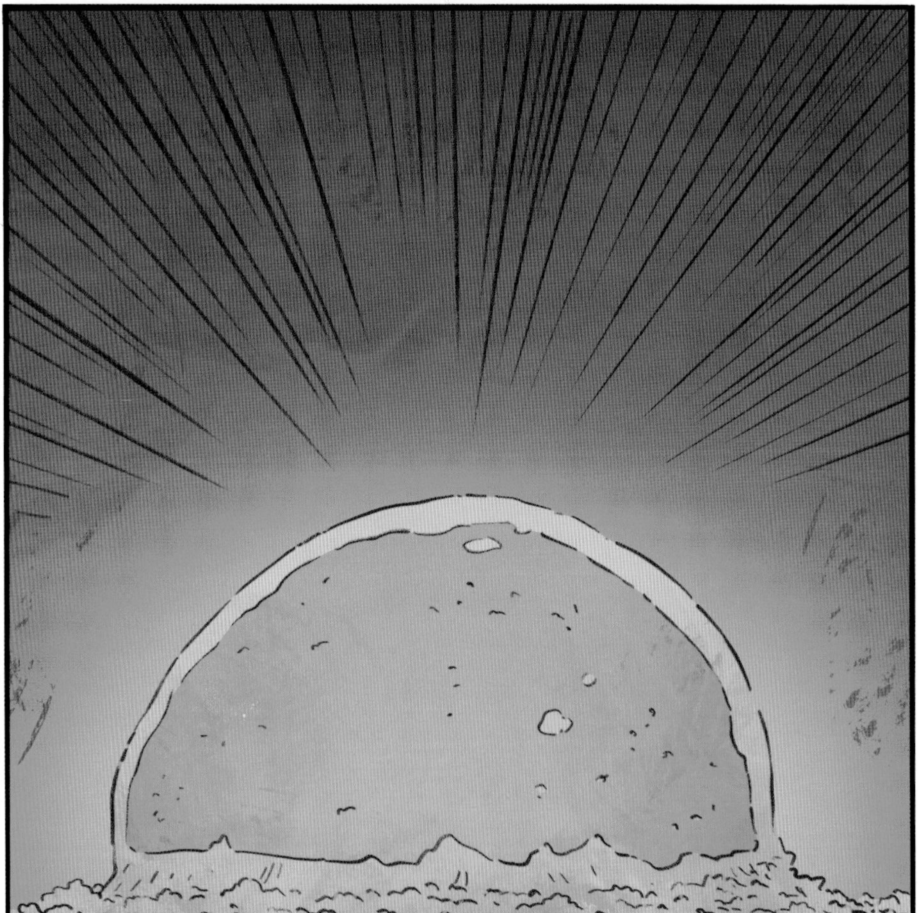

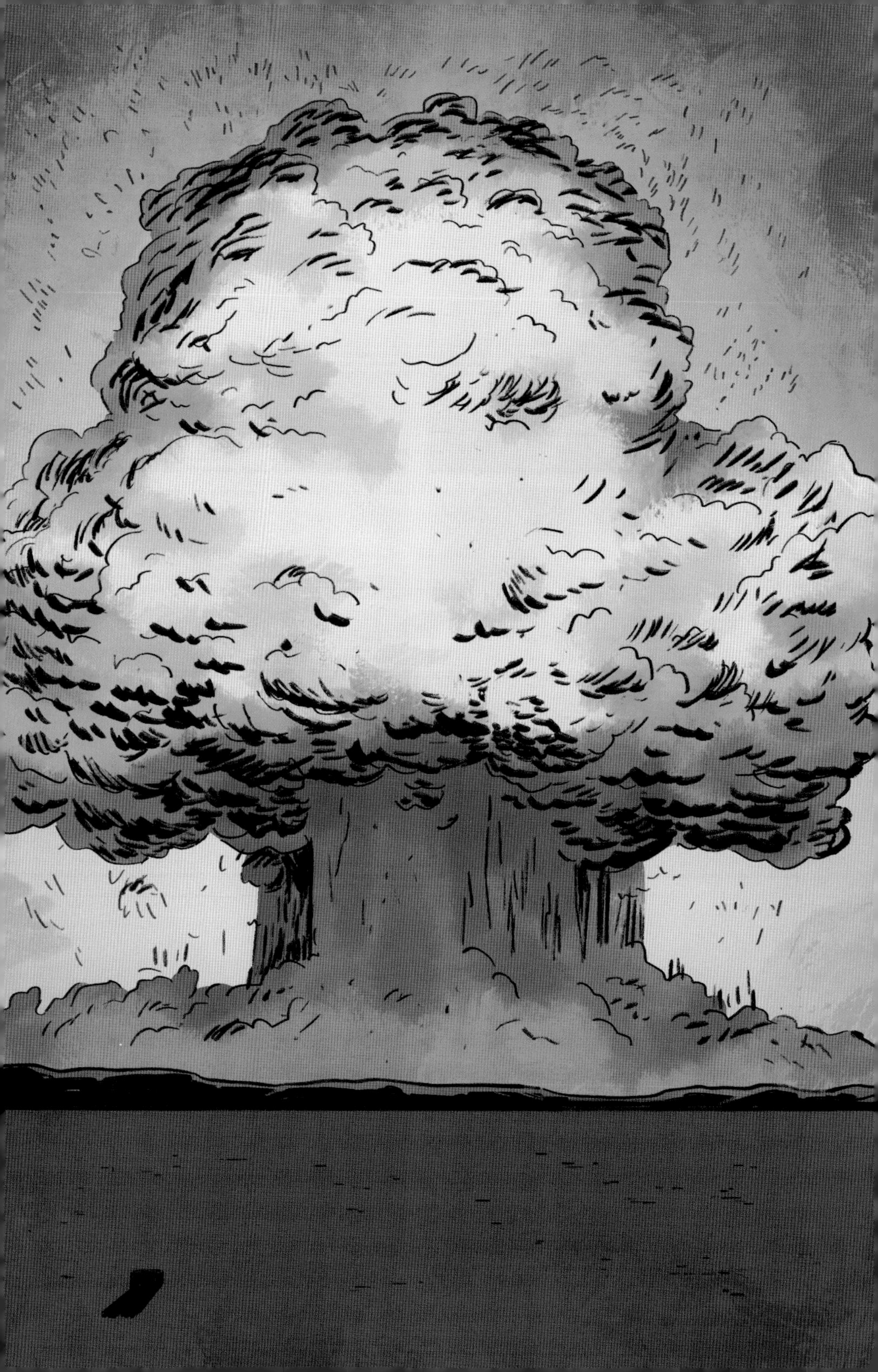

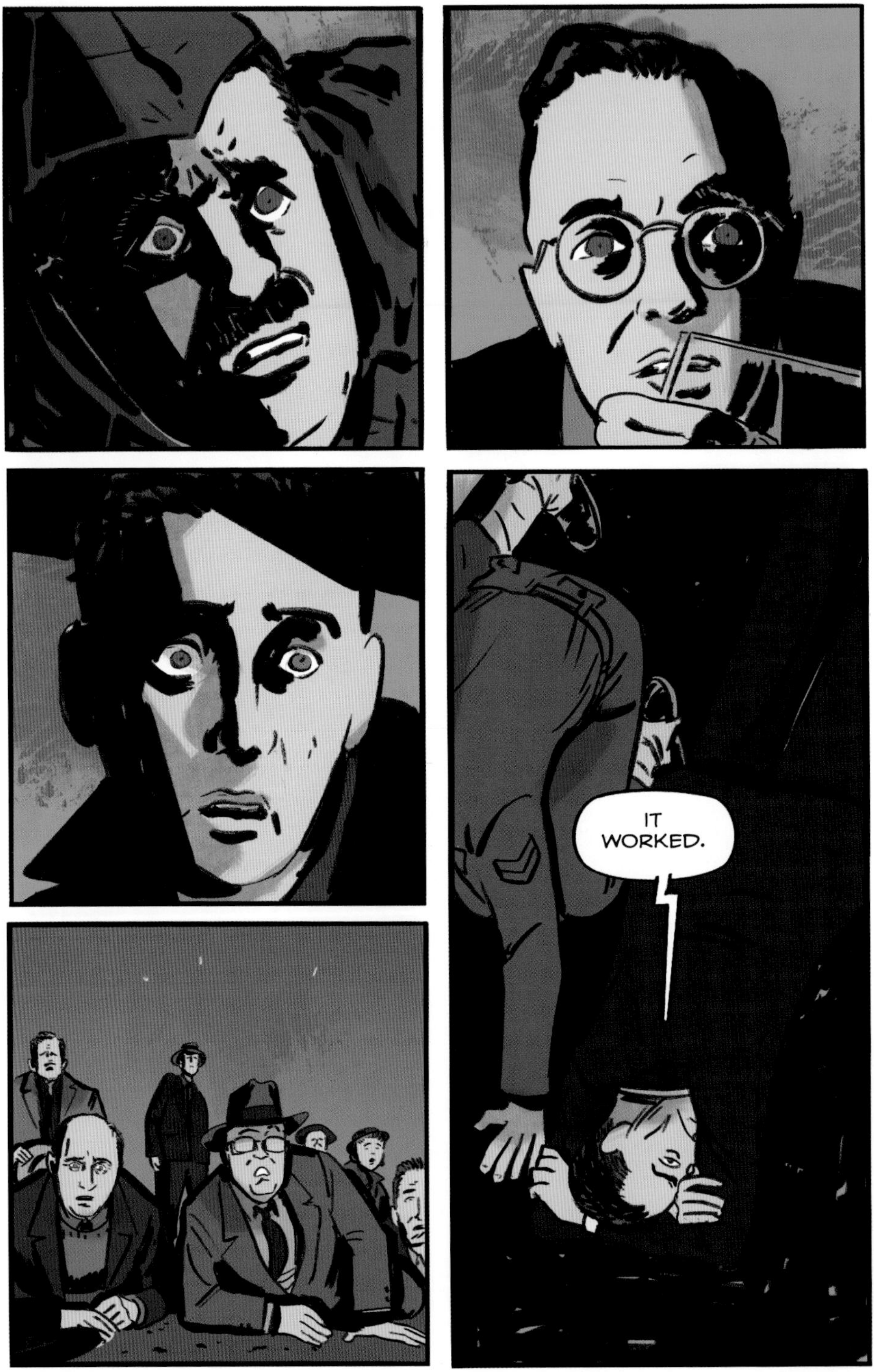
IT WORKED.

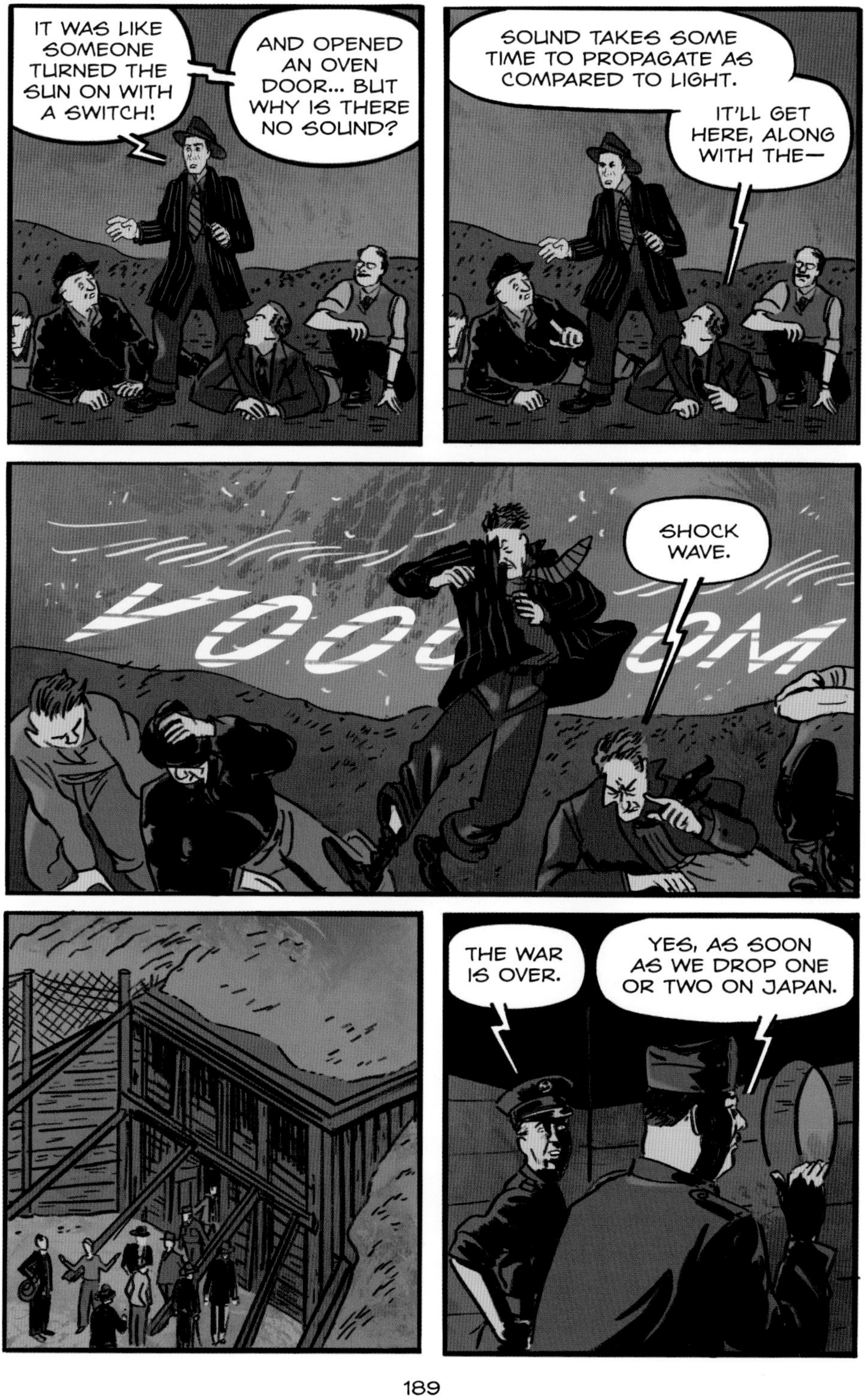
IT WAS LIKE SOMEONE TURNED THE SUN ON WITH A SWITCH!
AND OPENED AN OVEN DOOR... BUT WHY IS THERE NO SOUND?
SOUND TAKES SOME TIME TO PROPAGATE AS COMPARED TO LIGHT.
IT'LL GET HERE, ALONG WITH THE—
VOOOOOM
SHOCK WAVE.
THE WAR IS OVER.
YES, AS SOON AS WE DROP ONE OR TWO ON JAPAN.

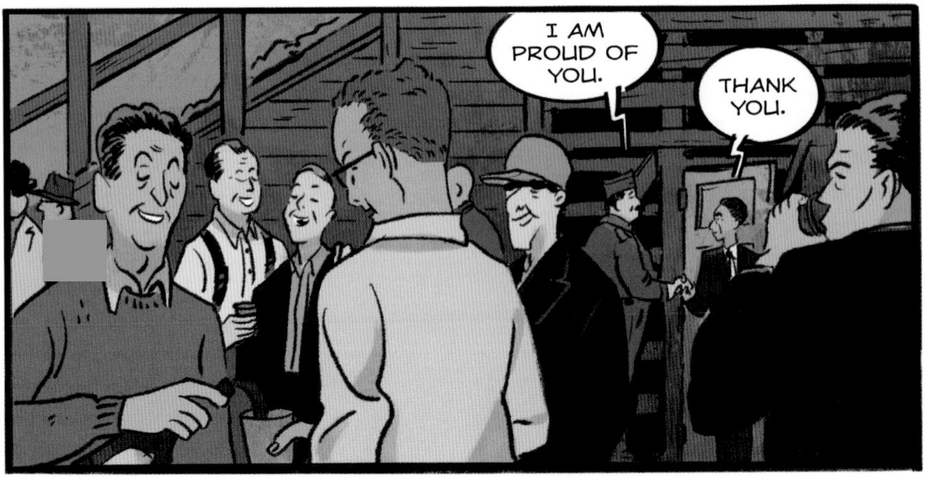
I AM PROUD OF YOU.
THANK YOU.

The feeling of celebration died quickly. The scientists felt a chill that was not the morning cold.

It was the chill of knowing they had used their life's passion—the study of physics—to build the deadliest weapon in human history.

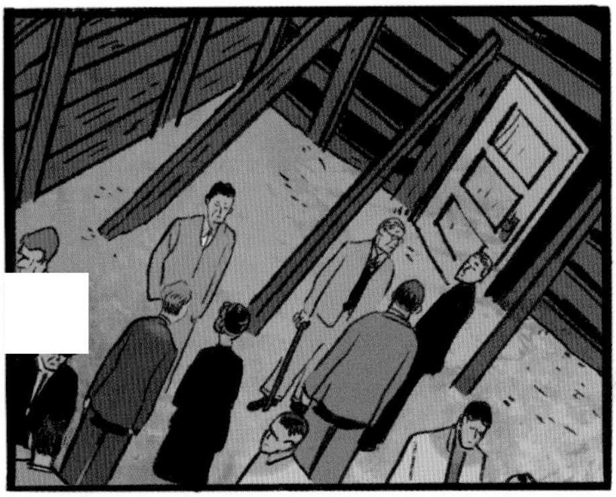

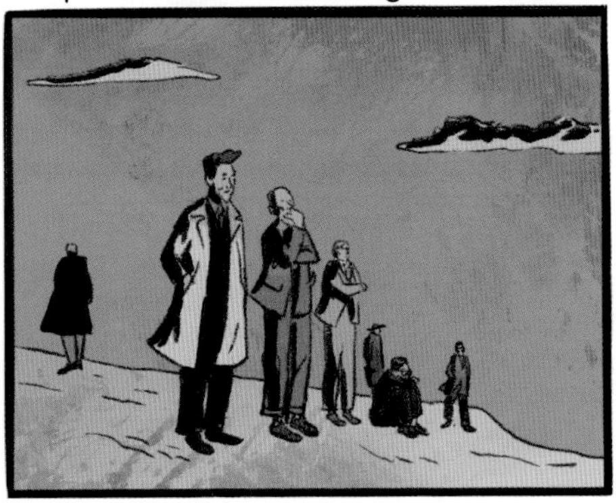

Robert Oppenheimer thought of a line from the ancient Hindu scripture the Bhagavad Gita, a dramatic moment in which the god Vishnu declares:

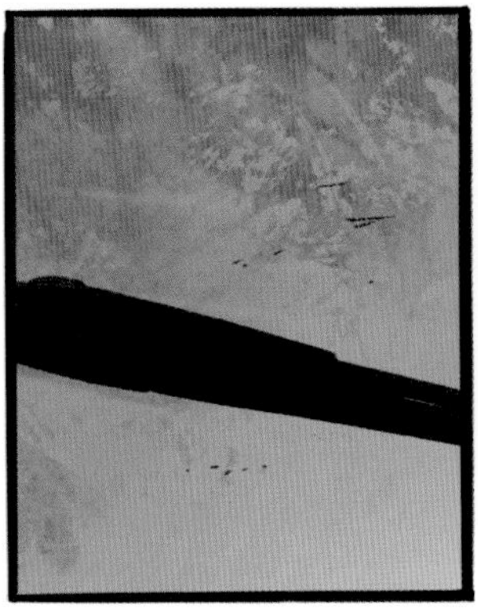

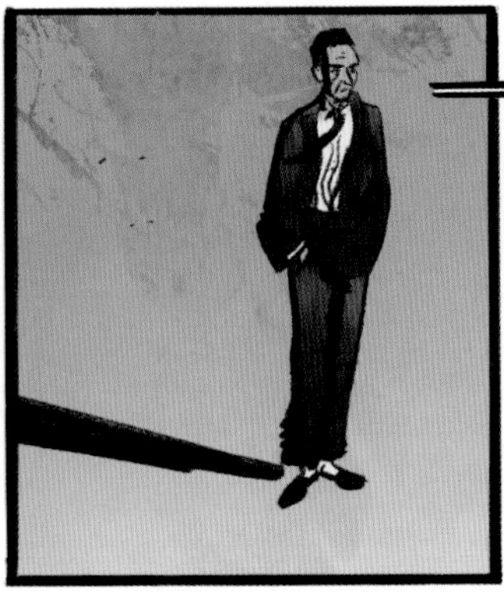

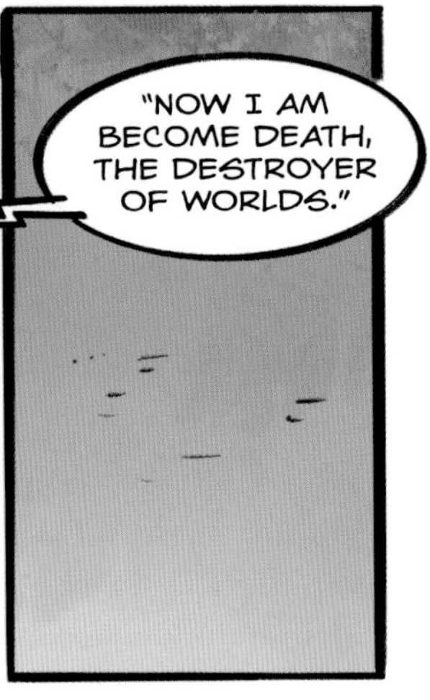
"NOW I AM BECOME DEATH, THE DESTROYER OF WORLDS."

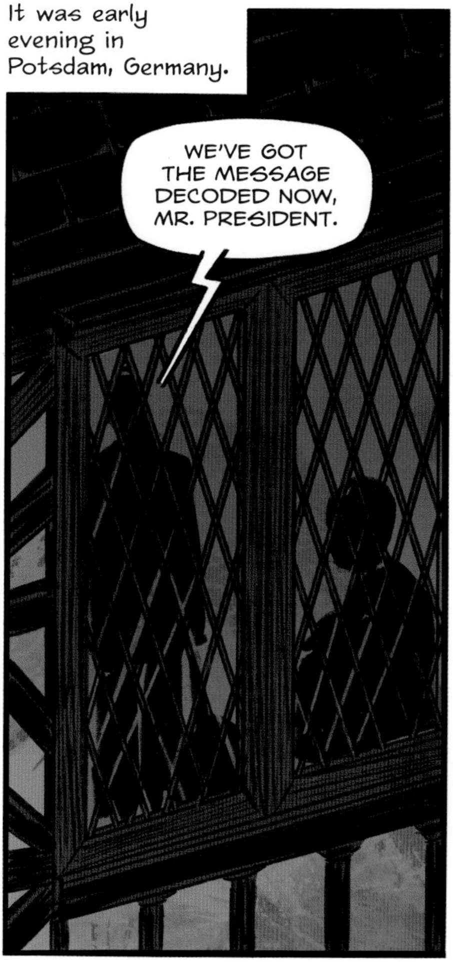
It was early evening in Potsdam, Germany.
WE'VE GOT THE MESSAGE DECODED NOW, MR. PRESIDENT.

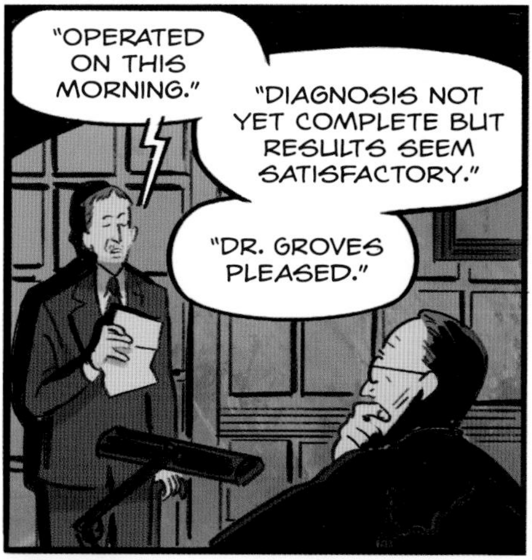
"OPERATED ON THIS MORNING."
"DIAGNOSIS NOT YET COMPLETE BUT RESULTS SEEM SATISFACTORY."
"DR. GROVES PLEASED."

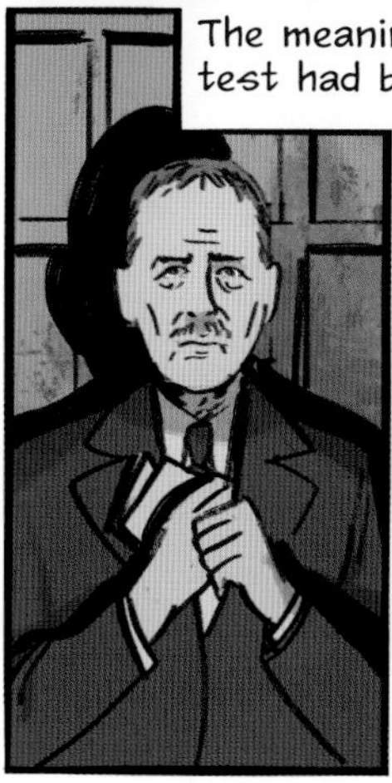
The meaning was clear—the test had been a success.

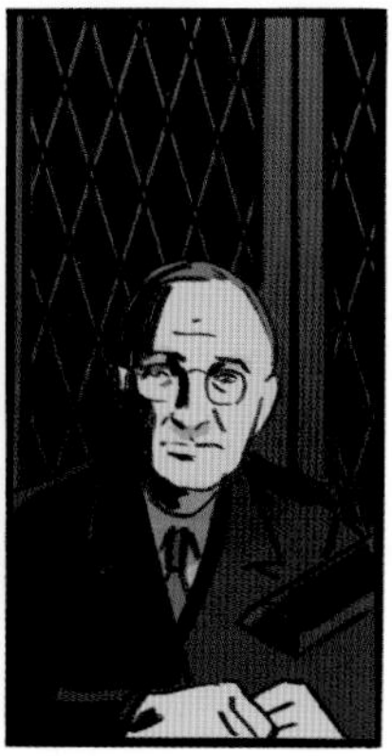

Nearly 6,000 miles to the west, at Hunter's Point Naval Shipyard on San Francisco Bay, sailors loaded a large crate aboard the USS *Indianapolis*.

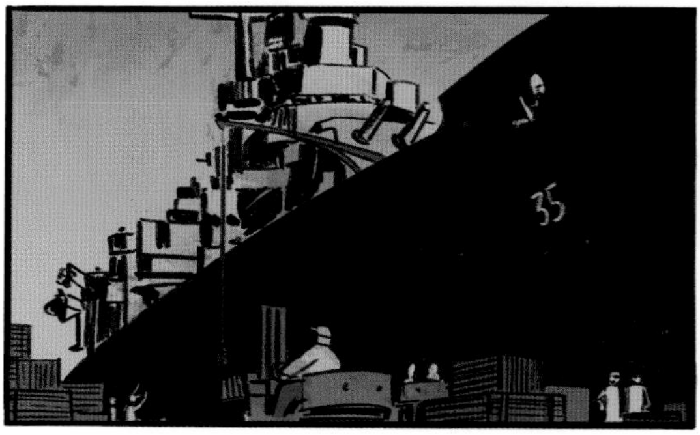
35

Inside was the gun assembly for the uranium bomb designed at Los Alamos.

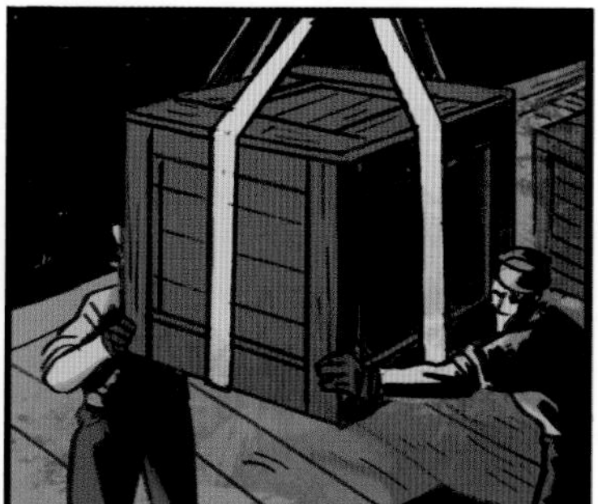

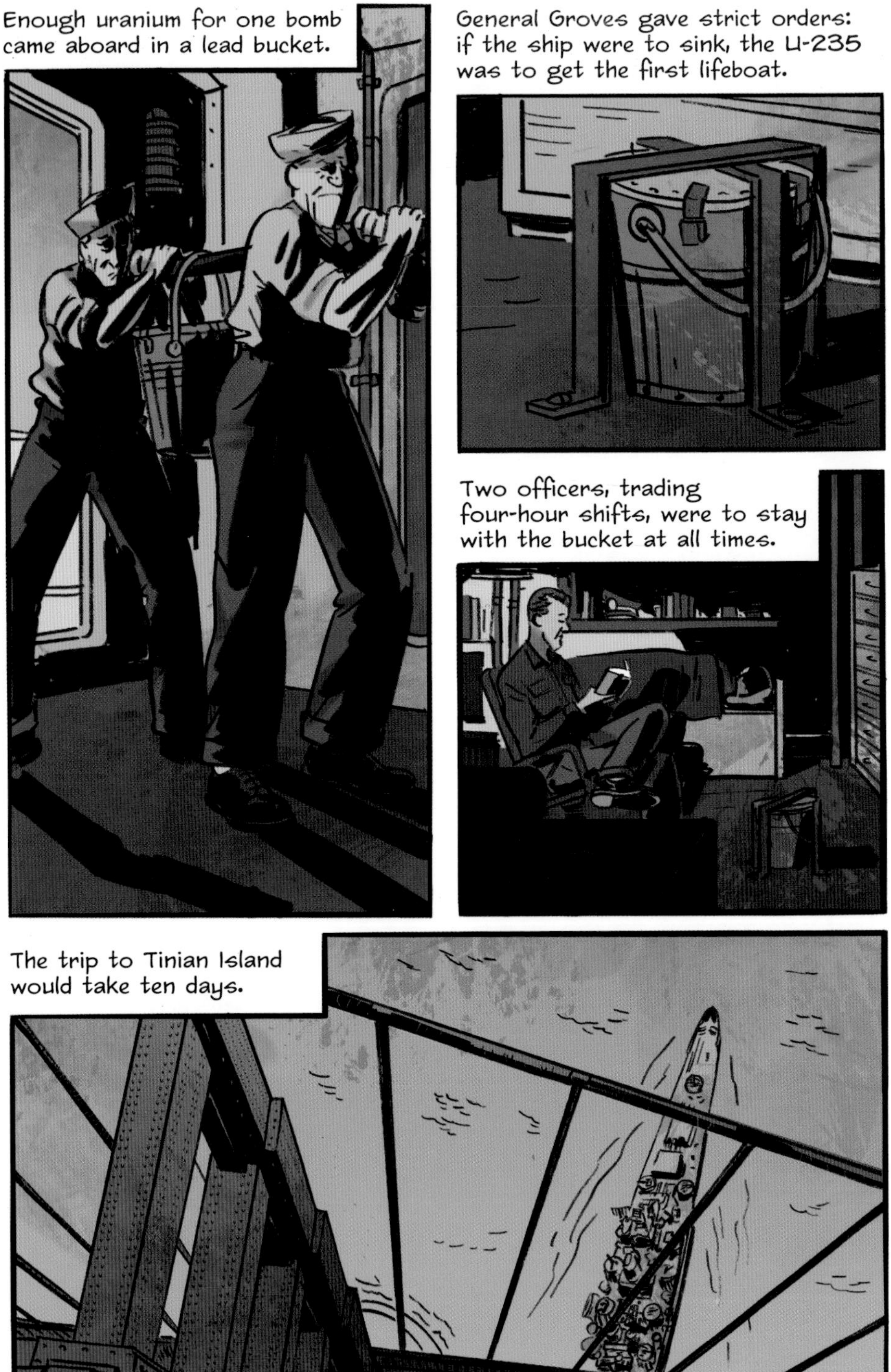
Enough uranium for one bomb came aboard in a lead bucket.
General Groves gave strict orders: if the ship were to sink, the U-235 was to get the first lifeboat.
Two officers, trading four-hour shifts, were to stay with the bucket at all times.
The trip to Tinian Island would take ten days.

Chapter 5

Scorpions in a Bottle

"Little Boy" bomb design

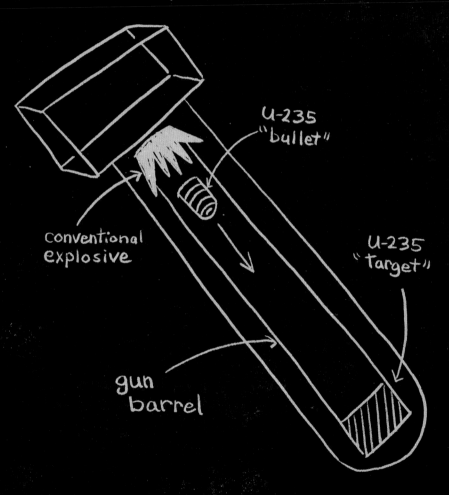

U-235 "bullet"

conventional explosive

U-235 "target"

gun barrel

In Potsdam, Germany, Harry Truman and Winston Churchill prepared for their meeting with Joseph Stalin.

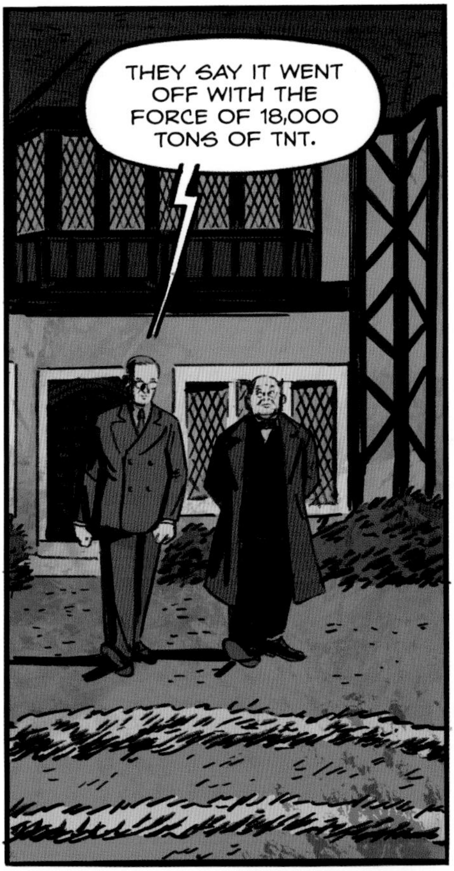
THEY SAY IT WENT OFF WITH THE FORCE OF 18,000 TONS OF TNT.

They reviewed a more complete report from the Trinity test.

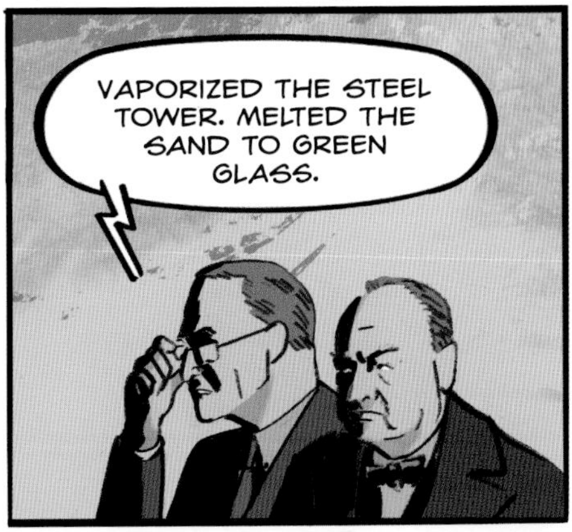
VAPORIZED THE STEEL TOWER. MELTED THE SAND TO GREEN GLASS.

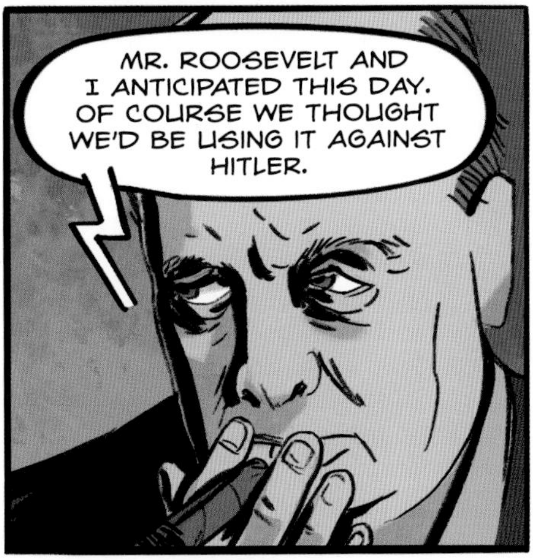
MR. ROOSEVELT AND I ANTICIPATED THIS DAY. OF COURSE WE THOUGHT WE'D BE USING IT AGAINST HITLER.

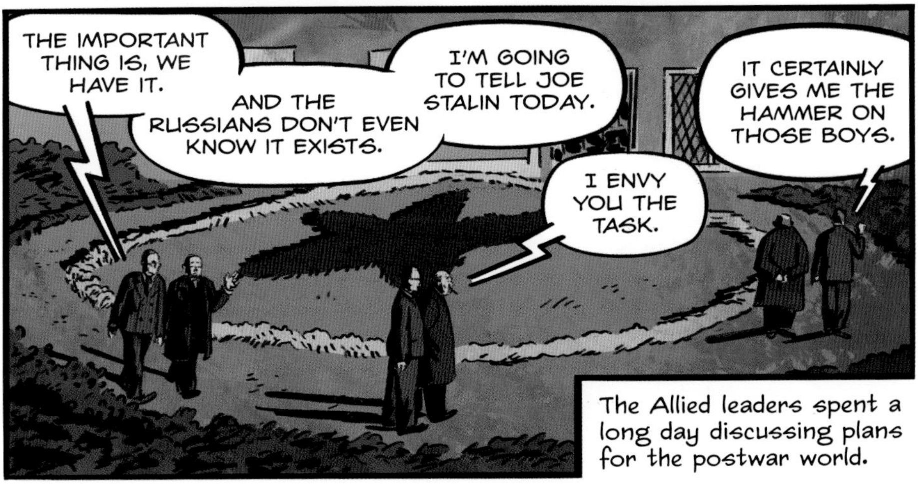
THE IMPORTANT THING IS, WE HAVE IT.
AND THE RUSSIANS DON'T EVEN KNOW IT EXISTS.
I'M GOING TO TELL JOE STALIN TODAY.
I ENVY YOU THE TASK.
IT CERTAINLY GIVES ME THE HAMMER ON THOSE BOYS.

The Allied leaders spent a long day discussing plans for the postwar world.

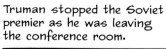

Truman stopped the Soviet premier as he was leaving the conference room.

WE HAVE DISCOVERED A WEAPON OF UNUSUAL DESTRUCTIVE FORCE.

A NEW KIND OF BOMB.

GLAD TO HEAR IT.

I HOPE YOU MAKE GOOD USE OF IT AGAINST JAPAN.

Then Stalin left the room.

HOW DID IT GO?

HE NEVER ASKED A QUESTION.

I'M NOT SURE HE UNDERSTOOD...

Truman never guessed that Stalin already knew all about the Manhattan Project.

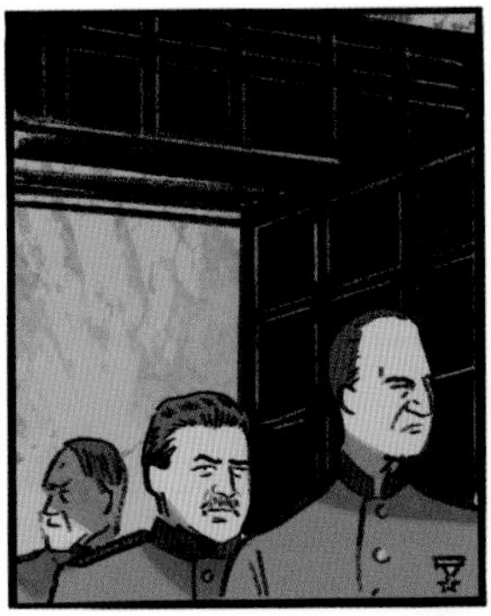

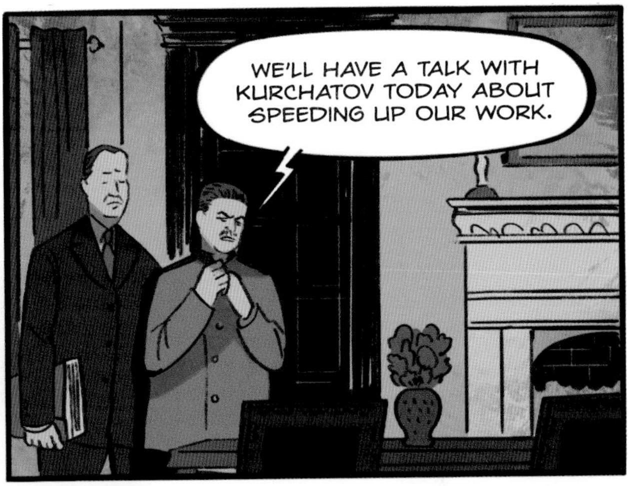
WE'LL HAVE A TALK WITH KURCHATOV TODAY ABOUT SPEEDING UP OUR WORK.

The *Indianapolis* cruised steadily toward Tinian.

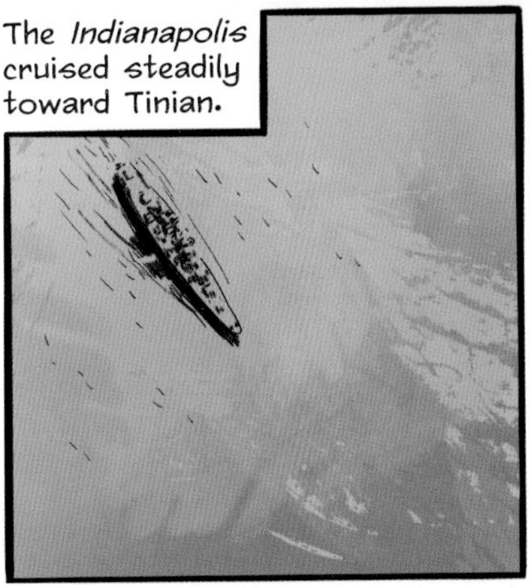

American bombers pounded Japan night after night, flattening and burning entire cities.

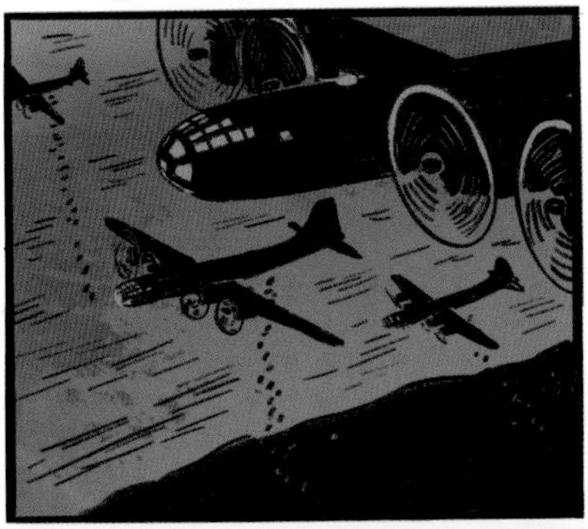

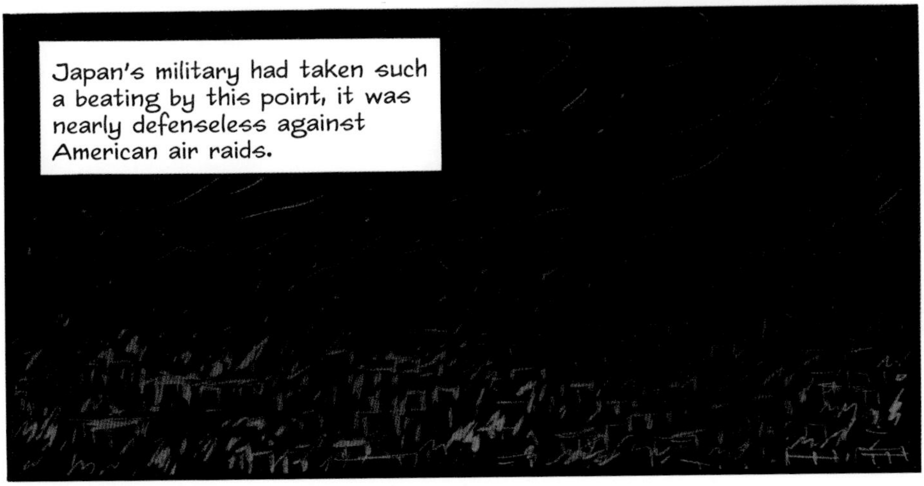
Japan's military had taken such a beating by this point, it was nearly defenseless against American air raids.

At Potsdam, Truman met with his top advisers.

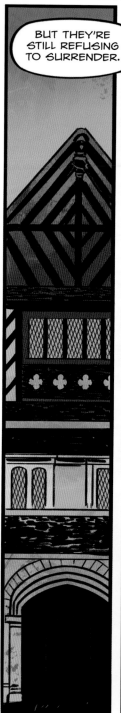

BUT THEY'RE STILL REFUSING TO SURRENDER.

WE'LL HAVE A MILLION MEN READY TO INVADE JAPAN BY NOVEMBER.

MILLIONS MORE TO FOLLOW.

HOW MANY AMERICANS ARE LIKELY TO BE KILLED OR WOUNDED?

WE'VE LOST 50,000 DEAD IN THE PACIFIC JUST SINCE MARCH.

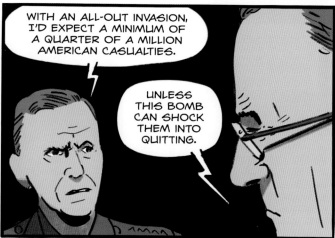

WITH AN ALL-OUT INVASION, I'D EXPECT A MINIMUM OF A QUARTER OF A MILLION AMERICAN CASUALTIES.

UNLESS THIS BOMB CAN SHOCK THEM INTO QUITTING.

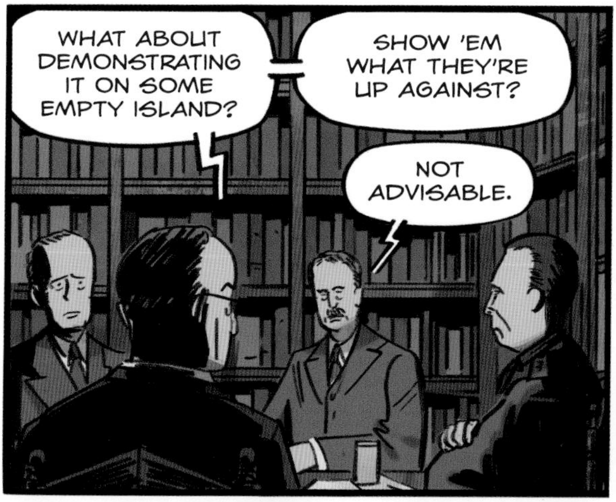
WHAT ABOUT DEMONSTRATING IT ON SOME EMPTY ISLAND?
SHOW 'EM WHAT THEY'RE UP AGAINST?
NOT ADVISABLE.

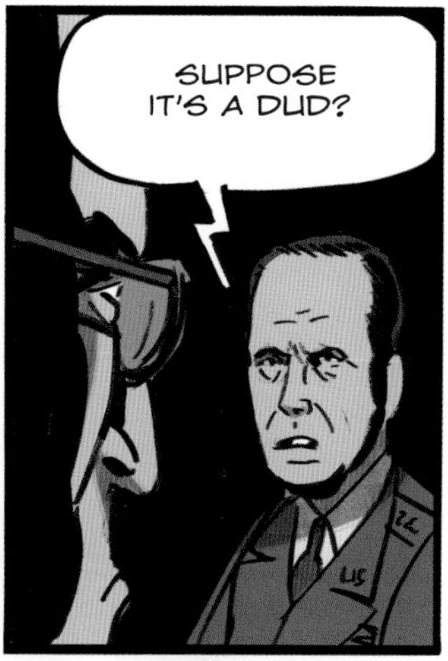
SUPPOSE IT'S A DUD?

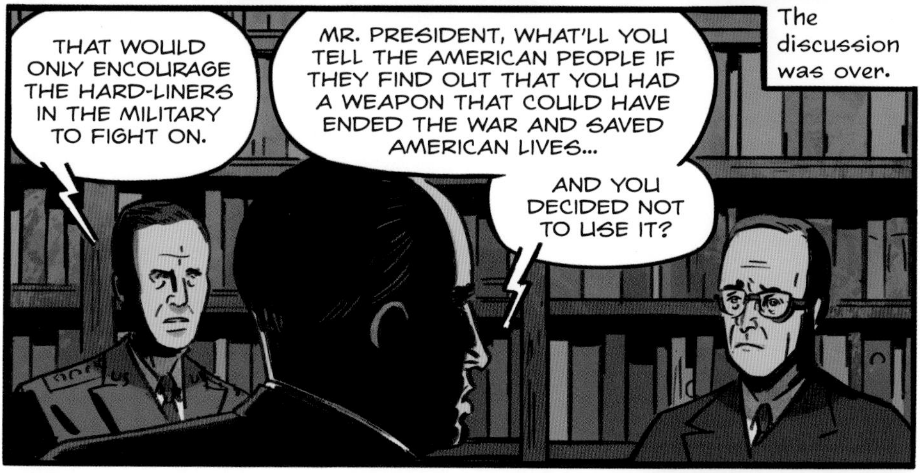
The discussion was over.
THAT WOULD ONLY ENCOURAGE THE HARD-LINERS IN THE MILITARY TO FIGHT ON.
MR. PRESIDENT, WHAT'LL YOU TELL THE AMERICAN PEOPLE IF THEY FIND OUT THAT YOU HAD A WEAPON THAT COULD HAVE ENDED THE WAR AND SAVED AMERICAN LIVES...
AND YOU DECIDED NOT TO USE IT?

On July 26, Truman and Churchill issued the Potsdam Declaration—a final demand that Japan end the fighting.

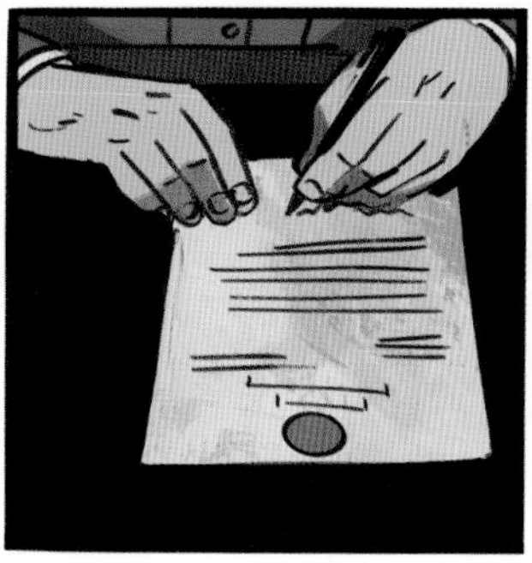

There was no mention of the atomic bomb, but the document closed with a harsh warning.

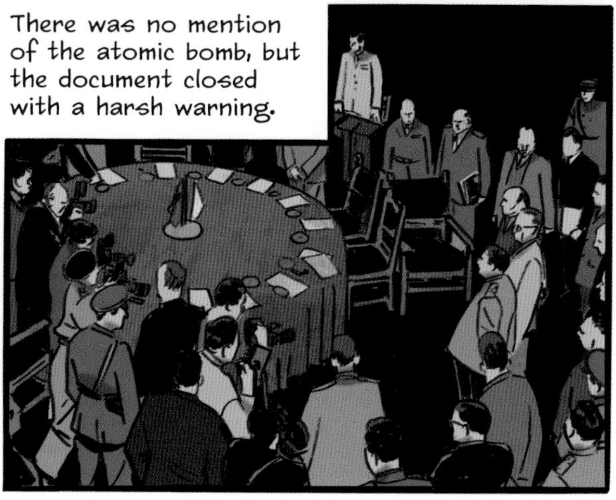

The six members of Japan's Supreme Council considered their options.

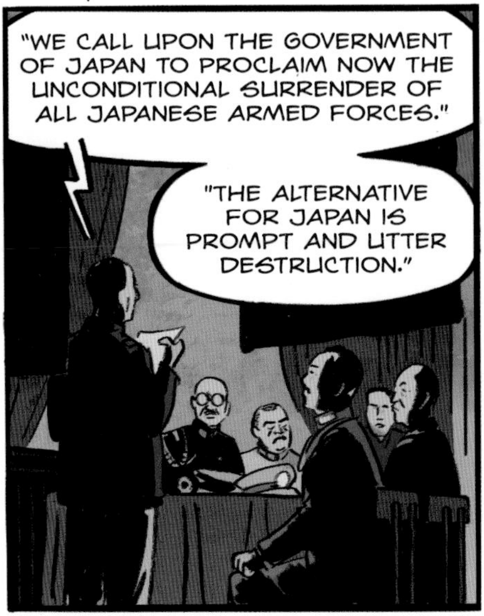
"WE CALL UPON THE GOVERNMENT OF JAPAN TO PROCLAIM NOW THE UNCONDITIONAL SURRENDER OF ALL JAPANESE ARMED FORCES."
"THE ALTERNATIVE FOR JAPAN IS PROMPT AND UTTER DESTRUCTION."

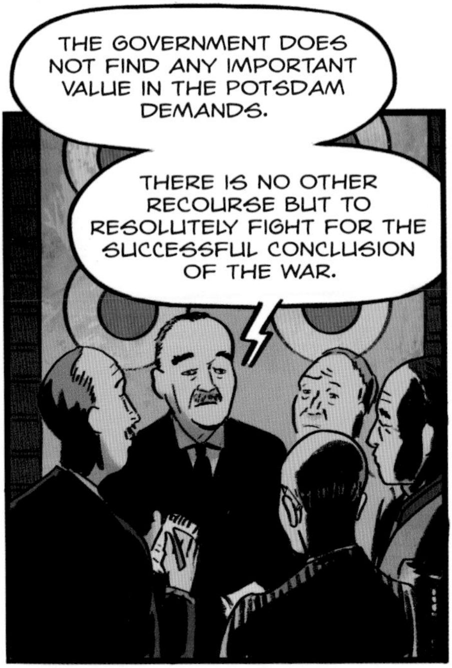
THE GOVERNMENT DOES NOT FIND ANY IMPORTANT VALUE IN THE POTSDAM DEMANDS.
THERE IS NO OTHER RECOURSE BUT TO RESOLUTELY FIGHT FOR THE SUCCESSFUL CONCLUSION OF THE WAR.

In an air-conditioned hut on Tinian Island, a team from Los Alamos assembled the uranium bomb.

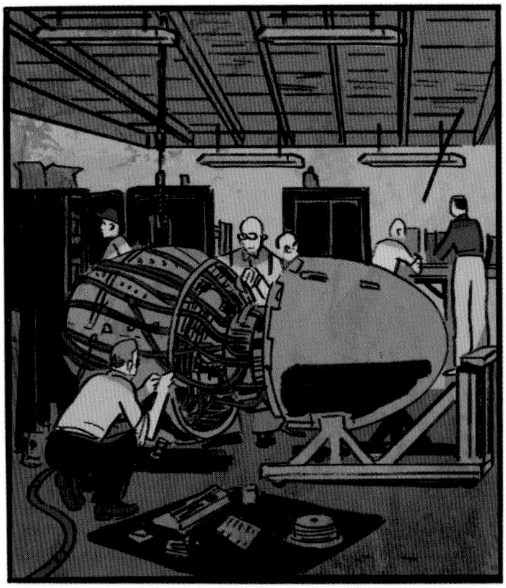

They nicknamed the bomb Little Boy. It was ready on August 2.

Now Paul Tibbets was just waiting on the weather.

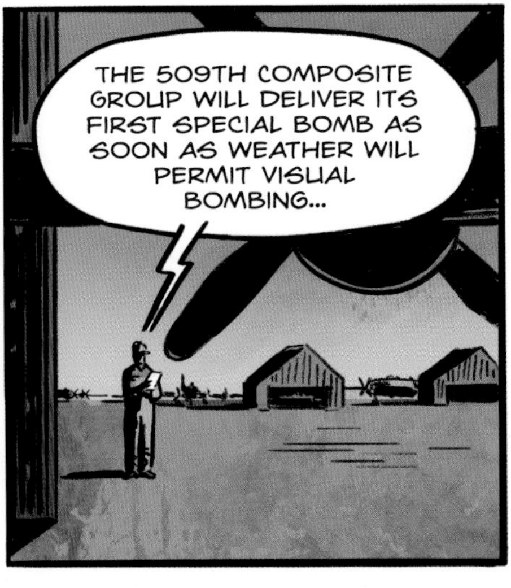
THE 509TH COMPOSITE GROUP WILL DELIVER ITS FIRST SPECIAL BOMB AS SOON AS WEATHER WILL PERMIT VISUAL BOMBING...

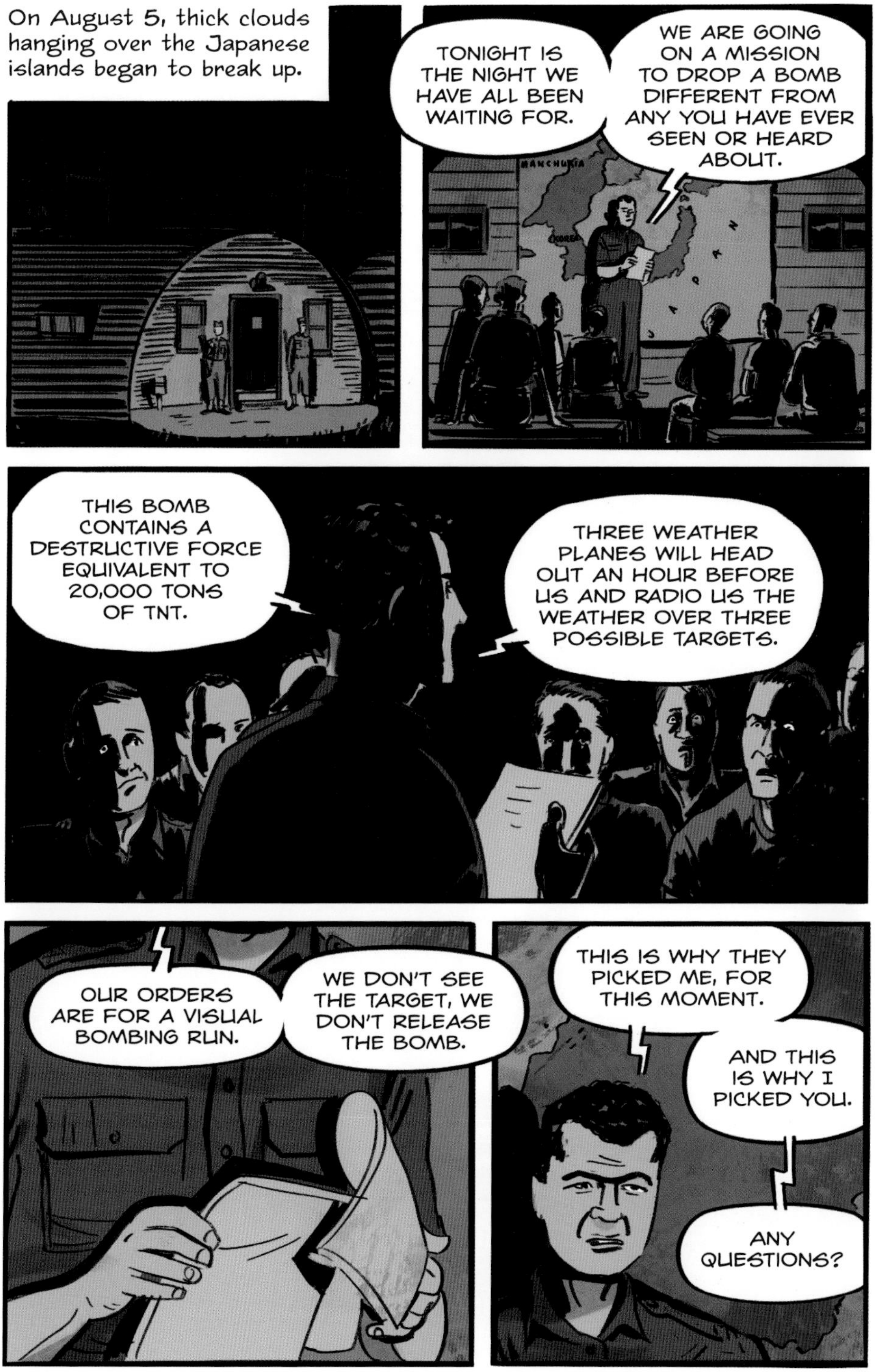
On August 5, thick clouds hanging over the Japanese islands began to break up.
TONIGHT IS THE NIGHT WE HAVE ALL BEEN WAITING FOR.
WE ARE GOING ON A MISSION TO DROP A BOMB DIFFERENT FROM ANY YOU HAVE EVER SEEN OR HEARD ABOUT.
THIS BOMB CONTAINS A DESTRUCTIVE FORCE EQUIVALENT TO 20,000 TONS OF TNT.
THREE WEATHER PLANES WILL HEAD OUT AN HOUR BEFORE US AND RADIO US THE WEATHER OVER THREE POSSIBLE TARGETS.
OUR ORDERS ARE FOR A VISUAL BOMBING RUN.
WE DON'T SEE THE TARGET, WE DON'T RELEASE THE BOMB.
THIS IS WHY THEY PICKED ME, FOR THIS MOMENT.
AND THIS IS WHY I PICKED YOU.
ANY QUESTIONS?

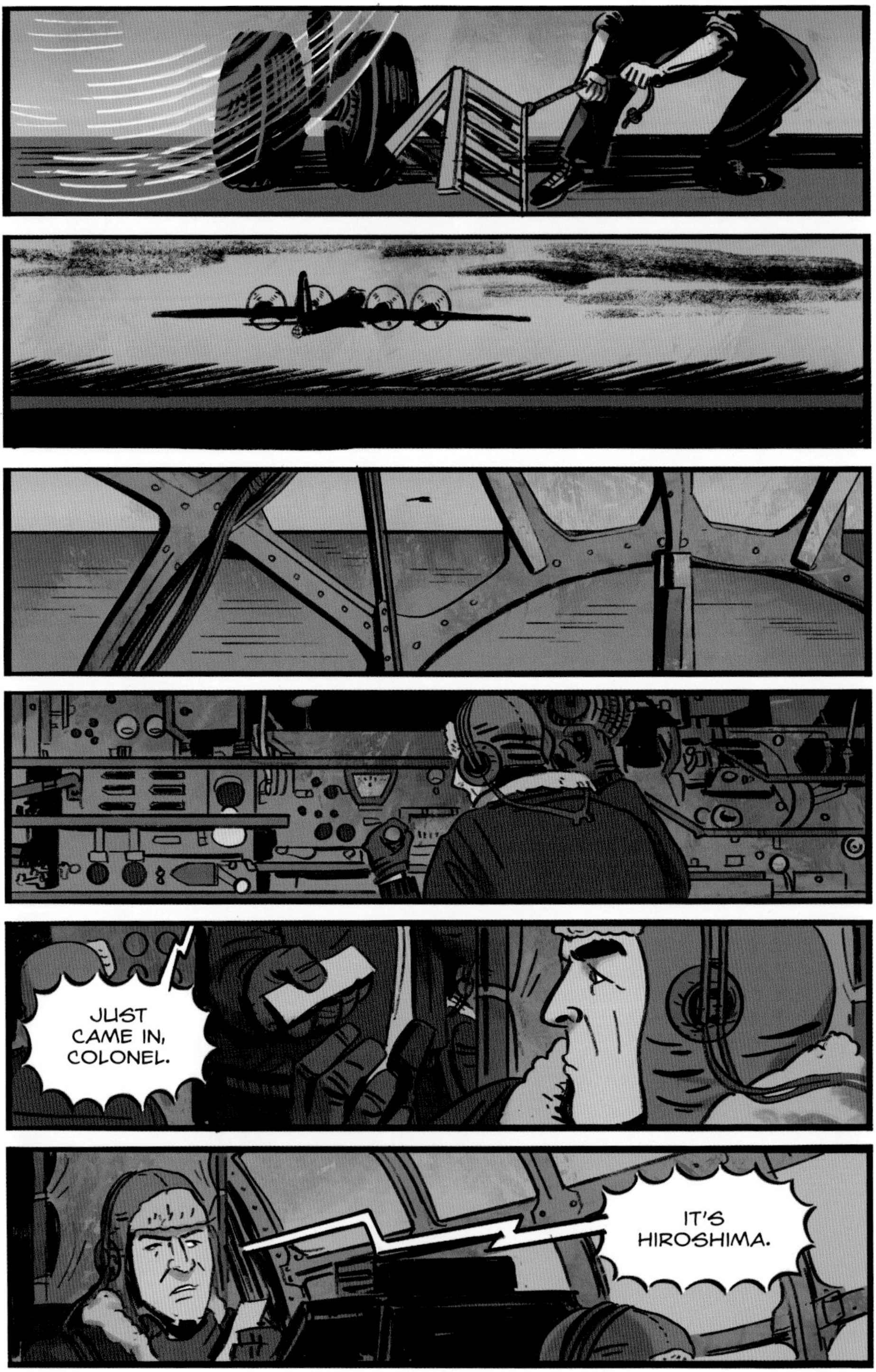
JUST CAME IN, COLONEL.
IT'S HIROSHIMA.

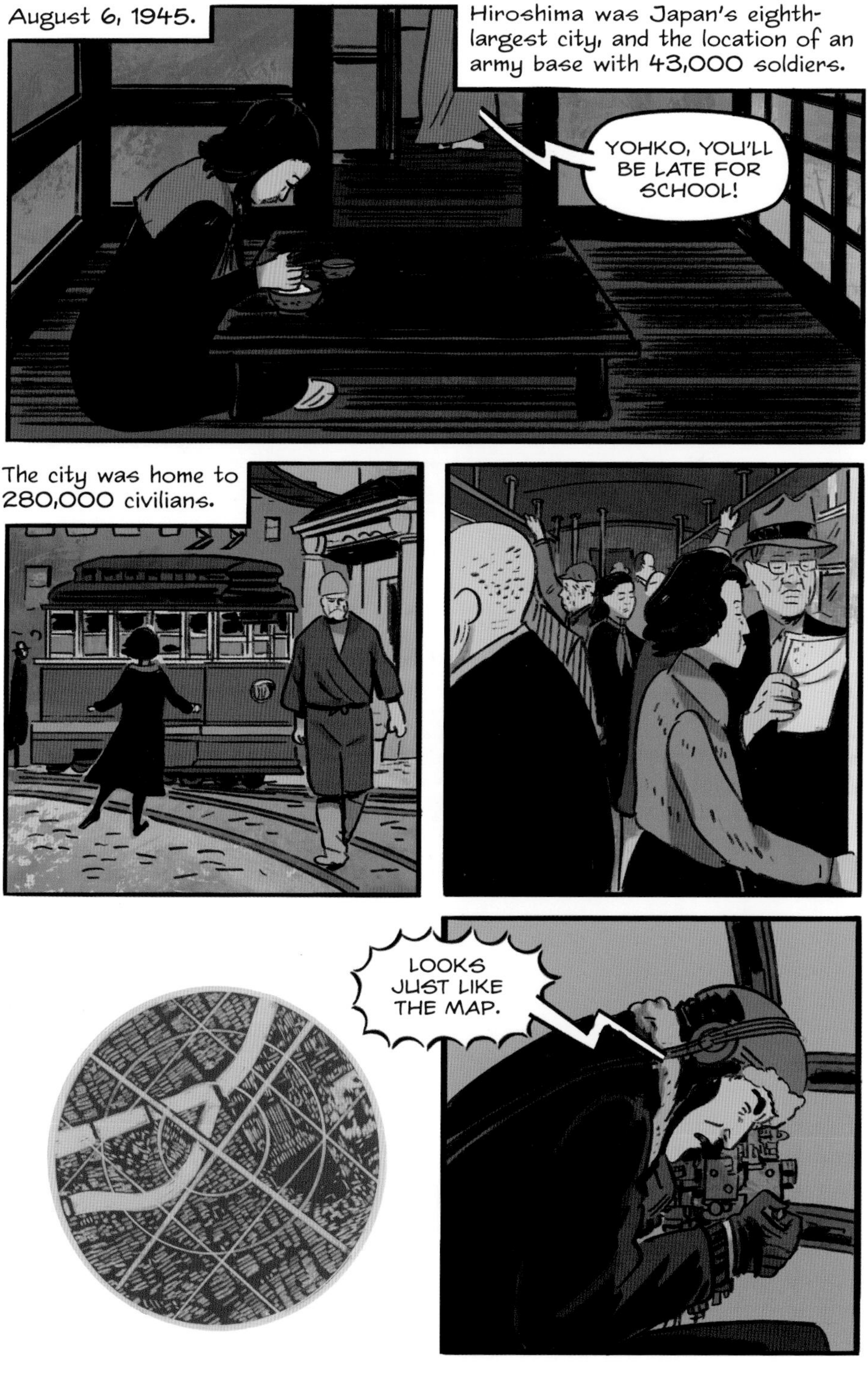
August 6, 1945.
Hiroshima was Japan's eighth-largest city, and the location of an army base with 43,000 soldiers.
YOHKO, YOU'LL BE LATE FOR SCHOOL!
The city was home to 280,000 civilians.
LOOKS JUST LIKE THE MAP.

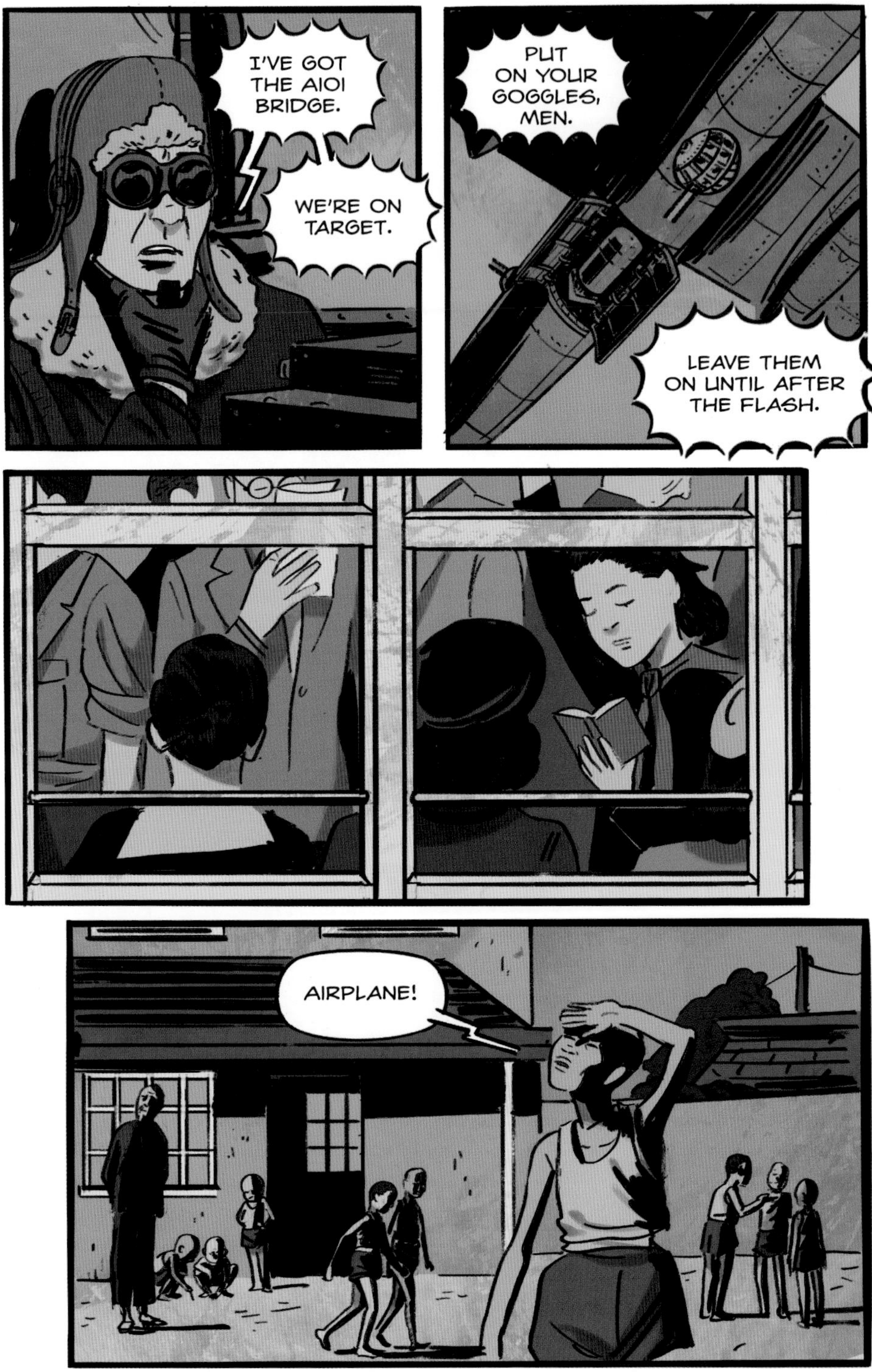
I'VE GOT THE AIOI BRIDGE.
WE'RE ON TARGET.
PUT ON YOUR GOGGLES, MEN.
LEAVE THEM ON UNTIL AFTER THE FLASH.
AIRPLANE!

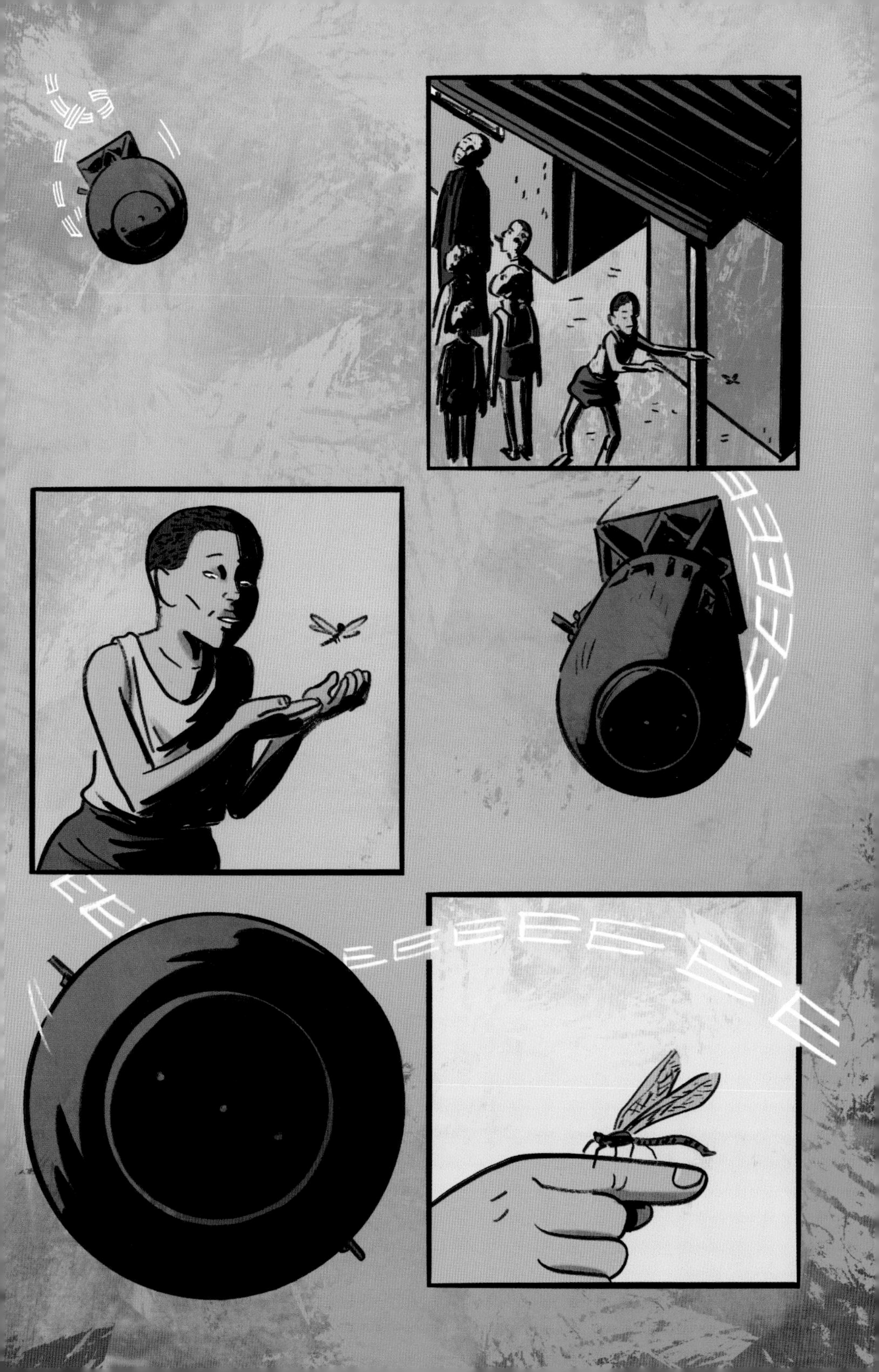

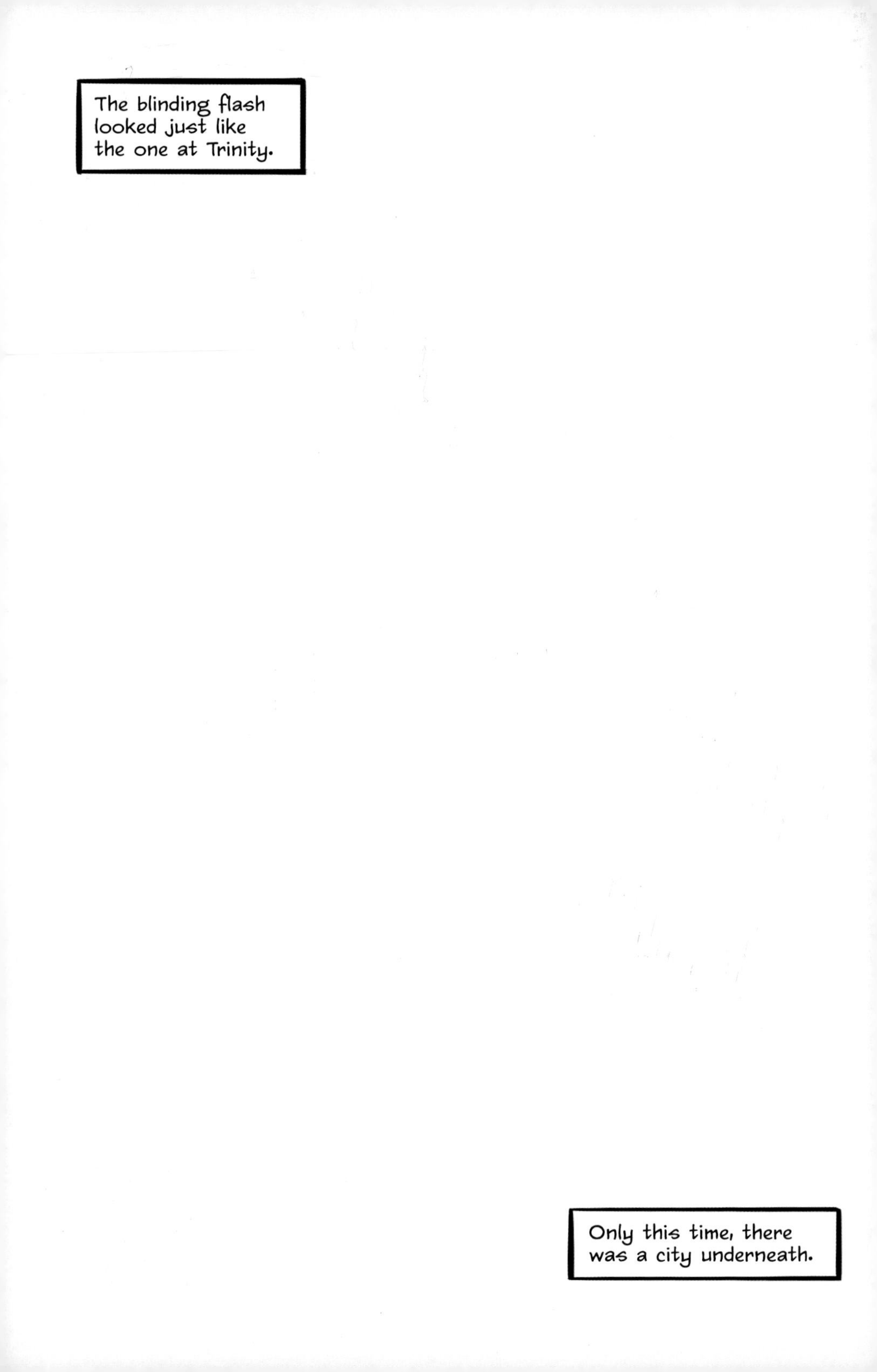
The blinding flash looked just like the one at Trinity.
Only this time, there was a city underneath.

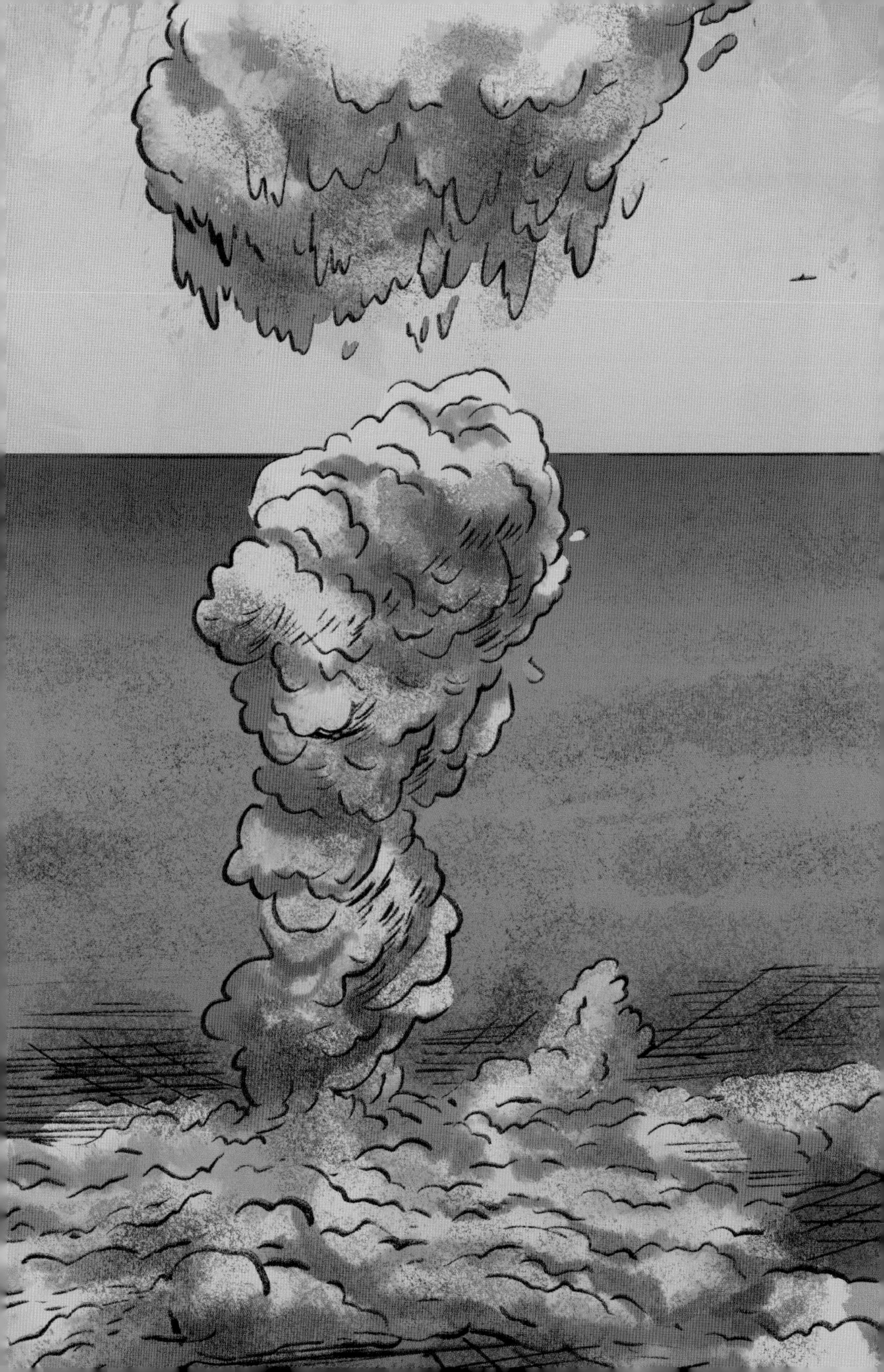

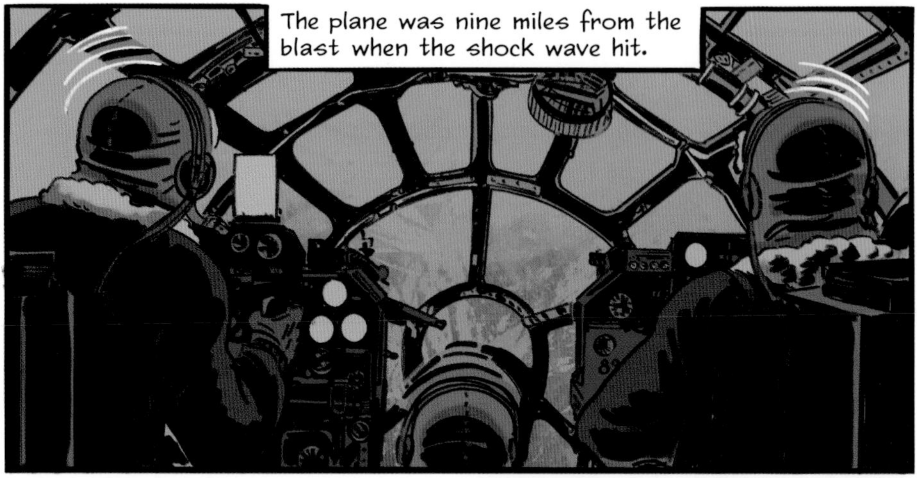
The plane was nine miles from the blast when the shock wave hit.

When Tibbets knew they were safe, he turned back and circled the city.

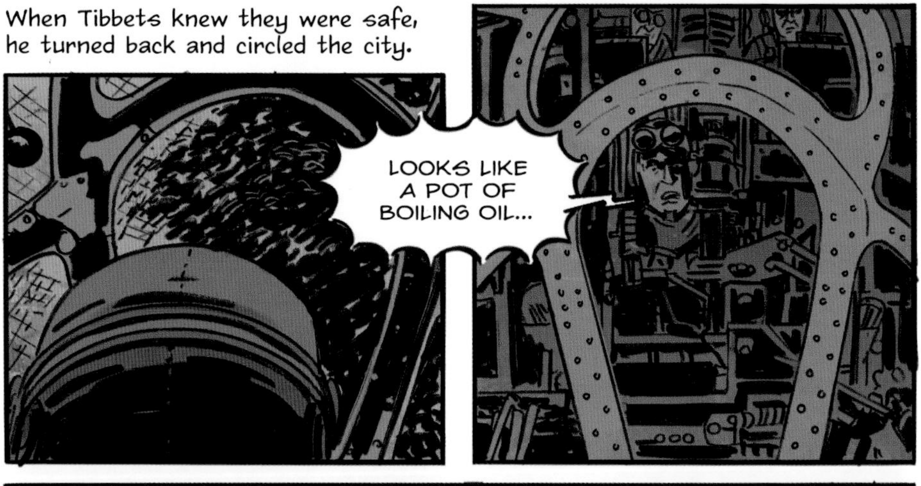
LOOKS LIKE A POT OF BOILING OIL...

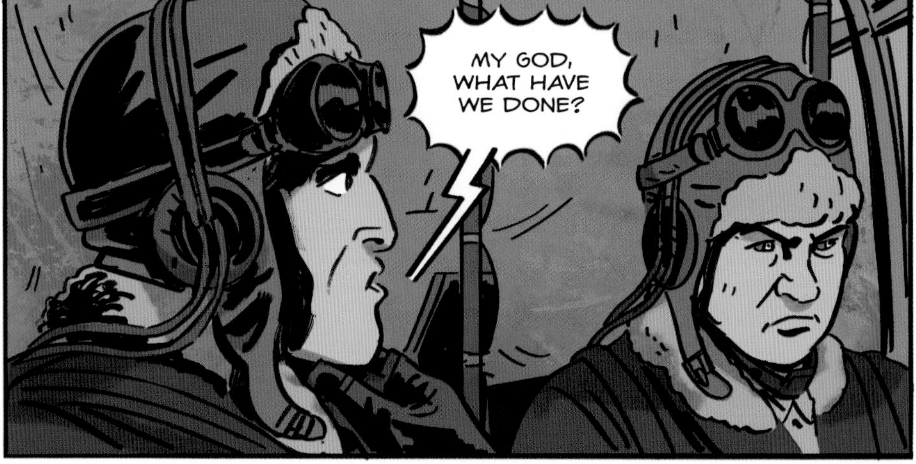
MY GOD, WHAT HAVE WE DONE?

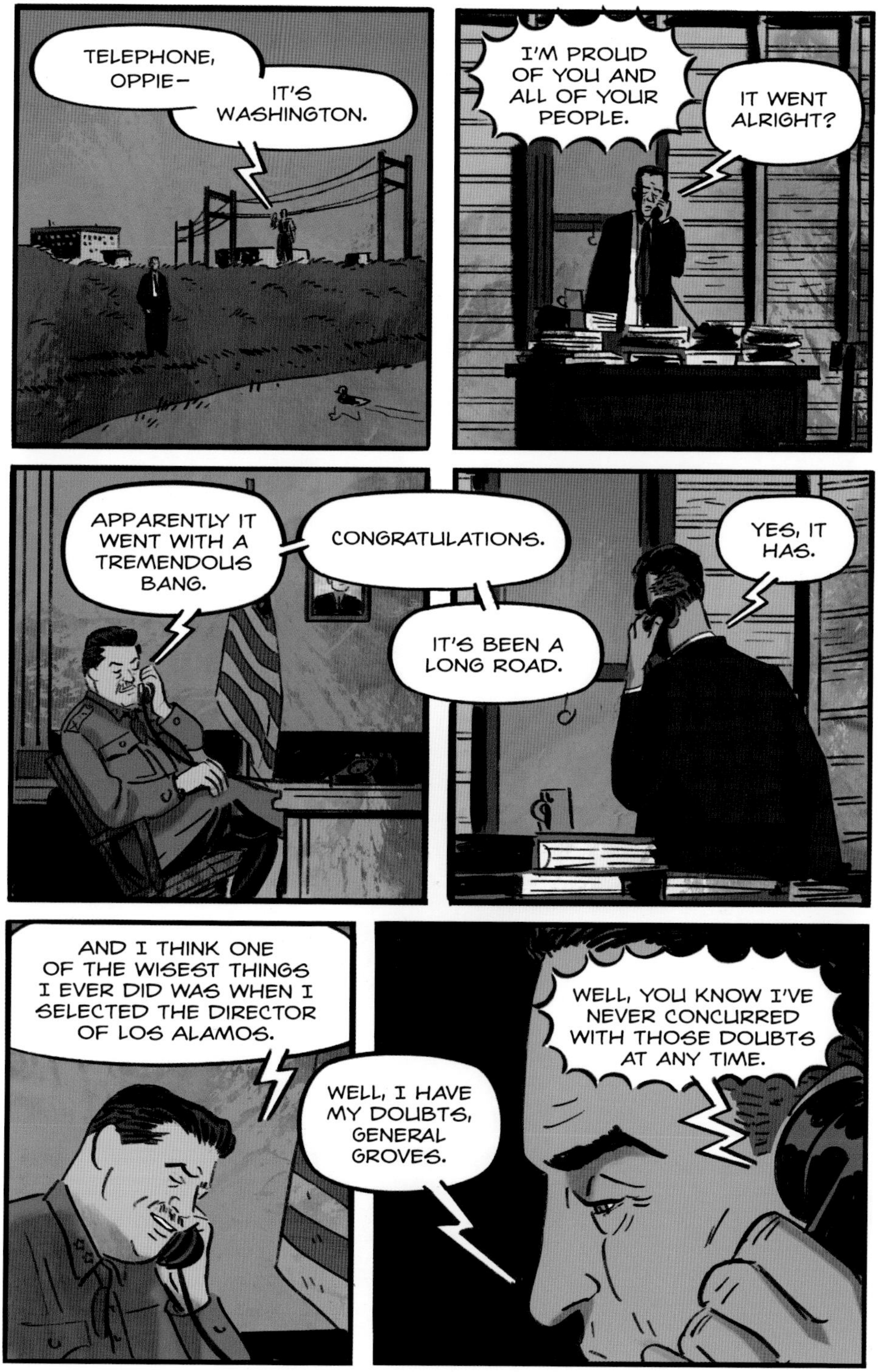
TELEPHONE, OPPIE–
IT'S WASHINGTON.
I'M PROUD OF YOU AND ALL OF YOUR PEOPLE.
IT WENT ALRIGHT?
APPARENTLY IT WENT WITH A TREMENDOUS BANG.
CONGRATULATIONS.
IT'S BEEN A LONG ROAD.
YES, IT HAS.
AND I THINK ONE OF THE WISEST THINGS I EVER DID WAS WHEN I SELECTED THE DIRECTOR OF LOS ALAMOS.
WELL, I HAVE MY DOUBTS, GENERAL GROVES.
WELL, YOU KNOW I'VE NEVER CONCURRED WITH THOSE DOUBTS AT ANY TIME.

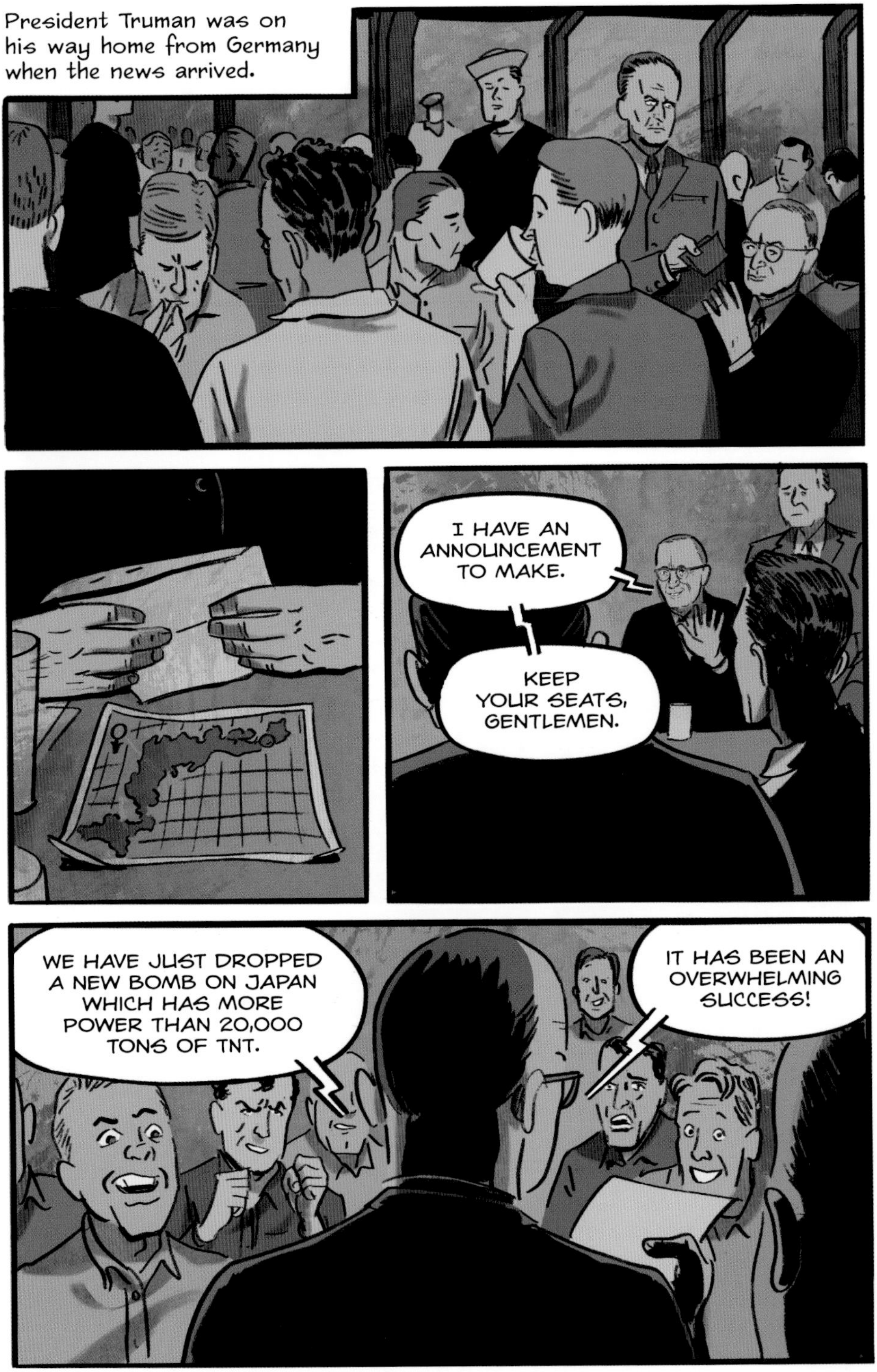
President Truman was on his way home from Germany when the news arrived.
I HAVE AN ANNOUNCEMENT TO MAKE.
KEEP YOUR SEATS, GENTLEMEN.
WE HAVE JUST DROPPED A NEW BOMB ON JAPAN WHICH HAS MORE POWER THAN 20,000 TONS OF TNT.
IT HAS BEEN AN OVERWHELMING SUCCESS!

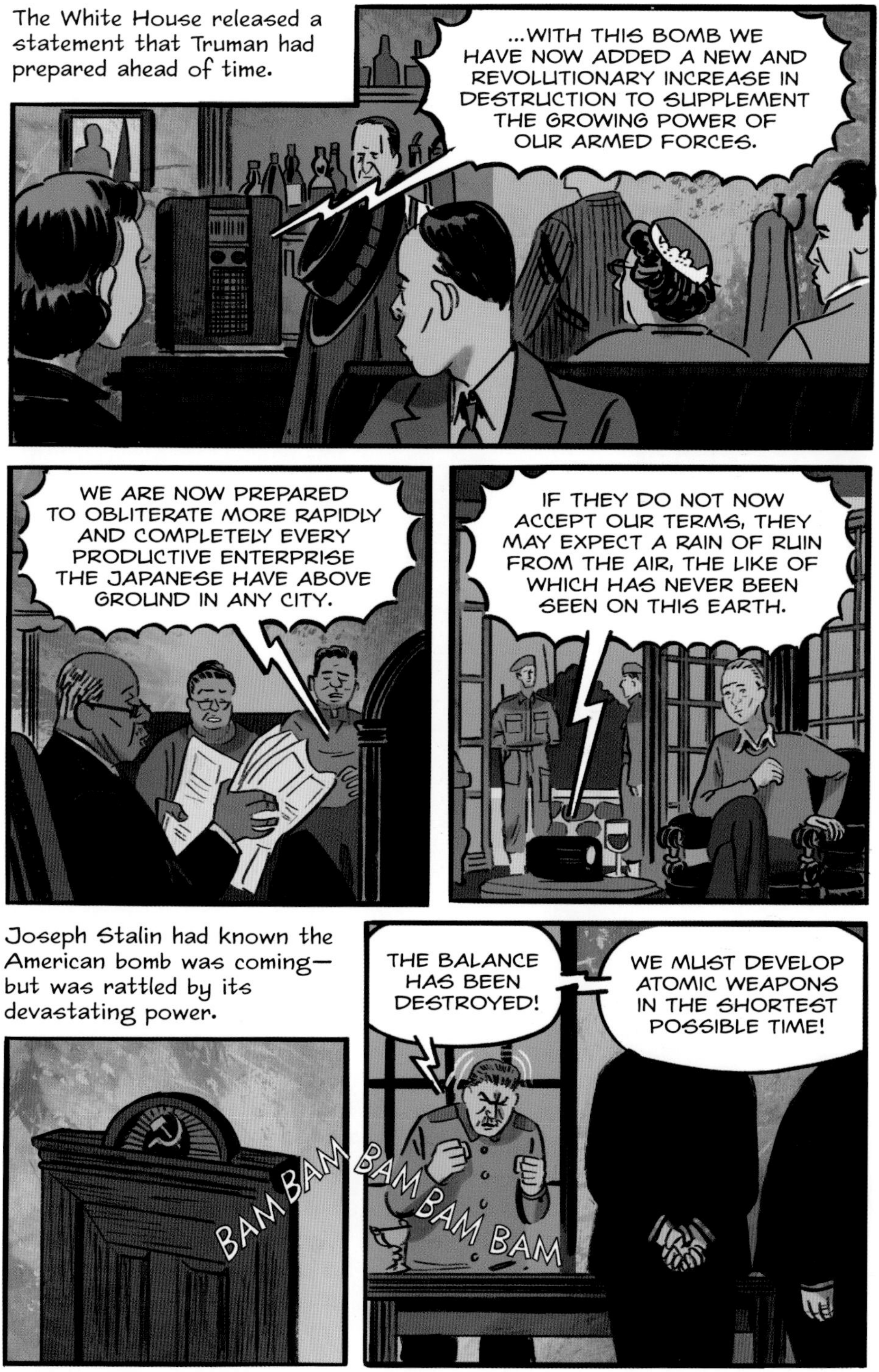
The White House released a statement that Truman had prepared ahead of time.
...WITH THIS BOMB WE HAVE NOW ADDED A NEW AND REVOLUTIONARY INCREASE IN DESTRUCTION TO SUPPLEMENT THE GROWING POWER OF OUR ARMED FORCES.
WE ARE NOW PREPARED TO OBLITERATE MORE RAPIDLY AND COMPLETELY EVERY PRODUCTIVE ENTERPRISE THE JAPANESE HAVE ABOVE GROUND IN ANY CITY.
IF THEY DO NOT NOW ACCEPT OUR TERMS, THEY MAY EXPECT A RAIN OF RUIN FROM THE AIR, THE LIKE OF WHICH HAS NEVER BEEN SEEN ON THIS EARTH.
Joseph Stalin had known the American bomb was coming—but was rattled by its devastating power.
BAM BAM BAM BAM BAM BAM
THE BALANCE HAS BEEN DESTROYED!
WE MUST DEVELOP ATOMIC WEAPONS IN THE SHORTEST POSSIBLE TIME!

Los Alamos.

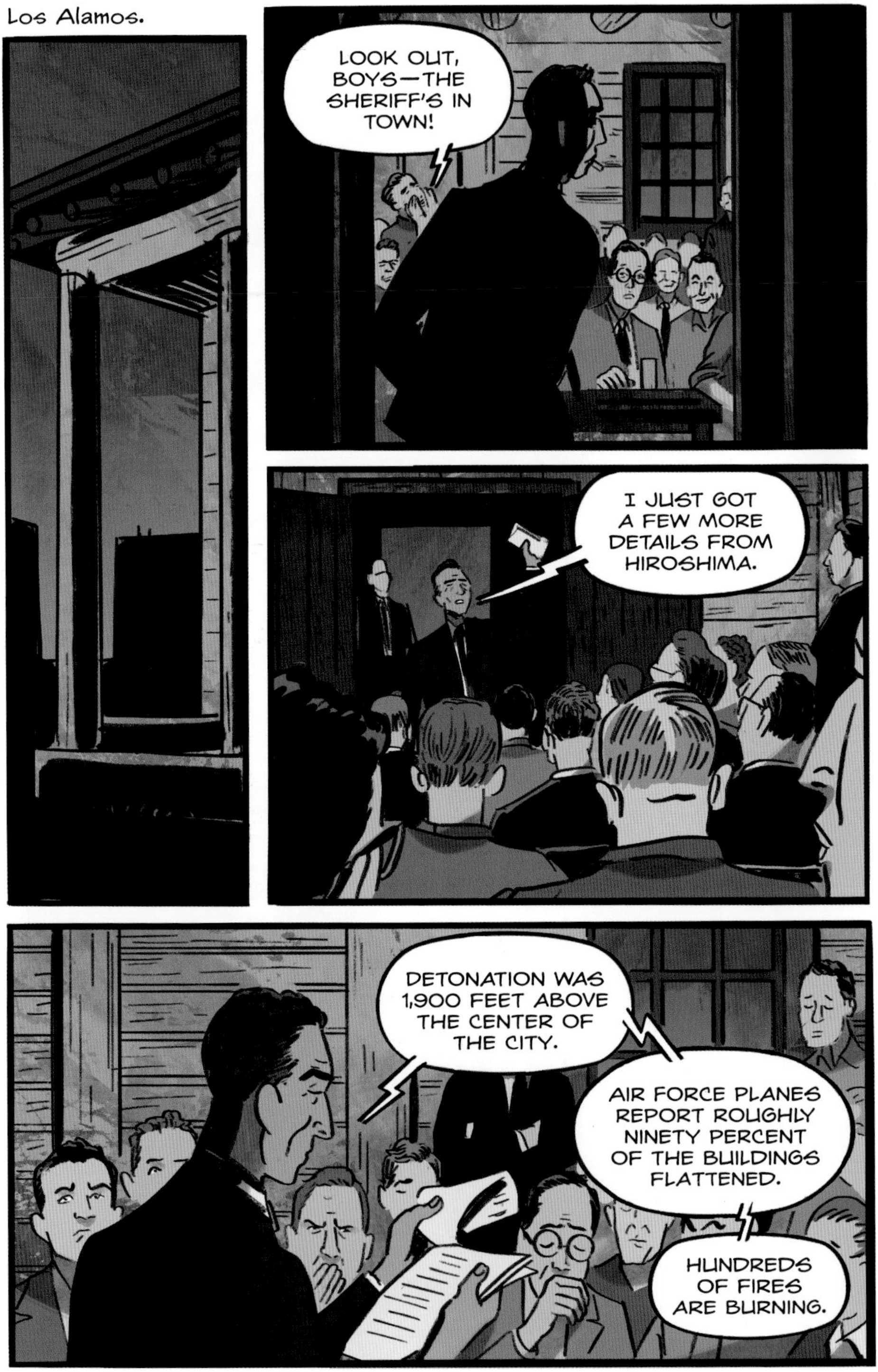
LOOK OUT, BOYS—THE SHERIFF'S IN TOWN!
I JUST GOT A FEW MORE DETAILS FROM HIROSHIMA.
DETONATION WAS 1,900 FEET ABOVE THE CENTER OF THE CITY.
AIR FORCE PLANES REPORT ROUGHLY NINETY PERCENT OF THE BUILDINGS FLATTENED.
HUNDREDS OF FIRES ARE BURNING.

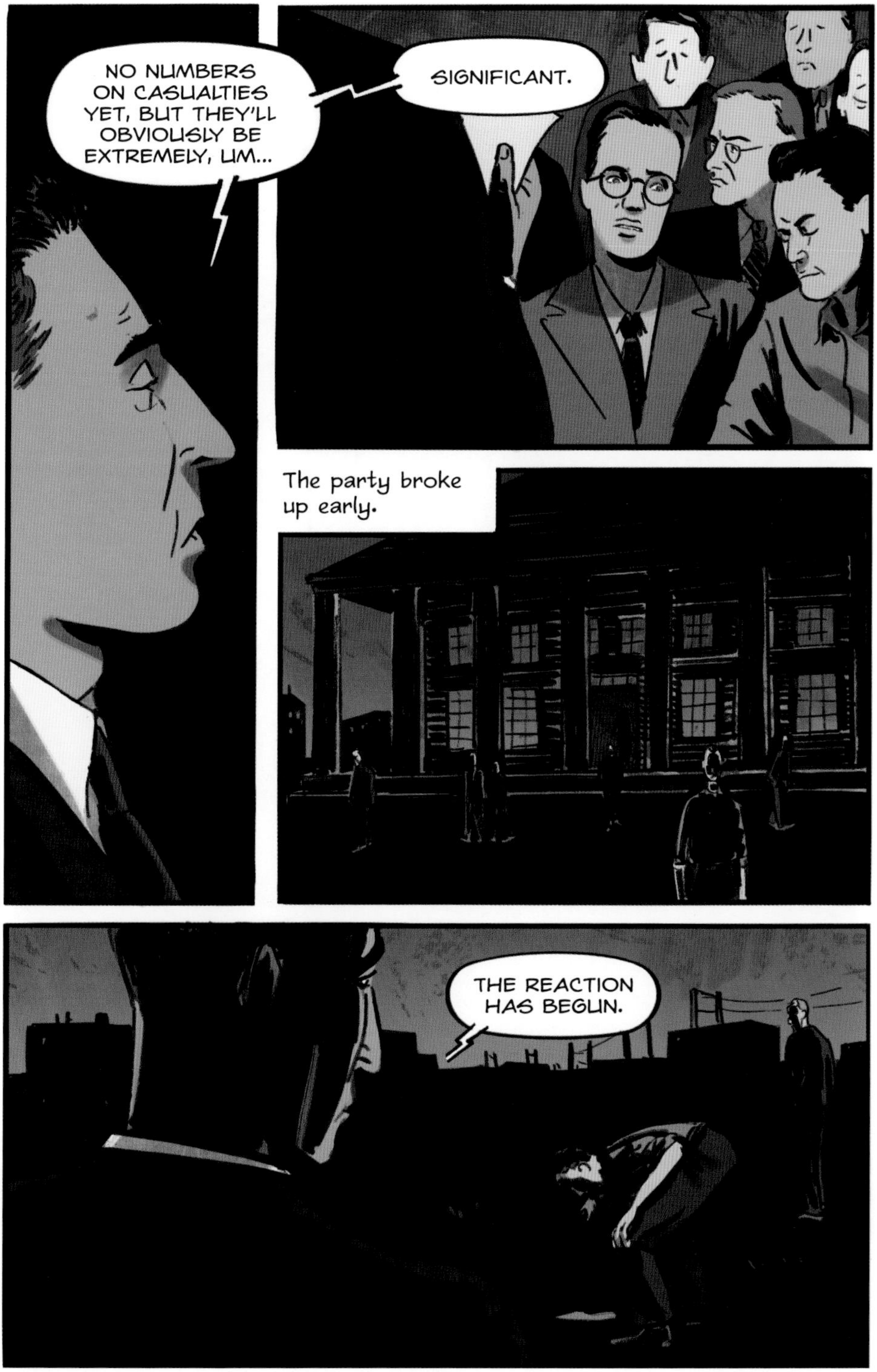
NO NUMBERS ON CASUALTIES YET, BUT THEY'LL OBVIOUSLY BE EXTREMELY, UM...
SIGNIFICANT.
The party broke up early.
THE REACTION HAS BEGUN.

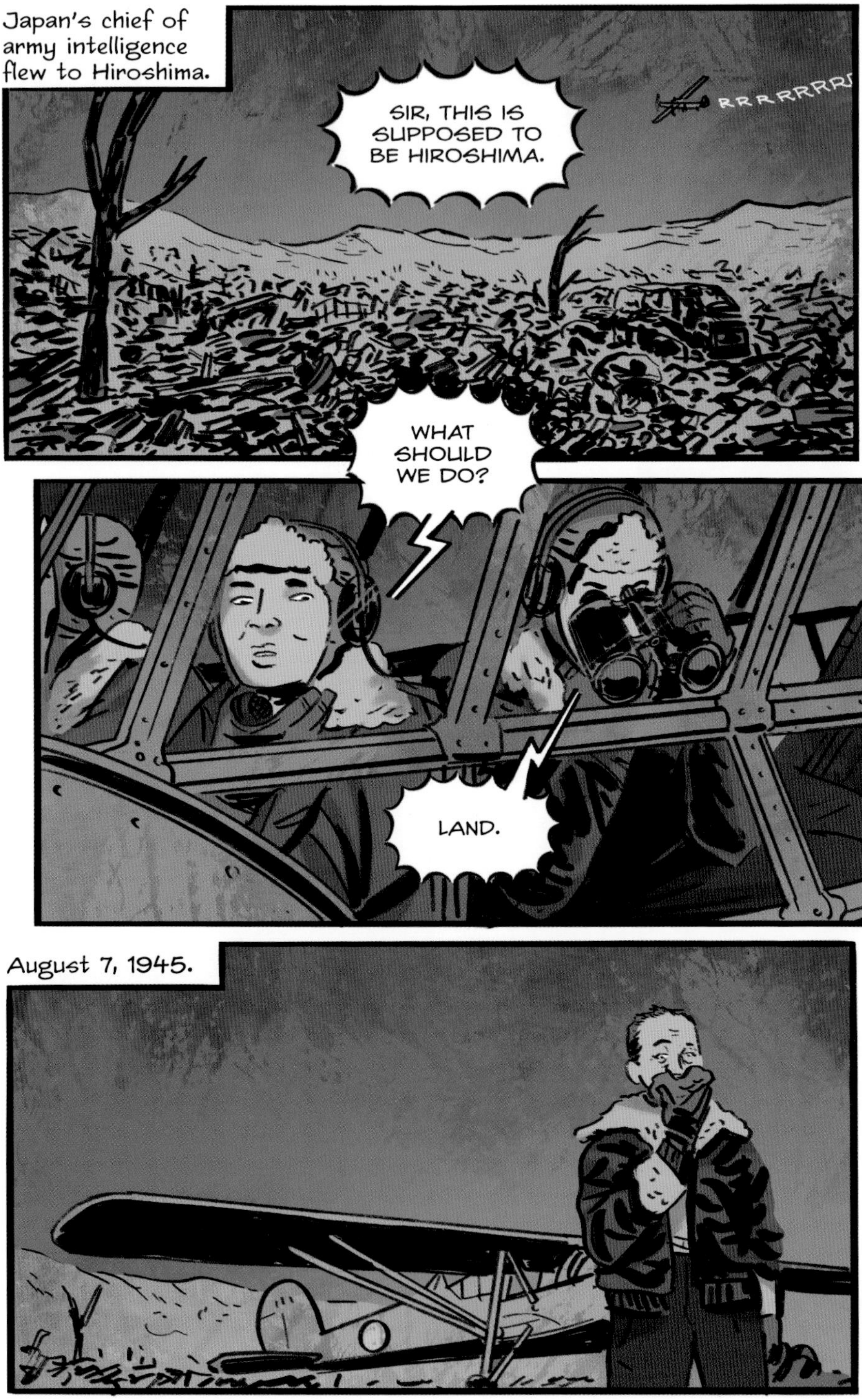
Japan's chief of army intelligence flew to Hiroshima.
RRRRRRR
SIR, THIS IS SUPPOSED TO BE HIROSHIMA.
WHAT SHOULD WE DO?
LAND.
August 7, 1945.

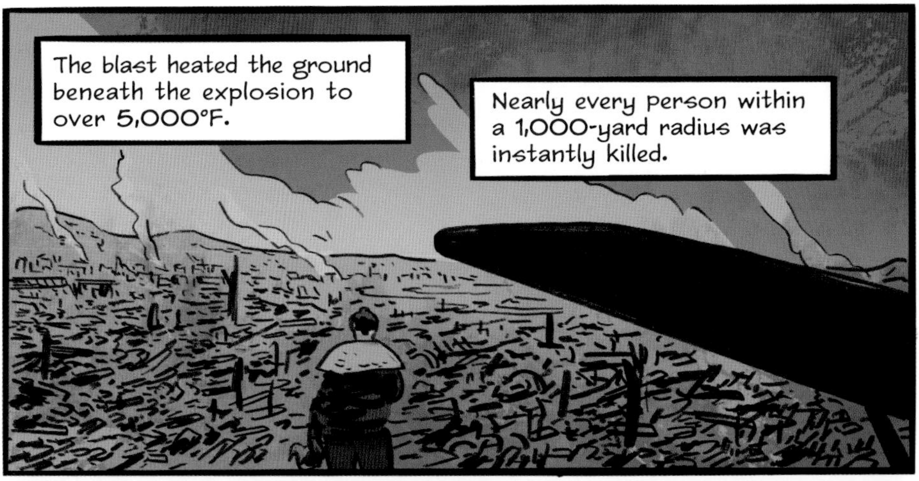
The blast heated the ground beneath the explosion to over 5,000°F.
Nearly every person within a 1,000-yard radius was instantly killed.

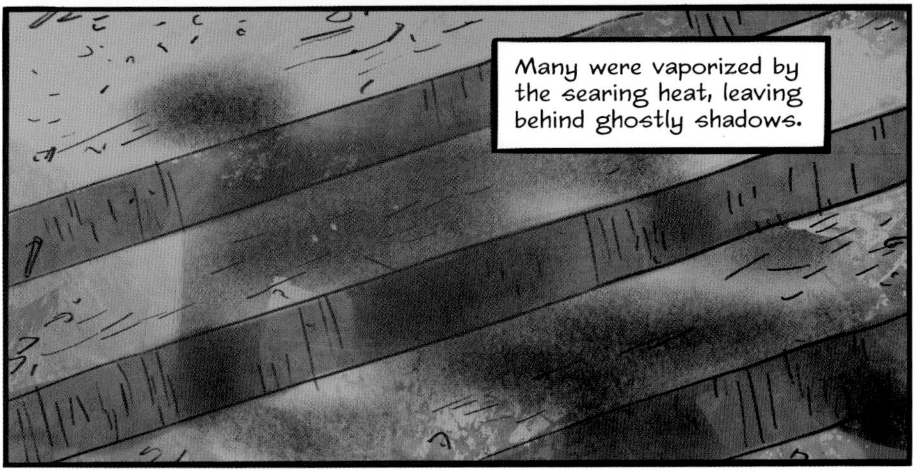
Many were vaporized by the searing heat, leaving behind ghostly shadows.

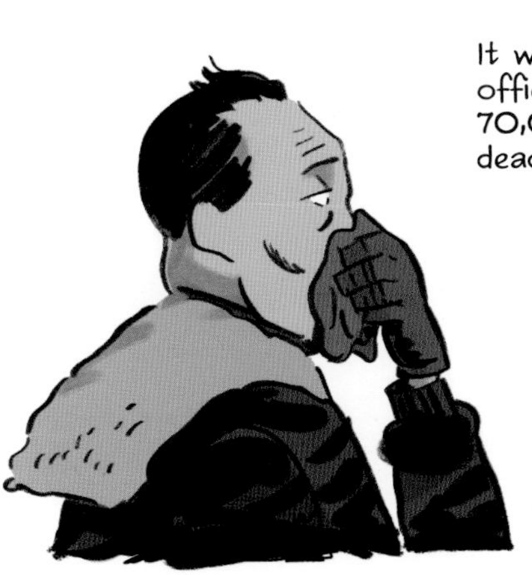

It would take time to compile official statistics, but about 70,000 people were already dead.

Over 100,000 more would die of wounds, burns, and radiation poisoning.

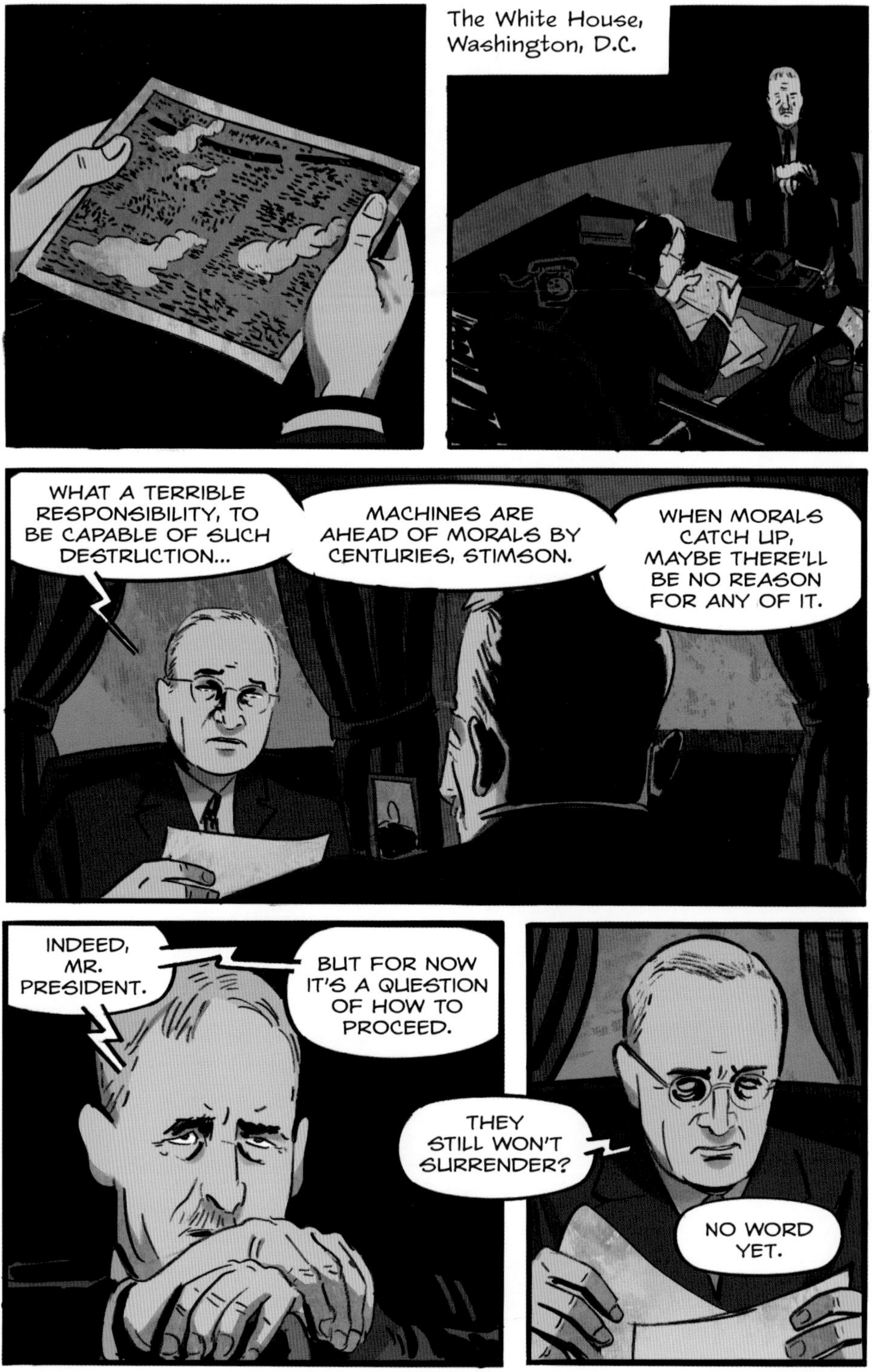
The White House, Washington, D.C.
WHAT A TERRIBLE RESPONSIBILITY, TO BE CAPABLE OF SUCH DESTRUCTION...
MACHINES ARE AHEAD OF MORALS BY CENTURIES, STIMSON.
WHEN MORALS CATCH UP, MAYBE THERE'LL BE NO REASON FOR ANY OF IT.
INDEED, MR. PRESIDENT.
BUT FOR NOW IT'S A QUESTION OF HOW TO PROCEED.
THEY STILL WON'T SURRENDER?
NO WORD YET.

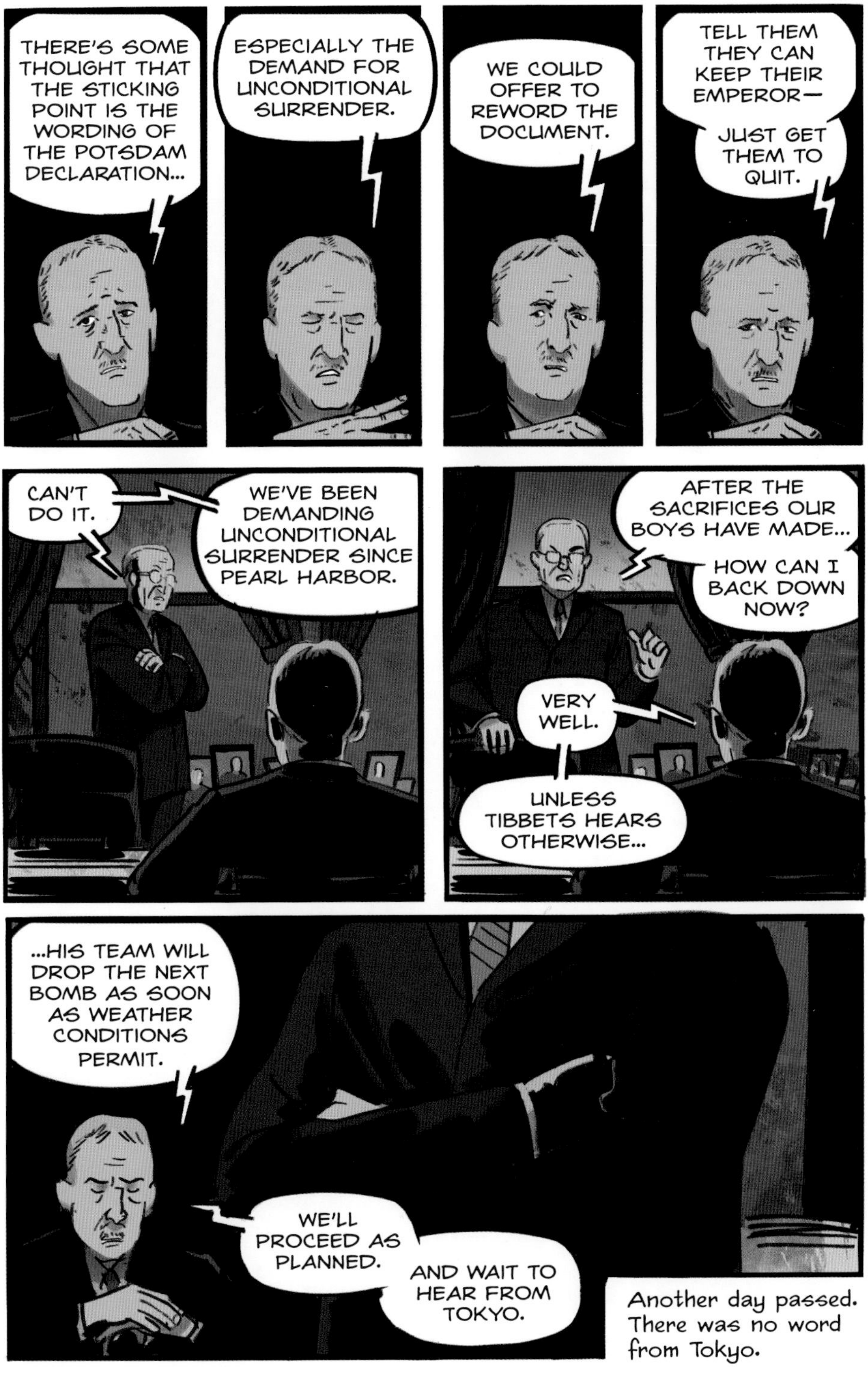
THERE'S SOME THOUGHT THAT THE STICKING POINT IS THE WORDING OF THE POTSDAM DECLARATION...
ESPECIALLY THE DEMAND FOR UNCONDITIONAL SURRENDER.
WE COULD OFFER TO REWORD THE DOCUMENT.
TELL THEM THEY CAN KEEP THEIR EMPEROR—
JUST GET THEM TO QUIT.
CAN'T DO IT.
WE'VE BEEN DEMANDING UNCONDITIONAL SURRENDER SINCE PEARL HARBOR.
AFTER THE SACRIFICES OUR BOYS HAVE MADE...
HOW CAN I BACK DOWN NOW?
VERY WELL.
UNLESS TIBBETS HEARS OTHERWISE...
...HIS TEAM WILL DROP THE NEXT BOMB AS SOON AS WEATHER CONDITIONS PERMIT.
WE'LL PROCEED AS PLANNED.
AND WAIT TO HEAR FROM TOKYO.

Another day passed. There was no word from Tokyo.

Tinian Island, August 9, 1945.

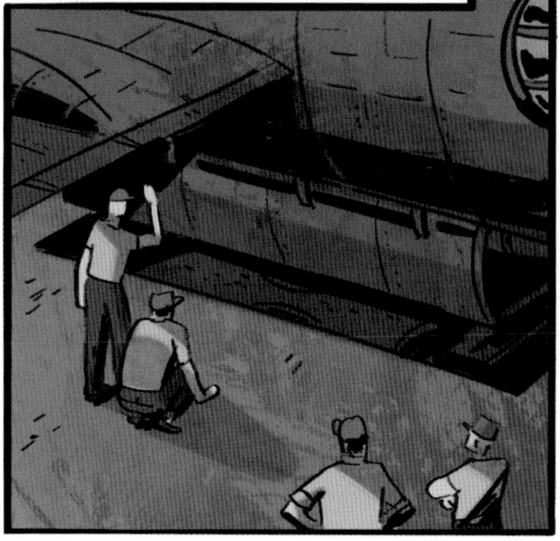

The world's second plutonium bomb, known to the crew as Fat Man, was loaded into Major Charles Sweeney's B-29.

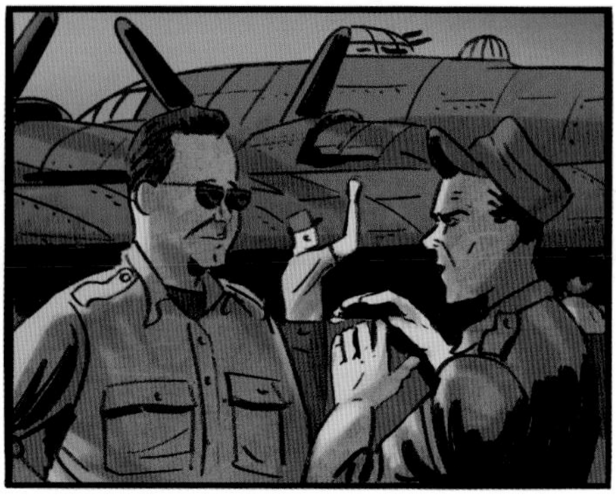

Sweeney's plane reached its primary target, the city of Kokura. It was covered with clouds.

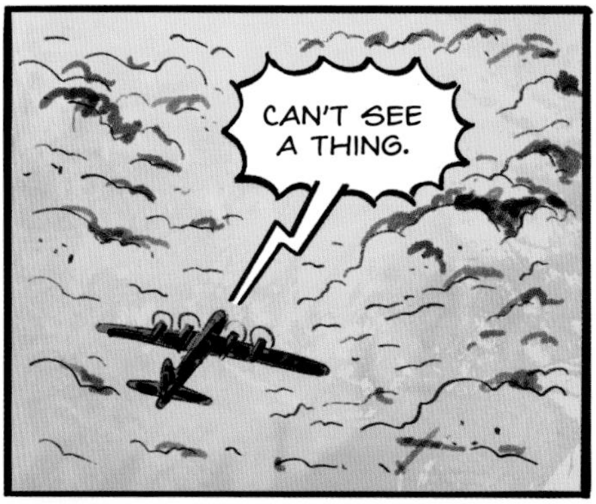
CAN'T SEE A THING.

As the bomber circled Kokura, looking for an opening, anti-aircraft guns opened fire.

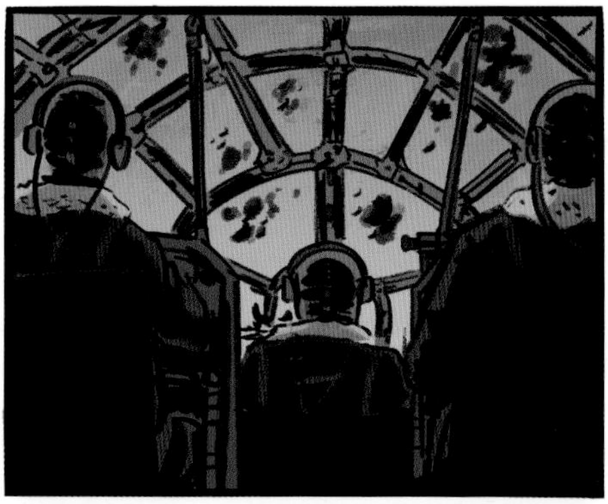

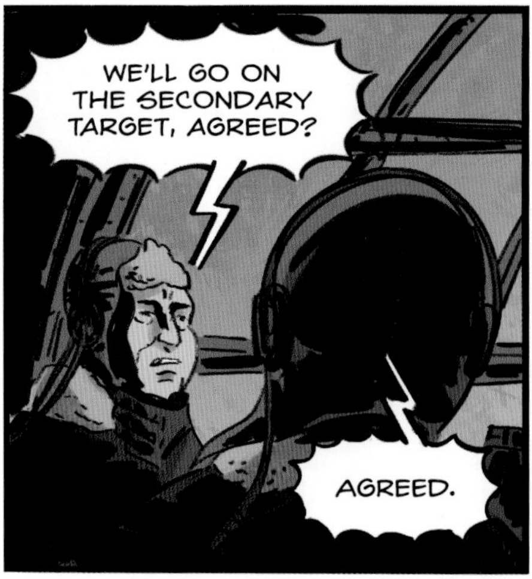
WE'LL GO ON THE SECONDARY TARGET, AGREED?
AGREED.

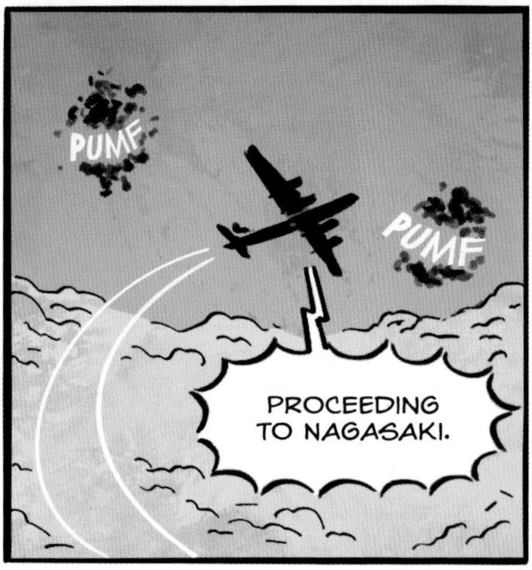
PUMF
PUMF
PROCEEDING TO NAGASAKI.

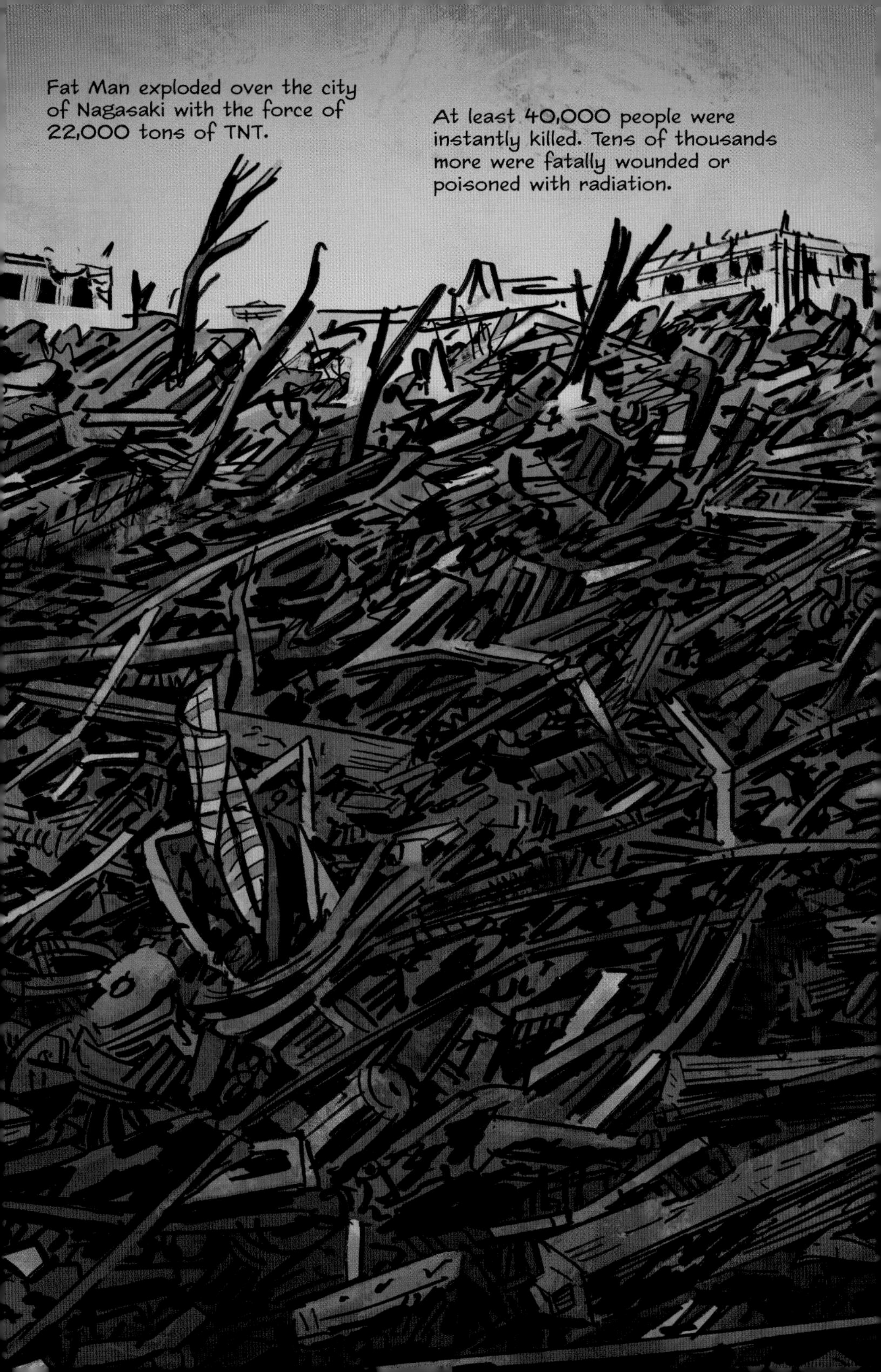
Fat Man exploded over the city of Nagasaki with the force of 22,000 tons of TNT.
At least 40,000 people were instantly killed. Tens of thousands more were fatally wounded or poisoned with radiation.

Everyone expected Tokyo—what was left of it—to be next.

The U.S. had already built a third bomb that would be ready in days.

Japan's Emperor Hirohito attended the Supreme Council's emergency meeting.

OUR ONLY ALTERNATIVE NOW IS TO ACCEPT THE POTSDAM DECLARATION AND TERMINATE THE WAR.

The leaders debated late into the night.

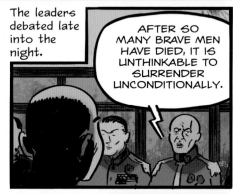

AFTER SO MANY BRAVE MEN HAVE DIED, IT IS UNTHINKABLE TO SURRENDER UNCONDITIONALLY.

WITH THE GREATEST REVERENCE, I MUST NOW ASK THE EMPEROR TO EXPRESS HIS WISHES.

Japan's emperor did not normally make policy decisions. But in times of crisis, his word was final.

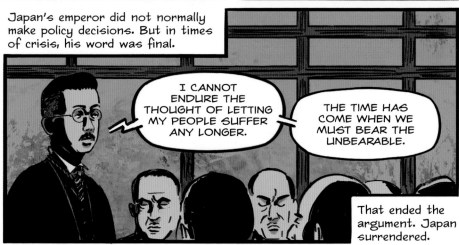

I CANNOT ENDURE THE THOUGHT OF LETTING MY PEOPLE SUFFER ANY LONGER.

THE TIME HAS COME WHEN WE MUST BEAR THE UNBEARABLE.

That ended the argument. Japan surrendered.

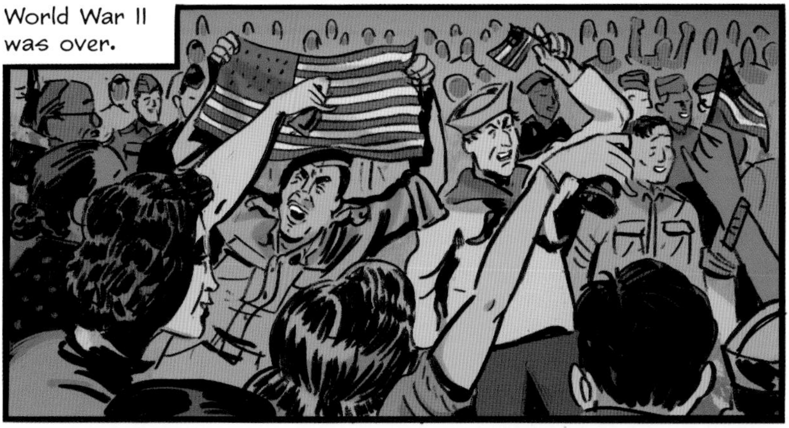
World War II was over.

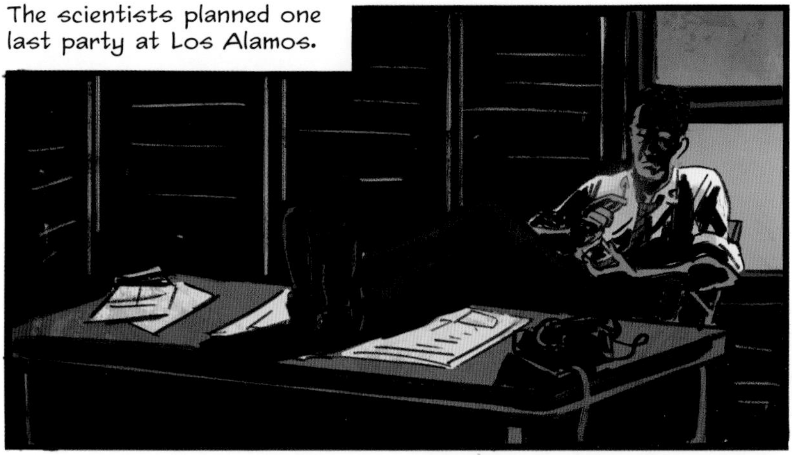
The scientists planned one last party at Los Alamos.

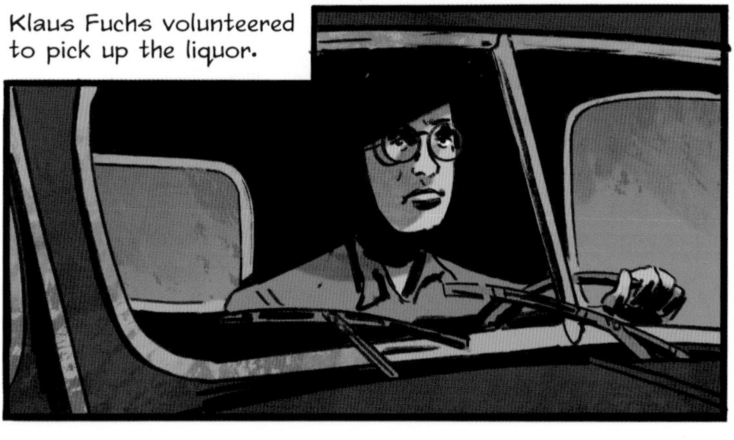
Klaus Fuchs volunteered to pick up the liquor.

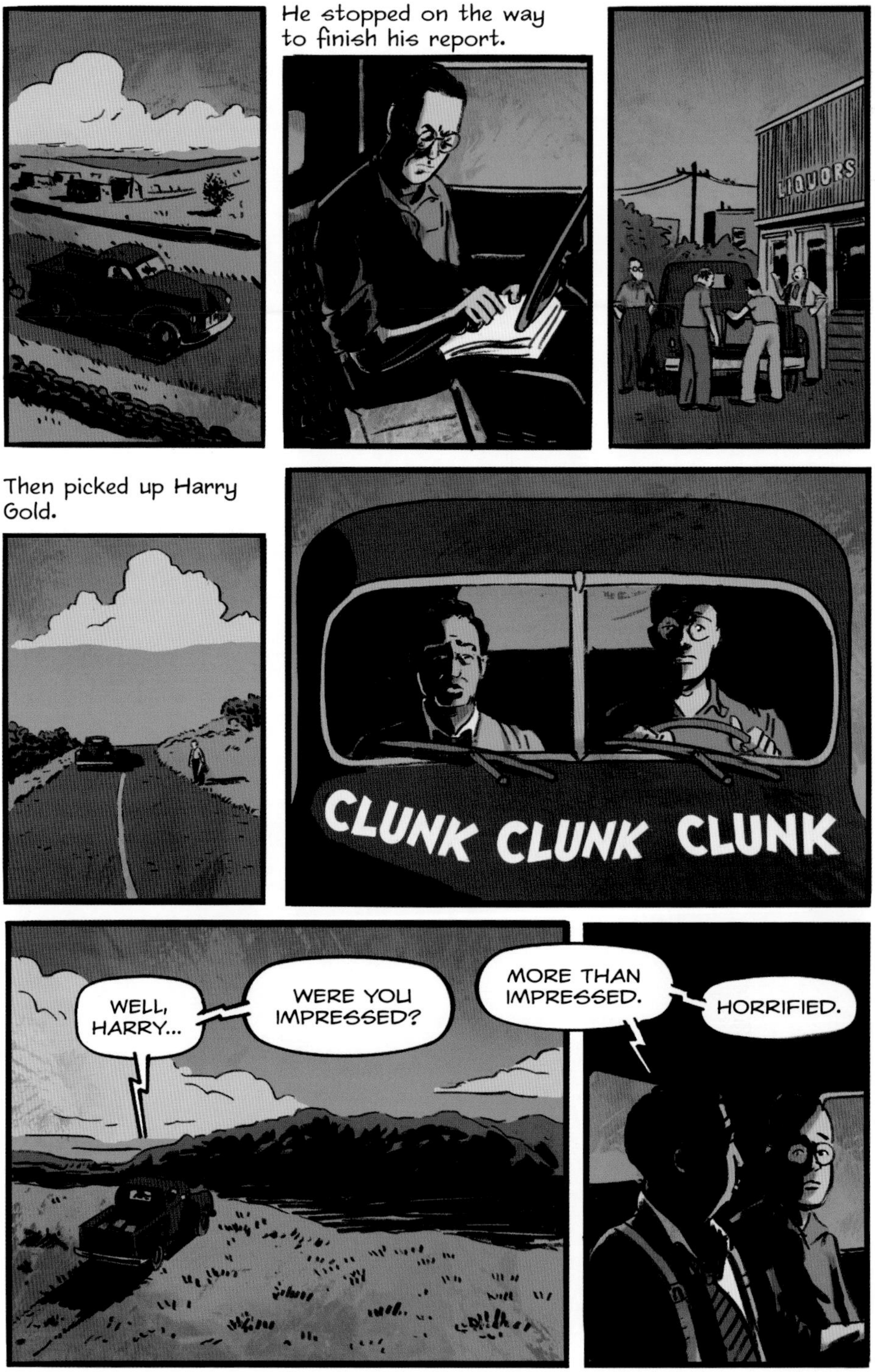
He stopped on the way to finish his report.
LIQUORS
Then picked up Harry Gold.
CLUNK CLUNK CLUNK
WELL, HARRY...
WERE YOU IMPRESSED?
MORE THAN IMPRESSED.
HORRIFIED.

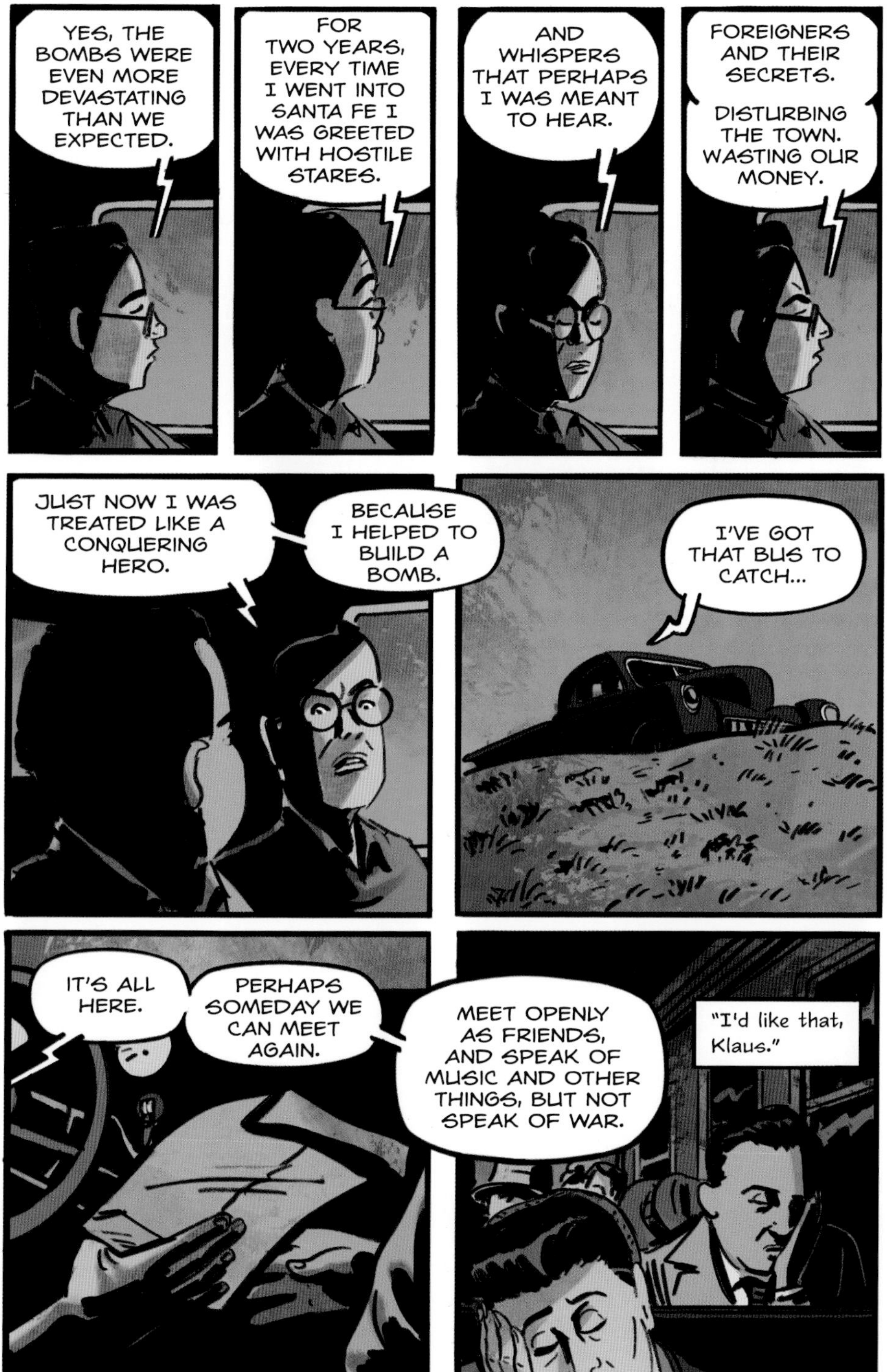

YES, THE BOMBS WERE EVEN MORE DEVASTATING THAN WE EXPECTED.
FOR TWO YEARS, EVERY TIME I WENT INTO SANTA FE I WAS GREETED WITH HOSTILE STARES.
AND WHISPERS THAT PERHAPS I WAS MEANT TO HEAR.
FOREIGNERS AND THEIR SECRETS.
DISTURBING THE TOWN. WASTING OUR MONEY.
JUST NOW I WAS TREATED LIKE A CONQUERING HERO.
BECAUSE I HELPED TO BUILD A BOMB.
I'VE GOT THAT BUS TO CATCH...
IT'S ALL HERE.
PERHAPS SOMEDAY WE CAN MEET AGAIN.
MEET OPENLY AS FRIENDS, AND SPEAK OF MUSIC AND OTHER THINGS, BUT NOT SPEAK OF WAR.
"I'd like that, Klaus."

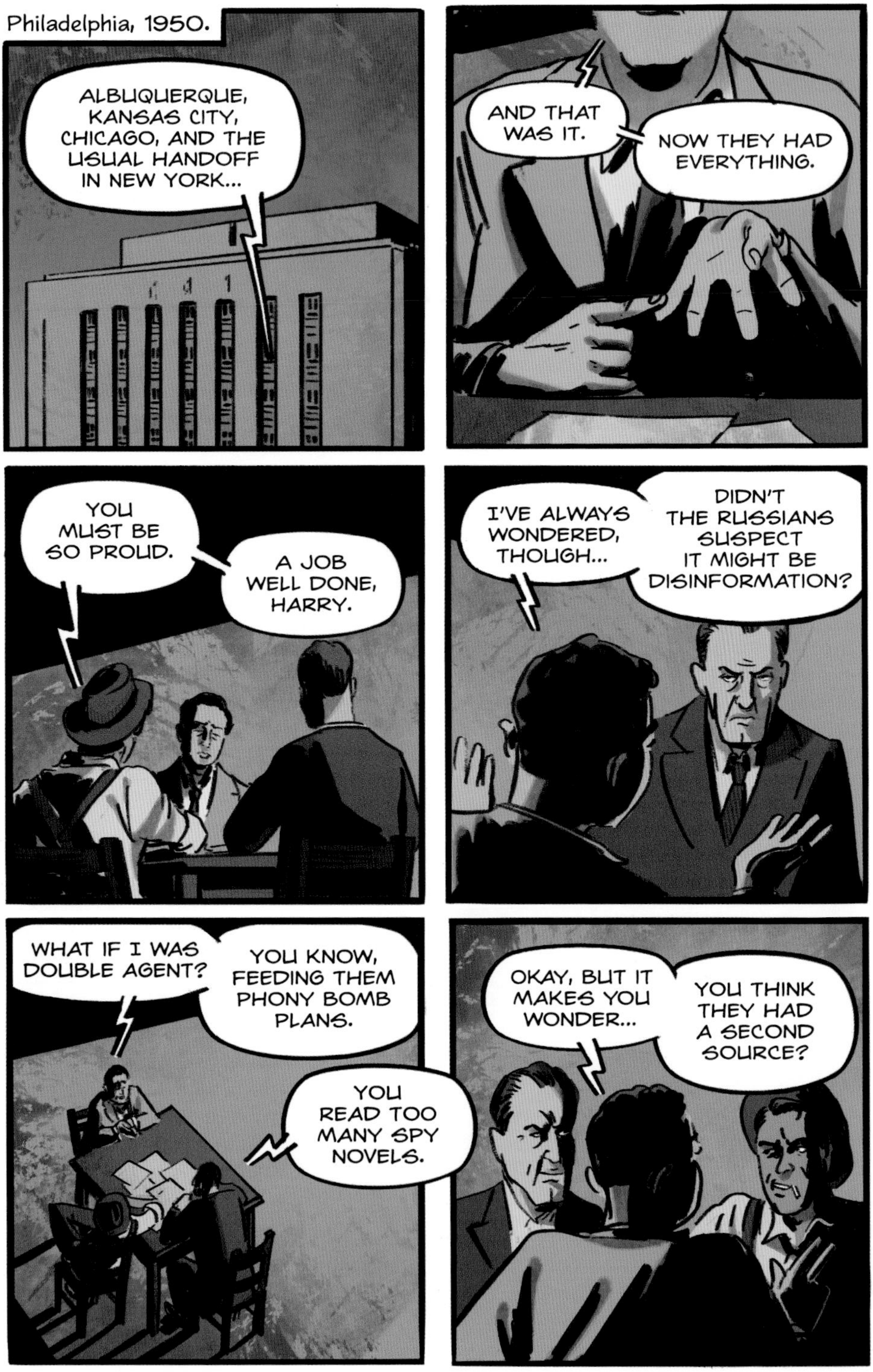
Philadelphia, 1950.
ALBUQUERQUE, KANSAS CITY, CHICAGO, AND THE USUAL HANDOFF IN NEW YORK...
AND THAT WAS IT.
NOW THEY HAD EVERYTHING.
YOU MUST BE SO PROUD.
A JOB WELL DONE, HARRY.
I'VE ALWAYS WONDERED, THOUGH...
DIDN'T THE RUSSIANS SUSPECT IT MIGHT BE DISINFORMATION?
WHAT IF I WAS DOUBLE AGENT?
YOU KNOW, FEEDING THEM PHONY BOMB PLANS.
YOU READ TOO MANY SPY NOVELS.
OKAY, BUT IT MAKES YOU WONDER...
YOU THINK THEY HAD A SECOND SOURCE?

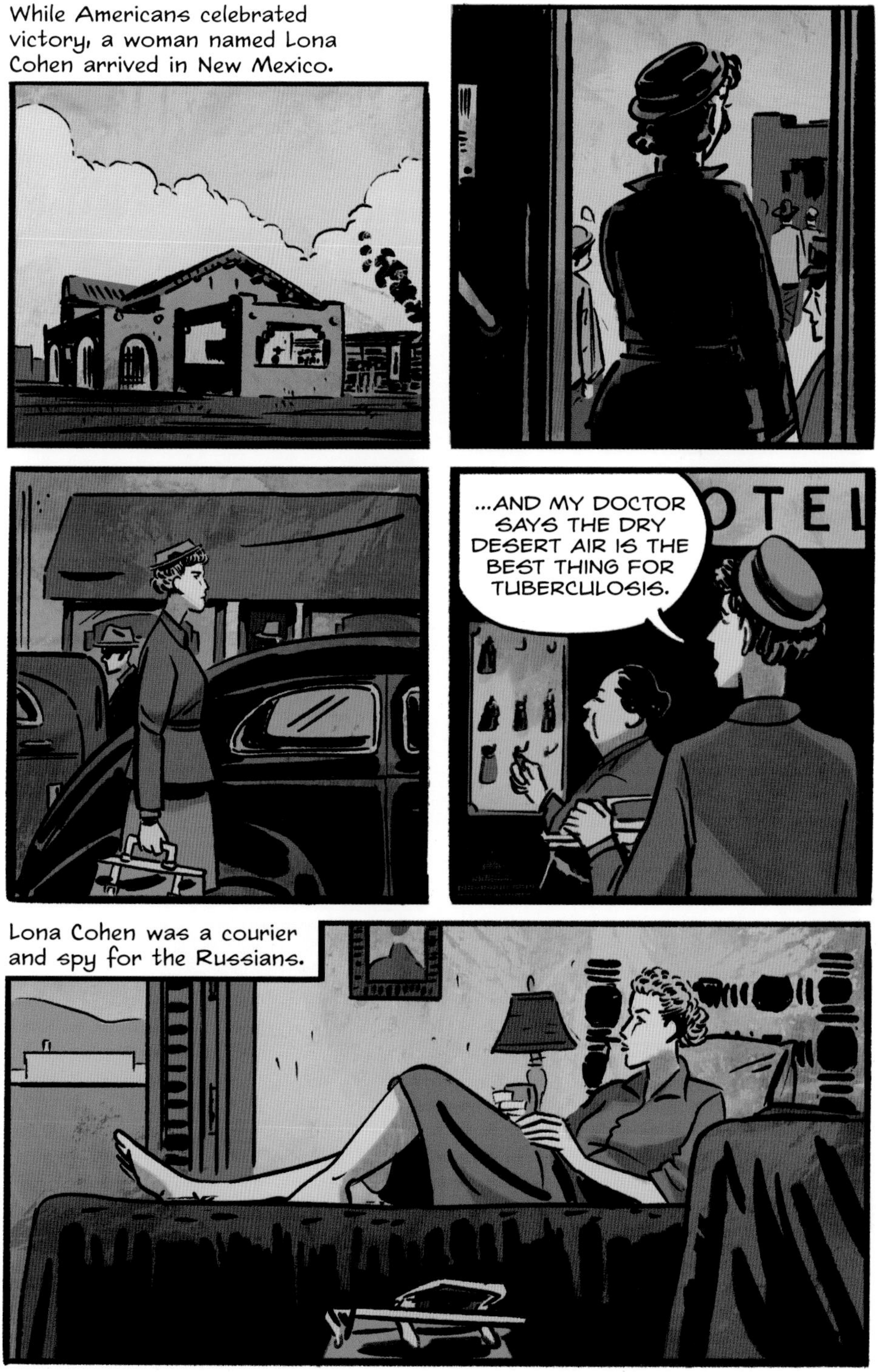
While Americans celebrated victory, a woman named Lona Cohen arrived in New Mexico.
...AND MY DOCTOR SAYS THE DRY DESERT AIR IS THE BEST THING FOR TUBERCULOSIS.
OTEL
Lona Cohen was a courier and spy for the Russians.

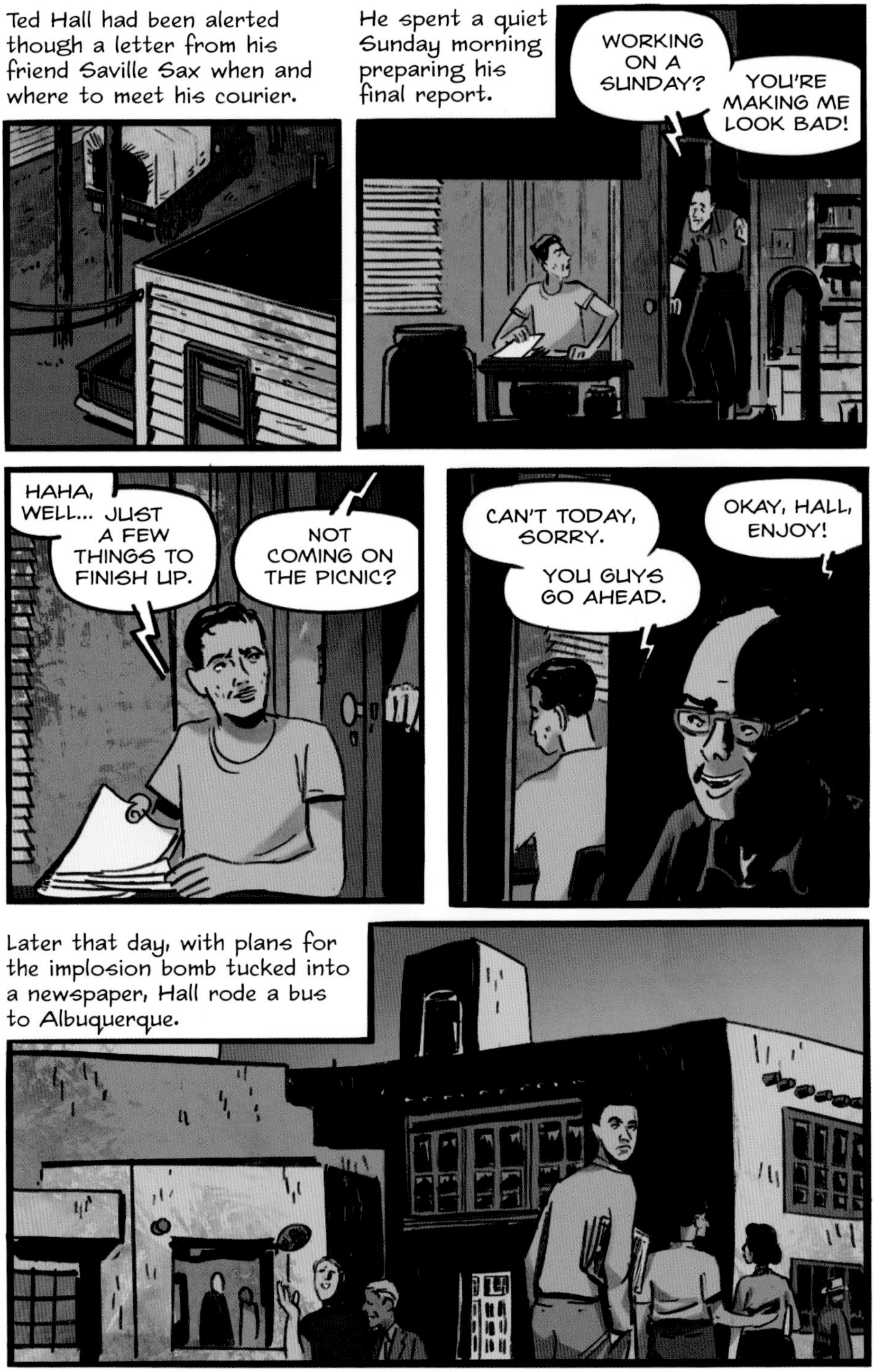
Ted Hall had been alerted though a letter from his friend Saville Sax when and where to meet his courier.
He spent a quiet Sunday morning preparing his final report.
WORKING ON A SUNDAY?
YOU'RE MAKING ME LOOK BAD!
HAHA, WELL... JUST A FEW THINGS TO FINISH UP.
NOT COMING ON THE PICNIC?
CAN'T TODAY, SORRY.
YOU GUYS GO AHEAD.
OKAY, HALL, ENJOY!
Later that day, with plans for the implosion bomb tucked into a newspaper, Hall rode a bus to Albuquerque.

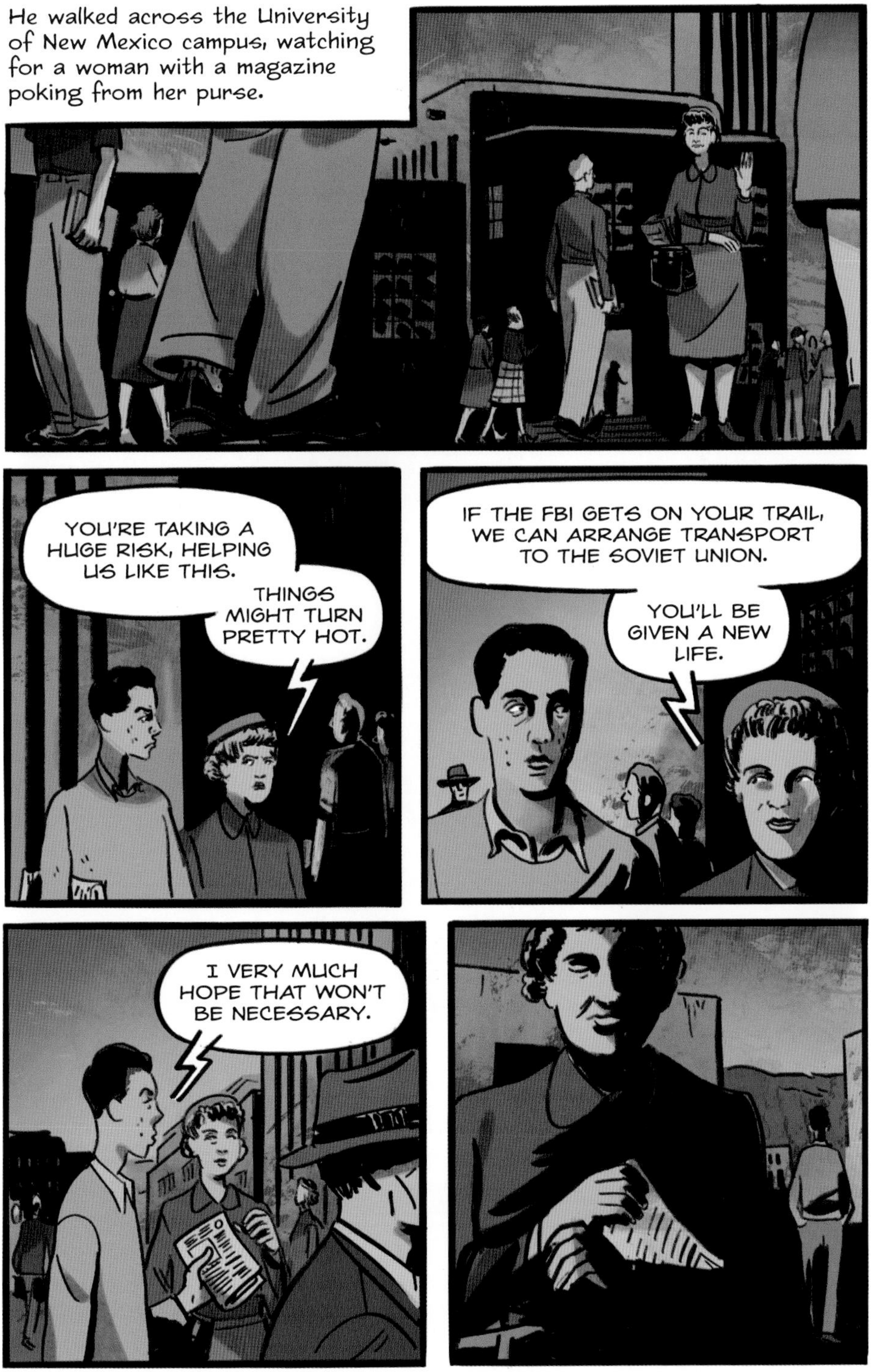
He walked across the University of New Mexico campus, watching for a woman with a magazine poking from her purse.
YOU'RE TAKING A HUGE RISK, HELPING US LIKE THIS.
THINGS MIGHT TURN PRETTY HOT.
IF THE FBI GETS ON YOUR TRAIL, WE CAN ARRANGE TRANSPORT TO THE SOVIET UNION.
YOU'LL BE GIVEN A NEW LIFE.
I VERY MUCH HOPE THAT WON'T BE NECESSARY.

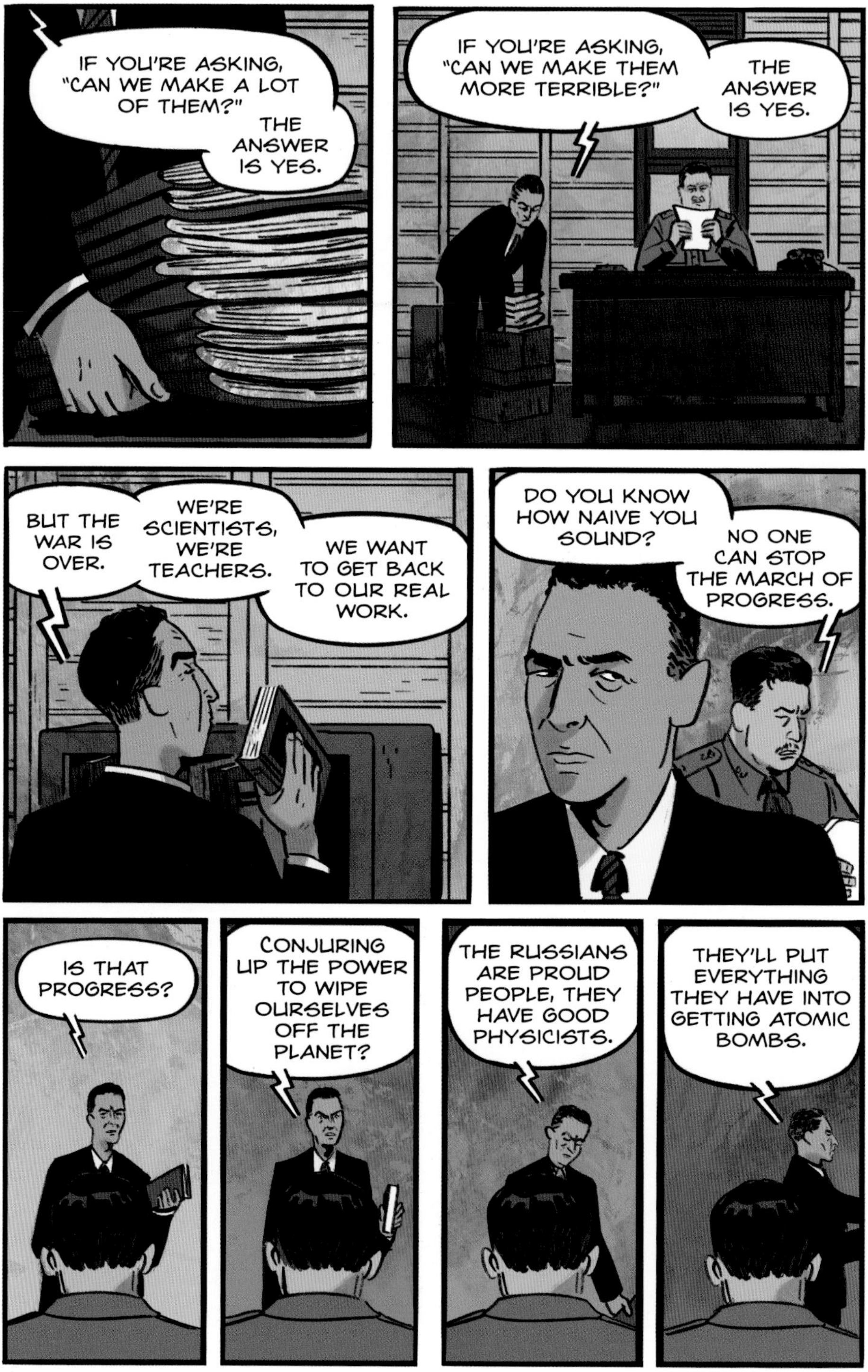
IF YOU'RE ASKING, "CAN WE MAKE A LOT OF THEM?"
THE ANSWER IS YES.
IF YOU'RE ASKING, "CAN WE MAKE THEM MORE TERRIBLE?"
THE ANSWER IS YES.
BUT THE WAR IS OVER.
WE'RE SCIENTISTS, WE'RE TEACHERS.
WE WANT TO GET BACK TO OUR REAL WORK.
DO YOU KNOW HOW NAIVE YOU SOUND?
NO ONE CAN STOP THE MARCH OF PROGRESS.
IS THAT PROGRESS?
CONJURING UP THE POWER TO WIPE OURSELVES OFF THE PLANET?
THE RUSSIANS ARE PROUD PEOPLE, THEY HAVE GOOD PHYSICISTS.
THEY'LL PUT EVERYTHING THEY HAVE INTO GETTING ATOMIC BOMBS.

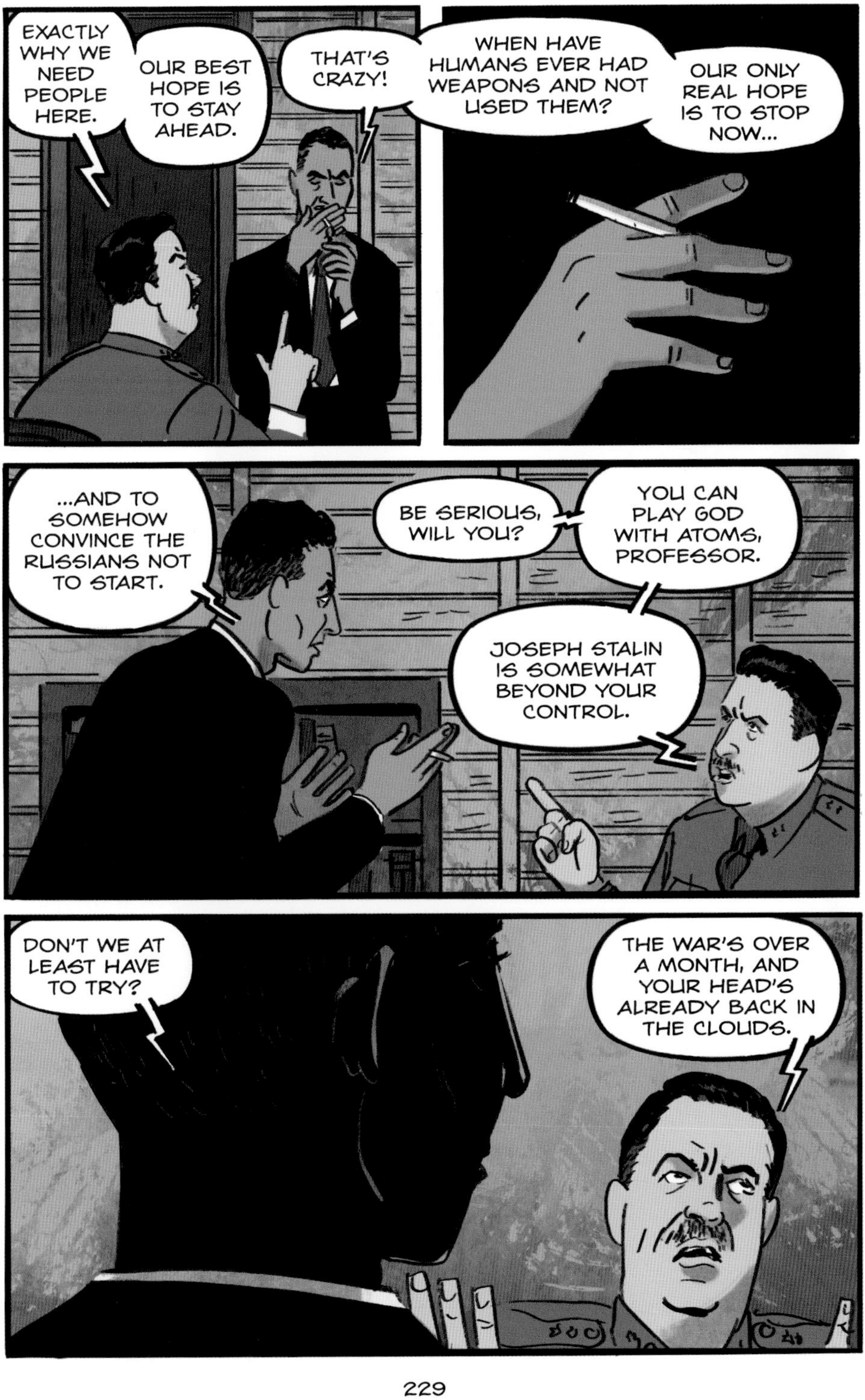
EXACTLY WHY WE NEED PEOPLE HERE.
OUR BEST HOPE IS TO STAY AHEAD.
THAT'S CRAZY!
WHEN HAVE HUMANS EVER HAD WEAPONS AND NOT USED THEM?
OUR ONLY REAL HOPE IS TO STOP NOW...
...AND TO SOMEHOW CONVINCE THE RUSSIANS NOT TO START.
BE SERIOUS, WILL YOU?
YOU CAN PLAY GOD WITH ATOMS, PROFESSOR.
JOSEPH STALIN IS SOMEWHAT BEYOND YOUR CONTROL.
DON'T WE AT LEAST HAVE TO TRY?
THE WAR'S OVER A MONTH, AND YOUR HEAD'S ALREADY BACK IN THE CLOUDS.

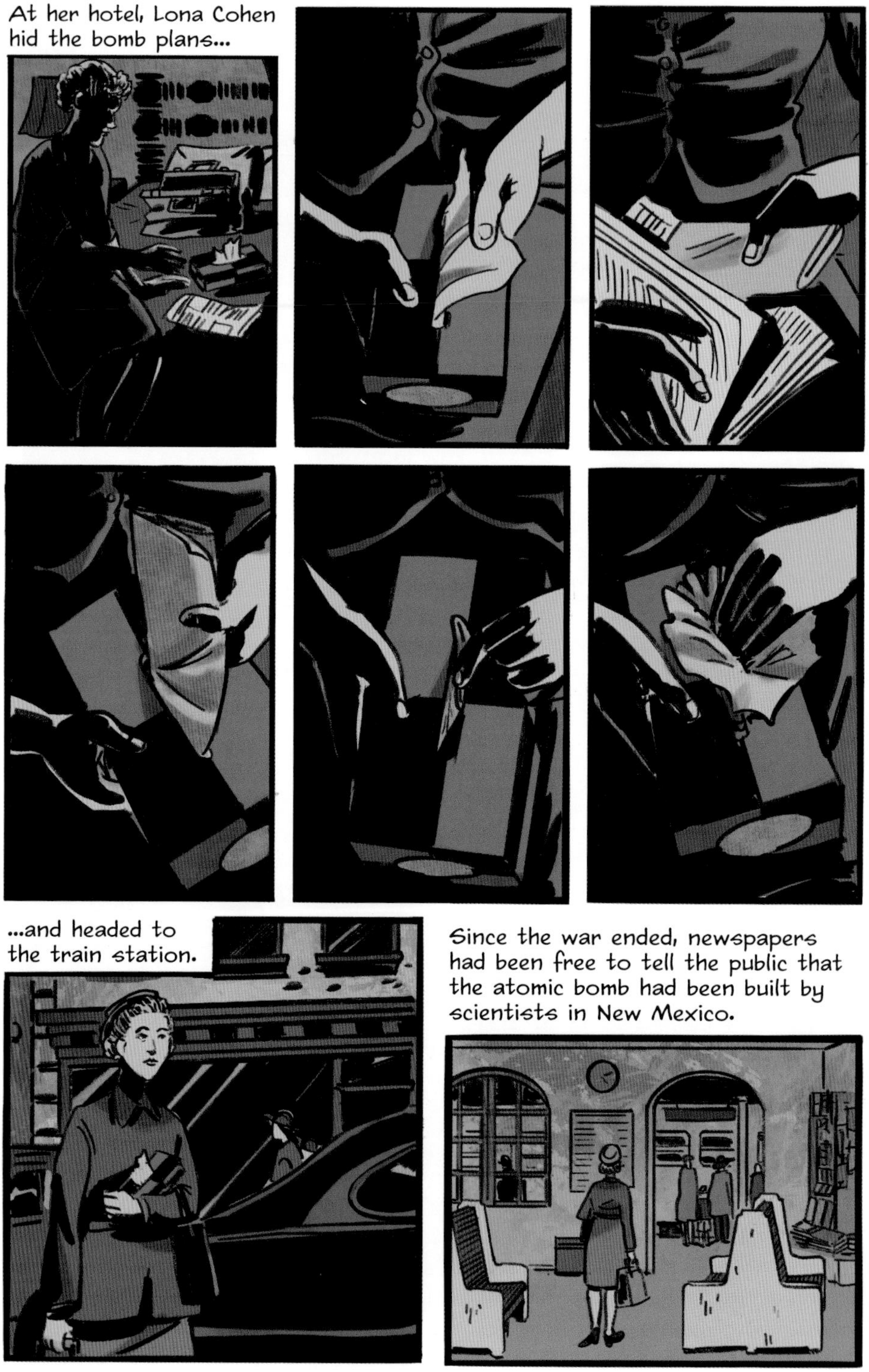
At her hotel, Lona Cohen hid the bomb plans...
...and headed to the train station.
Since the war ended, newspapers had been free to tell the public that the atomic bomb had been built by scientists in New Mexico.

The government was determined to protect its bomb-making secrets.

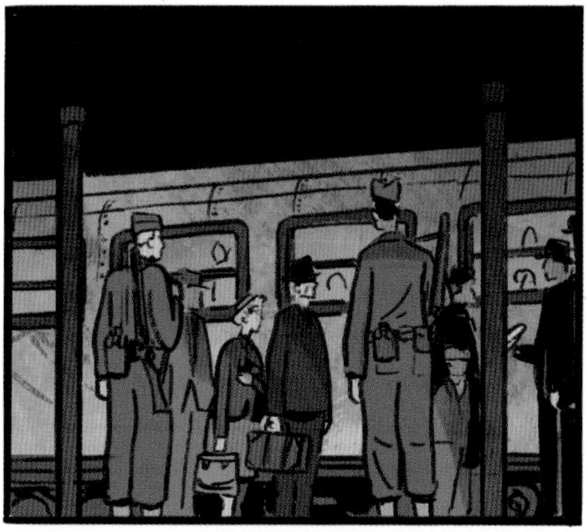

FBI agents were checking everyone. Cohen was too well trained to panel. She told herself:

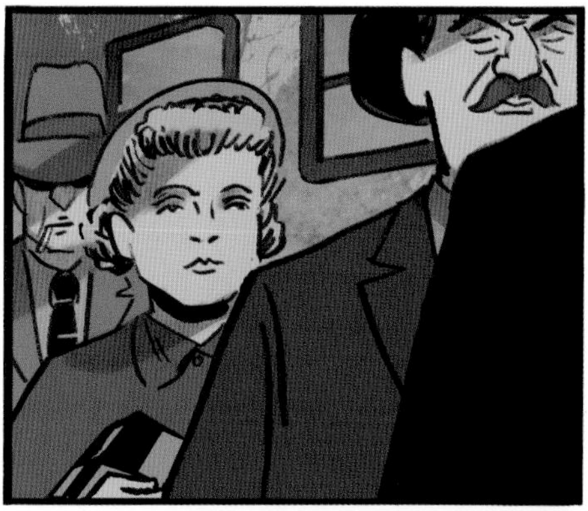

"I'm an absent-minded tuberculosis patient on her way home from the desert."

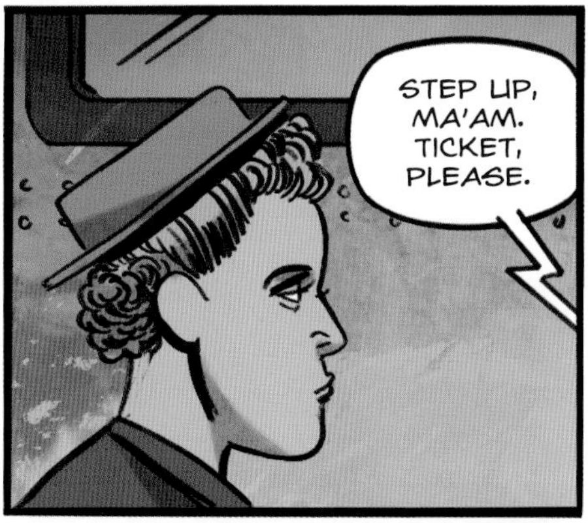
STEP UP, MA'AM. TICKET, PLEASE.

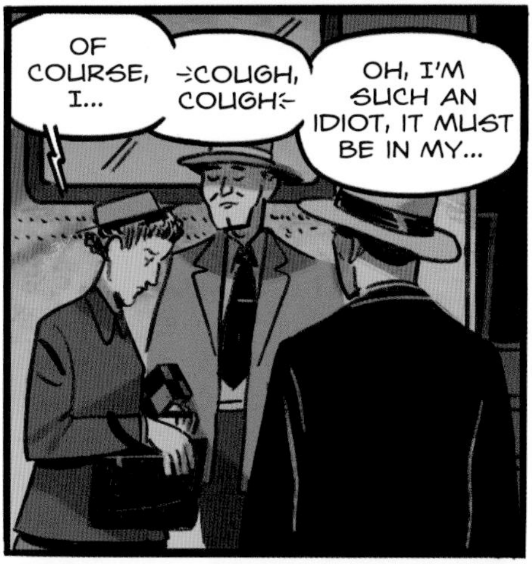
OF COURSE, I...
⇾COUGH, COUGH⇽
OH, I'M SUCH AN IDIOT, IT MUST BE IN MY...

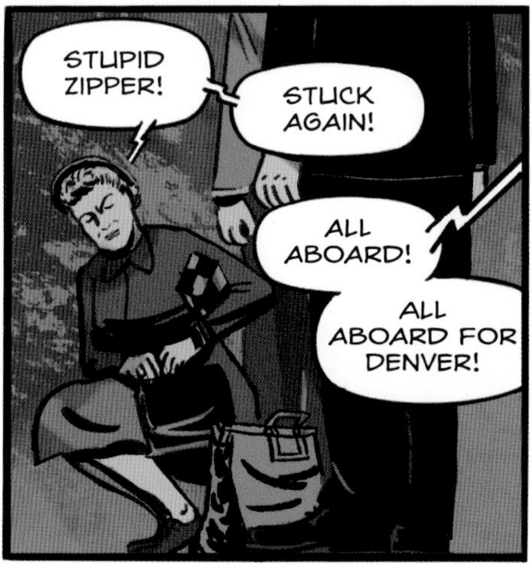
STUPID ZIPPER!
STUCK AGAIN!
ALL ABOARD!
ALL ABOARD FOR DENVER!

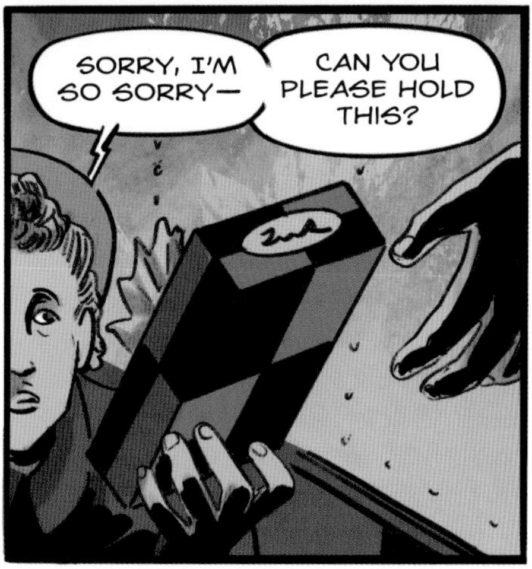
SORRY, I'M SO SORRY—
CAN YOU PLEASE HOLD THIS?

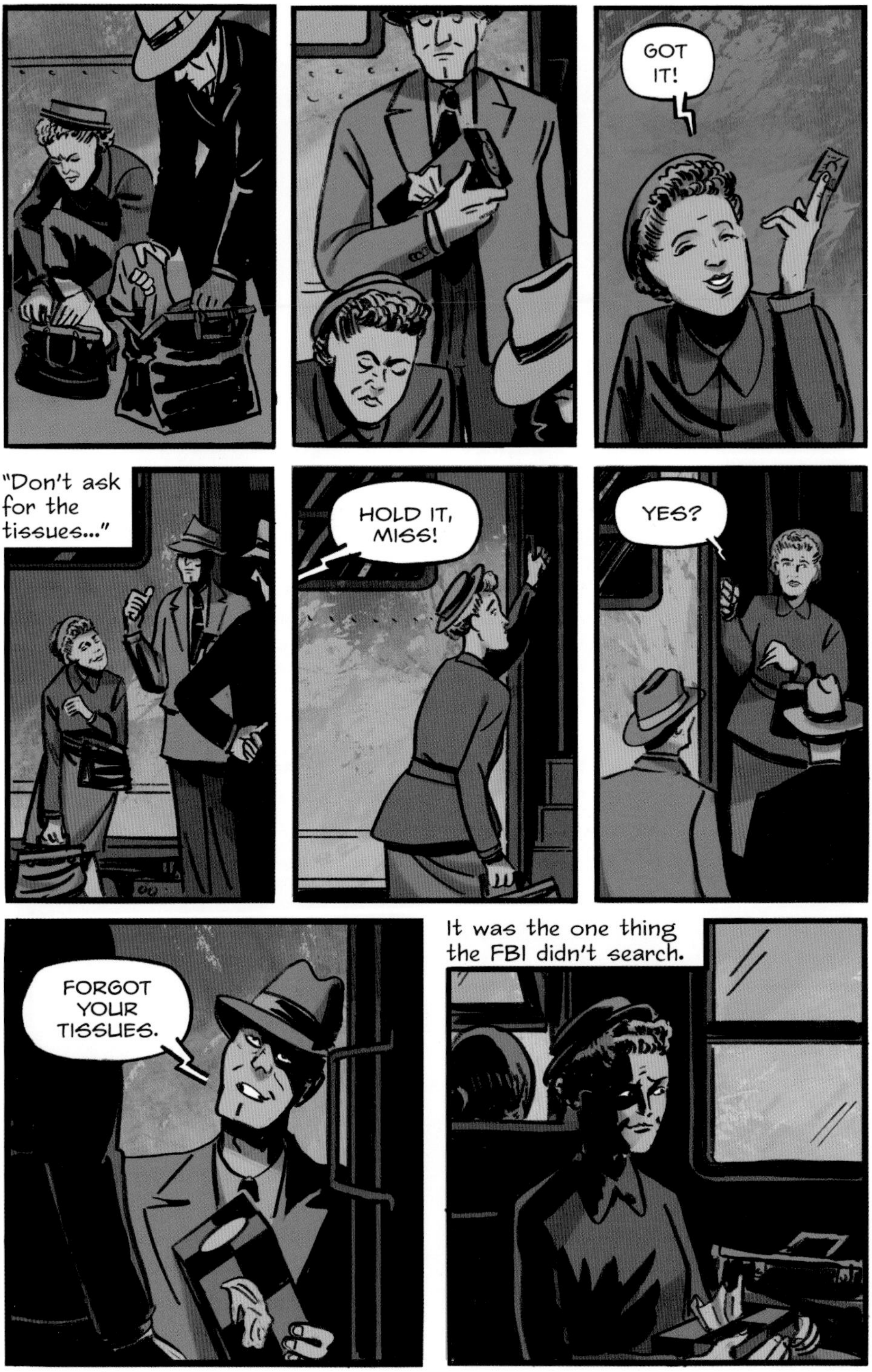
GOT IT!
"Don't ask for the tissues..."
HOLD IT, MISS!
YES?
FORGOT YOUR TISSUES.
It was the one thing the FBI didn't search.

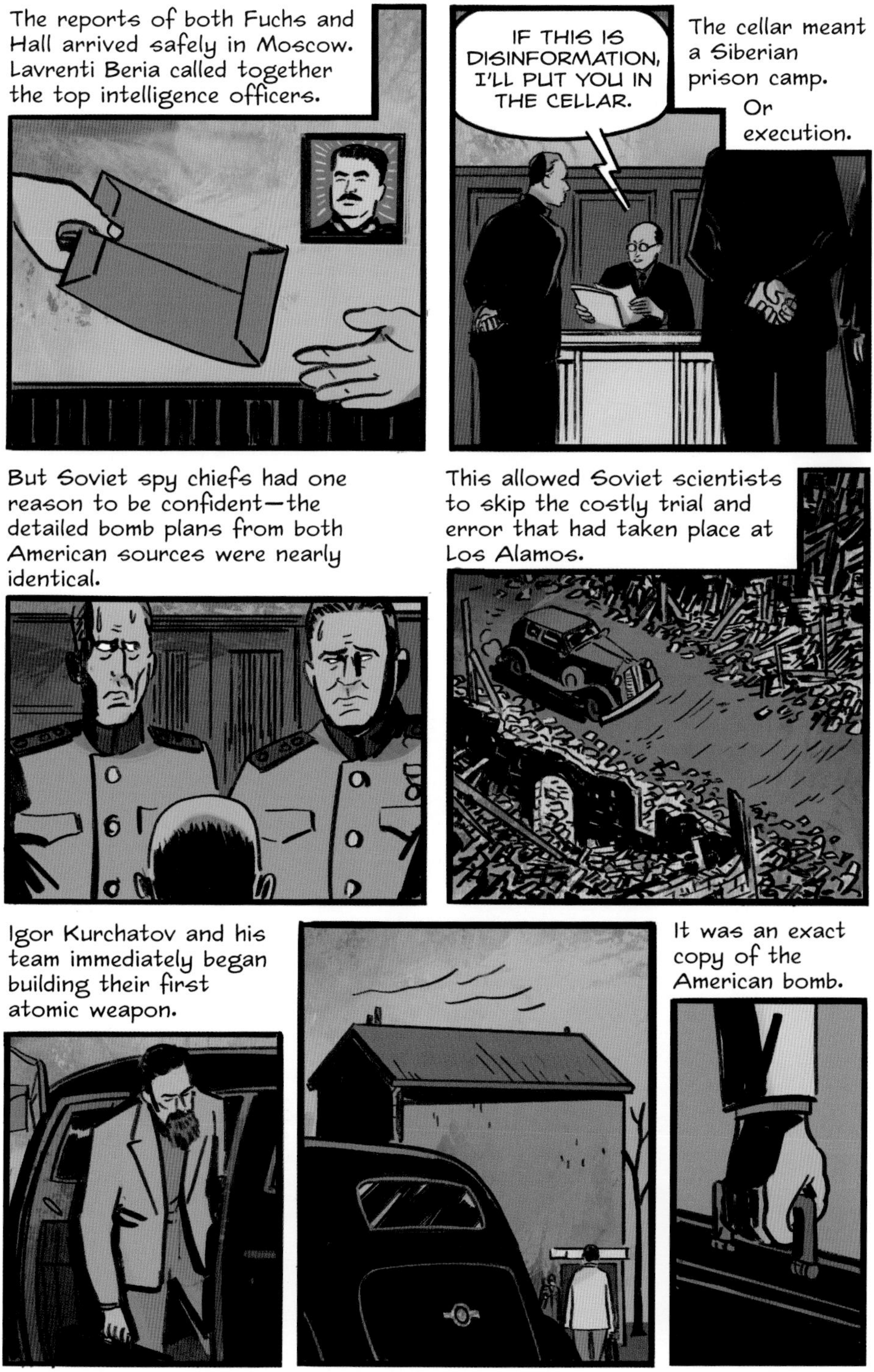
The reports of both Fuchs and Hall arrived safely in Moscow. Lavrenti Beria called together the top intelligence officers.
IF THIS IS DISINFORMATION, I'LL PUT YOU IN THE CELLAR.
The cellar meant a Siberian prison camp.
Or execution.
But Soviet spy chiefs had one reason to be confident—the detailed bomb plans from both American sources were nearly identical.
This allowed Soviet scientists to skip the costly trial and error that had taken place at Los Alamos.
Igor Kurchatov and his team immediately began building their first atomic weapon.
It was an exact copy of the American bomb.

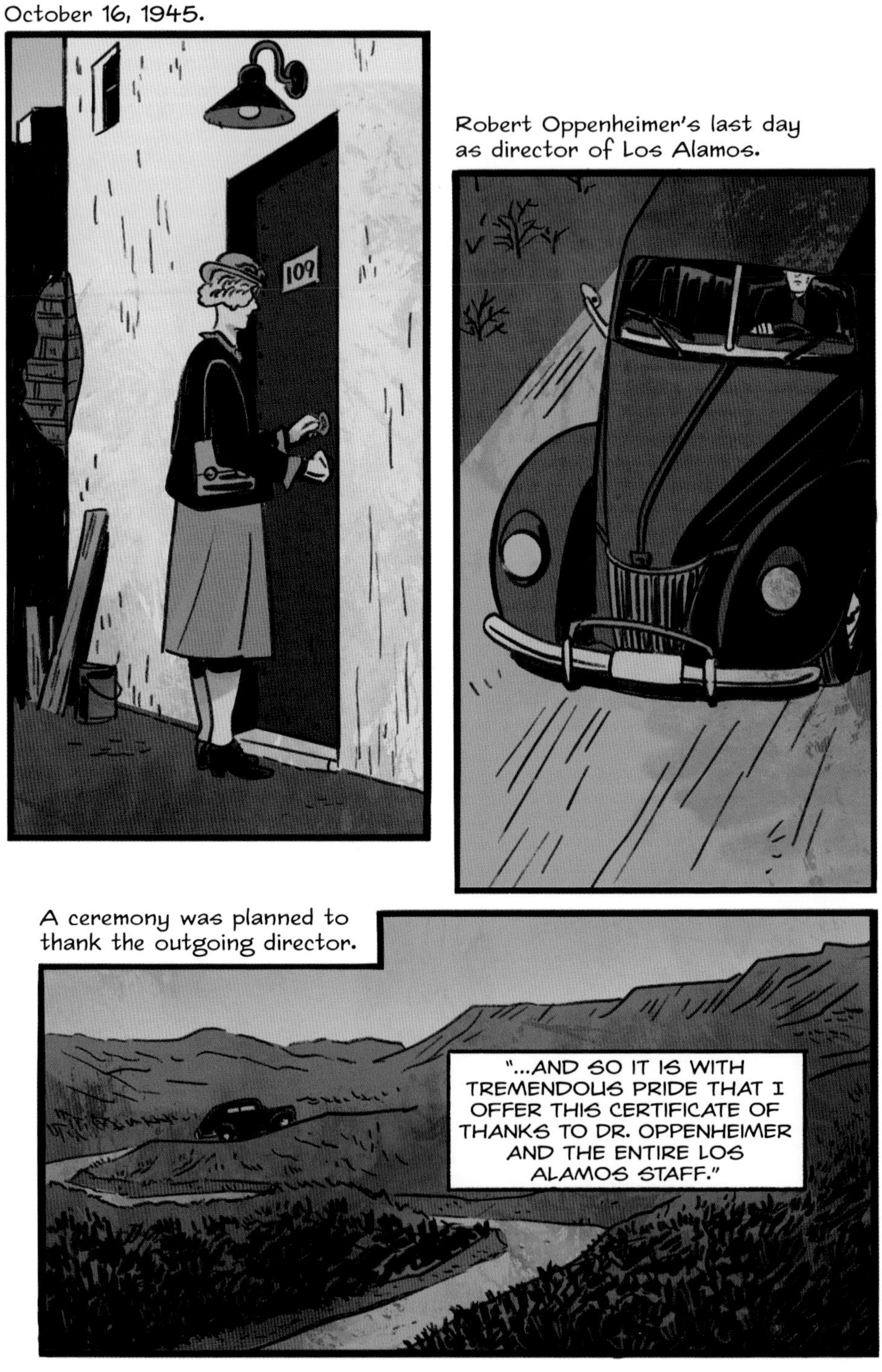
October 16, 1945.
109
Robert Oppenheimer's last day as director of Los Alamos.
A ceremony was planned to thank the outgoing director.
"...AND SO IT IS WITH TREMENDOUS PRIDE THAT I OFFER THIS CERTIFICATE OF THANKS TO DR. OPPENHEIMER AND THE ENTIRE LOS ALAMOS STAFF."

THANK YOU, GENERAL GROVES.

IF YOU ARE A SCIENTIST, YOU BELIEVE THAT IT IS GOOD TO FIND OUT HOW THE WORLD WORKS.

OUR LOVE OF SCIENCE BROUGHT US TOGETHER HERE.

WE WERE AT WAR, AND IT WAS NECESSARY FOR US TO CONTRIBUTE.

IT IS OUR HOPE THAT IN YEARS TO COME WE MAY LOOK AT THIS SCROLL, AND ALL THAT IT SIGNIFIES, WITH PRIDE.

BUT TODAY THAT PRIDE MUST BE TEMPERED WITH A PROFOUND CONCERN.

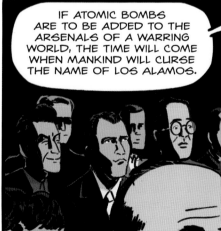

IF ATOMIC BOMBS ARE TO BE ADDED TO THE ARSENALS OF A WARRING WORLD, THE TIME WILL COME WHEN MANKIND WILL CURSE THE NAME OF LOS ALAMOS.

THE PEOPLE OF THIS WORLD MUST UNITE—

OR WE WILL PERISH.

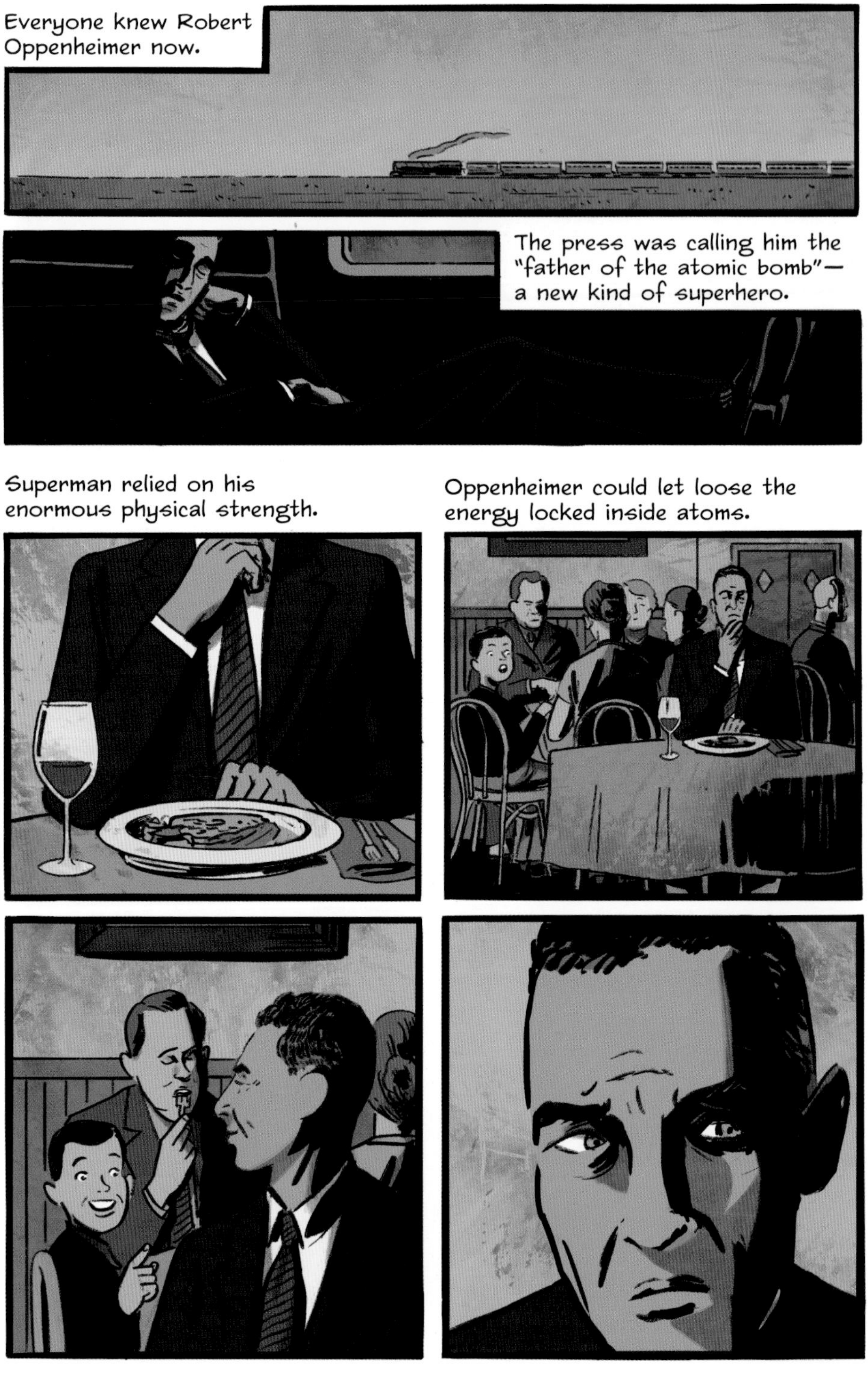
Everyone knew Robert Oppenheimer now.
The press was calling him the "father of the atomic bomb"— a new kind of superhero.
Superman relied on his enormous physical strength.
Oppenheimer could let loose the energy locked inside atoms.

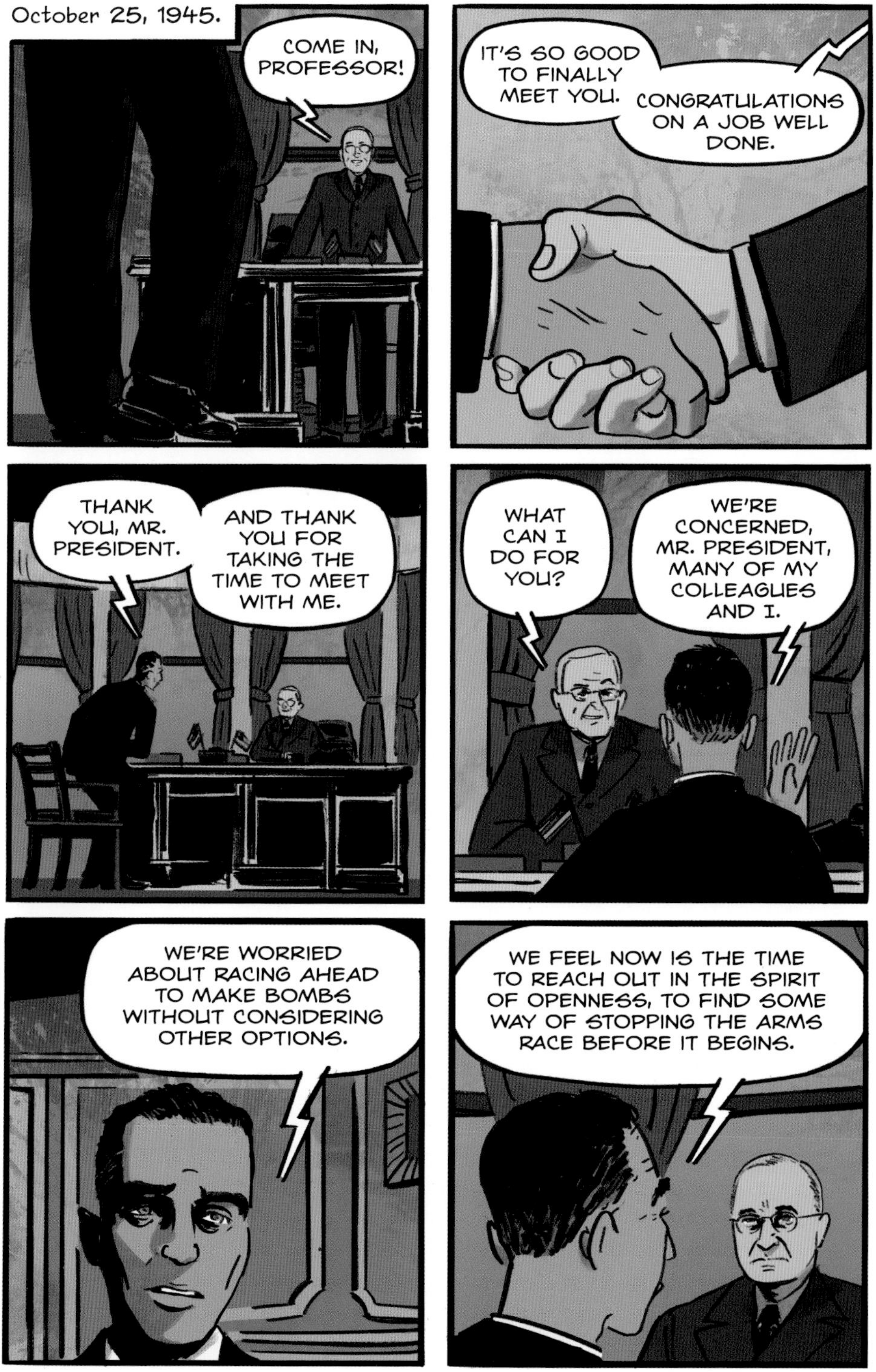
October 25, 1945.
COME IN, PROFESSOR!
IT'S SO GOOD TO FINALLY MEET YOU.
CONGRATULATIONS ON A JOB WELL DONE.
THANK YOU, MR. PRESIDENT.
AND THANK YOU FOR TAKING THE TIME TO MEET WITH ME.
WHAT CAN I DO FOR YOU?
WE'RE CONCERNED, MR. PRESIDENT, MANY OF MY COLLEAGUES AND I.
WE'RE WORRIED ABOUT RACING AHEAD TO MAKE BOMBS WITHOUT CONSIDERING OTHER OPTIONS.
WE FEEL NOW IS THE TIME TO REACH OUT IN THE SPIRIT OF OPENNESS, TO FIND SOME WAY OF STOPPING THE ARMS RACE BEFORE IT BEGINS.

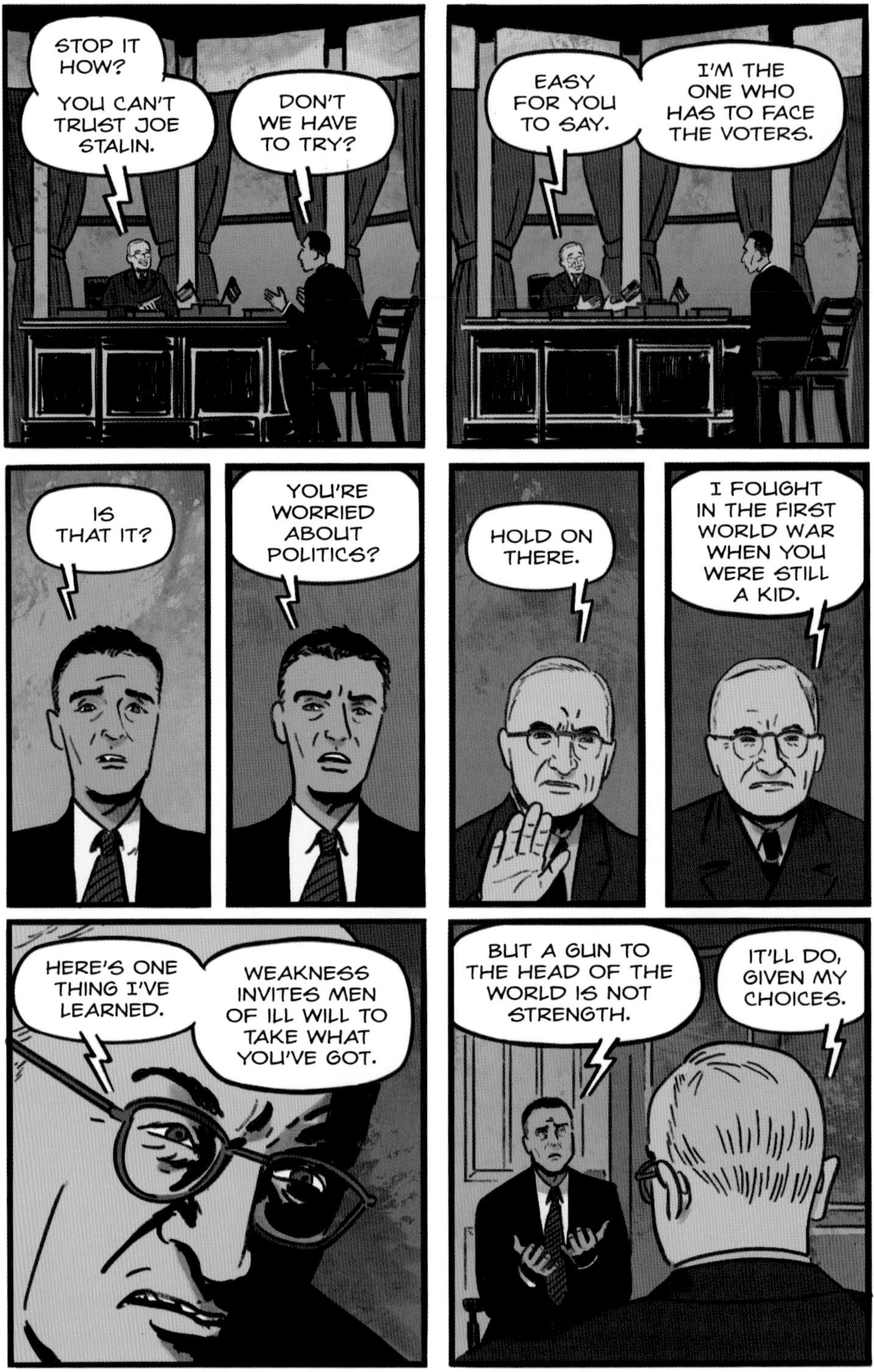
STOP IT HOW?
YOU CAN'T TRUST JOE STALIN.
DON'T WE HAVE TO TRY?
EASY FOR YOU TO SAY.
I'M THE ONE WHO HAS TO FACE THE VOTERS.
IS THAT IT?
YOU'RE WORRIED ABOUT POLITICS?
HOLD ON THERE.
I FOUGHT IN THE FIRST WORLD WAR WHEN YOU WERE STILL A KID.
HERE'S ONE THING I'VE LEARNED.
WEAKNESS INVITES MEN OF ILL WILL TO TAKE WHAT YOU'VE GOT.
BUT A GUN TO THE HEAD OF THE WORLD IS NOT STRENGTH.
IT'LL DO, GIVEN MY CHOICES.

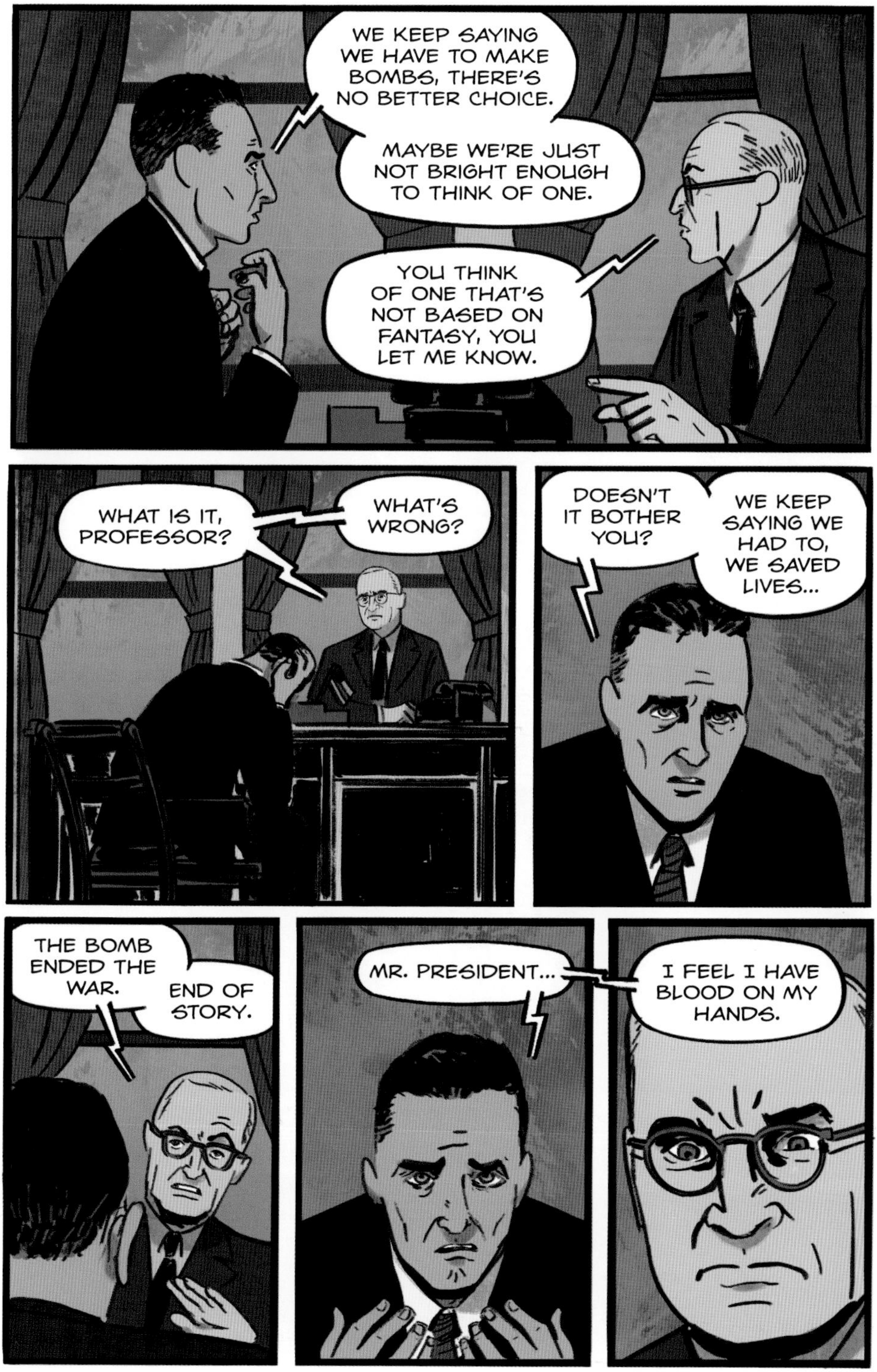
WE KEEP SAYING WE HAVE TO MAKE BOMBS, THERE'S NO BETTER CHOICE.
MAYBE WE'RE JUST NOT BRIGHT ENOUGH TO THINK OF ONE.
YOU THINK OF ONE THAT'S NOT BASED ON FANTASY, YOU LET ME KNOW.
WHAT IS IT, PROFESSOR?
WHAT'S WRONG?
DOESN'T IT BOTHER YOU?
WE KEEP SAYING WE HAD TO, WE SAVED LIVES...
THE BOMB ENDED THE WAR.
END OF STORY.
MR. PRESIDENT...
I FEEL I HAVE BLOOD ON MY HANDS.

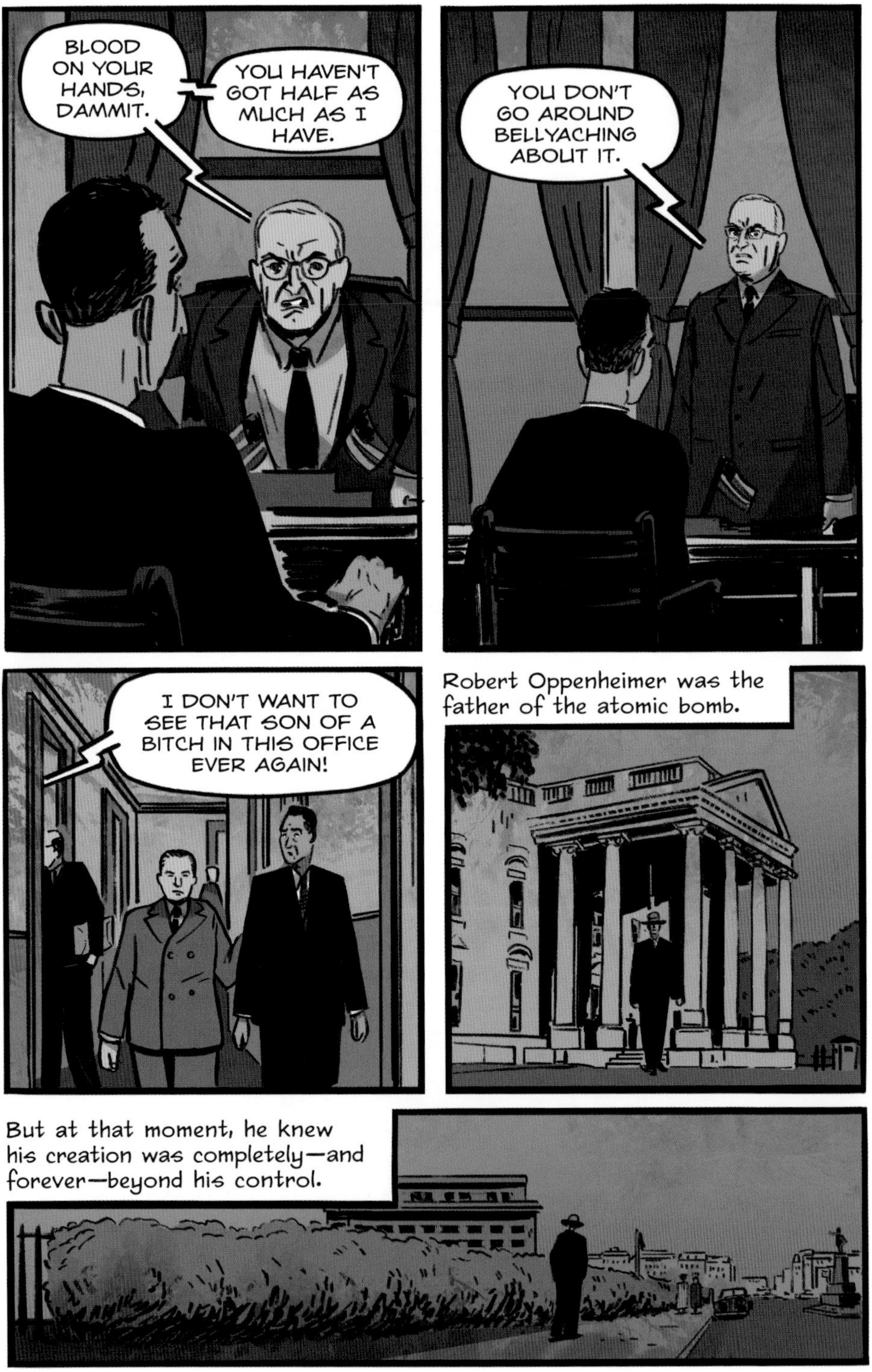
BLOOD ON YOUR HANDS, DAMMIT.
YOU HAVEN'T GOT HALF AS MUCH AS I HAVE.
YOU DON'T GO AROUND BELLYACHING ABOUT IT.
I DON'T WANT TO SEE THAT SON OF A BITCH IN THIS OFFICE EVER AGAIN!
Robert Oppenheimer was the father of the atomic bomb.
But at that moment, he knew his creation was completely—and forever—beyond his control.

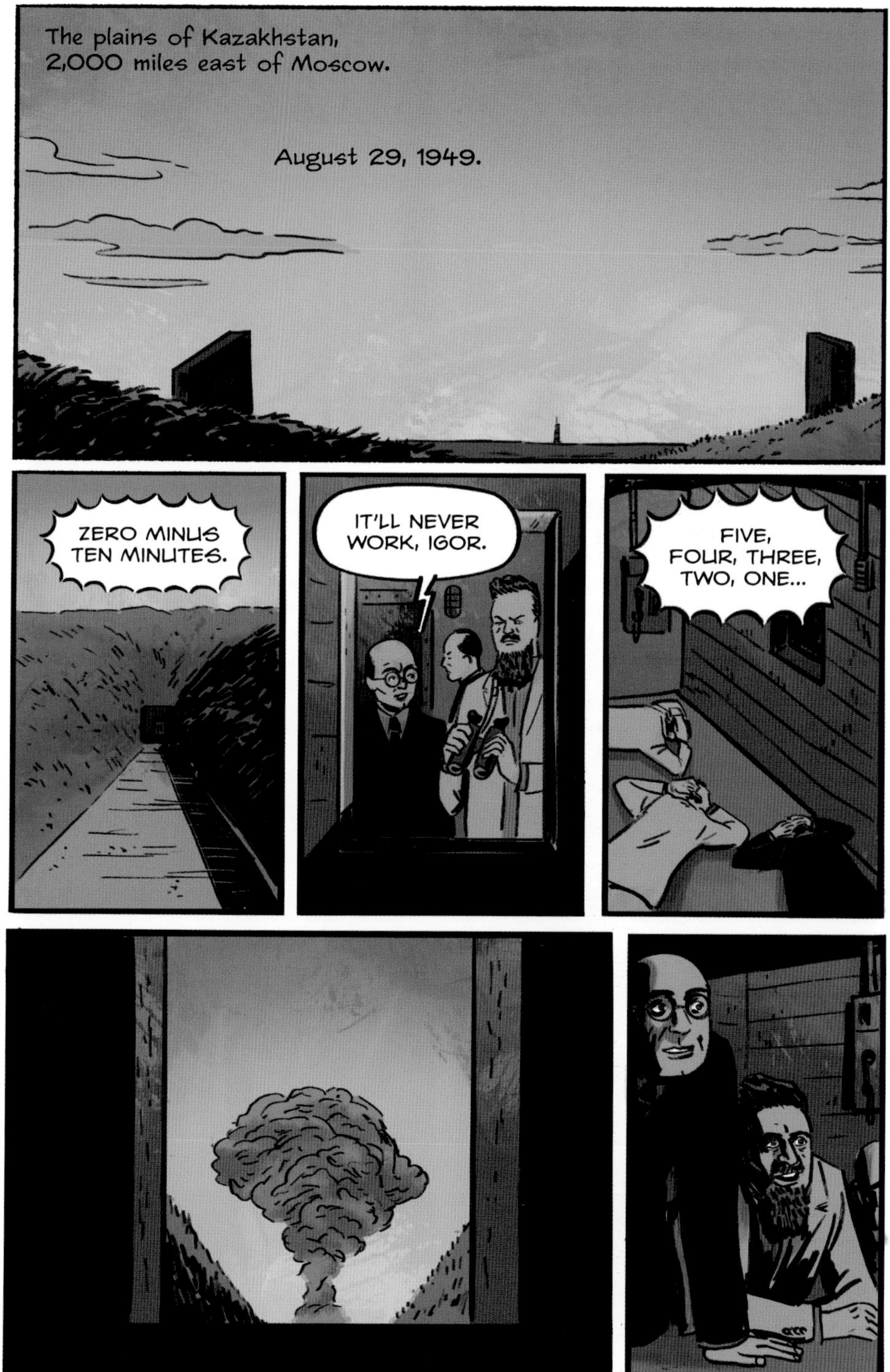
The plains of Kazakhstan, 2,000 miles east of Moscow.
August 29, 1949.
ZERO MINUS TEN MINUTES.
IT'LL NEVER WORK, IGOR.
FIVE, FOUR, THREE, TWO, ONE...

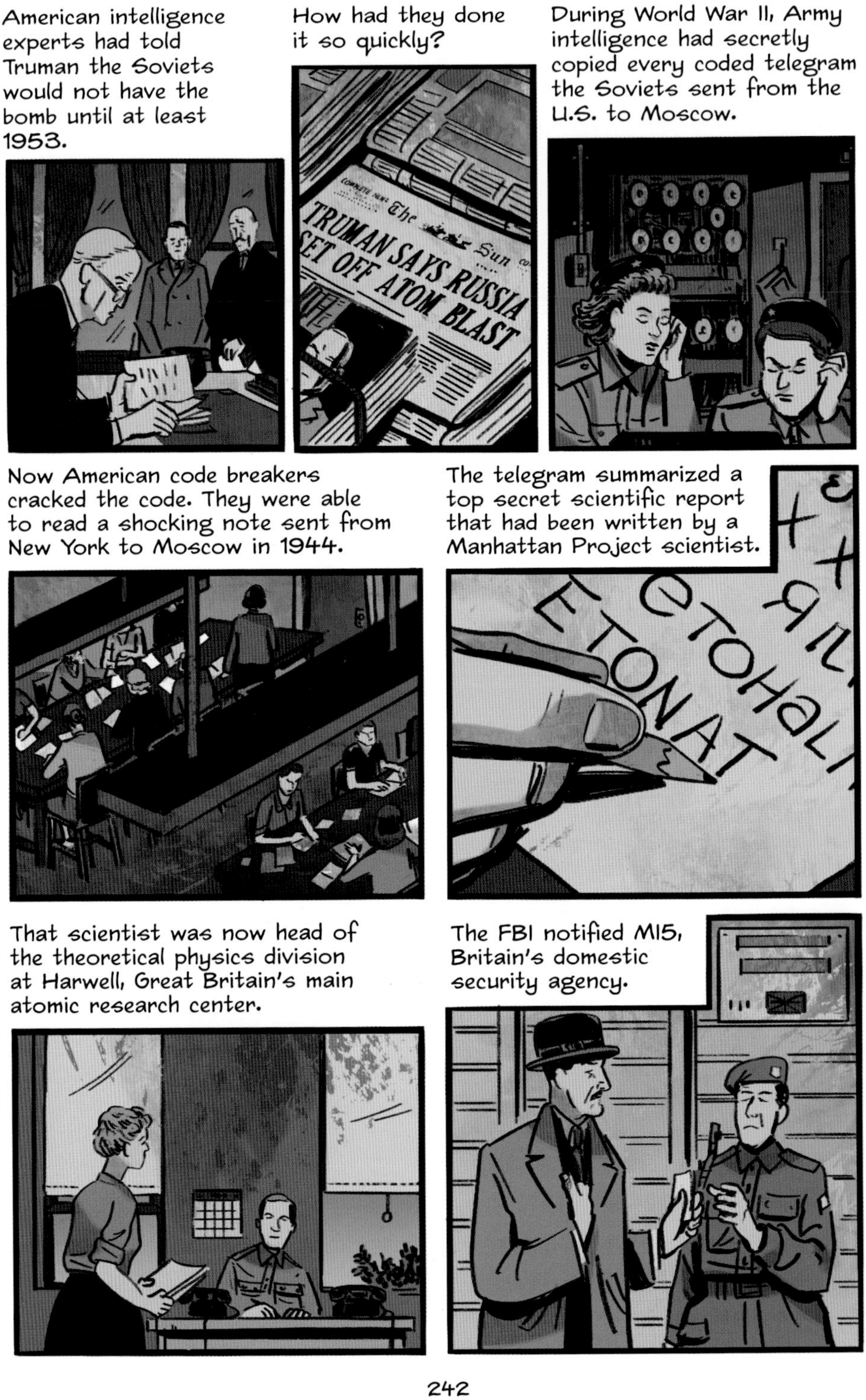
American intelligence experts had told Truman the Soviets would not have the bomb until at least 1953.
How had they done it so quickly?
The Sun
TRUMAN SAYS RUSSIA SET OFF ATOM BLAST
During World War II, Army intelligence had secretly copied every coded telegram the Soviets sent from the U.S. to Moscow.
Now American code breakers cracked the code. They were able to read a shocking note sent from New York to Moscow in 1944.
The telegram summarized a top secret scientific report that had been written by a Manhattan Project scientist.
That scientist was now head of the theoretical physics division at Harwell, Great Britain's main atomic research center.
The FBI notified MI5, Britain's domestic security agency.

MI5, investigator William Skardon paid the scientist a visit.

Then, after an hour of friendly chatter:

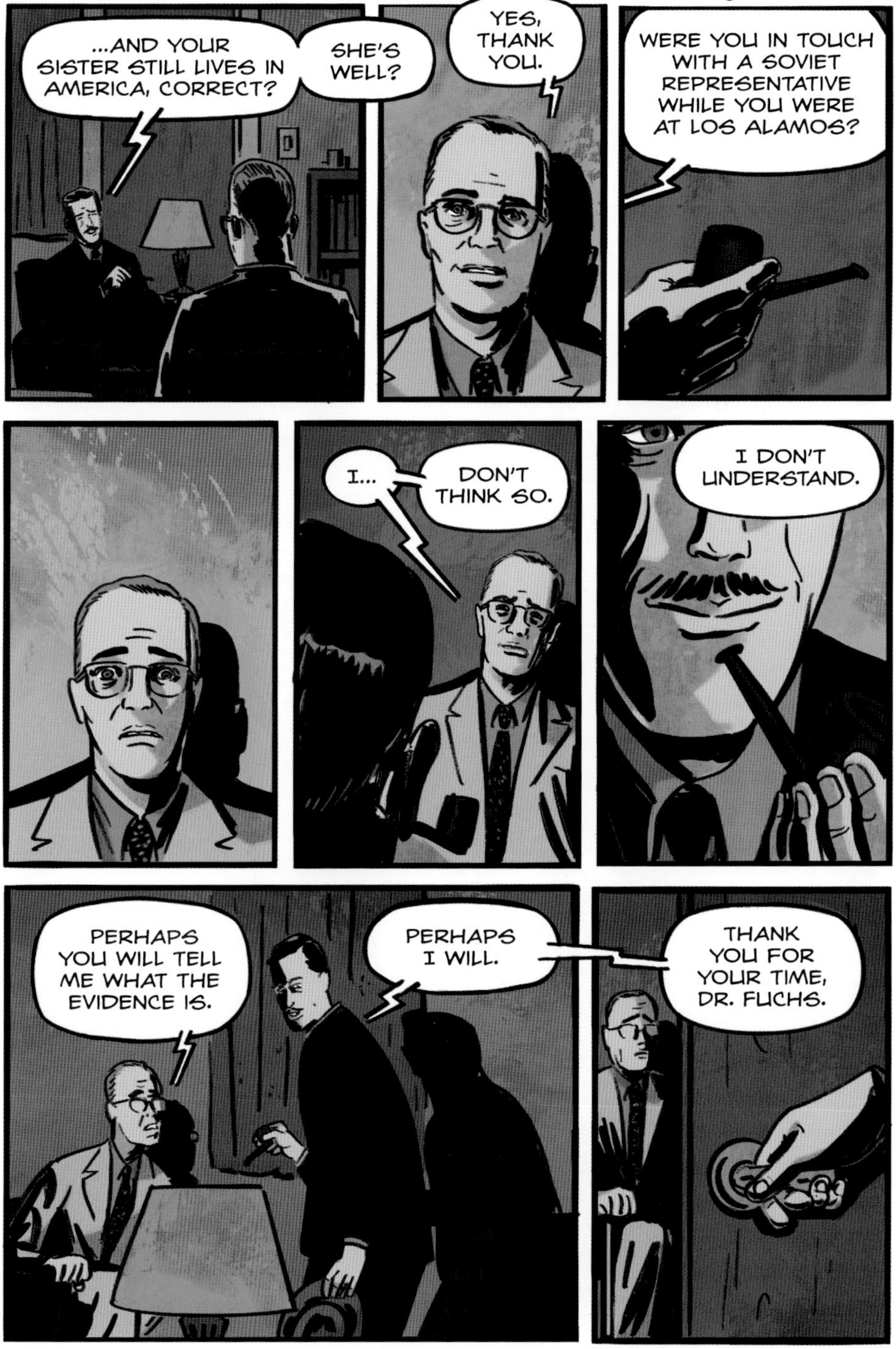
...AND YOUR SISTER STILL LIVES IN AMERICA, CORRECT?
SHE'S WELL?
YES, THANK YOU.
WERE YOU IN TOUCH WITH A SOVIET REPRESENTATIVE WHILE YOU WERE AT LOS ALAMOS?
I...
DON'T THINK SO.
I DON'T UNDERSTAND.
PERHAPS YOU WILL TELL ME WHAT THE EVIDENCE IS.
PERHAPS I WILL.
THANK YOU FOR YOUR TIME, DR. FUCHS.

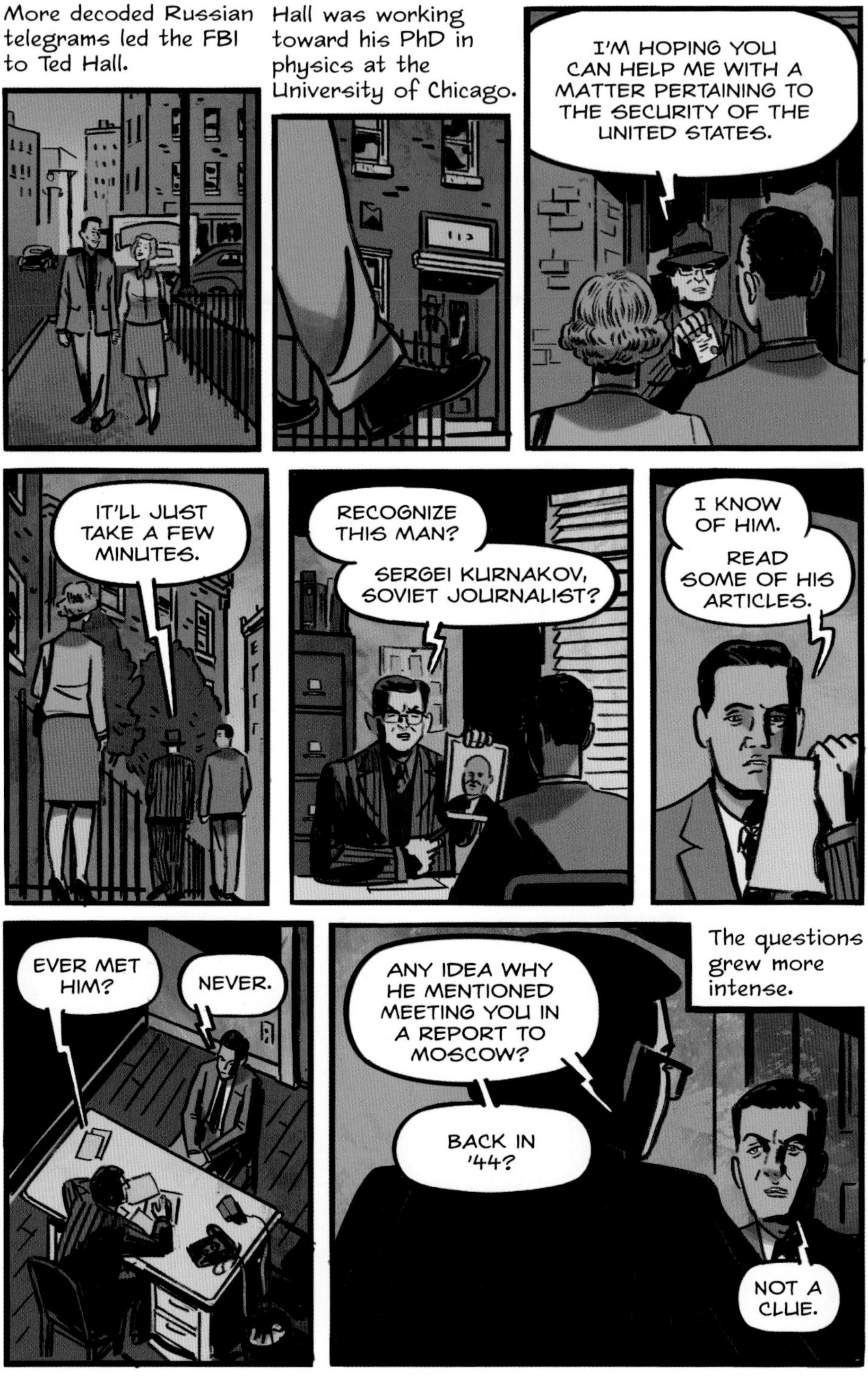
More decoded Russian telegrams led the FBI to Ted Hall.
Hall was working toward his PhD in physics at the University of Chicago.
I'M HOPING YOU CAN HELP ME WITH A MATTER PERTAINING TO THE SECURITY OF THE UNITED STATES.
IT'LL JUST TAKE A FEW MINUTES.
RECOGNIZE THIS MAN?
SERGEI KURNAKOV, SOVIET JOURNALIST?
I KNOW OF HIM.
READ SOME OF HIS ARTICLES.
EVER MET HIM?
NEVER.
The questions grew more intense.
ANY IDEA WHY HE MENTIONED MEETING YOU IN A REPORT TO MOSCOW?
BACK IN '44?
NOT A CLUE.

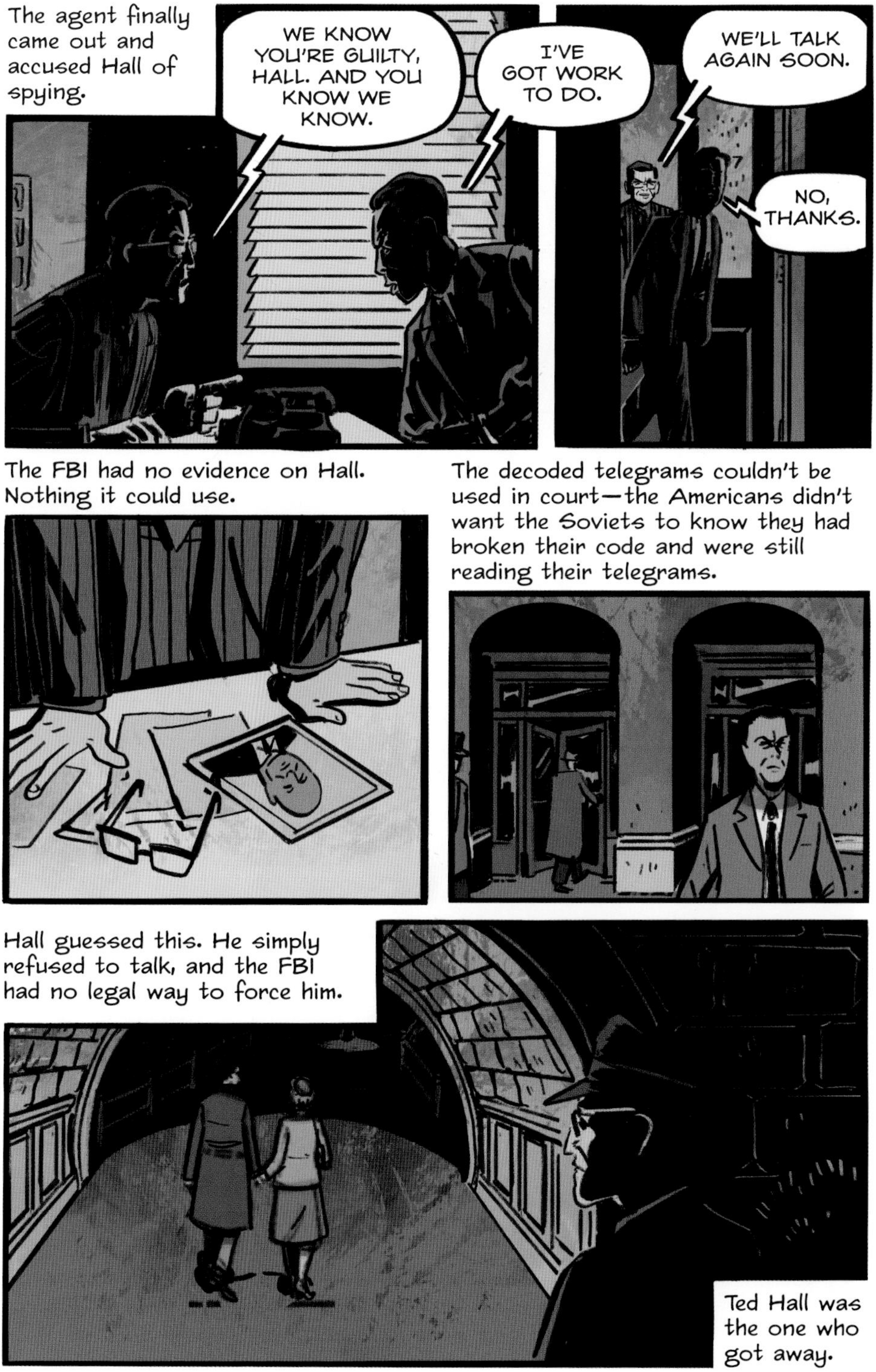
The agent finally came out and accused Hall of spying.
WE KNOW YOU'RE GUILTY, HALL. AND YOU KNOW WE KNOW.
I'VE GOT WORK TO DO.
WE'LL TALK AGAIN SOON.
NO, THANKS.
The FBI had no evidence on Hall. Nothing it could use.
The decoded telegrams couldn't be used in court—the Americans didn't want the Soviets to know they had broken their code and were still reading their telegrams.
Hall guessed this. He simply refused to talk, and the FBI had no legal way to force him.
Ted Hall was the one who got away.

Klaus Fuchs did not handle the heat as well. Skardon questioned Fuchs several more times.

Fuchs denied everything—but the pressure was getting to him.

At home, alone at night, he considered suicide.

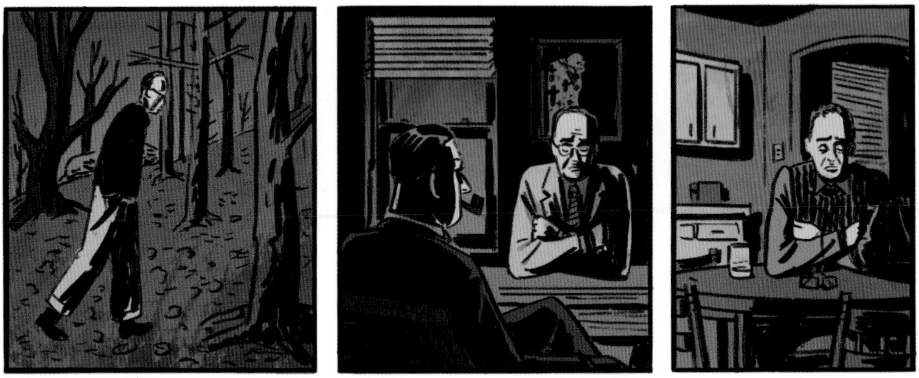

Finally, Fuchs called Skardon. He said he wanted to talk.

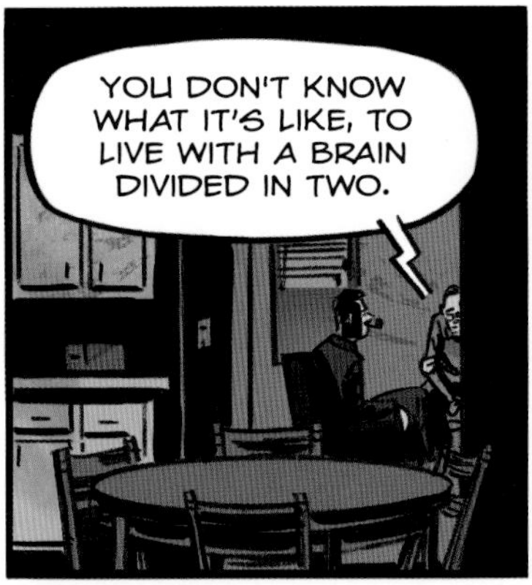
YOU DON'T KNOW WHAT IT'S LIKE, TO LIVE WITH A BRAIN DIVIDED IN TWO.

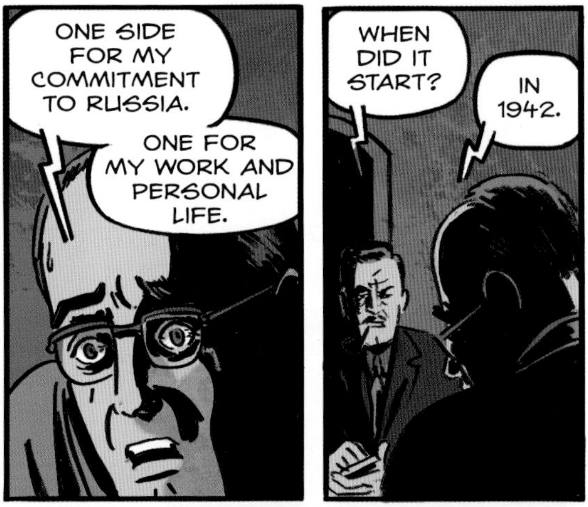
ONE SIDE FOR MY COMMITMENT TO RUSSIA.
ONE FOR MY WORK AND PERSONAL LIFE.
WHEN DID IT START?
IN 1942.

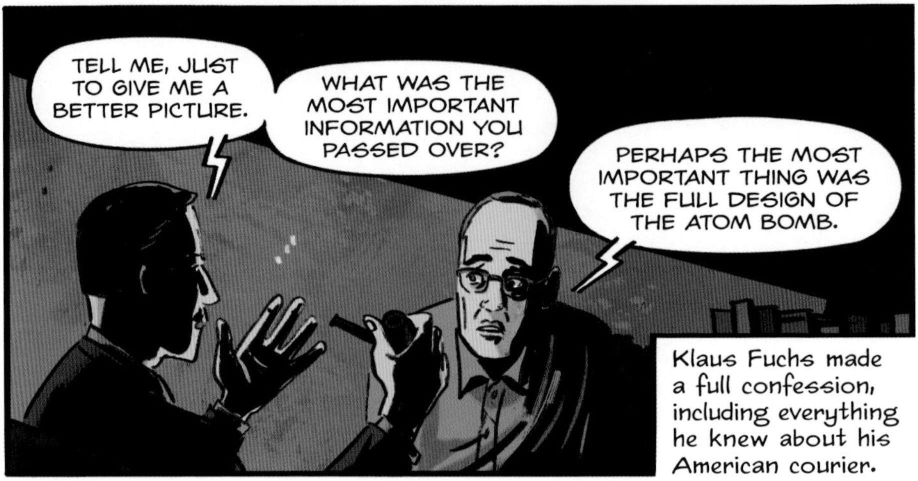
TELL ME, JUST TO GIVE ME A BETTER PICTURE.
WHAT WAS THE MOST IMPORTANT INFORMATION YOU PASSED OVER?
PERHAPS THE MOST IMPORTANT THING WAS THE FULL DESIGN OF THE ATOM BOMB.
Klaus Fuchs made a full confession, including everything he knew about his American courier.

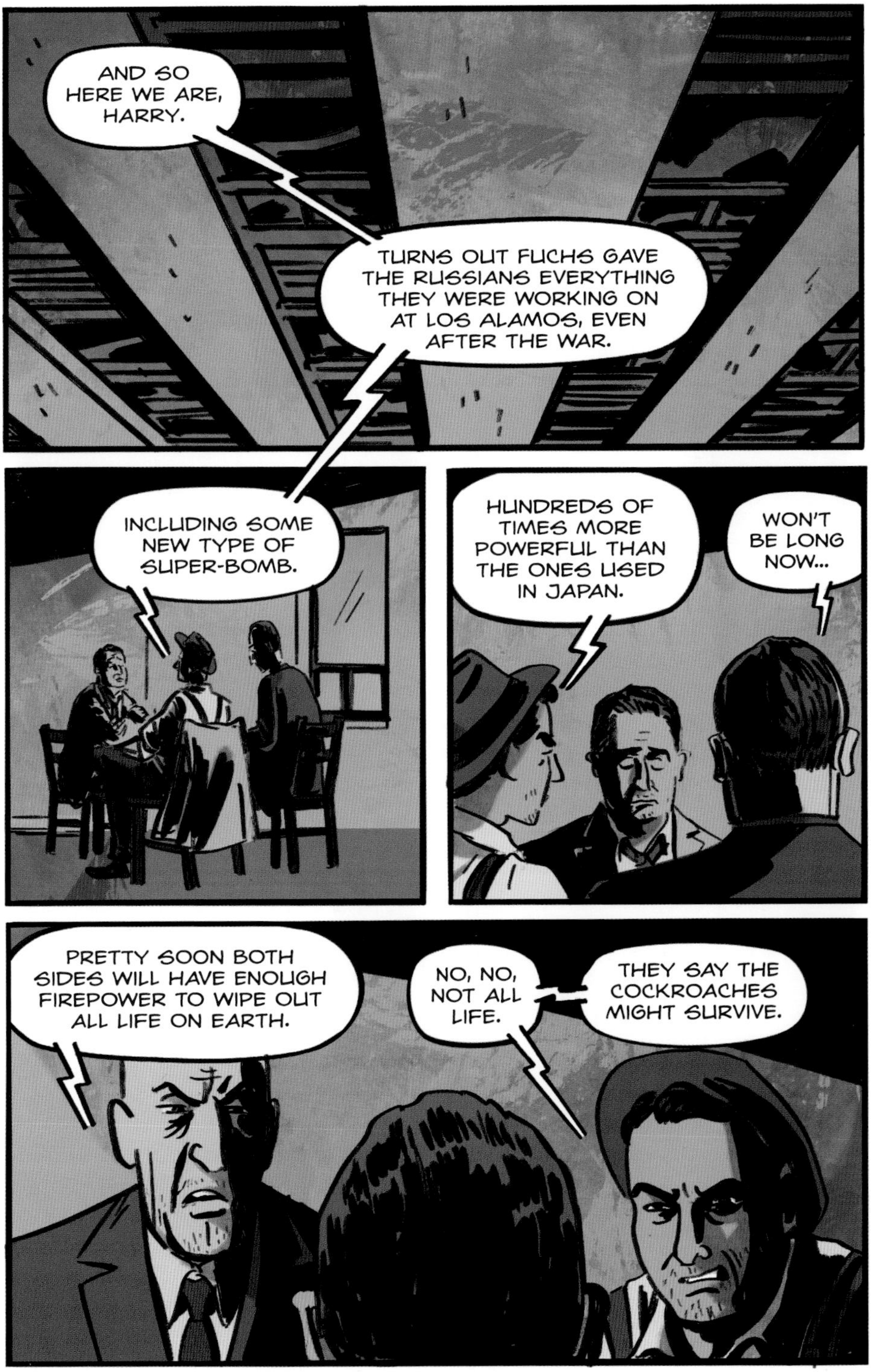
AND SO HERE WE ARE, HARRY.
TURNS OUT FUCHS GAVE THE RUSSIANS EVERYTHING THEY WERE WORKING ON AT LOS ALAMOS, EVEN AFTER THE WAR.
INCLUDING SOME NEW TYPE OF SUPER-BOMB.
HUNDREDS OF TIMES MORE POWERFUL THAN THE ONES USED IN JAPAN.
WON'T BE LONG NOW...
PRETTY SOON BOTH SIDES WILL HAVE ENOUGH FIREPOWER TO WIPE OUT ALL LIFE ON EARTH.
NO, NO, NOT ALL LIFE.
THEY SAY THE COCKROACHES MIGHT SURVIVE.

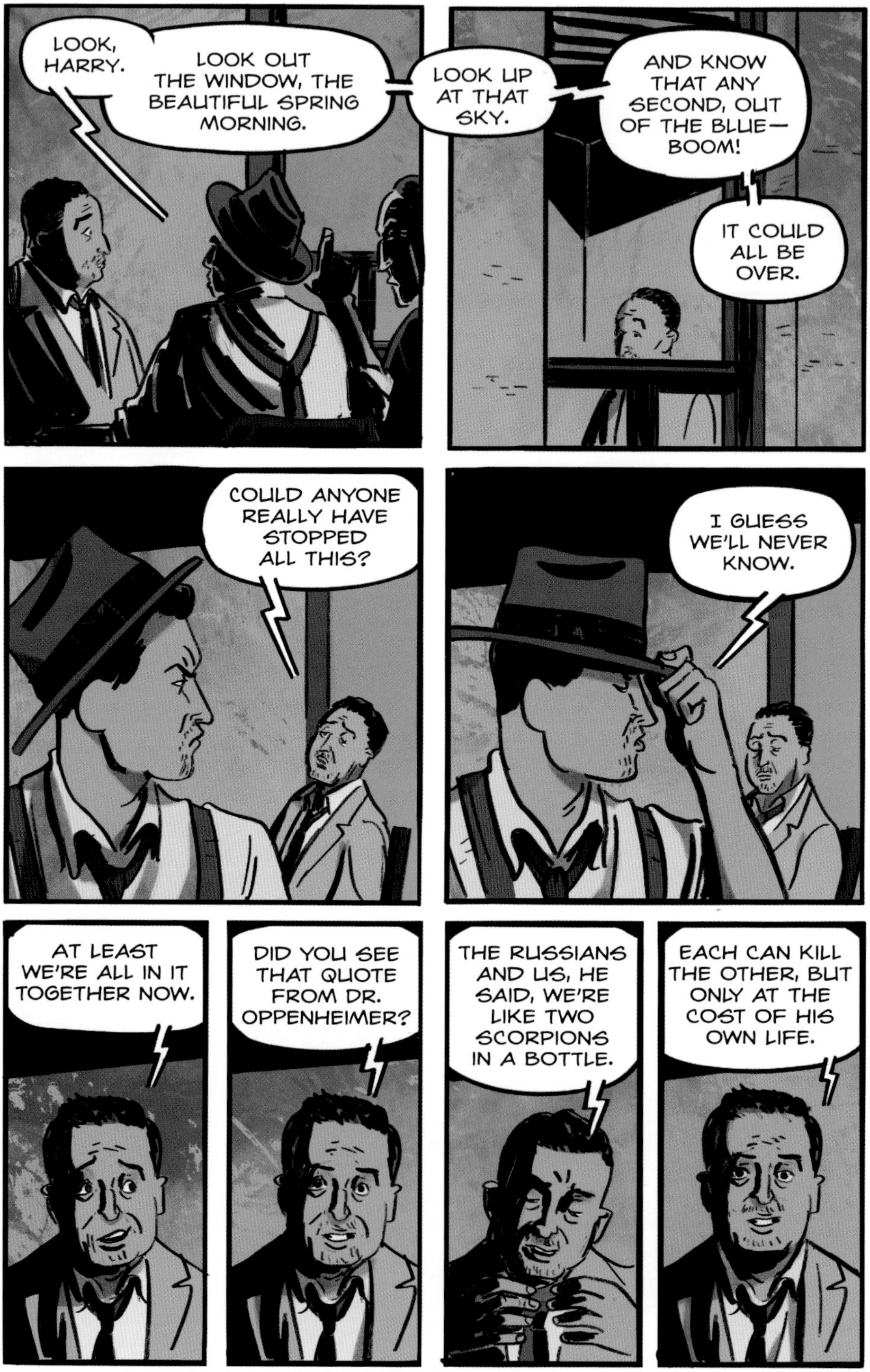
LOOK, HARRY.
LOOK OUT THE WINDOW, THE BEAUTIFUL SPRING MORNING.
LOOK UP AT THAT SKY.
AND KNOW THAT ANY SECOND, OUT OF THE BLUE— BOOM!
IT COULD ALL BE OVER.
COULD ANYONE REALLY HAVE STOPPED ALL THIS?
I GUESS WE'LL NEVER KNOW.
AT LEAST WE'RE ALL IN IT TOGETHER NOW.
DID YOU SEE THAT QUOTE FROM DR. OPPENHEIMER?
THE RUSSIANS AND US, HE SAID, WE'RE LIKE TWO SCORPIONS IN A BOTTLE.
EACH CAN KILL THE OTHER, BUT ONLY AT THE COST OF HIS OWN LIFE.

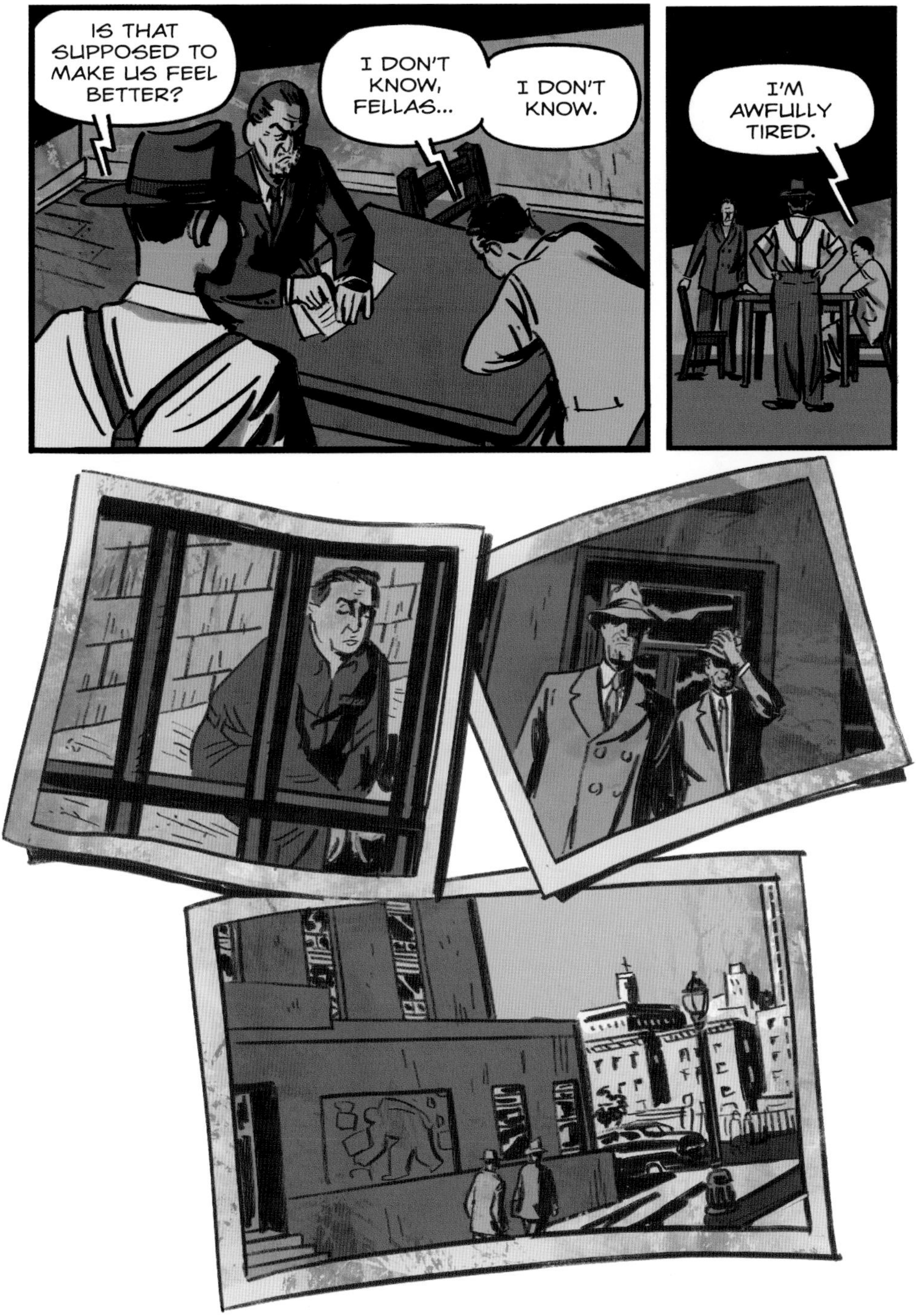
IS THAT SUPPOSED TO MAKE US FEEL BETTER?
I DON'T KNOW, FELLAS...
I DON'T KNOW.
I'M AWFULLY TIRED.

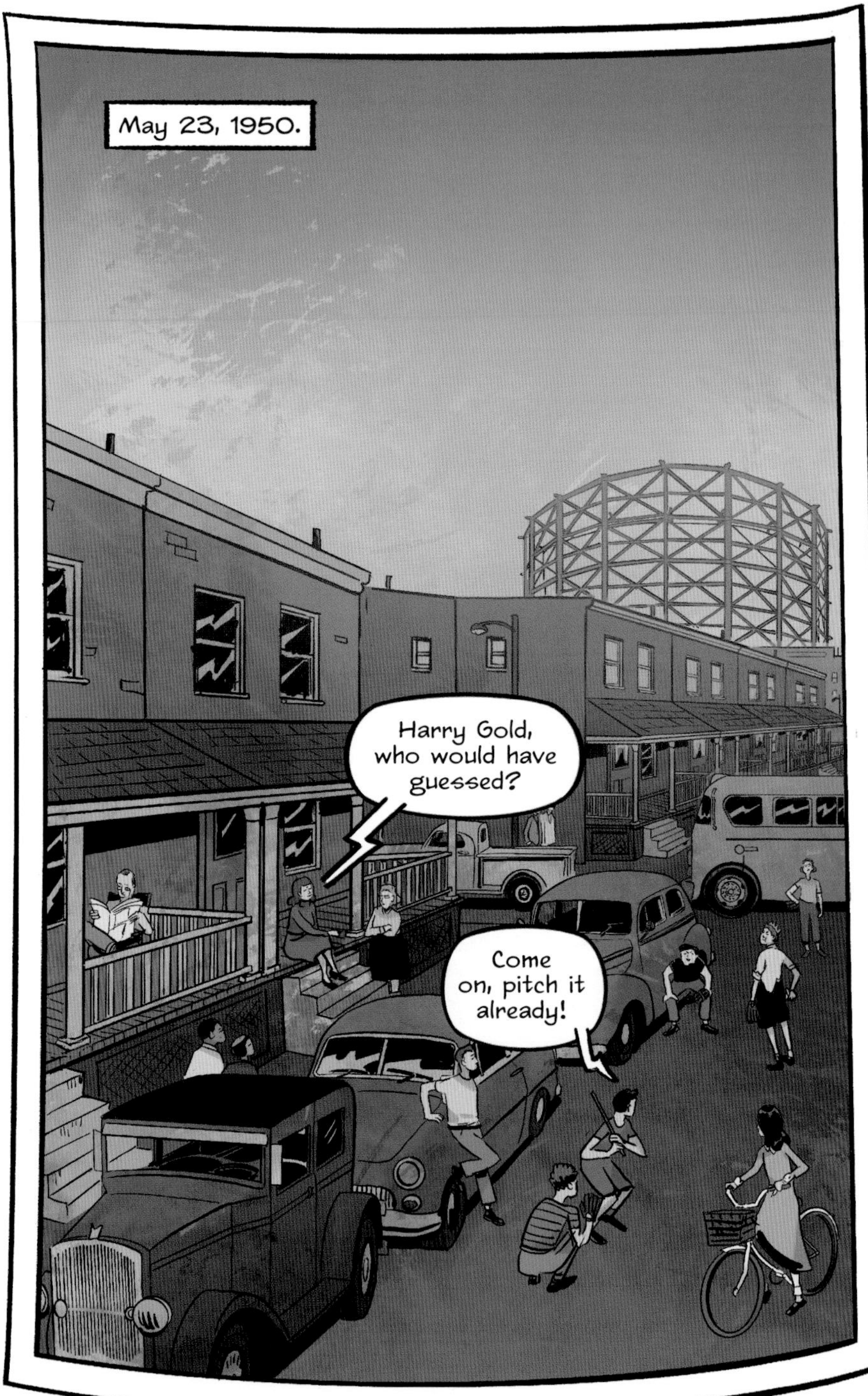
May 23, 1950.
Harry Gold, who would have guessed?
Come on, pitch it already!

EPILOGUE:
WHAT EVER HAPPENED TO . . . ?

Following his arrest in Philadelphia, Harry Gold endured countless hours of FBI interrogations and was hauled before Congress to testify about his spying activities. Seventeen years of secrets came pouring out. "Every time you squeeze him, there is some juice left," said one of the interrogating agents.

By cooperating with authorities, Gold avoided the electric chair, getting a thirty-year sentence instead. "I am calm," he said during his prison term, "and my mind is at peace for the first time in more than a decade and a half." Gold was paroled from prison in 1965 and returned home to Philadelphia, where he died in 1972, at the age of sixty-one.

Klaus Fuchs was certain he was going to be executed for spying, but was saved by a detail in British law. Had he committed treason to help an enemy, that *would* have been punishable by death. But at the time Fuchs committed treason—during World War II, that is—Great Britain and the Soviet Union were allies. The maximum sentence for passing secrets to an ally was fourteen years, which is what Fuchs got. He later settled in Communist East Germany, where he married and continued atomic research. Fuchs died in 1988, at the age of seventy-six.

Lona Cohen continued working for the Russians until the discovery of her spy ring necessitated a quick getaway in 1950. Cohen and her husband (and fellow spy), Morris, resurfaced in the suburbs of London, posing as quirky Canadians named Helen and Peter Kroger. They resumed spying for the Russians until their arrest in 1961. Sentenced to twenty years in prison, Lona and Morris were eventually exchanged for British prisoners held in the Soviet Union. Lona lived the rest of her life near Moscow, training younger spies. She died in 1992, at age seventy-nine.

Theodore Hall earned his PhD in physics at the University of Chicago and, with his wife, Joan, and three children, moved to Britain, in part to escape the attention of the FBI. Hall was never arrested and managed to avoid the subject of his wartime spying until much later in life. Looking back, he called himself a "a rather arrogant 19-year-old" and added: "Of course the situation was far more complicated than I understood at the time, and if confronted with the same problem today I would respond quite differently." Hall died in 1999, aged seventy-four.

Knut Haukelid and the other members of the Operation Gunnerside team were welcomed home as heroes in Norway, celebrated in books, movies, and museums. Haukelid's own book, *Skis Against the Atom,* details his part in wartime sabotage operations and was a valuable source for this book. Haukelid died in 1994, at the age of eighty-two. The last surviving Gunnerside member, Joachim Ronnenberg, lived to the age of ninety-nine, dying in 2018.

The qualities that made Leslie Groves a successful director of the Manhattan Project also proved to be his downfall in the army. Groves's final performance appraisal captured it well: "he often irritates his associates, but he has extraordinary capacity to get things done." Groves retired from the army in 1948, after twenty-nine years of service. He died in 1970, at the age of seventy-three.

The dramatic turns in the post-war life of Robert Oppenheimer could fill a whole other book, but the short version is that he made powerful enemies in the U.S. government. This was partly due to his opposition to the development of the hydrogen bomb, and partly a result of the Red Scare of the 1950s—the aggressive, at times paranoid, search for Communists everywhere in American life. Oppenheimer's association with Communists before World War II was dragged up, his loyalty to America questioned, and the government eventually stripped him of his security clearance.

"I think it broke his spirit, really," his colleague Robert Serber said.

Oppenheimer worked as director of the Institute for Advanced Study in Princeton, New Jersey, until his retirement in 1966. He died the following year, at the age of sixty-two.

Meanwhile, as Oppenheimer predicted, both the United States and the Soviet Union raced to develop much more powerful nuclear weapons. In November 1952, the U.S. tested its first "super-bomb"—more accurately, a hydrogen bomb, or fusion bomb. Fusion is the reaction that occurs in the core of stars, where atoms of hydrogen are fused to form helium, releasing vast amounts of energy. The first hydrogen bomb exploded with the force of ten million tons of TNT—more than five hundred times more powerful than the bomb dropped on Hiroshima in 1945. The Soviets tested their first hydrogen bomb less than a year later. The consequences of this arms race, and the superpower showdown that nearly led to World War III, are the subject of my 2021 nonfiction book *Fallout.*

Today, there are about 13,000 nuclear weapons in the world—down from nearly 70,000 in the 1980s. The United States and Russia have by far the biggest stockpiles. Seven other countries possess nuclear arsenals: China, France, the United Kingdom, Pakistan, India, Israel, and North Korea.

How does this story end? We don't know—because it's still going on.

And, like it or not, you're in it.

AUTHOR'S NOTE

This graphic novel is an adaptation of my narrative nonfiction book *Bomb: The Race to Build—and Steal—the World's Most Dangerous Weapon*. Basically, I started with the text of that book, pulled out key scenes and central characters, and used those elements to construct an outline for the graphic novel script. The one original addition was the series of interrogation scenes with Harry Gold and the FBI. This seemed like a useful way to bring in background information and tie the strands of the story together. Plus, that kind of hard-boiled banter is really fun to write.

The story Gold tells the FBI is entirely based on interrogation records, as well as Gold's testimony before Congress. Gold's dialogue is a combination of his actual words and my own take on what he *might* have said in such a situation, based on everything I learned about him, his manner of speaking, his voice.

Actually, the whole book presented this challenge. How do you craft dialogue for historical figures while staying true to what it's possible to know? In narrative nonfiction, of course, you can't invent any dialogue at all—but it felt necessary in the comics format, in order to create the kind of dramatic scenes I wanted the story to have. My solution was to mix in as many direct quotes as possible from primary sources. Where such sources don't exist, I tried to write lines that fit as seamlessly as possible with the quotes we do have.

All of that said, writing this book was the easy part. The real challenge went to Nick Bertozzi, who had the monumental task of turning words on a page into a full book of vibrant comics. It's as if he took my script and turned it into a movie, providing the actors, the sets, the lighting, everything.

I guess that would make Connie Hsu our tireless producer. She not only edited the story but oversaw the entire multi-year creative process with her usual clear vision and expert eye.

I'm grateful to Jen Besser for first suggesting the idea of a *Bomb* graphic novel. Thanks also to the entire creative team: Colorist Irene Yeom, Designer Sunny Lee, Associate Creative Director Kirk Benshoff, Production Editor Sarah Gompper, Managing Editor Jen Healey, Production Manager Alexa Blanco, and Editors Nico Ore-Giron and Mekisha Telfer.

STEVE SHEINKIN is the acclaimed author of fast-paced, cinematic nonfiction histories, including *Fallout*, *Undefeated*, *Born to Fly*, *The Port Chicago 50*, *Bomb*, and *The Notorious Benedict Arnold*. His accolades include a Newbery Honor, three Boston Globe–Horn Book Awards, a Sibert Medal and Honor, and three National Book Award finalist honors. He lives in Saratoga Springs, New York, with his wife and two children.

stevesheinkin.com

ALSO BY STEVE SHEINKIN

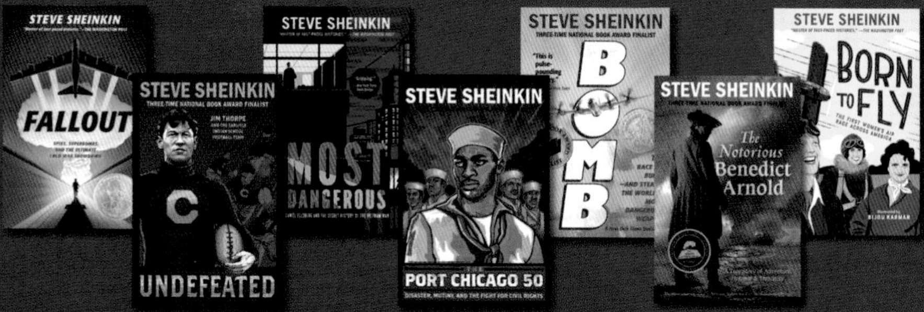
STEVE SHEINKIN
FALLOUT
STEVE SHEINKIN
THREE-TIME NATIONAL BOOK AWARD FINALIST
UNDEFEATED
STEVE SHEINKIN
MOST DANGEROUS
STEVE SHEINKIN
PORT CHICAGO 50
DISASTER, MUTINY, AND THE FIGHT FOR CIVIL RIGHTS
STEVE SHEINKIN
THREE-TIME NATIONAL BOOK AWARD FINALIST
BOMB
STEVE SHEINKIN
The Notorious Benedict Arnold
STEVE SHEINKIN
BORN TO FLY
THE FIRST WOMEN'S AIR RACE ACROSS AMERICA

NICK BERTOZZI has written and drawn many comics over the years, including *Becoming Andy Warhol*, *The Salon*, *Lewis & Clark*, and the *New York Times* bestselling *Shackleton: Antarctic Odyssey*. Bertozzi has won two Harvey Awards and has taught cartooning at the School of Visual Arts since 2003. He lives in Queens, New York, with his wife and daughters.

nickbertozzi.com

ALSO BY NICK BERTOZZI

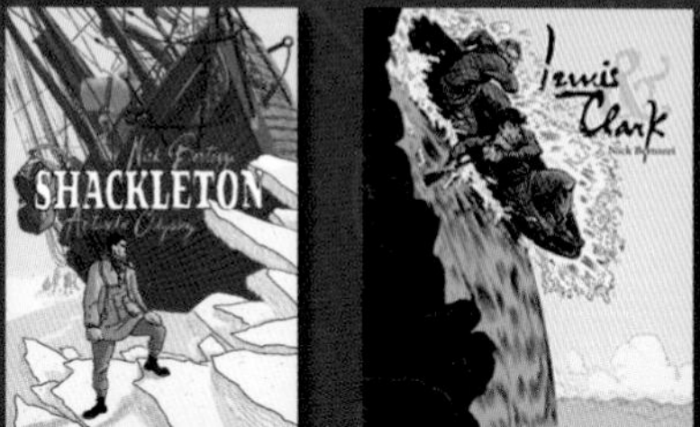
SHACKLETON
Lewis & Clark